The Rough G

Cuba

There are more than one hundred and fifty Rough Guide titles
covering destinations from Amsterdam to Zimbabwe

Forthcoming titles include

Beijing • Cape Town • Croatia • Ecuador • Switzerland

Rough Guide Reference Series

Classical Music • Drum 'n' Bass • English Football • European Football
House • The Internet • Jazz • Music USA • Opera • Reggae
Rock Music • Techno • World Music

Rough Guide Phrasebooks

Czech • Dutch • Egyptian Arabic • European Languages • French
German • Greek • Hindi & Urdu • Hungarian • Indonesian • Italian
Mandarin Chinese • Mexican Spanish • Polish • Portuguese • Russian
Spanish • Swahili • Thai • Turkish • Vietnamese

Rough Guides on the Internet

www.roughguides.com

Rough Guide Credits

Text Editor:	Ann-Marie Shaw and Kate Berens
Series Editor:	Mark Ellingham
Editorial:	Martin Dunford, Jonathan Buckley, Jo Mead, Amanda Tomlin, Paul Gray, Helena Smith, Judith Bamber, Orla Duane, Olivia Eccleshall, Ruth Blackmore, Sophie Martin, Geoff Howard, Claire Saunders, Gavin Thomas, Alexander Mark Rogers, Polly Thomas, Joe Staines, Lisa Nellis, Andrew Tomičíc, Polly Thomas, Richard Lim, Claire Fogg, Duncan Clark, Peter Buckley (UK); Andrew Rosenberg, Mary Beth Maioli, Don Bapst, Stephen Timblin (US)
Online Editors:	Kelly Cross, Loretta Chilcoat (US)
Production:	Susanne Hillen, Andy Hilliard, Link Hall, Helen Ostick, Julia Bovis, Michelle Draycott, Katie Pringle, Robert Evers, Niamh Hatton
Cartography:	Melissa Baker, Maxine Repath, Nichola Goodliffe, Ed Wright
Picture Research:	Louise Boulton, Sharon Martins
Finance:	John Fisher, Gary Singh, Edward Downey, Mark Hall, Tim Bill
Marketing & Publicity:	Richard Trillo, Niki Smith, David Wearn, Jemima Broadbridge (UK); Jean-Marie Kelly, Myra Campolo, Simon Carloss (US)
Administration:	Tania Hummel, Charlotte Marriott, Demelza Dallow

Acknowledgements

The authors would like to thank Darren Bills for the wildlife piece and Jan Fairley for her account of Cuban music. **At Rough Guides**, thank you to Sam Cook for setting us on the right road; and many thanks to Ann-Marie Shaw and Kate Berens for scrupulous editing, with help from Polly Thomas and James McConnachie. Thanks also to Robert Mackey and Stephen Townshend for extra Basics research; Ed Wright for unscrambling the maps; Sharon Martins for tireless picture research; and Margaret Doyle for proofreading.

In Cuba thanks from both authors to Yaquelin Triana at Publicitur for exhaustive help and Omar Mendoza at the Ministerio de Relaciones Exteriores.

Fiona: In Havana, the biggest thank you to Marivi Veliz and Albilio Guillot for food, laughter and conversation, also Lydia Flores Castro and Pepe Breuil Galigarcía for fact-filled emails. In Camagüey thanks to Francisco Luna Marrero; Marcos Tamames Henderson, Héctor Juárez Figueredo and Esmeralda Ávila Vázquez at Rumbos; and Arnaldo Iglesias. In Guantánamo thanks go to José Sánchez Yuerra; Miguel Angel Castro and Sudah Yehuda Shahéb in Baracoa deserve a special mention, as do Nieves and her family in Santiago. At home, many thanks to Alina Moat and Rodolfo Herrero Balmaseda for valuable insights and the family for endless encouragement. Final thanks to Martin for long-suffering support and love.

Matt: Thanks to Miriam Rodríguez Domínguez, Sinai Solé Rodríguez and Karen; Abelito and Bartutis; Julio Cárdenas; Ricardo Morales; Jorge Díaz; Hildegard, Aurara and Nimueh; Martha for the information on radio and TV; Gerardo Griñan; Arturo and Pompa in Pinar del Río; Raul and Raulito; Joe and Katie for feedback; Jamie for chauffeur skills; Lenin the taxi driver in Caibarién; the whole Rumbos team in the Península de Zapata; Julio Caravia Barbery; Lizette Castillo of the Cuba Tourist Board; my mum and dad for support throughout; Anna for last-minute information on Habana Vieja; Cath for the book review; and Rob for early morning courier duties. Shouts to RCA and El Piquete in Havana and all my boys in Kent and London.

This first edition published May 2000 by Rough Guides Ltd, 62–70 Shorts Gardens, London WC2H 9AB.
Distributed by the Penguin Group:
Penguin Books Ltd, 27 Wrights Lane, London W8 5TZ.
Penguin Books USA Inc, 375 Hudson Street, New York, NY 10014, USA.
Penguin Books Australia Ltd, 487 Maroondah Highway, PO Box 257, Ringwood, Victoria 3134, Australia.
Penguin Books Canada Ltd, 10 Alcorn Avenue, Toronto, Ontario M4V 1E4, Canada.
Penguin Books (NZ) Ltd, 182–190 Wairau Road, Auckland 10, New Zealand.
Printed in England by Clays Ltd, St Ives Plc
Typography and original design by Jonathan Dear and The Crowd Roars.
Illustrations throughout by Edward Briant.

The Rough Guide to
Cuba

Written and researched by
Fiona McAuslan and Matthew Norman

ROUGH
GUIDES

Help us update

We've gone to a lot of trouble to ensure that this first edition of *The Rough Guide to Cuba* is accurate and up-to-date. However, things inevitably change, and if you feel we've got it wrong or left something out, we'd like to know: any suggestions, comments or corrections would be much appreciated. We'll credit all contributions and send a copy of the next edition – or any other Rough Guide if you prefer – for the best correspondence.

Please mark letters "Rough Guide to Cuba" and send to:
Rough Guides, 62–70 Shorts Gardens, London WC2H 9AB or
Rough Guides, 375 Hudson St, New York, NY 10014.

Email should be sent to:
mail@roughguides.co.uk

Online updates about Rough Guide titles can be found on our Web site at *www.roughguides.com*

The Authors

Fiona McAuslan and Matthew Norman first visited Cuba in 1995 when they spent a year living with Cuban families and attending courses at the University of Havana. **Fiona** now lives in London where she is a freelance writer and television researcher, as well as an inept salsa dancer. **Matt** has established links with the growing hip-hop scene in Havana and has been working recently in a record shop. He carries an ongoing debt to the Cuban health service.

Rough Guides

Travel Guides • Phrasebooks • Music and Reference Guides

We set out to do something different when the first Rough Guide was published in 1982. Mark Ellingham, just out of university, was travelling in Greece. He brought along the popular guides of the day, but found they were all lacking in some way. They were either strong on ruins and museums but went on for pages without mentioning a beach or taverna. Or they were so conscious of the need to save money that they lost sight of Greece's cultural and historical significance. Also, none of the books told him anything about Greece's contemporary life – its politics, its culture, its people and how they lived.

So with no job in prospect, Mark decided to write his own guidebook, one which aimed to provide practical information that was second to none, detailing the best beaches and the hottest clubs and restaurants, while also giving hard-hitting accounts of every sight, both famous and obscure, and providing up-to-the-minute information on contemporary culture. It was a guide that encouraged independent travellers to find the best of Greece, and was a great success, getting shortlisted for the Thomas Cook travel guide award, and encouraging Mark, along with three friends, to expand the series.

The Rough Guide list grew rapidly and the letters flooded in, indicating a much broader readership than had been anticipated, but one which uniformly appreciated the Rough Guides' mix of practical detail and humour, irreverence and enthusiasm. Things haven't changed. The same four friends who began the series are still the caretakers of the Rough Guide mission today: to provide the most reliable, up-to-date and entertaining information to independent-minded travellers of all ages, on all budgets.

We now publish 150 titles and have offices in London and New York. The travel guides are written and researched by a dedicated team of more than 100 authors, based in Britain, Europe, the USA and Australia. We have also created a unique series of phrasebooks to accompany the travel series, along with the acclaimed series of music guides, and a best-selling pocket guide to the Internet and World Wide Web. We also publish comprehensive travel information on our Web site: *www.roughguides.com*

Contents

List of maps

MAP SYMBOLS

━━━	Railway	⛽	Fuel station
▬▬▬	Motorway	Ⓗ	Hospital
═══	Road	⌂	Shelter/lodge
━━━	Dirt road	♦	Military checkpoint
�fٟ̄	Steps	Ⳡ	Campsite
- - - - -	Footpath	◉	Accommodation
▬▬▬	Waterway	■	Restaurant
– – –	Provincial boundary	✈	Airport
━ ━ ━	Chapter division boundary	Ⓟ	Parking
♦	Point of interest	ⓘ	Tourist information office
▲	Peak	⊠	Post office
⌃⌃	Mountain range	Ⓒ	Telephone office
⚘	Viewpoint	▨	Building
⌒	Cave	⊞	Church (town maps)
�fāُ	Ruins/archeological site		Park
♯	Castle		Mangrove swamp
⛳	Golf course		Marsh
♦	Museum		Beach
⍭	Gardens	⊞	Cemetery
⊙	Statue/memorial		

Introduction

I solated from the Western world for over thirty years, **Cuba** burst back onto the international tourist scene in the early 1990s and hasn't looked back since. Shaped by one of the twentieth century's longest surviving revolutions, until recently Cuba's image had been inextricably bound up with its politics. Even five decades after Fidel Castro and the rebels seized power, Cuba's long satiny beaches, offshore cays and jungle-covered peaks – the defining attractions of neighbouring islands – played almost no part in the popular perception of this communist state in the Caribbean. Now, having opened the floodgates to global tourism, the country is changing and Cuba today is characterized as much as anything by a frenetic sense of transition as it shifts from socialist stronghold to one of the Caribbean's major tourist destinations, running on capitalist dollars. Yet at the same time, it can seem to visitors that nothing has changed for decades, even centuries. Cut off from the capitalist world until the end of the Cold War, and only just emerging from a chronic economic crisis, the face of modern-day Cuba is in many respects frozen in the past – the classic American cars, moustachioed cigar-smoking farmers, horse-drawn carriages and colonial Spanish architecture all apparently unaffected by the breakneck pace of modernization, brought on by the country's desperate need for dollars following the collapse of the Soviet bloc. Newly erected department stores and shopping malls, state-of-the-art hotels and entire resorts created from scratch are the hallmarks of this new, emerging Cuba. This improbable combination of transformation and stasis is symbolic of a country riddled with contradictions and ironies. In a place where taxi drivers earn more than doctors, and where capitalist reforms are seen as the answer to preserving socialist ideals, understanding Cuba is a compelling but never-ending task.

Despite the hard-to-swallow favourable treatment of tourists and the crippling US trade embargo, there is surprisingly little resentment directed at foreign visitors, and your overwhelming impression is likely to be that Cubans are outgoing, sociable and hospitable, notwithstanding the queues, food rationing and restrictions on free speech. What's more, in most of Cuba it's difficult not to come into contact with local people: the common practice of renting out rooms and opening restaurants in homes allows visitors stronger impressions of the country than they might have thought possible in a short visit. The much-vaunted Cuban capacity for a good time is best expressed through music and dance, both vital facets of the island's culture. As originators of the most influential Latin music styles, such as *bolero*, *rumba* and *son*, thereby spawning the most famous of them all – *salsa* – people in Cuba seem always ready to party.

There are occasional reminders that Cuba is a centralized, highly bureaucratic one-party state, which can give a holiday here an unfamiliar twist. Naturally this becomes more apparent the longer you stay, but one of the quickest ways of finding out is when things go wrong. Going to the police, finding your hotel room double-booked or simply needing to make an urgent phone call can prove to be unnecessarily and frustratingly complicated. These are the times when you discover Cuba has its own special logic and that common sense doesn't count for much here. This is not to say you're more likely to experience mishaps in Cuba than anywhere else – not only are all the major resorts as well equipped as you might hope, but violent crime is remarkably absent from Cuban cities. On the other hand, a certain determination and a laid-back attitude are essential

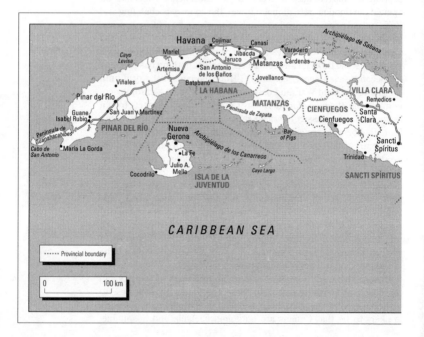

requirements for exploring less visited parts of the country, where a paucity of facilities and public transport problems can make travelling hard work. Things are becoming easier all the time, though, with the introduction of more efficient bus services, simplified currency systems and a wider variety of consumer goods. Ironically, these improvements also mark an irreversible move away from what makes Cuba unique. Though the nation's culture and character will always ensure that Cuba is more than just another island paradise, the determination to sell the country to a worldwide market means the time to go is now rather than later.

Where to go

No trip to Cuba would be complete without a visit to the potent capital city, **Havana**. A unique and personable mini-metropolis, characterized by a small-town atmosphere, its time-warped colonial core, Habana Vieja, is crammed with architectural splendours, some laced with Moorish traces and dating as far back as the sixteenth century. Elsewhere in the city there are handsome streets unspoilt by tawdry multinational chain stores and restaurants: with relatively little development since the revolution, the city retains many of its colonial mansions and numerous 1950s hallmarks.

The provinces to the immediate east and west of Havana, together with the capital itself, are where tourist attractions are most

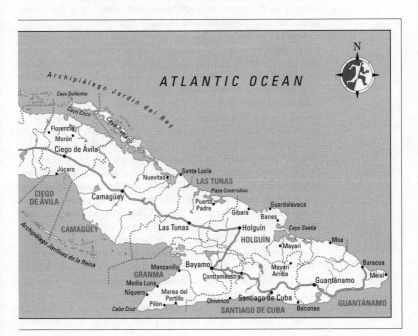

densely concentrated. Visited frequently by day-trippers from Havana, **Pinar del Río**, the centre of nature tourism in Cuba, offers more than enough to sustain a longer stay. The most accessible resorts for walking are **Las Terrazas** and **Soroa**, focused around the subtropical, smooth-topped mountain ranges of the Sierra del Rosario and Sierra de los Organos, but it's the peculiar *mogote* hills of prehistoric **Viñales** valley that attract most attention. Beyond, out of sight of the mountains, on a gnarled rod of land pointing out towards Mexico, there's unparalleled seclusion and outstanding scuba diving at **María la Gorda**.

There are **beach resorts** the length and breadth of the country but none is more complete than **Varadero**, the country's long-time premier holiday destination, two hours' drive east from Havana, in **Matanzas province**. Based on a highway of dazzling white sand, stretching almost the entire length of the 25-kilometre Península de Hicacos, this is where most tourists come for the classic package-holiday experience. For the tried-and-tested combination of disco-nightlife, watersports, sunbathing and relaxing in all-inclusive hotels, there is nowhere better in Cuba. On the opposite side of the province, the **Península de Zapata**, with its diversity of wildlife, organized excursions and mixture of hotels, offers a mélange of different possibilities. The grittier unpolished towns of **Cárdenas** and the provincial capital **Matanzas** contrast with the made-to-measure appeal of Varadero, but it's the nearby natural attractions of the **Bellamar caves** and the verdant splendour of the **Yumurí valley** that provide the focus for most day-trips.

Across the eastern border from Matanzas into next-door **Cienfuegos province**, tourist attractions begin to appear less frequently. Travelling east of here, either on the *autopista* or the island-long Carretera Central, public transport links become weaker and worn-out yet picturesque towns take over from brochure-friendly tourist hot spots. There is, however, a concentration of tourist activity around the historically precious **Trinidad**, a small colonial city brimming with symbols of Cuba's past, which attracts coach parties and backpackers in equal numbers. If you're intending to spend more than a few days in the centre of the island, this is by far the best base, within short taxi rides of a small but well equipped beach resort, the **Península de Ancón**, and the **Topes de Collantes** hiking centre in the **Sierra del Escambray**. Slightly further afield are a few larger cities: sociable **Santa Clara** with its convivial main square and thronging crowds of students is the liveliest of the lot, whilst laid-back **Cienfuegos**, next to the placid waters of a sweeping bay, is sprinkled with colourful architecture, including a splendid nineteenth-century theatre. Further east, the workaday cities of **Sancti Spíritus** and **Ciego de Ávila**, both capitals of their namesake provinces, provide excellent stop-offs on a journey along the Carretera Central. Two of the most popular destinations in this part of the country are off the north coast of Ciego de Ávila province.

With their reams of creamy white beaches and tranquil countryside, the luxurious resorts of **Cayo Coco** and **Cayo Guillermo**, on the secluded cays of the same name, are growing month by month.

Continuing eastwards into **Camagüey province**, the smaller, rather remote resort of **Santa Lucía** is a much promoted though less well equipped option for sun-seekers, while there's an excellent alternative north of here in tiny **Cayo Sabinal**, with long empty beaches and romantically rustic facilities. Back on the Carretera Central, the romantic and ramshackle city of **Camagüey**, the most populous city in the central part of the island, is a sightseer's delight, with numerous churches and intriguing buildings, as well as a lively nightlife, while the amiable city of **Holguín** is the threshold to a province containing the biggest concentration of pre-Columbian sites in the country. **Guardalavaca**, on the northern coast of Holguín province, is one of the liveliest and most attractive resorts in the country, spread along a long and shady beach with ample opportunities for watersports.

While **Guantánamo province**, forming the far eastern tip of the island, is best known for its infamous US naval base, it is the jaunty seaside town of **Baracoa** that is the region's most enchanting spot. Isolated from the rest of the country by a high rib of mountains, the quirky town freckled with colonial houses and populated by friendly and hospitable locals is an unrivalled retreat, popular with long-term travellers.

With a sparkling coastline fretted with golden-sand beaches such as **Chivirico**, the undulating emerald mountains of the **Sierra Maestra**, made for trekking, and **Santiago**, the country's most vibrant and energetic city after Havana, **Santiago de Cuba province**, on the island's southeast coast, could make a holiday in itself. Host to the country's most exuberant **carnival** every July, when a deluge of loud, sweet and passionate sounds surge through the streets, it is testimony to the city's musical heritage that you can hear some of the best Cuban musicians here all year round. Trekkers and revolution enthusiasts will want to follow the Sierra Maestra as it snakes west of here along the south coast into **Granma** province, offering various revolutionary landmarks and nature trails.

Lying off the southwest coast of Havana province, the **Isla de la Juventud** is often overlooked despite its immense though low-key charms. Easily explored over a weekend, the island promises leisurely walks, some of the best diving in the country and a personable capital town in Nueva Gerona. In the same archipelago is luxurious and anodyne **Cayo Largo**, the only sizeable beach resort off the southern coastline of Cuba.

When to go

Cuba has a hot and sunny tropical climate with an average yearly temperature of 24ºC, but in the winter months of January and February temperatures can drop as low as 15ºC, and even lower at night. This is during the **dry season**, which runs roughly from November to April, when if you intend to go into the mountains it's advisable to pack something warmer than a T-shirt. If you visit Cuba in the summer, and more broadly between May and October, considered the **wet season**, expect it to rain on at least a couple of days of a two-week holiday. Don't let this put you off, though: although it comes down hard and fast, rain rarely stays for very long in Cuba, and the clouds soon break to allow sunshine through to dry everything out. Eastern Cuba tends to be hotter and more humid during this part of the year whilst the temperature in the area around Trinidad and Sancti Spíritus also creeps above the national average. September and October are the most threatening months of the annual **hurricane** season that runs from June to November. Compared to other Caribbean islands and some Central American countries, Cuba holds up relatively well even in the fiercest of hurricanes, though rural areas are more vulnerable.

The **peak tourist season** in Cuba runs roughly from December to March and July to August. Prices and crowds are most rampant in high summer when the holiday season for Cubans gets underway. As much of the atmosphere of the smaller resorts is generated by tourists, Cuban and foreign, out of season they can seem somewhat dull – although you'll benefit from lower prices. Compared to the all-out celebrations in other countries, **Christmas** in Cuba is a low-key affair. For a long time it was banned on anti-religious grounds and even now the festivities are confined predominantly to the hotels. **New Year's Eve**, also the eve of the anniversary of the revolution, is much more fervently celebrated and a better time for experiencing party spirit. The cities, however, particularly Havana and Santiago, are always buzzing and offer good value for money all year round. For festivals, July and August are the best times to be in Havana and Santiago, while the capital is also enlivened in November by the Latin American International Film Festival.

CLIMATE CHART: HAVANA				
	Average daily maximum temperature		Average monthly rainfall	
	°C	°F	mm	inches
January	25	78	71	2.8
February	25	78	46	1.8
March	27	80	46	1.8
April	29	84	58	2.3
May	29	85	119	4.7
June	30	87	165	6.5
July	32	89	125	4.9
August	32	89	135	5.3
September	30	87	150	5.9
October	29	84	173	6.8
November	27	80	79	3.1
December	25	78	58	2.3

Part 1

Basics

Getting there from Britain and Ireland

Having come from relative obscurity in the early 1990s Cuba is now the fastest-growing tourist destination in the Caribbean, and for anyone in Britain and Ireland the choice of ways to get there has never been greater. With an ever-increasing number of travel agents, tour operators and airlines offering anything from flight-only to all-inclusive accommodation and travel packages, it pays to shop around.

Flights and fares

Flights to Cuba are gradually becoming cheaper but the majority still involve a change somewhere in Europe. It's certainly worth comparing prices, and the best place to start is with one of the **flight agents** listed on p.4. Though Cuba now regularly features in the brochures of all high-street travel agents, the experience of the smaller agents, particularly those specializing in Latin American destinations, such as Journey Latin America and South American Experience, gives them an edge over their better-known rivals. More familiar with the details specific to Cuba, such as airport departure tax and tourist cards (see "Visas and Red Tape", p.13), they can also usually find the cheapest flights. Other good sources of information include the classifieds section of London's *Time Out* magazine, the travel supplements in the Sunday broadsheets, Teletext and Ceefax.

Ticket prices and availability are of course affected by the season. This will differ from airline to airline but **high season** tends to be July, August, a week either side of Easter Sunday and, the most expensive of all, the last two weeks of December.

The only airline with **direct scheduled flights** to Cuba from Britain is **Cubana**, the national Cuban carrier, departing from London Gatwick for Havana on Tuesdays, Thursdays and Saturdays, with a stop en route in Cayo Largo on Tuesdays. Though Cubana tends to offer the least expensive flights on the market, it is notoriously unreliable (ranked lowest in a poll of fifty airlines in the *Guardian* and *Observer* travel awards in 1999), and you should be prepared for delays or, even more likely, over-booking. Overbooked passengers are normally provided with a hotel room until the next available flight, at least in Cuba, but Cubana does not have a good customer service record, and getting compensation can be a struggle. Return fares start at as little as £380 in low season and average out at about £450 in high season. British Airways flies once a week, on Saturdays, via Nassau in the Bahamas; tickets cost around £200 more than Cubana at peak times, though there is less of a mark-up in low season with return fares at between £450 and £550. If you need to be back home on a particular day this extra cost can easily be justified as countless hard-luck stories from Cubana passengers will testify.

Less convenient but better-value alternatives are the flights offered by **Iberia** and **Air France**. Iberia flies daily from London Heathrow and Manchester with a change of plane in Madrid, whilst on Monday, Thursday, Friday and Saturday Air France flies from London Heathrow or London City Airport to Paris, where another plane takes you on to Havana. Both airlines have return fares for between £400 and £500 for most of the year, with the glaring exception of late December when a ticket is more likely to cost you £800 or more. Finally, you could always try **Aeroflot**, which flies on Wednesday and Saturday to Havana via Moscow, though a ticket is likely to cost in the region of £550.

AIRLINES

Aeroflot ☎ 020/7355 2233.
Air France ☎ 0845/0845 111; *www.airfrance.fr.*
British Airways ☎ 0345/222111;
www.british-airways.com.

Cubana ☎ 020/7734 1165; *www.cubana.cu.*
Iberia ☎ 020/7830 0011; *www.iberia.com.*

FLIGHT AND DISCOUNT AGENTS

Flightbookers, 177–178 Tottenham Court Rd, London W1P 0LX ☎ 020/7757 2444; *www.ebookers.com.* Low fares on an extensive offering of scheduled flights.

Interchange, Interchange House, 27 Stafford Rd, Croydon, Surrey CR0 4NG ☎ 020/8681 3612; *www.interchange.uk.com.* Specialists in package holidays and flight-only deals for independent travellers.

Journey Latin America, 12 & 13 Heathfield Terrace, London W4 4JE ☎ 020/8747 8315; 28–30 Barton Arcade, 2nd Floor, 51–63 Deansgate, Manchester M3 2BH ☎ 0161/832 1441; *www.journeylatinamerica.co.uk.* Well versed in the various flight deals to Cuba and usually able to dig out some of the best-value flights on the market.

The London Flight Centre, 131 Earl's Court Rd, London SW5 9RH ☎ 020/7244 6411; 47 Notting Hill Gate, London W11 3JS ☎ 020/7727 4290; Shop 33, The Broadway Centre, Hammersmith tube, London W6 9YE ☎ 020/8748 6777. Long-established agent dealing in discount flights.

North South Travel, Moulsham Mill Centre, Parkway, Chelmsford, Essex CM2 7PX ☎ 01245/608 291; *www.nstravel.demon.co.uk.* Friendly, competitive travel agency, offering discounted fares worldwide – profits are used to support projects in the developing world, especially the promotion of sustainable tourism.

South American Experience, 47 Causton St, Pimlico, London SW1P 4AT ☎ 020/7976 6908; *www.sax.mcmail.com.* Experts in travel all over Latin America who can arrange internal Cuban flights as well as the transatlantic crossing.

STA Travel, 86 Old Brompton Rd, London SW7 3LH; 117 Euston Rd, London NW1 2SX; ☎ 020/7361 6262; *www.statravel.co.uk.* Worldwide specialists in low-cost flights and tours for students and under-26s, though other customers welcome. Dozens of branches throughout the UK, and over 200 offices abroad.

Trailfinders, 42–50 Earl's Court Rd, London W8 6FT ☎ 020/7938 3366 or 7937 5400; *www.trailfinders.com.* One of the best-informed and most efficient agents for independent travellers, with offices throughout the UK.

Travel Cuts, 295a Regent St, London W1R 7YA ☎ 020/7255 2082; *www.travelcuts.co.uk.* Budget, student and youth travel and round-the-world tickets, with offices in London and abroad.

The Travel Bug, 125 Gloucester Rd, London SW7 4SF ☎ 020/7835 2000; 597 Cheetham Hill Rd, Manchester M8 5EJ ☎ 0161/721 4000; *www.flynow.com.* Large range of discounted tickets.

Usit Campus, 52 Grosvenor Gardens, London SW1W 0AG ☎ 0870/240 1010; *www.usitcampus.co.uk.* Student/youth travel specialists, with branches all over Britain, some of them in YHA shops and on university campuses.

Air France also flies from **regional airports**, namely Birmingham, Glasgow, Manchester, Newcastle, Edinburgh, Southampton, Teeside and Humberside. Iberia and British Airways offer excellent-value connections from Aberdeen, Edinburgh and Glasgow, amongst other places.

There are also a number of **charter operators and airlines**, such as **Airtours** (☎ 01706/240033) and **Monarch** (☎ 01582/400 000), flying predominantly to Varadero or Holguín as part of an inclusive accommodation package, but sometimes offering flight-only fares to fill seats. These

are usually cheaper, if you can get them, but offer very little flexibility in terms of return dates.

Packages and tours

A high proportion of visitors to Cuba are on **package holidays**, a hassle-free and relatively inexpensive alternative to paying separately for your flight, accommodation and transfers. Packages work best for anyone happy to stay at the same resort for the entire two weeks, the timescale on which most deals are based, but some include

Captivating Cuba, 26 Crown Rd, St Margarets, Twickenham, Middlesex TW1 3EE ☎020/8891 2222. Specialist branch of Travelcoast Ltd. offering mostly resort-based packages but also tailor-made tours and a seven-day tour of Havana and Pinar del Río.

Exodus, 9 Weir Rd, London SW12 0LT ☎020/8675 5550; *www.exodus.co.uk*. Smoothly run and professionally packaged holidays with welcome raw edges from this experienced adventure holiday specialist. Highlights include the two-week biking holidays covering the best of the east, including some strenuous biking in the Sierra Maestra.

Gane & Marshall, 98 Crescent Rd, New Barnet, Herts EN4 9RJ ☎020/8441 9592; *www.ganeandmarshall.co.uk*. Organized tours and tailor-made itineraries starting at £750 from this specialist in Cuba, Ecuador and Venezuela. They can arrange cycling, trekking and cultural or historical tours.

Havanatour, 3 Wyllyotts Place, Potters Bar, Herts EN6 2HN ☎01707/646463. One of the longest-established Cuban state-run tour operators with branches all round the island and one of the most extensive ranges of resort-based stays. Also offers tailor-made packages as well as special-interest tours including cycling, salsa and birdwatching.

The Holiday Place, 240 West End Lane, London NW6 1LG ☎020/7431 0670. Escorted fourteen-day tours of the island taking in an impressive range of the island's major attractions plus shorter, four-night tours and a wide selection of all-inclusive resort holidays.

Interchange, Interchange House, 27 Stafford Rd, Croydon, Surrey CR0 4NG ☎020/8681 3612; *www.interchange.uk.com*. Specialist in multi-hotel holidays and tailor-made itineraries, with a catalogue of over two dozen hotels across the island.

Journey Latin America, 12 & 13 Heathfield Terrace, London W4 4JE ☎020/8747 8315;

28-30 Barton Arcade, 2nd Floor, 51–63 Deansgate, Manchester M3 2BH ☎0161/832 1441; *www.journeylatinamerica.co.uk*. Very well established specialist in Latin American travel, offering reliable and well thought-out escorted group tours and individual itineraries. Detailed fourteen-night tours for individuals covering the western half of Cuba or island-wide group tours.

Progressive Tours, 12 Porchester Place, Marble Arch, London W2 2BS ☎020/7262 1676. The emphasis is on grassroots visits, including study tours designed to provide close contact with Cuban people. It can also arrange more traditional but very reasonably priced seven-day or two-week hotel-based holidays.

Regal Holidays, 22 High St, Sutton, Ely, Cambs CB6 2RB ☎01353/778096; *www.regal-diving.co.uk*. Accomplished scuba diving specialists operating in an excellent choice of locations including remote María La Gorda in western Pinar del Río, Cayo Largo, and the Península de Ancón near Trinidad.

Regent Holidays, 15 John St, Bristol BS1 2HR ☎0117/921 1711; *www.regent-holidays.co.uk*. Cycling holidays and coach tours including a nature-based tour of the Sierra Maestra.

South American Experience, 47 Causton St, Pimlico, London SW1P 4AT ☎020/7976 6908; *www.sax.mcmail.com*. Well-priced deals on flights and hotels with an emphasis on good deals for independent travellers. The staff have a down-to-earth approach and are in touch with the unique aspects of travel in Cuba.

Special Places, Brock Travel Ltd., 4 The White House, Beacon Rd, Crowborough, East Sussex TN6 1AB ☎01892/661157; *www.specialplaces.co.uk*. Tailor-made holidays tending towards the more traditional package-holiday format but more flexible than the mainstream operators. Ready-made itineraries include a one-week cigar tour and an all-inclusive sailing yacht cruise.

---

day-trips to locations around the island. They range from all-inclusives – where one price covers everything (theoretically, at least – see p.30) from meals and unlimited drinks to hotel nightlife and entertainment – to self-catering options.

Most of the four- and five-star hotels in Varadero, the package-holiday capital of Cuba, operate on an all-inclusive basis, whilst the self-catering apartments tend to be at the less sophisticated end of the market. Increasingly popular are two-

AIRLINES AND OPERATORS IN IRELAND

AIRLINES

Aer Lingus ☎ 01/705 3333; Northern Ireland ☎ 0645/737 747.

Air France ☎ 01/844 5633.

British Airways ☎ 0141/222 2345; Northern Ireland ☎ 0345/222 111.

British Midland ☎ 01/283 8833; Northern Ireland ☎ 0345/554 554.

Iberia ☎ 01/677 9846.

AGENTS AND TOUR OPERATORS

Apex Travel, 59 Dame St, Dublin 2 ☎ 01/671 5933. Specialists in worldwide airfares with some reasonable deals to Cuba.

Cubatravel (GET Holidays), 11 South Anne's St, Dublin 2 ☎ 01/671 3422. The most experienced agent in Ireland for holidays and flight deals to and in Cuba. The emphasis is on flexibility and independent travel, though they do offer resort-based packages, with a variety of interests catered for including scuba diving. This is also the only agent in Ireland able to issue tourist cards on the spot.

Exodus, Colette Pearson Travel, 64 South William St, Dublin 2 ☎ 01/677 1029; *www.exodus.co.uk*. See p.5.

Trailfinders, 4–5 Dawson St, Dublin 2 ☎ 01/677 7888; *www.trailfinders.com*. One of the best-informed and most efficient agents for independent travellers.

Usit Now, Fountain Centre, College St, Belfast BT1 6ET ☎ 01232/324 073; 19 Aston Quay, Dublin 2 ☎ 01/602 1777 or 677 8117; *www.usitnow.ie*. Student and youth specialist, with branches throughout Ireland.

World Travel Centre, 35 Pearse St, Dublin 2 ☎ 01/671 7155. Good deals with all the major airlines flying to Cuba via else-where in Europe.

---

week packages which offer a seven-day tour of the country, staying overnight in hotels around the island, followed by a second week relaxing by the pool at your chosen resort.

For a two-week all-inclusive package in July or August expect to pay upwards of £850 per person, whilst room-only prices start around the £450 mark. Self-catering deals, which are much harder to come by, cost between £400 and £500. All of these options include a return flight and transfer to and from the airport.

People looking for a more adventurous stay or those with specific requirements and preferences might prefer to arrange a trip through a **specialist tour operator**, many of which offer trips combining hikes with town visits and avoiding the main tourist resorts. Alternatively, there are trips that focus on a particular **activity**, such as diving or cycling, put together by operators with years of experience and the kind of in-depth knowledge necessary to make the most of your time in the country.

Flights from Ireland

No airline flies nonstop from Ireland to Cuba. This means you'll have to change planes, usually in London, Paris or Madrid. **Aer Lingus** and **British Midland** are the principal carriers to London, from where there are flights on to Cuba with **British Airways** or **Cubana** (see p.3). Return flights to Havana from Dublin combining Aer Lingus and British Airways flights start at around £540. Alternatively you can make the whole journey with a single airline. **Iberia** flies from Dublin to Havana via Madrid for as little as £430, whilst **Air France** offers similar fares for its flights via Paris. The British Airways equivalent is somewhat more expensive with standard prices at around £580.

The relatively small size of the market and the comparatively low demand for flights to Cuba from Ireland means that most flight agents are unable to issue **tourist cards** as part of their packages. The Cuban authorities supply agents with tourist cards only if the agent can meet their minimum number requirements, and until now only Cubatravel in Dublin (see box above) has been able to do that. Other agents can nonetheless still sell you the flight and in some cases obtain a tourist card for you, either through Cubatravel or through the Cuban authorities themselves, but otherwise you will have to visit the Cuban Embassy yourself.

Getting there from North America

Since the United States continues to maintain a Cold War-era embargo on trade with Cuba (see p.471), US citizens are not allowed, by their own government, to travel there freely. The basic idea behind the prohibition is to keep the Cuban economy from benefiting from its most precious and obvious resource – the beauty of the island – and so to prevent what Washington sees as an intolerable situation: a successful Communist country, less than ninety miles off the coast of Florida, thriving on US tourist dollars. That said, it is actually possible for US citizens to go to Cuba, and something like 150,000 of them do so every year.

Canadians, of course are not directly affected by the US embargo and are as free to travel to Cuba as to any other country. In fact, there are regular flights from Toronto and Montréal to Havana on Cubana, as well as on a number of charter carriers. Travelling via Canada is one of the obvious alternatives for US citizens; nationals of other countries can also travel from Canada without problem.

Travelling from the US

The majority of US visitors to Cuba go legally by obtaining a "licence" from the US Treasury Department (the procedure for this is outlined overleaf). There is something of an ongoing tug-of-war between the conservative and the liberal factions of the US government about the provisions and enforcement of the embargo, but at the present time it is not as difficult as it used to be to make a case that you should be given permission to travel to Cuba. Journalists, businesspeople and official guests of the Cuban government have been getting licences for some time, but increasingly it is possible to get one if you intend to engage in some sort of study or humanitarian mission during your stay.

For everyone else who wants to visit Cuba for reasons less acceptable to the US government, like tourism, a degree of ingenuity is required. Usually this means doing little more than travelling via a third country, and there are a number of well-established routes to choose from should you decide to do this: including travel via other Caribbean islands, Canada or Mexico. The Cuban authorities make it easier for US citizens to get around the travel ban by agreeing to requests not to stamp the passports of American tourists entering or leaving Cuba (stamping their tourist cards instead).

However, if you are a US national, be aware that you will be operating outside the law in some sense by going to Cuba without a licence. It is probably a good idea to find out exactly what the restrictions are, and the possible consequences to you of ignoring them, before you decide to make the trip.

Since a key element of the economic embargo is the ban on US citizens conducting business with Cuba – which of course extends to tourists spending money on the island – one of the first obstacles Americans wishing to make the journey will encounter is the total absence of airlines, travel agents and tour operators in the US engaged in the business of organizing trips to Cuba. For businesses in the US, making such arrangements, even for travel through a third country, is illegal.

This means that arranging your trip from the US will involve a long-distance call or two to an airline, travel agent or tour operator in another country,

Obtaining permission to travel to Cuba

If you think you have a case for being granted permission to travel, perhaps as a journalist, student or on some sort of humanitarian mission, contact the **Licensing Division**, Office of Foreign Assets Control, US Department of the Treasury, 1500 Pennsylvania Avenue NW, Washington DC 20220 ☎ 202/622-2480; *www.treas.gov/ofac*. You can also get information from the Cuban government at the **Cuban Interests Section** at 2630 16th St NW, Washington DC 20009 ☎ 202/797-8518; or the **Cuban Consulate Office** at 2639 16th St NW, Washington DC 20009 ☎ 202/797-8609. You can also contact one of the specialist tour operators in the US for help in getting your licence.

most likely in Canada, Mexico, or one of the other Caribbean islands. Of course, you can also take a less direct route through Europe or South America if you like.

If you do succeed in obtaining a licence to travel to Cuba, you can call **Marazul Tours** in New Jersey or Miami (see box on p.10) about booking a place on one of the permitted direct charter flights to Havana, but if you don't have a licence, don't bother calling them, as they are prohibited by law from advising you on getting around the restrictions. There is little possibility of getting bargain fares, but then it may be worth paying a little more for the convenience of taking a direct flight to Havana. Marazul Tours runs flights from Miami for US$300 and from New York for US$625. Note that non-US citizens cannot use these routes if they are travelling as tourists or without official approval.

Flights from Canada, Mexico and the Caribbean

Regardless of how you travel or where you buy your ticket, fares to Cuba will vary depending on the **season** – although perhaps not as much as to other destinations in the Caribbean, which are more attuned to the rhythms of the US tourist industry. Seasonal definitions vary from airline to airline, but the period from Christmas to Easter, or mid-December to mid-April, is generally classified as the **high season**. In the **low season** it is possible to get APEX **fares** from Montréal or Toronto to Havana on **Cubana** for as little as US$210, though the published full fare is about US$530. While Cubana is the only airline with regularly scheduled flights to Cuba from Canada, there are a number of charter companies flying the route, so there are alternatives to check out. Since the charter operators are not allowed to deal directly with the public, to find out about these flights you must go through a travel agent.

The following are sample APEX **fares** for round-trip travel from Mexican and Caribbean cities to Havana: Mexico City (US$400); Cancún (US$280); Kingston or Montego Bay (US$226); Nassau (US$179). Flights to Nassau in the Bahamas (the least indirect route from the US for blockade-busting Americans or non-US citizens who want to move onto Cuba from the States) are frequent and quite cheap, starting as low as US$150. From there it is a simple step to make your own connection to one of the daily Cubana flights to Havana.

Shopping for tickets

Since it is essentially just another Caribbean destination for the rest of the (non-US) world, there are occasionally **cheap flights** to Cuba. As with travel elsewhere, apart from special promotions advertised from time to time, the cheapest of the airlines' published fares is usually an **APEX** ticket, although this will carry certain restrictions: you have to book – and pay – 7, 14 or 21 days before departure, spend at least 7 days abroad (maximum stay 3 months), and you tend to get penalized if you change your schedule.

Again as with travel to other parts of the world, you can normally cut costs further by going through a **discount travel agent**, who in addition to dealing with cut-price flights may also offer complementary services such as travel insurance, car rental and tours. With all reduced-rate operations, withdrawal penalties are high (check the refund policy). Local travel agents in Mexico or on other islands of the Caribbean should also be able to help in finding decent fares to Cuba, and charter flights from other tourist destinations, like the Cayman Islands or the Turks and Caicos Islands, may be offered regularly at certain times of the year.

For US citizens attempting to dodge the blockade, it is even more essential to find a travel agent outside America to help arrange your trip. Canadian tour operators can be contacted directly for information on packages and charter flights, but they prefer not to actually make bookings

directly with members of the US public, to avoid
incurring the wrath of angry US legislators. So the
best strategy is to work through a Canadian travel agent, either one that has a history of getting
good deals to other parts of the world, or one of
those that specializes in travel to Cuba. Another
source of travel agents in Canada is the Saturday
travel section of the *Toronto Star* newspaper,
which has regular listings and is widely available
in the US.

Packages and tours

Although flights from Canada, Mexico and the
Caribbean are frequent and quite reasonably priced,
and it is surprisingly easy to explore Cuba independently, you might well be tempted by the comfort
and convenience of a vacation **package**. If so, there
are many all-inclusive deals available, comprising
flights, transfers, accommodation and airport taxes.
If you are looking for packages for departures from

Canada, be advised that you'll need to go through
a travel agent, as most tour operators are not permitted by Canadian law to deal directly with the
public. While some operators take this very literally
and won't even speak with you, others will at least
give you an idea of their services if you call.

Many of the Canadian tours are geared around
lying on a beach for a week or two, but if this is
not your idea of a trip to Cuba, there are alternatives. A few specialist operators offer themantical-
ly designed **tours**, with itineraries geared around
special interests. This is particularly so with tour
operators in the US, as those groups who do
organize trips have, by definition, to be engaged
in one of the specific activities, like study tours,
permitted by the US government. The definition
of "studying" Cuba on one of these tours can be
quite broad, however, and if you check into
what's available, you may find that it's possible
to educate and vacate at the same time. US

TOUR OPERATORS

IN CANADA

Canadian-Cuban Friendship Association
☎ 416/742-6931; *www.lefca.com/ccfatoronto*. A non-profit NGO volunteer organization setting up exchanges in areas such as health, education and culture, as well as material aid to Cuba.

Hola Sun Holidays ☎ 905/882-9445; *www.holasunholidays.com*. A company handling bookings through travel agents only for eight destinations in Cuba.

Sunquest Vacations ☎ 416/482-3333; *www.sunquest.ca*. Takes bookings through travel agents only, mainly for beach holidays, but packages that combine resort stays with trips to Havana are available, as are flight-only options.

World of Vacations ☎ 416/620-8687 or 1-800/661-8881; *www.worldofvacations.com*. Offers packages to beach resorts only.

Worldwide Quest Nature Tours ☎ 416/633-5666 or 1-800/387-1483; *www.worldwide-quest.com*. Mountain resort and lodge stays for hiking or cycling tours with ecotourist agendas.

IN THE USA

Center for Cuban Studies ☎ 212/242-0559; *www.cubaupdate.org*. An excellent information resource, the Center arranges all-inclusive study tours on special interests such as the environment, education, museums and culture, and will even help you to plan an individual trip of your own. It also sends regular expeditions to the island on humanitarian missions, such as administering eye tests and distributing glasses, and arranges trips for professionals from a variety of fields, including lawyers, artists, architects, and filmmakers (who can attend the international film festival; see p.46). Prices from $1300.

Global Exchange ☎ 415/558-9490; *www.globalexchange.org*. A not-for-profit organization that leads "reality tours" to Cuba, giving participants the chance to learn about the country while seeing it. Check out the detailed Web site for information on "travel seminars" looking at issues such as culture, music, health, religion or agriculture in Cuba, to sign up for a class on Cuban rhythms or Spanish language, or book a place on a bicycle tour. Prices start at around $1000.

Marazul Tours ☎ 201/319-9670 or 305/644-0255. Books air tickets on charter flights, for the officially sanctioned, to Havana from Miami or New York, and can arrange hotel accommodation.

IN MEXICO

AS Tours ☎ 52/5-575-9814. Spanish-speaking agency with flights and packages.

Mexicana de Aviacion ☎ 52/5-448-0990; *www.mexicana.com*. Airline also arranges tours and packages.

Tip's Travel ☎ 52/5-584-1557; *ttravel@net-service.com.mx*. Mexico City-based company arranging flights and packages.

---

citizens who do obtain a "licence" from the Treasury Department to travel to Cuba (see p.8) can arrange their trips through one of the US companies or NGOs listed above, but the default option seems to be Marazul Tours, which actually does the booking for a number of different groups and has recently started selling tickets on charter flights with direct service from New York or Miami to Havana.

By sea

Out of deference, or fear, of the US blockade, very few **cruise ships** stop at Cuban ports. It is, however, quite possible to sail by private yacht or cruiser to a number of spots on the island.

With a history of confrontation at sea between Cuban exile groups based in Florida and the Cuban maritime authorities, obviously just turning up unannounced can be a very bad and even dangerous idea. However, there are a number of ways to alert the proper Cuban authorities of your plans and if you work things out in advance, you could arrive at the Marina Hemingway in Havana, or at one of the many other ports around Cuba.

One good place to start gathering detailed information about this option is a book called *The Cruising Guide to Cuba*, written by Simon Charles and published by Cruising Guide Publications (US$24.95).

Getting there from Australia and New Zealand

Cuba is hardly a **bargain destination** from Australasia. There are no direct flights from Australia or New Zealand, so you'll have to take a flight to Canada, the Caribbean, Central or South America, Europe, or the US (but only if you have permission from the US government to travel to Cuba; see "Getting there from North America" for details), and pick up onward connections from there.

The least expensive and most straightforward **route** is via Tokyo to Mexico City, from where there are frequent flights to Havana. Otherwise, Canadian Airlines has six flights each week from Sydney to Toronto, from where you can take connections to Havana via Mexico City.

If you're planning to see Cuba as part of a longer trip, **round-the-world** (RTW) tickets are worth considering, and are generally better

value than a simple return flight.. Whatever kind of ticket you're after, your first call should be one of the **specialist travel agents** listed in the box overleaf. If you're a **student** or **under 26**, you may be able to undercut some of the prices given here; STA is a good place to start.

Fares and air passes

The **fares** quoted below are for travel during **low season**, and exclude airport taxes; flying at peak times (primarily Dec to mid-Jan) can add substantially to these prices.

From Australia, Japan Airlines has flights from Melbourne and Sydney to Tokyo (where you stay overnight), then on to Mexico City and Havana for A$2499. More expensive still, Canadian Airlines flies from Melbourne/Sydney to Honolulu, on to Vancouver and Toronto, then connecting with Mexico City to Havana for A$3475. **From New Zealand**, Air New Zealand flies from Auckland to Mexico City, with connections on to Havana, starting at around NZ$2578. Lan Chile in conjunction with Qantas also has flights from Auckland to Papeete and Santiago and on to Havana for NZ$3850.

RTW tickets

Given these fares and routings, **RTW tickets** that take in Canadian or Latin American destinations are especially worth considering; you can then take an add-on flight to Cuba from there.

Your choice of route will depend on where else you want to go besides Cuba, but here are a few sample itineraries to whet your appetite: starting

AIRLINES

Air New Zealand Australia ☎ 02/9223 4666; New Zealand ☎ 09/336 2424; *www.airnz.com*.

Canadian Airlines Australia ☎ 1300/655 767; *www.cdnair.com*.

Japan Airlines Australia ☎ 02/9272 1111 or 03/9654 2733; *www.jal.co.jp*.

Lan Chile Australia ☎ 03/9920 3881 or 1300/361 400; *www.lanchile.com*.

Qantas Australia ☎ 02/9691 3636 or 03/9285 3000; New Zealand ☎ 09/357 8900; *www.qantas.com.au*.

DISCOUNT AGENTS

Anywhere Travel, 345 Anzac Parade, Sydney ☎ 02/9663 0411; *anywhere@ozemail.com.au*.

Budget Travel, 16 Fort St, Auckland ☎ 09/366 0061; other branches around the city (toll-free ☎ 0800/808 040).

Destinations Unlimited, Level 7, FAI Building, 220 Queen St, Auckland ☎ 09/373 4033.

Flight Centres, Level 11, 33 Berry St, Sydney; 19 Bourke St, Melbourne; plus other branches nationwide ☎ 13/1600; National Bank Towers, 205–225 Queen St, Auckland ☎ 09/309 6171; and other branches countrywide. *www.flightcentre.com.au*.

Northern Gateway, 22 Cavenagh St, Darwin ☎ 08/8941 1394; *oztravel@norgate.com.au*.

STA Travel, 855 George St, Sydney; 208 Swanston St, Melbourne; other offices in state capitals and major universities ☎ 13/1776,

fastfare telesales ☎ 1300/360 960; Travellers' Centre, 10 High St, Auckland ☎ 09/309 0458, fastfare telesales ☎ 09/366 6673, toll-free ☎ 0800/874 773; and other offices countrywide. *www.statravel.com.au*.

Thomas Cook, 175 Pitt St, Sydney; 257 Collins St, Melbourne; branches in other state capitals ☎ 13/1771 or toll-free 1800/063 913; 96-98 Anzac Ave, Auckland ☎ 09/379 3920. *www.thomascook.com.au*.

Topdeck Travel, 65 Grenfell St, Adelaide ☎ 08/8232 7222.

Travel Direct Pty Ltd, Level 3, 349 Queen St, Brisbane ☎ 07/3221 4933.

Travel Shop, Suite 13, 890 Canning Highway, Perth ☎ 08/9316 3888 or 1800/108 108.

Tymtro Travel, Level 3, 355 Bulwara Rd, Sydney ☎ 1300/652 969.

SPECIALIST AGENTS AND TOUR OPERATORS

Adventure World, 73 Walker St, Sydney ☎ 02/9956 7766; elsewhere ☎ 1300/363 055; *www.adventureworld.com.au*.

Caribbean Destinations, Level 1, Rialto Tower

North, 525 Collins St, Melbourne ☎ 03/9618 1128; elsewhere ☎ 1800/354 104.

Contours Travel, Level 1, 84 William St, Melbourne ☎ 03/9670 6900.

---

from **Sydney**, you could fly to Auckland to Papeete to Los Angeles to London to Frankfurt to Bangkok to Sydney (from A$2799); from **Melbourne**, flying to Bangkok to Rome to Boston to Honolulu to Christchurch to Melbourne (from A$2799); or, starting from **Perth**, flying to Bangkok to London to Rio de Janeiro to Los Angeles to Auckland to Perth (from A$3799). **From New Zealand**, you could fly from Auckland to Nadi to Vancouver to Miami to London to Bangkok to Brisbane and back to Auckland; fares for this route start at around NZ$4050.

Packages and tours

Package holidays from Australia and New Zealand to Cuba are few and far between, although some

operators (see "Specialist agents and tour operators" above) can arrange worthwhile deals. To give you some idea, Contours Travel has accommodation plus meal packages starting around A$325/$NZ410 for three days in Havana, while Adventure World has similar three-day holidays in Santiago de Cuba for A$280/NZ$350, or twelve-day holidays taking in Havana, Santiago de Cuba, Camagüey, Trinidad and Matanzas costing upwards of A$2025/$NZ2565 (based on per person three-star accommodation and low-season airfares from Australia). Another operator, Caribbean Destinations, also has reasonable deals, including a high-end airfare and accommodation package at around A$3490/NZ$4420 for seven nights in Havana.

Visas and red tape

Citizens of most Western countries must have a ten-year passport, valid for at least six months after your departure from Cuba, plus a tourist card (*tarjeta de turista*) to enter Cuba. Tourist cards are valid for a standard thirty days and although you can buy one from the Cuban consulate you will get immeasurably swifter and more efficient service if you buy it from your tour operator or travel agent when you purchase your flight. The charge in the UK is £15, in Australia A$35, in New Zealand NZ$44.

US CITIZENS

Strangely enough, the letter of US law does not actually prohibit US citizens from being in Cuba, just from spending money there. In practical terms, of course, this amounts to a ban on travel, by all except those approved and "licensed" by the US government. While many Americans see the embargo as cruel and unusual, or at least dated, there are no signs of it being lifted any time soon. As recently as 1996 it was in fact tightened, thanks to the power exerted by wealthy Cuban exiles in the US, combined with that of old Cold Warriors in Congress, like Senator Jesse Helms. The Helms-Burton Act of 1996, signed into law by President Clinton despite his objections – for reasons of election-year politics – allows for fines of up to US$50,000 and the confiscation of property of US citizens who visit Cuba without permission and at their own expense. This is in addition to the already standing threats contained in the Trading with the Enemy Act, which make fines of up to US$250,000 and prison terms of up to ten years theoretically possible. This is why it is more than a good idea for American citizens to get their hands on the most up-to-date information about the embargo and its enforcement before deciding to ignore it. For the lowdown on the current situation, check out the update offered on the Web site of the Center for Cuban Studies (*www.cubaupdate.org*) or talk to one of the groups organizing legal tours to the island. Things change quite often, depending on the direction of the prevailing political winds in the US. President Clinton's administration, for instance, actually took a number of steps to make it easier for Americans to visit Cuba legally, and also to send money or humanitarian aid to the country. The exact terms of the sanctions against Cuba are available from the US Treasury Department, Office of Foreign Assets Control in Washington DC (☎202/622-2480; *www.treas.gov/ofac*). Another detailed US government Web site, dedicated as much to defending as to explaining the regulations governing travel to Cuba, is at *www.state.gov/www/regions/wha/cuba/index.html*.

TOURIST CARDS

American citizens can travel to Cuba on **tourist cards** purchased in Canada, Mexico or other countries, and the Cuban authorities will on request stamp the card instead of your passport on entering and leaving Cuba. Most US citizens who travel to Cuba illegally do not bring the stamped tourist card back to the US with them, as this in itself can serve as proof of having been to Cuba – as, of course, can airline tickets, souvenirs, cigars, and photos of yourself at recognizable monuments. The kitsch value of any of these objects to you may pale in comparison to their meaning to zealous US immigration officers with their minds on the heavy fines and even jail time stipulated in the regulations for embargo busters. Strangely enough, non-US citizens can get tourist cards quite easily in the US, from the Cuban Consulate Office in Washington DC.

See "Getting there from North America", p.7, for more on travel to Cuba from the US.

Cuban bureaucracy

Cuba is a quagmire of bureaucracy. It is characterized by endless waiting, lost paperwork, low levels of competence and high levels of indifference, so dealing with any aspect of Cuban bureaucracy can feel like an unprecedented nightmare. Largely a product of an over-centralized system, it is often the case that the person with whom you are dealing has no authority over the situation so is powerless to help you anyway – their main function is to stand between the public and whoever is actually in control who, incidentally, is always out at lunch.

Every aspect of life in Cuba is governed by state laws and directives – this is how the revolution has managed to achieve its most laudable achievements, but these same laws can be extremely disadvantageous when you step outside the role assigned to you as a visitor in Cuba. Though you probably won't be affected during the course of a straightforward, trouble-free holiday, you are likely to encounter problems if you have to report a theft, renew a visa outside of Havana, change your visa status anywhere in the country, or visit areas not specifically designated as tourist regions.

Should you encounter problems, the first rule is to keep your cool. Getting cross will not impress anyone – Cubans have been coping with this situation for years and, understandably, don't see why you should get any special treatment. The second rule is to always make sure you leave at least double the time suggested by Cuban authorities to resolve a matter. Do both these things and you'll make life much easier for yourself.

Once in Cuba, you can **renew** a tourist card for another thirty days (bringing the total stay allowed to sixty days) for a fee of $25. Immigration offices in various provinces are listed throughout the guide, but you will find it far easier to renew your card in Havana, where the immigration officer in the *Hotel Habana Libre* (see p.76) will process it in a matter of minutes.

Should you wish to stay longer as a tourist you will have to leave Cuban territory and return with a new tourist card. Many people do this by island-hopping to other Caribbean destinations or Mexico and getting another tourist card from the Cuban consulate there.

Incidentally, the passport number listed on the tourist card must correspond to the number on the passport you bring with you to Cuba. So if you get a new passport for some reason, be sure to get a new tourist card as well.

You must fill out on the tourist form the address of where you first intend to stay on arrival in Cuba. Although you can put the name of a registered *casa particular* you will pass through customs much more smoothly if you have entered the name of a state hotel. If you don't have any address you may have to pay on the spot for three nights' accommodation in a hotel of the state's choosing. Putting the address of a friend is similarly likely to cause you – and them – problems. You must also be able to show an onward airline ticket when you enter the country.

CUBAN CONSULATES AND EMBASSIES ABROAD

Australia: Consulate-General, 18 Mainwaring Ave, Sydney ☎02/9311 4611; fax 9311 1255.

Canada: Embassy, 388 Main St, Ottawa, Ontario K1S 1E3 ☎613/563-0141.

Consulate-General, 5353 Dundas St West, Toronto, Ontario M9B 6H8 ☎416/234-8181.

Consulate-General, 1415 Pine Ave West, Montréal, Québec H3B 1B2 ☎514/843-8897.

Mexico: Embassy, Presidente Masarik 554, Colonia Polanco, 11560 Mexico, DF ☎52/5-280-8039.

UK: Embassy, 167 High Holborn, London WC1 ☎020/7836 3895; 24-hour visa and information service ☎0891/880 820.

USA: Cuban Interests Section, 2630 16th St NW, Washington DC 20009 ☎202/797-8518.

Consulate Office, 2639 16th St NW, Washington DC 20009 ☎202/797-8609.

FOREIGN CONSULATES AND EMBASSIES IN CUBA	
Canada: Embassy, Calle 30 no. 518, Miramar, Playa, Havana ☎ 7/24-12-22; fax 24-20-44.	**USA**: Special Interests Section, Calle Calzada y L, Vedado, Havana ☎ 7/ 33-35-31; fax 33-37-00.
United Kingdom: Embassy, Calle 34 no. 702–704, Miramar, Playa, Havana ☎ 7/24-17-71; fax 24-81-04.	There are no consulates or embassies for Australia or New Zealand; citizens are advised to go to either the Canadian or UK embassies.

Working and student visas

Anyone planning to **work** in Cuba must have the relevant visas organized before they arrive. You will need to have ready the name of the organization that will be sponsoring and be answerable for you ready to fill in on your form.

Journalists need to apply for a special journalist visa. The Cuban authorities advise you to apply at the consulate in your country of departure, and indeed broadcast journalists must do so as it is prohibited to enter Cuba with unauthorized professional camera equipment. Print journalists may find it easier to enter the country on a tourist card and then apply to the International Press Centre in Havana (Calle 23 esq. 0 ☎ 7/32-74-91) to change their status, though this is not without its own problems (see box opposite). Similarly, **students** must have a student visa entitling them to stay in the country; these can be arranged through the Cuban consulate.

Insurance

Cuba's world-famous health service may be free for Cuban citizens, but it's funded at least partly by the growing number of foreigners who come here solely to take advantage of Cuban medical expertise. If you'd rather not pay through the nose for treatment that may be unavoidable, an insurance policy is pretty much essential.

In Britain and Ireland, most travel agents and tour operators have their own **insurance** packages which they will offer you with your flight or holiday. For a two-week stay you should expect a minimum cost of around £40 but premiums with the mainstream operators will be more like £60 for the same period of time. Both South American Experience (see p.5, and Journey Latin America (see p.5, offer comprehensive insurance packages. Good-value policies are also issued by Usit Campus or STA Travel (see p.4 for addresses) and the specialist operators listed overleaf.

Before buying an insurance policy, **North Americans** should check they're not already covered. Some homeowners' or renters' policies are valid on vacation, while most Canadians' provincial health plans typically provide limited overseas medical coverage. If you're not covered – or for additional precautions – you might want to contact a specialist travel insurance company; see the box or ask your travel agent for a recommendation.

INSURANCE COMPANIES

UK

Columbus Direct Insurance ☎020/7375 0011; *www.columbusdirect.co.uk.*
Endsleigh Insurance ☎020/7436 4451.

Marcus Hearne & Co Ltd ☎020/7739 3444.
Worldwide Travel Insurance Services Limited ☎01892/833 338; *www.wwtis.co.uk.*

CANADA

Desjardins Travel Insurance ☎1-800/463 7830.

STA Travel ☎1-800/777-0112.
Travel Guard Canada ☎715/345-0505.

AUSTRALIA AND NEW ZEALAND

AFTA ☎02/9956 4800 in Sydney; elsewhere ☎1800/066 758.
Cover More ☎02/9202 8000 in Sydney; elsewhere ☎1800/251 881.

Ready Plan Australia ☎02/9650 5700 in Sydney; elsewhere ☎1300/555 018; ☎0800/441 678 in New Zealand.

The cheapest coverage is currently with *STA Travel*, but they only sell policies to travellers who book their flights to Cuba with them as well. As with every other aspect of travel to Cuba, American companies cannot sell insurance for travel to the island.

In **Australia and New Zealand** travel insurance is put together by the airlines and specialist groups such as those listed below, in conjunction with insurance companies. Policies are broadly comparable in premium and coverage, though Ready Plan usually gives the best value for money. A typical policy for Cuba costs A$189/NZ$239 for one month.

Information and maps

eat. A trustworthy **map** is also a scarcity in Cuba, whilst street maps for anywhere other than the largest town in each province are unavailable.

Before you leave home, it's worth contacting the nearest branch of the **Cuban Tourist Board**, which has information on the country and maps that might come in handy. Similarly, the **Caribbean Tourism Organization** (*www.caribtourism.com*), based in Barbados with branches in Britain, the US and Canada, can help with general enquiries about travel to and in Cuba, one of the 32 member states of the organization set up to increase the value, volume and understanding of tourism flowing into the region.

Information

Currently there is no independent nationwide **tourist board** in Cuba and getting hold of both impartial and detailed tourist information can be difficult, particularly away from the heavily visited areas. Although the tourist guides published in Cuba up until now are widely available they tend to be sketchy and unreliable. The only tourist information network is **Infotur**, which has been whittled down to just two branches, both in Havana – at Obispo no. 358 e/ Habana y Compostela in Habana Vieja (☎7/33-33-33), and at 5ta. Ave. y 112 in Playa (☎7/24-70-36) – but also has desks in many

There is a disabling shortage of printed travel literature in Cuba and getting hold of any kind of **tourist information**, particularly outside of the major resorts, can be difficult. You should find out as much as you can before you leave, as printed information is often more readily available abroad. The **Internet** is a good place to start, the state-run site offering more information than any booklet you will find inside Cuba.

Be aware that all information outlets and travel agents in Cuba, like everything else, are run by the state and are unlikely to offer impartial advice on, for example, accommodation deals or places to

---

CUBAN TOURIST BOARD OFFICES ABROAD

Canada: 440 Blvd Rene Levesque, Suite 1105, Montréal H2Z 1V7 ☎514/875-8004; 55 Queen St East, Suite 705, Toronto M5C 2R6 ☎416/362-0700.

Mexico: Insurgentes Sur 421 y Aquascalientes, Complejo Aristos, Edificio B, Local 310, Mexico DF 06100 ☎52/5-574-9651.

UK: 154 Shaftesbury Ave, London WC2H 8JT ☎020/7240 6655; *cubatouristboard.london@virgin.net* (Mon–Fri 10am–7pm).

CARRIBEAN TOURISM ORGANIZATION

Britain: 42 Westminster Palace Gardens, Artillery Row, London SW1P 1RR ☎020/7222 4335.

Canada: Taurus House, 512 Duplex Ave, Toronto, Ontario, Canada M4R 2E3 ☎416/485 7827.

USA: 80 Broad St, 32nd Floor, New York, NY 10004 ☎212/635 9530.

MAP OUTLETS

As well as over-the-counter sales, most of the outlets listed below allow you to order and pay for maps by mail, over the phone and sometimes via the Internet.

AUSTRALIA AND NEW ZEALAND

Foreign Language Bookshop, 259 Collins St, Melbourne, VIC 3000 ☎03/9654 2883; *www.languages.com.au.*

Mapland, 372 Little Bourke St, Melbourne, VIC 3000 ☎03/9670 4383; *www.mapland.com.au.*

The Map Shop, 6 Peel St, Adelaide, SA 5000 ☎08/8231 2033.

Perth Map Centre, 884 Hay St, Perth, WA 6000 ☎08/9322 5733; *www.perthmap.com.au.*

Specialty Maps, 58 Albert St, Auckland ☎09/307 2217.

Travel Bookshop, 175 Liverpool St, Sydney, NSW 2000 ☎02/9261 8200.

UK AND IRELAND

Blackwell's Map and Travel Shop, 53 Broad St, Oxford OX1 3BQ ☎01865/792792; *bookshop.blackwell.co.uk.*

Daunt Books, 83 Marylebone High St, London W1M 3DE ☎020/7224 2295; fax 020/7224 6893; 193 Haverstock Hill, London NW3 4QL ☎020/7794 4006.

Easons Bookshop, 40 O'Connell St, Dublin 1 ☎01/873 3811.

Fred Hanna's Bookshop, 27–29 Nassau St, Dublin 2 ☎01/677 1255.

Heffers Map and Travel, 3rd Floor, 19 Sidney St, Cambridge CB2 3HL ☎01223/568467; *www.heffers.co.uk.*

Hodges Figgis Bookshop, 56–58 Dawson St, Dublin 2 ☎01/677 4754.

James Thin Melven's Bookshop, 29 Union St, Inverness IV1 1QA ☎01463/233500; *www.jthin.co.uk.*

John Smith and Sons, 57–61 St Vincent St, Glasgow G2 5TB ☎0141/221 7472; *www.johnsmith.co.uk.*

The Map Shop, 30a Belvoir St, Leicester, LE1 6QH ☎0116/2471400.

National Map Centre, 22–24 Caxton St, London SW1H 0QU ☎020/7222 2466; *www.mapsworld.com.*

Newcastle Map Centre, 55 Grey St, Newcastle upon Tyne, NE1 6EF ☎0191/261 5622; *nmc@enterprise.net.*

Stanfords, 12–14 Long Acre, London WC2E 9LP ☎020/7836 1321; Campus Travel, 52

hotels and at the José Martí International Airport. Concentrating on booking organized excursions, hotel room reservations and car rental, it has very little information on public transport, other than the Víazul bus service (see p.24), nor can it supply information on *paladares* or *casas particulares.* Despite these limitations, however, it is the best place to go for practical information, and the friendly staff are generally willing to try and help with all sorts of different queries, though they do try to steer visitors towards the tourist apparatus set up by the state.

There are also state-run **tourist travel agents**, principally Rumbos, Cubatur and Tour y Travel, which can supply you with general information on local attractions, advise on eating and enter-

tainment options, and book hotel rooms. You will find the office of at least one of them in most of the major resorts and largest towns and cities, whilst Rumbos and Cubatur have desks in most hotel lobbies. Each has its own set of excursions and tours, though the basic packages and prices differ very little.

Maps

Maps of Cuba are infrequently updated and there are large sections of the country for which there are no detailed maps at all. The exception is the *Guía de Carreteras,* the only available national road map, which also carries basic street maps for Havana and Varadero. It costs $6 and will prove invaluable if you plan to make any long-distance journeys around the

BASICS

Grosvenor Gardens, London SW1W 0AG
☎020/7730 1314; British Airways, 156 Regent
St, London W1R 5TA ☎020/7434 4744; 29 Corn
St, Bristol BS1 1HT ☎0117/929 9966;
sales@stanfords.co.uk.

The Travel Bookshop, 13–15 Blenheim
Crescent, London W11 2EE ☎020/7229 5260;
www.thetravelbookshop.co.uk.

Waterstone's, 91 Deansgate, Manchester, M3
2BW ☎0161/837 3000; *www.waterstones
-manchester-deansgate.co.uk*; and branches
throughout Britain.

USA AND CANADA

Book Passage, 51 Tamal Vista Blvd, Corte
Madera, CA 94925 ☎415/927-0960;
www.bookpassage.com.

The Complete Traveler, 3207 Fillmore St, San
Francisco, CA 94123 ☎415/923-1511;
www.completetraveler.com.

The Complete Traveler Bookstore, 199
Madison Ave, New York, NY 10016 ☎212/685-
9007; *completetraveler@worldnet.att.net*.

Elliot Bay Book Company, 101 S Main St,
Seattle, WA 98104 ☎206/624-6600 or
1-800/962-5311; *www.elliotbaybook.com\ebbco*.

International Travel Maps & Books, 552
Seymour St, Vancouver, V6B 3J5 ☎604/687-3320;
www.itmb.com.

Map Link Inc., 30 S La Patera Lane, Unit 5,
Santa Barbara, CA 93117 ☎805/692-6777;
www.maplink.com.

The Map Store Inc., 1636 I St NW, Washington
DC 20006 ☎202/628-2608 or 1-800/544-2659.

Open Air Books and Maps, 25 Toronto St,
Toronto, ON M5C 2R1 ☎416/363-0719.

Phileas Fogg's Books & Maps, #87 Stanford
Shopping Center, Palo Alto, CA 94304
☎1-800/533-FOGG; *www.foggs.com*.

Rand McNally, 444 N Michigan Ave, Chicago, IL
60611 ☎312/321-1751; 150 E 52nd St, New York,
NY 10022 ☎212/758-7488; 595 Market St, San
Francisco, CA 94105 ☎415/777-3131;
☎1-800/234-0679 for nearest store and direct
mail; *www.randmcnallystore.com*.

Sierra Club Bookstore, 6014 College Ave,
Oakland, CA 94618 ☎510/658-7470;
www.sierraclubbookstore.com.

Travel Books & Language Center, 4437
Wisconsin Ave, Washington DC 20016 ☎1-
800/220-2665.

Traveler's Choice Bookstore, 22 W 52nd St,
New York, NY 10019 ☎212/941-1535;
tvlchoice@aol.com.

Ulysses Travel Bookshop, 4176 St-Denis,
Montréal H2W 2M5 ☎514/843- 9447;
www.ulysses.ca.

island. Geographical and orienteering maps
have been published for Topes de Collantes
but are otherwise nonexistent.

Other than the *Guía de Carreteras* the maps in
this guide should be all you need, but if you do
decide to purchase a locally produced version, the
best map shop in the country is *El Navegante* at
Mercaderes no. 115, e/ Obispo y Obrapía in
Habana Vieja (☎7/57-10-38). It's a good idea to
buy any maps you think you might need whilst you
are in Havana as it can be a frustrating and often
fruitless business trying to find one in the provinces.

The Internet

The vast majority of **Web sites** on Cuba have
been set up in the US, many of them politically
orientated and making stimulating reading. Some

of the best ones are listed in the box overleaf.
The best places for tourist information on just
about anything run by the Cuban state, from car
rental to specialized tours, are the official government sites, *www.cubaweb.cuk* and, more
specifically aimed at tourists, *www.cubatravel.cu*.

In a country as yet bereft of cybercafés, there
are very few places in Cuba where the general
public can get access to the Internet, and private
home connections to the World Wide Web are
forbidden by law. The most straightforward way
to have a quick surf is to visit the Playa branch of
Infotur (see p.17). You may also be able to gain
access at the *Parque Central* and *Meliá Cohiba*
hotels in Havana (see p.75 and p.76 respectively), though strictly speaking their business facilities are for guests only.

WEB SITES

www.afrocubaweb.com Fantastically detailed site covering absolutely anything even remotely connected to Afro-Cuban issues, from history and politics to music and dance. Balanced discussion and cutting-edge awareness characterize this excellent site which also features global tour news for Cuban musical outfits.

www.closeup.org/cuba.htm Detailed discussion of US-Cuban relations from a US perspective. This site links into the CIA's factbook on Cuba which is impressively well informed and surprisingly non-political with a myriad statistics on TV set numbers, railways, the military and all kinds of information about the structure of the country.

www.cubanet.org Devil's advocate Web site, presenting the point of view of the Miami exiles, plus links to other related sites and an engaging collection of photographs.

www.cubatravel.cu The Cuban Ministry of Tourism Web site with practical information and advice on a wide range of issues from customs regulations to accommodation and transport.

www.cubaupdate.org A really excellent source of information that details tours organized by the Center for Cuban Studies, offers advice about planning your own trip and brings you the latest information on the state of play on the embargo, its enforcement and attempts to have it relaxed or lifted.

www.cubaweb.cu The Cuban government's official site, offered in cooperation with a Canadian Internet service provider, includes news reports from the Cuban press, plus information on travel, investment, trade, aid and many other subjects.

www.discuba.caribbeansources.com Previews and sale of the latest Cuban music on the market covering over twenty categories of music from rock and pop to *salsa*. This site also features occasional information on musical events and festivals in Cuba.

www.dtcuba.com Currently in Spanish only, though there are plans to offer parallel text in English, this well laid-out site has up-to-date news of the latest goings-on in Cuban sport, culture, health and business.

www.globalexchange.org A source of information on study tours, as well as information about the legality of travelling to Cuba during the embargo.

www.granma.cu The national Cuban newspaper in digital format providing an insightful look at the Cuban take on international and domestic affairs. Updated on a daily basis, and you can look back at previous issues.

www.igc.org/cubasoli Information about the activities of InfoMed, a humanitarian aid organization furnishing computers to Cuban hospitals.

www.state.gov/www/regions/wha/cuba /index.html A US government site dedicated to explaining – and seeking to legitimize – the terms of the embargo to Americans. Not to be missed for the casual attitude to the cruelty of the embargo's impact on the lives of Cubans, illustrated perfectly by a photograph of Cubans riding pushbikes with the caption: "as the transportation sector deteriorated, Cuba's love affair with the automobile was gradually replaced by resignation to the bicycle".

www.treas.gov/ofac The US government's official contribution to the debate – with a detailed presentation of the terms of the sanctions against Cuba and other information on US policy and regulations.

www.zpub.com This picture-based site is dedicated to post-revolutionary poster art in Cuba. Their archive is growing steadily and it's well worth checking out for a taste of the instantly recognizable Cuban style, commonly seen in cinemas throughout Cuba.

Costs, money and banks

Cuba is not a particularly cheap place to visit, and for the package tourist the costs of eating in restaurants and staying in hotel rooms will require a budget only slightly lower than you'd need back home. However, it is possible to survive on very little given the availability of fresh food sold for pesos and the relatively inexpensive private room market. The existence of three currencies can make things confusing, but on the whole visitors stick to using straightforward US dollars.

Currency

Cuba's national unit of currency is the Cuban **peso**, or, in Spanish, the *peso cubano*, divided into 100 **centavos**. Referred to in this book simply as pesos, banknotes are issued in denominations of 50, 20, 10, 5, 3 and 1. The lowest value coin is the worthless 1c, followed by the 5c, 20c, 1-peso and 3-peso coins, this last adorned with the face of Che Guevara. Though virtually obsolete you may also see the 2c and 40c coins.

The Cuban government publishes the **rate of exchange** at one peso per US$1, but this serves only to confuse matters. At the time of writing US$1 is, for all practical purposes, worth twenty Cuban pesos, and although it has been more or less at this level for a number of years now, there have been severe fluctuations in value since August 1993, when the US dollar became legal tender. To confuse matters further, in 1995 the government introduced the **convertible peso**, again divided into centavos, which, though completely worthless outside of Cuba, is interchangeable with the dollar and has exactly the same value. Don't be surprised to receive convertible pesos as change for a purchase made with dollars. The banknote denominations are 100, 50, 25, 10, 5 and 1, whilst there are 50c, 25c, 10c and 5c coins.

This complicated three-currency system has its own vocabulary, consisting of a collection of widely used terms and slang words (see box). The first thing to learn when trying to make sense of it all is that pesos, convertible pesos and dollars are all represented with the dollar sign ($). Sometimes common sense is the only indicator you will have to distinguish whether this means pesos or dollars, but the most commonly used qualifiers are *divisas* for dollars and *moneda nacional* for pesos. Thus one peso is often written $1MN. However, many Cubans refer to either currency as pesos, in which case you may have to ask if they mean *pesos cubanos*. Unless otherwise stated, any references to pesos in this book will be to Cuban pesos and not convertible pesos, while we use the $ symbol to signify the US dollar only.

All official tourist-oriented facilities, including all state-run hotels, most state-run restaurants and pretty much all shop products, are charged in **US dollars**. You'll also be expected to pay for a room in a house, meals in *paladares* and most private taxis in dollars, though there is some flexibility in these cases. Entrance to cinemas and sports arenas, rides on local buses, snacks bought on the street and food from *agromercados* are all paid for with pesos. There are also goods and services, such as stamps, entrance to museums and, most notably, long-distance transport, that can be paid for with either pesos or dollars. In these instances tourists are often advised and sometimes obliged to pay in dollars, and by doing so occasionally enjoy some kind of benefit, such as being able to bypass a waiting list or getting a guaranteed seat. It should be noted, however, that it is nonetheless perfectly legal for a non-Cuban to pay for meals and private taxis with pesos, despite the funny looks or contrary advice you might well receive. The general rule for the visitor is to assume that everything will be paid for with dollars or convertible pesos, but should you ever pay for anything with pesos – which will usually be in situations where you are the only non-Cuban – expect it to cost you the equivalent of a few cents or less.

It's best to carry dollars in low denominations as many shops and restaurants simply won't have enough change. Be particularly wary of this at bus and train stations or you may find yourself unable to buy a ticket. If you do end up having to use a $50 or $100 note, you will usually be asked to show your passport for security.

Costs

You're unlikely to find a **hotel room** for less than $25, though some of the older, more basic hotels that cater to both Cubans and foreign visitors offer much lower rates. **Private rooms** can be negotiated down to as little as $10, although this is unlikely in Havana, and it is generally more realistic to expect to pay between $15 and $25 depending on where in the country you are staying.

Discounting accommodation, your **daily budget** can vary quite considerably. If you're content with eating pizzas, sandwiches and snacks bought from street vendors, or buying fresh fruit, vegetables and the occasional piece of meat from food markets, and are prepared to muck in with the locals for night-time entertainment, then you can get away with a daily budget of just $5 or about 100 pesos. In the more likely event that you will want to eat out at restaurants and *paladares* you should allow $5–15 for food and at least another $5 if you want to attend a live performance or go to a club. A daily budget of $50 is high-rolling but easily spendable in Havana or the major resorts.

If you **travel** by Víazul or another tourist bus service, the most comfortable and efficient way to get around, then expect to pay upwards of $15 for most journeys (the 335km journey from Havana to Trinidad, for example, is $25). Private taxis can sometimes work out cheaper than buses if you share them with three or four other dollar-paying travellers, with a 100km trip costing as little as $5–10 each (see p.27).

Travellers' cheques and credit cards

Hard currency is king in Cuba, and although you'll generally be OK in the major tourist areas and big hotels, when dealing with any kind of private enterprise, from *paladares* to puncture repairs, anything other than cash isn't worth a centavo.

Although **travellers' cheques** are easily exchangeable for cash in many banks, subject to a small commission (2.5–4%), they are not as convenient as they can be in other countries, with a significant number of shops and restaurants still refusing to accept them. Travellers' cheques issued by a US bank are unusable in Cuba, though American Express cheques issued outside of the US are now accepted.

Credit cards – Visa and Mastercard in particular, but no cards issued by a US bank (including American Express, regardless of country of issue) – are more widely accepted, especially around the large tourist resorts, but in most small to medium-sized towns plastic is absolutely useless as a method of payment. Credit cards are more useful for obtaining **cash advances**, most efficiently through branches of the Banco Financiero Internacional, for which you'll need to show your passport. There is a minimum withdrawal, currently set at $20.

There are very few **ATMs** in Cuba and most of them accept only cards issued by Cuban banks, which means that at weekends, when most banks are closed, it is virtually impossible to obtain money.

Banks and exchange

Banking hours in Cuba are generally Monday to Friday 8am to 3pm, but in the larger tourist resorts, particularly Varadero, some banks stay open until 6 or 7pm and a tiny minority open Saturday mornings. As a general rule, make sure you have any money you'll need for the weekend by Friday.

The **Banco Financiero Internacional** is the most efficient and experienced at dealing with foreign currency transactions, with a branch in each of the major cities. Be warned that many other banks are only equipped to deal with pesos, and are therefore useless as far as foreign visitors are concerned.

Most of the larger hotels have *cambios* where you can exchange money, with more flexible hours than the banks – indeed, the *cambio* at the *Hotel Nacional* in Havana (daily 8am–noon & 1–7pm) is one of the few places in the country where you can withdraw or exchange money on a Sunday. Commission for changing foreign cash to dollars ranges from 2 to 4%.

For changing dollars into Cuban pesos, the government body CADECA runs its own *casas de cambio*, often in the shape of white kiosks at the side of the road. There is no minimum or maximum quantity restriction and you can use a credit card. Opening hours are generally Monday to Saturday 9am to 6pm and often Sunday 8.30am to 12.30pm, though in Havana some are open much later. The exchange rate seems to have stabilized in recent years so that now you can expect all *casas de cambio* to exchange at a rate of 20 pesos per dollar. No commission is charged for buying pesos.

Black market dollar salesmen often hang around outside *casas de cambio* and may offer a favourable exchange rate or, sometimes more tempting, the opportunity of buying pesos without having to queue. Whilst there is very little financial risk involved, black market rates being usually no more than a couple of pesos below or above the official rate, be aware that exchanging dollars for pesos with anyone other than the state is strictly illegal, and though you are unlikely to get into any trouble, it could result in a prison sentence for the Cuban. You may also be approached by people on the street offering to exchange your dollars for convertible pesos, sometimes at an exceptionally good rate. This is almost always a con: they are actually trying to sell you Cuban pesos hoping you won't notice the difference.

Emergency cash

For money problems of all kinds most people are directed to **Asistur**, set up specifically to provide assistance to tourists with financial difficulties, as well as offering advice on a number of other matters, legal and otherwise. It can arrange to have money sent to you from abroad as well as providing loans or cash advances. Branches, however, are still not that commonplace; the main one is at Paseo del Prado no. 212 esq. Trocadero in Havana (☎7/33-89-20 or 33-85-27 or 33-83-39).

One of the most efficient ways of getting hold of emergency cash is to have money from your home bank account or that of a friend or family member sent by **wire transfer** to a bank in Cuba, but note that only the Banco Financiero Internacional, and the Banco Internacional de Comercio in Havana, can handle money transfers from abroad. The person sending you the money will need to know your address in Cuba, whether at a hotel or in a *casa particular*, and your passport number. Be aware that the bank from which the money is sent will charge a hefty commission fee. The Havana International Bank in London, the National Australia Bank in Melbourne and the Canadian Imperial Bank of Commerce in Toronto all have links with the Banco Internacional de Comercio and may prove to be better prepared than others for this kind of transaction.

Getting around

Mastering the different ways to get around Cuba can be a fascinating if sometimes frustrating experience, and understanding the nuances of hitching a lift and catching a private taxi can take years. With the introduction of a new bus service, a proliferation of car-rental agencies and an increase in the number of state-run taxis, in recent years it's become much easier for the dollar-paying traveller, who can bypass the waiting lists, endless queues and uncomfortable conditions which characterized public transport, particularly the bus system, until the latter years of the 1990s.

If you are willing to pay the extra cost for getting around quickly and efficiently there is now a sufficiently well-maintained infrastructure to allow you to do so. On the other hand, in Cuba the journey is all part of the fun, especially when it's a 200-kilometre ride in a 1957 Chevrolet or any one of the thousands of classic American cars from the 1940s and 50s which have survived in isolation from the outside world since the 1959 revolution and have become one of the defining images of modern Cuba. Some are beautifully maintained, others are rolling scrapheaps, but almost all of them are now employed by their owners as taxis.

Whilst public transport improves from the tourist's point of view, Cubans continue to struggle with overcrowding, constant delays and interminable waiting lists. Having made a marginal recovery from the petrol shortages caused by the Special Period, which hit hardest in the early 1990s, things started to go backwards again by the end of the decade. The demands of the ever-expanding tourist industry are given priority so that, for example, the number of tourist buses between Havana and Varadero tripled from 1998 to 1999, whilst the peso service used by Cubans was cut by half.

Buses

With a relatively low percentage of car owners on the island, **buses** are at the heart of everyday Cuban life and by far the most commonly used form of transport. However, petrol shortages and a paucity of vehicles mean long queues and overcrowding which, coupled with the complicated system of timetables and buying tickets, can make using them a nightmare.

There are, however, two separate and distinct services for interprovincial routes, one operated by Astro, the other by the more recently formed Víazul. Though technically available to anyone willing and able to pay dollars, **Víazul** (☎7/81-14-13) is effectively a bus service for tourists. Set up so that visitors don't have to contend with the confusion and inefficiencies of the Astro system (see opposite), Víazul buses are equipped with air-conditioning, toilets and in some cases television sets. The number of routes is strictly limited, with a total of only fifteen towns, cities and resorts forming the entire network. It is, however, the quickest, most reliable and most hassle-free way to get about the country independently. Though it's set to increase, the current size of the fleet means that only the Havana–Varadero and the Havana–Trinidad connections operate on a daily basis whilst connections not involving the capital are, on the whole, even more infrequent. If you don't have enough time to wait for the next Víazul bus but would rather not sacrifice any comfort, one possible solution is to book a seat on a **tour bus**, paying for the journey only on an organized excursion. Known as a *transfer*, this can be arranged through most of the main travel agents, but it's an expensive way to travel; a one-way transfer with Cubatur from Havana to Viñales, for example, costs over twice as much as it would with Víazul. **Tickets** are always one-way, requiring you to book the return ticket when you get to your destination. Costs range from $10 between Havana and Varadero to $51 between Havana and Santiago.

Most bus routes are still the exclusive domain of **Astro** (☎7/70-33-97), and if you intend to travel even slightly off the beaten track then the chances are you will make a journey in one of its rusting vehicles. Even if you choose a destination covered by Víazul you may decide that the Astro fare, usually between half and two-thirds of the price of a Víazul ticket, justifies the less comfortable conditions. Most Cubans have no choice, the determinant factor being that they can pay their fare in pesos, even if this means, as it usually does, joining a waiting list which can last weeks.

Foreign passport-holders are obliged to pay for their ticket in **dollars** but by doing so they forgo the rigmarole of queuing to get into another queue, joining waiting lists and all the other confusing rituals which dominate the public transport system. Most big-town or city bus stations have a separate office where dollar tickets are sold. The buses used for the most popular routes have two or more seats specifically reserved for dollar-customers, and though this means you will usually get a seat there is no guarantee that a bus will not already have met its dollar quota. Staff will always advise you to arrive at the bus station at least an hour before departure. Before you do that, however, you should ring to check whether the bus is actually leaving, particularly if you are catching it in an untouristed area. Chalkboard timetables can be found on the walls of most bus stations, but they should be taken with a giant pinch of salt. There are occasions when buses don't leave simply because there's not enough gasoline to go round, with those running the most heavily used routes naturally given priority. It's also worth bearing in mind that buses going to the same place don't always go by the same route. Check beforehand whether the bus is going via the *autopista* (the motorway) or the slower Carretera Central (the most common variation) as this will significantly affect the journey time.

In Havana there are separate **bus stations** for Víazul and Astro services but elsewhere for either you should head for the *Terminal de Omnibus Nacionales* or *Interprovinciales*. This is not to be confused with the intermunicipal station which may look very similar but in most towns is in an entirely different location and serves only those towns within the provincial borders.

Whilst foreign travellers have become a familiar sight on long-distance buses, catch a **local town bus** and you're bound to attract a few stares. The lack of timetables, information-less bus stops and overcrowding are more than enough to persuade most people unfamiliar with the workings of the local bus system to stay well away. However, as most journeys cost less than half a peso you may be tempted to try your luck. The only written information you will find at a bus stop are the numbers of the buses that stop there. The front of the bus will tell you its final destination but for any more detail you'll have to ask. Once you know which one you want, you need to mark your place in the queue, which may not appear to even exist. The unwritten rule is to ask aloud who the last person is; so, for example, to queue for bus #232 you should shout "*¿Ultima persona para la 232?*". When the bus finally pulls up make sure you have within a peso of the right change – there's a flat fee of 40c. Other than the familiar-looking single-deck buses, many of them imported from Europe, called *gua-guas*, there are *camellos*, the converted juggernauts employed throughout Cuba but especially in Havana. Almost always heaving with passengers, they tend to cover the longer city journeys but actually charge less, usually just 20c.

Trains

At present Cuba is the only country in the Caribbean with a functioning **rail** system, and although trains are slow they are a good way of getting a feel for the landscape as you travel about. The main line, which links Havana with Santiago, is generally reliable and the trains operating on it are surprisingly comfortable given their apparent age. The other cities served by this route are Matanzas, Santa Clara, Ciego de Ávila, Camagüey and Las Tunas. There are branch lines to other towns and cities and a few completely separate lines, but anything which does not fall directly in between Havana and Santiago will be subject to more delays and even slower trains. Standards vary even on the main line with essentially two different kinds of services. Normal trains, which are perfectly comfortable, leave once daily, stopping at all the mainline stations and fares work out at around $4 per 100km; Havana to Santiago, for example, costs $35. The *especial* service runs every three days and is more expensive (for example, $43 from Havana to Santiago), but the trains have air conditioning and are significantly quicker.

The two most obvious routes beside the main line are the **Havana–Pinar del Río line**, one of the slowest in the country, and the **Hershey line**, an electric train service running between Havana and Matanzas (see p.205). Some of the trains on these and other lesser routes are no more than a single carriage and, like the buses, only sometimes run in accordance with their timetables.

You'll need your passport to buy a ticket, which you should do at least an hour before departure, direct from the train station. Fail to turn up an hour beforehand and the ticket office will refuse to sell you a ticket. Strictly speaking all foreign travellers must pay for tickets in dollars but on some of the less-travelled routes you may get away with a peso ticket.

Driving

The best way to get around the island is undoubtedly in your own **rental car**. Traffic jams are almost unheard of and away from the cities many roads, including the *autopista*, are almost empty. Driving a car allows you more flexibility and avoids the hassles that catching buses and trains often entails in Cuba, and also opens up the possibility of visiting the numerous places that still have no formal public transport links at all with major urban centres. Even resort areas such as Topes de Collantes near Trinidad or the Sierra del Rosario in Pinar del Río are pretty much unreachable for the independent traveller without a car.

There is a confusing proliferation of different car rental agencies given that they are all state-run firms. Apart from prices, which are rarely less than $35 a day and more often between $50 and $70, the essential difference is the type and make of car, ranging from chauffeur-driven limousines to two-door hatchbacks. **Havanautos** and **Transautos** have the most branches throughout the island as well as the widest range of vehicles, and in general their prices, which are middle of the range, do not differ a great deal. However, it is worth shopping around even between these two as agencies can often only offer one or two of the cars in their fleet, demand usually far outweighing supply. For any chance of getting a car that isn't the most expensive model, it's essential to book at least a day in advance. All agencies require you

to have held a driving licence from your home country or an international driving licence for at least a year and that you are 21 or over. Internationally recognized companies like Avis and Hertz do not exist in Cuba.

Most agencies offer myriad different packages which are usually split into two groups: those which allow unlimited distance and those which set a daily maximum, usually 100km, with a charge for every kilometre above that limit. Unless you intend to stay within the limits of a city, the latter option is likely to work out unnecessarily expensive. The average **prices** for the most basic unlimited-distance deals are around $50 a day, with an extra $10–15 a day for insurance and a deposit of $200. Costs go down by about $5 a day if you rent the car for a week or more. Be prepared for extra charges, legitimate or otherwise, which won't appear in the agency brochure. The most usual is a charge for the cost of the gas already in the car, but if you are charged for this then you should be able to return it with an empty tank. It pays to be absolutely clear from the start about what you are being charged for as scams are common. By the same token, if you want your deposit back in one piece you should check the car over thoroughly before setting off to make sure every little scratch is recorded in the log-book by the agent.

The cost of **gas** is 90c per litre for *especial*, which most rented cars require by law, 65c for *regular* and 45c for diesel, still used in one or two models. Black-market prices hover around 50c per litre for *especial*, but getting hold of it can be tricky unless you have a trusted contact. By far the most detailed **road map** of the island is the *Guía de Carreteras* (see p.19).

Roads, rules and safety

As there is only one **motorway** in the whole of Cuba it is known simply as *el autopista*, literally "the motorway". From Havana it cuts directly through the country down to the eastern edge of Sancti Spíritus province and in the other direction to the provincial capital of Pinar del Río. Supposedly it fluctuates between six and eight lanes but road markings are almost nonexistent and the 100km/hr speed limit would undoubtedly lead to accidents were there more traffic. As it stands, the *autopista* is amongst the most deserted major roads in Cuba and there is as much chance of colliding with a cow as with another vehicle. The main alternative route for

CAR RENTAL AGENCIES IN CUBA

Cubacar, Head Office: Calle 1ra no. 16401, Miramar, Havana ☎ 7/33-22-77 or 33-72-33. Most central branch in Havana is in the *Meliá Cohiba* hotel ☎ 7/33-46-61. Offices all over the island, many of them based in hotels; standard prices.

Havanautos, Head Office: Calle 1ra esq. 0, Miramar, Havana ☎ 7/23-98-15 or 23-96-57, reservations 24-06-47 or 24-06-48. Most central branch in Havana is at the Cupet-Cimex gas station at Malecón y 11, Vedado ☎ 7/33-46-91. Offices all over the island, with a fleet ranging from beach buggies to jeeps, hatchbacks and saloons.

Micar, Head Office: Calle 13 no. 562, Vedado, Havana ☎ 7/33-67-25 or 33-61-38. Most central branch in Havana is at Malecón y Príncipe in Centro Habana ☎ 7/33-58-10. The best-value agency with the most flexible price packages, but a fairly limited number of offices and a relatively small fleet.

Palcocar, Palacio de Convenciones, Calle 146 e/ 11 y 13, Playa, Havana ☎ 7/33-72-35. Part of the service package offered at this centre for international business visitors. Reasonable rates but strictly limited choice of cars.

Panautos, Línea y Malecón, Vedado, Havana ☎ 7/55-32-55. The most expensive of the island-wide agents, specializing in Citroëns and luxury jeeps.

Rex, Head Office and reservations: Ave. de Rancho Boyeros y Calzada de Bejucal, Havana ☎ 7/33-91-60, fax 33-91-59. Most central branch in Havana is at Línea y Malecón, Vedado ☎ 7/33-77-88; fax 33-77-89. One of the most professionally run services, offering luxury Volvos at extortionate prices. Branches in Havana only and a minimum age requirement of 25.

Transautos, Head Office: Calle 40-a esq. 3ra, Miramar, Havana ☎ 7/24-76-44, reservations 24-55-32. Most central branch in Havana is at Calle 21 e/ N y O ☎ 33-40-38. The largest car rental agency in Cuba, with a desk in most dollar hotels.

---

most long-distance journeys is the two-lane **Carretera Central**, an older more congested road with an 80km/hr speed limit. This tends to be a more scenic option, which is just as well, as you can spend hours on it stuck behind tractors, trucks and horse-drawn carriages.

The quality of **minor roads** varies enormously and potholes are commonplace, particularly in Pinar del Río province. Take extreme care on mountain roads, many of which are littered with killer bends and have few crash barriers. The absence of street lighting means driving anywhere outside the cities is dangerous at night, but to mountain resorts like Viñales or Topes de Collantes it's positively suicidal. The high proportion of cyclists on the road, the vast majority without lights, and the array of horse-drawn transport are also cause for caution.

Taxis

Taxis come in all shapes and sizes in Cuba and have become one of the most popular expressions of private enterprise in response to the tourism boom and the deterioration of public transport. There are essentially three different kinds of taxi, although it often seems that merely owning a car qualifies a person as a taxi driver.

The official **metered state taxis** are the easiest to spot and, along with rental cars, make up the vast majority of imported models on Cuban roads. Most towns with a dollar hotel have a tourist taxi service, often run from the hotels themselves, and getting hold of one by telephone isn't usually a problem. As with rental cars the fact that they are all run by the state does not mean state taxis can be considered one homogeneous service. Your prime concern, however, will be the size of the car as it is this more than anything else which determines the cost; the smaller the car, the lower the rate. For the smallest hatchback taxi in a provincial town you will be charged just 30c per kilometre, whilst in Havana a saloon car can cost as much as 90c per kilometre, with luxury taxis a grade above that.

Equally as common are the individually owned cars, predominantly 1950s American classics or Ladas, which have been converted into taxis by their owners – the conversion usually consisting of a piece of cardboard in the front window reading "Taxi". The local name for these is *máquinas* or *taxis particulares* but those that carry tourists are referred to throughout this guide as **private taxis**. Finding a private taxi in the towns and cities is easy, as every other person with their own car seems to have turned it into a taxi, but understanding the mechanics of the system takes more time. Drivers register their vehicles with the government but must declare whether they intend to charge their passengers in pesos or dollars, as separate licence fees apply. There is no way of telling from outward appearances which currency the taxi is licensed for – a point worth remembering if you have no luck in flagging one down, as it is assumed that as a foreigner you will be paying in dollars. Illegality is not enough to deter most drivers, and the suspicious behaviour and strange routes which characterize many a private taxi ride reflect the small proportion of dollar-charging drivers who actually have a dollar licence. This should not put you off, however, as you do not stand to get into any trouble if the driver of your taxi is caught out by the police, a frequent occurrence. Most journeys within a city will cost between $2 and $5, but negotiation is part and parcel of the whole unofficial system, and if you don't haggle the chances are you'll end up paying more than a state taxi would have cost you. Often drivers are willing to take you long distances and there is usually a specific area of a town, invariably next door to a bus station, where taxis waiting for long-distance passengers congregate. As a rough indicator, a driver will be looking for between $20 and $30 per 100km but this depends heavily upon whether the car is a gas-guzzling antique, in which case you should expect to pay more, or something more efficient like a Lada, the usual alternative.

Peso taxis are known as *colectivos* and more akin to a privately run bus service. A driver will pack as many people into his car as will fit, replacing anyone who gets out as quickly as possible with the next passer-by who waves them down. It is generally accepted in Havana that a trip in a *colectivo* within the city, however long or short, will cost ten pesos and the rest of the country follows along similar lines. You may find, however, that if a driver realizes you are foreign he'll insist on charging you in dollars.

Planes

Domestic flights in Cuba are a somewhat mixed bag as an alternative to the much slower road and rail routes. The national airline **Cubana** (☎7/33-39-11) operates regular flights from Havana's José Martí Airport (☎7/33-57-77) to most of the much smaller airports around the

---

Main domestic airports

Baracoa ☎21/42-52-80.
Camaguey ☎322/6-10-00.
Ciego de Ávila ☎33/3-25-25 or 4-36-95.
Granma ☎23/42-36-95.
Guantánamo ☎21/34-81-6.
Havana ☎7/33-57-77.
Holguín ☎24/4-39-34 or 4-32-55.
Las Tunas ☎31/4-24-84 or 4-29-00.
Manzanillo ☎23/5-49-84.
Nueva Gerona ☎61/2-26-90 or 2-21-84.
Santiago de Cuba ☎226/9-10-14.
Trinidad no phone
Varadero ☎5/61-30-16.

---

island (see box above). Apart from the capital only Varadero, Holguín and Santiago de Cuba have direct timetabled links with one another. Most fares are around the $90 mark. The vast majority of domestic flights are on old Russian biplanes, and the experience of flying in them is no more reassuring than you would expect given Cubana's poor record for safety over the last thirty years.

Chartered flights, which are no safer, can be arranged through the other national airlines, Aerotaxi (☎7/32-81-27, fax 33-26-21), Aerogaviota (☎7/81-30-68 or 81-30-86, fax 33-26-21) and Aerocaribbean (☎7/33-45-43, fax 33-50-16). All of them mostly use out-of-date single-engine biplanes seating eight to twelve people.

Bicycles and scooters

Cycling is one of the best ways of getting around Cuba if you have the stamina for the heat. Tens of thousands of bicycles were imported from China in the early 1990s and the streets are still full of these basic no-gear models. However, though bicycles are common as an alternative to waiting for a bus or owning a car, cycling for recreation is less popular and there are only limited opportunities for visitors who want to cycle but don't come on a prepackaged cycling tour. A minority of hotels rent out bicycles, mostly at the beach resorts, but there are no cycling shops or specialist rental firms. The hotel chain Horizontes (☎7/33-40-42 or 33-42-38; *www.horizontes.cu*) offers packages of *ciclo-*

turismo but they tend to be resort-based or for large groups. The best place to go if you want to rent out bikes individually and independently is Cubamar at Calle 15 no. 752 esq. Paseo, Vedado, Havana (☎7/30-55-36 to 39).

One of the conveniences of cycling in Cuba, especially in the cities, is the proliferation of private **bicycle-repair** workshops. If you get a puncture or your brake cable snaps you won't have to travel far before you come across a *ponchera*, usually run from a front room or a roadside shelter, where for a few pesos you can get your puncture repaired or replace anything they have spare parts for, which often isn't actually that much. If you do intend to cycle in Cuba it's worth bringing a pad-lock as they are rarely supplied with rental bikes and are difficult to find for sale. Most Cubans use the commonplace *parqueos de ciclos*, privately run bike-parks, often down the side of houses or actually inside them, where the owner will look after your bike for a peso or two until you get back.

Hitchhiking

Hitching a lift in Cuba is as common as catching a bus and some people get around exclusively this way. The petrol shortages following the collapse of trade with the former Soviet Union meant every available vehicle had to be utilized by the state effectively as public transport. Thus a system was adopted whereby any private vehicle, whether a car or a tractor, was obliged to pick up anyone hitching a lift. The yellow-suited workers employed by the government to hail down vehicles at bus stops and junctions on the *autopista* can still be seen today, though their numbers have decreased somewhat. Nevertheless the culture of hitching, or *coger botella* as it is known in Cuba, remains. Crowds of people still wait by bridges and junctions along the major roads waiting for trucks or any-thing else to stop. Drivers often ask for a few pesos now and tourists, though they are likely to attract a few puzzled stares, are welcome to join in.

Accommodation

Broadly speaking, accommodation in Cuba falls into two types: state and private. You'll find at least one state hotel in every large town for which you should budget at least $20 per night. Private accommodation, in *casas particu-lares*, works out cheaper at between $10 and $20. Only in major tourist areas like Havana will you need to pay more.

State tourist hotels

State-owned **tourist hotels** are the most conve-nient type of accommodation in Cuba – every town has at least one and you can usually get a room by turning up on spec, although tele-phone reservations are recommended to be on the safe side. On arrival, it's a good idea to state how many days you intend to stay to avoid hav-ing your room booked by someone else. Although in smaller places state hotels tend to be marooned on the town outskirts in run-down monolithic concrete constructions, in bigger cities like Havana or tourist centres like Varadero, state hotels can be splendid. Establishments that are owned and run in part-nership with international hotel chains are par-ticularly luxurious, with all mod cons and inter-national-quality restaurants, and, although at the top end of the price range, offer good value for money.

There are three main **hotel chains**, of which *Islazul* is the only one to cater for national as well as international tourists. Its hotels are the least expensive and the least luxurious, with simple rooms, usually without hot water, and workaday restaurants. In smaller towns the

ACCOMMODATION PRICE CODES

All accommodation listed in this guide has been graded according to the following price categories.

① peso hotel equivalent to $5 or less   ④ $30–50   ⑦ $100–150
② $5–20   ⑤ $50–70   ⑧ $150–200
③ $20–30   ⑥ $70–100   ⑨ $200 and above

Rates are for the cheapest available double or twin room during high season, usually May–September and the end of December. During low season some hotels lower their prices by roughly ten percent.

tourist hotel (if there is one at all) is likely to be *Islazul*. **Horizontes**, on the other hand, offer better quality mid-range accommodation and are in the process of refitting many of their hotels across the country. Rooms often have cable television, while their pleasant restaurants and bars are stocked with a reasonable choice of food and drink.

The luxury end of the market falls under the **Gran Caribe**, umbrella with the majority of the all-inclusives and smart city hotels belonging to this group. Hotel rooms are on a par with international luxury hotels with all mod cons including mini-bars, multi-channel television, hot water and a full complement of miniature bath products. Hotels generally have several restaurants, often serving some of the best food Cuba has to offer; huge pools; and an array of other services.

The major downside of staying in a hotel is that your contact with Cubans will be limited: many hotels discourage Cubans from entering, particularly at night, and you certainly won't be able to entertain Cuban friends in your room unless they are residents in another country or have a passport.

All-inclusives

The first fact to grasp about **all-inclusives** in Cuba is that many aren't inclusive of everything at all. Although billed as a complete package of room, meals, drinks, watersports and entertainment, some include only nationally produced drinks and charge extra for motorized watersports, so you should check the conditions at each hotel carefully. With cheaper deals for those on package tours, prices are generally upwards of $70 a night. They can still be excellent value if you are looking for a sun-sea-sand holiday with minimum hassle, and as many dominate the best beaches in the country, they're often your only accommodation option.

However, as many of the prime resorts, like Santa Lucía, Guardalavaca and Cayo Coco, tend to revolve around a deserted beach, they can be rather remote with no real infrastructure of a town to support them. In effect the resorts really consist of a series of all-inclusive hotels and a few purpose-built tourist restaurants and attractions, and consequently can feel a little contrived. A two-week stay in an all-inclusive here certainly won't give you a real impression of Cuba.

Peso state hotels

Most commonly found in less cosmopolitan towns away from the tourist centres, **peso state hotels** are the cheapest accommodation in Cuba, sometimes working out at the equivalent of a couple of dollars a night, although they are often extremely dilapidated, with bare-bones facilities running only to a very poor bathroom and ripped bedsheets. They are intended to be exclusively for Cubans, and the state does not promote them for visitor use; if you go to one you may well be told that all rooms are full, whether they are or not. Despite this, if you're looking for an absolute budget option it's always worth asking, as admission often depends on the whim of the person on reception – a donation to whoever is in charge sometimes helps.

Casas particulares

For many visitors, staying in *casas particulares* – literally "private houses" – is an ideal way to gain an insight into the country and its people. Operating like guesthouses, with proprietors renting out rooms in their home for private income, they are becoming more common throughout Cuba, found in all major towns and many smaller ones; they'll often as not find you, with touts (called *jineteros* or *intermediarios*) waiting to meet potential customers off the bus.

Because they are in direct competition with state hotels, the laws governing their operation vary from province to province according to the general demand for tourist accommodation and how many hotels are in an area – for example, they're banned completely in top tourist areas like Varadero and Guardalavaca, legal but heavily taxed in places where hotels are plentiful, and more lightly taxed in areas where state accommodation is sparse. Similarly, laws differ from province to province as to whether or not *casas particulares* may advertise their services – those permitted to do so are identifiable by a small blue-and-white sticker, reading *"Arrendador Inscripto"*, outside the premises. Prices vary according to area and level of taxation, but all are reasonably priced and as a rule $25 is the most you will ever pay. The law requires proprietors to register the names and passport numbers of all guests.

Most *casas particulares* offer breakfast and an evening meal for an extra cost, which can be anything between $1 and $10, with $5 the average. If you're brought to the *casa particular* by a tout, you can expect an additional cost of roughly $5 per night.

In addition to registered *casas particulares* there are many that operate **illegally** without paying taxes. You are not breaking the law by staying in one, and they can be as viable an option as their registered counterparts, if usually no cheaper, but if you stay in this type of accommodation and encounter a problem you will get little sympathy from the authorities.

Campismos

Often overlooked by visitors to Cuba, *campismos*, quasi-campsites, are an excellent countryside accommodation option. Although they are not prolific, all provinces have at least one and they are often set in sweeping countryside near a sparkling ribbon of river or small stretch of beach, making them perfect for a relaxing break. Whilst some have an area where you can pitch a tent, they are not campsites in the conventional sense, essentially offering basic accommodation in rudimentary concrete cabins. Some have barbecue areas while others have a canteen restaurant. They are all extremely reasonably priced, at around $5 a night per cabin. Although visitors are welcome, Cubans have priority and *campismos* are sometimes block-booked in June and July for workers' annual holidays. For more details contact Cubamar, Calle 15 no. 752 esq. Paseo Vedado, Havana (☎7/66-25-23 or 30-55-36; *cubamar@.mit.cma.net*), which runs the best sites.

Health

Providing you take common-sense precautions, visiting Cuba poses no particular health risks. In fact some of the most impressive advances made by the revolutionary government since 1959 have been in the field of medicine and the free health service provided to all Cuban citizens. Cuba now has one of the lowest infant mortality rates in the world – 7.2 per thousand live births – and a life expectancy at birth of 75.2 years, statistics all the more impressive given the shortages in the health service as a result of the US trade embargo and the exodus of around half of all the doctors on the island following the revolution. Vaccination programmes since 1959 have eliminated malaria, polio and tetanus whilst advances in medical science have attracted patients from around the world who come for unique treatments developed for a variety of conditions such as night blindness, psoriasis and radiation sickness.

No **vaccinations** are legally required in order to visit Cuba unless you're arriving from a country where yellow fever and cholera are endemic, in which case you'll need a vaccination certificate. It is advisable, however, to get inoculations for hepatitis A, polio, tetanus, rabies and typhoid, all of which are rare on the island but nevertheless exist.

It is essential to bring your own **medical kit** (see box), painkillers and any other medical supplies you think you might need as they are difficult to buy on the island and choice is extremely limited.

Heat problems

Cuba has a **hot and humid climate** which, for people used to cooler conditions, is harder to adjust to than a hot and dry climate. The temperature remains relatively high even at night and so the body sweats more. Generally speaking this means you will need an increased intake of salt and water, a lack of which can lead to **heat exhaustion**. Fatigue, headaches and nausea are all symptoms of **dehydration** and should be treated with rest and plenty of water, preferably with added salt. If sweating diminishes and the body temperature rises this could be a sign of **heatstroke**, also known as sunstroke and potentially fatal, in which case immediate professional treatment is essential.

A common skin disorder caused by hot climates is **prickly heat** – symptoms consist mainly of rashes and sore skin – which can be guarded against by taking frequent showers, keeping yourself clean and dry and wearing loose cotton clothing. It can be treated with calamine lotion and you should avoid applying sunscreen or moisturizer to affected areas.

All the usual common-sense precautions should be taken when exposing yourself to the **sun**; most importantly you should take care not to stay out in it for too long. Sunscreen protection factor numbers will give you an idea of how long you can sunbathe for but factor 15 is generally recommended as a minimum if you'll be spending time in the sun. Away from the hotels and the big dollar shops you may find sunscreen difficult to come by so be sure to have some packed before any trips into less-visited areas. If you do burn, apply calamine lotion to the affected areas or, in more severe cases, a mild antiseptic.

Food and water

Drinking **tap water** is not a good idea in Cuba, even in the swankiest hotels. Whenever you are offered water, whether in a restaurant, *paladar* or private house, it's a good idea to check if it has

---

A travellers' first-aid kit

Following are some of the items you might want to carry with you – especially if you're planning to go hiking (see p.54).

Antihistamines
Antiseptic cream
Insect repellent
Plasters/Band-aids
Lint and sealed bandages
Imodium (Lomotil) for emergency diarrhoea treatment
Paracetamol/aspirin
Multivitamin and mineral tablets
Rehydration sachets
Calamine lotion
Hypodermic needles and sterilized skin wipes
Thrush and cystitis remedies

---

been boiled – in most cases it will have been. This has become more of an issue since the hardships of the Special Period led to a breakdown of the purification system and some fairly short-sighted sewage disposal methods. **Bottled water** is available in dollar shops and most tourist bars and restaurants, but there are a number of ways that you can purify water yourself. If you boil your water make sure that once it reaches boiling point (100°C) you allow it to stay bubbling for a full two minutes. The two main alternatives are filters and purification tablets, neither of which are widely available in Cuba. To be extra safe you can combine the two methods but if you do so make sure you filter first as this can remove some of the active chemicals in the tablets.

Although reports of **food poisoning** are few and far between there are good reasons for exercising caution when eating in Cuba. Food bought on the street is in the highest risk category and you should be aware that there is no system of checks ensuring acceptable levels of hygiene. Self-regulation does seem to be enough in most cases but take extra care when buying pizzas, meat-based snacks or ice cream from street-sellers. If you can, find out how long the seller has been doing business on that spot; generally speaking, the longer the better. Peso restaurants can be equally suspect, particularly those where the near-absence of both tourists and competition means neither nonchalance nor negligence have any repercussions. The food is often very basic and, even when properly cooked, can be quite a shock to the untrained stomach. Dollar restaurants and *paladares*, on the other hand, tend to be much more reliable, although the state-run fast-food places are sometimes poorly maintained.

The most common food-related illness for travellers is **diarrhoea**, possibly accompanied by vomiting or a mild fever. Try to avoid antibiotics unless prescribed by a doctor, and stick to the basic principles of rest and rehydration, drinking plenty of liquid (though not alcohol or sugary drinks) and trying to replace lost salts. Eat plain foods like rice or bread and avoid fruit, fatty foods and dairy products. If symptoms persist for more than a few days, then salt solutions containing a small amount of sugar are recommended. If you haven't brought rehydration sachets, you can prepare your own solution by adding eight level teaspoons of sugar and half a teaspoon of salt to one litre of water.

Pests, bites and stings

Despite its colourful variety of fauna there are no dangerously venomous animals in Cuba, the occasional scorpion being about as scary as it gets, whilst the chances of contracting diseases from bites and stings are extremely slim. There are a number of insects whose bites are potentially very irritating but rarely if ever lethal.

Mosquitoes are the biggest pests, found throughout the island but particularly prevalent in Viñales, the Península de Zapata and the Isla de la Juventud, and although Cuba is not malarial there is a slight risk of **dengue fever**. There is no vaccine for this viral infection, most common during the rainy summer season, but serious cases are rare. Symptoms develop rapidly following infection and include extreme aches and pains in the bones and joints, severe headaches, dizziness, fever and vomiting. Rest is the best treatment but as with all disease, prevention is better than cure. Long-sleeves and trousers significantly reduce the chances of being bitten as do lotion, cream and spray repellents that contain DEET (diethyltoluamide). It's a good idea to pack repellents and mosquito coils, two of the most effective easy-to-carry insect-busters, before you leave for Cuba as they are impossible to get hold of in quite a few areas. Air conditioning and fans also act as deterrents. If you do get bitten try to resist scratching, which can encourage infection and will increase irritation. Apply antihistamine cream or calamine lotion to the affected areas or take antihistamine tablets.

In some areas **ticks** are also a problem, burrowing into the skin of any mammal they can get hold of and therefore more widespread wherever there is livestock. They lie in the grass waiting for passing victims, making walking about barefoot a risky business. Repellent is ineffective against these creatures so your best form of defence is to wear trousers, which you should tuck into your socks. It is possible to remove ticks from your skin with tweezers but care should be taken to make sure the head, which can get left behind, is plucked out along with the body. Smearing them with Vaseline or even strong alcohol leaves less of a margin for error. Minuscule **sand flies** can make their presence felt on beaches at dusk by inflicting bites which cause prolonged itchiness.

AIDS and HIV

Cuba has a very low incidence of **HIV positive** citizens but it has achieved this using controversial prevention techniques, though criticism has come from outside rather than from within the country where in general the people have supported the government response to the worldwide AIDS epidemic. Between 1986 and 1989 the government compulsorily tested 75 percent of the adult population, and those people who tested positive were effectively quarantined in residential parks, the most famous being Finca Los Cocos in Havana, where they live comfortably but are denied their freedom. The influx of foreign tourists now threatens state-control of the disease, but for now at least the risk of contracting AIDS in Cuba remains very low. All the usual common-sense precautions do of course still apply, whilst the poor quality of Cuban condoms means it's worth bringing your own supply.

Hospitals, clinics and pharmacies

Don't visit Cuba assuming that the country's world-famous free health service extends to foreign visitors – far from it. In fact, the government has used the advances made in medicines and medical treatments to earn extra revenue for the regime, through a system of **health tourism**. This includes a small network of anti-stress clinics, such as the one at Topes de Collantes, offering massage and various other therapies, but also entails some pretty unhealthy medical fees for visitors who spend time in Cuban hospitals. The health service has been hit hard by a combination of the US trade embargo and the shortages caused by the loss of trade with the former Soviet bloc. The worst affected area is the supply of medicines, and some hospitals now simply cannot treat patients through lack of resources. There are specific hospitals, most of them run by Servimed (the institution set up to deal with health tourism), which accept foreign patients. Foreigners on the whole remain immune from the hardships affecting the health service, though

it can cause considerable stress should you be unlucky enough to wind up in a Cubans-only institution. Some hospitals, such as the Hospital Hermanos Ameijeiras in Havana, considered the best of its kind in Cuba, have designated sections for dollar-paying patients. In these, unlike in the Cuban sections, patients are not expected to supply their own towels, soap, toilet paper and even their own food.

If you do wind up in hospital in Cuba one of the first things you or someone you know should do is contact **Asistur** (☎7/33-89-20 or 33-85-27 or 33-83-39), who usually deal with insurance claims on behalf of the hospital. However, for minor complaints you shouldn't have to go further than the hotel doctor, who will give you a consultation. If you're staying in a *casa particular* things are slightly more complicated. Your best bet, if you feel ill, is to inform your hosts, who should be able to call the family doctor, the *médico de la familia*, and arrange a house-call. This is common practice in Cuba where, with one doctor for every 169 inhabitants, it's possible to visit all the patients personally.

As with much else on the island there are two types of **pharmacy** in Cuba: tourist pharmacies operating in dollars and peso pharmacies for the population at large. Tourists are permitted to use the peso variety – antiquated establishments with shelves of bottled medicine – but will rarely find anything of any use in them besides aspirin, as they primarily deal in prescription-only drugs. You may have to ask to be directed to the dollar equivalents, which only exist in some of the largest towns, as detailed throughout the guide. The majority are run by Servimed (☎07/24-01-41 or 42) and you should ask for the nearest *Clínica Internacional* within which they are normally located. Even in these there is not the range of medicines that you might expect and if you have a preferred brand or type of painkiller, or any other everyday drug, you should bring it with you. A small number of hotels, such as the *Hotel Nacional* in Havana, have their own pharmacies, whilst some tourist hospitals have a pharmaceutical counter selling medicine.

Food and drink

While you'll often be able to feast well on simply prepared, good food in Cuba, mealtimes are certainly not the gastronomic delight enjoyed on other Caribbean islands. Other than garlic and onion, spices are not really used in cooking, and most Cubans have a distaste for hot spicy food altogether. The main culinary influence is North American, with fast food popular and readily available, as the fried chicken and pizza outlets you'll find everywhere bear witness to.

In some ways the country is still suffering from the aftershock of the Special Period when severe food shortages rocked the local and foreign population alike and empty supermarket shelves were a common sight. Shortages have slackened off and although everyone has enough to eat choice is still rather limited, meaning that meals can seem rather repetitive and formulaic – you'll find the same platters cropping up time and again. However, whatever people may tell you, Cuba's culinary blandness is not all down to the revolution; a brief glance through a typical 1950s Cuban cookbook, in which housewives are extolled to serve but one carbohydrate per meal and urged to make more of the spices available, indicates a problem long entrenched.

Where to eat

Restaurants in Cuba are divided into two categories: state restaurants and cafés, and privately run *paladares*. Covering both dollar establishments and peso eateries, **state restaurants** differ greatly in quality – the best offer up tasty meals in congenial settings while the worst are diabolical. As a visitor you are more likely to stick to the dollar establishments which, particularly in the large cities and tourist areas, tend to have better-quality and wider-ranging food – often with some international cuisine like Chinese and Italian – as well as being cleaner and more pleasant. The other viable option for international-standard meals is the restaurants in the tourist hotels, although the food dished up in these is quite removed from Cuban cuisine. There are also various state **café chains**, Rumbos and El Rápido being the two most common, serving cheap fried chicken, fries, hot dogs and occasionally burgers.

At the other end of the scale, **peso restaurants**, which you'll find away from the tourist areas, cater essentially to Cubans. Whilst undeniably lower in quality than dollar restaurants, these are still worth checking out as you can occasionally get a decent meal very cheaply. In contrast, state-run **roadside cafés** are unhygienic and poorly run and should be avoided wherever possible.

Paladares and street stalls

Run privately, usually from a spare room in the proprietor's house, *paladares* – a 1990s Cuban phenomenon – are a godsend. Introduced by the state in response to calls from Cubans for the right to earn money through private enterprise, they offer visitors a chance to sample good Cuban home cooking in an informal atmosphere. They're allowed to seat no more than twelve people, and are subject to tight restrictions on what food they can serve: beef and seafood are always prohibited, although you may be offered them anyway, and lamb and mutton are banned in some provinces. Chicken and pork, however, are always on the menu, generously dished up in well-cooked meals. Although the menu will have few, if any, set **vegetarian** options, *paladares* are more accommodating than state restaurants to off-menu ordering, making them a good choice for non-meat-eaters. *Paladares* are plentiful in Havana but while most large towns have at least one, some smaller towns may not have any at all. Prices are usually uniform with a main meal costing $5–10.

A GLOSSARY OF FOOD AND DRINK

THE BASICS

Aceite	Oil	*Comedor*	Dining room	*Mesa*	Table
Ají	Chilli	*Cuchara*	Spoon	*Miel*	Honey
Ajo	Garlic	*Cuchillo*	Knife	*Pan*	Bread
Almuerzo	Lunch	*La cuenta*	The bill	*Pimienta*	Pepper
Arroz	Rice	*Desayuno*	Breakfast	*Queso*	Cheese
Azúcar	Sugar	*Ensalada*	Salad	*Sal*	Salt
Botella	Bottle	*Huevos*	Eggs	*Tenador*	Fork
Carta	Menu	*Mantequilla*	Butter or	*Vaso*	Glass
Cena	Dinner		margarine		

FISH (*PESCADOS*) AND SEAFOOD (*MARISCOS*)

Aguja	Swordfish	*Merluza*	Hake
Atún	Tuna	*Paella*	Classic Spanish dish
Calamares	Squid		with saffron rice, chicken,
Camarones	Prawns, shrimp		seafood, etc.
Cangrejo	Crab	*Pargo*	Red snapper (tilapia)
Langosta	Lobster	*Pulpo*	Octopus

MEAT (*CARNE*) AND POULTRY (*AVES*)

Albondigas	Meatballs	*Conejo*	Rabbit	*Pierna*	Leg
Bistec	Steak (rarely	*Escalope*	Escalope	*Pollo*	Chicken
	beef)	*Hamburguesa*	Hamburger	*Rana*	Frog's meat
Cabra/Chivo	Goat	*Hígado*	Liver	*Res*	Beef
Cerdo	Pork	*Lomo*	Loin (of pork)	*Sesos*	Brains
Chorizo	Spicy sausage	*Oveja*	Mutton	*Venado*	Venison
Chuleta	Chop	*Pavo*	Turkey		

FRUITS (*FRUTAS*)

Albaricoque	Apricot	*Limón*	Lime/Lemon	*Manzana*	Apple
Cereza	Cherry	*Mamey*	Mamey	*Melocotón*	Peach
Ciruelas	Prunes		(thick,	*Melón*	Melon
Coco	Coconut		sweet red	*Naranja*	Orange
Fruta bomba	Papaya		fruit with a	*Piña*	Pineapple
Guanábana	Soursop		single stone)	*Plátano*	Banana
Guayaba	Guava	*Mango*	Mango	*Toronja*	Grapefruit

Also privately run, from front gardens and driveways, the peso **street stalls** dotted around cities and towns are invariably the cheapest places to eat and an excellent choice for snacks and impromptu lunches, serving fritters, pies and sweets that are home-made daily.

What to eat

Whether you eat in a restaurant, a *paladar*, or enjoy a meal cooked by friends you will find that there is essentially little variety in Cuban cuisine, which revolves around a basic diet of pork or chicken, accompanied by rice and beans and generally known as *comida criolla*. Cubans don't tend to eat as many fruit and vegetables as Westerners do, but these are plentiful and available in the markets.

Breakfast

Breakfast in Cuba tends to be light, consisting of toast or, more commonly, a bread roll eaten with fried, boiled or scrambled eggs. The better hotels do buffet breakfasts that cover cooked eggs and

VEGETABLES (*VERDURAS*)

Aguacate	Avocado	*Frijoles*	Black beans
Berenjenas	Aubergine/ eggplant	*Hongos*	Mushrooms
		Lechuga	Lettuce
Calabaza	Pumpkin	*Papa*	Potato
Cebolla	Onion	*Pepino*	Cucumber
Col	Cabbage	*Pimiento*	Capsicum pepper
Congrí	Rice and black beans (mixed)	*Remolacha*	Beetroot
Chícaro	Pea (pulse)	*Tomate*	Tomato
Esparragos	Asparagus	*Zanahoria*	Carrot

SWEETS (*DULCES*) AND DESSERTS (*POSTRES*)

Arroz con leche	Rice pudding	*Galleta*	Biscuit/cookie
Churros	Long curls of fried batter similar to doughnuts	*Helado*	Ice cream
		Merengue	Meringue
Cocos	Sweets made from shredded coconut and sugar	*Pasta de Guayaba*	Guava jam
Empanada de Guayaba	Guava jam in pastry	*Pay*	(Fruit) pie
		Tortica	Shortbread-type biscuit
Flan	Crème caramel		

DRINKS AND BEVERAGES (*BEBIDAS*)

Agua	Water	*Jugo*	Juice
Agua mineral	Mineral water	*Leche*	Milk
...(con gas)	...(sparkling)	*Limonada natural*	Fresh lemonade
...(sin gas)	...(still)	*Prú*	Fermented drink flavoured with spices
Batido	Milkshake		
Café	Coffee	*Refresco*	Flavoured soft drink
Café con leche	Coffee made with hot milk	*Refresco de lata*	Canned drink
Cerveza	Beer	*Ron*	Rum
Chocolate	Drinking chocolate	*Té*	Tea
Cuba Libre	Rum, Coke and a twist of lime	*Vino blanco*	White wine
		Vino tinto	Red wine

meats, cold meat cuts and cheeses, and cereals, and, even if you're not a guest, are the best places to head if you're hungry.

Lunch and dinner

Lunch also tends to be light, and although all restaurants serve main meals at lunchtime, following the locals' lead and snacking on maize fritters, *pan con pasta* – bread with a garlic mayonnaise filling – or cold pasta salad from the peso street stalls is the best bet for a midday meal. Widely available and cheap, at between six and ten pesos, a **pizza** is a good basic option, but can differ wildly in quality with the best topped with cheese, onion and chorizo sausage and the worst a doughy mass thinly spread with tomato sauce – it's a good idea to look at what's being served up before you buy.

Cubans eat their main meal in the evening. The basis for a typical **dinner** is fried chicken or a pork chop or cutlet fried in garlic and onions, although some restaurants and *paladares* also serve goat, mutton and lamb. Although there is not as much fresh **fish and seafood** as you may expect, what you can get is excellent, particularly the lobster, prawns and fresh tuna.

Invariably accompanying the meal are the ubiquitous **rice and beans** (black or kidney) which come in two main guises: *congrí*, where the rice and beans are served mixed (also known as *moros y cristianos*), and *arroz con frijoles*, where white rice is served with a separate bowl of beans, cooked into a soupy stew, to pour over it. Other traditional **vegetable** accompaniments are fried plantain; mashed, boiled or fried green bananas, which have a buttery almost nutty taste; cassava, a starchy carbohydrate; and a simple salad of tomatoes, cucumber and avocado.

Fruit

Although **fruit** is plentiful in Cuba, much is for export and the top end of the tourist market. The best places to buy fruit are the *agromercados*, where you can load up cheaply with whatever is in season. Particularly good are the various types of mangoes, juicy oranges and sweet pineapples, while delicious lesser-known fruits include the prickly green soursop, with its unique sweet but tart taste, and the mamey, the thick, sweet red flesh of which is made into an excellent milkshake.

Sweets

As you might expect from a sugar-producing country there are several delicious **sweets and desserts** which you are more likely to find on a street stall than served up in a restaurant. Huge slabs of sponge cake coated in meringues are so popular at parties that the state supplies them for children's birthdays to make sure no one goes without. Also good are *torticas*, small round shortcake biscuits; *cocos*, immensely sweet confections of shredded coconut and brown sugar; and thick, jelly-like *guayaba pasta* that is often eaten with cheese.

Drinking

It's a good idea to stick to bottled **water** in Cuba, which is readily available from all dollar shops and hotels – or follow the lead of prudent locals and boil any tap water you plan to drink (see p.32). Canned **soft drinks** are readily available from all dollar shops, and in addition to Coke and Pepsi you can sample Cuba's own brands of lemonade (*Cachito*), cola (*Tropicola*, refreshingly less sugary than other cola drinks) and orangeade (the alarmingly Day-Glo *Najita*). Peso food stalls always serve non-carbonated soft drinks made from powdered packet mix – these cost just a couple of pesos, a fraction of a dollar shop drink, though you should be cautious about hygiene and the water supply. With the same caveats, try *granizado* (slush), served in a paper twist from portable street wagons; *guarapo*, a super-sweet frothy drink made from pressed sugar cane and mostly found at *agromercados*; and, a speciality in the east of the island, *Prú*, a refreshing drink fermented from sweet spices and tasting a little like spiced ginger beer. If you are in a bar, fresh lemonade (*limonada*) is rarely advertised but almost always available.

Coffee and tea

Served most often as pre-sweetened espresso, **coffee** is the beverage of choice for many Cubans and is served in all restaurants and bars and at numerous peso coffee stands dotted around town centres. Cubans tend to add sugar into the pot when making it so there is little chance of getting it unsweetened other than in hotels and tourist restaurants. Aromatic packets of Cuban ground coffee and beans are sold throughout the country, and it's well worth buying a few packets to take home.

Tea is less common but is available in the more expensive hotels and better restaurants as an often unsuccessful marriage of lukewarm water and limp tea bag or a very stewed brew.

Alcohol

If you like *ron* or **rum** you'll be well away in Cuba – the national drink is available everywhere in several manifestations and is generally the most inexpensive tipple available. Havana Club reigns supreme as the best brand, but also look out for Caribbean Club and Siboney. White rum is the cheapest form, generally used in cocktails, while the darker, older rums are best appreciated neat. As well as the authorized stuff sold bottled in hotels and dollar shops there is also a particularly lethal bootleg white rum, usually just called street rum (*ron de la calle*), which is guaranteed to leave you with a fearful hangover and probably partial memory loss. Thick and lined with oily swirls, it is usually sold in most neighbourhoods in the bigger cities; *jineteros* will certainly know where to go but

don't let them charge you more than a couple of dollars a litre. Apart from rum itself, Cuba's most famous export is probably its **cocktails**, including the ubiquitous Cuba Libre. Made from white rum, Coke and a twist of lime, it's second only in popularity to the Mojito, a refreshing combination of white rum, sugar, sparkling water and mint.

Spirits other than rum are also available and are generally reasonably priced in all bars and restaurants, other than those in the prime tourist areas. The bottles on sale in many dollar shops usually work out cheaper than in Europe.

Lager-type **beer** (*cerveza*) is plentiful in Cuba and there are some excellent national brands, particularly Cristal, Hatuey and Bucanero. These are all sold in cans and less commonly in bottles, even when served in bars and restaurants – you can't get beer on draught in Cuba.

Communications

The telephone system in Cuba is inefficient and antiquated, requiring a considerable degree of patience especially when calling within the country. Improvements have been made in recent years and international call rates have actually fallen since Italian investors helped to

untangle the mess which decades of underinvestment had caused. Much the same can be said of the postal service; it now takes weeks instead of months for airmail to leave the island. Some hotels and businesses now have email addresses, but most people don't know what email is and it remains a strictly "official" means of communication.

Phones

There are increasing numbers of **payphones** appearing all over the island, and in the major cities and resorts you should be able to locate one relatively easily. There are, however, two distinct kinds, both operated by the only national telecommunications network, ETECSA. The newer kind, which you are most likely to use, only accept prepaid phone cards, available in denominations of $10 and $20 from post offices, hotels, national travel agents, some banks and the glass-walled phone cabins where a significant proportion of these dollar phones are located.

National rates are reasonable, starting at 5c per minute for calls within the same province. The older, rustier kind of phones, which only accept 5c peso coins, are useless for international calls and have about a one-in-five chance of working for any kind of call whatsoever. They are, however, still the only kind of public phone in the majority of Cuban towns and villages.

A telling indication of the chaos into which the Cuban telephone system slowly descended following the revolution of 1959, picking up the pace when the Special Period took hold in the early 1990s, is the state of its **telephone numbers**. Numbers generally contain either four, five or six digits but in areas of particularly small populations there are two- and even single-digit numbers. Frustratingly there is often a whole series of different numbers for the same place and nothing to determine which one is most likely to get you connected. Thus you may see a number written as "48-77-11 al 18", which means when dialling the final two digits you may have to try all the numbers in between and including 11 and 18 before you get through. To top it all, numbers change at an astonishingly quick rate, especially now that the transition is finally being made to a new, digital system. Thankfully the numbers for dollar hotels, restaurants and much of the rest of the country's tourist infrastructure have been simplified and standardized so that you are most likely to encounter six-digit numbers with only one or two alternative combinations. Look out for numbers beginning with either 33 or 66 as these belong to the newly established, more efficient sections of the system.

International calls made from Cuba are charged at exorbitant rates. The cheapest method is to call from a payphone, as opposed to calling from a hotel where it is likely to be as much as one and a half times more expensive. Currently a payphone call to the USA or Canada costs $2 per minute, whilst to Britain or Australia it's $4.40 per minute. Making an overseas phone call from a **private phone** in a house has its own special procedure and can be quite confusing. If you are staying at a *casa particular* and ask to ring abroad be aware that a direct call will probably not be possible and that you will be obliged to reverse the charges (call collect). Ideally you should get the person you are trying to contact to ring you as it could cost them up to ten times more to receive a reverse-charge call from Cuba.

What's more, calls are charged by the minute and not the second, so that a ten-second call at the rate of $10 a minute will cost $10. If you do make an international call from a Cuban household then you should first ring the international operator, the number for which differs from place to place (see box). The operator will ask for the name and number of the person you are calling, the number you are calling from and your name, usually in that order.

Making a call

To make a call within the same province you will not need to dial the area code of the place you are calling but instead you will need the **exit code** for the place from where you are making the call. The exit code, available either through the operator or from the telephone directory, can itself depend upon where you are calling to. However, if calling from a prepaid card phone simply dial 0 followed by the area code and number.

For **interprovincial** calls you will need to dial first the appropriate prefix (usually 0 but there are a number of variations depending on where you are in the country) to get onto the national grid, then the area code, followed finally by the number. Some interprovincial calls are only possible through the operator. If you are consistently failing to get through on a direct line dial ☎ 00.

For international calls without the assistance of an operator, possible from the newer payphones but only on a relatively small proportion of private phones, dial the international call prefix, which is ☎ 119, then the country code, the area code and the number.

Mail

There's a good chance you'll get back home from Cuba before your postcards do. Don't expect airmail to reach Europe or North America in less than two weeks, whilst it is not unknown for letters to arrive a month or more after they have been sent. Inland mail is equally slow, and a letter from Havana to Santiago is likely to take between one and two weeks to get there. If you send anything other than a letter, either inland or overseas, there's a significant chance that it won't arrive at all as pilfering is widespread within the postal system. You should also be aware that letters and packages coming into Cuba are sometimes opened as a matter of policy.

USEFUL NUMBERS

Directory enquiries ☎113.

Operator ☎00 from most places, including major towns,
cities and resort areas. The most common alternative is ☎110.

INTERNATIONAL OPERATOR

In Bayamo	☎182	In Guantánamo	☎111	In Pinar del Río	☎030
In Camagüey	☎90 or	In Havana	☎09	In Sancti Spíritus	☎112
	83540	In Holguín	☎180	In Santa Clara	☎180
In Cayo Coco	☎180	In Las Tunas	☎06	In Santiago de Cuba	☎180
In Ciego de Ávila	☎180	In Matanzas	☎180	In Trinidad	☎110
In Cienfuegos	☎180	In Nueva Gerona	☎08	In Varadero	☎180

Stamps are sold in both US dollars and pesos at post offices, from white and blue kiosks marked *Correos de Cuba* and in many hotels, though in the last they will only be available for dollars. Dollar-stamped mail does not receive preferential treatment so it's worth buying peso stamps if you can, especially if you are sending large numbers of postcards or letters. Dollar rates are reasonable at 40c for postcards to the USA or Canada and 50c to Britain or Australia, whilst letters cost 25c more in all cases. However, at between 40c and 75c in pesos for postcards and marginally more for letters to the same countries it can work out at over fifteen times cheaper to pay for stamps with the national currency.

All large towns and cities have a **post office**, normally open Monday to Saturday from 8am to 6pm. Most provincial capitals as well as Varadero and Cayo Largo have a branch with DHL services and in some cases the cheaper Cuban equivalent, EMS. At a few select branches, such as the one at Paseo del Prado esq. San Martín in Havana, there are **poste restante** facilities – letters or packages should be marked *lista de correos* (poste restante) and will be held for about a month; you'll need your passport for collection. A more reliable alternative is to have mail sent to a hotel, which you need not nec-

essarily be staying in, marked *esperar* followed by the name of the addressee. The full range of postal services, including DHL and EMS, is offered in some of the larger hotels, usually at the desk marked *Telecorreos*. In smaller towns and villages, post offices, where they exist, offer services in pesos only and are more likely to be closed at the weekend.

Email

Email is in its infancy in Cuba and is of relatively limited use, the vast majority of the population still being without access to a computer let alone email facilities. The number of businesses, especially hotels, with email addresses, is growing but still very much a minority. There are very few places from where you can send or receive an email whilst in Cuba and outside of Havana it will be more or less impossible. The Playa branch of Infotur, at 5ta. Ave. y 112 (☎7/24-70-36), is one of the most straightforward options. The charges are $1 per email sent and $1 to receive each item of incoming mail. Alternatively the luxury *Parque Central, Meliá Habana* and *Meliá Cohiba* hotels have access to email amongst their other business facilities, whilst the Palacio de las Convenciones at Calle 146, e/ 11 y 13 in Playa is also connected but is strictly for business visitors.

The media

All areas of the media in Cuba are subject to tight censorship and are closely controlled by the state. Whilst on the one hand this means the range of information and opinion is severely restricted it has also produced a media geared to producing what the government deems to be socially valuable, refreshingly free of any significant concern for high ratings and commercial success.

Newspapers and magazines

There may be some significance in the fact that *Granma*, Cuba's only national daily **newspaper**, works out considerably cheaper than buying toilet paper, and certainly there are sections of the population who feel this is the only positive thing that can be said of it. Such a judgement, though harsh, reflects the disillusionment many Cubans feel with the role of the press in Cuba as a propaganda tool for the state. The government does little to hide this fact; the front page of *Granma* openly declares it the official mouthpiece of the Cuban Communist Party. Whilst this means that amongst its eight tabloid-size pages you are unlikely to find much breadth of opinion, technically speaking the journalism is of a reasonably high standard and if treated as a political manuscript it can make for an interesting read. Reports are almost exclusively of a political or economic nature, usually publicizing meetings with foreign heads of state, denouncing US policy towards Cuba, or announcing developments within some sector of industry or commerce. Castro's speeches are often published in their entirety whilst international news takes a firm back seat. The occasional article challenging the official party line does appear, but these are usually short pieces on the inside pages, directed at specific events and policies rather than overall ideologies. There are two other national papers, *Trabajadores*, a weekly representing the workers' unions, and *Juventud Rebelde*, claiming to be the newpaper of the Cuban youth, which is published daily between Wednesday and Sunday. These are effectively repackaged versions of *Granma*. Though officially all three newspapers cost just 20c in pesos each, you have to be quick to pick one up for that price, quicker than the street-vendors who

> ### Listings
>
> Finding out about forthcoming events is a somewhat hit-and-miss business in Cuba. Although the free weekly **listings newspaper** *Cartelera*, only available in Havana, where you'll find it in most of the larger hotels, carries information on a variety of goings-on in the capital, it is far from comprehensive and many local events, particularly those organized principally by and for Cubans, don't get a mention. The national newspaper, *Granma*, has details of baseball games and is one of the only sources of information on television programming schedules. Radio Taíno often broadcasts details of major shows and concerts as well as advertisements for the tourist in-spots. For the less mainstream events the principal method of advertising is word-of-mouth, with posters and flyers seldom if ever seen.

buy stacks of them at the start of the day and sell them around town for a peso each. Some post offices and the white-and-blue *Correos de Cuba* kiosks hold copies but short of that you should try any dollar hotel.

Hotels are more likely to stock *Granma International* (50¢), published weekly, twice as thick as its daily counterpart and tailored to a foreign readership. Printed in five languages including English, it offers a round-up of the week's stories but sometimes comes off like a political brochure, extolling the virtues of the Cuban state to a supposedly impressionable foreign public. There is a disproportionate number of articles based on tourism, though, to its credit, it usually carries a couple of pages of culture-oriented reporting.

There are two weekly business papers, *Opciones* ($1) and *Negocios en Cuba* ($1), which are unlikely to catch your attention unless you're interested in trading with the government, although *Opciones* does have a listings page geared to tourists.

There are very few **international newspapers** available in Cuba, a couple of Spanish and Italian dailies being the only ones that appear with any regularity. Away from the more sophisticated hotels you're unlikely to find even these, and certainly tracking down an English-language newspaper of any description is an arduous, usually unrewarding task. The *Hotel Nacional* and the *Meliá Habana* hotel, both in the capital, are two of the best places in the whole country for picking up bits and pieces of foreign press. There is also a growing number of bookshops, mostly in the capital, stocking non-Cuban newpapers and magazines, though editions are often months, even years out of date. The most often-seen titles for English-speakers are *Time, Newsweek, Rolling Stone, Sports Illustrated* and *Cosmopolitan*.

Presenting a rather more diverse picture of Cuban society are its **magazines**. Amongst the most cultured is *Bohemia*, Cuba's oldest surviving periodical, whose relatively broad focus offers a mix of current affairs, historical essays and regular spotlights on art, sport and technology. The best of the more specialist publications are the bimonthly *Revolución y Cultura*, concentrating on the arts and literature, and *Récord*, dedicated entirely to sport. Appearing at sporadic intervals with an average of three or four issues a year, the latter not only provides top-quality journalism but is also an interesting insight into the elevated importance of sport in Cuba and the proud place that sporting achievement occupies in the national consciousness. Aimed at foreign visitors, the insipid reporting in *Cuba Internacional*, a monthly publication with an emphasis on economic and political issues, will attract far fewer readers than the more lively *Prisma*, billed as Cuba's tourism magazine. With articles written in Spanish and English it adopts a relatively light-hearted, very readable tone, drawing on all kinds of topics and areas of anecdotal interest, often spotlighting particular cities or featuring interviews with musicians and artists.

All of these magazines are sold in dollars, though some, most notably *Bohemia*, have a corresponding edition for sale in pesos, and are most commonly found in bookshops and hotels, far more readily available in Havana, Varadero and Santiago de Cuba than elsewhere. However, you can sometimes pick up out-of-date editions, as well as the peso equivalents, from the *Correos de Cuba* kiosks at a fraction of the dollar cost.

Radio

There are six national **radio stations** in Cuba but tuning into them isn't always easy as signal strength tends to vary quite considerably. You're most likely to hear broadcasts from **Radio Taíno**, the official tourist station to which most sets in public places are tuned. Playing predominantly mainstream pop and Cuban music, the station is also a useful source of up-to-date tourist information such as the latest nightspots, forthcoming events and places to eat. Tune in between 4 and 5pm on Saturday or Sunday for *La Gran Jugada*, a show carrying the results of sporting events from around the globe, including European football, NBA and MLB.

Musically speaking, other than the ever-popular sounds of Cuban salsa, stations rarely stray away from safe-bet US, Latin and European pop and rock, with entire genres, such as reggae and jazz, all but ignored. The predominantly classical music content of **Radio Musical Nacional** is about as specialist as it gets.

Of the remaining stations there is little to distinguish one from the other. The exception is **Radio Reloj**, a 24-hour news station with humourless reports read out to the ceaseless sound of a ticking clock in the background as the exact time is announced every minute on the minute.

RADIO STATIONS AND FREQUENCIES

Radio Enciclopedia (1260MW/94.1FM)
Strictly instrumental music drawn from various genres.

Radio Habana Cuba (106.9FM) News and chat in a number of languages.

Radio Musical Nacional (590MW/99.1FM) Internationally renowned classical music.

Radio Progreso (640MW/90.3FM) Music and drama with current hits both in Cuba and abroad broadcast between 3 and 6pm every day.

Radio Rebelde (670 and 710MW/96.7FM) Sport, current affairs and music.

Radio Reloj (950MW/101.5FM) National and international news 24 hours a day.

Radio Taíno 1(1290MW/93.2–93.4FM) Tourist station playing popular Cuban and international music.

On the northern coast of the island, particularly in and between Havana and Varadero, it is quite possible to tune into stations broadcasting from southern Florida, a fact which has not escaped the attention of the exile community in Miami who set up **Radio Martí** specifically for that purpose.

Television

There are two national **television channels** in Cuba, Cubavisión and Telerebelde, both commercial-free and littered instead with public service broadcasts, revolutionary slogans and daily short slots commemorating historical events and figures. Other than a short newscast around midday neither channel begins its transmissions until 6pm, though in July, August and every weekend there are programmes throughout most of the day. Surprisingly for some, given the relationship between Cuba and the US, Hollywood films are a staple on both channels, sometimes preceded by a discussion of the film's value and the central issues. Many are impressively recent, the result of pirating from US satellite channels, whilst the frequent use of subtitles makes them watchable for non-Spanish speakers. Other than this, however, North American culture has penetrated very little into programming schedules. **Cubavisión** shows the majority of the films, of which rarely more than six are screened in a single week. For years there have been two films broadcast on Saturday nights, usually well-known blockbusters, from around 10pm onwards. The same channel hosts another long-standing television tradition in Cuba, the staggeringly popular *telenovelas*, usually Brazilian or Colombian soap operas, going out on Mondays, Wednesdays and Fridays at around 9.30pm. Their melodramatic characters and outlandish plots, which capture the attention of the whole nation, are offset by the consistently more sober, homegrown soaps on Tuesdays and Thursdays. There are several weekly music programmes showcasing the best of contemporary Cuban music as well as giving space to popular international artists. Saturday evenings are the best time to catch live-broadcast performances from the cream of the national salsa scene. For music videos and a taste of the predominantly Latin and US artists who make it into Cuban homes, *Colorama* goes out late on Monday nights. **Telerebelde** is where you'll find all the sport, with live national-league baseball games shown almost daily throughout the season with basketball, volleyball, athletics and boxing making up the bulk of the rest. Tune in on Sunday afternoons for a full five or six hours of it.

Officially, satellite television is the exclusive domain of the hotels, which are also the recipients of **Cubavisión Internacional**, the tourist channel showing a mixture of films, documentaries and music programmes. In Varadero, Havana and the other major resort areas, most hotel rooms come with a broad range of satellite channels including at least one music and one film channel. However, a significant proportion of hotels still have only two or three, ESPN and CNN amongst the most common. The government has ensured that TV Martí, set up for the same purpose as its radio namesake, rarely if ever gets through, by jamming the signal.

The best places to look for **programme times** are in the pages of *Granma*, for Cubavisión and Telerebelde, and *Opciones* for Cubavisión Internacional. The plusher hotels usually carry a television schedule magazine for the satellite channels.

Opening hours, festivals and entertainment

Cuban offices are normally open for business between 9am and 5pm Monday to Friday, with many of them closing for a one-hour lunch break anywhere between noon and 2pm. Shops are generally open 9am to 6pm Monday to Saturday, sometimes closing for lunch, while the shopping malls and department stores in Havana stay open as late as 8pm. Sunday trading is increasingly common, with most places open until noon or 1pm, longer in the major resorts. Hotel shops stay open all day. Banks generally operate Monday to Friday 8am to 3pm, but this varies – see p.22 for more details.

Museums are usually open six days a week (Mon–Sat or Tues–Sun) from 9am to between 5pm and 7pm, with an hour (or two) for lunch. Those open on Sunday generally close in the afternoon. You may also arrive at a museum to find it shut for another reason, the person with the keys having failed to turn up, for instance.

Entertainment

Music forms the pulsing backdrop to virtually all entertainment in Cuba, and to everyday life as it booms from crackling taxi stereos, upmarket salsa palaces, markets and free-for-all street parties alike; although nowadays you are just as likely to hear imported Latino disco or the latest boy band as home-grown salsa. Despite this, in the large cities there are plenty of live music and dance clubs to satisfy ardent aficionados. Best are the **Casas de la Trova**, atmospheric music halls specializing in traditional Cuban tunes that often have live groups. In the smaller cities you may find nightlife surprisingly low-key, though no less enjoyable. At beach resorts, entertainment tends to revolve around the discos and professional entertainment put on at the hotels.

Cuban **theatre** and **cinema** are also hugely enjoyable, visual and atmospheric enough for even non-Spanish speakers to enjoy, particularly during the festival season.

A key event during the Cuban festive calendar is **carnival** – an explosion of sound and colour that takes place in many of the main towns around the country, with the most celebrated versions happening in Santiago and Havana.

Street parties

There's nothing to equal the atmosphere of a Cuban **street party**, uniquely riotous events when the streets teem with partygoers, beer trucks and food stalls sprawl across closed-off roads and live salsa bands expertly tease seductive moves from a heaving crowd. State organized, they take place on national holidays, anniversaries and at carnival, with revellers bussed in from the suburbs for the parties in larger towns. Some towns also have a mini-street party weekly at weekends; these are just as jubilant although live music is not a regular feature. The friendly atmosphere should present no problems for visitors wanting to join in, but taking the minimum of money is a good idea in case of pickpockets.

National holidays

Jan 1 Liberation Day. Anniversary of the triumph of the revolution.
May 1 International Workers' Day.
July 25–27 Celebration of the day of national rebellion.
Oct 10 Anniversary of the start of the Wars of Independence.

CALENDAR OF EVENTS

JANUARY

Cubadanza, Gran Teatro, Habana Vieja
(☎ 7/31-13-57; *paradis@turcult.get.cma.net*).
Cuban contemporary dance festival featuring performers from around the country.

Winter Cuballet, Gran Teatro, Habana Vieja
(☎ 7/20-86-10;
paradis@turcult.get.cma.net). The winter season of the national ballet.

FEBRUARY

Havana Carnival (☎ 7/62-38-83;
rosalla@cimex.com.cu). Festivities in Havana get under way in the second week of February with parades and street parties around the city centre for about three weeks.

Havana Jazz Festival, Teatro Nacional, Havana (☎ 7/ 79-60-11). See the best of Cuban jazz, including the legendary *Irakere* with Chu Chu Valdés, play around the town at a range of different venues. International guest stars also feature.

MARCH

Ciego de Ávila International Carnival, Ciego de Ávila (☎ 33/23-33-35). A more tourist-oriented version of the traditional carnival.

JULY

Fiesta of Fire Festival, Santiago de Cuba
(☎ 226/2-35-69; *upec@mail.infocom.
etecsa.cu*). Santiago's week-long celebration of Caribbean music and dance culture takes place at the beginning of July.

Santiago Carnival, Santiago de Cuba
(☎ 226/2-33-02; *burostgo@binanet.lib.cult.cu*). Cuba's most exuberant carnival holds Santiago in its thrall in the first two weeks of July with costumed parades and congas, salsa bands and late-night parties.

Camagüey Carnival, Camagüey. Smaller than Santiago's version but exciting nonetheless.

AUGUST

Cubadanza, Gran Teatro, Habana Vieja
(☎ 7/31-13-57; *paradis@turcult.get.cma.net*).
The summer season of the Cuban contemporary dance festival which draws performers from all over the country to Havana.

Summer Cuballet, Gran Teatro, Habana Vieja
(☎ 7/20-86-10; *paradis@turcult.get.cma.net*).
The national ballet's summer season.

SEPTEMBER

Havana International Theatre Festival,
Havana (☎ 7/31-13-57; *paradis@turcult.get
.cma.net*). Excellent ten-day theatre festival showcasing classics and contemporary Cuban works at various theatres around the city.

DECEMBER

International Festival of New Latin American Film, Havana (☎ 7/55-28-54;
rosalla@cimex.com.cu). One of Cuba's top events, the ten-day film festival combines the newest Cuban films with the finest classics, as well as providing a networking opportunity for leading independent film directors.

Live music clubs

Traditional Cuban music, as popularized by the group Buena Vista Social Club, is making a resurgence in the West, and those who come to Cuba to catch the real thing won't be disappointed. Live music is the backbone of the culture, and particularly in Havana, Santiago and Varadero, there's a variety of places in which to soak it up: from lavish salsa palaces and open-air venues to hotel salons where you can enjoy an evening of live music for around $10–20. Although the most renowned stars frequently tour abroad, they also play the mainstream Cuban circuit and are supported by lesser-known but equally capable musicians and bands.

You can hear all the soulful *son, boleros* and *guajiras* (as well as salsa) in **Casas de la Trova** throughout the country (see Contexts, p.485). These are always worth checking out, as even the smallest one in the most pedestrian town will have live music at least once a week and recorded salsa at other times.

Discos, rock and hip-hop venues

Discos in Cuba tend to draw a younger crowd keen to show off their salsa, casino and merengue – dauntingly complicated dance steps – to the strains of Ricky Martin and the like. They are generally dark sweaty places where dancers wiggle and slink to a limited repertoire of music played so loudly over the substandard speakers that the tunes are distorted almost beyond recognition. However what they lack in quality they make up for in atmosphere, and as long as you can handle the persistent attentions of amorous admirers they are good for a laugh. The entrance fee rarely exceeds $5, and most start around 8pm, heat up at around 11pm and wind down by 2am.

Other non-Cuban music is growing in both popularity and availability and home-grown **rock** and **hip-hop** bands have an increasing youth following. Although enthusiasm sometimes outstrips talent the concerts are frenetic and now form the unofficial stamping ground of alternative Cuban youth. In Havana, the listings paper *Cartelera* carries details of gigs, while in the provinces, information offices, hotels and, most reliably, word of mouth are the best ways to find out what's on.

Theatre, dance and cinema

With **theatre** in Cuba of such a high standard, it's well worth catching at least one performance of this typically highly visual art form, even if you're a non-Spanish speaker. The best time to sample the culture is during Havana's superb International Theatre Festival in September (see box), but even small towns have a theatre and/or a Casa de Cultura (literally "cultural house") where performances and recitals are staged throughout the year – from locally written avant-garde groundbreakers to European classics. Actors are highly trained, sets and costumes display an imaginative use of limited resources and direction is uniformly excellent. The largest and most professional theatres are in Havana, notably the Gran Teatro in Habana Vieja and the Teatro Nacional in Plaza de la Revolución; however, there are smaller venues in Havana and throughout the country that are well worth checking out. Typical Cuban theatre is put on by a small company, between five and ten people, and both contemporary and classic plays tend towards the heavy and dramatic. Whether elaborate or stark, sets are often chimerical creations with covert jabs at the state hidden in the symbolism.

For many visitors and locals alike, **cabaret**, with its bevy of scantily clad women, is the height of sophisticated entertainment. Cabaret has been a part of the Cuban cultural scene since the 1930s, with the dancers supplemented by comedians, musicians, magicians, acrobats and crooners. However, you can be sure that the staple of any show, whether it be at the best Havana venues or a small-town club, will be the phalanx of all-singing all-dancing women wearing their own weight in sequins and fluff and high kicking their way through elaborate routines. The *Tropicana* open-air cabaret in Havana is the most famous and offers the most spectacular show with star turns by the most popular musicians of the moment. Prices range from $5 for a provincial show to $60 for the Havana nightspots.

Widely considered the flagship of Cuba's cultural life, the **national ballet** was formed in 1948 by prima donna Alicia Alonso, who took the ballet into exile from 1953, returning after the revolution – with which the ballet is still associated. The company comprises over a hundred members, some of whom perform abroad, and its reputation has gained in strength, with several members having won international awards for their artistic interpretation and technique. Based at the Gran Teatro in Habana Vieja, the ballet performs a winter and summer season.

Cinemas are widespread, ranging from huge auditoriums to tiny flea pits. In all venues the film is screened continuously: Cubans enter at any point and leave again when the film has come full circle. The atmosphere is often riotous, especially when there is a popular film showing, and raucous cat-calls, loud cheers and appreciative clapping are all the norm. Although there are some heavyweight Cuban films like *Memorias de Subdesarrollo*, the most popular ones are the burlesques typified by *Guantanamera* and *La Muerte de un Burócrata* by director Tomás Gutiérrez Alea. Tickets cost 1 or 2 pesos, although as a foreigner in Havana you may be charged the equivalent in dollars. If you're particularly keen to see some Cuban cinema, visit during Havana's **film festival**, when new work showcases, offering up-to-date insights into the heart of Cuban culture, in addition to the current arthouse films from all over the world. Dubbed and subtitled North American and European films show regularly, usually reaching the Cuban screens about twelve to eighteen months after their domestic release. You can catch more recent films in the ubiquitous **Salas de Video,** literally "video rooms", although as a rule viewing quality leaves much to be desired.

Festivals, special events and carnival

Cultural **festivals** like the International Theatre Festival and world-celebrated International Festival of New Latin American Film have won Havana global applause, though there are plenty of lesser-known festivals celebrating Afro-Cuban dance, literature, ballet and other arts, and a whole host of smaller but worthwhile events in other provinces. Catching one of these can make all the difference to a visit to a less than dynamic town.

With exuberant floats and conga parades, Cuba's main **carnival** takes place in Santiago de Cuba in July and is an unmissable experience if you're around. As well as numerous parades featuring dramatically costumed carnival queens waving from floats, and more down-to-earth neighbourhood percussion bands, several stage areas are set up around the town and live salsa bands play nightly. Perhaps the most enjoyable aspect of carnival, though, is the *conga* parades, unique to Santiago de Cuba. Signalling the unofficial start to carnival, the *conga* usually takes place on the first evening, and locals and visitors alike can join in. Each neighbourhood forms its own parade, led by its own percussion band. Amid a mad cacophony of sound, with musicians blowing shrill Chinese horns, beating drums and general uproar, men and women (children borne aloft) flood from their houses to form an unruly parade that weaves around the town. Also worth checking out are the smaller carnivals held in Havana in February and Camagüey in July, which also feature parades and boisterous street parties.

Shopping

Cigars, rum, music and arts and crafts remain the really worthwhile purchases in Cuba, and though the range of consumer products available in the shops is constantly expanding, the quality and choice is still generally poor. The late 1990s saw the first modern shopping malls emerge, predominantly in Havana, but outside of these and a few of the grandest hotels, shopping comes with none of the convenience and choice you're probably used to. Almost all shops actually carrying any stock now operate in dollars, but a pocket full of pesos as back-up allows you the slim chance of picking up a bargain.

In any dollar shop where the locals outnumber the tourists you should be prepared for some idiosyncratic **security measures**, as hilarious as they are infuriating. Don't be surprised to be asked to wait at the door until another customer leaves and don't expect to be able to enter carrying any kind of bag – if you have a bag with you look for the *guardabolso* where you can leave it, with some identification, to be collected afterwards. If you purchase anything, make sure you pick up your receipt at the cash till as your shopping will be checked against it at the exit. It's also possible that your carrier bag will be sealed with tape at the till only to be ripped open when you get to the door so that the contents can be checked – ripping it open yourself will leave not only your bag but the whole precious system in tatters.

Where to shop

A shopping expedition will draw up very short anywhere other than Havana – with by far the widest choice – Varadero or Santiago, but any town with a dollar hotel will usually have a couple of shops worth checking out. Most of the largest towns have an indoor **craft market**, at least a couple of **bookshops** and somewhere to buy **CDs and cassettes**, but more common are the single-floor **department stores** run by Tiendas Panamericanas, stocking household goods, groceries and poor-quality clothing.

The best places for a selection of good shops in one place are the **hotels** and the **shopping malls** in Havana and Varadero. The total number of malls in the country is unlikely to exceed double figures for a few years to come. The hotels *Habana Libre*, *Meliá Cohiba* and *Comodoro* have the best choice, especially of name-brand clothing, which is still scarce in Cuba.

Though you will rarely find anything of value, it is sometimes worth taking a look inside those **peso shops** which have remained open. Poorly lit and badly maintained, some understandably won't allow foreign custom, giving priority to the peso-earning public. Most, however, are open to anyone who cares to take a look and though they are often half-empty, it is still possible to unearth the odd antique camera or a long-since deleted record. The best of these are in Centro Habana; Variedades on the Avenida de Italia is a classic of its kind. Also worth looking out for are the **casas de comisiones**, the nearest thing Cuba has to a pawnbrokers. These can be delightful places to poke around, frequently full of 1950s paraphernalia ranging from pocket watches to transistor radios. One of the most exciting is in Sancti Spíritus.

What to buy

The most successful shopping itinerary for the Western visitor to Cuba will be one which features only those items that are, in one sense or another, home-grown. Don't come to the country hoping to pick up bargain-priced sneakers or cut-price electrical goods – nine times out of ten anything readily available at home will cost more in Cuba and won't come with the same kind of guarantees.

Cigars

Now that **cigars** are in vogue again and with the price of the world's finest tobacco at half what you would pay for it outside of Cuba, it's crazy to not at least consider buying some *habanos* (the frequently used term for Cuban cigars) whilst on the island. There are at least five excellent cigar emporiums in Havana and numerous others around the island, with most half-decent hotels stocking at least a few boxes. The industry standard is for cigars to be sold in boxes of 25, for which prices vary enormously according to brand, strength, length and circumference. For anything less than $50 a box you'd be entitled to question the quality of the product whilst prices go as high as $300 and beyond for the top brands. The most coveted brand is Cohiba, unusual in that it was established after the revolution of 1959, a black-market favourite and top of many a connoisseur's list. However, there are no duff brands as such and if you're buying cigars as souvenirs or for a novelty smoke you'd do as well to go for

---

Spotting fake cigars

What makes a Cuban cigar a fake and what makes it genuine can be fairly academic, and some fakes are so well made that even once they are lit it is difficult to tell the difference. If you intend to sell them rather than smoke them, however, it may be more important to be certain whether or not you have been sold a bunch of duds. No method is foolproof but if your cigars pass the following checks you'll know that at the worst you have some well-made copies.

• All the cigars in a box should be the same colour and shade.

• There should be no loose bits of tobacco falling from the cigar when rolled between the fingers.

• There should be the same strength smell from all the cigars in a box.

• There should only be extremely slight variations in the length of cigars, no more than a few millimetres.

• Genuine boxes should be sealed with two labels: a banknote-style label at the front and a smaller label reading *Habanos* in the corner.

• The bottom of the box should be stamped: *Habanos SA*, *Hecho en Cuba* and *Totalmente a mano*.

---

such world-famous names as Monte Cristo, Romeo y Julieta, Punch or Hoyo de Monterrey, all classics but available at more affordable prices than Cohiba. First-time smokers hoping to find a new hobby should start with a light smoke for their initiation ceremony and take it from there; good beginners' cigars include most of the H.Upmann range, whilst for a fuller but still manageable flavour try a Churchill from the Romeo y Julieta brand. Bear in mind that without receipts you are permitted to take only fifty cigars out of the country – with receipts the limit is a total value of no more than $2000. This will be of particular relevance if you have bought your cigars on the black market (see box on p.51).

Rum and coffee

Along with cigars, **rum** is one of the longest established Cuban exports and comes with a worldwide reputation. There are a few specialist rum shops around the island; the Casa del Ron on Obispo in Habana Vieja carries as comprehensive a range as anywhere. However, you can pick up most of the recognized brands in any large supermarket without fear of paying over the odds. The most renowned name is Havana Club, owned by Bacardi until the 1960s when the distillery was nationalized and the firm effectively driven abroad. Rum is available in several different strengths, according to how long it was distilled; the least expensive, Silver Dry, is pleasantly smooth and will set you back between just $3 and $5 depending on where you shop. The strength of the more potent brews is expressed in years on the label as *Añejo* 3, 5 or 7 *Años*. The maximum number of bottles permitted by customs is six.

Coffee, first introduced to the island by French plantation owners fleeing from the 1798 Haitian revolution, is one of the lesser-known traditional products in Cuba. It's easy to find, and again supermarkets are as good as anywhere, but for one of the few specialist shops head for the Plaza de Armas in Habana Vieja. Just off the square, on the corner of Baratillo, La Casa del Café has a modest selection of different coffees, including *Cubita*, the top name, but nevertheless a greater choice than anywhere else.

Books and music

Ironically there has been a far greater variety of books on Cuban topics published abroad in recent years than in the country itself. Few of these are for sale in Cuban **bookshops**, where the speciality is political writings. From the prolific works of the nineteenth-century independence-fighter José Martí to the speeches of Fidel Castro, there are endless lists of titles, all unwavering in their support of the revolution. Also popular, and perhaps more universally appealing, are the coffee-table books of photography covering all aspects of life in one of the most photogenic countries in the world.

Havana has some fantastic **book markets**. The best is on the Plaza de Armas, where amongst the revolutionary pamphlets you can find vintage copies of rarely seen early twentieth-century Cuban books and even colonial-era literature. The markets are the places to uncover written material, such as US-printed tourist brochures reflecting life before Castro, which have no place on the shelves of the official state-run stores.

English-language books are few and far between but two or three bookshops in Havana and at least one in Varadero have a foreign-language literature section, usually consisting of crime novels and old Penguin paperbacks.

As with books there is not necessarily a better choice of Cuban **music** inside the country than in London, New York or Montréal. There are, however, all sorts of titles that are unavailable elsewhere and for the most up-to-date, fresh-out-the-studio *salsa* this is the only place to shop. Some of the most comprehensive catalogues of CDs and tapes are found in **Artex** stores, the chain responsible for promoting culture-based Cuban products. Most provincial capitals now have a branch, and in Varadero there are two with sizeable stocks, though in terms of quantity none resembles anything like what many visitors will have come to expect from the average record shop in their own country. Other than these, in Havana, the record stores in the hotel *Habana Libre* and Longina on Obispo are well stocked with everything from Cuban jazz to obscure *rumba* outfits to remastered 1950s recordings by Beny Moré.

Arts and crafts

One of the most rewarding shopping experiences to be had in Cuba is looking around the **outdoor markets** in Havana, where the full range of local arts and crafts, generally referred to as *artesanía*, are on sale. The tacky tailored-to-tourism Che ashtrays and garishly coloured pictures from the school of painting-by-numbers are more than balanced out by the expressive African-style wood carvings, wide choice of jewellery, hand-made shoes and everything else from ceramics to textiles. Haggling is par for the course and often pays dividends but shopping around won't reveal any really significant differences in price or product.

The three main **craft markets** in Havana are on Tacón, just outside the Plaza de la Catedral, La Rampa and the Malecón, a few blocks east of the *Meliá Cohiba* hotel. In the island's other tourist towns, the work of local artisans can be found in specially designated shops, usually called a Fondo de Bienes Culturales or, more misleadingly, a Galería de Arte. Artex shops also make a good port-of-call, though they tend to have more mass-produced items.

Clothing

Cuba has a thriving T-shirt market which, thankfully, has yet to be overrun by the *Life's a Beach* design trends so prominent elsewhere. The

The black market

The **black market**, or the *bolsa negra*, is an integral part of life for most Cubans, who rely on it to supply them with the long list of products put out of their reach both by shortages and by the introduction of the dollar as the only effective currency. From paint to pillowcases the hotels, where so many of the available resources are found, are the inadvertent suppliers of much of what changes hands under the state table. The attraction of a job connected in any way with tourism or dollars, whether it be as a shop assistant, waiter, construction worker or anything else, is, for many Cubans, inextricably linked with the opportunities it will throw up for illicit dealings. Theft from the workplace is common and not surprising given that a few towels or a map of Havana will sell for a week's wages.

The biggest business on the black market is in the selling of cigars to foreign visitors, the average price of a box representing at least as much as the average monthly wage. If you spend any time at all in a Cuban town or city you will inevitably be offered a box of cigars on the street. You can find boxes for as little as $10 but no self-respecting salesman is likely to sell the genuine article at that price and they will almost certainly be fakes (see box on p.49). Realistically you should expect to pay between $20 and $40, depending on the brand and type, for the real thing. Ideally you should speak to someone you know, most obviously the owner of a *casa particular*; even if they don't have a direct contact the chances are that they will be able to help you out – everyone knows someone who can get hold of a box of Cohibas or Monte Cristos.

---

obvious choice is a Che T-shirt, of which there are hundreds of different kinds, but there are plenty of more original alternatives and it's worth shopping around. You'll be pushed to find a better selection than the ones in the Palacio de la Artesanía or the T-shirt shop outside the entrance to the *Habana Libre* hotel, but they are sold in shops and hotels up and down the island. The most archetypal item of Cuban clothing is the *guayabera*, a lightweight shirt usually characterized by four pockets and worn in all walks of life. It makes a good souvenir and is sold in tourist shops and, less expensively, in department stores such as La Epoca in Centro Habana.

If you're looking for name-brand or designer clothing then you'll do better to get it all out of the way at the airport before you leave. An increasing number of recognizable names are creeping into Cuban shops, particularly those located inside hotels, but you're still more likely to see poor-quality, amusingly named fakes such as *Dodios*, the Cuban answer to Adidas, than a reasonably priced foreign brand.

Sport and outdoor activities

In terms of participatory sports and outdoor pursuits in Cuba much, like golf and hiking, is still in the development stages. Watersports are the exception, with dive sites and diving centres all over the island and some of the richest and most unspoilt waters in the world. Live spectator sport costs next to nothing, and whether in baseball or basketball you can't beat a Havana versus Santiago match-up.

Spectator sports

Like *salsa*, **baseball** is in the blood for most Cubans and with a tradition in the sport going as far back as 1874, when the first ever game took place on the island, between Matanzas and Havana, there are few better places outside of the USA to appreciate this most American of pastimes. The national league, the Serie Nacional de Beisbol, takes place between sixteen teams over a regular season which usually begins in October and finishes with the playoffs in March and April. Every provincial capital has a baseball stadium and, during the season, teams play five times a week so there's a good chance of catching a game if you're in the country during the winter months. There are rarely capacity crowds and though the atmosphere at games doesn't quite equal the emotion of a British football match or the hype of the NBA the crowds are unintimidating and friendly, making it pleasantly accessible to all. Historically the best team has been Industriales, one of the two Havana teams, but Pinar del Río and Santiago de Cuba have been at least as strong in recent years and the battle for the title is never a foregone conclusion.

The other league which generates enough excitement to make a live game worth catching is the Liga Superior de Baloncesto, the national **basketball** league. Though everything is on a smaller scale compared to baseball, from the number of teams to the size of the crowds, the smaller arenas and the faster pace of the game itself often give live basketball an edge over the national sport. There are only four teams in the league, with Havana's Capitalinos and Santiago's Orientales usually the strongest title contenders. The best places to see a game are in the Sala Polivalente Ramón Fonst, near the Plaza de la Revolución, or the Ciudad Deportiva, on the way to the airport, both in Havana. The **season** usually lasts from October to January.

There are amateur **boxing** bouts throughout the year in cities all over Cuba, with the main international fights usually held in the Ciudad Deportiva or the Sala Polivalente Kid Chocolate, one of the country's oldest sporting arenas, opposite the Capitolio building in Habana Vieja. Held in Villa Clara in recent years, the Giraldo Córdova Cardín Tournament usually takes place in April and is one of the most prestigious annual competitions. Boxing has been one of Cuba's most successful Olympic sports but the strictly non-professional policy of the government has kept Cuban names out of the international limelight. Two of the most respected Cuban boxers of late and still names to look out for are the heavyweight Félix Savón and Ariel Hernández.

Participatory sports

Public sports centres where facilities can be rented out do not exist in Cuba and the easiest way to get a game of football, basketball or baseball is simply to turn up at the **local park** and join in with the locals. Where there are open spaces in towns and cities there's a good chance that a game of baseball is going on, and most places have an outdoor basketball court. Football or soccer, despite the poor national standard, has become significantly more popular since the 1998 World Cup, and it's now almost as easy to find a bunch of locals kicking a ball as swinging a bat. Outdoor squash courts are also popular, though you may find that *cancha*, the version played in Cuba, differs slightly from what you are used to. Any physical activity you participate in, however, is more likely to be of the kind organized by a tour operator or based around a resort area.

Watersports

With 5745km of coastline, an average water temperature of 24°C and a thirty-year break from the potentially damaging effects of the international tourist market, Cuba is a **scuba diving and snorkelling** paradise. There is a fantastic variety of dive sites all over the island, many still virtually untouched, though now that word of the uniqueness of Cuba has spread throughout the global diving community this is changing rapidly. As well as reefs there are numerous underwater caves and tunnels, whilst wrecks are also common.

Most of the major beach resorts, including Varadero, Santa Lucía and Guardalavaca, have well-equipped diving centres. Varadero, where there are three marinas and two diving clubs, is one of the best places for novice divers. For a more secluded expedition María La Gorda, in western Pinar del Río, and Guajimico, between Cienfuegos and Trinidad, operate on a smaller scale but sacrifice nothing in the quality of the diving.

The two main **dive operators**, who also run most of the marinas, are Marlin (☎7/24-66-75, fax 24-70-20), a branch of Cubanacan, and Puertosol (☎7/24-59-23 to 26, fax 24-59-28; *www.puertosol.cubaweb.cu*). Some diving centres are run as joint ventures with foreign companies, a development which has led to the availability of internationally recognized PADI and ACUC courses. There are countless opportunities for all levels of diving, from absolute beginners to hardened professionals, but the best place to start is in a hotel-based diving resort where you can take your first lesson in the safety of a swimming pool. Typically a beginners' course involving some theory, a pool lesson and an open-water dive costs between $60 and $80, whilst a week-long ACUC course costs in the region of $375. For one single-tank dive expect to pay $25–30 but bear in mind that there is usually an extra charge for rental of equipment which will add approximately $5 per day to any diving you do.

Facilities for sports like **water-skiing** and **kayaking** are available at the major resorts, but don't expect every beachfront hotel to be well catered for in this respect. Everything from **parasailing** to **glass-bottomed boats** to **jet-skis** can be found at Varadero, Guardalavaca, Santa Lucía and Cayo Coco, but generally where resorts, total just two or three hotels, like the Península de Ancón, there is less chance of finding motorized equipment. Cuba does not usually experience much **surf**, and though boards are rented out at a number of resorts you're more likely to catch a cold than a wave at most of them.

Fishing

The lakes, reservoirs and coastal areas of Cuba offer excellent **fishing** opportunities and there are numerous possibilities for organized fresh- and saltwater fishing trips throughout the island. Bass and trout are particularly abundant inland, at places like Lake Hanabanilla in Villa Clara, the Zaza Reservoir in Sancti Spíritus and the several artificial lakes in Camagüey province. The best saltwater fishing is off the northern coast where blue marlin, sail fish, white marlin, barracuda and tuna are amongst the most dramatic potential catches. There is no bad time for fishing around Cuba but for the biggest blue marlin, July, August and September are the most rewarding months, whilst April, May and June attract greater numbers of white marlin and sail fish. The best bass catches usually occur during the winter months when the average temperature drops to 22°C.

The **hotels** and **marinas** are your main points of contact, many of them working in conjunction with one another. The hotel chain Horizontes (☎7/33-40-42 or 33-42-38; *www.horizontes.cu*) is better prepared than most and operates several hotels designed specifically for freshwater fishing holidays. Before you start you will need a fishing licence, which costs $20, whilst a three- to four-hour session typically costs $40, rising to $70 for six to eight hours. Horizontes also organizes the annual **International Bass Fishing Tournament** every February, which draws enthusiasts from overseas. Other chains offering fishing-based holidays and excursions are Cubasol, based at Calle 154 no. 332 e/ 3raC y 3raD, Reparto Naútico, Havana (☎7/33-68-68 or 33-68-73); Cubamar at Calle 15 no. 752 esq. Paseo, Vedado, Havana (☎7/30-55-36 to 39); and Havanatur at 5ta Ave. no. 8409 e/ 84 y 86, Miramar, Playa, Havana (☎7/24-01-66 or 24-05-85).

For **saltwater** fishing excursions, usually on motorized yachts, the two chains operating the most extensive network of marinas and fishing programmes are Puertosol at Calle 1ra. no. 3001 esq. 30, Miramar, Playa, Havana (☎7/24-59-23); and Marlin, Calle 184 no. 123, Reparto Flores, Playa, Havana (☎7/24-66-75). The cost of a day trip, typically with four to six hours of fishing, starts at around $200 for four people and can go up to as much as $350. The marinas always supply a boat crew and any necessary equipment.

Golf

Its associations with the ruling classes prior to the 1959 revolution made **golf** something of a frowned-upon sport in Cuba once Castro and his supporters took over the country. The advent of mass tourism has brought it back, and though

CALENDAR OF SPORTING EVENTS AND ACTIVITIES IN CUBA

JANUARY
National Basketball League Playoffs and Finals

MARCH
International Trout Fishing Tournament, Moron, Ciego de Ávila ☎ 335/45-63.
Trans-Caribbean Yachting Regatta, Marina Hemingway, Havana ☎ 7/24-66-53 or 24-66-89.
Black Bass Fishing All Star Open Tournament, Lake Hanabanilla, Villa Clara ☎ 7/24-75-20.
National League Baseball Finals

APRIL
Giraldo Cordova Cardin Tournament, Villa Clara ☎ 7/81-56-79. Boxing tournament.
Marathon in the Sea Tournament, Varadero ☎ 7/57-70-78. Long-distance swim.

MAY
Havana Cup International Yachting Regatta, Marina Hemingway, Havana ☎ 7/24-66-53 or 24-66-89.
International Triathlon Week, Cayo Coco and Cayo Guillermo, Ciego de Ávila ☎ 33/2-33-35.

Tournament Barrientos, Estadio Panamericano, Havana ☎ 7/97-21-01.
Morro Castle Yachting Regatta, Marina Hemingway, Havana ☎ 7/24-66-53 or 24-66-89.
International Ernest Hemingway Marlin Fishing Tournament, Marina Hemingway, Havana ☎ 7/24-66-53 or 24-66-89.

JUNE
Gregorio Fuentes Marlin Fishing Tournament, Varadero ☎ 7/24-59-23 to 26.
Caribbean Open Water-Skiing Contest, Varadero.

JULY
Big Island Boating Grand Prix and International Formula T1 Boats Championship, Cienfuegos ☎ 7/33-78-83.
The Old Man and the Sea International Marlin Fishing Tournament, Marina Tarará, Havana ☎ 7/24-59-23 to 26.

NOVEMBER
Marabana Marathon, Havana ☎ 7/81-46-98 or 41-32-88.

currently there are only two courses on the island there are plans for more. The biggest, best equipped and more expensive is the eighteen-hole course run by the Varadero Golf Club (☎ 5/66-77-88), established in 1998. Less taxing are the nine holes of the Club de Golf Habana (☎ 7/33-88-80 or 45-45-78), just outside the capital. Green fees range from $20 to $60 whilst a caddy and equipment rental together will cost you around $15. Both clubs offer 30- to 45-minute golf classes costing $10 in Havana and twice as much in Varadero.

Hiking

All three mountain ranges in Cuba feature resorts set up as bases for **hiking**, and certainly these mostly unspoilt routes are a wonderful way to enjoy some of the most breathtaking of Cuban landscapes. Designated hikes tend to be quite short, rarely more than 5km, and trails are often unmarked and difficult to follow without a guide. Furthermore, orienteering maps are all but non-existent. This may be all part of the appeal for some people but it is generally recommended that you hire a guide, especially in adverse weather conditions. In the Cordillerra de Guaniguanico in Pinar del Río the place to head for is Las Terrazas, where there are a series of gentle hikes organized mostly for groups. The Topes de Collantes resort in the Escambray Mountains offers a similar programme, whilst serious hikers should head for the Gran Parque Nacional Sierra Maestra, host to the tallest peak in Cuba, Pico Turquino.

Crime and harassment

Registered *casas particulares* are, as a rule, safe but you stay in an unregistered one at your peril. Also avoid leaving personal possessions on view in a rental car, as these are also a prime target. There is little **violent crime** in Cuba but should you be mugged do not resist, just comply with your attackers' demands. Avoid walking down poorly lit alleys or deserted streets, particularly at night.

You should always carry a photocopy of your **passport** (or the passport itself) as the police sometimes ask to inspect them. This is especially likely if you are spending time with Cubans or are black.

Despite increasing reports about crime on the island and the opinions of many Cubans themselves, Cuba is still one of the safest destinations in the Caribbean and Latin America, and the majority of visitors will experience a trouble-free stay. The worst you're likely to experience is incessant and irritating attention from *jiniteros*, *jineteras* and hustlers. However, following a few simple precautions will help ensure that you don't fall prey to any petty crime.

The most common assault upon tourists is **bag-snatching** or **pickpocketing**, so always make sure you sling bags across your body rather than letting them dangle from one shoulder, keep cameras concealed whenever possible, don't carry valuables in easy-to-reach pockets and always take the minimum amount of cash out with you. A common trick is for thieves on bicycles to ride past and snatch at bags, hats and sunglasses, so wear these at your discretion. Needless to say don't leave bags and possessions unattended anywhere, but be especially vigilant on beaches where it can take a skilful thief a mere moment to be off with your possessions. While there's no need to be suspicious of everyone who tries to strike up a conversation with you (and many people will), a measure of caution is advisable.

Some **hotels** are not entirely secure, so be sure to put any valuables in the hotel security box, if there is one, or at least stash them out of sight.

Emergencies

Should you be unfortunate enough to be robbed and you want to make an insurance claim, you *must* report the crime to the **police** and get a statement. The police in Cuba are generally indifferent to crimes against tourists – and may even try blame you for not being more vigilant. Don't expect them to take your plight seriously: at best you will spend several hours waiting to be seen and at worst they will attempt to withhold your copy of your statement, assuring you they will send the details on to you when you return home. You *must* insist upon the statement there and then; there is little chance of receiving anything from them at a later date. Unfortunately, the chance of your possessions being recovered is equally remote.

After seeing the police, you may find it more useful to contact **Asistur** (☎7/33-85-27 or 33-89-20), the 24-hour assistance agency, based in Havana and Santiago, which can arrange replacement travel documents, help with financial difficulties and recover lost luggage. In the case of a serious emergency you should notify your **foreign consul** (see p.15).

> **Police**
>
> The **emergency number** for the Cuban **police** differs from place to place; see the listings in the respective chapters.

Jineterismo or the escort industry

Everywhere you go in Cuba, you'll see Western men – or less commonly women – laden down with shopping bags and with a dazzling, dolled-up young Cuban hanging off their arm. There is no single issue in Cuba today as complex or contentious as **jineterismo** or the escort and hustler culture, widely perceived as the re-emergence of prostitution in Cuba. A way of life for some poorer, less educated Cubans prior to the revolution, prostitution was immediately banned by Castro's regime and, officially at least, wiped off the streets, with prostitutes and pimps rehabilitated into society.

However, the revolutionary regime is only forty years old, and the experience of widespread prostitution, embedded in the nation's consciousness, has proved difficult to shift. The resurgence of the tourist industry in recent years has seen it slink back into business since the mid-1990s, with purveyors of both genders, although now, rather than the brazen selling of sex only, the exchange of services is rather more hazy.

As a general definition, a *jinetero* – a pejorative term – is a male hustler or someone who will find girls, cigars, taxis or accommodation for a visitor and then take a cut for the service. He – though more commonly this is the preserve of his female counterpart, a *jinetera* – is often also the sexual partner to a foreigner, quite often for material gain. In the eyes of Cubans, this can mean anything along a sliding scale of prostitute, paid escort, opportunist or simply a Cuban boyfriend or girlfriend.

As an obvious foreign face in Cuba you will often be pursued by persistent *jineteros* and *jineteras*, and indeed you may well find yourself using their services – at least to get a taxi – so it's as well to be polite even when the hustling reaches fever pitch. Many Cubans are desperate to leave the country and see marrying a foreigner as the best way out, while others simply want to live the good life and are more than happy to spend a few days (or hours) pampering the egos of middle-aged Western swingers in order to go to the best clubs and restaurants and be bought the latest fashions. Don't be flattered – it's your money they're after, not your heart, but single foreign men may find that the ceaseless attention of sometimes stunning Cuban women may well be the defining experience of their trip.

It's not a phenomenon unique to Cuba by any means, but the state is now making stringent attempts to limit these activities. In February 1999 a law was passed that increased police powers of arrest, resulting in large numbers of women, some as young as twenty, receiving prison sentences of up to four years for associating with foreigners. Not surprisingly, many former *jineteros* have thrown in the towel or have at least become wary of even talking to foreigners, leaving the path clear for the more hard-nosed and professional to continue with less competition. However, as foreigners themselves are not penalized in any way, even when obviously soliciting, it remains to be seen how successful Cuba will be at stamping out the oldest trade in the world a second time.

Drugs

Drugs, specifically marijuana and cocaine, are increasingly common in Cuba and you may find that you are offered them, especially in Havana and the main tourist areas, with frequency. If you are not interested a firm "no" should suffice.

Should you choose to indulge, do so with extreme caution, as the authorities take a very dim view of drug abuse – one of the triumphs of the revolution was to rid the country of dealers and users – and prison sentences are often meted out for possession of small amounts of marijuana alone.

Women travellers

Though violent sexual attacks against female tourists are virtually unheard of, women travelling in Cuba should brace themselves for a quite remarkable level of attention. Casual sex is a staple of Cuban life and unaccompanied women are generally assumed to be on holiday for exactly that reason, with protestations to the contrary generally greeted with sheer disbelief. The non-stop attention can be unnerving, but in general, Cuban men manage to combine a courtly romanticism with wit and charm and at worst the persistent come-ons will leave you irritated rather than threatened. It's worth knowing, too, that many of your would-be suitors are likely to be *jineteros* (see box opposite).

If you are not interested, there's no surefire way to stop the flow of comments and approaches, but saying "no" decisively, not wearing skimpy clothing and avoiding eye contact with men you don't know will lessen the flow of attention a little. However, it's as well to remember that this will be the defining factor of most of your relationships with Cuban men. Even a few hours of friendship can lead to pledges of eternal love and flattering though this may be, it's most likely nothing to do with your personal charms but because marriage to a foreigner is a tried-and-tested method of emigrating.

For this reason, if you do succumb, you may find events moving along at an alarming rate, and before you know it you could be introduced to family and friends as the fiancée as well as finding yourself paying for everything. Establish your position at the outset – in so far as you can – and don't allow yourself to be bullied into any course of action you'd rather not follow through. Having said that, don't be put off relationships altogether: there are of course plenty of Cubans looking for more genuine relationships.

Cuban women

The stylized image adopted by the Federación de Mujeres de Cuba (Cuban Women's Federation; see box) of a woman cradling a baby with one hand and holding a rifle in the other is a defining one – strong woman are part of the revolution. Women make up almost forty percent of the Cuban workforce and although a glass ceiling still exists for women in many areas, there are significant numbers of women in previously male-dominated professions like medicine. Although machismo is alive and kicking in Cuba, women's rights are respected and free healthcare, abortion on demand and low levels of violent crime have given women a freedom not usually enjoyed in Latin America and the Caribbean. However, despite legislation introduced in 1974 designed to give men a greater share in responsibility in the home, household chores and child care still tend to be the lot of women, and although three months' leave is allowed if a child is ill, it falls to women, rather than their partners to take the time off.

Women's organizations

The main women's organization is the Federación de Mujeres de Cuba (FMC), which has a branch in each province and promotes the interests of women within the revolution. If you want to make contact with or get information on specific groups this is the place to start. The Havana office is at Paseo no. 260, Vedado ☎ 7/55-27-71.

Directory

ADDRESSES AND STREET NAMES Most addresses are written down as being located between one street, or *calle* in Spanish, and another, with the Spanish word for between, *entre*, abbreviated to e/. Thus the address of a hotel located on street L between street 23 and street 25 would normally be written as Calle L e/ 23 y 25. If a building is on a corner, then the abbreviation *esq.*, short for *esquina*, is used. So the address of a house on the corner of San Lázaro and the Avenida de Italia would appear as San Lázaro esq. Ave. de Italia. You may also see this written as San Lázaro esq. a Ave. de Italia or even San Lázaro y Ave. de Italia. When an address incorporates the *autopista* or the Carretera Central it may often include its distance from Havana. Thus the address Autopista Nacional km 142, Matanzas is 142km down the *autopista* from Havana. These distances are often marked by signs appearing every kilometre at the roadside.

CIGARS Theoretically, should you wish to leave the country with more than fifty cigars they must be declared at customs, and you must show your receipts for all cigars on request (although usually you are not checked leaving) or risk having them confiscated.

DEPARTURE TAX The airport departure tax is $20.

DISABLED TRAVELLERS Most of the upmarket hotels are well equipped for disabled travellers, with at least one specially designed room and all the necessary lifts and ramps. However, away from the resorts there are very few amenities or services provided for disabled people and in fact you rarely see anyone in a wheelchair in the street in Cuba.

ELECTRICITY AND GAS The electricity supply is generally 110V 60Hz but always check as in some hotels it is 220V. Private houses are often prey to organized power cuts for both electricity and gas, an energy-saving device introduced during the Special Period to help conserve limited fuel resources. If you stay in a tourist hotel you are unlikely to be affected by this.

ETIQUETTE There are a few cultural idiosyncrasies worth bearing in mind. Many shops restrict entrance to a few people at a time and although as a tourist you may bypass the queue you'll win more friends if you ask "*¿el ultimo?*" (who's last?) and take your turn. Avoid asking questions which include a possible answer, as people often give the response they think you are looking for, thus "What time does the bus leave?" is better than "Does the bus leave at noon?" Finally, Cubans tend to be fairly conventional in their appearance, and view some Western fashions, especially traveller garb, with circumspection, mainly because Cubans in similar dress (and there are a number around, particularly in Havana) are seen as anti-establishment. Anyone with piercings, dreadlocks or tattoos may find themselves checked rigorously at customs and occasionally asked to show their passport to the police.

LAUNDRY There are few public laundry services in Cuba and only Havana has a laundry delivery service. Most people do their own or rely on the hotel service, although if you are staying in a *casa particular* your landlady is likely to offer to do yours for you.

LESBIAN AND GAY TRAVELLERS Cubans in general are not particularly accommodating towards gays and lesbians, although matters have moved on from the days when gay men were rounded up into camps to rid them of their unmanly (and unrevolutionary) tendencies. Open displays of affection are likely to earn you at the least a few sniggers from passers-by and at worst demands to produce identification from the police.

PHOTOGRAPHY Cuba is an immensely photogenic country and keen snappers will have a field day. Don't try to photograph anything military, and remember that some people prefer not to be photographed, so always ask first. Kodak, Fuji and Agfa standard films are widely available (although as yet there are no APS films) but always check the expiry date on the box before buying. You can get film developed but it may not turn out as well as it might back home.

TIME DIFFERENCES Cuba is on Eastern Standard Time in winter and Eastern Daylight Time in summer. It is five hours behind London, fifteen hours behind Sydney and on the same time as New York.

TIPPING Service charges are not included in restaurant bills so you should tip at your discretion; in *paladares* tips aren't expected but always welcome. There's no need to tip when you've negotiated a fare for a taxi, but you should normally tip when you use a state-run taxi. And it's worth knowing that a tip of a dollar or two can sometimes open previously closed doors – getting you into a museum without the minimum-size group, for example.

TOILETS Public toilets are few and far between in Cuba and even fast-food joints often don't have a washroom. The best places for public toilets are hotels and petrol stations but even in these you should not necessarily expect there to be toilet paper – carry your own supply. Train and bus stations usually have toilets but conditions are often appalling, leaving you wondering whether the attendants waiting on the doors have ever gone inside.

WORK Although you won't find casual work in Cuba, the chance to carry out agricultural and construction work alongside Cubans is offered on

---

Things to take

Most things are easy to find in Cuba but here is a miscellaneous list of items you might consider taking from home:

Envelopes

A supply of rolling papers and tobacco if you like to roll your own, as these products are totally unavailable

Toilet paper – you can buy it in Cuba but it's rarely there when you need it

A small flashlight

A multi-purpose penknife

A selection of herbs and spices if you intend to do any self-catering

A supply of disposable nappies as required

Some basic medication (see p.32)

A waterproof overcoat

A supply of candles

Soap – if you intend to stay in *campismos* or peso hotels

Water bottle or flask – invaluable, since drinks are usually sold in returnable containers

A padlock – if you intend to use bikes

Tampons

Condoms

---

trips organized in association with the Cuban authorities, as a way to see the achievements of the revolution first hand. Contact Cuba Solidarity Campaign (Brigade), 129 Seven Sisters Rd, London N7 7QG (☎020/7561 0191, fax 7561 0191), or Rock around the Blockade, c/o FRFI, BCM Box 5909, London WC1N (☎020/7837 1688) for more details. Also see p.10.

The Guide

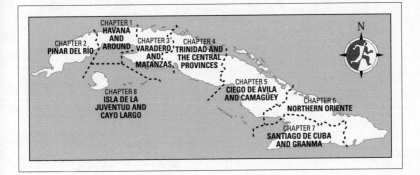

Chapter 1

Havana and around

With five times as many inhabitants as the next biggest city, **Havana** is in a class by itself in Cuba. Nowhere else are the contradictions which have come to characterize the country, particularly since the advent of mass tourism and the introduction of the US dollar, as pronounced as they are in the capital. The emerging middle classes, most of whom have made their money through the latest wave of tourism, drift around the brand-new shopping malls, whilst down the road long queues of people clutching ration books form outside the local *bodega*. Restoration projects have returned some of the finest colonial architecture in the Caribbean to its original splendour, whilst whole neighbourhoods, overcrowded and dirty, wait for their first coat of paint since the early 1990s. There is a sense that Havana is on the move, with dollars pouring in, new nightspots appearing regularly and an increasing variety of products in shops which not long ago either didn't exist or stood empty. Yet on the other hand, time stands still, or even goes backwards, in a city where 1950s Chevrolets, Buicks and Oldsmobiles ply the roads, locals fish from tyres floating within sight of the ageing seawall and significant numbers of people seem to spend most of the day in the street or on their crumbling nineteenth-century doorsteps.

Havana doesn't jump out at you with all-night parties or flashing lights but works its magic slowly and subtly. It may not be the first thing you notice, but the fact that the main tourist areas are residential neighbourhoods is one of the city's most striking characteristics. It allows an unusually close, though often quite tiring, contact not just with the buildings and monuments but with the people, who are more often than not willing to share it all with you. Life unfolds openly and un-self-consciously in Havana: from domino players sitting at tables on the kerb, kids playing ball games in the road, conversations shouted across balconies, and streetside barbershops with their doors open, an infectious vitality pervades every neighbourhood.

Though the tourist industry and US dollar are infiltrating every level of life in the capital, the city is far from a slave to tourism.

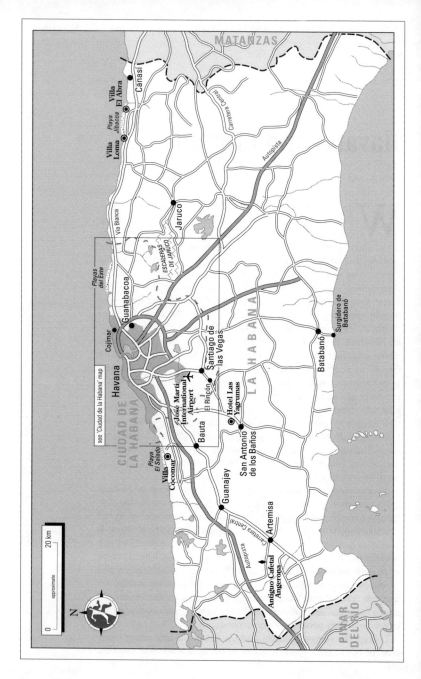

Cuban **culture** is at its most exuberant here, with an abundance of theatres, cinemas, concert venues and art galleries. Along with Santiago, Havana is host to the country's most diverse **music scene** where world-famous *salsa* and *bolero* orchestras and bands ply their trade and, bubbling under the surface, the newer rock and hip-hop subcultures, almost nonexistent elsewhere on the island, are gaining momentum. The sounds spill out onto the streets in an ever-present musical accompaniment to daily life, smoothing off some of the capital's rougher edges and injecting an irresistible sense of celebration.

The city's **suburbs** stretch out for miles and bleed gently into Havana province, known simply as **La Habana**, offering a range of possible day-trips. Though many of them are within the political boundaries of the city, they feel far removed, a sense that's reinforced by the extremely poor public transport links.

East of the city, past the uncomplicated provincial-style towns of **Cojímar** and **Guanabacoa** are the province's best beaches, including the top-notch **Playas del Este**, the more subdued **Playa Jibacoa** and the even lower-key **Canasí**. The wild and mysterious **Escaleras de Jaruco** hills, classic Indiana Jones territory, are the only draw inland on this side of the province.

South of the city is the neatly packaged **Museo Ernest Hemingway**, the writer's long-time Cuban residence, while slightly further west, the landscaped expanse of **Parque Lenin** and impressive **Jardín Botánico Nacional** offer some of the most picturesque scenery in the city. In the same area are the **Parque Zoológico Nacional** and **ExpoCuba**, a cross between an industrial estate, a museum and a theme park, where the achievements of the revolution are displayed in exhaustive – and exhausting – detail. The **Santuario de San Lázaro** and nearby town of **Santiago de las Vegas** won't occupy a whole day but are worth making a short journey for, while the town of **San Antonio de los Banos**, on the other hand, is one of the only places in Havana province where it's worth staying the night.

Most people travelling **west** from Havana are making their way to Pinar del Río (see Chapter Two) and indeed the time and energy it takes to see most of what there is out this way would be better spent going marginally further to the neighbouring province's nearest attractions, Las Terrazas and Soroa. **Playa El Salado**, however, is easily reached by car, whilst small towns like **Guanajay** serve best as stopping-off points or components of a wider tour rather than the sole reason for a day-trip.

Havana

HAVANA is a stunning city, its glorious diversity of architecture and neighbourhood design littered with reminders of this heterogeneous nation's history. Founded on the western banks of a fabulous natural harbour, it had, by the end of the seventeenth century, established itself as a fortified urban port, protected by the water on one side and

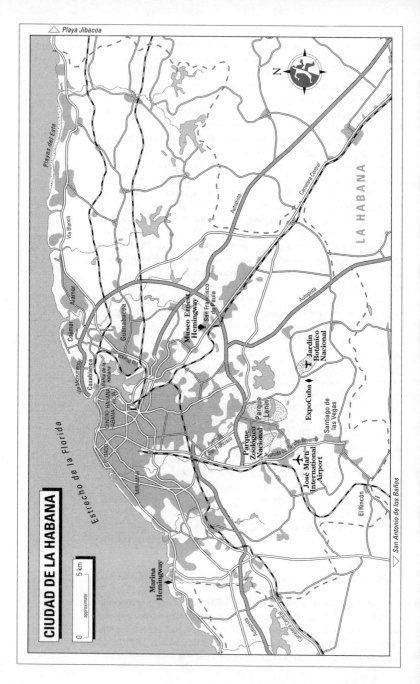

CIUDAD DE LA HABANA

0 approximate 5 km

a ten-metre city wall on the other. The bay is now dominated by heavy industry whilst what was once contained within the city walls forms the most captivating part of **Habana Vieja**, the old city, which has long since breached its own defences and is now the capital's tourist centre, a UNESCO-declared World Heritage Site of crumbling magnificence and restored beauty. Any sightseeing you do will fan out from here, where the main brace of fine museums and immaculately renovated colonial buildings form elegant plazas, sweeping boulevards and, most of all, narrow atmospheric streets bristling with life.

Most visitors restrict themselves to Habana Vieja and the other two most central *municipios* (boroughs) running the length of the classic oceanfront promenade, the **Malecón**. West of the old city, predominantly residential **Centro Habana** is often bypassed by those on their way to more tourist-friendly parts of town. This, however, is a mistake, for though Centro Habana is low on specific attractions it pulsates with energy, and wandering its busy nineteenth-century streets reveals an intrinsically Cuban side to the city. **Vedado**, the heart of the *municipio* known locally as Plaza, is the city's 1950s postmodern centre. Many of the magnificent postcolonial mansions that jostle for attention amongst the tower blocks have been converted into public works or ministry offices and a few are museums. The area is compact enough to negotiate on foot – and in fact that's the best way to appreciate the quiet suburban streets. From here you could walk the couple of kilometres to the vast and famous **Plaza de la Revolución**, where giant monuments to the two most famous icons of the Cuban struggle for independence, Che Guevara and José Martí, present archetypal photo opportunities.

Beyond Vedado to the west, on the other side of the Río Almendares, **Miramar** ushers in yet another change in the urban landscape. Modelled on mid-twentieth-century Miami, this is a fairly anonymous part of the city but ideal as an escape from the more frenzied atmosphere of Habana Vieja. A commercial district is emerging on its western fringes, accompanied by a number of luxury hotels, whilst some of Havana's most sophisticated restaurants are scattered around Miramar's leafy streets. South of the seafront districts, the city appears to merge into one giant residential neighbourhood, the different *municipios* less discernible and the hotels and restaurants absent almost immediately.

East of the bay, the city per se soon bleeds into a large, sparsely populated area forming part of the capital's official territory only as a result of the arbitrary shifting of political boundaries. However, immediately over the other side of the channel connecting the bay to the sea, and visible from Habana Vieja, is Cuba's most extensive network of colonial military fortifications, known collectively as the **Parque Morro-Cabana**, forming an integral part of the capital and its history.

Amongst the city's highlights, the tours around the **Fábrica de Tobacos Partagas** cigar factory are as stimulating as they are revealing, whilst the imposing **Capitolio** displays a phenomenal variety of architectural styles. Don't miss out on a visit to the **Nacional**, the best hotel in the city with its beguiling gardens caressed by the sound of waves crashing against the Malecón down below. As in many of the major cities in Cuba, Havana's **hotels** play a prominent role in its social life and provide much of the focus for visitors. With many of the best restaurants, shops, bars, nightlife and pretty much all of the usable swimming pools located within hotel grounds, there's a strong chance you'll spend some time in or around them even if you're not staying in one.

Some history

Blessed with the largest natural port in the Caribbean, Havana's success and riches were founded on the strength and position of the **harbour** spotted by Sebastián de Ocampo in 1509 when he took advantage of its deep and sheltered waters to repair his ship during his circumnavigation of Cuba.

It was Sebastián de Ocampo who dispelled Columbus's earlier notion that Cuba was a continent.

However, it was not until 1519 that the city arrived at its present site and not until 1556 that it became the Cuban capital. The original site of the **San Cristóbal de La Habana** settlement was established on St Christopher's Day – 25 July, 1515 – on the south coast at Batabanó, 50km from where the city now stands. This first *villa* was an unmitigated disaster zone: problematic swampland rife with mosquitoes and tropical diseases, with a flat coastline and shallow port which left ships unable to drop anchor close to shore. The settlement limped along under these testing conditions for four years before relocating in 1519 to the north coast, at the mouth of the freshwater Río Chorrera (now the Almendares), until rising seas and the lack of a sheltered harbour forced another move less than a year later. On November 25, 1519, the city shifted a few kilometres east to the banks of the large deep-water bay, backed by heavy forests, now known as the **Bahía de la Habana**.

The *villa* began to ripple out into what is now Habana Vieja, with the first streets established down on the seafront between the present-day Plaza de Armas and Plaza de San Francisco. However, it was with the discovery of a deep navigable channel through the treacherous shallow waters between Cuba and the Bahamas – a major step in the establishment of **trade routes** between Spain and the New World – that Havana really took off and, helped by the presence of its marvellous harbour, Cuba rose in global importance throughout the sixteenth and seventeenth centuries.

As the Spanish conquistadors plundered the Americas, gathering fairytale cargoes of gold and emeralds, pearls and indigo, and even parrots, Havana became a convenient port of call, with captains of the Spanish fleet steering their galleons in to have sails stitched and hulls remade, and sailors allowed to let rip one last time before setting off for Seville. An infrastucture of brothels, inns and gambling houses sprang up to cater for the seamen, and harlotry and syphilis were rife. With ships disgorging new sailors and merchants daily, pirates drawn by tales of wealth were able to wander anonymously through the town, planning their attacks with admirable precision. Inadequately armed and with few resources, Habaneros were forced to hand over town riches under threat of having their mud and thatch homes razed to the ground, as was the case when French pirate Jacques de Sores attacked and burned Havana in July 1555.

It took Spain three years to take action but in 1558 it centralized operations in the area by making Havana the only port authorized to engage in commerce and then constructing the first military stone building in the Americas, the impressive **Castillo de la Real Fuerza**, which stands by the harbour mouth. As the capital of Cuba, Havana became known as *Llave del Nuevo Mundo y Antemural de las Indias Occidentales* (Key to the New World and Bulwark of the West Indies), and Spain was understandably keen to safeguard her money-spinning colony. Wattle and daub houses had been banned following the fire of 1555 and there now followed a long period of fortification. Work started on the Castillo de San Salvador de la Punta and the formidable Castillo de Los Tres Reyes del Morro in 1589 and was finally completed in 1630. And in 1663, after more than a hundred years of discussion, a protective wall began to be built around the city, and was completed in 1740.

Attacks, however, persisted, and in 1762 the **British** made a successful two-pronged assault on the city. Whilst part of the fleet sailed up the Río Almendares to lure the Spanish there as a decoy, the rest of the fleet landed to the east of El Morro castle at Cojímar (see p.128) and attacked. This cunning paid off, and after a six-week siege Havana fell to the British. Although only in occupation of the city for eleven months – the British swapped Havana for Florida and left the island's shores suitably enriched – the free trade that the port enjoyed kickstarted the island's **sugar trade**; previously restricted to supplying Spain, it was now open to the rest of the world. The consequential influx of wealthy Spanish sugar families propelled Havana into a new age of affluence.

The **nineteenth century** was a period of growth, with some of the most beautiful buildings around Habana Vieja constructed and the city enjoying a new-found elegance. At the same time, prostitution, crime and corruption amongst city officials were reaching new heights, and many of the new bourgeoisie abandoned the old city to the poor and began to colonize what is now the district of Vedado. By the 1860s the framework of the new suburbs stretching west and south was in place.

In 1902, after the wars of independence, North American influence and money flowed into the city and the first half of the twentieth century saw tower blocks, magnificent hotels and glorious

Art Deco palaces like the Bacardí building creep into the main areas to serve the booming tourist industry. The **revolution** put an abrupt end to all this, and throughout the 1960s the new regime cleaned the streets of crime, prostitution and general debauchery, and laid out the basis of a socialist capital. Fine houses, abandoned by owners fleeing back to the States, were left in the hands of erstwhile servants, and previously exclusive neighbourhoods changed face overnight. With the emphasis on improving conditions in the countryside, city development was haphazard and the post-revolution years saw many fine buildings crumble while residential overcrowding increased, prompting Fidel Castro himself to admit that action had to be taken. Happily the last few years have seen slow but steady improvements, with redevelopment work now much in evidence, especially in the worst-affected areas of Habana Vieja.

Arrival and information

All international flights land at **José Martí International Airport**, about 15km south of the city centre. The vast majority deposit passengers at Terminal Three where most of the airport services are concentrated, though there are **car rental desks** in each of the three teminals. The only public transport into the city is an unreliable **bus shuttle service** with no fixed pick-up point or regular departure times – ask at the airport information desk for what details there are. It's most likely you'll be forced to pay for a **taxi**; the half-hour journey into Havana shouldn't cost much more than $15.

Arriving by **bus**, you'll be dropped off at either the **Víazul terminal** (☎81-14-13 or 81-56-52), over the road from the city zoo, or the Astro-operated **Estación de Omnibus** (☎79-24-56), near the Plaza de la Revolución, depending on which bus service you've used. Both stations are a $3–5 taxi ride from most of the centrally located hotels, and there's a car rental desk at the Víazul terminal.

Trains pull in at the **Estación Central de Ferrocarriles** (☎62-19-20 or 61-29-59) in Habana Vieja, where picking up a taxi is slightly more problematic and you'll probably have to find yourself a private cab or one of Havana's army of bicitaxis (see opposite).

In the less likely event that you arrive on one of the two or three **cruise ships** that dock in Havana every week, you will disembark at the splendid **Terminal Sierra Maestra** (☎62-19-25), facing the Plaza de San Francisco in Habana Vieja. Here there's a bar and souvenir shop, car and scooter rental services, and branches of two of the national travel agent chains, Fantástico and Rumbos, both of which arrange city tours and other excursions.

There is no independent tourist board in Havana, but Infotur operates two **information centres** at Obispo no. 358 e/ Habana y Compostela in Habana Vieja (daily 9am–7pm; ☎33-33-33), and in Playa at 5ta. Ave. y 112 (daily 9am–6pm; ☎24-70-36). Both sell a few maps and basic guides but are generally low on free literature or any kind of written information, especially regarding accommodation. You can, however, book rooms and excursions through them. For a better choice of **maps and guides**, head for El Navegante at Mercaderes no. 115 e/ Obispo y Obrapía, Habana Vieja (☎57-10-38).

Details of what's going on in the city are difficult to come by, though the free weekly **listings guide** *Cartelera* makes it easier here than anywhere else in Cuba. You should be able to pick it up in most of the four- and five-star hotels, but the most reliable supplier is the *Hotel Nacional*. Keep an eye out, also, for *Opciones*, a weekly business newspaper which usually has a page or two dedicated to cultural events in the capital.

Orientation and city transport

Most of the central sections of Havana are laid out on a grid system and finding your way around is relatively simple, particularly in Vedado, where the vast majority of streets are known by either a number or a letter: streets running roughly north to south are known either by an even number or a letter between A and P, whilst those running east to west have odd numbers. Habana Vieja and Centro Habana are a little more complicated, not least because the narrower, more densely packed streets allow less forward vision. The best place for **orientation** is the Parque Central, with the landmark Capitolio building just off to the side. This area spans the border between the two oldest *municipios*, and most sightseeing generally takes place to the north and east of it. The obvious compass reference is the seafront to the north, whilst familiarizing yourself with just a few of the main streets, namely the Malecón, the Paseo del Prado, Linea and Calle 23 in Vedado, all of which cut through the most heavily visited areas, simplifies things considerably. The problem of old and new street names is no different in Havana than in the rest of Cuba but the box on p.73 should prevent too much confusion.

Taxis

There's only one way to experience Habana Vieja and that's on foot, but **getting around** the city will almost inevitably involve a **taxi** ride of some kind, especially if you intend to experience the full range of Havana's neighbourhoods. There are plenty of official tourist taxis which will take you across the city for around $5. It shouldn't take long to flag one down in the main hotel districts and particularly along the Malecón, but to be certain head for the *Hotel Nacional* in Vedado or the Parque Central in Habana Vieja. The most stylish way to travel, however, and no more expensive, is in a 1950s Oldsmobile, Chevrolet or any number of vintage pre-revolutionary cars found all over the city, the vast majority of which have turned themselves over as both official and unofficial taxis. To take in the surroundings at a slower pace, **bic-itaxis**, the three-wheeled, two-seater bicycle cabs found all over Havana, are ideal, and considerably more pleasant than a car. They are not, however, necessarily any cheaper; a fifteen-minute ride is likely to cost in the region of $2 to $3. The newest addition to Havana's taxi ranks are the **cocotaxis**, three-wheeled novelty motor-scooters encased in large yellow spheres, usually found waiting outside the *Hotel Inglaterra*. Their numbers are still extremely limited but you pay no extra for their comedy value, with fares cheaper than for normal state-taxis.

Buses

Buses are overcrowded and infrequent and there is no information at bus stops to indicate which route each bus takes, though if you brave it and get lucky your journey will cost no more than 40 centavos (less than 3¢). The converted juggernauts, known as **camellos**, tend to cover the longer routes, many leading right out of town, usually stopping short of the provincial boundary. Most of them converge on the Parque de la Fraternidad in Habana Vieja, where, along with some of the normal buses, they begin their journeys. Make sure you have roughly the right change and don't bother trying to pay with a note unless you intend to buy tickets for everyone on the bus. To be honest, unless you're desperately short on cash or fancy a taste of real Habanero life, it's difficult to justify the hassle of public transport in the capital. You have as much chance of walking to wherever you are going in the same time that you'll spend waiting at a bus stop. The most obvious exception is the seven-kilometre journey from Habana Vieja to Miramar, best made on bus #232 from the Parque de la Fraternidad.

There is, however, a **tourist bus** service, the Bus Turístico Vaivén, which operates between the Palacio de Convenciones in Playa and the Parque Morro Cabaña. Running every hour between 9am and 10pm on a daily basis, it will take you, for $1, any distance to any one of the 23 stops, which include the *Cohiba* and *Riviera* hotels, the Plaza de la Revolución, Coppelia and Parque Central.

Car, scooters and bikes

Generally speaking, if you stay put in Havana **car rental** is a relatively expensive way of getting around, but if you intend to make regular trips to the beach, or you are staying in one of the hotels in Miramar, it could work out cheaper than the taxi rides which you'll almost certainly otherwise have to take. There is a particular concentration of rental agencies on or within a few blocks of the Malecón, between the Parque Antonio Maceo in Centro Habana and the Cupet-Cimex Tángana petrol station in Vedado. The same agencies have desks in the lobbies of most of the four- and five-star hotels. See p.126 for addresses.

Almost all the **scooter rental** outlets in the city are located at the Playas del Este, with the exception of the Transautos office in the Terminal Sierra Maestra, opposite the Plaza de San Francisco in Habana Vieja (see p.84). Though the wide spread of Havana's main tourist districts means travelling by **bicycle** can be quite tiring, it is a

Havana's new and old street names	
New name	**Old name**
Agramonte	Zulueta
Aponte	Someruelos
Avenida Antonio Maceo	Malecón
Avenida de Bélgica (northern half)	Monserrate
Avenida de Bélgica (southern half)	Egido
Avenida Carlos Manuel de Céspedes	Avenida del Puerto
Avenida de España	Vives
Avenida de Italia	Galiano
Avenida Salvador Allende	Carlos III
Avenida Simón Bolívar	Reina
Brasil	Teniente Rey
Capdevila	Cárcel
Leonor Pérez	Paula
Máximo Gómez	Monte
Padre Varela	Belascoaín
Paseo de Martí	Paseo del Prado
San Martín	San José

See p.58 for an explanation of Cuban addresses.

fantastic way to see the city and there are special lanes for cyclists on most of the main roads, including the entire length of the Malecón. Despite the huge number of bicycles in the city, there are no specialist bicycle shops or rental agencies and your best bet is to contact Cubamar at Calle 15 no.752 esq. Paseo, Vedado (☎30-55-36 to 39), the chain responsible for many of Cuba's *campismos* but which also rents bicycles.

Accommodation

Likely to be the biggest daily expense of your trip to Havana, **accommodation** in the capital is abundant, and in most of the main areas you'll find rooms starting from $25 as well as those charging upwards of $200. You can usually find a hotel room on spec but you'd do well to make a **reservation**, particularly in high season (roughly November to April), when the town is chock-full.

The telephone area code for Havana is ☎7.

Many visitors choose to stay in the state hotels in **Habana Vieja**, handy for many of the key sights and well served by restaurants and bars. Hotels here are appearing at a phenomenal rate, with developments on the Plaza Vieja in particular set to bring the square further into the limelight. Many of the established state hotels are charismatic colonial properties, overflowing with history and patronized in the 1950s by the likes of Ernest Hemingway and Graham Greene. Quieter, leafy **Vedado** is a more relaxed place to stay, although you'll need transport to make the trip to Habana Vieja. Though usually the preserve of visiting businesspeople, the slick, towering hotels in **Miramar** are a defining part of that neighbourhood's landscape. It's a bit inconvenient for sightseeing but if money is no object and Western-style luxury a priority, this is the best the city has to offer.

Accommodation price codes

All accommodation listed in this guide has been graded according to the following price categories.

① peso hotel equivalent to $5 or less   ④ $30–50   ⑦ $100–150
② $5–20   ⑤ $50–70   ⑧ $150–200
③ $20–30   ⑥ $70–100   ⑨ $200 and above

Rates are for the cheapest available double or twin room during high season, usually May–September and the last two weeks of December. In Havana premium rates are also charged during the week of the annual international trade fair, the Feria de La Habana, usually the first week in November, and during Easter week. In low season some hotels lower their prices by roughly ten percent.

Unsurprisingly Havana boasts the broadest range of **casas particulares** in the country, from several houses run more like small hotels to a significant number of illegal places, some best avoided. Finding even the legitimate options independently isn't as easy as it can be elsewhere, as they are spread throughout the city and the current law still prevents the use of display boards advertising their existence, but touts to take you to them are hard to avoid. The three central *municipios* boast the main concentration of rooms to rent, with prices steepest in Habana Vieja and Vedado. Things are cheaper in Centro Habana, where the tax payable on each room is roughly halved, while many places in the outer boroughs are unregistered and so often relatively inexpensive.

Habana Vieja

Ambos Mundos, Obispo no. 153 esq. Mercaderes ☎66-95-29 to 31; fax 66-95-32. Once home to Ernest Hemingway, this stylishly artistic 1920s hotel features an original metal cage elevator and a fantastic rooftop terrace. Rooms are well equipped and comfortable. ⑥.

Caribbean, Paseo del Prado no. 164 e/ Colón y Refugio ☎33-82-33; fax 66-94-79. One of several cheaper options within easy walking distance of the Parque Central, but the rooms are a bit poky and many have no windows. ④.

Casa del Científico, Paseo del Prado no. 212 esq. Trocadero ☎62-45-11 or 63-35-91; fax 33-01-67. Unlike most of Havana's remodelled colonial buildings, the opulent columned interior of this three-floor aristocratic residence has barely been touched. Rooms are sufficiently well equipped, though some share bathrooms, and there's a spacious rooftop terrace. ④.

Hostal Conde de Villanueva, Mercaderes esq. Lamparilla ☎62-92-93. Despite its relatively small size this place packs in a host of charming communal spaces including a fantastic cellar-style restaurant, a delectable courtyard and a relaxing smokers' lounge and bar. Also known as the *Hostal del Habano*. ⑤.

Hostal Valencia, Oficios no. 53 esq. Obrapía ☎57-10-37; fax 33-56-28. Plain but pleasant rooms in a beautiful building that feels more like a large house than a small hotel. Attractions include a cobbled-floor courtyard with hanging vines. ⑤.

Inglaterra, Paseo del Prado no. 416 esq. San Rafael, Parque Central ☎33-85-93 to 97; fax 33-82-54. This classic nineteenth-century hotel in a superb location on the lively Parque Central has become rather complacent and could do with a little inspiration. However, the atmospheric if slightly gloomy interior is full of genuine colonial hallmarks and the rooms are of a high standard. ⑦.

Parque Central, Neptuno e/ Paseo del Prado y Agramonte, Parque Central ☎66-66-27; fax 66-66-30. Unbeatable in the old city for its range of facilities, this five-storey luxury hotel is aimed predominantly at business guests. The sophisticated but inconsistent interior features a graceful glass-ceiling lobby, two restaurants – one aristocratic, one 1950s retro – and there's a swimming pool on the roof. ⑧.

Plaza, Agramonte no. 167 esq. Neptuno ☎33-85-83. With more finesse than neighbouring hotels on the Parque Central, the *Plaza* has a bar in the colourful lobby area, complete with fountain, mosaic floor and detailed ceilings, which is a great place to hang out. There's an equally stylish restaurant and the rooms are well equipped. ⑥.

Santa Isabel, Baratillo no. 9 e/ Obispo y Narcisco López, Plaza de Armas ☎66-97-42 or 33-82-01; fax 33-83-91. One of the more formal and refined of Habana Vieja's hotels, this impressively restored, graceful eighteenth-century building features colonial-style furnishings in all the rooms and a fountain in the idyllic, arched courtyard. ⑧.

Sevilla, Trocadero no. 55 e/ Paseo del Prado y Agramonte ☎33-85-60; fax 338582. Large hotel with an eclectic mix of architecture, one of Havana's most spectacular rooftop restaurants and a certain amount of grace. ⑦.

Casas particulares

Casa de Eugenio Barral García, San Ignacio no. 656 e/ Jesús María y Merced ☎62-98-77. Deep in southern Habana Vieja, this large apartment is clean and beautifully furnished, with three double bedrooms, all with a/c and one with a TV, and very hospitable landlords. The price includes full breakfast. ③.

Casa de Fefita y Luís, Aguacate no. 509, apto.403, e/ Sol y Muralla ☎61-41-97, 61-32-10 or 61-64-33. Situated on the fourth floor of a modern building in the heart of the old city, this small self-contained unit provides fantastic views over Habana Vieja. The double bedroom is equipped with a/c, while the lounge has a TV, video and fridge-freezer. ③.

Casa de Migdalia Caraballé Martín, Luz no. 164, apto.F, e/ Cuba y San Ignacio ☎61-73-52. Opposite a convent, this large, airy apartment is more of a guest house than a *casa particular*, with the owners living in a separate apartment next door. There are three double rooms and one with three single beds. One of the doubles is windowless and all but one of the others have their own bathroom. It's very popular, so reservations are recommended. ③.

Centro Habana

Deauville, Ave. de Italia esq. Malecón ☎33-88-12 or 62-80-51; fax 33-81-48. The only seafront hotel in Centro Habana, this recently overhauled high-rise offers rooms with great views and is one of the few places around here with a swimming pool. ⑤.

Lido, Consulado no. 210 e/ Animas y Trocadero ☎33-88-14. On a run-down street in a lively local neighbourhood, this hotel has dark rooms and rickety furniture, but is an inexpensive option so close to Habana Vieja. ③.

Lincoln, Virtudes no. 164 esq. Ave. de Italia ☎33-82-09. One of the more characterful budget hotels with reasonably equipped though unsophisticated rooms and good views over some of the grittier parts of the city. ④.

New York, Dragones esq. Amistad ☎62-52-60. The inner-city back-street feel of this five-floor neo-colonial hotel will put off more people than it attracts, but it's one of the few places regularly accepting both Cubans and foreign visitors and boasts the cheapest rooms available to tourists this close to the old city. Only a few rooms have TVs and there are fans instead of a/c. ②.

Casas particulares

Casa de Jorge Díaz, Gervasio no. 209 e/ Concordia y Virtudes ☎70-04-89. This impressively well run, deceptively large *casa particular* has five rooms and good facilities. With an affable, multilingual owner, and guests congregating in an attractive leafy courtyard, it's a particularly sociable option. ③.

Casa de Luis Bermúdez, Soledad no. 204, apto. 4e, e/ San Lázaro y Animas ☎79-13-04. An attractive bedroom with en-suite bathroom and a/c in a spick-and-span fourth-floor apartment in a characterful block predating the revolution. You can rent the whole apartment for only marginally more money, but be prepared to scale three flights of stairs. ③.

Casa de Miriam Rodríguez Domínguez, San Lázaro no. 621 e/ Gervasio y Escobar ☎78-44-56. A popular, smartly furnished first-floor balcony apartment just a block from the Malecón. Two comfortable double bedrooms, one with a/c, run by one of the friendliest, hardest-working landladies in the city. ③.

Casa de Roberto Blanco, Ave. de Italia no. 123, apto. 103, e/ Animas y Trocadero; no phone. One-bedroom first-floor apartment on one of the principal streets in Centro Habana, a few minutes' walk from an old cinema. The kitchen is tiny but the place is in better condition than the building might suggest, and you can see the sea from the bedroom balcony. Call at apto. 203 on the second floor for arrangements. ③.

Vedado

Bruzón, Calle Bruzón no. 217 e/ Pozos Dulces y Boyeros ☎57-56-84. More like a youth hostel than a hotel, though the small, dark room and paucity of frills or hot water are all redeemed by the reasonable price. Near the Plaza de la Revolución. ③.

Habana Libre, Calle 23 esq. L ☎33-40-11; fax 33-31-41. Large, slick city hotel with lots of shops, a terrace pool, three restaurants, numerous bars and a cabaret, making it a solid, if somewhat anonymous, choice. ⑦.

Meliá Cohiba, Calle Paseo e/ 1ra y 3ra ☎33-36-36; fax 33-45-55. Close to the Malecón this good-looking modern hotel caters predominantly for the business visitor, with uniformed bellhops, indoor fountains and a mini-mall. The tasteful but unimaginative rooms are full of mod-cons. ⑧.

Nacional, Calle O esq. 21 ☎33-35-64; fax 33-51-71. The choice of visiting celebrities, this handsome hotel looks like an Arabian palace and is deservedly recognized as one of Havana's best hotels. Beautiful rooms, smooth service and excellent facilities. ⑧.

Riviera, Paseo y Malecón ☎33-40-51; fax 33-37-39. Built by the Mafia in the 1950s as a casino hotel, the *Riviera* retains much of its cool style and many original features, like its long, sculpture-filled lobby, rooms boasting original furniture and fittings, and dark, atmospheric bars. Together, they more than compensate for the frayed edges. ⑦.

Vedado, Calle O no. 244 e/ 23 y 25 ☎33-40-72; fax 33-41-86. Modest but amiable downtown hotel just off the central Rampa. It's currently being renovated, but is still a reasonable option despite the disorganization. ⑥.

Victoria, Calle 19 esq. M ☎33-35-10; fax 33-31-09. Small and extremely friendly, with only 28 rooms and attentive service, the *Victoria* feels like a private hotel, and features a small swimming pool. ⑥.

Casas particulares

Casa de Aurora Ampudia, Calle 15 no. 58 altos e/ M y N ☎32-18-43. Two double rooms in a friendly household on the first floor of a beautiful mock-colonial house within a stone's throw of the Malecón, with very helpful owners and two expansive balconies tailor-made for chilling out. A superb choice. ③.

Casa de Deisy Pérez Santos, Calle K, no. 361 altos e/ 19 y 21 ☎32-91-13. One double room in a pleasantly bohemian house with a balcony onto a picturesque Vedado street. ③.

Casa de Enrique Oramas, Calle J no. 512 e/ 23 y 25 ☎35-9-13. Well positioned on an appealing quiet street in Central Vedado, this house offers a self-contained room with its own entrance, private bathroom with electric shower and off-road parking. ③.

Casa de Pablo González Carrillo, Zapata no. 906 e/ Infanta y Basarrate ☎79-58-67. A 1920s-built house in a closely packed neighbourhood one block from Centro Habana with two simple, clean double bedrooms, one much larger than the other, both with en-suite bathroom and a/c. The independent entrance from the street allows plenty of privacy. ③.

Miramar and the western suburbs

El Boque, Calle 48a e/ 49a y 49c, Reparto Kohly ☎24-92-32; fax 24-56-37. Hidden away beside a pretty wood about 7km from Habana Vieja on the edge of Miramar, this small and intimate hotel has a homely feel and, despite the smallish rooms, is an excellent choice for those looking for a suburban retreat. ⑤.

Chateau Miramar, Ave. 1a e/ 60 y 62, Miramar ☎33-19-51; fax 33-02-24. This fairly smart, luxurious hotel is one of several that line the seafront. It has an excellent view over the ocean and is near a small rocky beach popular with Cubans, though it also boasts its own pool. Handy for the businesses centred in the area. ⑦.

Kohly, Ave. 49 y 36, Reparto Kohly ☎24-02-40; fax 24-17-33. An unremarkable property with a friendly atmosphere in a quiet neighbourhood. The pleasant airy rooms are a little worn but serviceable and there's a small pool that fills up with the local kids at weekends. It's rather far from all amenities and sights, so is only an option with your own transport. ⑤.

Meliá Habana, Calle 3ra e/ 76 y 80, Miramar ☎24-85-00; fax 24-85-05. Very professional hotel in the heart of the business district. The impressive marble reception area (with fountain), well-stocked international restaurants, smoking room and huge pool make this the best anti-stress centre for visiting VIPs. ⑨.

Habana Vieja

Bursting with centuries-old buildings and buzzing with a strong sense of the past, **Habana Vieja** – or Old Havana – is by far the richest and most densely packed sightseeing area in the city. Its narrow streets, refined colonial mansions, countless churches, cobblestone plazas

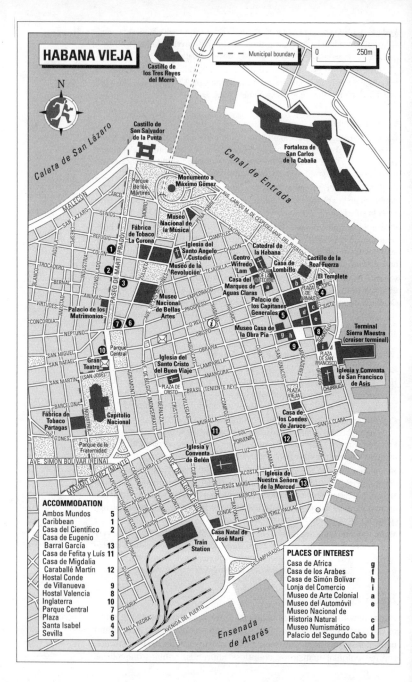

HABANA VIEJA

--- Municipal boundary

0   250m

Castillo de los Tres Reyes del Morro

Castillo de San Salvador de la Punta

Fortaleza de San Carlos de la Cabaña

Caleta de San Lázaro

Canal de Entrada

N

Parque de los Mártires

Monumento a Máximo Gómez

AVE. CARLOS M. DE CÉSPEDES (AVE. DEL PUERTO)

Museo Nacional de la Música

Fábrica de Tobaco La Corona

Iglesia del Santo Angelo Custodio

Catedral de la Habana

Castillo de la Real Fuerza

Centro Wifredo Lam

Casa de Lombillo

El Templete

Museo de la Revolución

Casa del Marques de Aguas Claras

Palacio de los Capitanes Generales

1
2
3

Palacio de los Matrimonios

Museo Nacional de Bellas Artes

4

5

Terminal Sierra Maestra (cruiser terminal)

7 **6**

Museo Casa de la Obra Pía

8

9

10

Gran Teatro

Parque Central

Iglesia del Santo Cristo del Buen Viaje

Iglesia y Conventa de San Francisco de Asis

Fábrica de Tobaco Partagas

Capitolio Nacional

Casa de los Condes de Jaruco

11

12

Parque de la Fraternidad

AVE. SIMÓN BOLÍVAR (REINA)

Iglesia y Conventa de Belén

Iglesia de Nuestra Señora de la Merced

13

Casa Natal de José Martí

Train Station

Ensenada de Atarés

ACCOMMODATION

Ambos Mundos	**5**
Caribbean	**1**
Casa del Científico	**2**
Casa de Eugenio Barral García	**13**
Casa de Fefita y Luís	**11**
Casa de Migdalia Caraballé Martín	**12**
Hostal Conde de Villanueva	**9**
Hostal Valencia	**8**
Inglaterra	**10**
Parque Central	**7**
Plaza	**6**
Santa Isabel	**4**
Sevilla	**3**

PLACES OF INTEREST

Casa de Africa	**g**
Casa de los Arabes	**f**
Casa de Simón Bolívar	**h**
Lonja del Comercio	**i**
Museo de Arte Colonial	**a**
Museo del Automóvil	**e**
Museo Nacional de Historia Natural	**c**
Museo Numismático	**d**
Palacio del Segundo Cabo	**b**

and sixteenth-century fortresses make it one of the most complete colonial urban centres in the Americas. Not surprisingly, then, for many people it's the old city as a whole, rather than the individual attractions within it, that leaves the most penetrating impression.

Yet there is much more to Habana Vieja than its unforgettable physical makeup. Unlike many of the world's major cities the tourist centre of Havana is also home to a large proportion of the city's residents, with some of its poorest families crammed into the very buildings that tourists stare up at, instilling the vibrant, sometimes hectic atmosphere that brings the area to life.

Prior to the Cuban tourism boom of the 1990s this was a fast-decaying part of town – as trade with the Soviet Union collapsed so the oldest, most fragile sections of the city began to collapse with it. Today the streets teem with foreign visitors whose dollars have brought a new sense of vigour to the area. A massive restoration project has seen some of the most impressive buildings converted into hotels, whilst museums and residential apartment blocks alike are being treated to their first coat of paint in years.

With so many historic buildings and museums to choose from, tackling the old city can seem a daunting task. However, it's relatively easy to prioritize your options and in fact trying to see everything can be counter-productive. If you intend to do all your sightseeing in one chunk you should restrict yourself to a maximum of three or four museums, as the half-hearted displays and incoherent collections which occupy a large number of them can become disheartening. The **Plaza de Armas** and the nearby **Plaza de la Catedral** are both good starting points, with numerous options in all directions (we start from the latter). For the other unmissable sights head up **Obispo**, Habana Vieja's busiest street, to the **Parque Central**. Bordered by some of the finest hotels in the city and just a few paces away from the awesome Capitolio building this is also the easiest, though not the quickest, route to the **Museo de la Revolución**, the country's most comprehensive celebration of the revolution. Different in feel from the rest of the old town, the wide streets and grand buildings on this western edge of Habana Vieja date predominantly from the first thirty years or so of the twentieth century. Heavily influenced by the United States, these early decades of reconstruction in Havana saw many colonial buildings demolished and replaced with flamboyant palaces and imposing Neoclassical block buildings, in tune with the ambition and growing confidence of the emerging superpower. The most untouched part of Habana Vieja is the southern half, mostly unreached by the restoration projects and still displaying the battered charm that gives this district so much of its unique character.

A word of warning: Habana Vieja is the **bag-snatching** centre of the city, with an increasing number of petty thieves working the streets, so take the usual precautions. Even at night, however, there is very rarely any violent crime.

Plaza de la Catedral

The **Plaza de la Catedral**, in northeastern Habana Vieja, is one of the most historically and architecturally consistent squares in the old city. Perfectly restored and pleasantly compact, it's enclosed on three sides by a set of simplistically symmetrical eighteenth-century aristocratic residences. The first houses were built on the site – which was swampland when the Spanish found it – around the turn of the sixteenth century. It wasn't until 1788 that the Plaza de la Ciénaga, or Swamp Square, as it was then known, was renamed the Plaza de la Catedral, when in that year the Jesuit church on its north face was consecrated as a cathedral and subsequently remodelled into its current elaborate shape.

The striking yet relatively small **Catedral de la Habana**, hailed as the consummate example of the Cuban Baroque style, dominates the plaza with its swirling detail, curved edges and cluster of columns. Curiously, however, the perfect symmetry of the detailed exterior was abandoned in the design of the two towers, the right one noticeably and unaccountably wider than the left. The less spectacular cathedral **interior** (Mon–Sat 10.30am–4pm, Sun 9.30am–noon; Mass at 10.30am; free) bears an endearing resemblance to a local church. It features a set of lavishly framed portraits by French painter Jean Baptiste Vermay, copies of originals by artists such as Rubens and Morillo, which were commissioned by Bishop José Díaz de Espada at the beginning of the nineteenth century in an attempt to replace anything in the newly consecrated cathedral which he considered to be in bad taste. Other than these and an unspectacular altar, featuring imported silverwork and sculptures completed in 1820 by the Italian artist Bianchini, the three naves are relatively empty. This is due in part to the removal of one of the cathedral's principal heirlooms, a funeral monument to Christopher Columbus said to have contained his ashes. It now stands in the cathedral in Seville, where it was taken when the Spanish were expelled from the island in 1898.

Opposite the cathedral, the Casa de los Condes de Casa Bayona, built in 1720, houses the **Museo de Arte Colonial** (daily 9.30am–7pm; $2). Its comprehensive collection of well-preserved, mostly nineteenth-century furniture and ornaments offers more insight into aristocratic living conditions during the later years of Spanish rule in Cuba than any other interior on the plaza, particularly because many of the rooms have been laid out as if they were still lived in. The predominantly European-made artefacts have been collected from colonial residences around the city and include elaborately engraved mahogany dressers, ostentatious gold and porcelain vases and crystal candlesticks; examples of the brightly coloured stained-glass arches, known as *vitrales*, used to crown doorways and windows and a classic of colonial Cuban design; as well as wrought-iron door-knockers and silver cutlery. The small exhibition of twentieth-century sculpture and art on the ground floor looks quite out of place and would be more at home displayed in the **Galería Victor Manuel**, an art shop occupying one half of the west side of the plaza.

Next door to the shop, and thoroughly deserving of a visit, is the **Casa del Marques de Aguas Claras**, the most sophisticated of the colonial mansions on the plaza. Its serene fountain-centred courtyard encompassed by pillar-propped arcs and simple coloured-glass portals is actually part of the delightful *El Patio* restaurant (see p.116), so you'll need to eat there to see it. Across from here, the **Casa de Lombillo** dates from 1741 and was originally home and office to a sugar factory owner before housing the Museo de la Educación (now on Obispo; see p.83). It's currently being renovated, so the only part you can visit is the small post office-cum-gift shop inset in one of its hallways.

At the end of Callejón del Chorro, a short cul-de-sac on the southwestern corner of the plaza, is the low-key **Taller Experimental de Gráfica** (Mon–Fri 9am–4pm; free), where a small selection of artwork, more innovative than most of what's on offer around this area, is exhibited in front of the large workshop where it is produced. The **Centro Wifredo Lam** (Mon–Sat 10am–5pm; $2), at San Ignacio esq. Empedrado, in the shadow of the cathedral, has a much larger though often quite bare gallery showing equally off-centre contemporary art, including photography, painting and sculpture. All exhibitions are temporary; previous shows have included huge, bizarre-looking amalgamations of modern household objects.

Plaza de Armas and the Castillo de la Real Fuerza

A couple of blocks southeast of the Plaza de la Catedral, on San Ignacio and then on O'Reilly, the area around the **Plaza de Armas**, the oldest and most animated of Habana Vieja's squares, was where Havana established itself as a city in the second half of the sixteenth century. There's still a sense, particularly for the visitor, that life emanates from this square, the focal point for the old city's more tangible tourist attractions. Based around an attractive landscaped leafy core, at its busiest the plaza seethes with tourists as live music wafts from *La Mina* restaurant in the corner. The three brick streets and, uniquely, the single wooden one which make up the outer border, are dominated, from Monday to Saturday, by Havana's biggest and best secondhand **book market**. This is the place to find publications of Fidel Castro's speeches or Che Guevara's theories, as well as collectable pre-revolutionary and even some colonial-era literature.

Once the political heart of Havana, the plaza is also host to some distinguished colonial architecture. The robust, refined **Palacio de los Capitanes Generales** on the western, wooden-street side was the seat of the Spanish government from the time of its inauguration in 1791 to the end of the Spanish-American War in 1898. It's now home to one of Havana's best museums, the **Museo de la Ciudad** (daily 9.30am–7pm; $3, $1 extra for guided tour), a fine illustration of the city's colonial heritage. A number of the upstairs rooms have been precisely restored to their original splendour, including the magnificent Salón de los Espejos (Hall of Mirrors), lined with glorious gilt looking-glasses, and the sumptuous Salón del Trono (Throne Room) with its dark-red; satin-lined walls intended for royal visits, though in fact no Spanish king or queen ever did visit colonial Cuba. Most striking is the Salón Dorado, where the governor of the city used to receive his guests amidst golden furniture and precious porcelain. Downstairs, exhibits range from horse-drawn carriages to an impressively detailed model of a nineteenth-century sugar mill and railway.

In the same corner of the plaza, at Tacón and O'Reilly, is the **Palacio del Segundo Cabo**, dating from the same period and similarly characterized by elegant, stern-faced architecture. It served its original purpose as home to the Royal Post Office for only a few years, and has been used by a whole host of institutions since, including the Tax Inspectorate, the Supreme Court of Justice and the Cuban Geographical Society, and currently acts as the headquarters of the **Instituto Cubano del Libro**, the Cuban Book Institute (Mon–Fri 8.15am–4.30pm). Based around an attractive shadowy patio, it's not really set up to receive visitors but you can wander through into the courtyard for a peek at the august Baroque architecture, where the ageing stone archways shoulder an iron-girdered wraparound balcony complete with wooden shutters and colourful portals. In the entrance hall are posted details of readings, workshops and conferences which take place periodically inside the building, open to the public and usually free. There's also a relatively well-stocked **bookshop** (daily 8am–5pm).

There's more to see around the rest of the square, particularly in the **Museo Nacional de Historia Natural** (Tues–Sun 9.30am–6.30pm; $3), on the corner of Obispo and Oficios. Relocated from the ground floor of the Capitolio Nacional (see p.91) and reopened in 1999, it has a smarter, more professional feel than most other museums in the area. The essentials are covered on the ground floor, where models and interactive video displays help tell the history of life on earth and light-and-sound effects bring the mammals of the five continents to a semblance of life, whilst one floor up Cuban wildlife is the dominant theme.

In the square's northeastern corner, the incongruous classical Greek architecture of **El Templete**, a curious, scaled-down version of the Parthenon in Athens, marks the exact spot of the foundation of Havana and the city's first mass in 1519. Inside the tiny interior (daily 9.30am–6pm; $1), two large paintings depict these two historic ceremonies, both by nineteenth-century French artist Jean Baptiste Vermay, whose work can also be seen inside the Catedral de la Habana (see p.80).

In the same corner, just beyond the plaza's northern border, is the **Castillo de la Real Fuerza**, a heavy-set sixteenth-century fortress surrounded by a moat. Built to replace a more primitive fort which

Plaza de la Revolución, Havana

Necrópolis Colón, Havana

Malecón, Havana

Farmer and ox-drawn plough, Viñales

Playa Ancón

Gran Teatro, Havana

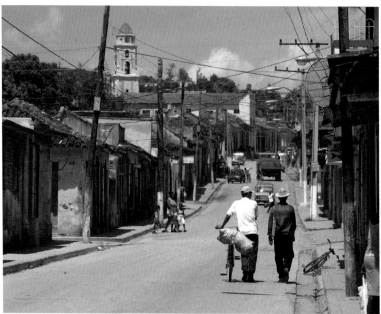

Trinidad

Palacio de Valle, Cienfuegos

El Mural de la Prehistoria, Viñales

Parque Josone, Varadero

Lamp, Trinidad

Tobacco in drying house, Pinar del Río

Diver explores colonial shipwreck

stood on the same site but was destroyed by French pirates in 1555, the building, though stronger than its predecessor, never really got into its role as protector of the city. It is set well back from the mouth of the bay, and its location deemed it useless against the English who, in 1762, took control of Havana without ever coming into the firing-range of the fortress's cannon. Today the ground floor houses an excellent collection of ceramic art, the **Museo de la Cerámica** (daily 8.30am–6.30pm; $1), where pre-Columbian-style vases sit alongside quirkier modern pieces, like the pottery typewriter, made by Fernando Velázquez Vigil, complete with a clay piece of paper between its jaws. It's worth looking out for the innovative temporary exhibitions, which in the past have included a collection of miniature dinosaur-clad pots. A wooden staircase leads up to the ramparts where, disappointingly, little has been made of the building or its history. Instead there's a gift shop and a café with reasonable views across the harbour.

Obispo

Shooting west from the Plaza de Armas, and linking it with the Parque Central (see p.91), is the tightly packed shopping street of **Obispo**, scene of some of the most intense redevelopment in Habana Vieja since the mid-1990s. Crowded with foreign visitors, and one of the most animated thoroughfares in the entire city, Obispo is a lively mix of dollar shops, street vendors, open-front bars, secondhand book stalls in doorways, hotels, *paladares* and a plethora of private front-room art galleries and workshops. Away from the new shopping malls which have sprung up in recent years, this is the best place in Havana for a relatively wide variety of at least half-decent shops in the same place, including Longina, one of the better places for Cuban music on CD or cassette, situated between Compostela and Habana.

See "Shopping" (p.123) for more on Obispo's shops.

Near the Plaza de Armas end of the street is a small concentration of quick-stop distractions. On the corner of Aguiar, the **Drogueria Johnson**, a dimly lit pre-revolutionary pharmacy, may not date back further than the 1950s but its dark-wood shelves and cabinets and even medicines reek of a bygone era. Untouched by renovation, it's the sole preserve of prescription-wielding Cubans, and its authenticity is far more intriguing than the manufactured charm of the **Farmacia Taquechel** (daily 9.30am–6.30pm), a couple of blocks further down, between San Ignacio and Mercaderes. Founded in 1898 and perfectly restored in 1996, this fully functioning but clearly tourist-focused pharmacy specializes in natural medicines, but attracts a constant stream of visitors with its admirable attention to detail – from the shelves of porcelain medicine jars down to the cash register, there isn't a piece out of place. Bang opposite the pharmacy is the humdrum **Museo de Educación** (Tues–Sat 10am–5pm; $1), whose exhibition attempting to chart the history of education in Cuba, with the usual emphasis on the revolution, belongs to the document-dominated old school of Cuban museums. Infinitely more interesting is the hotel **Ambos Mundos** next door, **Ernest Hemingway**'s base in Cuba for ten years from 1932 and allegedly where he began writing *For Whom the Bell Tolls*. Thoroughly renovated in the mid-1990s, the hotel is one of the best places for a drink in the old city, in the rooftop garden bar. On the way up, in the original 1920s cage-elevator, stop off on the fifth floor and visit Room 511, where Hemingway invariably stayed. The original furniture and even his typewriter have been preserved, and there's usually a guide on hand to answer any questions.

Along Oficios to Plaza de San Francisco

Heading south from the Plaza de Armas is **Oficios**, the oldest street in the city, lined with colonial residences, several of which now house small museums. The **Museo del Numismático** at no. 8 (Tues–Sat 11am–6pm; free) is unlikely to interest anyone but the most ardent currency collector, with its several rooms of encased banknotes and coins, some dating back centuries. There are pieces from Asia and the Middle East, and a disproportionate amount of drachma, but the primary focus is on the history of Cuban coinage. Further along at no. 16, the **Casa de los Arabes** (daily 9.30am–7.30pm; $1) is housed in what was, in the late 1800s, a religious school. The building was actually constructed in the seventeenth century and is one of the most striking single examples of the Moorish influence on Spanish – and therefore Cuban – architectural styles. The red-brick arches, wooden-frame ceilings and patio draped in plantlife rather outshine the sketchy collection of heavily patterned rugs, Arabian furniture, some of it sixteenth-century, and robes once worn by Saharan nomads, which are impressive but displayed too haphazardly to be effective.

Across the street, and of wider appeal, is the **Museo del Automóvil** (daily 9am–7.30pm; $1) where, amongst the two dozen or so cars parked inside, dating mostly from the first half of the twentieth century, the 1902 Cadillac in the window is one of the most attention-grabbing. The 1981 Chevrolet donated to the museum by the Peruvian ambassador, classic Harley Davidson motorbikes, 1920s Fords and a number of other models deliver a rather succinct history of the automobile, which you can't help feeling should be more comprehensive given the number of old cars still on the streets in Cuba.

Two blocks beyond the car museum, Oficios opens out onto the **Plaza de San Francisco**, opposite the colourful **Terminal Sierra Maestra** where the two or three luxury cruisers that include Cuba in their Caribbean tour come to dock. With the main port road running the length of its west side and two of its main buildings given over to offices the square is the most open and functional of Habana Vieja's main plazas, and attracts fewer sightseers than its counterparts nearby. The surrounding architecture, however, exercises a commanding presence, particularly the impressive five-storey **Lonja del Comercio** on the north side. This corpulent construction, clasped by rows of columns and stone-arched window frames, could be a classical Roman theatre but in fact was built in 1909. It originally served as the Chamber of Representatives but now houses the Brazilian Embassy and a variety of commercial companies in a spankingly modern office complex better suited to Wall Street than Habana Vieja. Across the port road, the yellow-painted Terminal Sierra Maestra, with its pointed brick-coloured tiled roof, looks vaguely Japanese in design and manages to appear homely despite its size.

Hogging the entire southern side of the square, the **Iglesia y Convento de San Francisco de Asís** (daily 9.30am–7pm; $1) was built in 1739 on the site of a late sixteenth-century structure, which from 1579 was one of the most prestigious religious centres in Havana, a kind of missionary school for Franciscan friars who set off from here to convert the ignorant masses throughout Spanish America. Wonderfully restored in the early 1990s, the monastery now contains a neatly condensed **museum** (same opening hours; $2) of religious art, featuring wooden and ceramic figurines of the saints, church furniture and pottery found on the site. The real pleasure, however, comes from wandering around the beautifully simple interior, admiring the solid curves of the north cloister, and, for a dollar extra, climbing the wooden staircase up the 46-metre-tall bell tower for magnificent views across the bay and over most of Habana Vieja.

At Oficios no. 162, opposite the entrance to the church, is the **Casa de la Pintora Venezolana Carmen Montilla Tinoco** (Mon–Sat 9.30am–5pm; free), a delightful colonial town house restored in the mid-1990s from scratch by the Venezuelan artist and friend of Fidel Castro, and used for exhibitions of Cuban and overseas artists alike. Tinoco's own surreal and sometimes quite morbid paintings hang on the interior balcony whilst outside, on the far wall of the patio garden, is a huge, ceramic mural, made up of hundreds of leafy and mollusc-like shapes to represent Cuban flora and fauna, the work of renowned Cuban artist Alfredo Sosabravo.

Around Plaza de Simón Bolívar

A few blocks before the Plaza de San Francisco, a right turn off Oficios onto Obrapía leads to the intersection with Mercaderes, where a mixed group of museums and galleries huddle around the tiny **Plaza de Simón Bolívar**. The most exceptional is the **Casa de África** at Obrapía no. 157 e/ Mercaderes y San Ignacio (daily 9am–7pm; $2), with three floors of displays relating to African and Afro-Cuban arts, crafts and religion. The top floor is dedicated to the symbolism and imagery of Santería, Palo Monte and Abaku, three of the more widely practised Afro-Cuban religions. There are ceremonial costumes, some quite eerie-looking, in the various earthy colours which represent the different *orishas* (see box overleaf), as well as ornate hatchet-like instruments, maracas,

Orishas and syncretism in Afro-Cuban religion

Walking the streets of Havana you may notice, from time to time, people dressed head to foot in white, a bead necklace providing the only colour in their costume. These are practitioners of Santería, the most widely endorsed of Afro-Cuban religions, and the beads represent their appointed *orisha*, the gods and goddesses at the heart of Santería worship.

With its roots in the religious beliefs of the Yoruba people of West Africa, Santería evolved in Cuba with the importation of slaves from that region. Forbidden by the Spanish to practise their native religion, the slaves found ways of hiding their gods behind the backs of the Catholic saints to whom they were forced to pay homage. From this developed the open syncretism of African *orishas* with their Catholic counterparts, which forms such an integral part of Santería today.

Though there are countless *orishas*, most Cubans know only a few, with around a dozen or more commonly deferred to in religious ceremonies. Each has a specific Catholic equivalent, originally determined by characteristics and attributes which the Yoruba identified as being shared by both and duly interchangeable. Thus, for example, the Virgen de la Caridad del Cobre, the patron saint of Cuba, embodies the *orisha* known as Oshún, the goddess of femininity, in part because both are believed to provide protection during birth. Similarly, Yemayá, goddess of water and queen of the sea, considered the mother of all *orishas*, was the natural equivalent of the Virgen de Regla, whom Spanish Catholics believed protected sailors. Other pairings include San Lázaro, patron saint of the sick, with Babalu-Ayé, Santa Bárbara with Changó, and San Cristóbal with Aggayú.

cloth-covered drums and all sorts of ceramic and wooden pots and receptacles. The rest of the museum, on the lower two floors, covers everything from tribal weapons to engraved elephant tusks, and trying to see everything becomes slightly overwhelming. There is, however, an added fascination to the huge collection on the first floor as every single piece once belonged to Fidel Castro, most of it given to him by leaders of the African countries he has visited.

Opposite the Casa de Africa, and distinguished by its ornately framed front entrance, is the more eclectic **Museo Casa de la Obra Pía** (Tues–Sat 10.30am–5.30pm, Sun 9am–1pm; $1). Effectively three museums under one roof, it features a section devoted to Alejo Carpentier (1904–1980), Cuba's most famous novelist, including the Volkswagen Beetle he used when he lived in France, and another detailing the era of the Spanish monarch Carlos III. If you can't read Spanish, skip this ground floor and head upstairs, where the house itself, a prestigious seventeenth-century mansion, becomes the point of interest, comprehensively furnished to reflect the tastes of its colonial owners. A room full of Chinese furniture features some particularly elaborate chairs, whilst the dining-room walls are lined with plates given to the owners of the house by guests, as was the fashion in eighteenth-century aristocratic circles. Many of the rooms are impressively complete, as is the record of its occupants, represented by a huge family tree going back as far as the late seventeenth century.

Simón Bolívar and Latin American independence

One of the few men in history to have had a country named after him, and honoured throughout Latin America for the prominent role he played in the independence struggles of the early nineteenth century, **Simón Bolívar** received widespread commemorations on the bicentenary of his birth in 1983, confirming him as one of the region's most enduring icons, revered in Cuba as much as anywhere.

Born into an aristocratic family on July 24, 1783, in Caracas, Venezuela, Bolívar was orphaned by the age of nine, his father dying when he was only three and his mother six years later. At the age of sixteen he was sent to Europe where he saw out the final years of his formal education. He returned to Venezuela a married man, but his wife, the daughter of a Spanish nobleman, died of yellow fever within a year of the wedding. Grief-stricken, he returned to Europe and immersed himself in the writings of Montesquieu, Jean Jacques Rousseau and other European philosophers. It was under such influences in Paris and Rome that Bolívar developed a passion for the idea of American independence.

He returned once again to Venezuela in 1807 in time to witness the effects of the Napoleonic invasion of Spain in 1808. Suffering enormous domestic problems, Spain was forced to loosen its grip on the colonies, providing independence movements all over Spanish America with the perfect opportunity for an insurrection. Over the next twenty years all mainland South American countries were to break free of their colonial shackles and declare themselves independent, leaving the Spanish clinging onto Cuba and Puerto Rico as the last vestiges of a once-vast empire.

Bolívar was to be the single most influential man during these wars of independence, involved personally in the liberation of Venezuela, Colombia, Ecuador, Peru and Bolivia. His military career began in 1811 when he enrolled himself in the army of the recently declared independent Venezuela. The Spanish were soon to claim back their lost territory and during the ensuing war Bolívar fought hard in six battles to regain control of the capital in 1813, where he assumed the political leadership of the separatist movement. The fighting was far from over, however, and it wasn't until 1821, following numerous military manoeuvres, time spent in exile in Jamaica and Haiti and the expansion of his ambitions to incorporate the freeing of the whole of the northern section of Spanish South America, that Bolívar was to see his vision of a truly independent Venezuela a reality. Perhaps the most important and heroic of all the military campaigns that he waged during these eight years was the taking of New Granada, modern-day Colombia. Against all the odds he led an army of some 2500 men through the Andes, enduring icy winds and assailing the seemingly unnegotiable pass of Pisba. When Bolívar and his men descended into New Granada the colonial army was completely unprepared and on August 10, 1819, after victory at the battle of Boyacá, they marched triumphantly into Bogotá.

Around the corner, facing the plaza at Mercaderes no. 156, the **Casa de Simón Bolívar** (Tues–Sat 10.30am–6pm, Sun 9.30am–12.30pm; $1) informatively and originally details the life and times of the Venezuelan known throughout Latin America as *El Libertador de las Américas* (see box above). It depicts the life of Bolívar, born in 1783, through a series of often comic cartoonish clay models, each representing a significant or symbolic event – such as his birth, baptism and first sexual experience – whilst he is also shown in battle and dancing with a black general in an act of solidarity. Display screens in a separate room go into greater depth with useful written explanations in English, as well as prints of some great paintings from the period providing a lively visual context. The entrance fee also entitles you to take a look around the excellent gallery upstairs, which includes some impressionistic paintings relating to Bolívar as well as a reproduction of Picasso's *Guernica* made from coloured fabric.

Facing the plaza from the Obrapía side is the missable **Casa de Benito Juárez** (Tues–Sat 10.30am–5.30pm, Sun 9.30am–12.30pm; $1), also known as the Casa de México. There are some paintings and a few pre-Columbian artefacts from various regions of Mexico but this is essentially the museum of unused space. The **Casa de Guayasimín**, on the same block at Obrapía no. 111 (Tues–Sat 10.30am–5.45pm, Sun 9am–12.45pm; $1), feels only slightly less bare but can claim a more palpable subject matter. Set up in 1992, the house doubles as a studio and a gallery for the Ecuadorian painter Oswaldo Guayasimín, a friend of Fidel Castro. Upstairs – where there's a bedroom and dining room set up for the man in case he pops over – are examples of his work, including the portrait of Castro which Guayasimín presented to him on his seventieth birthday. The best place, though, to get a flavour of the artist's distinctive and likeable style is in the shop, which you can enter independently. There are more original paintings at **Casa Quitrin** (Tues–Sat 10am–5pm, Sun 9am–1pm; free), a gallery on the corner of Obrapía and San Ignacio that exhibits the dream-like works of Orlando Hernández Yanes, considered one of Cuba's premier portrait painters, and the flower specialist Isabel Rodríguez Jardines, another Cuban artist, who paints under the pseudonym Casiguaya.

Plaza Vieja and Plaza del Cristo

Despite its name, **Plaza Vieja**, three blocks south of the Plaza de Simón Bolívar, is not the oldest square in the city. It was first used as an official public space in the 1580s when the Plaza de Armas was commandeered for military use. It was renamed when the newer Plaza del Cristo was built around 1640, by which time it had firmly established itself as a centre for urban activity, variously used as marketplace and festival site. Today, more than any of the other main old town squares, it reflects its original purpose as a place for the local community, with predominantly residential buildings and, as yet, relatively little for the visitor to do. However, newly repaved, with two hotels opening up on its borders and a central fountain installed in the late 1990s, the square is being primed for tourism, as well as being improved for its residents. There is already a minor **art gallery** and a small **shopping arcade**, featuring a couple of so-called boutiques selling arts and crafts, wooden cigar boxes and a few items of clothing, in the Casa de los

Condes de Jaruco, an eighteenth-century mansion on the southern face of the square. Many of the simple but likeable two- and three-storey buildings, with their uncomplicated curved arches, are already fully restored and colourfully painted.

Six blocks west along Brasil, smaller, more local **Plaza del Cristo** contains the **Iglesia del Santo Cristo del Buen Viaje**, a handsome little neighbourhood church. The surrounding apartment buildings and school are run-down and you're unlikely to stop here other than to savour a taste of real-life Havana, something you can do all over southern Habana Vieja.

Southern Habana Vieja and the Casa Natal de José Martí

Immediately south of plazas Vieja and del Cristo, Habana Vieja becomes much more residential, devoid of hotels or shopping centres and home to only one museum of note. A wander around this as yet undeveloped part of town offers an undiluted taste of old Havana, and despite a pro-liferation of churches and other religious buildings, the main appeal of a visit here is the chance to enjoy some undisturbed street life.

There is no particular route more or less interesting than any other; the narrow crowded streets are all equally enchanting, with the ever-present chance of running across an old convent or church. However, for a variety of experience it's worth including the colour-ful fruit and vegetable **street market** on Compostela, in between Luz and Acosta, running alongside the shabby **Iglesia y Convento de Belén** and, a couple of blocks further south, the surprisingly grand **Iglesia de Nuestra Señora de la Merced**, slotted into the local neighbourhood on the corner of Merced and Cuba. If you're lucky enough to arrive when this faded orange church is open (it keeps unpredictable hours), don't miss the opportunity to marvel at the magnificently decorated interior with frescoed ceilings and tapestried arches looming tall between the three naves, once a choice location for lavish society weddings.

The most tangible and best-kept tourist attraction in this part of town is the **Casa Natal de José Martí** (Tues–Sat 9am–5pm, Sun 9am–1pm; $1), a few blocks southwest from the church at Leonor Pérez no. 314. This modest, two-storey house was the birthplace of Cuba's most widely revered intellectual and freedom fighter, though he only lived here for the first three years of his life. Though dotted with the odd bit of original furniture, the rooms of this compact and per-fectly preserved little blue and yellow house don't strive to recreate domestic tableaux, but instead exhibit photographs, documents and other items relating to Martí's dramatic life (see box overleaf). There are images of his arrest, imprisonment and exile on the Isla de Pinos, now the Isla de la Juventud, and details of his trips to New York, Caracas and around Spain. In tune with the endearing simplicity of the house it will take no more than fifteen minutes to see everything here.

Havana

José Martí

It doesn't take long for most people who spend any time touring round Cuba to start wondering, if they don't already know, who **José Martí** is. Almost every town, large or small, has a bust or a statue of him somewhere, usually at the centre of the main square. Born José Julián Martí y Pérez to Spanish parents on January 28, 1853, this diminutive man, with his bushy moustache and trademark black bow tie and suit, came to embody the Cuban desire for self-rule and was a figurehead for justice and independence, particularly from the extending arm of the US, throughout Latin America.

An outstanding pupil at the San Anacleto and San Pablo schools in Havana, and then at the Instituto de Segunda Enseñaza de la Habana, Martí soon proved himself equally a man of action, and it didn't take him long to become directly involved in the separatist struggle against colonial Spain. Still a schoolboy when the first Cuban war of independence broke out in 1868, by the start of the following year he had founded his first newspaper, *Patria Libre*, contesting Spanish rule of Cuba. His damning editorials swiftly had him pegged as a dissident, and he was arrested a few months later on the trivial charge of having written a letter to a friend denouncing him for joining the Cuerpo de Voluntarios, the Spanish volunteer corps. Aged just sixteen, Martí was sentenced to six years' hard labour in the San Lázaro stone quarry in Havana, though thanks to the small amount of influence his father, a Havanan policeman, was able to use, the sentence was mitigated and the now ailing teenager was exiled to the Isla de la Juventud, then known as the Isla de Pinos (see p.90), and finally, in 1871, exiled to Spain.

Martí wasted no time, studying law and philosophy at the universities in Madrid and Zaragoza, all the time honing his literary skills and writing poetry, his prolific output evidenced today in countless compendiums and reprints in bookshops around Cuba. By 1875 he was back on the other side of the Atlantic, reunited with his family, now living in Mexico. Settling down, however, was never an option for this tireless man who, wherever he was, rarely rested from his writing or his agitation for an independent Cuba. When, in 1877, he returned to Havana under a false name, he began a series of moves that was to take him to Guatemala, back again to Havana, back to Spain for a second period of exile, Paris, Caracas and New York, where he managed to stay for the best part of a decade. His years in New York were to prove pivotal. Initially swept away by what he perceived to be the true spirit of freedom and democracy, he soon came to regard the US with intense suspicion, regarding it as a threat to the independence of all Latin American countries.

The final phase of Martí's life began with his founding of the Cuban Revolutionary Party in 1892. He spent the following three years drumming up support from around Latin America for Cuban independence, raising money, training for combat, gathering together an arsenal of weapons and planning a military campaign to defeat the Spanish. In 1895, with the appointed general of the revolutionary army, Máximo Gómez, and just four other freedom fighters, he landed on Cuban soil at Playitas on the south coast. Disappearing into the mountains of the Sierra Maestra, just as Fidel Castro and his rebels were to do almost fifty years later, they were soon joined by hundreds of supporters. On May 19, 1895 Martí went into battle for the first time and was shot dead almost immediately. Perhaps the strongest testament to José Martí's legacy is the esteem in which he is held by Cubans on both sides of the Florida Straits, his ideas authenticating their vision of a free Cuba and his dedication to the cause an inspiration to all.

Parque Central and Paseo del Prado

From the Casa Natal de José Martí it's a five- to ten-minute walk north on busy Avenida de Bélgica to the grandest square in Habana Vieja. Flanked by some of the old city's most prestigious hotels, the **Parque Central**, two-thirds of it shrouded in shade, straddles the border between Habana Vieja and Centro Habana and lies within shouting distance of one of Havana's most memorable landmarks, the Capitolio Nacional. Though the traffic humming past on all sides detracts a little, the grandeur of the surrounding buildings, characteristic of the celebratory early twentieth-century architecture in this section of town, lends the square a stateliness that's quite distinct from the residential feel which pervades elsewhere in Habana Vieja. The attention-grabber is undoubtedly the **Gran Teatro**, between San Martín and San Rafael, an explosion of balustraded balconies, colonnaded cornices and sculpted stone figures striking classical poses. There's been a theatre on this spot since 1838, though the building standing today actually dates from 1915. For a proper look inside, you'll have to attend a performance, which usually take place at weekends. Next door is the renowned **Hotel Inglaterra**, the oldest hotel in the country, founded in 1856; past guests include Antonio Maceo, widely considered the bravest general in Cuban history, who lodged here in 1890 during a five-month stay in Havana. The pavement café out front belonging to the hotel, *La Acera de Louvre*, is one of the few places around the park where you can sit and take it all in. While you're here, check out the crowd of local men who congregate every day, usually in the afternoon, always in the same shady spot, zealously discussing the topic of the moment.

See p.123 for details of performances at the Gran Teatro.

Cutting through the park's western edge is the **Paseo del Prado**, one of the prettiest main streets in the old town. Also known as the Paseo de Martí but more often simply as El Prado, it's the boulevard section north of the park, beginning at the *Hotel Parque Central* and leading down to the seafront, which gives it its reputation. A wide walkway lined with trees and stone benches bisects the road, while either side are the hundreds of columns and arches of the mostly residential neo-colonial balcony buildings, painted in a whole host of colours, some recent recipients of face-lifts, others long since in need of one. Look out for the illustrious **Palacio de los Matrimonios** on Animas – showered in sculpted stone detail it looks ready to receive royal guests but is in fact one of the city's many wedding ceremony buildings, the popular Cuban alternative to a church. Encouragingly, despite its position in the city's touristic centre, El Prado still belongs to the locals and is usually overrun with newspaper sellers, chattering Cubans and children playing ball games.

Capitolio Nacional

Just beyond the southwestern corner of the Parque Central, visible above the sublime detail of the Gran Teatro on the same corner, looms the familiar-looking dome of the **Capitolio Nacional** (daily

9am–7.30pm; $3). Bearing a striking resemblance to the Capitol Building in Washington DC, though little is made of this in Cuban publications, its solid, proudly columned front gloriously dominates the local landscape. It is arguably the most architecturally complex and varied building in the country, and any doubters will be silenced once inside, where the classical style of the exterior is replaced with flourishes of extravagant detail and a selection of plushly decorated rooms. Built in just three years by several thousand workers under the instructions of a dozen architects and engineers, it was opened in 1929 amidst huge celebrations. The seat of the House of Representatives and the Senate prior to the revolution, the two fantastically ornate main chambers now make up the centrepieces for visitors. The walk round, with or without a free tour guide, is surprisingly brief and shouldn't take you longer than twenty minutes as only one floor is open to the public, much of it behind ropes. Nevertheless the sheer size of the magnificent polished entrance hall known as the Salón de los Pasos Perdidos (The Room of Lost Steps) and the breathtaking gold and bronze Rococo-style decoration of the Hemiciclio Camilo Cienfuegos, a theatrical, echoing conference chamber dripping with detail, are enough in themselves to leave a lasting impression. Though there's not, strictly speaking, a bar here, you can sit on the simple terrace off the main hall and order a drink, a great way to take in the hustle and bustle of one of the busiest parts of Habana Vieja.

Fábrica de Tobacos Partagás

Behind the Capitolio stands the **Fábrica de Tobacos Partagás** (tours Mon–Fri 10am & 2pm; $10), one of the country's oldest and most productive cigar factories. Disputably just inside the Centro Habana municipal border but generally regarded, spiritually at least, as part of Habana Vieja, the factory was founded in 1849 and now churns out such famous makes of Cuban cigars as Cohiba, Bolívar and Partagás. Though steeply priced compared to most museum entrance fees, the 45-minute tours here are easily among the most fascinating things to do in the city, with English-speaking guides taking you through the various stages of production – drying, sorting, rolling and boxing – all performed in separate rooms under one roof. There's even an area used as a kind of cigar school, from where, after a nine-month course, those who graduate will move upstairs and join the hundred or so workers making some of the finest cigars in the world. It's on this top floor that the most lasting images are formed, where the sea of expert workers, expected to produce between 80 and 250 cigars during their eight-hour shifts, are read to, from a newspaper in the mornings and from a book in the afternoons. Entirely uncontrived, there's a very genuine sense of looking on at an everyday operation, with most of the workers almost oblivious to the stares of tourists and the flashing of cameras.

Museo de la Revolución and around

From Parque Central it's a two-minute walk along Agramonte to the **Museo Nacional de Bellas Artes** on the corner of Trocadero, closed until at least 2001 but well worth checking out once it reopens (details on ☎61-18-64). It houses the country's finest collection of art, displaying paintings of a breadth of period and style unequalled on the island – from the large Cuban collection dating right back to the seventeenth century, to originals by the likes of Velázquez, Rubens and Goya, and ancient Egyptian and Greek pieces. Just a couple of blocks further down is Havana's most famous museum, the **Museo de la Revolución** (Tues 10am–6pm, Wed–Sun 10am–5pm; $3). Defiantly housed in the sumptuous presidential palace of the 1950s dictator General Fulgencio Batista, the museum manages to be both unmissable and overrated at the same time. The events leading up to the triumph of the revolution in 1959 are covered in unparalleled detail, but your attention span is unlikely to last the full three storeys. Visitors work their way down from the top floor, the most engaging part of the museum and where you should concentrate your efforts. The events of the revolutionary war and the urban insurgency movements during the 1950s were surprisingly well documented photographically and there are some fantastically dramatic pictures, such as one of the police assault on the Socialist Party headquarters. Some of the classic photos of the campaign waged in the Sierra Maestra by Castro and his band of followers might look familiar, but even serious students of Cuban history will struggle to keep track of the chronology of the revolution as they overdose on models of battles and vaguely relevant exhibits such as miscellaneous firearms. It comes as a relief, then, to find the monotony of exhibits broken by the sensationalist **Memorial Camilo-Che**, a life-sized wax model of Che Guevara and Camilo Cienfuegos, both heroes of the revolution, portrayed in guerrilla uniform striding out over some rocks from a bushy thicket. Most of the second floor is given over to tiresome depictions of battle plans and would be missable altogether if it weren't for the captivating and colourful mural on the ceiling of the Salón de los Espejos, a mesmerizingly dramatic celebration of the republic, with an angel at its centre carrying the Cuban flag amidst a fanfare of heavenly and worldly onlookers.

Joined to the building but located outside to the rear of the museum is the **Granma Memorial**, where the boat which took Castro and his merry men from Mexico to Cuba to begin the revolution is preserved in its entirety within a giant glass case. Also here are military transports, whole or in bits depending on which side they belonged to, used during the 1961 Bay of Pigs invasion. These include a US B-26 bomber shot down during the attack and a T-34 Soviet tank from which Fidel Castro opened fire on the advancing counter-revolutionary brigade.

Across the road from the museum, on the other side of Agramonte, is the **Fábrica de Tobaco La Corona** (tours Mon–Fri 9am; $10), one of the two cigar factories in the capital open to visitors. Similar to the more renowned Partagás factory (see p.92), the factory offers fascinating **guided tours** lasting about 45 minutes, giving hands-on insight into the entire production process. In the same building but with a separate entrance is the **Palacio del Tobaco** (Mon–Sat 9am–5pm), an excellent cigar shop which features a lounge and a bar, making a visit worthwhile even if you don't intend to buy a box of *habanos*.

Facing the opposite side of the museum, on the corner of Avenida de las Misiones and Cuarteles, is the nineteenth-century neo-gothic **Iglesia del Santo Angel Custodio** (Mon, Wed & Sat 3–6pm, Tues, Thurs & Fri 9am–noon). Distinctive for its rampart-like set of spires, the church boasts a strikingly well-kept, if unremarkable, interior and some gorgeously colourful stained-glass windows.

La Punta and around

La Punta, the paved corner of land at the entrance to the bay, capping one end of the official border between Habana Vieja and Centro Habana, can be considered as the outer limit for sightseeing tours in this part of town. Just above the junction of the busy Malecón and the Avenida Carlos Manuel de Céspedes, its position is less than enchanting, though it attracts groups of chattering locals and youngsters who gather to throw themselves off the Malecón into the rocky pools which jut out from the sea wall here. In addition, the **Castillo de San Salvador de la Punta**, the sixteenth-century fortress occupying a large proportion of this space, is one of the oldest military fortifications in the city and will be well worth a visit when restorations are finally completed.

Standing at the entrance to the **tunnel** which joins the two sides of the bay, the wide open space linking La Punta with the rest of Habana Vieja is dominated by heavy traffic. The road winding down into the tunnel encircles the neoclassical **Monumento a Máximo Gómez**, one of the grandest memorials in Havana, yet, due to its location, relegated to no more than a fleeting curiosity for most visitors. Dedicated to the venerated leader of the Liberation Army in the nineteenth-century Cuban wars of independence, the statue has the general sitting on a horse held aloft by marble figures representing the People.

The aristocratic mansion facing the monument houses the **Museo Nacional de la Música** (Mon–Sat 9am–4.45pm; $2), a showcase for the surprising variety of contraptions made and used to produce music over the last two hundred years. The most coherent single collection is in the Sala Fernando Ortíz, where several dozen Afro-Cuban drums – mostly nineteenth-century instruments from Africa, Haiti and Cuba – have been gathered together by the country's most renowned scholar of Afro-Cuban culture. In other rooms the displays are more disjointed but there are some eye-catching exhibits, such as the strange-looking violin from China or the boat-shaped xylophones from Laos. There's also a beautiful little upstairs courtyard, lined with plants, where you can sit down, and a shop on the ground floor selling CDs and sheet music.

A one-minute walk from the music museum, also on the road encircling the monument, is the pretty little **Parque de los Mártires**, marking the spot where a now notorious prison, the Cárcel de Tacón, built in 1838, held such political prisoners as José Martí (see p.90). It was pretty much demolished in 1939, and all that remains are two of the cells and the chapel in what is little more than a large concrete box.

Centro Habana

For many visitors the crumbling buildings and bustling streets of **Centro Habana**, crammed between the hotel districts of Habana Vieja and Vedado, are glimpsed only through a taxi window en route to the city's more tourist-friendly areas. Yet this no-frills quarter has a character all of its own, as illuminating and fascinating as anywhere in the capital. Overwhelmingly residential, though a number of Havana's classic shopping streets fall within its borders, its late eighteenth- and nineteenth-century neighbourhoods nevertheless throb with life, particularly **El Barrio Chino**, Havana's Chinatown, and there's no better place to really savour the essence of the city, particularly because here it's not put on display but is up to you to discover.

*Just across the water is **Habana del Este**, which you could easily fit into your itinerary while you're in this part of Habana Vieja; it's described in more detail on p.113.*

Still very run-down, Centro Habana it has not yet enjoyed the degree of investment and rejuvenation that Habana Vieja has gained so much from, save for the **Malecón** where there are at last visible signs of part of the famous seafront promenade returning to its former glory. For now, the most impressive sight in Centro Habana is the **Iglesia del Sagrado Corazón**, a glorious neo-gothic church rarely visited by tourists.

El Barrio Chino

A block inside Centro Habana from the Habana Vieja western border, the grand entrance to **El Barrio Chino**, Havana's version of Chinatown, is likely to confuse most visitors, placed as it is three blocks from any visible change in the neighbourhood. The entrance, a rectangular concrete arch with a pagoda-inspired roof, is south of the Capitolio Nacional, on the intersection of Amistad and Dragones, and marks the beginning of the ten square blocks or so which, at the start of the twentieth century, were home to some ten thousand Chinese immigrants. Today only a tiny proportion of El Barrio Chino, principally the small triangle of busy streets comprising Cuchillo, Zanja and San Nicolás – collectively known as the **Cuchillo de Zanja** – three blocks west of the arched entrance, is discernibly any more Chinese than the rest of Havana. Indeed, the first thing you are likely to notice about El Barrio Chino is a distinct absence of Chinese people, the once significantly sized immigrant population having long since dissolved into the racial melting pot. If features its own tightly packed little back-street **food market** composed mostly of

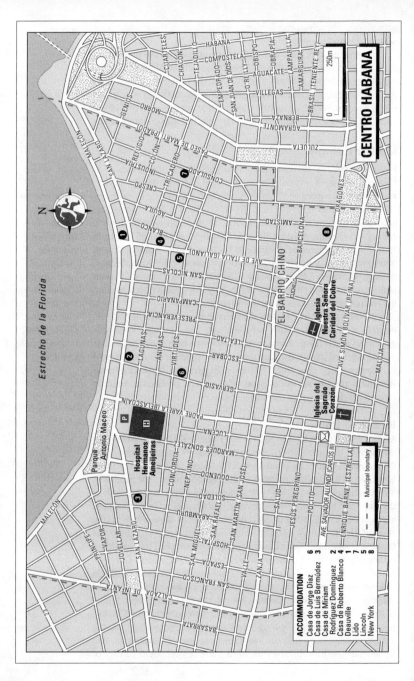

CENTRO HABANA

0   250m

ACCOMMODATION

Casa de Jorge Díaz	6
Casa de Luis Bermúdez	3
Casa de Miriam	
Rodríguez Domínguez	2
Casa de Roberto Blanco	4
Deauville	7
Lido	5
Lincoln	1
New York	8

- - - - Municipal boundary

simple fruit and vegetable stalls and lined with eccentric-looking restaurants, many still charging in pesos, and the curious mixture of tastes and styles is as much Cuban as oriental but nevertheless lends the place a unique feel.

Iglesia Nuestra Señora Caridad del Cobre and Iglesia del Sagrado Corazón

Three blocks southwest of the Cuchillo de Zanja, occupying the length of the block between Manrique and Campanario, embedded in the local neighbourhood, is the simple though appealing **Iglesia Nuestra Señora Caridad del Cobre** (Tues–Sun 7am–6pm). The construction of the church began in 1802 and involved the joining of two existing temples, but its restoration in the 1950s has given it a distinctly modern feel, its soft light and dusty-coloured stone walls engendering an atmosphere of soothing tranquillity. Circular portholes with stained-glass windows featuring star-shaped designs line the edges and are clearly relatively recent additions. Perched on top of the golden altar is the Cuban national badge, an unusually secular touch somehow in keeping with the overall orig- inality of this characterful city church.

Walk a block south of the Iglesia Nuestra Señora Caridad del Cobre on Manrique, then five blocks west on Simón Bolívar, to reach the **Iglesia del Sagrado Corazón** (daily 8am–noon & 3–5pm), shoot- ing out from a block of worn-out neo-colonial apartment buildings. Built between 1914 and 1923, this is arguably the most magnificent church in the whole country. Its unlikely location in the grime of Centro Habana, with heavy traffic passing by outside, contrasts effectively with its neo-gothic splendour and makes a wander through its imposing entrance irresistible. Inside, a second surprise awaits, as the church interior is infinitely more impressive than that of the much more heavily visited cathedral: the cavernous vaulted roof of the three naves is supported by colossal columns and the huge central altar incorporates a dazzling array of detail. Wherever you look, something catches the eye, from the skilfully sculpted scenes etched into the central pillars to the stained-glass windows at different levels on the outer walls.

The Malecón

The most picturesque way to reach Vedado from Centro Habana is to stroll along the **Malecón**, Havana's famous seawall, which snakes along the coastline west from La Punta for a distance of 4km. Chequered with schoolchildren hurling themselves into the churning Atlantic, crowds of sun-worshippers and wrinkled anglers, it's the definitive image of the city, and ambling along its length, drinking in the panoramic views, with the city's rich architecture laid out before you in a visual time line, is an essential part of the Havana experience. But don't expect to stroll in solitude: the Malecón is Havana's front room and you won't be on it for long before someone strikes up a conversation. People head here for free entertainment, particularly at night-time when it fills up with guitar-strumming musicians, peanut sellers offering cones of fresh-roasted warm nuts, and star-gazing couples, young and old alike. Shutterbugs should visit in the early evening when a good sunset bathes the wall (and locals) in a photogenic glow.

Photos of the Malecón usually feature the fifteen blocks of Centro Habana between the Paseo del Prado and Padre Varela, an archetypal stretch.

Pot-holed, sea-beaten and lined with battered old buildings, the Malecón looks much older than its hundred years, but construction only began in 1901 after nearly a century of planning. As with many public works projects in colonial Cuba, it was beset with funding problems and it wasn't until after independence that building got slowly under way, and the seawall advanced the length of Havana in slow sections. Each decade saw another chunk of wall erected, until in 1950 it reached the Río Almendares. Today, after decades of neglect, it's slowly being spruced up again, with a number of its buildings conspicuously freshly painted. Reports from the US reveal that the fast-food giants, anticipating the end of the trade embargo, have already staked their claim on various buildings. Until they move in, this is the most Havanan part of Havana, so enjoy it while you can.

Vedado

The cultural heart of the city, graceful **Vedado** draws the crowds with its palatial hotels – the backbone of so much of Havana's social scene – and contemporary art galleries, its original, exciting (and sometimes incomprehensible) theatre productions and live music concerts, and its glut of restaurants, bars and nightspots. Loosely defined as the area running west of Calzada de Infanta up to the Río Almendares, it's less ramshackle than other parts of the city and more intimate – after a couple of trips you'll notice the same faces going about their business. Tall 1950s buildings and battered hotrods parked outside ultra-modern stores lend a strongly North American air, though the nineteenth-century mansions work against it; the general impression is of an incompletely sealed time capsule, the decades and centuries all running together. Plenty of crowds lend a veneer of activity but look closely and you'll see that many people are actually part of a bus queue, waiting their turn to enter Havana's massive ice-cream parlour, *Coppelia*, or *jineteros* keeping watch for the next buck.

Vedado divides into three distinct, easy-to-negotiate parts intersected by four main thoroughfares: the broad and handsome boulevards Avenida de Presidentes (also known as Calle G) and Paseo, running north to south, and the more prosaic Linea and Calle 23 running east to west. The most obvious part is modern, whizzy **La Rampa** (Calle 23), and the streets immediately north and south, racing with gunning Ladas and battered Chevrolets and Buicks and landscaped in high-rise 1950s hotels and blocky utilitarian buildings, all presenting a rather bland uniformity that's absent from the rest of the area. It's a relatively small

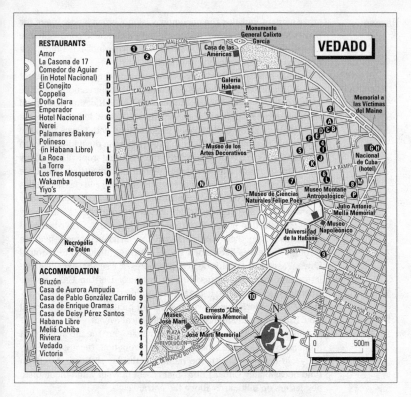

RESTAURANTS

Amor	N
La Casona de 17	A
Comedor de Aguiar	
(in Hotel Nacional)	H
El Conejito	D
Coppelia	K
Doña Clara	J
Emperador	C
Hotel Nacional	G
Nerei	F
Palamares Bakery	P
Polineso	
(in Habana Libre)	L
La Roca	I
La Torre	B
Los Tres Mosqueteros	O
Wakamba	M
Yiyo's	E

ACCOMMODATION

Bruzón	10
Casa de Aurora Ampudia	3
Casa de Pablo González Carrillo	9
Casa de Enrique Oramas	7
Casa de Deisy Pérez Santos	5
Habana Libre	6
Meliá Cohiba	2
Riviera	1
Vedado	8
Victoria	4

space, trailing along the eastern part of the Malecón and spanning just a couple of streets inland, but it dominates your immediate impression of Vedado, firstly because the skyscrapers – even these fifty-year-old, peeling-paint tower blocks – are such a rarity in Cuba that they scream for attention, and secondly because as a visitor you end up spending a fair amount of time here – confirming or booking flights in the airline offices, changing money in the urbane hotels, souvenir-shopping in the homespun street markets and dollar shops or eating at the restaurants. It's an area for doing rather than seeing, though you will find some worthy museums, including the **Museo Napoleónico**, a treasure trove of extravagant artefacts relating to the erstwhile French emperor and, nearby, the **Universidad de La Habana**, a series of beautiful buildings in elegant verdant grounds, attended by well-behaved and orderly students who personify the virtues of post-revolutionary education.

Beyond here, to the south, is the second of Vedado's sectors, the **Plaza de la Revolución** with its immense monuments to twin heroes José Martí and Ernesto "Che" Guevara. Although generally considered part of Vedado, this area is actually a municipality in its own right, and with its huge utilitarian buildings has a flavour quite distinct from the other parts of Vedado. The uncompromisingly urban landscape of the plaza itself – a huge sweep of concrete – is a complete contrast to the area's other key attraction, the atmospheric Necrópolis de Cólon, one of the largest cemeteries in the Americas.

Vedado shows its third face further west and north. This quieter area is less distinct but broadly encompasses the area north of Calle 23 up to the Malecón, bordered to the west by the Río Almendares and stretching east roughly as far as Avenida de los Presidentes, where the back streets narrow and avenues are overhung with leaves from the pine, rubber and weeping fig trees planted here in the mid-nineteenth century to create a cool retreat from the blistering tropical sun. Many of the magnificent late- and post-colonial buildings that line these streets – built in a mad medley of Rococo, Baroque and classical styles – are now converted into state offices and museums. Particularly noteworthy is the **Museo de los Artes Decorativos**, a dizzyingly detailed collection of fine furniture and *objets d'art*. Other beautiful mansions retain their role as lavish but stricken homes, peeking through the leaves like ruined ghosts. Further afield, dotted around Linea, Paseo and Avenida de los Presidentes, are several excellent galleries and cultural centres. Not to be missed is the **Casa de las Américas**, a slim and stylish Art Deco building that was set up to celebrate Pan-Americanism, which displays quality artworks from all over Latin America and hosts regular musical events.

Another attraction – of Vedado as a whole – are the threadbare but immensely personable **cinemas** dotted throughout the area, endearingly old-fashioned, with the names of the latest North American (and occasionally Cuban) films picked out in wonky and incomplete peg letters on billboards above the entrance.

La Rampa and Central Vedado

Halfway along the Malecón, the striking **Memorial a las víctimas del Maine** marks the start of Vedado proper. It was erected by the US government in memory of 260 crew members of the US battleship *The Maine* which was blown up in Havana harbour on February 15, 1898, and so is studiously ignored by Cuban maps and guidebooks.

The Maine had been despatched to Cuba in December 1897 to protect US interests during Cuba's war of independence with Spain. The incident did nothing to improve the relationship between the US and Cuba, with both sides quick to assign blame to the other. The North American press used the opportunity to whip up jingoistic feeling against Spain, and a hastily concocted US enquiry pointed the finger at "unknown conspirators".

Modern interpretation has it that the US, keen to tighten control over Cuba's destiny, sabotaged its own ship as an excuse to enter the war, and indeed, navy officials have since admitted the explosion took place on board. Following the revolution crowds attacked the monument, toppling and destroying the heavy iron eagle that once perched on the top (the smashed and twisted pieces are displayed in the Museo de la Ciudad; see p.81). What remains is still impressive: above the two marble Corinthian columns, great rusted cannons clad in iron chains are flanked by a dolorous, despairing mourner and solemn female figures standing almost to attention in star-spangled dresses, with stylized Art Deco griffins and sea monsters carved into the base. The present government has stamped its presence with the terse inscription: "To the victims of *The Maine* who were sacrificed by imperialist voraciousness in its zeal to seize the island of Cuba from February 1898 to 15 February 1961."

Within view of the memorial is the **US Special Interests Office** – the organization that has acted in lieu of the US embassy since diplomatic relations between Cuba and the US ended in 1961. In front of the building is a large billboard with a much-photographed colourful cartoon depicting a Cuban revolutionary shouting across the ocean at an enraged Uncle Sam, "Mr Imperialists, we have absolutely no fear of you!" It's a long-standing poster campaign although, perhaps due to Special Period cutbacks, it no longer features the glowing neon it had during the 1980s. Round the side of the building queues of hopeful Cubans wait to apply for a US visa.

Looming behind the memorial, the twin-towered **Hotel Nacional** – near an artificial waterfall that doubles as a paddling pool for Havana juniors – marks the start of **La Rampa** (The Slope), the road into the centre of Vedado. Once the debauched pre-revolutionary home of Chinese theatres, casinos and pay-by-the-hour knocking shops, La Rampa is now lined with airline offices and official headquarters, its seamy side long gone (or at least well hidden).

See p.76 for a full review of the Hotel Nacional.

Set on a precipice above the now inaccessible Tanaganana cave (allegedly named after an Indian seeking refuge from pursuing conquistadors), and with a magnificent view of the ocean, the world-famous stately hotel is a must-see landmark in its own right, with a princely tiled lobby and an elegant and airy colonnaded veranda looking out to sea across an expanse of well-tended lawn commandeered by two tame peacocks: the perfect cinematic backdrop for a *mojito* cocktail. Built in 1930, it soon became a favourite with visiting luminaries – amongst them Ava Gardner, Winston Churchill, Josephine Baker and John Wayne – and since its refit in 1992 has added the likes of Naomi Campbell, Matt Dillon and Jack Nicholson to its clientele.

Just west around the corner from the hotel, in the middle of a vast park which spans a whole block of Calles 21 and 23, is **Coppelia**, Havana's mighty ice-cream emporium. Looking like a giant space pod, with a circular white chamber atop a podium, the multi-chamber restaurant was built during the revolution as an egalitarian eating place with prices within the reach of every Cuban. It's hugely popular, serving over a thousand visitors a day with Cubans, who consider the ice cream the equal of the finest Italian confections, regularly

To really appreciate Coppelia's space age architecture go up to La Torre restaurant (see p.118) for a panoramic view.

waiting in line for over an hour – though, contrary to its ethics, paying in hard currency lets you jump the queue. Cuban film buffs will recognize the park from the opening scenes of Tomás Gutiérrez Alea's seminal 1993 film, *Fresa y Chocolate*, which takes its name from the most popular and available flavours.

Universidad de la Habana

Regal and magnificent, the **Universidad de la Habana** sits on the brow of the Aróstegui (or Pirotecnia) Hill, three blocks or so south of La Rampa, overlooking Centro Habana. Founded in 1728 by monks of the Dominican Order, the university educated Havana's white elite; mulattos, blacks, Jews and moors were all banned, though by a surprising oversight, women weren't, and by 1899 one-seventh of its students were female. It counts among its alumni many of the country's famous political figures, including Cuban liberator José Martí (see p.90), independence fighter Ignacio Agramonte (see p.323), and Fidel Castro, who studied law here.

Originally based in a convent in Habana Vieja, it was secularized in 1842 but did not move to its present site, a former Spanish army barracks, until 1902, spreading out across the grounds over the next forty years. Today, it's an awesome collections of buildings, and home to some of the city's most unusual **museums**.

Directly in front of a sweeping stone staircase capped by twin observation points, the rubbly pile of oversized grey and whitewashed concrete blocks is actually the **Memorial a Julio Antonio Mella**, a modern tribute to this former student, first secretary of the University Students' Federation (FEU), political agitator and early member of the Communist Party, thought to have been murdered for his beliefs by the government of the day (see box). Off to one side, a bust captures his likeness while the words on the main column are his: "To fight for social revolution in the Americas is not a utopia for fanatics and madmen. It is the next step in the advance of history." More conventional is the serene, Junoesque alma mater figure halfway up the stairs. Sculpted in bronze by Czechoslovak artist Mario Korbel, this symbol of wisdom presides over the steps with outspread arms upturned to the sky, while the bronze-panelled stone base, cast in New York, features more studious and berobed women bearing symbolic globes and feathered quills. At the top of the stairs, beyond the lofty open-ended entrance chamber, lavishly feted with Corinthian columns, lies the Ignacio Agramonte courtyard, with a central lawn scattered with marble benches and bordered on four sides by grandiose faculty buildings.

The scene of countless student protests, including one led by Julio Antonio Mella in 1922, the university was long seen as a hotbed of youthful radicalism, and during the Batista administration, when it was the only site where political meetings could take place unhindered, it was actually used as a place to stash guns. The present administration, however, keeps the university on a firm rein and firebrand protests are a

Julio Antonio Mella, the student hero

Born in 1905 to an Irish mother and a Dominican father, charismatic, good-looking **Julio Antonio Mella** was a leading light in the Cuban student movement. After a comfortable middle-class childhood, he enrolled in the Universidad de la Habana in 1921, aged sixteen, and soon became one of the organizing forces behind the formation of the University Student's Federation (FEU), his rousing speeches stirring a generation of students to protest against university corruption. His campaign against the appointment of incompetent and unqualified professors to well-paid posts through nepotism and political favours paid off, and in 1923 over a hundred hapless professors were dismissed. After graduation, his influence spread further and he became something of a national figure, famed for roaming Havana giving lectures on Marxism to workers. In 1927, fearful that his outspoken diatribes against Machado's government had earned him serious enemies, he fled to Mexico to live in exile. His fears were proved correct and he was shot in the street in Mexico City on January 10, 1929, whilst with his girlfriend, Italian photographer Tina Modotti. Although never proved, it was widely assumed that Machado was responsible.

thing of the past, though its political past is evoked in some quirky details scattered throughout the grounds: the original American tank captured in 1958 during the civil war and placed here by the Union of Young Communists as a tribute to youth lost during the struggle, and, opposite, an "owl of wisdom" made of bits of shrapnel gleaned from various battle sites. A respected seat of learning, the university has a rather serious air: earnest students sit on the lawn and steps in front of faculty buildings locked in quiet discussion, while inside a library-like hush reins. With few leisure facilities student hipsters go elsewhere to relax, leaving the grounds to their geekier counterparts and sightseers.

To the left of the main entrance is the **Museo de Ciencias Naturales Felipe Poey** (Mon–Fri 9am–noon & 1–4pm; $1), the most bewitching of all the university buildings, with a beautiful central atrium from which, as though from a marble swamp, rises a towering palm twisted with vines. Named after an eminent nineteenth-century naturalist, and with the musty atmosphere of a zoologist's laboratory, the dimly lit room holds an assortment of stuffed, preserved and pickled animals, its walls lined with the remains of sharks and reptiles, while a whale dangles from the ceiling. The highlight is the collection of Polymita snails' shells, delicately ringed in bands of egg-yolk yellow, black and white, while other notables are a (deceased) whistling duck, a stuffed armadillo and Felipe Poey's death mask, incongruously presented along with some of his personal papers. Modern parents and their offspring may wish to check out the children's corner and pet the stuffed duck, squirrel and iguana.

Those unmoved by the charms of taxidermy can press on up the right-hand staircase along the cloistered balcony to the **Museo Montane Antropológico** (Mon–Fri 9am–noon & 1–4pm; $1), home to an extensive collection of pre-Columbian pottery and idols from Cuba and beyond. Though padded out with apparently indiscriminately selected pieces of earthenware bowls, the collection contains some excellently preserved artefacts, like the Peruvian Aztec pots adorned with alligator heads and the fierce stone figurine of the Maya god Quetzalcoatl, the plumed serpent, tightly wrapped in a distinctive clay coil design.

Star attractions include a lignum vitae **Taino tobacco idol** from Maisí in Guantánamo; roughly 60cm tall and clearly male, the elongated, grimacing, drum-shaped idol with shell eyes is believed to have been a ceremonial mortar used to pulverize tobacco leaves. Also fascinating is the delicate Haitian two-pronged wooden reproduction **inhaler** carved with the face of a bird, which the Taino high priest would use to snort hallucinogenic powder in the *Cohoba* ceremony, a religious ritual for communicating with the dead. Suitably empowered, he would enter into direct communication with the spirits and give divine answers to questions from the assembled community. He would also cure illness, possibly with the aid of a **vomiting stick**, such as the one on display nearby, made from manatee ribs, inserting it into the throats of the afflicted to make them vomit up impurities of the soul. Although from different countries, the inhaler and vomiting stick correspond in shape and design and are thought to come from similar cultures. Finally, check out the stone axe found in Banes, Holguín, engraved with the stylized figure of Guabancex, a female deity governing the uncontrollable forces of nature, her long twisted arms wrapped around a small child.

Museo Napoleónico

Just behind the university on San Miguel, spread over four storeys of a handsome nineteenth-century house, the **Museo Napoleónico** (Mon–Sat 10am–5pm; $3, guided tour $3 extra) boasts an eclectic collection of ephemera on the French emperor, gathered at auction by Orestes Ferrara, an Italian ex-anarchist who became a colonel in the rebel army of 1898 and subsequently a politican in Cuba. Ranging from state portraits, *objets d'art* and exquisite furniture to military paraphernalia and sculpture, it will appeal to anyone with even a passing interest in the era.

Eighteenth-century sketches of Voltaire, Rousseau and Diderot crowd the narrow staircase up to the first floor, but most fascinating is Marie Antoinette's plaintive farewell note to her children, written in a shaky hand and marked with the date of her execution. The expansive first-floor chamber is awash with heavily engraved ornamental swords and bronze sabres, many belonging to Napoleon himself, and lined with stately oil portraits and large canvases depicting the Battle of Waterloo, the victory in Egypt and the Duke of Wellington. The room is filled with opulent furniture: a marble-topped sideboard with swan-shaped drawer handles laden with Sèvres china competes for attention with a hideous imperial carriage clock adorned with two golden Europeans borne along by bronze slaves. The best piece is a grandiose *guéridon* table designed after Napoleon's Egyptian campaign. Made of bronze, it's inlaid with fourteen Sèvres china miniatures of the general along with a larger picture of an ermine-clad Napoleon perched on a throne clutching a staff.

On the second floor there's more Sèvres china from the Napoleonic family treasure chest, along with portraits of his first wife Josephine and his fashionably attired daughters, and an extremely pompous, self-serving portrait by Pierre Alexander Tardieu, which has the little man dressed up as a Roman emperor. The best painting is a large work by Jean-Georges Vibert which depicts Napoleon and entourage discussing his forthcoming coronation ceremony using a set of miniature mannequins to represent the guests, with Napoleon sweeping aside the figures of the cardinals he no longer wishes to attend.

The third floor consists of recreations of Napoleon's study and bedroom, with a sombre painting of the great man's death above a bed laid with his personal bedspread; on a table sits his surprisingly smooth and wrinkle-free death mask. It's worth continuing on up to the fourth floor, not to see the collection of books about the French revolution, but to step out on the terraces: the back one has a good view over the Capitolio and Calzada de Infanta, while the front one is simply gorgeous, with richly tiled walls and a floor decorated with shields.

Plaza de la Revolución

From the Museo Napoleónico, Calle 17 de Noviembre, which flanks the university stadium, heads south up and over the hill into Avenida Ranchos Boyeros and then on for a kilometre to the **Plaza de la Revolución**. Best visited on May Day and other annual parade days, when legions of loyal Cubans come to wave at Fidel Castro saluting the crowds at the foot of the Martí memorial, the plaza comes as a bit of a letdown at other times, revealing itself to be a prosaic expanse of concrete bordered by policed government buildings and the headquarters of the Cuban Communist Party. However, throughout the year, tourists still flock to its twin attractions: the Memorial Ernesto "Che" Guevara and the Memorial José Martí tower.

Memorial and Museo José Martí

Although widely seen as a symbol of the revolution, the sleek, star-shaped **Memorial José Martí** had been in the pipeline since 1926 and was completed a year before the revolution began. Its 139-metre marble super-steeple is even more impressive when you glance up to the seemingly tiny crown-like turret, constantly circled by a dark swirl of birds. Near the base sits a gigantic seventeen-metre sculpture of José Martí, the eloquent journalist, poet and independence fighter who missed his chance to be Cuba's first inspirational president by dying in his first ever battle against the Spanish on April 11, 1895 (see p.90). Carved from elephantine cubes of white marble, the immense monument captures him hunched forward in reflective pose.

Behind the statue, the stately ground floor of the tower houses the exhaustive **Museo José Martí** (Tues–Sat 10am–6pm; $5), which charts Martí's luminary career mainly through letters and photographs, with an additional room dedicated to the achievements of the revolution. The lavish entrance hall, its walls bedecked with green and gold mosaic interspersed with Martí's most evocative quotes, certainly befits a national hero and is the most impressive aspect of a museum that tends to stray off the point at times.

As many of Martí's more substantial artefacts are housed in his birthplace in Habana Vieja (see p.89), much of what's on display in the first room is photographic, with pictures of his parents in sombre nineteenth-century fashions and several sepia prints of Martí at various stages of youth, curiously always wearing the same pensive, unsmiling expression. One of the most interesting exhibits is a reproduction of the fifteen-metre mural *Sueño de una tarde dominical en la Alameda Central* (Dream of a Sunday Afternoon in Alameda Park) by the Mexican artist Diego Rivera. It shows Martí standing in the Mexico City park next to Frida Kahlo, Rivera's soulmate and fellow artist, with the artist himself in front of them depicted as a boy; Martí's inclusion reflects Rivera's interest in Marxism and Pan-Americanism.

In the second room, photographs of Martí in Spain, Mexico and North America hang next to wholly superfluous images of those countries today. Also on show is an assortment of artillery, most notably Martí's six-shooter Colt revolver engraved with his name, and the Winchester he took with him on his only battle. A wall-length colour photograph of Fidel Castro planting a flag on La Playita de Cajobabo beach, where Martí and fellow Independenista Maximo Gomez disembarked for that fateful April battle, tie the revolutionary to the present regime.

The collection begins to falter in the third room, and worthwhile exhibits thin out in the face of numerous pre-construction plans of the tower, alternative propositions to the final choice of monument and a large commemorative coin collection. But wade through these and the eminently missable video re-enactment of Martí's death and you'll be rewarded with plenty of atmospheric shots of the crowd-filled plaza in the early years of the revolution. Another vintage photo shows several of the core rebels, including Raul Castro, Haydee Santermaría and Celia Sánchez, standing beside a bust of Martí at the peak of Pico Turquino.

Never slow to trumpet the achievements of the revolution, the state has pulled out the stops in the fourth, and arguably most interesting, part of the museum, where a thoughtfully presented gallery of photographs and exhibits chart breakthroughs in medical research – such as the cure found by Cuban scientists for meningitis and advances in laser treatment – Cuba's high standards in education, with a particular emphasis on schools in the most rural parts of the country; and achievements in the arts, with prima ballerina Alicia Alonso's frayed ballet shoes worn to pieces when she danced *Giselle* at the Gran Teatro in 1962. Also on show are **Fidel Castro**'s most memorable photos: standing with the Pope, embracing Nelson Mandela, and, famously, leaping to the ground from a tank at the Bay of Pigs. The most impressive photo captures one of Castro's myth-making moments: upon his triumphant arrival in Havana in the early days of the revolution, he stood before the excited Habaneros to make his first speech when two doves released into the crowd circled and spontaneously landed upon his shoulders. In an unchoreographed moment, Castro was endowed with the universal symbols of peace and unity.

When you've finished in the museum you can take the elevator to the top floor to the highest **lookout point** in Havana – on a clear day you can see the low hills in the east and out as far as Miramar in the west. The room is divided into segments corresponding to the five spines of its star shape, so you can move around to take in five separate views, while a mosaic compass on the ground with distances from several capital cities lets you know how far you are from home.

If you're in need of refreshment, there's a café hidden to the back of the José Martí museum.

Memorial Ernesto "Che" Guevara

Back on the ground, on the opposite side of the square, the ultimate Cuban photo opportunity is presented by the **Memorial Ernesto "Che" Guevara**, a stylized steel frieze replica of Alberto "Korda" Gutierrez' famous photo of Guevara – the most widely recognized image of Guevara in existence. Taken during a speech on Calle 23 in 1960, the photo, with Guevara's messianic gaze fixed on some distant horizon and hair flowing out from beneath his army beret, embodies the unwavering, zealous spirit of the revolution, but it was only in 1967 after his capture and execution in Bolivia by CIA agents (for more on Ernesto "Che" Guevara see pp.282–283) that the photo passed into iconography, immortalized in T-shirts and posters throughout the 1970s as an enduring symbol of rebellion. As a tribute to the Argentinian whom the Cubans had taken to their hearts, the image was printed onto a huge sheet of cloth and draped over the side of the Ministry of Industry building where he had served as a minister and where millions of Cubans came to pay their last respects. In 1993 the sculpture that you see now was forged from steel donated by the French government.

The original photograph can be seen, along with many others, at the Museo Memorial al Che, in Santa Clara; see p.281.

Enjoying a revival, this image of Che is lately the height of postmodern chic, appearing on bottles of beer and even modelled by Kate Moss in British *Vogue*. Though Che disapproved of the cult of personality, Cubans themselves (government included) have not been slow to put him to good use, and street vendors and dollar shops throughout Cuba make a quick buck from flogging T-shirts, key-rings, cartoon figurines, black berets and even CDs of soulful memorial ballads.

Havana

The tourist office is in the gatehouse to the right of the entrance.

Necrópolis de Colón

Five blocks west from Plaza de la Revolución along tree-lined Paseo, there's a worthwhile detour on the left at the Calle Zapata junction: the **Necrópolis de Colón** (daily 8am–5pm; $1), one of the largest cemeteries in the Americas. With moribund foresight the necropolis was designed in 1868 to have space for well over a hundred years' worth of corpses, and the neatly numbered "streets", lined with grandiose tombstones and mausoleums and shaded by large trees, stretch out over five square kilometres. A tranquil refuge from the noise of the city, it is a fascinating place to visit – you can spend hours seeking out the graves of the famous, including the parents of José Martí (he is buried in Santiago), celebrated novelist Alejo Carpentier and a host of revolutionary martyrs.

Originally a farm, the land was bought by the church and construction began in 1871 according to a design by Calixto Aureliano de Loira y Cardoso, a Spanish architect who won the job in a competition. He had little time to celebrate, however, having been struck by illness shortly after completing the project and dying at 33, a premature denizen of his own creation. His most magnificent achievement is the neo-gothic entrance portal: a vision of overwrought piety, it comprises three arched gateways representing the Trinity, an excessive marble sculpture depicting Faith, Hope and Charity, and a plaque high above the central arch showing the Crucifixion.

The main avenue sweeps past tall Italian marble tombstones draped in lachrymose Madonnas and maidens, including a copy of Michelangelo's *Pietà*. Particularly noteworthy is the mausoleum, just behind the main avenue on Calle 1 y Calle D, of a group of medical students executed in 1871 on the charge of desecrating the tomb of a Spanish journalist, draped with marble maidens depicting justice and innocence. Also outstanding is the firemen's mausoleum on the main avenue, dedicated to those who died in a city fire in 1890. Encrusted with shields, garlands, flags and a finely worked cameo of each man who died, it features life-sized allegorical figures, including a pelican which symbolizes the self-sacrifice (the pelican traditionally fed its young from its own breast) of those who perished.

In the centre of the necropolis is the fanciful, Romanesque **octagonal chapel**, opened in 1886, which consists of three tiers, each iced in a frill of contrasting curlicues and crowned with a delicate cupola. Masses are held every day at 8am but the chapel is also open at varying times during the day, and you should seize the chance to peek inside and admire the beautiful, luminous German stained-glass windows and, towering above the altar, Cuban artist Miguel Melero's fresco *The Last Judgement*, which has Christ presiding over winged devils and other reprobates as they plummet to their peril.

Close to hand, at Calle 1 e/ F y G, engulfed by a constant cornucopia of flowers and guarded by an attendant, the **tomb of Amelia Goyri de la Hoz** and her child is an arresting sight. A Havanan society woman,

Goyri de la Hoz died in childbirth on May 3, 1901, and was buried with her child, who survived her by only a few minutes, placed at her feet. During a routine exhumation the following year, she ws found to be cradling the child in her arms. The story spread immediately, Goyri de la Hoz was dubbed "La Milagrosa" (the miracle worker), and the event was attributed to the power of a mother's love working beyond the grave. Soon La Milagrosa was attributed with universal healing powers, and to this day supplicants queue round the block to have their wishes granted. A strict etiquette controls the ritual: to stand a chance of success you must knock on the tombstone three times with the brass handles to alert the saint within, cover the tomb with flowers before mentioning the wish and finally leave without turning your back.

In the southern half of the cemetery, marked by large plots of as yet unused land, veterans of the revolution including luminary figures Celia Sánchez, Fidel Castro's companion, and poet Nicolás Guillén (see p.324), lie in an extensive and faintly austere pantheon house just off the main avenue, while a little way behind this, those who accompanied Fidel Castro on the yacht *Granma* and were slain in the first revolutionary battle at Alegría de Pío (see p.423) repose in slightly more ornate style.

The rest of Vedado

North of the Necrópolis de Colón lies the rest of Vedado, quieter than the boisterous La Rampa area and more scenic than Plaza de la Revolución. To walk through the silent streets of suburban Vedado, once the exclusive reserve of the wealthy, is one of the richest pleasures Havana holds, the air scented with sweet mint bush and jasmine, and, at night, the stars, untainted by street lamps, forming an eerie ceiling above the swirl of ruined balconies and inky trees. No less attractive in the daytime, with few hustlers it is also one of the safest areas to stroll, and the added attraction of several museums and art galleries will give extra purpose to a visit.

Museo de los Artes Decorativos

Housed in a mansion at no. 502 Calle 17, a ten-minute walk northeast from Necrópolis de Colón, the beautifully maintained **Museo de los Artes Decorativos** (Tues–Sat 11am–7pm; $2; $1 extra with guide, $3 extra with camera) contains one of the most dazzling collections of pre-revolutionary decorative arts in Cuba. Built towards the end of the 1920s, the house was the private estate of Count and Countess of Revilia de Camargo who fled Cuba in 1961, whereupon it was appropriated by the state as the ideal showcase for the nation's cultural treasures. With its regal marble staircase, glittering mirrors and high ceilings, it is a perfect backdrop for the sumptuous if overwrought collection of Meissen and Sèvres china, Chinese vases and *objets d'art*, and fine furniture – a tantalizing glimpse of Vedado's erstwhile grandeur. The rooms are divided according to period and

The necropolis is the site of the funniest scenes in Tomás Gutiérrez Alea's revolutionary farce La Muerte de un Burócrata (Death of a Bureaucrat).

style and each is crammed with such a dizzying display of exhibits that it becomes quite hard to appreciate each individual piece. Guides are knowledgeable and friendly but tend to bombard you with information, and with such a massive collection in a small space you may feel more comfortable setting your own agenda and seeing the rooms unattended.

To the left of the grand entrance hall paved in multicoloured marble, the Principal Salon, richly panelled in gold and cream, is full of expensive Rococo knick-knacks, like the pair of stylishly ugly eighteenth-century German dog-lions, while in the Chinese Room next door exquisite silkscreens and porcelain compete for your attention with a lacquered table inlaid with mother-of-pearl branches and mandarin ducks. In the Neoclassical Room, an eighteenth-century mantle clock by Jean Andre Lepaufe, swarming with golden cherubs, takes over-the-top interior design to new heights, as do the faintly unnerving bronze French male and female candelabra by Claudio Michel Clodión. The Sèvres Room is a better exercise in restraint, with a small but splendid display of rich royal blue porcelain finely painted with pastoral scenes. Equally delicate is the Salon Boudoir with a battery of intricately painted fans, a prime tool in the flirting tactics of nineteenth-century ladies. Finally, the subtlety of the English Room's Wedgwood china and eighteenth-century Chippendale chairs goes somewhat unappreciated amongst the crowd of showier pieces, but it's worth taking the time to examine these and the half-moon sideboard by Robert Adam, which boasts unusual painted panels.

Galería Habana

From the Museo de los Artes Decorativos it's a short stroll through the pleasant Vedado streets towards the east end of the Malecón, home to some of the city's best contemporary art galleries. Emerging from the suburbs onto busy Linea you'll find the Galería Habana (Mon–Fri 10am–4pm, Sat 10am–1pm; free) at no. 460, which has been showcasing exclusively Cuban talent since 1962. Many of the artists who exhibit here go on to receive worldwide acclaim, as did Fernando Rodríguez, whose wall built from life-sized bricks of miniature uniformed workers, Bloque, speaks volumes about the duality of the revolution; and Belki Ayón with her subtle and mysterious etchings exploring the secret world of the Afro-Cuban religious cult Abukuá. Other names such as Wilfredo Lam, Cuba's best-known twentieth-century painter, and lesser-known René Peña with his menacingly nightmarish portrait photography, have also shown and the gallery is a good stable of up-and-coming talent. Those looking for an investment can snap up canvases at competitive prices and the gallery takes care of all tax and paperwork for export. There are two satellite galleries in Havana, one in Vedado's Nacional hotel, the other in Miramar's Mélia Habana.

Casa de las Américas and Galería Haydee Santermaría

Further down Linea, the road joins regal Avenida de Presidentes where, at the junction with Calle 3ra, you'll find the **Casa de las Américas**, housed in a slender dove-grey Art Deco building inlaid with panes of deep blue glass. Previously a private university, it was established as a cultural institute – with its own publishing house, one of the first in the country – in 1959 by Haydee Santermaría to promote the arts, history and politics of the Americas. Since then, its promotion and funding of visual artists, authors and musicians has been successful enough to command respect throughout the continent and to attract endorsement from such international literary figures as Gabriel García Márquez. Today it hosts regular conferences, concerts and talks and boasts two worthwhile galleries: the **Sala Contemporánea** (Mon–Fri 10am–5pm; free), showing modern Cuban pieces, and the **Galería Latinoamericana** (Mon–Thurs 10am–5pm, Fri 10am–noon; $2), showing high-quality temporary exhibitions, usually of painting, from other Latin American countries.

On the opposite corner of Avenida de los Presidentes is the institute's sister gallery, **Galería Haydee Santermaría** (Tues–Sat 10am–5pm, Sun 9am–1pm; $2), which displays large canvases, sculptures and installations from around Latin America in an expansive clean white space. The exhibitions tend towards the experimental and unknown artists with the emphasis on innovation, enthusiasm and raw talent rather than big names.

Within view of Casa de las Americas on the Malecón is the aristocratic **Monumento General Calixto García**. Set in a walled podium, it's an elaborate tribute to the war of independence general who led the campaign in Oriente see p.347, and has him dynamically reining in his horse surrounded by friezes depicting his greatest escapades, and would warrant closer inspection were it not widely used as a public toilet.

Miramar and the western suburbs

Miramar and the western suburbs are Havana's alter ego: larger than life, with super-sleek, ice-white, Miami-style residences, flash new business developments, spanking new hotels and curvy Japanese cars streaking along wide avenues. The last suburbs to be developed before the revolution, this is where the wealth was then concentrated, and it's slowly trickling back, with Miramar, at least, home to the city's growing clique of foreign investors and ambassadors.

Though the wonderful houses and embassies are good for a gawp, most visitors who venture over the river do so for the **entertainment**, particularly the famous *Tropicana* cabaret in Marianao on the borders of Almendares, and the swanky international **restaurants**, a welcome respite from pork, rice and beans. The **Marina Hemingway** on the outskirts of Miramar also pulls in scores of yachties, and a couple of minor sights will help you spin out a pleasant day.

Havana

See "Drinking, nightlife and entertainment" (p.121) for details of activities at the Casa de las Américas.

See "Drinking, nightlife and entertainment" (p.122) for an account of the Tropicana.

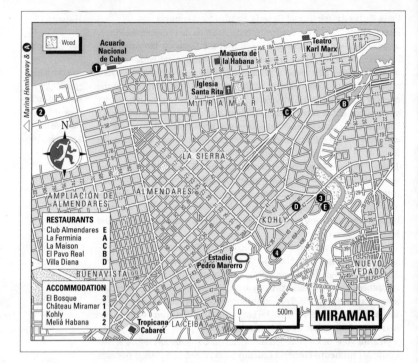

The area is divided into four main suburbs: oceanfront **Miramar**, reached from the Malecón through the tunnel bridging under the Río Almendares; **La Sierra** to its immediate south; **Kohly** tucked underneath; and **Almendares** to the west; but you'll often hear the whole area referred to as **Playa** and sometimes addresses are listed as such.

Maqueta de la Habana and the Acuario Nacional de Cuba
Near to Avenida 5ta on Calle 28 e/ 1ra y 3ra in Miramar, the **Maqueta de la Habana** (Tues–Sat 9.30am–5.30pm; $3) is a scale model of the whole of Havana, with tiny replicas of every single building the size of Monopoly houses. Built as an aid to the offices of city planning and development, the tiny city's various eras of construction are colour coded: colonial buildings are brown, twentieth-century pre-revolutionary structures are ochre, post-revolutionary ones are cream. Some of the white buildings are monuments, while others represent buildings in the pipeline. With a scale of 1:1000 it is colossal, and much of the detail in the centre is difficult to see, although the unwieldy telescopes available for public use in the viewing gallery above do remedy this a little.

THE GUIDE: CHAPTER 1

Also a good bet for a fun half-day is the recently refurbished **Acuario Nacional de Cuba**, a fifteen-minute walk west on Avenida 1ra (Tues–Thurs, Sat & Sun 10am–6pm, Fri 10am–10pm; $5 adults, $4 children), featuring sea life indigenous to Cuban waters in tanks organized into categories of sea depth. Although the aquarium is largely well maintained, some of the more sizeable creatures – the crocodiles, dolphins and sharks – seem crushed into inadequate spaces; the extension currently being built should sort this out. Shows are laid on throughout the day with trained sea lions, dolphins and moray eels performing various stunts.

Marina Hemingway

Further west along the coast, just beyond the small suburb of Jaimantias, the **Marina Hemingway**, Ave. 5ta y Calle 248 Santa Fe (☎33-11-49), despite the name, has little connection with Ernest Hemingway. Several restaurants and a shopping centre make it a draw for visitors looking for a deluxe spot to relax, while yacht owners can dock in one of the four parallel canals, each 1km long, 15m deep and 6m wide. If you are docking you should notify your arrival through VHF channel 16 or 7462 SSB. As well as hosting billfish and marlin **fishing tournaments** annually (see p.54), the marina is one of the only places in Havana to offer any **diving**, with a dive centre here (☎33-11-49) and two dive sites offshore.

The marina is about a fifteen-minute taxi ride from Vedado ($6–8 in an unmetered taxi).

Habana del Este

While many people omit the sights in **Habana del Este**, across the bay from Habana Vieja, from their itinerary, erroneously believing them to be inconveniently located, those visitors who do make it this far are rewarded by uncrowded sights that are a telling link in the city's history.

Even if you don't make it as far as the Cristo de La Habana, a visit to the castles and fortifications that collectively make up the **Parque Morro-Cabaña** is really worthwhile. A stalwart part of the Havana skyline, they dominate the view across the harbour, and, along with the fortifications in Habana Vieja, comprise the city's oldest defence system. The **Castillo de los Tres Reyes Magos del Morro** (daily 8am–8.30pm; $2, $2 extra for lighthouse) was built between 1589 and 1630 to form an impeding crossfire with the **Castillo de San Salvador de la Punta** on the opposite side of the bay, a ploy which failed spectacularly when the English invaded overland in 1762 and occupied the city for six months. Today the castle has an eerie, just-abandoned feel, its cavernous billet rooms and cannon stores empty but in near-perfect condition. Particularly fine are the high parade grounds studded with rusted cannons and the circular Moorish bartizans in the corners, from wihch you could easily spend a hour or so surveying the bay. A highlight of the visit is watching the sun set over the sea from the summit of the **lighthouse** that was built on the cliff edge in 1844.

Both sights within the Parque Morro-Cabaña charge $2 extra to enter with cameras, $5 for camcorders.

Roughly 250m further east, the **Fortaleza San Carlos de la Cabana** (daily 8am–11pm; $2) needs a full day to do it justice, and despite being the more interesting of the two sights it's the lesser visited, so more relaxing. Built to be the most complex and expensive defence system in the Americas, the fortress was started in 1763 as soon as the Spanish traded the city back from the English. However, its defensive worth has never been proved, as takeover attempts by other European powers had largely died down by the time it was finished. It took eleven years to finish, and you can see why with one look at the extensive grounds, complete with impeccable cobbled streets lined with houses where soldiers and officers were originally billeted – now a miscellany of workshops, artisanal boutiques and restaurants – lawns, private gardens and even a chapel.

Further east, on the hill above the picturesque village of Casablanca, and lying on the same axis as the cathedral in Habana Vieja, is the **Cristo de La Habana**. Seventeen metres high, the gigantic Christ figure was commissioned by Marta Batista, wife of the dictator, in one of the couple's last contributions to the city before departing, and sculpted from Italian marble by Jilma Madera in 1958. Although impressive close up, when you can ponder the massive scale of the huge sandalled feet and the perfectly sculpted hands, each said to weigh a ton, there's precious little to do on the hillside other than drink at the refreshment kiosk. This is one sight best enjoyed from Habana Vieja in the evening, when you can gaze across the bay and enjoy its floodlit grandeur.

The easiest way to **get to** Habana del Este is to take a metered taxi ($4) or a private one ($2–3); or a bus (40c) from the bus stop near the Monumento Máximo Gómez (see p.94) – get off at the first stop after the tunnel. From the fortifications it's a brisk half-hour walk to the Cristo de La Habana, or a pleasant ride on the foot-and-bicycle ferry (1 peso) that leaves every thirty minutes from Avenida del Puerto e/ Sol y Luz, ten minutes' walk south from Plaza San Francisco and the main Sierra Maestra Terminal.

Eating

In restaurant listings, we've only included phone numbers for those places where you might need to reserve a table.

Although not a city famed for its cuisine, Havana offers the most varied eating scene in Cuba, with a reasonable supply of well-priced international and local **restaurants**, although the settings of these are often more notable than the food: dining in a high-rise tower restaurant with panoramic city views or in one of the quirky charismatic eateries typical to the city often compensates for the somewhat staid and repetitive menus. Foodwise, the best restaurants tend to be in Miramar and the western suburbs, where you'll find such luxuries as lobster and king prawns. Numerous *paladares* dish up good-value portions of *comida criolla* – and the competition between them ensures good quality. There are several **ethnic** restaurants in Havana; the most common are Chinese, Italian and Spanish, though you'll also find Turkish and French cuisine represented. Every major hotel usually has at least two quality restaurants, the best of which are listed below, and although most are much of a muchness, they offer dependably edible meals.

Vegetarians will find decent though predictable choices (pizza and omelettes featuring heavily) at most places, but vegans should resign themselves to a diet of salad and fries. Stick to the hotels for **breakfast** as elsewhere the choice is a bit patchy; the *Habana Libre* does a particularly fine buffet for about $12. The best option for **lunch** is to grab a snack from one of the **street stalls** dotted around Centro Habana and Vedado, which sell tasty fritters and pizzas for just a few pesos. Otherwise most restaurants, state and private, are open from noon onwards, with those in the main tourist centres offering meals from about $5–8.

Habana Vieja and Centro Habana

Al Medina, Oficios no. 12 e/ Obispo y Obrapía. Relatively spicy Arabic and Turkish food, including some excellent kebabs, falafel and hummus. Part of a larger Arab-themed complex in a superbly restored colonial mansion, the long narrow room with its tiled floor, wooden beam ceiling and glass lanterns has the atmosphere of a spruced up wine-cellar.

Bar Monserrate, Ave. de Bélgica esq. Obrapía. This characterful roadside bar is a good place for a simple and familiar-looking breakfast – eggs, bacon, toast and coffee – against a backdrop of wood panelling, ceiling fans and a traditional-style bar. See also "Drinking, nightlife and entertainment", p.119.

El Baturro, Ave. de Bélgica e/ Merced y Jesús María. Good-value Spanish cuisine and quick simple meals in one of the few restaurants in southern Habana Vieja. Sealed off from the street by blue-tinted windows, and with a pleasant indoor balcony section, this is a good place for lunch on a scorching hot day. The Spanish theme is tastefully underdone.

El Bodega de los Vinos, Fortaleza San Carlos de la Cabaña, Parque Morro-Cabaña ☎66-91-32. Friendly, moderately priced Spanish restaurant with a tasty selection of traditional tapas and more substantial seafood and steak main courses. Bench seats and heavy wooden tables over flagstones lend a banqueting hall ambience and there's usually flamenco dancing of an evening, though you'll have to pay the $2 entrance fee for the fort.

La Bodeguita del Medio, Empedrado e/ San Ignacio y Mercaderes ☎57-13-75. An immensely popular Havana classic which relies more on its unique, secret-hideout ambience and Ernest Hemingway associations than its standard though fairly priced *comida criolla*. Hemingway was a regular member of the literary and bohemian crowd that drank here and his usual tipple, a *mojito*, has become the house speciality. The tightly packed closeness is all part of the appeal, the walls covered in autographs and scribbled messages.

Café O'Reilly, O'Reilly no. 203 e/ San Ignacio y Cuba. Simple, reasonably priced set meals, sandwiches and fast food in a plain but smartly arranged restaurant-cafeteria. Good for an easy-going lunch.

Castillo de Farnés, Ave. de Bélgica esq. Obrapía. With a refreshingly original menu by local standards, the Spanish cuisine here includes the tasty *Arroz Indiana*, a mixed meat and rice dish, and well-prepared seafood. The deliberately uncomplicated interior evokes an archetypal French bistro.

Havana

D'Giovanni, Tacón esq. Empedrado. Relatively authentic Italian cuisine by Cuban standards in an aristocratic colonial mansion with views over the nearby streets to the bay.

Dona Blanquita, Paseo del Prado no. 158 e/ Colón y Refugio. Pricey *paladar* in a roomy first-floor apartment with characterful interior arches and a wide selection of *comida criolla* dishes, particularly pork and chicken.

El Floridita, Monserrate esq. Obispo ☎57-12-99 or 57-13-00. Expensive seafood dishes in one of the most formal and exclusive restaurants in the old city and another Hemingway heritage site. A velvet-curtain doorway leads through from the equally famous bar (see p.120) to an elegant circular dining area punctuated by two central marble pillars.

Gentiluomo, Obispo esq. Bernaza. Basic pasta sauces and pizzas plus a few meat and seafood dishes. The food and the restaurant itself lack any sophistication but it works well as a relatively inexpensive lunch spot for sightseers.

Hanoi, Teniente Rey esq. Bernaza. Some of the cheapest *comida criolla* meals in the city are dished up here in a sociable and informal atmosphere.

La Julia, O'Reilly no. 506a e/ Bernaza y Villegas. Top-quality cooking and flavourful *comida criolla* are the main attractions of this homely little *paladar* which has pork dishes down to a science.

La Marina, Brasil esq. Oficios. Simple omelettes and modest meat dishes on a shady open-air patio surrounded by hanging plants. Near the Plaza de San Franciso and best incorporated into a tour of this area rather than approached as the target of an outing.

La Moneda Cubana, San Ignacio no. 77 e/ O'Reilly y Empedrado. This tiny *paladar* near the cathedral, so narrow it almost spills onto the street, offers four set meals, each around the $10 mark and all with *congrí*, salad, fried bananas and bread. Choose from ham, pork steak, omelette or fish whilst you admire the walls plastered with banknotes and coins from around the world.

La Paella, *Hostal Valencia*, Oficios no. 53 esq. Obrapía. Authentically prepared, good-quality Spanish food including six different kinds of paella and an ample selection of light meals and aperitifs in this artistic yet down-to-earth hotel restaurant. Main dishes are moderately priced.

El Patio, Plaza de la Catedral. The serenity of this leafy eighteenth-century mansion courtyard goes a long way to justifying the above-average prices, as does the excellent choice of main dishes, with an emphasis on seafood, set vegetarian meals and plenty of optional extras.

El Rincón de Elegguá, Aguacate no. 257 e/ Obispo y Obrapía. Pork, chicken and fish in one of several *paladares* on or around Obispo where the convenient location means rather inflated prices. Plain interior but very friendly people.

La Terraza, *Hotel Inglaterra*, Paseo del Prado no. 416 esq. San Rafael, Parque Central. Cuban cuisine in small quantities on the fairly ordinary roof terrace of this famous colonial hotel. It is, however, pleasantly breezy, and looks right onto the Capitolio and Gran Teatro and over the Parque Central.

La Torre de Marfil, Mercaderes e/ Obispo y Obrapía. Tasty Chinese cuisine with a high proportion of chow mein and chop suey dishes in an authentically decorated if slightly threadbare colonial building. Set meals start at around $10.

Torre del Oro, *Hotel Sevilla*, Trocadero no. 55 e/ Paseo del Prado y Agramonte ☎33-85-60. Also known as the *Roof Garden Restaurant*, this place serves finely prepared meat and seafood, with an attention to style and detail that sets it apart from its rivals. The large, regal hall with views across the city lends itself perfectly to special occasions.

Torresson, Malecón no. 27 e/ Prado y Cárcel, Centro Habana. Chicken, pork and fish dishes for average prices in a basic balcony *paladar* overlooking the seafront with a good view of El Morro.

La Zaragozana, Ave. de Bélgica no. 352 e/ Obispo y Obrapía. Havana's oldest restaurant, established in 1830, is relatively formal and moodily atmospheric, serving fish, lobster, shrimp, pork, beef and chicken at prices both moderate and expensive.

Vedado

Amor, Calle 23 No. 759 e/ B y C. A sumptuous *paladar* in a beautiful Baroque apartment where the innovative menu includes peanut-fried chicken and smoked meats. A little pricier than the average private restaurant, with a main meal costing around $10, but perhaps worth it for the luxurious surroundings. Closed Mon.

La Casona de 17, Calle 17 no. 60 e/ M y N. The house speciality is a substantial paella and although the restaurant serves fairly average food at rather high prices, dishes like barbecued beef and fries ($9) are dependable options.

Comedor de Aguiar, *Nacional*, Calle O esq. 21. Regal à la carte restaurant serving suitably toothsome dishes, including lobster ($35) and fresh fish ($15), and mouthwatering desserts like profiteroles. One of two restaurants in the hotel (see below).

El Conejito, Calle 17 esq. M. Quirky, moderately priced restaurant with mock-Tudor panelling, staff inexplicably costumed in Teutonic regalia, incongruous live piano music and a house speciality of rabbit, prepared in several ways. A few standard seafood options may tempt the less adventurous.

Coppelia, Calle 23 esq. L. Havana's massive ice-cream emporium contains several peso-paying cafés and a dollar open-air area, serving rich and creamy sundaes in a constantly changing menu of exotic flavours like coconut, mango and guava. Closed Mon.

Dona Clara, Calle 21 no. 107 e/ L y N. The best stall for lunch snacks at rock-bottom prices. Ice-cold soft drinks, *papas rellenas* and moreish guava pies.

Emperador, Calle 17 e/ M y N. A dark, red-and-gold restaurant with a good range of cheap eats – including soup, tasty tortillas and pasta – and more substantial dishes like fillet of fish in breadcrumbs and beef steak, along with splendid desserts such as baked Alaska.

Nacional, Calle O esq. 21. The $18 all-you-can-eat buffet restaurant in the basement is the second of two restaurants in the hotel (see above) and is one of Havana's best feeds, with an extensive range of fish and meat and a welcome array of green vegetables.

Nerei, Calle 19 esq. L. Elegant mid-range *paladar* where you can dine al fresco on escalope of pork, pork cooked in garlic or fried chicken all served with yucca, fried banana and salad. The house speciality of rubbery squid is best avoided.

Palamares Bakery, Calle 25 e/ O y Infanta. Just the place for tea and cakes, with a small seating area and a large and tempting selection of pastries and savoury breads, most for under a dollar.

Polineso, *Habana Libre*, Calle 23 e/ L y M. This quasi-Chinese hotel complex restaurant serves up standard dishes like chow mein with chicken and shrimp at middling prices, with a special-offer set meal for $15.

La Roca, Calle 21 esq. M ☎33-45-01. This recently refurbished restaurant has a tranquil atmosphere and specializes in seafood, and although somewhat pricey is great for a blow-out meal of lobster or delicious grilled red snapper.

La Torre, Calle 17 no. 55 Edificio Focsa piso 36. Mesmerizing views from the city's second tallest building are matched by the excellent French menu at this stylish restaurant. Definitely worth splashing out $40 or so to dine on foie-gras, fillet of beef with rosemary, shrimps caramelized in honey, and profiteroles.

Los Tres Mosqueteros, Calle 23 no. 6607 Altos e/ E y F. Atmospheric little terrace *paladar* popular with a local hippy-chic crowd, where you can get well-prepared *comida criolla* and local beer at low prices.

Wakamba, Calle 0 e/ 23 y Humbolt. Speedy but basic pizzas and sandwiches are served at this modern café whose central location and low prices make up for its somewhat mundane menu.

Yiyo's, Calle L no. 256 e/ 17 y 19. Apartment block *paladar* doling out generous portions of basic Cuban food, with good lunchtime tuna sandwiches and natural juices and shakes for under $5.

Miramar and the western suburbs

Club Almendares, Calle 49c y 28a, Reparto Kohly. A country club-style venue with two restaurants. The popular outdoor pizza house serves excellent Italian-style thin-crust pizzas and pasta dishes for less than $5, whilst the fancier *Restaurant Almendares* offers decent lobster, paella, fried rice and Cuban cuisine for upwards of $7 per dish.

La Ferminia, 5ta Ave. no. 18207 esq. 184, Miramar ☎33-65-55. One of Havana's swankiest restaurants, operating a strict dress code and serving Cuban and international food, like well-prepared spaghetti bolognese and juicy steaks, for suitably inflated prices.

La Maison, 16 esq. 7ma Ave., Miramar ☎24-15-43. Set in an elegant mansion, and widely hyped as the height of Cuban chic, *La Maison* serves Cuban food – chicken, pork and turkey served with rice and salad – similar to that available in quality places elsewhere, with the $30 set charge (exclusive of drinks) paying for the slick nightly fashion and music shows.

El Pavo Real, Calle 7ma no. 205 esq. 2, Miramar. Elegant, upmarket restaurant in an Oriental folly serving tasty, well-cooked Chinese food, including excellent vegetable chop suey and honeyed shrimp.

Villa Diana, Calle 49 e/ 28A-47, Reparto Kohly. A newly opened, classy establishment offering a $12 set meal of grilled and roast meats and some good live music.

Drinking, nightlife and entertainment

A typical night out in Havana is a giddy whirl of thumping *salsa* or soulful *boleros*, well-oiled with rum and often a chunky bill attached for you and all your newly acquired Cuban friends. What Cuba does best is **live music**, so you should definitely try to catch at least one of the excellent *salsa*, jazz or *son* groups that regularly do the rounds of the best-known clubs. Old-timer bands like Buena Vista Social

Club are hard to beat and you can pick up information on their gig dates at the *Nacional* hotel's information desk or in the free weekly listings paper *Cartelera*, which also lists *salsa* groups and venues. It's worth keeping an eye on the big Vedado hotels, which have their own cabaret shows and sometimes host big-name Cuban stars. **Discos** are generally best avoided unless you're desperate to dance to last year's Euro-pop and Latino house tunes.

A more spontaneous night out is a bit difficult, as there's no single area with a buzz. **Bar crawls** will involve a lot of walking, although the Plaza de la Catedral district is usually quite lively at night with most of the attention focused on *El Patio* bar and restaurant. Again, hotels feature prominently on any drinker's itinerary – the *Habana Libre* is central Vedado's best starting point for night-time drinking, with the *Riviera* another option. However, for sheer *joie de vivre* action you can't beat Havana's best option, taking some beers or a bottle of rum down to the Malecón and mingling with the crowds beneath the stars.

Costing just a few pesos, **cinema** is a popular form of entertainment with Cubans, and there are plenty of atmospheric fleapits dotted particularly around Vedado. Although as a visitor you may be charged in dollars ($2–3), it is still well worth the experience. Havana's cinemas usually have a selection of Cuban, North American and European films showing end to end, with the English-speaking ones generally subtitled in Spanish or if you are unlucky, badly dubbed. Havana also has the cream of the country's **theatres** and especially during the international festival in September (see Basics, p.46) you can catch excellent avant-garde and traditional performances.

Bars and cafés

Aire Mar, *Nacional*, Calle O esq. 21, Vedado. Seasoned visitors swear a cooling daily *mojito* on the palatial terraces of this hotel is the way to beat the languid afternoon heat. The *Salón de la Fama* bar just inside is a bit tackier, but intriguing for all the photos of the hotel's famous guests.

Ambos Mundos, Obispo no. 153 esq. Mercaderes. Looking out over the Palacio de los Capitanes Generales and with the cathedral visible further off, lolling on the tasteful garden furniture amongst the potted plants of this hotel's fabulous rooftop patio-bar is as relaxing an option as you could wish for in Habana Vieja.

Bar Dos Hermanos, San Pedro no. 304 esq. Sol. A cool saloon bar opposite the more run-down section of the Terminal Sierra Maestra, attracting at least as many Cubans as tourists with its distinguished yet workman-like character.

Bar Monserrate, Ave. de Bélgica esq. Obrapía. A traditional bar that's on the tourist circuit but feels very much like a local drinkers' haunt, with none of the song-and-dance used elsewhere to attract custom. A good place for a no-nonsense rum. See "Eating", p.115.

Bar Nautilius, San Rafael e/ Consulado y Paseo del Prado, Centro Habana. This dark and shady-looking local hangout based on a submarine theme is refreshingly untouristy, surprisingly so given that it's right next to the swanky *Inglaterra* hotel. There's a limited selection of drinks, though.

La Bodeguita del Medio, Empedrado e/ San Ignacio y Mercaderes. Made famous by Ernest Hemingway, this sometimes hectic, usually overcrowded but always atmospheric bar no longer attracts Havana's bohemian set as it did in the 1930s and 1940s, but retains some of the spirit of that era despite the queues of tourists.

Café Habano, Mercaderes esq. Amargura. A popular café-bar fuelling the caffeine cravings of a mostly Cuban clientele. Light snacks are served in the airy seating area and although the drinks list consists entirely of cappuccino and soda, at less than a peso a throw they won't get too many complaints. Open 10am–9pm.

Café del Oriente, Oficios esq. Amargura, Plaza de San Francisco. Despite looking like a high-class restaurant, this is essentially a bar where food is served. Plush *Oriental Express*-style decor, bow-tied waiters, live piano and violin all make for an aristocratic ambience more closely associated with the 1920s and 1930s than anything in contemporary Cuba. The selection of cocktails is outstanding and there are over fifteen types of coffee.

Café de Paris, San Ignacio esq. Obispo. Always packed with an even mix of tourists and locals, this little bar has a worn simplicity that belies the party atmosphere stirred up by a live band on a nightly basis.

La Casa del Café, Baratillo esq. Obispo. A shop-cum-coffee bar that's an inviting place for a quiet chat over a coffee cocktail – try the Daiquiri de Café.

Delirio Habanero Piano Bar, Teatro Nacional de Cuba, Paseo y 39, Plaza de la Revolución ☎ 33-57-13. This sultry and atmospheric late-night jazz hangout is popular with Cuban sophisticates and visitors alike, with low-key piano music and live jazz bands nightly. Limited table space makes reservations essential at weekends. Bands play between 10.30pm and 3am though the place stays open till 6am when it's busy.

El Floridita, Monserrate esq. Obispo. Home of the daiquiri, this was another of Hemingway's favourite hangouts. A completely different experience to *La Bodeguita del Medio*, the comfy chairs, flowery wallpaper and velvet curtains make it feel like a posh living-room, albeit one crammed with people trying to look cool while sampling a range of fifty-odd cocktails which includes over fifteen types of daiquiri.

Gato Tuerto, Calle O e/ 17 y 19, Vedado ☎ 55-26-96. The recently reopened pre-revolutionary Beatnik jazz bar, whose name translates as "One-eyed Cat", has kept its cool edge despite a complete renovation. Excellent live Feeling (trova jazz fusion) is played nightly from midnight to 4am. Entry is free but subject to a $5 consumption minimum. There's a stylish restaurant upstairs.

Habana Café, *Meliá Cohiba*, Paseo y Malecón ☎ 33-36-36. Expensive retro cabaret-café filled with Cubamericana: classic Chevrolets and photos of Cuba at its Vegas best. Very *Planet Hollywood*, with an overpriced burger-and-fries menu. A flashy and brash variety show entertains the largely tourist clientele. Free entry with a $5 surcharge on your first drink.

Lluvia de Oro, Obispo esq. Habana. One of the liveliest and most reliably busy bars in Habana Vieja but depends heavily on a live band for atmosphere.

Puerto de Sagua, Ave. de Bélgica (Egido) esq. Acosta. This classy 1930s-style bar could easily be a set for a Hollywood gangster movie. The sleek black bar is a fantastic throwback and the excellent selection of drinks, including plenty of cocktails, are surprisingly reasonably priced. Attached is a restaurant with nothing like the same character.

El Relicario, *Meliá Cohiba*, Calle Paseo e/ 1ra y 3ra. With its wide selection of luxurious cigars and liquors, this stylish little bar feels like a gentleman's drinking club, perfect for an expensive post-prandial Cohiba and scotch.

Taberna del Galeon, Baratillo no. 53 e/ Obispo y Jústiz. Just off the Plaza de Armas and a good place to avoid the sometimes frenzied atmosphere of the Obispo bars and the plaza itself, in an attic-like upstairs balcony above a rum and cigar shop. Open 10am–5pm.

Cabarets, discos and live music

Bar de las Estrellas, Calle A e/ 15 y 16 no. 507 Lawton. A unique late-night *paladar*-cum-cabaret in south Havana where portly transvestites lip-synch to *I Will Survive* and other diva favourites. Blending decent food, exorbitant beer-prices and quality entertainment, it's off the beaten track but worth the trip. Opens at 8pm, but doesn't get going until 10pm.

Cabaret Nacional, San Rafael esq. Paseo del Prado. Below the Gran Teatro, this seedy basement cabaret and disco is more than just a pick-up joint, though it is certainly that. Less glamorous and much cheaper than the average cabaret, the show follows the usual routines, but the place has a strong character, the low ceiling and abundance of dark red lending it a clandestine flavour. The show starts around 11pm and the disco usually gets going at about 1am.

Cabaret Turquino, *Habana Libre*, Calle L e/ 23 y 25. On the top floor of the *Habana Libre*, one of two nightspots in the hotel, this expansive disco/cabaret ($15) boasts a roll-back roof that reveals the stars but still manages to look like a student bar with rather ordinary black chairs and tables. However, it puts on a cracking show, with live *salsa* on Mon, Tues, Thurs and Sat.

Café Cantante Mi Habana, Teatro Nacional de Cuba, Paseo y 39 Plaza de la Revolución ☎ 33-57-13. The club to show off your *salsa* and *merengue* moves to all the latest tunes. Top artists like Paulito F. G. and Los Van Van headline here sometimes; prices depend on who's playing but are upwards of $10 with a cheaper Thursday matinee. Arrive early at weekends when the small basement gets jam-packed and the queue can be enormous.

Café Tertulia, Centro Cultural Habana, San Rafael e/ Ave. de Italia y Aguila. A makeshift café hosting good live music most nights in a bizarre setting, at the back of a bookshop, and attracting plenty of locals. Entrance is free but there is an obligatory set meal costing around $5.

Casa de la Amistad, Paseo no. 406 esq. 17, Vedado ☎ 30-31-14. Resident troubadour groups gently perform well-executed *salsa*, *son* and *boleros* in the majestic grounds of a Rococo building that was once a private house. Compay Segundo's group plays on Tuesdays although he's usually touring ($5), while Saturdays are livelier with old-school *salsa* ($7). Closed Mon.

Casa de las Américas, Esq. Calle 3ra y Avenida de los Presidentes ☎ 55-27-06. This cultural institution regularly hosts bands in its large first-floor function room, playing anything from rap, *salsa* or rock.

Casa de la Cultura, Aguiar no. 509 e/ Amargura y Brasil, Habana Vieja ☎ 63-48-60. In the converted Convento de San Francisco, this centre for local talent runs a full programme of evening performances ranging from folk music to rap. Entrance is usually between two and five pesos.

Disco Galicia, Agramonte no. 658 e/ Apodaca y Gloria. Inauspicious disco-bar at the top of a battered neo-colonial building. Plenty of local flavour and a laid-back crowd. Entrance $5.

Havana

Havana Club, Calle 86 y 1ra Miramar Playa ☎24-29-02. The most upmarket disco in Havana, and the haunt of visiting movie stars and supermodels. An even mix of up-to-the-minute *salsa* tunes and last year's house music get the fashion pack up and dancing. Open nightly from 11pm to 5am; entrance is $15.

La Maison, Calle 16 no. 701 esq. 7ma, Miramar ☎24-15-43. An elegant mansion containing shops, a piano bar and restaurant. The $30 fee covers a meal and entrance to the nightly fashion and music shows. A popular spot for wedding receptions, it's generally considered to be the height of elegance by Cubans.

Palermo, San Miguel esq. Amistad. The nightly shows put on in this untouristy, no-frills venue vary from cabaret to live music and usually include a disco. Doors open around 10.30pm.

La Pampa, Parque Maceo, Centro Habana. Distinguished by a music policy of swing and hip-hop, a rarity in Cuban clubs, *La Pampa* attracts an enthusiastic finger-on-the-pulse local crowd. At just 20 pesos to get in, you can't go wrong.

Salon de los Embajadores, *Habana Libre*, Calle L e/ 23 y 25. Cuba's finest music stars, including Chu Chu Valdés, Los Van Van and a host of hot *salsa* acts, play in this regal reception room, one of two salons in the hotel (see *Cabaret Turquino*, p.121). Well worth the costly price tag ($15–20). Ask at reception for details of performances.

Tropicana, Calle 72 no. 504 Mariano. Possibly the oldest and most lavish cabaret in the world, Cuba's much-hyped open-air venue hosts a pricey extravaganza in which class acts, such as Pablo Milanes, and a ceaseless flow of dancing girls (under)clad in sequins, feathers and frills regularly pulls in a full house. Starts at 8.30pm with the show from 10 to 11pm. You can arrange all-inclusive bus trips from $50 from most hotels, otherwise entrance is $35–55. Closed Mon. Unmissable.

Villa Diana, Calle 49 e/ 28A-47, Reparto Kohly. A newly opened, classy establishment that makes the most of the elegant mansion in which it is set. Quality live music includes classic Cuban *son*, *boleros* and *danzón*.

La Zorra y el Cuervo, Calle 23 No. 155 e/ N y O, Vedado ☎55-26-96. A cool and stylish basement venue, with contemporary decor and a European feel, that puts on superior live Latin jazz nightly. Doors open at 9pm but it doesn't heat up till the band starts at 11pm. $5 entrance.

Cinemas and theatres

Cine Actualidades, Ave. de Bélgica no. 362 e/ Animas y Virtudes, Habana Vieja. Cinema offering one of the more varied monthly programmes, with performance times for the whole month usually posted in the front window.

Cine Chaplin, Calle 23 e/ 10 y 12, Vedado. An appealing arts cinema that shows vintage Cuban and incomprehensible Russian films.

Cine la Rampa, Calle 23 esq. O, Vedado. A rather run-down cinema that shows predominantly North American films.

Cine Payret, Paseo del Prado esq. San José, Habana Vieja. The principal cinema in Habana Vieja showing Cuban films and the occasional Hollywood blockbuster. One of the main venues for the Havana Film Festival.

Cine Riviera, Calle 23 e/ G y H, Vedado. A stylish cinema painted cobalt blue that shows a range of films from North American and English to Cuban and Spanish.

Cine Yara, Calle L esq. 23, Vedado. A large old-fashioned cinema with a lofty auditorium showing the latest Spanish and Cuban releases and a small video room showing special interest films.

Gran Teatro, Paseo del Prado esq. San Rafael, Habana Vieja ☎62-94-73. This outstandingly ornate building on the Parque Central is the home of the Ballet Nacional de Cuba but also hosts operas and works of contemporary dance. There are performances most weeks, usually from Fri to Sun. Entrance is usually $10.

Teatro América, Ave. de Italia no. 253 e/ Concordia y Neptuno, Centro Habana ☎62-54-16. Smaller than its more renowned counterparts, this humble but happening theatre lends itself well to the comedy shows, live jazz and traditional music performances which are its mainstays.

Teatro Hubert de Blanck, Calzada e/ A y B, Vedado ☎3-59-60. This very small theatre has a good repertoire of contemporary Spanish and Cuban theatre. Entrance is a snip at $3–5.

Teatro Karl Marx, Calle 1ra e/ 8 y 10, Miramar ☎30-07-20. Impressively ugly 1960s building hosting all kinds of music and dramatic arts events including rock concerts and classical theatre. Definitely worth checking what's on.

Teatro Nacional de Cuba, Calle Paseo y 39, Plaza de la Revolución ☎79-60-11. Havana's biggest theatre puts on some of the best events all year round, from ballet to guitar and jazz. Spanish-speakers should check out the avant-garde drama, especially during the February theatre festival.

Shopping and galleries

Havana is no shoppers' paradise, and most visitors are happy enough to just buy bottles of rum, a handful of cigars and a souvenir T-shirt or two: a demand met by all the large hotels and the **Artex** state chain stores on Calle 23 y L and in Habana Vieja. Those intent on shopping will find that **Obispo**, in Habana Vieja, offers the widest choice of shops in the most congenial setting, with the best of the bunch being the Casa del Ron, the rum and cigar shop between Bernaza and Avenida de Bélgica; the Librería Internacional, one of Havana's two best-stocked bookshops along with the Librería Fernando Ortíz; and Longina, for a good selection of Cuban music on CD as well as musical instruments. There are also a number of clothing boutiques and the gimcrack trinket/toiletry/electrical appliances/toy shops which Cuban retail has made its own.

Elsewhere, whilst new shopping malls and boutiques are mushrooming steadily around the city, the general standard of merchandise is low, with dime-store items like doe-eyed ceramic animals featuring heavily. That said, the goods available are well-priced and you can often pick up inexpensive shoes and clothes in the large malls, though these won't necessarily win you many admiring glances back home. The biggest **malls** are the North American-style *Tiendas Carlos Tercero* (Mon–Sat 10am–6pm) on Carlos Tercero in Centro Habana, and *La Tienda Primer de Paso Galerias de Paseo*, on the corner of Paseo and Calle 1ra, Vedado (Mon–Sat 10am–6pm), both replete with clothes, shoes, groceries and beauty products.

If you are prepared to put in the hours running the gauntlet of the eager hawkers in the **street markets** you can spot surprising one-off bargains, especially in the **art and crafts** market on the Malecón e/ C y D near the *Hotel Riviera* (Tues, Wed & Fri–Sun 9am–5pm), where you can pick up a range of souvenirs from crocheted dresses and recycled jewellery to burnished wood sculptures of buxom women, something of a theme amongst Cuban artists. Likewise there is a small craft market (closed Mon) on La Rampa, its miscellaneous merchandise including inflated and lacquered puffer fish, highly suspect fat-black-mama sculptures, pumpkin seed necklaces and handmade leather items. However, the largest and best market (closed Sun), especially for souvenirs, is in Habana Vieja, on Tacón, near the Plaza de la Catedral,which has all of the above as well as several types of unique and original hand-crafted jewellery, like shell earrings and clay-bead necklaces, and attractive ornaments such as jade-coloured polished marble statues.

Secondhand bookshops are very popular in Cuba, and proliferate in Havana, with plenty of stalls around the central tourist areas selling books in Spanish, English and sometimes French and German, some of which pre-date the revolution. For new titles, check out the shop in Obispo (see p.123), various outlets along Calle L, the *Habana Libre* hotel's tourist shop and, for a wide selection of history and politics titles in English and Spanish, as well as a decent selection of novels, Fernando Ortíz, at the corner of Calle 27 (Mon–Fri 10am–5pm, Sat 9am–3pm).

Fans of Cuban **music** will be delighted by the expansive range of CDs and tapes in Havana's shops, with a wider choice of *salsa, son* or *bolero* than the rest of the country; the best place to browse for these is in the *Habana Libre* shopping mall (Calle L e/ 23 y 25) or the souvenir shop *L y 23* opposite.

As far as basics like **toiletries** go, things have moved on since the Special Period and you can pick up most things easily enough so long as you're equipped with dollars. It's worthwhile checking out the big-name perfumes available from hotels like *Cohiba* and *Habana Libre*, as they often work out cheaper than they are back home.

You can buy original **artwork** from several of Havana's excellent galleries but remember to make sure you have the correct export certificates. The Galería Habana, no. 460 Linea (Mon–Fri 10am–4pm, Sat 10am–1pm; free), always has an impressive collection of contemporary art, while the Galería Victor Manuel in Habana Vieja (see p.80) offers a good range of *artesanía*, as well as paintings.

The best places to buy **cigars** are the factory shops detailed on p.92 and p.94, and the Casa del Habano, Mercaderes e/ Obispo y Obrapía.

Sport

You only need to spend a few hours wandering the streets of any part of the capital to appreciate the prominent role that **sport** plays in the lives of Habaneros. Fierce arguments strike off every evening on basketball courts all over the city and rarely will you see an open space, at any time of the day, not hosting a game of baseball. The virtually traffic-less streets of much of Centro Habana witness local neighbourhood clashes on a daily basis – using rope for volleyball nets and hands for baseball bats, nothing stops the locals coming out to compete.

On a professional level, Havana is the finest place for live sport in Cuba, with the best stadia in the country and several big-league teams. The city has two major **baseball** teams and both play at the **Estadio Latinoamericano** (☎70-65-26) on Zequeira in Cerro. Industriales, traditionally the most successful team in Havana, attract the biggest crowds, especially when they play their arch-rivals Santiago de Cuba. Expect five games a week during the regular season, usually October to March; if Industriales are playing away, Metropolitanos, the capital's second team, are playing at home. There is always plenty of banter in the crowd and a real feel-good vibe, but be warned that with so many games the stadium is often half-empty, the big crowds only coming out for the big games and even then they don't generate the kind of atmosphere you would expect from, say, an English football match. Check the back pages of *Granma* for details of forthcoming games.

Live **basketball**, the other big spectator sport, is harder to find out about, but the smaller arenas mean there's often more of a buzz. Capitalinos, the local team, spend the winter months in weekly combat with the other three teams in the national league. The **Sala Polivalente Ramon Fonst**, on the Avenida de Rancho Boyeros near the Plaza de la Revolución (☎81-42-96), is the only purpose-built basketball arena, but currently most games are played at the **Ciudad Deportiva** (☎57-71-56), sitting to one side of the roundabout where the airport road meets the Vía Blanca in Cerro. Occasional host to a game is the **Sala Polivalente Kid Chocolate** (☎61-15-48) opposite the Capitolio Nacional on the Paseo del Prado between Brasil and San Martín, but this rickety old sports hall is more used to staging boxing matches. A number of international tournaments have been held here in recent years but there is no regular boxing season or schedule so catching a fight can be quite difficult.

Entrance to any sports arena costs one peso and booking in advance is unnecessary and rarely possible.

There are no public sports centres as such in Havana; instead, the best places for **participatory sports** are the local neighbourhood courts and pitches where all comers are usually welcome. The most reliable place for a game of football is the university stadium, the Estadio Juan Abrantes, which has several games going on almost every evening. One of the best places to pick up a game of basketball is the Parque Martí, within sight of the Malecón next to the Avenida de los Presidentes in Vedado.

Listings

The telephone area code for Havana is ☎7.

Airlines Aeroflot, Calle 23 no. 64, Vedado ☎33-32-00 or 33-37-59; Aerotaxi, Calle 27 no. 102, Vedado ☎32-81-27; Air France, Calle 23 no. 64, Vedado ☎66-26-42; Air Jamaica, *Habana Libre*, Calle L e/ 23 y 25, Vedado ☎33-40-11; Cubana, Calle 23 no. 64, Vedado ☎33-39-11; Iberia, Calle 23 no. 74, Vedado ☎33-50-41 or 42.

Airport Ring the José Martí International Airport switchboard on ☎33-57-77 and ask for information. You can call information direct on ☎33-56-66 but it tends to be harder to get through to.

Banks and exchange Of all the places where you can withdraw money with a foreign credit card and cash travellers' cheques, the *cambio* in the *Nacional* hotel has the longest opening hours (daily 8am–noon & 1–7pm). The Banco Internacional de Comercio (Mon–Fri 8.30am–3pm), at Empedrado esq. Aguiar, is the best bank in the old city for foreign currency transactions, whilst for more or less the same services in Centro Habana the Banco de Crédito y Comercio is centrally located at Zanja esq. Padre Varela (Mon–Fri 8.30am–3pm); in Vedado the Banco Financiero Internacional, at Linea no. 1 esq. Calle O (Mon–Fri 8am–3pm), is within walking distance of at least four hotels. For purchasing pesos there are Cadeca *casas de cambio* all over the city, including one at Obispo esq. Compostela, Habana Vieja (8am–5.30pm).

Car rental Micar is the cheapest and has offices at the Fiat showroom, Malecón esq. Príncipe, Centro Habana ☎33-58-10, and Calle 1era esq. Paseo, Vedado ☎55-35-35 (open 24hr). Alternatives include Havanautos at Malecón esq. Calle 11 ☎33-46-91; Panautos at Línea esq. Malecón, Vedado ☎55-32-55; and Transautos at Calle 21 e/ Calle N y Calle O ☎33-40-38.

Embassies The vast majority of embassies and consulates are based in Miramar. They include the British Embassy, Calle 34 no. 702/704 ☎24-17-71, fax 24-81-04; and the Canadian Embassy, Calle 30 no. 518 ☎24-25-16 or 24-25-17, fax 24-20-44. The United States is represented by the Special Interests Section at Calle Calzada esq. Calle L, Vedado ☎33-35-31 to 33-35-59, fax 33-37-00.

Immigration and legal Asistur, Paseo del Prado no. 212 esq. Trocadero ☎33-89-20, 33-85-27 or 33-83-39, is open 24hr. Otherwise, try the Consultoria Juridica Internacional, Calle 16 no. 314 e/ 3ra y 5ta ☎24-24-90 or 24-26-97 (Mon–Fri 8.30am–noon & 1.30–5.30pm).

Laundry Aster, Calle 34 e/ 3ra y 5ta, Miramar ☎24-16-22 (Mon–Sat 8am–5pm).

Left luggage There is no official left-luggage office in Havana but the administration office on the first floor of the building housing *D'Giovanni* restaurant, Tacón esq. Empedrado, Habana Vieja ☎33-59-79, will look after your luggage at the rate of $5 per day. Ask for Orlando.

Library The well-maintained Biblioteca Rubén Martínez Villena on the Plaza de Armas (Mon–Fri 8am–9pm & Sat 9am–4pm) has a foreign literature section on the second floor but non-residents are not permitted to take books outside the building.

Medical Call ☎40-50-93 or 40-45-51 for a state ambulance, or contact Asistur on ☎57-13-15 for a tourist ambulance. The switchboard number for the Hospital Hermanos Ameijeras is ☎57-60-77.

Newspapers and magazines There are usually copies of *Time*, *Newsweek*, *National Geographic* and *Rolling Stone* for sale in the lobby of the *Nacional* hotel, but the only foreign newspapers tend to be Italian and Spanish. The small shop in the lobby of the *Habana Libre* hotel is also worth checking out for similar publications.

Pharmacies Farmacia Taquechel at Obispo no. 155 e/ Mercaderes y San Ignacio in Habana Vieja stocks basic pain-relief tablets including aspirin but specializes in natural medicines. The small pharmacy in the basement of the *Nacional* hotel is equipped with most of the essentials.

Photography The largest branch of Photoservice is at Calle 23 esq. Calle 0, in Vedado, for films and developing. Trimagen is at Neptuno esq. Industria, Centro Habana.

Police The main station in Centro Habana is at Dragones e/ Lealtad y Escobar ☎62-44-12. In an emergency ring ☎82-01-16.

Post offices The branch at Ave. Salvador Allende esq. Padre Varela, Centro Habana (Mon–Sat 8am–6pm) offers peso services only. The branch in the Gran Teatro building at Paseo del Prado esq. San Martín offers fax and telegram services as well as poste restante facilities (daily 8am–6pm), while the one at Obispo no. 518 e/ Bernaza y Villegas (daily 8am–6pm) has DHL, fax and photocopying facilities.

Public toilets There is one on Obispo between Bernaza and Villegas in Habana Vieja. Your best bet in Vedado is the washrooms on the ground floor of the *Habana Libre*.

Scooter rental Transautos in the Terminal Sierra Maestra opposite the Plaza de San Francisco in Habana Vieja.

Taxis Turistaxi ☎33-66-66; Habanataxi ☎41-96-00; Panataxi ☎55-55-55.

Telephone ETECSA telephone cabins are located at Ave. de Italia esq. Ave. Simón Bolívar, Centro Habana.

Travel agents The main branches of Cubatur, at Calle 23 esq. Calle L ☎33-41-35 or 33-35-69, and Tour y Travel, at Calle 23 esq Calle M ☎33-40-82 or 83, are next door to one another in Vedado. For information on *campismos* throughout the country contact Cubamar at Calle 15 esq. Paseo ☎66-25-23 or 24, also in Vedado. For specialized historically and culturally oriented excursions, try the San Cristóbal Agencia de Viajes at Oficios no. 110 e/ Lamparilla y Amargura ☎33-95-85.

East of Havana

Taking the tunnel in Habana Vieja under the bay and heading east on the Via Monumental, past El Morro and parallel to the coast, leads you straight to **Cojímar**, a fishing village famed for its Hemingway connection. Past here the road dips inland to become the Vía Blanca and heads south towards **Guanabacoa**, a quiet provincial town with numerous attractive churches and a fascinating religious history. For many the big attraction east of Havana will be the boisterous **Playas del Este**, the nearest beaches to the city, where clean sands and a lively scene draw in the crowds. In contrast, **Playa Jibacoa**, 32km further east, offers a quieter, less glitzy beach resort, while the inland hills of the **Escalera de Jaruco** present a scenic diversion. The hippy retreat at **Canasí**, tucked away on the cliffs overlooking the ocean, is perfect for a back-to-basics camping experience and represents the final outpost in the province before the border with Matanzas.

The scarcity and unreliability of **public transport** becomes even more pronounced once outside the city proper, and you'll need a car to see many of these sights.

Cojímar

Just 6km east of Havana the tiny fishing village of **COJÍMAR** is a world apart from the bustling city – tailor-made for enjoying such simple pleasures as watching fishing boats bob about in the calm, hoop-shaped bay, or wandering the tidy streets fringed with bright bougainvillea.

Cojímar's sole claim to fame revolves around one of its oldest residents, one Gregorio Fuentes, the old man upon whom Ernest Hemingway based Santiago, the protagonist of his Pulitzer- and Nobel Prize-winning novel *The Old Man and the Sea*. Fuentes was actually only in his forties when Hemingway, who used to berth his fishing boat *The Pilar* here, started the tale in 1951, but is now nearly 100, and until recently could be seen sitting outside his house or in *La Terraza de Cojímar* restaurant, charging $10 for a consultation with fans eager for Hemingway stories. Now, however, the years are beginning to take their toll and often a notice on his simple clapboard house pleads: "Please don't knock, I'm sleeping."

The village pays homage to Hemingway's memory in the **Monumento a Hemingway**, a weatherbeaten construction close to the small *malecón* that looks a bit like a dwarf Acropolis, with a ring of six classic columns on a stately plinth, crowned with an entablature like a big open hoop. In the middle is Hemingway himself, represented by a rather meagre bust on top of a block and looking rather comical in contrast with the august surroundings. The whole thing has the air of a misplaced garden ornament and manages to invest the nearby **Torreón de Cojímar** with a similarly spurious air.

Overhanging the water's edge, the fort, built between 1639 and 1643 as part of the Spanish colonial fortification, is so small it looks rather like a well-crafted toy. A squat and sturdy building, with sharp, clean angles and Moorish sentry boxes, it was designed by the engineer Juan Bautista Antonelli – who also designed the not dissimilar El Morro castle (see p.113) – as an early warning system for attacks on Havana harbour, and only needed to accommodate a couple of sentries rather than a whole battalion. Even so, it was usually left unmanned, a defensive weakness fully exploited by the British in 1762, who bombarded it with cannon-fire, routed the peasants' and slaves' attempts at retaliation and romped off to capture the city. The fort is still in military use, so there's no access to the building, although you are free to examine the outside.

There's no state-sanctioned **accommodation** at present, though you may be able to find an unlicensed *casa particular*. Cojímar's flagship **restaurant**, *La Terraza de Cojímar*, on the east side of the village in Calle Real (☎7/65-34-71), is airy, pleasant and full of black-and-white photos of Hemingway and Fuentes, although the food isn't all it could be: go for the simple dishes and avoid the soggy paella and over-salted Lobster Thermidor. Reservations are recommended as the place is sometimes booked out by bus tours.

Otherwise, there's a *Rumbos* café on the *malecón* serving chicken and chips, and the *El Golfito* on the east side of the river that runs through the town, offering basic eats for Cuban pesos.

Guanabacoa

Less than 2km inland from the turnoff to Cojímar is **GUANABACOA**, a little town officially within the city limits but with a distinctly provincial feel. The site of a pre-Columbian community and then one of the island's first Spanish settlements, it is historically important, though the disproportionately large number of churches and strong tradition of Afro-Cuban religion hold the most appeal for visitors, especially after a visit to the town's most coherent attraction, the **Museo Histórico de Guanabacoa** (Mon & Wed–Sat 10.30am–6pm; $2), at Martí no. 108 e/ Quintin Bandera y E.V.Valenzuela, two blocks from the understated main square, Parque Martí. The collection of cultish objects relating to the practices of Santería, Palo Monte and the Abakuá Secret Society give the museum its edge. One room is moodily set up to reflect the mystic environment in which the *babalao*, the Santería equivalent of a priest, would perform divination rituals, surrounded by altars and African deities in the form of Catholic saints (see p.86). Equally poignant are the representations of Elegguá, one of the most powerful of Afro-Cuban *orishas*, with their almost threatening stares. There are also some interesting bits and pieces, including furniture and ceramics, relating to the town's history.

The town's five **churches** make up the remainder of its sights, and though none has reliable opening times there's usually a member of staff on hand willing to let you take a wander inside. The most accessible and intact are the run-down **Iglesia Parroquial Mayor** on Parque Martí, with its magnificent, though age-worn, wooden gilted main altar; the eighteenth-century **Iglesia de Santo Domingo** and adjoining monastery, on the corner of Lebredo and Santo Domingo, with a lovely leafy courtyard; and the huge monastery, now a school, attached to the still-functioning **Iglesia de San Francisco**, a block south of Martí on Quintin Bandera. Otherwise, once you've checked out the Afro-Cuban-style knick-knacks in the Bazar de Reproducciones Artísticas, two blocks down from the museum at Martí no. 175, and eaten at *El Palenque*, the basic outdoor restaurant next door, you've done the town justice.

Playas del Este

Fifteen kilometres east of Cojímar, the Vía Blanca reaches Havana's nearest beaches – Playa Santa María del Mar, Playa Boca Ciega and Playa Guanabo, collectively known as the **Playas del Este**. Hugging the Atlantic coast, the three fine-sand beaches form a long, twisting ribbon of ochre which vanishes in summer beneath the crush of

Cojímar is served by the #58 bus from Prado, Habana Vieja, by the mouth of the tunnel, while an unmetered or a metered taxi will cost around $10.

After a long period of restoration, the museum should be open again by the time you read this, though it's worth checking with Infotur (see p.70) before setting out.

A metered taxi from the centre of Havana to Guanabacoa will cost around $10. Alternatively the #295 bus leaves from Calle 23 and G.

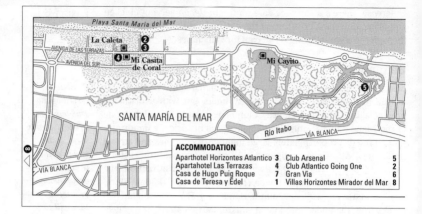

ACCOMMODATION

Aparthotel Horizontes Atlantico	**3**	Club Arsenal	**5**
Apartahotel Las Terrazas	**4**	Club Atlantico Going One	**2**
Casa de Hugo Puig Roque	**7**	Gran Via	**6**
Casa de Teresa y Edel	**1**	Villas Horizontes Mirador del Mar	**8**

weekending Habaneros and tourists. There's not a whole lot to distinguish between them, geographically, although as a general rule the sand is better towards the western end.

There is an abundance of really good self-catering and hotel **accommodation** around the beaches, and if you're based in Havana for most of your holiday this could be an excellent mini-break. Those craving creature comforts should head for the big hotels in Santa María, though budget travellers will find the best value in the inexpensive hotels and *casas particulares* in Guanabo. Other than the rather anonymous all-inclusive *Club Arsenal*, there's nowhere to stay in Playa Boca Ciega. Although a number of restaurants serve cheap meals, these all tend to be much of a muchness, and your best bet is to eat at the *paladar* in Guanabo; otherwise, see if a *casa particular* can recommend somewhere, or stick to the rather standard fare in the hotels.

Playa Santa María del Mar

Due to its proximity to Havana, **Playa Santa María del Mar**, usually just called Santa María, is the busiest and trendiest of the eastern beaches, with canned *salsa*, watersports and bodies beautiful on sun loungers making it the hip place to hang out. It extends for about 4km from the foot of Santa María Loma, a hill to the mouth of the Río Itabo, with the bulk of hotels dotted around the main **Avenida de las Terrazas**, just behind the beach. Arguably the most beautiful of the three beaches, with golden sands backed by grasslands and a few palm trees, it's also the most touristy and can feel a bit artificial. Studded with palm-thatch sun shades and sun loungers ($2 a day), and patrolled by eager beach masseurs (roughly $5–7 for 30min), it's the best bet for beach activities: the only place you can play volleyball or rent a catamaran ($5 per hour) or snorkelling equipment ($3 per hour), though sadly you'll see more empty beer cans than fish. With thatch-hut beach bars at intervals

along the beach and roving vendors selling rum-laced coconuts, there's no shortage of **refreshment**, while a big dollar shop on Avenida de las Terrazas sells the makings of a picnic.

Accommodation

Aparthotel Horizontes Atlantico, Ave. de las Terrazas e/ 11 y 13 ☎ 7/97-12-03. Spotless, spacious and airy self-catering apartments ($5 extra for a cooker and fridge) in slick, ice-cream coloured buildings with views over the beach. Good value for several people sharing. There's a Transtur moped rental desk. ③/④.

Aparthotel Las Terrazas, Ave. de las Terrazas e/10 y Rotunda ☎ 7/97-13-44; fax 80-23-96. Despite a holiday camp vibe that's emphasized by the huge busy swimming pool, this is a good option, with decent two- and three-bed apartments with kitchen, sitting room and mini bar. ⑥.

Club Atlantico Going One, Avenida Norte ☎ 7/97-10-85; fax 80-39-11. Old-fashioned concrete hotel right on the beach that's been recently renovated into an all-inclusive. Facilities include a large swimming pool, gym, tennis court, and relentlessly jolly interactive entertainment. ⑦.

Villas Horizontes Mirador del Mar, Calle 11 e/ 1a y 3ra ☎ 7/97-13-54; fax 97-12-62. A complex with good-quality hotel rooms and apartment bungalows (sleeping up to 5), some with splendid sea views, on the hillside overlooking the beach. ④/⑤.

Eating

El Brocal, Calle 5ta C Avenida esq. 500. Almost on the town's eastern limits, this fresh and bright open-air state restaurant, with tables on a wooden veranda, has the feel of a *paladar*. It's pricier than its rivals, with even basic meals between $6 and $10, but worth it, with a good range of seafood and meat dishes, plus the occasional catch of the day. All meals come with cassava, salad and fried green banana.

La Caleta, Ave. de las Terrazas s/n. Central to the beach, this open-air restaurant has a thatched palm roof, music at weekends and a lively air. The decent menu includes lobster brochette for $8, pork dishes for $5 and steak for $6.50.

Mi Casita de Coral, Ave. de las Terrazas s/n. A carbon-copy sister restaurant to *La Caleta*, with exactly the same menu, on the other side of the road.

Playa Boca Ciega

A bridge across the Río Itabo leads to **Playa Boca Ciega**. The least appealing of the three beaches, it's marred by the presence of *Club Arsenal* (☎ 7/97-12-72; ⑦), a large all-inclusive hotel catering almost exclusively to pre-booked package holidays, and a lack of public facilities, with just one rather grubby café, *Mi Cayito*. However, the beautiful sherbet-yellow beach is open to all, and the waters around the estuary mouth are usually quite busy and cheerful, with Cuban kids and adults paddling and wading in the river currents.

Playa Guanabo

Far pleasanter than Playa Boca Ciega is laid-back **Playa Guanabo**, roughly 2.5km further east, where the sun-faded wooden houses and jaunty seaside atmosphere go a long way to compensate for the slightly poor brownish-sand beach. With fewer crowds and no big hotels, it feels much more authentic than Santa María, especially towards the east end of town where tourism has hardly penetrated at all. Whilst not idyllic, it has its charms; palm trees offer welcome shade on the generous stretch of beach, and if you're not bothered about the odd bit of seaweed clouding the sea this is a refreshingly unaffected spot to hang out.

Guanabo village has an existence beyond the immediate tourist industry and many people commute daily into Havana to work, and as most tourists stay on the better beaches further west, Guanabo is pretty much left to the Cubans. Avenida 5ta, the appealing main street, has a clutch of cafés and shops, while around the side streets and near the beach are a couple of excellent *paladares*.

Accommodation

Casa de Hugo Puig Roque, Calle 5ta Avenida no. 47203 e/ 472 y 474 ☎ 7/96-34-26. Two rooms with shared bathroom and a/c in an appealing red and white house with a balcony over the street, not far from the beach. ③.

Casa de Teresa y Edel, Calle 5ta Avenida no. 49816 e/ 498 y 500 ☎ 7/96-32-94. Two rooms with a/c in an attractive, well-run house with hot running water, a kitchen and sitting room and the use of a phone. ③.

Gran Via, Calle 5ta Avenida esq. 462 ☎ 7/96-22-71. Pleasant but very basic rooms with cold water in a small hotel close to the beach and the town centre. ③.

Eating

Coppelia, Calle 5ta Avenida e. 478 y 480. Guanabo's small and dainty branch of the ice-cream parlour chain also offers snack meals, with chicken and chips a firm favourite with locals. It has the added bonus of being open 24 hours.

Cuanda, 472 esq. 5ta D. A basic restaurant dishing up reasonable meals on the pork, salad, rice and beans theme. At $3.50 for a main meal, it's good value.

Parriada, Calle 5ta Avenida e/ 472 y 474. Very ordinary hamburger and fried chicken-type snacks served in an open-air dining area. A meal costs about $2.

Tropinini, Calle 5ta Avenida no. 49213 e/ 492 y 494. Excellent *paladar* open till 2am. Breakfast is a wholesome combination of eggs, toast and fruit juice, while lunch and dinner consist of well-prepared pork, chicken or spaghetti served with fried green bananas and salad for $5–6. Easily the best choice in the area.

Playa Jibacoa

Forty kilometres east from the Playas del Este, tucked behind a barricade of white cliffs, is **Playa Jibacoa**, a stretch of coastline basking in the relative anonymity it enjoys as a neighbour of the more popular, more developed beaches closer to Havana. Approaching from the capital on the Vía Blanca road, the first turning after the bridge over the Río Jibacoa leads down onto the coastal road which runs the length of this laid-back resort area. Predominantly the domain of Cuban holidaymakers, the beaches, mostly small and unspectacular but pleasantly protected by swathes of twisting trees and bushes, are the best in the province for combining a reasonable standard of sea and sand with quiet seclusion, and the sparsely wooded slopes pressed up against the cliffs which enclose this narrow strip of land cement the appealing sense of privacy. There are modest **coral reefs** offshore and basic snorkelling equipment can be rented at *Villa El Abra* (see below), though for better diving opportunities as well as boat trips and fishing facilities, you're better off heading 12km further east to the nautical centre at Puerto Escondido.

There are *campismo* sites all along the shoreline, many quite scrappy, reserved for Cubans and closed throughout the winter months; an exception is spacious and sociable *Villa El Abra* (☎692/8-33-44; ②), which has rather squat cabins, most without TV or air conditioning, but otherwise good facilities, including a huge swimming pool and a tennis court. The one complex in the immediate vicinity aimed at the international market and open all year is *Villa Loma* (☎692/8-33-16; ③), overlooking one of the widest sections of beach, at the mouth of the river, within sight of the bridge. Peering over the water's edge from a grassy platform, this twelve-house site is simple rather than basic with a charming little restaurant, a pool and a fantastic stone watchtower bar. In between these two places there's the *Discoteca Jibacoa* (Fri–Sun 2pm–2am; $1), a small **disco** attracting Cubans and foreign visitors, best visited on a Saturday night.

Canasí

Around 10km east of Playa Jibacoa, high upon a cliff-like precipice across the narrow Arroyo Bermejo estuary, the tiny hamlet of **CANASÍ** is the informal weekend campsite of a hippie-chic crowd of young Habaneros. In the summer, scores of revellers descend every

Friday to set up camp in the tranquil woodland around the cliff's edge, spending the weekend swimming and snorkelling in the clear Atlantic waters, exploring the woods and nearby caves, singing folk songs and generally communing with nature. It's a refreshingly uncontrived experience with a peace-festival kind of atmosphere. There are no facilities, so you'll have to take everything you need, most importantly fresh water, but don't worry too much if you don't have a tent as the summer nights are warm enough for you to bed down beneath the stars.

Regular visitors take the late-night **Hershey train** from Casablanca to Canasí on Friday night; this is not the most reliable form of transport, though, and you might be better off driving. The road down to the water's edge is badly signposted but look for a turning left off the Vía Blanca (a 5min walk from the station) and take the dirt track to the estuary mouth, where the fishermen who live in the waterside cottages will row you across the shallow waters to the site for about $2 a head, though the hardy can wade.

The inhabitants of the waterside houses may let you draw water from their standpipe but you will need to sterilize this water before drinking it.

Escaleras de Jaruco

Further inland, the **Escaleras de Jaruco**, a small crop of hills west of Jaruco, the nearest town of any significant size, make a stimulating detour on the way to or from the beaches, though only feasible with your own transport. There are lonely roads from any of the beach resorts east of Havana to **Jaruco**, the best place from which to venture into the hills. The dramatic change in the landscape is the first surprise as a steep-sided mini-mountain range covered in a kind of subtropical rainforest erupts from the surrounding flatlands, a terrain seemingly transplanted from a faraway land. Approaching from Jaruco, the lonely worn-out road which cuts through like a mountain pass leads directly up to the second surprise, a **restaurant**, *El Arabe* (no phone), here in the middle of nowhere. In its heyday, prior to the revolution, it was undoubtedly a classic, with its splendid Arabic-style interior and domed tower, but is now as low on food as it is on staff, and there's no guarantee it will be open when you turn up. Nonetheless it provides a focus for the area, and you can park up and stroll onto its superbly placed balcony terrace to enjoy views that stretch all the way to the northern coastline, taking in a vast tract of land occupied by tens of thousands of palms, like a huge army surrounding the hills.

Two minutes' drive up the road, at around about the hills' highest point, is the *Hotel Escaleras de Jaruco* (☎64/3-19-25; ②) – rundown and low on facilities but with water still in the reasonably sized pool. As with the restaurant, the location makes all the difference and in the unlikely event that you decide to spend the night here, waking up to the magnificent views will more than compensate for the dull and poorly equipped rooms. Exploring this area further is a hit-and-miss affair, with nothing officially marked out but tracks leading into the thick forest where there are ample opportunities for getting lost.

South of Havana

The airport road, the **Avenida de Rancho Boyeros**, is the least complicated route to most of the day-trip destinations in southern Havana. It makes sense to visit at least a couple of these on the same day, as seeing each one on its own is unlikely to last more than a few hours. A perfect preservation of the great writer's home in Havana, the **Museo Ernest Hemingway**, nearer the Vía Blanca than the road to the airport, is the most concrete option and one of the few that stands up well by itself; the views across Havana alone are enough to justify the trip. The relative proximity of **Parque Lenin**, an immense half-city, half-country park next door to the **zoo**, to the sprawling **Jardín Botánico**, over the road from **ExpoCuba**, makes these a convenient combination for anyone looking for a reasonable variety of experience. A few kilometres further south, beyond the airport, the town of **Santiago de las Vegas** and the nearby **Santuario de San Lázaro** make good stopping-off points on the way to **San Antonio de los Baños**, 15km further south, which, with its unique Museo de Humor, is the most visitable town in the province, its picturesquely set hotel making it worth spending more than a day there.

Museo Ernest Hemingway

Eleven kilometres southeast of Habana Vieja, in the suburb of San Francisco de Paula, is **La Vigía**, an attractive little estate centered around the whitewashed nineteenth-century villa where Ernest Hemingway lived for twenty years until 1960. Now the **Museo Ernest Hemingway** (Wed–Sat 9am–4pm, Sun 9am–noon; $3), it makes a simple but enjoyable excursion from the city. On top of a hill and with splendid views over Havana, this single-storey colonial residence, where Hemingway wrote a number of his most famous novels, has been preserved almost exactly as he left it – with drinks and magazines strewn about the place and the dining-room table set for guests. Brimming with character, it's a remarkable insight into the writer's lifestyle and personality, from the numerous stuffed animal heads on the walls to the thousands of books lining the shelves in most of the rooms, including the bathroom. The small room where his typewriter is still stationed was where Hemingway did much of his work, often in the mornings and usually standing up. Frustratingly, you can't walk into the rooms but must view everything through the open windows and doors, but by walking around the encircling verandah you can get good views of most rooms. In the well-kept gardens, which you can walk round, Hemingway's fishing boat is suspended inside a wooden pavilion and you can visit the graves of four of his dogs, next to the swimming pool.

The museum closes when it rains to protect the interior from the damp and to preserve the well-groomed grounds, so time your visit to coincide with sunshine. To **get there**, take the Vía Blanca through the southern part of the city and turn off at the Carretera Central, which cuts through San Francisco de Paula. Alternatively you can brave the M-7 *camello* from the Parque de la Fraternidad and walk from the bus stop.

Parque Lenin and Parque Zoológico Nacional

A train trundles around the park at weekends and every day in July and August. It can be picked up at various stopping points around the park on its hourly tours and costs $2.

Roughly a twenty-minute drive south of the city, about 3km west of the José Martí airport, are the immense grounds of **Parque Lenin** (Wed–Sun 10am–6pm; free). Founded in 1972, this was once a popular escape for city residents who came here, out of earshot of the roads, to lunch in the shade of the trees, ride horseback around the park and unwind through simple pleasures, like boating and fairground rides, in beautifully kept surroundings. However, the deterioration in public transport since the Special Period has led to a sharp drop in visitors, and a pervasive air of abandon blows around the now-empty park, with many of its former attractions lying desolate. Nonetheless, its sheer size, almost eight square kilometres, and scenic landscape make it a great place for a picnic or just a breath of fresh air.

Parque Lenin is currently only reachable by car. To get there, head towards the airport from the city on Avenida Rancho Boyeros, and turn left onto Avenida San Francisco, which, within 5km, leads to the park's main entrance, marked by a large billboard. You can drive right into and around the park, though a more exciting way to explore is on **horseback**; Club Hípico and Escuela de Equitación, both at the northern end of the park, along the first road on the right after the entrance, rent out horses for $3 an hour, though it's not guaranteed they'll have anything available. Also in this area is a now motionless little amusement park, while the sweeping, dried-out lawns and abundant trees in this section make it a good option for a wander about. For more concrete things to do, head for the southern part of the park, where you can take a **boat** out on the large **lake**; peruse the paintings, predominantly the work of the Cuban Amelia Peláez (1896–1968), at the **Galería de Arte** (10am–4pm; $1); visit the freshwater fish, turtles and crocodiles at the **aquarium** (10am–4pm; $1); or just admire the park's most famous monument, the nine-metre marble **bust of Lenin**. Also in this section are the park's swimming pools and rodeo, all, unfortunately, closed for the foreseeable future.

Until the various cafés dotted about the place crank back into life, **eating** options in Parque Lenin are limited to *Las Ruinas*, a hulk of a restaurant beyond the lake, built amongst some ruined, moss-covered walls around the entrance to the building. It specializes in expensive seafood, though with more reasonably priced spaghetti, pizza and *comida criolla*, and is more refined than you might expect from the outside, overlooking a tree-lined lawn and decked out with chandeliers and old dressers. There's also a piano **bar** downstairs.

Parque Zoológico Nacional

South of
Havana

Just over a kilometre west is the **Parque Zoológico Nacional** (July &
Aug Wed–Sun 9am–4.30pm; Sept–June Wed–Sun 9am–3.15pm; $3
adults, $2 children, $5 car, including passengers), a perpetually half-
finished safari park. The spacious three-and-a-half-square-kilometre
site, which includes a small lake, has a suitably natural feel and the
two enclosures which have been completed do allow good views of
the animals. Herbivores of the African savannah, including elephants, rhinos, giraffes and zebras, roam about in the **Pradera
Africana** enclosure whilst the **Foso de Leones**, a huge grass- and
tree-lined pit, allows excitingly close contact with the park's twenty
or so lions. However, the majority of the animals, mostly big cats and
apes, are kept in cramped conditions in the so-called **Area de
Reproducción**. The park suffered severe setbacks as a result of
Cuba's economic crisis in the early 1990s and is clawing its way back
to respectability at a relatively slow pace.

If you don't have your own car, **buses** leave from just inside the
main entrance every thirty minutes or so on tours of the park; they
include guides, but don't count on an English speaker.

Jardín Botánico Nacional and ExpoCuba

Three kilometres south of the entrance to Parque Lenin, along the
Carretera del Rocío, is the entrance to the **Jardín Botánico Nacional**
(Wed–Sun 8.30am–4.30pm; US60¢, $3 for guided tour), a sweeping
expanse of parkland that's a showcase for a massive variety of plants
and particularly trees from around the world.

Laid out as a savannah rather than a forest, the grounds are split
into sections according to continent, with the different zones blending
almost seamlessly into one another. Highlights include the collection
of 162 surprisingly varied species of **palm** from around the world, and
the picture-perfect **Japanese Garden**, donated by the Japanese government in 1989 on the thirtieth anniversary of the revolution – a
compact, colourful and meticulously landscaped area built around a
beautiful little lake and backing onto rocky terraced waterfalls and
fountains. The Japanese Garden is also the best place to stop for
lunch, in *El Bambú* (1–3.30pm), where $10 lets you eat your fill of a
tasty vegetarian buffet. Near the main entrance are the captivating
indoor **Pabellones de Exposiciones**, two large greenhouse-style
buildings with raised viewing platforms and twisting pathways, one
housing a fantastic collection of cacti, the other a landscaped jungle
of tropical plants and flowers.

Though you can explore the park yourself, a lack of printed literature and plaques means you'll learn far more by taking the **guided
tour**, whether in the tractor-bus or having a guide in your own car, at
no extra cost. The guides are impressively knowledgeable and make
the whole experience interactive; as well as teaching about the origins of the various species and their various medicinal uses, they let

*Mondays and
Tuesdays are
reserved for
prepaid orga-
nized excur-
sions which
can be
arranged
through Tour
y Travel on
Calle 23
(☎33-40-82
or 83) or
Fantástico on
Calle 146
(☎33-98-84,
33-99-20 or
33-60-44), both
in Havana.*

South of
Havana

*It's worth
reserving a
place at* El
Bambú *at the
ticket booth at
the entrance,
especially if
the park is
very busy or
very empty.*

you stop within reaching distance of trees to pick and eat cherries or smell leaves. There's usually at least one English-speaking guide available, but it's worth noting that the tractor-bus tours, which generally last from one to two hours, do not necessarily cover the whole park. Tours leave every hour or so from just inside the main entrance, near the useful **information office**. There's also a small **shop** selling ornamental plants; at weekends a bus takes passengers from here directly to the Japanese Garden (every 30min; $1).

ExpoCuba

On the other side of the road, directly opposite the gardens, what looks like a well-kept industrial estate is in fact **ExpoCuba** (Wed–Sun 9am–5pm; $1), a permanent exhibition of the island's achievements in industry, science, technology and commerce since the revolution. A series of huge pavilions, each showcasing a different area of achievement, it's impressively wide-ranging – with exhibits ranging from an entire aeroplane to a bottle of brake liquid – but only really manageable if you don't try to see everything; if you've come with a specific interest in, say, the Cuban health system or the sugar industry, you'll find plenty to occupy you in those areas alone. Despite its scope, displays are a little dry and the hordes of children here on school trips tend to be more interested in running about the place, riding on the mini-roller coaster (50¢) and boating on the small lake ($1). There's a fish **restaurant** by the lake and various cafeterias, including the *Bar Mirador*, a circular **revolving café** balanced on top of two giant concrete stilts from where you get an excellent perspective on the layout of ExpoCuba and views across to the Jardín Botánico.

*See p.46 for
details of
festivals and
events
throughout
Cuba.*

For one week every year, usually the first week in November, ExpoCuba hosts the **Feria Internacional de la Habana** (information from Hector Díaz on ☎21-07-58). This is by far the best time to visit as manufacturers from around the world come to exhibit their wares and promote their name, creating a livelier atmosphere and a more exciting range of exhibits. There are fashion shows, music concerts and all kinds of goods on display as well as a pitch for many of the most famous restaurants in the capital.

The Santuario de San Lázaro and Santiago de las Vegas

Ten kilometres south of central Havana, the **Santuario de San Lázaro** (daily 7am–6pm), on the edge of the tiny village of **EL RINCÓN**, is the final destination of a pilgrimage made by thousands of Cubans every December. Amidst scenes of intense religious fervour, they come to ask favours of San Lázaro, whose image appears inside the gleaming, lovingly maintained church, in exchange for sacrifices (see box opposite). Whatever the month, though, people drive here to cut deals with the saint and lay down flowers or make

> **El Día de San Lázaro**
>
> On December 17 the road between Santiago de las Vegas and El Rincón is
> closed as hordes of people from all over Cuba come to ask favours of San
> Lázaro in exchange for a sacrifice, or to keep promises they have already
> made to the saint. Some have walked for days, timing their pilgrimage so
> that they arrive on the 17th, but the common starting point is Santiago de
> las Vegas, 2km down the road. The most fervent of believers make their
> journey as arduous as possible, determined that in order to earn the favour
> they have asked for they must first prove their own willingness to suffer.
> In the past people have tied rocks to their limbs and dragged themselves
> along the concrete road to the church, others have walked barefoot from
> much further afield, whilst others bring material sacrifices, often money,
> as their part of the bargain.

a donation, and the road through the village is always lined with
people selling flowers and statuettes. Sitting peacefully in the
grounds of an old hospital, the building itself is striking only for its
immaculately kept simplicity, though there are several fine altars
inside, and the open doors and shutters let in the birds and sunlight.
San Lázaro stands in the main altar, which is made of wood with a
gold and marble finish, and also features, looking totally different,
in a squatter marble altar off to the side. These two distinctly separate images of the same saint are the result of an on-going muddling
of the real San Lázaro with what is essentially an imposter. The
character with crutches and a dog usually evoked by Cuban worshippers is in fact the subject of one of Jesus's parables and not the
saint officially recognized by the Catholic Church.

En route to the church, it's well worth calling in at **SANTIAGO
DE LAS VEGAS**, 2km south of José Martí airport. Half-provincial
town, half-city suburb, it doesn't offer a lot to do besides wander
aimlessly around the dusty streets and attractive central square, but
it's a pleasantly relaxing place to get a feel for Cuba beyond the big
city, entirely untouched by tourism. Avenida 409, leading off the
square, is full of peso snack-sellers, and with a *casa de cambio* on
the same street there's no excuse for not testing the local fast-food.
The M-2 *camello* from the Parque de la Fraternidad in Habana Vieja
drops you off on the square. El Rincón is a couple of kilometres
south of the town on the Carretera Santiago de las Vegas, the main
road running through it.

San Antonio de los Baños

Of all the small towns in Havana province, **SAN ANTONIO DE LOS
BAÑOS**, a 45-minute drive from Habana Vieja, about 20km due
south of Playa, is the only one with the right ingredients to make
more than a fleeting visit rewarding. This is due in no small part to
the appeal of *Las Yagrumas* (☎650/33-52-38, fax 33-50-11; ⑥),
a beautifully set family-oriented hotel just north of the town.

*The price per
person per
hour for
renting
rowing boats
and pedalos is
$1 and for
motor boats
it's $3.*

Refreshingly, there are always large numbers of Cubans staying here, most of them on the reward schemes offered to employees of the state. Set in their own private piece of countryside and based around a large pool, the palm-fringed grounds slope down to a bend in the Río Ariguanabo where you can rent rowing boats, motor boats and pedalos. Other activities include organized excursions, nature trails and a full programme of night-time entertainment.

The town itself, a minute's drive from the hotel, has the undisturbed nonchalant feel that characterizes so much of the Cuban interior. Unlike most places of this size, however, it boasts a novel little museum, one that for once is not a formulaic, Spanish-only plod through local history. Based in a colonial home at Calle 60 e/ 41 y 45, the excellent, seven-room **Museo de Humor** (Tues–Sun 10am–6pm; $2), founded in 1979, has a small permanent exhibition charting the history of graphic humour in Cuba. Though nothing is placed within any historical context, the museum illuminates the tradition of political satire in Cuban newspaper art, with one or two anti-Spanish cartoons from the last century, anti-imperialist drawings and some Punch-style creations. The museum also hosts a number of international competitions of comic art, easily the best time to visit. The most prestigious of these, the Evento de Humor y Sátira and the Bienal Internacional del Humor, take place in alternate years every March or April. Both follow similar lines, with entries drawn from a large number of countries, falling under categories such as political humour, caricatures, photography and comic strips. The standard is usually very high, and the best entries are displayed throughout the museum for the weeks surrounding the events. Also worth catching is the Evento de Caricatura Personal Juan David every September, a national competition attracting the best caricaturists in the country.

A few blocks away the relatively diverse collection in the modest **Museo de Historia** (Tues–Sat 10am–6pm, Sun 9am–1pm; $1), at Calle 66 e/ 41 y 45, includes some great photographs of local bands during the 1920s and 1930s as well as a room of colonial furniture. For **refreshment** there's a branch of the fast-food chain *El Rápido* on Calle 68, but for more atmosphere and an attractive setting follow Calle 68 uphill to its conclusion on the edge of town where a right turn leads to *La Quintica*, a simple peso **restaurant** leaning over a river, serving standard *comida criolla*. The stagnant waters and tree-lined banks of the river lend this spot a delightfully relaxing ambience which is occasionally shattered by music blared out from the restaurant itself.

West of Havana

Driving west through Miramar and the western suburbs is one of the more pleasant drives in the whole city and enough reason in itself to come out this way. The other appealing aspect of a drive out this way is the straightforwardness of the route. To get from Miramar to the only beach resort on the west side of Havana, **Playa El Salado**, the first turn you'll make will be down to the beach itself.

Playa El Salado

Fifteen kilometres west of the capital, straight along Avenida 5ta from Miramar, the province's only coastal resort of any significance is **Playa El Salado**, five minutes' drive beyond the lazy seafront hamlet of Baracoa. It's an unspectacular place with a rocky beach and an eyesore of a gutted restaurant, but its big attraction is the 1200-metre **go-cart track** (Mon–Sat 9am–5pm; $5 for 10min, $25 for an hour), one of only several in the whole country and a rare recreational facility so near to the city. There are competitions most Sundays, when local carters do battle, but all-comers are welcome the rest of the week. You're more likely to have someone to race against in the afternoons but don't come expecting to see a great spectacle – the fun here lies in taking part, not watching.

Go-carters must be sixteen or older.

A gently flowing river divides the go-cart track from *Villa Cocomar* (☎ 7/80-50-89 or 80-53-89, fax 80-50-89; ④), a spacious if slightly exposed cabin complex on the shore, struggling to attract tourists more interested in the sandier beaches and better facilities of the Playas del Este. Nevertheless, it's well suited to an uncomplicated overnight break and boasts a thirty-metre pool, tennis court and disco.

West along the Carretera Central

Most people travelling through this western half of Havana province are on their way to the more dramatic scenery of Pinar del Río. The buses speed along the four-lane *autopista* but for a closer look at rural provincial Cuba at a more relaxed pace head along the **Carretera Central**. The going is mostly flat, cutting through sugar cane territory and pleasant croplands with occasional glimpses of the south coast. The small towns along this animated route, principally Bauta, Guanajay and Artemisa, are all much of a muchness, with enough of interest in each to keep you occupied for a fifteen-minute leg-stretching break. The one detour worth making before crossing the provincial border is to the **Antiguo Cafetal Angerona**, 6km west of Artemisa, a nineteenth-century coffee plantation where 750,000 coffee plants once grew. Here you'll find the ruins of the Neoclassical mansion, where the owners lived alongside the slave quarters, and a ten-metre high watchtower. Occasionally a tour group will stop by for a look but you're more likely to be the only visitor, and with no formal visiting arrangements there's nothing to stop you taking a wander about.

Travel details

There are no Astro or Víazul buses from Havana to any of the worthwhile destinations around the outskirts of the city or in Havana province, and getting about without your own transport or a taxi involves either hitching lifts or chancing it with the local buses. The local buses listed overleaf do not follow any regular timetables and are particularly susceptible to delay, cancellation, route changes and desperate overcrowding. The Hershey train which leaves from Casablanca does stop at some dead-end places en-route to Matanzas and can take you within a few kilometres of Playa Jibacoa, but generally speaking trains leaving Havana don't stop until they reach one of the neighbouring provinces.

LOCAL BUSES

Havana to: Cojímar (every 20min; 40min); Guanabacoa (every 40min; 50min); Habana del Este (every 20min; 10min); Playas del Este (4 daily; 1hr); San Antonio de los Baños (2 daily; 1hr 30min); San Francisco de Paula (every 40mn; 1hr 30min); Santiago de las Vegas (every 40min; 1hr).

VÍAZUL BUSES

Havana to: Bayamo (2 weekly; 13hr); Camagüey (2 weekly; 8hr 15min); Ciego de Ávila (2 weekly; 7hr); Cienfuegos (daily; 3hr 45min); Holguín (2 weekly; 11hr 30min); Las Tunas (2 weekly; 10hr); Península de Zapata (6 weekly; 3hr); Pinar del Río (3 weekly; 2hr 30min); Sancti Spíritus (2 weekly; 6hr); Santa Clara (2 weekly; 4hr 30min); Santiago de Cuba (2 weekly; 16hr); Trinidad (daily; 5hr 30min); Varadero (3 daily; 2hr 45min); Viñales (3 weekly; 3hr 15min).

TRAINS

Havana to: Pinar del Río (3 weekly; 5hr 30min); Santiago de Cuba (daily; 14hr).

FERRY

Havana to: Casablanca (every 30min; 10min).

DOMESTIC FLIGHTS

Havana to: Baracoa (3 weekly; 2hr 45min); Camagüey (9 weekly; 1hr 30min); Holguín (7 weekly; 1hr 30min–2hr 50min); Nueva Gerona (2 daily; 40min); Santiago de Cuba (2 daily; 1hr 35min–2hr 30min); Varadero (6 weekly; 30min).

Chapter 2

Pinar del Río

Despite its relative proximity to Havana, life in the province of **PINAR DEL RÍO** is a far cry from the noise, pollution and hustle of the capital. Butt of a string of national jokes, native Pinareños are caricatured as the island's most backward country folk, a reputation that fits in with the slower, more relaxed feel to the region. There's a distinctly provincial feel to its towns and even to its laid-back capital, **Pinar del Río**, whose appeal lies less within the city itself and more in its location at the centre of the province's other attractions. Most of the highlights are well away from the population centres, the majority situated in and around the green slopes of the **Cordillera de Guaniganico**, the mountain range that runs like a backbone down the length of this narrow province, invitingly visible from the *autopista* running alongside.

Hidden within the relatively compact **Sierra del Rosario**, the eastern section of the *cordillera*, the peaceful, self-contained mountain retreats of **Las Terrazas** and **Soroa** provide perfect opportunities to explore the tree-clad hillsides and valleys. Both are set up as centres for **ecotourism**, though of the two Las Terrazas offers the chance to get a little bit closer to the local community.

Heading west along the *autopista* there are options to the north and south but it's unlikely you'll want to make much more than a fleeting visit to any of them. That is, unless you are a hunting enthusiast – in which case you should head for the **Maspotón** reserve – or in search of the type of healing afforded by the springs at **San Diego de los Baños**. Though the area around this small village is host to a large landscaped park and a set of caves of both geological and historical interest, their considerable potential is lost to neglect and isolation.

Most visitors to the province bypass the above altogether and head straight for what is justifiably the most touted location in Pinar del Río, the **Viñales valley**, whose unusual **flat-topped mountains** or *mogotes*, unique in Cuba, are worth the trip alone. Whilst heavily visited, Viñales remains unspoilt and blessed with some of the best hotels in Cuba. The valley provides a well balanced set of attractions, including the ambiguously named and slightly tacky **Mural de la**

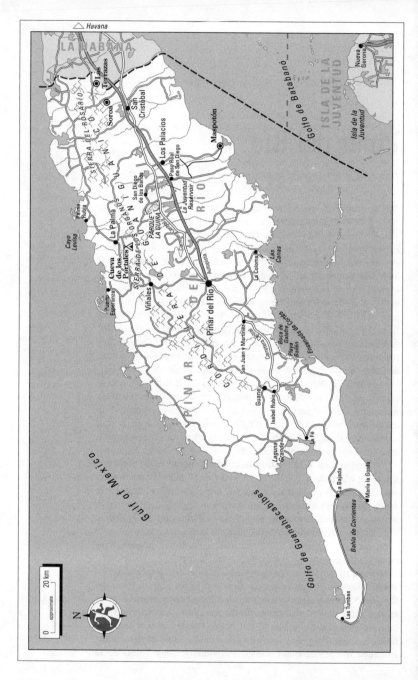

Accommodation price codes

All accommodation listed in this guide has been graded according to the following price categories.

① peso hotel equivalent to $5 or less   ④ $30–50   ⑦ $100–150
② $5–20   ⑤ $50–70   ⑧ $150–200
③ $20–30   ⑥ $70–100   ⑨ $200 and above

Rates are for the cheapest available double or twin room during high season, usually May–September and the last two weeks of December. During low season some hotels lower their prices by roughly ten percent.

Prehistoria; the reconstructed refuge of a group of runaway slaves at **El Palenque de los Cimarrones**; and a brief but worthwhile boat excursion in the **Cueva del Indio**. Easily visited on a day-trip from Havana, there is enough to see away from Viñales's official sites to satisfy you if you're planning a longer, more adventurous stay.

You'd need to be pretty determined in order to reach the country's westernmost locations; which are beyond the provincial capital and more or less out of reach unless you can rent a car. You won't find the **beaches** of **Playa Bailén** and **Boca de Galafre** on any postcards, though they should be enough to stave off any withdrawal symptoms that beach bums might be feeling this far down the province. The small tourist site at **Laguna Grande** serves as little more than a less-than-convenient stopover if you want to break the journey to the only really worthwhile – but still underdeveloped – tourist centre on the western tip, **Maria la Gorda**, whose crystal-clear waters rival any in Cuba and whose scuba diving is second to none.

Getting around

The most direct and convenient way, other than renting a car, to get to most of what's worth seeing in Pinar del Río is in a **private taxi**. Right next to the Astro bus station in Havana there's always a line of private cars waiting to take people to the neighbouring provinces, in particular Pinar del Río. Drivers usually expect around $25 to take foreign tourists as far as the provincial capital, but negotiating a cheaper price is not out of the question.

As with much of Cuba, relying on **public transport** in Pinar del Río is a hazardous, patience-testing business. Much of the province is quite simply out of range of any of the public services, which, where they do exist, are more often than not extremely unreliable. Luckily Víazul provide a **bus** from Havana to the provincial capital and then on to Viñales every other day, whilst there are daily Astro buses following the same route. Very few tourists ever take the **train** into Pinar del Río. The service is notoriously slow and other than the provincial capital itself the towns which it stops in are at least a few kilometres from anywhere worth visiting. It is, however, the closest you'll get to Soroa or Las Terrazas on public transport, though you'll need to hitch a lift from San Cristóbal, around 15km away, where the train drops you off, or try and find a private taxi – a scarcity around here.

Most drivers speed their way down the centre of the province on the **autopista**, which comes to an end at the provincial capital. Running roughly parallel to the north, the **Carretera Central** is a slower option, which takes you closer to the mountains and gives better views of the surrounding landscape. Once past the city of Pinar del Río, this is the only major road.

Sierra del Rosario

Heading west out of Havana on the *autopista*, the first tourist attractions you'll come to, only just inside the provincial border, are the isolated mountain valley resorts at **Las Terrazas** and **Soroa**. These are by far the best bases from which to explore the densely packed semi-deciduous forest slopes of the protected **Sierra del Rosario**. Both are centres for **ecotourism** designed to coexist harmoniously with their surroundings, in which regard Las Terrazas is the more successful. Soroa is considerably smaller but no less popular than Las Terrazas, as its compact layout makes it more accessible to day-trippers. The sierra was declared a Biosphere Reserve by UNESCO in 1985, and visitors are encouraged to explore their surroundings using official **hiking routes**: there's a comprehensive programme of hikes at Las Terrazas and some gentler but rewarding walks around Soroa. Though sometimes referred to as such, the peaks of the Sierra del Rosario don't quite qualify for mountain status, the highest point reaching just under 700 metres, and although there is some fantastic scenery it's rarely if ever breathtaking.

Las Terrazas

Eight kilometres beyond the turnoff at Km 51 of the *autopista* is **LAS TERRAZAS**, a wonderfully harmonious tourist resort and small community forming the premier **ecotourism site** in the province and one of the most important in the country. The motorway suddenly seems a long way behind as the turnoff road takes you into thickly wooded landscape and up to a junction where, after a left turn, you'll reach a **toll booth**. Tourists are often waved on without a charge, but you should be prepared to pay the $3 toll to drive into the resort. About 2km beyond the toll booth, a few hundred metres past a left-hand turn onto a side road, beautifully woven into the grassy slopes of a valley leading down to a lake, is a well-spaced complex of red-tile-roofed bungalows and apartment blocks. The housing is perched on terraced slopes which dip steeply down into the centre of the community, forming a smaller, more compact, trench-like valley within the valley-settlement itself. Though the cabins might look as if they're meant for visitors, they belong to the resident population, who number around a thousand and have lived here since the foundation of the community in 1971, as part of a government-funded conservation and reforestation project covering some 50 square kilometres of the Sierra del Rosario. The residents were encouraged to play an active role in the preservation and care of the local environment, and Las Terrazas was built as a kind of model settlement. The spirit of conservation persists and research into the area's ecosystems, studies of animal habitat and behaviour and related projects continue at the **Centro de Investigaciones Ecológicas**, set back from the road between the toll booth and the resort; guided tours of the centre can be arranged either at the administration offices or through the hotel.

Today a large proportion of the locals work in tourism, either directly or indirectly, many as employees at *Moka* (☎ & fax 7/33-55-16; ⑤, lakeside cabin ⑦), a **hotel** that's well worth a visit whether or not you intend to stay the night. Looking over the community from the wooded hillside that forms one of its borders, in the shadow of the Loma del Salón, one of the highest peaks around Las Terrazas, the hotel is hidden from view behind the trees and the main building, which tastefully combines a modern design with colonial style. The hotel fits in with its surroundings so perfectly, it seems to have been built around the trees, and indeed in some instances they penetrate the floor and ceiling of the building itself. This effect is best appreciated in the reception area, where the trunk and branches of one of the larger trees has been stunningly accommodated into the architecture. There's an adjoining bar and moderately priced restaurant with a variety of mostly meat-dominated dishes, whilst the swimming pool and tennis court area, set further back, provide the only open spaces within the complex. If you prefer to be amongst the locals and don't mind having to walk a bit further to use the hotel's facilities, you can also stay in a cabin down by the lake.

Several sets of steps lead from the hotel down the slopes into the local community, where there are a number of small, low-key **workshops** set up inside some of the apartment block buildings. Local artists churn out pottery, silkscreen prints, paintings and other works, which you can buy or simply watch being produced, though you can't help feeling that you're seeing something set up specifically for tourists. Also on this side of the village complex is the *Fondita de Mercedes*, a restaurant-cum-*paladar* on a balcony overlooking the community, serving tasty Cuban cuisine at cheaper prices than those in the hotel.

On the other side of the trench-like divide which separates the two halves of the village is the **Plaza Comunal**, with benches, trees and modest views of the lake and valley. It's a focal point for local residents, and gets quite sociable in the evening. In the three-storey building on one side of the plaza is the small but neat and concise **Museo**

Comunitario (daily except Wed 8am–1pm; $1), where photographs and documents offer further insights into Las Terrazas' brief but interesting history, including the pre-Columbian and colonial eras. If you're planning to do some hiking you should pick up any **picnic** supplies in the small Tienda Panamericana supermarket, in the same building, but don't expect much choice. There's a good chance that neither the shop nor the museum will be open on a Monday. Over on the other side of the village is a basic rodeo pen which occasionally comes into use, usually when a large tour group is staying at the hotel.

Hiking at Las Terrazas

Day-trips to Las Terrazas, which include a full programme of hiking and lunch, can be booked through Cubatur (☎ 7/33-41-35) or Tour y Travel (☎ 7/33-40-82) in Havana.

There are six official **hiking routes** around Las Terrazas, none more than 6km in length and each characterized by a different destination of historical or ecological interest (see box below). There is no better way to experience the diversity of the Sierra del Rosario than along these routes, which collectively offer the most comprehensive insight available into the region's topography, history, flora and fauna. Whilst you are free to follow the trails independently, some are not clearly marked and none is signposted, and though basic maps are available, it's quite easy to wander astray. It's generally better to hire a **guide** from the administra-

---

Hiking routes

Ruta del Cafetal Buenavista (2.5km). The route follows a trail barely distinguishable amid the dense foliage on one of the more back-breaking hikes. There are occasional views of the complex below on the way up to the coffee plantation (see opposite).

Ruta del Río San Juan (3km). The only hike starting in Las Terrazas itself, the route begins at the rodeo pen, descends into the valley between two of the local peaks and joins the Río San Juan. It passes the ruins of another of the area's old coffee plantations, La Victoria, as well as fresh and sulphurous water springs, and finishes up at the Baños del San Juan, a beautiful little set of pools and cascades where you can bathe.

Ruta de la Canada del Infierno (3km). On the road to Soroa, 6km from Las Terrazas, a dirt track next to the bridge over Río Bayate follows the river into the dense forest. Passing first the dilapidated San Pedro coffee plantation, it arrives at the Santa Catalina plantation ruins, a peaceful spot where you can take a dip in the natural pools.

Sendero Las Delicias (3km). This route starts on the same course as the Cafetal Buenavista trail, but bypasses the turn for the coffee plantation and continues up to a *mirador* at the summit of the Loma Las Delicias, for some magnificent panoramic views.

Sendero La Serafina (5km). This trail through rich and varied forest is the best route for bird-watching and much enhanced by going with a guide who'll be able to point out to you the red, white and blue tocororo, the endemic catacuba and the enchanting Cuban nightingale amongst the 73 species which inhabit the sierra.

Sendero El Taburete (1.5km). More of a stroll than a hike, the simplest of the six routes starts just off the main road and runs through the forest up gentle slopes before circling back round.

---

tion centre, as you'll learn a lot more and won't get lost. The several buildings that make up the small complex, which also acts as an **information centre**, where you can pick up a map, are several hundred metres off the main road cutting through this part of the valley, down a right-hand turn just before the left turn that leads down to the village and hotel. Guides cost between $15 and $40 per person on a prebooked excursion, depending on the size of the group and your specific requirements (see box on p.148). It works out considerably cheaper if you're in a group of six or more; if you call a day or so in advance, you may be able to join another visiting group. However, if you turn up without booking and get lucky you can hire a guide for just $3 per hike, though this may depend on your joining a prebooked group.

Two of the hikes end up at the **Cafetal Buenavista** (daily; noon–4pm), an excellent reconstruction of a nineteenth-century coffee plantation incorporating much of the original site. French immigrants who had fled Haiti following the 1798 revolution established over fifty coffee plantations across the sierra, but this is the only one which has been wholly reconstructed. The stone house has been superbly restored and its high-beamed ceiling now shelters a **restaurant**, the focal point for visitors, whilst the food is cooked in the original kitchen building behind the house. The terraces on which the coffee was dried have also been accurately restored and the remains of the slaves' quarters are complete enough to give you an idea of the incredibly cramped conditions in which the 126 slaves who worked on the plantation would have slept. Visitors are free to take a look around, and there's sometimes someone on hand to answer any questions, in Spanish.

Soroa

Sixteen kilometres southwest from Las Terrazas, the tiny village of **SOROA** nestles in a long narrow valley. It's very cosy, but as access into the hills is limited and the list of attractions brief, Soroa is best for a shorter break rather than a protracted visit. All of the official attractions are based around the **Villa Soroa** (☎85/21-22; ④), a well-kept little complex encircling a swimming pool, its comfortable, modern-looking cabins slightly out of tune with the ecological slant of tourism in the area. The hotel is the best local source of information for any of the sights or available activities, though you need not be a guest to enjoy them. Most of what you'll want to see is within ten minutes' walk of the reception building, but if you've driven up from the *autopista* the first place you'll get to, 100m or so from the hotel resort, is the car park for **El Salto** (daylight hours; $2), a twenty-metre waterfall and one of Soroa's best-known and most publicized attractions. If you've seen any of the official tourist bumph, you'll be disappointed when you reach the unspectacular cascade, especially after the long, winding walk through the woods, though it's worth taking a dip in the water, particularly refreshing if you've just walked from one of the two nearby *miradores* (see pp.150-51).

Ecotourism and the environment

There is a paradox within Cuban attitudes towards environmental issues that is accurately reflected by the leader-comment of an article which featured in a national business newspaper, *Negocios en Cuba*, in March 1999. This article, celebrating the success of a crocodile-breeding scheme on the Península de Zapata in Matanzas, began with the headline "Eliminated from the danger of extinction, the fearsome creature becomes a valuable export".

Like other governments around the world, Cuba has come to realize the benefit of promoting the country as a location for environmentally friendly tourism, and there are now what the Cuban tourist chains have labelled "ecotourism centres" up and down the country, the most prominent at Las Terrazas but also on the Península de Zapata, the Valle de Yumurí, Baconao and Gran Piedra in Santiago. Ecotourism in Cuba, however, fits a loose definition and though conservation projects do exist, in general the concept does not go far beyond building hotels in national parks and offering nature trails and birdwatching. However, there is a twist in this communist country's approach to ecotourism, further clouding the lines between image-driven conservationism and honest defence of the environment. The Cuban state quite simply sees no contradiction, and can thus put crocodile steak on the menu of a restaurant in a breeding farm famed for bringing the animal back from the brink of extinction; or make no attempt at hiding the dumping of industrial waste in the waters around Cuba, as anyone who has had a good look over the wall of the Malecón in Havana or dared to take a dip in the Bay of Cienfuegos will testify, whilst espousing the principles of *ecoturismo*.

Attitudes do appear to be changing slowly and it seems that the economic value of ecotourism to the Cuban state has led to a greater awareness amongst Cubans in general and a wider platform for campaigning naturalists like Antonio Núñez Jiménez, president of the Man and Nature Foundation, to bring environmental issues to public attention. There is a genuine move towards correcting some of the mistakes made in the past, such as the cleaning up of the Bay of Havana, one of the most contaminated in the world, and the careful maintenance of Varadero beach, one of the cleanest you are ever likely to see. There remains, however, a strong sense in Cuba that nature is to be respected not for its own sake but only because, if treated correctly, it can be harnessed to serve the interests of humans. The words of José Martí, perhaps the most revered of all Cuban intellectuals, strike at the heart of the Cuban attitude: "Studying the forces of nature and learning how to control them is the most direct route to solving social problems."

Back at the car park, follow the sign pointing in the direction of the small bridge to **El Mirador**, the most easily accessible point for views of the surrounding landscape. As you cross the bridge, on your right are the **Baños Romanos**, in an unassuming stone cabin, where massages, sulphurous baths and other treatments can be arranged through the hotel (prices from $2). El Mirador is the more challenging of the two climbable hills in the area, a thirty-minute hike scaling an increasingly steep and narrow dirt track, though it's mercifully shady and a set of steps have been installed for the final stretch.

There are a number of possible wrong turns on the way up and the best way to avoid them is simply to follow the track with the horse dung. At the summit you'll find vultures circling the rocky, uneven platform and the most impressive views to be had around Soroa.

El Castillo de las Nubes is the more developed of Soroa's two hilltop viewpoints and the only one you can drive to. The road up to the summit, which you'll have to follow even if walking as there are no obvious trails through the woods, is between the car park for El Salto and the hotel. It shouldn't take you more than twenty minutes on foot to reach the hilltop restaurant, housed in a building resembling a toy fortress with a single turret (the *castillo* – or castle – in question). It's worth stopping for a meal in the **restaurant** (daily 11.30am–4pm), as the views from the tables alongside the windows are fantastic. Alternatively, walk beyond the restaurant to the deserted house at the end of the road from where you can see all the way to the province's southern coastline. This tranquil spot shrouded by trees and bushes, with the abandoned stone house providing an air of mystery, is also a great spot for a picnic.

For the less energetic, horse rides up to El Mirador can be arranged at Villa Soroa *for $3 per person.*

At the foot of the road up to the *castillo* the 35,000 square metres of the well-maintained **Orquideario** (daily 9.30am–3.30pm; $3), a botanical garden specializing in orchids, spread across the slopes. Currently being used for research purposes by the University of Pinar del Río, it was originally constructed by a lawyer and botanist from the Canary Islands named Tomás Felipe Camacho. The obligatory tours are a little rushed, but take in flowers, plants, shrubs and trees from around the globe, including some 700 species of orchid, in grounds radiating out from a central villa, where Camacho lived prior to the Cuban revolution. Though you get the feeling you haven't seen absolutely everything, the tour offers enough to satisfy most people's interest in orchids, and there are sweeping views from the villa's terrace.

There are less well-trodden routes into the hills, though it's generally a case of guesswork as to where to start and you should be careful not to trample the sometimes inconspicuous crops; *Villa Soroa* offers three- to six-hour **guided treks** starting at $6 per person. There are also some slightly shorter muddy trails into the hills at the back of run-down *El Campismo La Caridad* (no phone; ①), 1km north of the tourist complex and the only other **accommodation** option in the area. It's very basic, with cabins containing just a narrow single bed and a bunkbed, a sink with no running water and a toilet which might have to be flushed with a bucket. There's no soap or toilet paper, though fans can be rented for $1.50 a night. To compensate for the lack of comfort, there's a friendly farmyard atmosphere as horses, pigs and goats roam freely about and the helpful staff, all locals, can advise on some of the lesser-known sights and hikes around Soroa. Simple but substantial home-cooked meals are available at *Merendero El Mango* (look out for the homemade sign, just before the turning to the cabins), basically just a room with a table, run by the family of one of the *campismo* staff.

Maspotón, San Diego de los Baños and around

Continuing along the *autopista* towards the provincial capital, about 40km beyond the turning for Soroa are a number of detours, all within a forty-minute drive of the main road. There are no bus routes currently operating to any of these destinations either from Havana or Pinar del Río, and making a day-trip out to any one of them without your own transport will almost certainly prove more hassle than it's worth. It's perfectly possible, however, to spend more than a day at **Maspotón** hunting reserve, though you'll only want to do this if you're here to shoot the birds unfortunate enough to pass through it. It's more likely that you'd actually *want* to spend more than a day in the sleepy town of **San Diego de los Baños**, famous for its health spa, said to be the best in the country. From here it's only a short drive to the area's other two attractions. **Parque La Güira**, although not what it used to be, is still a pleasant place to stop the car and stretch your legs, while slightly further north, the **Cueva de los Portales**, one-time military headquarters of Che Guevara and his army, is a modestly impressive cave cutting a dramatic hole straight through the Loma de los Arcos.

Maspotón

Forty kilometres beyond the turning for Soroa along the *autopista*, spread down to the southern coast of the province, 134 square kilometres of mostly flat, marshy, uninspiring terrain make up the grounds of the **Maspotón** hunting reserve (Oct–March daily). It's a bleak and desolate place whose dirt roads make it feel all the more hostile to the casual visitor and whose empty vistas would convince even the most curious observer that there's very little worth discovering in these southern lowlands. Sightseeing, however, is not what Maspotón is about. Situated close to the migratory routes between North and South America it is particularly rich in **birdlife** between September and February. Especially abundant are long-tail and white-wing doves, quails, guinea-fowl, pheasant and duck. Fresh- and saltwater **fishing** is also possible, with the coast less than 15km to the south and easy access to **La Juventud Reservoir,** north of the *autopista*.

Hunting expeditions leave in the early morning from the reserve's central **hunting club**, the *Coto de Caza Maspotón* (☎8/66-05-81 or 85/59-14; ④/⑤), which also houses the only **accommodation**: eight dull two-room bungalows just comfortable enough to send a weary hunter to sleep. The club has a tired-looking pool, a games room and a restaurant, where the chef will cook anything you catch during the day. Due to its specialist nature, the majority of Maspotón's visitors arrive on prearranged **package trips** which can be booked through either *Villa Soroa* (see p.149) or Horizontes in Havana (☎7/66-05-

81). If you turn up unannounced there may be a spare cabin, but priority is given to prebooked tours. You will have to pay $25 for a hunting licence plus $50 for each hunting session; shotgun rental is $15.

The 10km of unsignposted dirt track leading directly up to the complex should ideally be tackled in a four-wheel-drive vehicle, especially if it's raining. Approaching from Havana turn left at Km 103 on the *autopista* and head south, passing through the small town of Paso Real de San Diego, for 6km until you reach another left turn. Five kilometres beyond the turning you'll reach the dirt track which leads up to the club itself.

San Diego de los Baños

On the other side of the road at the turning for Maspotón is the road leading to the laid-back little town of **SAN DIEGO DE LOS BAÑOS**, on the borders of both the Sierra de los Organos and the Sierra del Rosario, and offering a retreat from the province's more heavily visited tourist locations. The draw for most visitors is the **Balneario San Diego** (Mon–Sat 8am–5pm; ☎8/3-78-12), whose reputation for medicinal powers dates back to 1632, when a slave, forced into isolation because of ill-health, took an afternoon dip in the natural springs here and was instantly cured. Word rapidly spread and the country's infirm began to flock here to be healed. By 1844 a town had been established to provide for the visitors, and eventually a health spa was built to house the healing waters, though this didn't take its current shape until after the revolution. Nowadays most visitors are tourists, or Cubans on a prescribed course of treatment.

The *balneario*, which has fairly basic massage and bathing facilities and is now in need of some modernization, continues to be the sole purpose for the town's existence, used for the treatment of skin disorders, rheumatic diseases, stress, obesity and even bone fractures, as well as for beauty therapy, though its drab, box-like exterior contrasts heavily with a more recent addition: the graceful *Hotel Mirador* (☎ & fax 7/33-54-10; ④) just over the road. Beautifully set in small-scale landscaped gardens, its naturally light and pleasantly furnished rooms and overall tranquillity make it the perfect place to stay while visiting the spa; in fact, many of its guests are here on a treatment-plus-accommodation package deal. Qualified medical specialists based in the hotel work in partnership with staff across the road and can arrange consultations and courses of treatment. When you've had your fill of the waters, you can rent out bikes and motorbikes or arrange hiking and fishing trips into the hundred square kilometres of protected **woodlands** that are just a leisurely stroll away. The only other things worth seeing are a couple of buildings within a stone's throw of the *balneario*, both elegant, neo-colonial Cuban-only hotels. The *Saratoga* is in slight disrepair, though the *Libertad* is well preserved and would make a great place for tourists to stay if they were allowed.

The cost of using the baths for non-hotel guests is $4 for the maximum allowed time of 15 minutes. Medical consultations are $25 whilst mud therapy and Swedish massages are $20 and $25 respectively.

Maspotón, San Diego de los Baños and around

There's not much else to do in town, though you could happily while away a few hours in the cinema, a couple of minutes' walk from the hotel, so long as you're not expecting to see the latest Hollywood blockbuster. The only place you can rely on for a **meal** is the hotel restaurant, offering a selection of fish, meat and basic spaghetti dishes, though you could try your luck at the unadorned front yard *paladar*, *La Sorpresa*, opposite the *Hotel Libertad*, where, during its sporadic working hours, wholesome, good-value *comida criolla* is served.

Parque La Güira

Originally a colonial estate known as Hacienda Cortina, **Parque La Güira** lies 5km west of San Diego de los Baños. Local legend has it that in 1908 the wealthy owner of the estate hired a lawyer, José Manuel Cortina, to take out a lawsuit against his wife, and gave him the property as payment. Once in Cortina's hands he converted it into an area for local recreation, importing truckloads of rock from the local mountains to aid in its construction and turn it into a large landscaped **park**, of the kind usually found in big cities. The medieval-style fortifications marking the entrance are promisingly grand, but the grounds show signs of neglect suffered in recent years. The park's former beauty is obvious, though, with all the hallmarks of a once picture-perfect scene: intricately landscaped gardens, artistic sculptures with limbs missing, winding paths which no longer lead anywhere, a rich and varied plant life starting to think for itself, and the remains of an elegant fortress-like mansion somewhere near the centre. It's far from overgrown, and its nostalgic, lonely charm makes it ideal for a quiet picnic or contemplative wander. Technically, the park extends beyond the landscaped gardens into remoter parts rich in wildlife, but there are no marked routes and unless you're feeling reckless there's nothing much to entice you any further.

If you're coming directly from Havana, leave the *autopista* at the sign for *Hotel Mirador*, follow the road for 12km, then turn left at the end. Once through the fortified arch at the entrance, take the first left turn into the car park. The dismal *Motel Dos Palmas* (no phone; ②) here is the only place to **stay** should you want to spend more time exploring the outer reaches of the park. It has a bar, a cheap but poor-quality restaurant and nine dark but adequate air-conditioned rooms, most of them housed in a long red-brick bungalow thankfully surrounded by greenery; supposedly there's a **disco** here at weekends but don't expect to have to queue to get in. The far more attractive *Villa La Güira* on the far side of the park is for military personnel only. It's near the park's biggest eyesore: the oversized *Restaurant Mirflores*, an ugly semicircular building reminiscent of a school dining hall. Don't rely on the opening times posted outside the doorway leading into the restaurant, which is low on both stock and quality. A quick drink at the empty **bar** is the most you're likely to get out of the place, whose clumsy size is testament to La Güira's long-departed heyday.

Cueva de los Portales

About 16km north of Parque La Guira along a heavily potholed road is the historically significant **Cueva de los Portales**, a gaping corridor through the hillside hidden beyond the lonely *Campismo Los Portales* – and the suitably remote **former headquarters** of Che Guevara and his army during the 32-day Cuban Missile Crisis of October 1962, when it was anticipated that the United States might make a direct attack on the island (see p.472, Contexts). As a result it was declared a national monument in 1987, though this status slightly outweighs its capacity to impress and there are more affecting, complex and accessible cave systems elsewhere in the province. Nevertheless, anyone can drive up and wander in free of charge, and if you're in the area it's well worth thirty minutes of your time. If you're lucky there'll be a guide about who'll offer you a free tour of the complex. Undoubtedly a tip would be appreciated.

From a clearing in the woods a stone path leads into and through a wide open tunnel, the full length of which is visible from outside the high arching entrance. Through the arch, running parallel with the path, is the **Río Caiguanabo**, a tributary of the Río San Diego. Off to the side is the cave itself, a giant chamber adorned with imposing stalactites and stalagmites. It's not unduly fascinating in itself, though there are some intriguing remnants of Guevara's occupation – the stone table where he worked and played chess, an unfinished little breeze-block hut which acted as his office and some stone staircases and paths hewn out of the rock.

Maspotón, San Diego de los Baños and around

The road from La Guira forks at a sign for the now abandoned Los Pinos complex. Take the left-hand fork and look out for the sign pointing to Campismo Los Portales.

Pinar del Río city

Despite its 125,000-strong population **PINAR DEL RÍO** has the feel of a much smaller town, with a pace of life that's slower than in other Cuban cities of similar size and an atmosphere more reminiscent of a residential neighbourhood than a town centre. Though both are common throughout Cuba, the vultures circling overhead are more noticeable and the horse-drawn carriages more at home here than in other cities, with the lush surroundings giving the place a distinctly non-urban feel. It's a good-looking town, too, adorned with palm trees and pines, and with a beautiful mountainous backdrop that's tantalizingly visible from parts of the city.

Though doubtless you'll be offered a box of cigars or a place to stay, the level of harassment is leagues below that of Havana, as despite being the capital of the province, the city is comparatively undeveloped for tourism: none of the international hotel chains is represented here, there are limited nightlife options and the museums could do with a rethink. However, none of this is necessarily a bad thing; this is a relatively undiluted taste of provincial Cuban life and a good opportunity to mix with the local people, with countless *casas particulares*

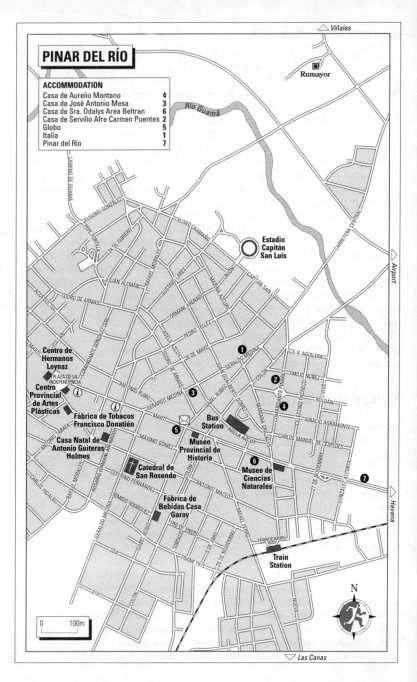

and hotels which cater to both nationals and tourists. Along with the Santiagueros, Pinareños have the reputation of being the most hospitable people in Cuba and there's no better place to test the theory.

You'll need no more than four or five days to get to know the place inside out, and it's an ideal base from which to explore many of the province's other attractions, particularly Viñales, just 25km to the north (see p.164), but also María La Gorda and the beaches Boca de Galafre and Playa Bailén to the south (see pp.172-74). The highlight in the town itself is the **Fábrica de Tobacos Francisco Donatién**, a diminutive cigar factory offering illuminating tours. Also, try to catch the *Cabaret Rumayor*, a taste of classic Cuban entertainment whose extravagance feels somewhat out of place here.

Arrival, orientation and information

Arriving by **bus**, whether Astro or Víazul, you'll be dropped at the Terminal de Omnibus on Adela Azcuy, one block from the city's main street, José Martí. It's within walking distance of most of the hotels and a good number of private rooms; although there are usually plenty of private taxis outside the station, they are usually looking to fill their cars for long-distance journeys.

There's a small **airport** on the northern outskirts of the city where the Russian biplanes operated by Aerotaxi land. There's no straightforward way of getting into the centre from here but the least complicated method is to ring for a **taxi** (Turistaxi ☎82/6-34-81), which should take you to any of the hotels in the centre for less than $5.

The centre itself is easily manageable on foot and it's unlikely you'll stray more than three or four blocks either side of Martí, which serves as a handy north–south division. The centre quickly becomes the outskirts, characterized on the north side by a huge housing estate, which dissolves equally rapidly into rich countryside.

The three **information offices** are all at or off the western end of Martí. The best is **Cubatur** (Mon–Fri 8am–noon & 1–5pm, Sat 8am–noon; ☎82/50-78), less than a block from the main street on Rosario e/ Martí y Máximo Gómez. It usually has maps and glossy but uninformative guides to the province, and can arrange excursions and accommodation. Next door, on the corner of Martí and Rosario, a similar service is available in **Rumbos** (Mon–Fri 9am–5pm, Sat 9am–noon; ☎82/51-33), whilst the information office of the hotel chain **Islazul**, at Martí 127 e/ Rafael Morales y Plaza de la Independencia, handles enquiries about the city's *Hotel Pinar del Río* and *Restaurante Cabaret Rumayor*, plus the *Villa Laguna Grande* (see p.174), the other hotel it operates within the province.

Accommodation

All the **hotels** in the city were built prior to Cuba's launch into international tourism at the start of the 1990s, with the most modern of them, and the only one promoted in official tourist brochures, the

Pinar del Río city

Hotel Pinar del Río, dating from 1978. There are therefore no luxury options and little variety amongst the state-run establishments, but this is compensated for by the plethora of **casas particulares**. Most of them are handily signposted, so finding them shouldn't be a problem. The *Lincoln*, on Máximo Gómez between Rosario and Berardo Medina, the *Vueltabajo* on Rafael Morales between Máximo Gómez and Martí, and *La Marina*, Martí no. 56, are for Cubans only.

Hotels

Hotel Globo, Martí esq. Isabel Rubio ☎82/42-68. Very central hotel that's a little run-down and displays too much concrete, but enjoys a lively atmosphere. Rooms are basic but quite spacious, with balconies looking onto the busy street, and there are good urban views from the third-floor restaurant. ③.

Hotel Italia, Gerardo Medina no. 215 at the junction with Isabel Rubio ☎82/30-49. A homely if somewhat cramped three-storey hotel within easy walking distance of the centre but away from the hustle and bustle. Six rooms are set aside for tourists, of a higher standard than the rest: not all have a TV but most come with a/c and a fridge. ②

Hotel Pinar del Río, end of Martí just before the *autopista* ☎82/50-70 or 50-77. The biggest hotel in the city and the one most used by tourists, this apartment block-style building has plenty of facilities but little style. There's a swimming pool, two restaurants, four bars, a pizzeria, car rental, shops and the best disco in town. Neither slick nor shabby, the hotel interior falls somewhere between the international standards set in Havana and those scraped elsewhere in town. ③

Casas particulares

Casa de Aurelio Montano, Ave. Comandante Pinares no. 106, e/ Roldán y Agramonte ☎82/31-96. Two simply furnished rooms with optional a/c ($5 extra) and hot water, and a messy garden with pleasant patio. Meals are offered for around $6. ②.

Casa de José Antonio Mesa, Gerardo Medina no. 56 altos, e/ Isidro de Armas y Adela Azcuy; ☎82/31-73. The nearest thing to a privately run hotel in Pinar del Río, this pleasantly furnished first-floor apartment is run by an ambitious couple. Three rooms – one with TV and video – plus a separate small apartment for two people; some rooms have a/c but cost $5 extra. There are plans to open a *paladar* and even a tiny nightclub. ②.

Casa de Servilio Afre Carmen Puentes, Ave. Comandante Pinares no. 157, e/ Roldán y Emilio Núñez ☎82/23-09. Of the three rooms available, one has a/c and two face a beautiful shady garden featuring a banana tree, a mango tree and a coffee plant. Meals, which are offered for between $3 and $6, are served on the garden patio. Other facilities include hot water and contacts with local drivers. ②.

Villa Odalys, Martí 158, e/ Comandante Pinares y Calle Nueva ☎82/52-12. A large room at the back of the house with en-suite bathroom, hot water, a/c, fridge and black-and-white TV. Ideal for those seeking privacy whilst also very sociable, with five people living in the house and plenty of young people always about. ②.

The Town

All of Pinar del Río's sights can be covered in a single day if so
desired, but it's a good idea to select just three or four to avoid what
can become a slightly monotonous tour as the town struggles to offer
much in the way of variety. A good starting point is at the top of town
near the summit of the small hill which leads up into suburban Pinar
del Río. Here, on the pint-sized square known as the **Plaza de
Independencia**, is the small **Centro Provincial de Artes Plásticas**
and the unprepossessing **Centro de Hermanos Loynaz**. High on
your list of priorities should be the **Fábrica de Tobacos Francisco
Donatién**, the town's cigar factory, one of the more stimulating
attractions and least like any of the others. The **Fábrica de Bebidas
Casa Garay** is also worth a visit for a look at the production process
behind Pinar del Río's renowned Guayabita rum. The best museums,
though only comparatively, are both on Martí: the **Museo de
Ciencias Naturales** and the **Museo Provincial de Historia**.

Plaza de la Independencia

At the western tip of Martí, the highest part of town, the **Plaza de la
Independencia** is a small square which, were it not surrounded by
roads, would make a relaxing spot for a sit down. As it is, the droop-
ing branches of the resident trees dousing this concrete patch in
shade and even the turquoise-trim concrete bandstand don't do
enough to elevate the square to social centre status.

On Antonio Guiteras, the street forming the plaza's eastern side,
the **Centro Provincial de Artes Plásticas** (Mon–Sat 8am–noon &
1–5pm; 50¢) has temporary exhibitions of sculptures, drawings and
paintings by artists from the province. The exhibitions vary considerably in terms of content, and there's as much chance of seeing
three nameless piles of sticks as the works of any local notables.

On the opposite side of the plaza, hidden away in the corner, is the
Centro de Hermanos Loynaz (Mon–Sat 8.30am–4.30pm; free), a lovingly run four-room museum and study centre dedicated to the four literary Loynaz siblings, all of whom wrote poetry and fiction in the earlier part of the twentieth century and have become prominent figures in
more recent years. Their poetry appears frequently in newspapers and
magazines and the most famous Loynaz, Dulce Maria, author of three
novels of which the best known is *Jardín*, has received numerous
awards, including the prestigious Premio Cervantes de Literatura. A
rather amateurish portrait of her, painted in 1986, now hangs in the
museum, along with display cabinets full of her prizes, a photograph of
her giving a public reading and photos of the rest of the family. It may
not look much like a museum from the outside but it's run and cared for
with more purpose and attention than most of the other museums in the
city, and if you can secure one of the assistants' attention for a few minutes they'll answer questions with knowledge and enthusiasm. More
engaging than the two exhibit rooms is the crowded and cosy library in

the two front rooms, crammed with publications from the 1830s to the present, including some English literature; you can browse at your leisure. One of the gems is an ornately covered version of *Alice's Adventures in Wonderland*.

Fábrica de Tobacos Francisco Donatién

Two blocks from the plaza on Antonio Maceo is the **Fábrica de Tobacos Francisco Donatién** (Mon–Fri 7.30am–noon & 1–4.30pm, Sat 7.30–11.30am; $2), home of Vegueros cigars, a lesser-known brand but well respected amongst connoisseurs. The imposing, high-arched 1859 building with its balustraded rooftop and unadorned queue of supporting columns, which has housed the cigar factory since its inauguration in 1961, belies the cosy atmosphere of the intimate, non-mechanized workshop inside, and the brief guided tour (available in English or French) offers a genuine insight into the care and skill involved in producing some of the world's finest cigars. The *tabaqueros* sit at wooden desks dextrously rolling and cutting the tobacco into shape whilst a *compañero* reads out articles from the national newspaper, *Granma*. The cigars are then passed on to be approved by some of the most experienced workers, then banded and boxed. A selection of brands is sold in the shop.

Casa Natal de Antonio Guiteras Holmes and Catedral de San Rosendo

Further down the hill on Antonio Maceo, on the corner with Ormani Arenado, the **Casa Natal de Antonio Guiteras Holmes** (Mon–Fri 9am–4.30pm, Sat 9am–noon; free) is only just worth the nonexistent entrance fee. A few exhibits have been scraped together in a half-hearted attempt at detailing the life of this 1930s rebel activist. There is no explanation, in Spanish or English, of who Holmes actually was and very little attention has been paid to any of the displays, which consist of little more than a few firearms and some old photographs. His brief tenure as Secretary of the Interior in Grau San Martín's left-leaning government of 1933 followed an active political life, particularly as a student in his native Pinar del Río. The only attention-grabber is the dramatic and quite graphic photograph of the dead bodies of Guiteras and the Venezuelan Carlos Aponte after they'd been shot by government forces in May 1935. This reversal of government attitude towards Holmes came after Grau allowed the future dictator Fulgencio Batista a prominent place in the running of the country and Holmes subsequently resigned.

Two blocks away, on the corner of Antonio Maceo and Gerardo Medina, is the relatively ordinary and weary-looking **Catedral de San Rosendo**, built in 1883. The unsophisticated facade, with two bell towers and four pillars providing just a hint of grandeur, has to be viewed from behind a set of iron railings, and you can only see the interior if you happen to arrive during public opening times (ostensibly between 3 and 6pm, but don't count on it).

Fábrica de Bebidas Casa Garay

Four blocks south of Martí on Isabel Rubio is the **Fábrica de Bebidas Casa Garay** (Mon–Fri 9am–4pm; $1), the rum factory, founded in 1891, where the popular Guayabita del Pinar brand is produced. The entrance charge includes a ten-minute guided tour of the three rooms and court-yard that make up the compact factory, beginning in the back room where barrels of fermenting molasses create a potent smell and finishing in the claustrophobic bottling and labelling room. Unsurprisingly bottles of Guayabita are on sale, and you get a free sample of both the dry and the sweet versions to help you make your decision.

Museo Provincial de Historia and Museo de Ciencias Naturales

The most central of the two museums on Martí is the **Museo Provincial de Historia** (Tues–Sat 8am–5pm, Sun 8am–1pm; $1), between Isabel Rubio and Colón. It contains some interesting bits and pieces but over-all it is too disparate to present any kind of coherent history of the region. There are some pre-Columbian tools and bones as well as poten-tially interesting displays on the history of tobacco, coffee and slavery in the province, which are all worth a look but fail to create any under-standing of how they developed. Whilst it is surprisingly brief on the history of tobacco there is, as with all history museums in Cuba, an overemphasis on the revolution. The low entrance fee means it can't hurt to whisk yourself round and see if anything catches your eye, but for a comprehensive history of the province this is not the place to come.

Down at the quieter end of Martí, at the corner with Comandante Pinares, the Palacio de Guach contains the city's **Museo de Ciencias Naturales** (Tues–Sat 9am–4.30pm, Sun 8–11.30am; $1). This eclectic building is the most architecturally striking in the city, its columned arches adorned with dragons and other monstrous figures and the whole place riddled with elaborate chiselled detail. Inside, each room has a spe-cific theme – from the ocean to mammals – and although the ocean and plant rooms seem to be made up of whatever the museum could get its hands on, like bottled fruits and some miscellaneous dried leaves, there are more complete collections of butterflies, moths, exotic insects, shells and birds. Kids will enjoy the convincing giant stone tyrannosaurus and stegosaurus in the courtyard, where there's also a mural depicting other prehistoric creatures. The attraction is admittedly limited, and some of the stuffed animals on display in the mammal and reptile sections look as bored as visitors might start to feel after half an hour.

Eating

There are very few good state-run restaurants in Pinar del Río – most of them lack both variety and ambience, with a concentration of par-ticularly poor ones right in the centre on Martí. For a decent meal, head away from the centre to the *paladares*, none more than five minutes' walk from Martí, or go the extra distance for the better state restaurants on the outskirts of the city. Good-value ice cream is served during the day at *Coppelia*, Gerardo Medina e/ Antonio Rubio y Isidro de Armas, whilst the fast-food chain *El Rápido* is represented at Martí 65 e/ Isabel Rubio y Colón.

Casa 1890, Rafael Ferro esq. Frank País. Minimalistic state-run restaurant aimed at tourists in one of the oldest buildings in town, near the train station. The stately surroundings are spoilt by the shop partitioned off but visible from the dining area and the audible traffic outside, but there's a good selection of pizzas, pastas, sandwiches and meat dishes for very reasonable prices.

Casa Don Miguel, Ceferino Fernández e/ Gerardo Medina y Isabel Rubio. A delightfully located *paladar* on the first-floor veranda of a house tucked behind the cathedral: the view and abundance of potted plants make it a good spot to unwind. There's no set menu, but the food is fine.

Errazina, Antonio Rubio esq. 20 de Mayo. Of a poor crop of state-run restaurants, this is arguably the best. The charming rockery- and plant-filled terrace compensates, for an uninspired interior, whilst the Italian cuisine, suitable for those on the tightest of budgets, is nevertheless as good as anything you'll get from its peso-charging counterparts. Limited opening hours, usually between 6 and 10pm.

El Mesón, Martí e/ Comandante Pinares y Celestino Pacheco. Unatmospheric *paladar* at the quieter end of Martí. The decor is dominated by a massive, simplistic mural, though there's more variety on the menu (lots of chicken, pork and salad dishes) than in the other *paladares*. Simple, good-quality food and reasonable prices.

Nuestra Casa, Colón no. 161 e/ Ceferino Fernández y 1ero de Enero. Rooftop *paladar* reached via a stepladder. Among the branches of a mature tree the netting which has been draped all over the place partly spoils the wonderful natural setting. The menu is limited to simple but filling meat dishes.

Paladar Restaurant Rodrigo, Colón no. 177. Pleasantly furnished, poorly decorated front-room *paladar* with chicken, ham and pork dishes priced in pesos.

Restaurante Rumayor, Carretera Viñales km 1 ☎82/6-30-07. The city's biggest and best restaurant, next door to the cabaret of the same name, boasting a large, rustic dining hall adorned with African tribal imagery and a spacious shady garden. The sensibly priced Cuban cuisine includes the recommended smoked chicken à la Rumayor.

Drinking, nightlife and entertainment

The hotels *Italia*, *Globo* and *Vueltabajo* all have low-key, shadowy little **bars** but otherwise there are very few places in the city specifically for drinking in. *Cadena Servicio* on the corner of Martí and Rafael Morales is one of the few places where you can get a drink and a snack in the open air, but it's nothing more than a spacious concrete patio. There are a few tables and chairs inside the *Doñaneli Dulcería*, on Gerardo Medina between Martí and Máximo Gómez, which sells mostly cakes and sweets but also stocks beer and soda.

Don't expect much **nightlife** during the week as the entire city seems to save its energy for Friday, Saturday and Sunday, when the main streets buzz with young people. The only **nightclub** in town is at the *Pinar del Río*, which though small has the slickest decor of all the nightspots, whilst the discos at the *Italia* and *Globo* amount to little more than loud music and dim lights in the bar. For traditional live music your best bet is the *Casa de la Música* on Gerardo Medina, an open-air enclosure packed with uncomfortable chairs. The pleasantly entertaining unpretentious shows cater to an undemanding audience and usually start at 9pm.

The most spectacular night out in town is the *Cabaret Rumayor*, Carretera Viñales km 1 (Tues–Sun 10pm–late; ☎82/6-30-07; $5, including one drink), where one of the best **cabaret** shows in the country draws crowds of raucous locals – who seem to know the show backwards – as well as tourists. Like most cabarets in Cuba, the show is a tribute to 1970s glamour, a throwback to the days of *Saturday Night Fever*, as frilly shirts, shiny loafers, stilettos, gel-drenched hairdos and neon colours abound. Desperately romantic, mostly ageing songsters take it in turns to strut out onto the open-air stage, backed up by their equally glitzy, scantily clad, all-smiling dancers, as a seemingly endless sequence of song and dance routines takes you into the early hours of the morning, switching back and forth from tearful ballads to button-busting showtime numbers.

For **cinema**, there's Cine Praga, at Gerardo Medina e/ Antonio Rubio y Isidro de Armas (☎82/32-71), and the **sala de video** run by UNEAC at Antonio Maceo 178 e/ Comandante Pinares y Rafael Ferro (☎82/45-72); details of what's showing at both are displayed in the window of Cine Praga. Pinar del Río has one of the most successful **baseball** teams in the national league. Games take place in the 14,000-capacity Estadio Capitán San Luis (☎82/42-90 or 38-90) near the road to Viñales, usually on a Tuesday, Wednesday, Thursday or at the weekend. Games start at around 7.30pm on weekdays and Saturdays, while Sunday games are held at 4pm; check beforehand in case the team's playing away. The Teatro Milanes on Martí has been closed for years.

Listings

Airport Served exclusively by Aerotaxi (☎82/6-32-48) and its antiquated small aircraft, which can be chartered for flights around the island. The only scheduled services are to Nueva Gerona on the Isla de la Juventud. Flights are $20 each way and leave in the morning on Monday, Wednesday, Friday and Saturday.

Banks and money The best bank for foreign currency transactions and credit card withdrawals is Banco Financiero Internacional at Rosario (Ormani Arenado) e/ Martí y Máximo Gómez (Mon–Fri 8am–3pm). Around the corner the Banco de Crédito y Comercio at Martí e/ Rosario (Ormani Arenado) y Rafael Morales also handles most foreign exchange transactions. Pesos can be purchased at the Cadeca *casa de cambio* on Gerardo Medina e/ Antonio Rubio y Isidro de Armas (Mon–Sat 8.30am–6pm, Sun 8.30am–12.30pm).

Books La Internacional at Martí esq. Colón has a poor selection of mostly old books, mainly Cuban literature and political history. Better is the library, the Biblioteca Provincial Ramón González Coro (Mon–Sat 8am–5pm) at Colón e/ Martí y Máximo Gómez, whose small foreign fiction section includes about twenty books in English.

Car and scooter rental Both the town's car rental agencies operate from the *Pinar del Río* hotel. Transautos (daily 8am–6pm; ☎82/35-41) has a desk in the lobby while Havanautos (daily 8am–6pm; ☎82/49-89), which also rents out scooters, has an office in the car park. Outside of office hours you should be able to contact a Havanautos representative by asking at the desk in the hotel.

Medical Hospital Abel Santamaria, Carretera Central km 3 ☎82/6-20-46. Ring ☎82/6-23-17 for an ambulance.

Pharmacy The only pharmacy for tourists is in the *Pinar del Río* hotel.

Photography There are branches of Photoservice at Martí 35 e/ Isabel Rubio y Gerardo Medina and opposite the library on Colón.

Police Dial ☎082/25-25, or ☎116 in case of emergency.

Post office The main branch is at Martí esq. Isabel Rubio where you can send and receive faxes and make photocopies. DHL and Cuban equivalent EMS services are also available.

Shopping There's a good selection of Cuban music on CD and cassette in the Caracol shop at Maceo esq. Antonio Tarafa. For arts and crafts the best place is the Fondo de Bienes Culturales, Martí esq. Gerardo Medina. All the supermarkets are on Martí.

Taxis The only taxi rank in town is outside the *Pinar del Río* hotel. You can call for a Turistaxi via the hotel on ☎82/50-71, or directly on ☎82/6-34-81.

Telephone National and international calls can be made at the 24-hour ETEC-SA office on Martí e/ Isabel Rubio y Gerardo Medina. Late at night, a knock on the door should rouse the sleeping staff.

Viñales

The jewel in Pinar del Río's crown, the valley of **Viñales** is by far the most visited location in the province. With two of the best hotels in the country, some striking and memorable landscapes and an atmosphere of complete serenity, a visit to Viñales is essential if you're in the province or anywhere near it.

Though only 25km from the city of Pinar del Río, the valley feels far more remote, with a weird, almost dream-like quality that's inextricably linked to the unique *mogotes*, the boulder-like hills which look like they've dropped from the sky onto the valley floor. These bizarre limestone hillocks were formed during the Jurassic period, some 160 million years ago, through a process of erosion. Rainfall slowly ate away at the dissolvable limestone and flattened much of the landscape, leaving a few survivors behind, their lumpy surface today coated in a bushy layer of vegetation. The most photographed example, **Mogote Dos Hermanas** or "twin sisters", appears on almost every piece of tourist literature for the province. Their almost vertical sides create a sense of being walled in, a feeling accentuated by the flatness of the valley floor. The rich soils and regular rainfall, especially during the summer months, make Viñales a very productive area, and much of the valley floor is carpeted with crops, most notably tobacco.

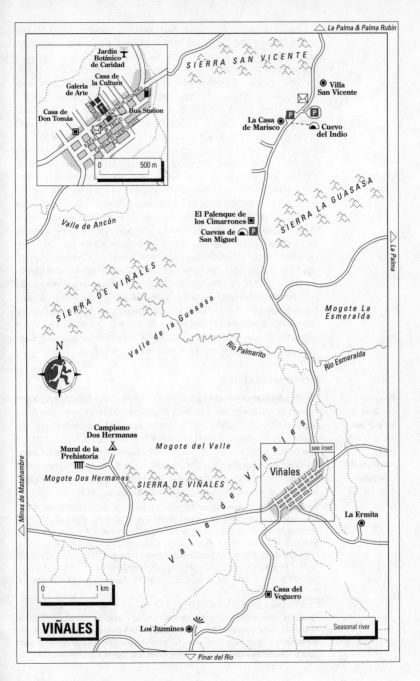

VIÑALES

Seasonal river

Despite the influx of visitors, the region has remained unspoilt. The tourist centres and hotels are kept in isolated pockets of the valley, often hidden away behind the *mogotes*, and driving through it's easy to think that the locals are the only people there. Most of them live in the small **village** of Viñales, which you'll enter first if you arrive from the provincial capital or Havana, and where there are plenty of *casas particulares*. From the village it's a short drive to all the official attractions, most of which are set up for tour groups, but it's worth doing the circuit just to get a feel of the valley and a close look at the *mogotes*. If time is limited, concentrate your visit on the **San Vicente** region, a valley within the valley, much smaller and narrower than Viñales, and home to the **Cueva del Indio**, the most comprehensive accessible cave system in the valley, a tour of which is the best chance you'll get to experience the *mogotes* close up. Also in San Vicente are the **Cueva de San Miguel** and **El Palenque de los Cimarrones**, a much smaller cave system leading through the rock to a rustic encampment where runaway slaves once hid, but now set up to provide lunch-time entertainment for coach parties. Difficult-to-explore and little-visited **Valle Ancón** lies on the northern border of this part of the valley. On the other side of the village, the **Mural de la Prehistoria** is by far the most contrived of the valley's attractions. There are a number of places in Viñales difficult to find or impossible to access if you're not on an **organized excursion** but, conversely, a stay in any of the *casas particulares* often yields information otherwise unavailable to the tourist. Either method reaps worthwhile rewards.

Accommodation

Mosquito repellent is a must if you're going to stay in one of the places on the valley floor.

There's an even spread of good **places to stay** in Viñales, with average costs relatively low – indeed, the most you're likely to pay for a night in the valley is $60. Furthermore, amongst the choices are two of the best located and most attractive hotels in Cuba, *Los Jazmines* and *La Ermita*, as well as a surprising abundance of rooms for rent. Finding the latter shouldn't be a problem, as most have signs outside and the bus that drops tourists in the valley's tiny village is usually met by a crowd of locals equipped with business cards.

Campismo Dos Hermanas, on the road to the Mural de la Prehistoria ☎8/9-32-23. This *campismo*, buried within the jagged borders of the surrounding *mogotes*, is better equipped than most, despite having no a/c or fans in its neat, well-kept white cabins. On the spacious site are a TV room, games room, bar and restaurant, swimming pool and a regional museum. There's a disco every night. The cheapest of the official options, this is the place to come if you want to share your stay with Cuban holiday makers, but be prepared for the constant blare of music in peak season. ②.

Casa de Dona Hilda, casa no. 4, Km 25 Carretera a Pinar del Río ☎8/9-33-38. There are three rooms for rent in this mini-home complex. The biggest is in its own small bungalow, next door to the main house where the two smaller rooms are located, with en suite bathroom, fridge and colour TV. A large dirt courtyard joins it all together and there is a drive where you can safely park your car. ②.

Casa de Ines Nunez Rodríguez, Salvador Cisnero no. 40 ☎8/9-32-97. Run by an elderly couple the two rooms, one with a/c, for rent in this *casa particular* in the heart of the village are in a separate apartment taking up the entire top floor of the house and accessed via an outside set of steps. With a wide balcony running around three sides of the apartment, this is one of the best places to stay in the village. ②.

La Casa de Marisco, over the road from the Cueva del Indio ☎8/93-60-62. Three rooms in a single bungalow with communal living room and dining room where meals are served. Simple, clean and good value. The whole bungalow can be rented out for $35 a night. ②.

Casa de Teresa Martínez Hernández, Camilo Cienfuegos no. 10 e/ Adela Azcuy y Seferino Fernández ☎8/9-32-67. Though there is only one room to rent in this attractive and compact *casa particular*, it has a capacity for up to four people, which can make it a bargain for the price. ②.

La Ermita, Carretera de Ermita km 2 ☎8/93-61-00 or 93-60-71, fax 93-60-91. Gorgeous open-plan hotel in immaculate grounds high above the valley floor. The panoramic views take in some of the best perspectives on the San Vicente valley and out beyond the *mogotes*. The tidy complex features three dignified apartment blocks with columned balconies, a central pool, a tennis court, a wonderful balcony restaurant and a comprehensive programme of optional activties and excursions including horse riding, trekking and bird watching. Rooms are tasteful and reasonably well equipped. ④.

Los Jazmines, Carretera de Viñales km 25 ☎8/93-62-05, fax 93-62-15. Run by the same chain as *La Ermita* and similarly handsome, this is the first hotel along the winding road into Viñales, in an unbeatable hillside location with stunning views of the most photographed section of the valley. The elegant colonial-style main building, built in 1959, houses a restaurant with balcony, and almost all of the 62 tastefully furnished rooms have panoramic views. Most rooms are in a separate, more modern block, with a few in red-roofed cabins. There's a good-sized pool, a well-stocked shop, two bars, a small disco and taxi and car rental facilities. ④.

Rancho San Vicente, opposite the abandoned *Hotel Ranchón* on the way out of San Vicente towards the Valle Ancón ☎8/9-32-00 or 9-32-01. Twenty attractive and comfortable a/c cabins spread out around the gentle, wooded slopes. There's a swimming pool and a bathhouse offering massage and mud therapy. ④.

Viñales village

Surprisingly, considering the number of tourists who pass through it, the village of **VIÑALES**, conveniently located for all the sights and hotels, has not been particularly developed for tourism, with only one official state restaurant and no official accommodation. Nestled on the valley floor, simple tiled-roof bungalows with sun-burnt paintwork and unkempt gardens huddle around its pine-lined streets, the occasional car or tour-bus disturbing the laid-back atmosphere as they ply their way up and down Salvador Cisnero, the main street sloping gently either side of a small square. Despite the village's diminutive size, there's no shortage of people offering you a place to stay or a taxi, though this doesn't constitute any kind of hassle. There's a genuine charm to the place, but whilst the village has been declared a national monument, there's actually little to hold your attention for very long, and its attractions, while worthy, are as brief as the town is small. The lazy little main square plays host to all but one of the noteworthy buildings, including the proud **Casa de la Cultura** (daily 7am–11pm; free), which dates from 1832 and houses a small, sporadically active theatre on the second floor. You're free to take a quick peek upstairs where there's still some old colonial-style furniture, including an elegant wood-framed mirror and some artistic-looking chairs. Next door, the diminutive **Galería de Arte** (Mon & Fri 3–11pm, Wed & Thurs 8am–5pm, Sat 1pm–9pm, Sun 8am–noon; free), which was a pharmacy prior to the revolution, displays small collections of paintings by local artists. The third of the square's trio of notable structures is the modest little **church**, often closed but worth a moment's contemplation, with its Islamic-style dome cap at the top of the bell tower.

The most intriguing of the village's attractions, a four-minute walk from the plaza, is the densely packed garden of two of its residents, referred to as the **Jardín Botánico de Caridad** in official tourist literature, though it seems likely this name has emerged as a handy term for something which can't be easily labelled. Just past the end of Salvador Cisnero on C. P. Esperanza, a gate adorned with pieces of real fruit marks the easily missable entrance of these almost fairy-tale gardens, the property of two sisters whose small brick cottage sits in the middle. The compact shady garden is a botanist's dream, squeezing in all kinds of trees, shrubs and plants – papaya, begonias, orchids, a mango tree, a starfruit tree and many others. One of the sisters is usually around to help you pick your way through, explaining and identifying all the plants and noting many of their medicinal qualities. As each one is pointed out and described, it becomes clear that there is order amongst this seeming chaos. The trees create a canopy which stretches back some way, and you're free to wander off and explore, though the garden becomes less varied as it merges into a small wood.

Mogote Dos Hermanas and the Mural de la Prehistoria

Less than a kilometre to the west of the village, the flat surface of the valley floor is abruptly interrupted by the magnificent hulking mass of the **Mogote Dos Hermanas**, the public face of Viñales as seen on the front of almost every tourist brochure printed about the area. It plays host to the somewhat misleadingly named **Mural de la Prehistoria** (daily 8am–7pm; $1), hidden away from the main road down a dust track. Rather than the prehistoric cave paintings that you might be expecting, the huge painted mural, measuring 120m by 180m, desecrating the face of one side of the *mogote* is in fact a modern depiction of evolution on the island, from molluscs to man. It's impressive only for its size; the garish colours and lifeless images are out of tune with the otherwise humble yet captivating valley hidden within the ancient walls of these fascinating rock formations. The mural was commissioned by Fidel Castro and painted in the early 1960s under the direction of the Cuban scientist and teacher Leovigildo González; nobody seems to know *why* it was thought necessary, and although in fact this wasn't the intention, you can't help feeling that its sole purpose is to attract tourists. The bar, restaurant and souvenir shop just off to the side of the mural do nothing to alleviate the contrived nature of the place, although it's not an unpleasant spot to have a drink and a bite to eat. The **restaurant**'s speciality is roast pork cooked "Viñales style", undoubtedly the highlight on an otherwise limited menu which also features a number of egg dishes.

The Cueva de San Miguel and El Palenque de los Cimarrones

By taking the left-hand fork at the petrol station at the northeastern end of the village, you can head out of Viñales through the heavily cultivated landscape to the narrower, arena-like San Vicente valley, around 2km away. Just beyond the *mogotes* on sentry duty at the entrance to the valley is the **Cueva de San Miguel** (daily 9am–4pm), also referred to as the Cueva de José Miguel and formerly known as the Cueva de Viñales. Unmissable from the road, the gaping mouth of the cave appears to promise drama and adventure, but inside it's disappointingly prosaic, with unnecessarily loud music blaring from a **bar** just inside the entrance which, though a bit tacky, does provide a welcome break from the sun's rays and has amusingly miniature tables and chairs.

Past the bar, you can pay $1 to investigate further by venturing down the corridor which disappears into the rock. After just 50m or so you emerge on the other side at **El Palenque de los Cimarrones**. This reconstruction of a runaway slave (*cimarron*) settlement provides limited insight into the living conditions of the African slaves who, having escaped from the plantations, would have sought refuge in a hideout (*palenque*) such as the one on display here. No more than some cooking implements and a few contraptions made of sticks and stones set up in a hollow section of the rock, it does, however, feature some original pieces used by the slaves. You're left to guess what each piece was used for and although there is a small plaque declaring its authenticity, it's not made clear whether this was actually the site of an original *palenque*. Back in the daylight, cut off on three sides by cliffs, there's a large **restaurant** (daily 9am–5pm) set under round *bohío* roofs. It's a pleasantly secluded spot for lunch, but becomes considerably less private in the afternoons when the tour parties arrive, though coinciding with group visits does bring the added bonus of being entertained by the Afro-Cuban folkloric show put on for guests.

The Cueva del Indio and the Valle Ancón

From the Cueva de San Miguel it's a two-minute drive or a twenty-minute walk north to San Vicente's most captivating attraction, the **Cueva del Indio** (daily 9am–6pm; $2, $3 with boat ride), 6km north of the village. Rediscovered in 1920, this whole network of caves is believed to have been used by the Guanahatabey Amerindians both as a refuge from the Spanish colonists and, judging by the human remains found here, as a burial site. On the path leading up to the caves' entrance you'll pass the uninspired *Restaurante Cueva del Indio* (daily 11am–4pm), which resembles a small school dining hall.

Well lit and well trodden enough not to seem ominous, the cool caves nevertheless inspire a sense of escape from the contrastingly humid and bright world outside. There are no visible signs of Indian occupation, but it's not difficult to imagine the cavernous corridors echoing with the sound of native-Cuban voices. Instead of paintings the walls are marked with natural wave patterns, testimony to the flooding which took place during the caves' formation millions of years ago. It's well worth paying the extra dollar for the **boat ride** as only the first 300m of the large jagged tunnel's damp interior can be explored on foot before a slippery set of steps leads down to a subterranean river, where a tour guide steers you for ten minutes through the remaining 400m of explorable cave (there exists at least another kilometre of unlit tunnels which haven't yet been secured for visitors), pointing out images – mostly indiscernible, but supposedly resembling everything from crocodiles to champagne bottles – which have formed naturally on the rock. The boat drops you off out in the open, next to some souvenir stalls and a car park around the corner from where you started. From here a small footbridge leads across the river to *El Ranchón* (daily noon–5pm), a restaurant hidden behind the trees where the set meal, featuring grilled pork, costs $11. The restaurant is part of a small **farm**, the Finca San Vicente, usually accessible only to tour groups, consisting mostly of orchards and coffee crops and host to the occasional cock fight.

A few hundred metres further up the road is an isolated **post office** and just past this *Rancho San Vicente* (see p.167). About 500m beyond the hotel, a left turn leads to the last stop in Viñales, the **Valle Ancón**. Mostly untouched by tourism, the least visited and unspoilt of the valleys is also the most complicated to explore and can become uncomfortably muddy in the rain. There's a small village of the same name, plenty of coffee plantations and a number of hard-to-find caves and rivers, but the rewards are usually outweighed by the effort needed to get there.

Cayo Levisa

Fifty kilometres northeast of Viñales, the lonely military outpost of Palma Rubia is the jumping-off point for **Cayo Levisa**, the only resort on the north coast of the province developed for international tourism.

Still relatively unspoilt, this three-kilometre-wide, densely wooded islet, within sight of the mainland, boasts some of the finest white sands and clearest waters in Pinar del Río, and unless you take advantage of its **diving centre**, there's blissfully little to do. Don't expect any wild nights out here – Cayo Levisa specializes in peace and quiet with more than enough beach for everyone to have their own private patch, even if the resort is full to its lowly twenty-cabin capacity.

The only regular **boat** to the island leaves Palma Rubia at around 11am every day (ring the resort on the cay beforehand to check). If you're staying at the resort there's no charge for the twenty-minute crossing, otherwise it's a hefty $25 though this does include a usually seafood-based lunch at the restaurant on the island. The return journey is at 5pm, which makes a day-trip fairly pointless unless you're going diving, and even then it's a little rushed.

The boat moors on a rickety wooden jetty, a two-minute walk from the twenty grey **cabins** of the *Villa Cayo Levisa* (☎7/66-60-75; ⑤), the only accommodation on the island, sprawled untidily along the gleaming white beach. Whilst not particularly attractive, the cabins are well equipped and furnished, with spacious interiors and large porches. Behind the beach, thick woodland reaches across the island to the opposite shore, forming a natural screen that encourages a delicious sense of escape and privacy. The coastline extends on both sides of the complex well beyond the main beach, although the scenery becomes increasingly monotonous. Most of the coastline is completely untouched on this uninhabited cay and although the beach is narrower and the washed-up seaweed more plentiful away from the resort area, the tranquillity is unparalleled.

The hotel has surfboards and catamarans for rent, and there's a separate **dive centre** within the small complex offering gear rental, courses and dives around the nearby coral reef, a short boat trip away. For experienced divers a single dive costs $25, or $45 for two; the centre runs its own courses from $65 per person. There's also a day-trip offered to nearby **Cayo Paraíso**, a similarly unspoilt islet once favoured by Ernest Hemingway, where you can dive or snorkel.

Southwest to the Península de Guanahacabibes

Heading southwest from Pinar del Río city on the Carretera Central, the only main road through this part of the region, the towns become more isolated and the resorts less developed. Getting around here without your own transport can be a real problem, though the unreliable and very slow train service and the occasional bus from the provincial capital do at least provide the possibility of getting to some of the beaches here on public transport. Even with a car the going can be tough, as the Carretera Central features very few signs, becomes increasingly potholed and hands over to minor roads just before the **Península de Guanahacabibes**, the highlight of this area. For the first 50km the relatively colourful and varied scenery makes the journey interesting, though it's unlikely you'll want to stop except perhaps to take the odd photo. The desolate towns along the route hold scant reward for even the most enthusiastic explorer, and twenty minutes in any one of them should suffice for the whole lot. After the small town of Isabel Rubio, 60km from the provincial capital, the landscape becomes increasingly monotonous and doesn't improve until the dense forest and crystalline waters of the peninsula move into view, well beyond the end of the Carretera Central at the fishing village of **La Fe**.

The most easily reachable of the places to visit are the **beaches** around the Ensenada de Cortés, a wide open bay, although the appeal lies more in their proximity to the provincial capital and their popularity with locals than in their negligible beauty. The large featureless lake at **Laguna Grande**, the site of one of the two hotels in this part of the province, does not warrant a trip for its own sake but is fairly well placed if you want to break up what is bound to have been a reasonably long journey, especially if you're heading to or from **María La Gorda** in Cuba's virtually untouched western tip, one of the best scuba diving locations in the country.

Boca de Galafre and Playa Bailén

*The only public transport to Boca de Galafre is the **train** from Pinar del Río city (daily; 1hr 30min), which will leave you 2km from the beach, and the bus to Cortés (daily; 1hr 15min), a nondescript little hamlet further southwest.*

There's very little to choose from when it comes to **beaches** on Pinar del Río's southern coastline, and the two around the **Ensenada de Cortés** are really the best of a bad bunch. If you make the journey by car you'll pass through the pleasant but uneventful town of San Juan y Martínez in the famed Vueltabajo region. The finest **tobacco** in the world comes from this area and it's worth stopping in the town to find out about visiting a plantation (see box). Fifteen kilometres beyond San Juan y Martínez there's a clearly signposted turn-off for **Boca de Galafre**, the smaller of the two beaches. The sand and sea leave a lot to be desired – the former full of seaweed, the latter murky and unappealing – but this doesn't deter either locals or Cuban holidaymakers and the beach is sociable if nothing else, the seaside equivalent of a big city backstreet. A few people live in simple concrete cabins along the beachfront, whilst home-made **snacks and drinks** are sold from a couple of makeshift kiosks. Between September and June sixteen of the **cabins** facing the shore can be rented for fifteen pesos a day.

Five kilometres past the turning for Boca de Galafre, an eight-kilometre side road leads down to a more substantial beach, **Playa Bailén**, the most popular seaside resort along the southern coastline – though the holidaymakers here are still Cuban rather than international. Here you get a real feel for the kind of tourism that predominated before foreign investment transformed the island's better-known resorts. The beach is wide and sandy, bordered by a beachfront path lined with

Tobacco

Tobacco is an intrinsic part of Cuban culture. Not as vital to the economy as sugar, the most widely grown crop in Cuba, tobacco farming and cigar smoking are nonetheless more closely linked with the history and spirit of this Caribbean country. When Columbus arrived, the indigenous islanders had long been cultivating tobacco and smoking it in pipes which they would inhale through their nostrils rather than their mouth. When the leaf was first taken back to Europe it received a lukewarm reaction, but by the nineteenth century it had become popular enough to list as one of the most profitable Spanish exports from its Caribbean territories. However, it was as early as the sixteenth century that Cuban peasants became tobacco farmers, known as *vegueros*, during an era in which sugar and cattle-ranching were the dominant forces in the economy. As it became more profitable to grow tobacco so the big landowners, most of them involved in the sugar industry, began to squeeze the *vegueros* off the land, forcing them either out of business altogether or into tenant farming. Many took their trade to the most remote parts of the country, out of reach of big business, and established small settlements from which many communities in places like Pinar del Río and northern Oriente now trace their roots. There nevertheless remained a conflict of interest which, to some extent, came to represent not just sugar versus tobacco but *criollos* versus *peninsulares*. The tensions which would eventually lead to the Cuban wars of independence first emerged between *criollo*, or Cuban-born, tobacco growers and the Spanish ruling elite, the *peninsulares*, who sought to control the industry through trade restrictions and price laws. Thus the tobacco trade has long been associated in Cuba with political activism. Today, when you visit a cigar factory and see the workers being read to from a newspaper or novel, you're witnessing the continuation of a tradition which began in the nineteenth century as a way of keeping the workers politically informed and aware.

Fernando Ortíz, the renowned Cuban historian, believed that the history of tobacco was a symbol of Cuban creativity. Both the patience involved in the time-consuming process of growing tobacco and the undivided attention that a connoisseur will give to the simple pleasure of smoking a cigar seem somehow intrinsically Cuban.

shady *uva caleta* – or sea-grape – trees, and the light breezes characteristic of this stretch of coastline make gentle waves on the warm but murky water. During the summer the resort teems with families and is a good place to meet people, but for much of the year it can be rather empty and a bit depressing. Look out for men pushing carts along the beachfront path selling cold meals and rapidly melting ice cream from their unrefrigerated trollies. If you're keen to stay, you could try the poorly equipped but affable *Villa Bailén* (no phone; ②), which has cabins of all shapes and sizes stretched along 2km of beach. The complex is split into three zones, with only Zone One, where visitors first arrive, available to dollar-paying foreign guests. There's a basketball court, a very basic children's playground and a number of poorly stocked cafeterias and restaurants, each offering the same basic Cuban cuisine – you're better off bringing your own **supplies**.

Laguna Grande

Ten kilometres beyond Isabel Rubio, opposite a military base, is the
turn-off to **Laguna Grande**, an artificial fishing lake and modest
resort. The road cuts through acres of citrus orchards which spruce
up an otherwise unremarkable flat landscape until, at a crossroads, a
left turn leads directly to the resort. Hidden away in a small wood,
Villa Laguna Grande (☎82/23-03 or 32-02; ③) is appealing in its
isolation. Facilities are basic but as comprehensive as it gets in this
part of the province, comprising a snack and souvenir shop, a cheap
restaurant, bicycle rental for only 50¢ an hour and horses to rent.
The twelve pink and blue cabins, only four of which have air conditioning, are reasonably comfortable. The off-the-beaten track appeal
of this site is complemented by its unkempt appearance, with scruffy
lawns and a few farmyard shacks dotted about the place. Laguna
Grande itself is right next to the complex, hidden from sight behind
a grassy bank. Large, round and bereft of features, the reservoir is
not much to look at, but you can go fishing for trout, swimming and
rent small rowing boats ($1 per hour).

María La Gorda and the Península de Guanahacabibes

Only the most determined make the trip down to Cuba's westernmost
tip, the forest-covered **Península de Guanahacabibes**, but the journey
is certainly not without its rewards. Some of the most beautiful and
most unspoilt coastline in Cuba is to be found around the **Bahía de
Corrientes**, in what has been declared a UNESCO Biosphere Reserve,
one of the largest national forest-parks in the country. It was here that
the Cuban Amerindians sought their last refuge, having been driven
from the rest of the island by the Spanish colonists. Virgin beaches and
water clear enough to compete with Cuba's most famous have been
relatively untouched by tourism, though this is unlikely to be the case
for much longer. The price for such unspoilt scenery is a fairly basic
set of facilities at the only resort currently open on or anywhere near
the peninsula.

The only way into the peninsula is along a potholed road through
a thick forest which begins where the Carretera Central ends, at the
tiny fishing village of **La Fe**. About 30km beyond here is the first
checkpoint guarding the protected territory, no more than a hut by
the side of the road where you should slow down so that the forest
warden can note your number plates. On the edge of the forest, as
the large bay looms into sight, is the official checkpoint, La Bajada,
where your passport should be enough to get you through. Turn
left down the road to **María La Gorda**, an international dive centre
and host to what is currently the area's sole place to stay. The
relaxing drive follows the shoreline of the bay, with dense forest on
one side and the open expanse of brilliant blue-green water on the

other. There are a few slightly scrappy but likeable little beaches along this road, which you can make your own if you want complete privacy, but it's unlikely you'll have too many rivals even on the much larger beach belonging to the resort at the end of the road. Don't expect to be pampered at *Motel María La Gorda* (☎84/31-21; ③), which is used more as a base camp for divers than a hotel for beach bums. The small, sea-facing collection of wood-panelled bungalows and two-storey concrete apartment blocks are comfortable enough for a good night's sleep and all equipped with air conditioning and televisions. *Las Gorgonias*, the resort's functional **restaurant**, serves $5 breakfasts and $15 lunches and dinners – each meal a good-quality, all-you-can-eat buffet. A souvenir shop and outdoor bar make up the rest of the patchy resort, whilst much of the area in which it is set, backing onto the forest, has received very little care or attention. The fine white sand beach is limited to the immediate surrounds of the hotel, interrupted at its centre by the wharf where the dive centre moors its yachts. The beach stretches around the cape into the distance, providing plenty of opportunity to escape the hotel area, though it becomes significantly narrower and more pebbly.

The virgin waters around María La Gorda are widely regarded as among the best for **diving** in the whole of Cuba, with over fifty sites around the bay taking in coral reefs, sunken Spanish galleons and various underwater caves and tunnels. Yachts belonging to the **Centro Internacional de Buceo María La Gorda** (daily 8.30am–5.30pm), the resort's diving club run by Puertosol, depart every day at 9.30am and 3.30pm. One dive for experienced divers will cost you $30, or $57 for two, with equipment rental an extra $7. Snorkelling gear is sold at the equipment-cum-souvenir shop.

Back at La Bajada the road to **El Cabo de San Antonio**, the westernmost tip of the peninsula, is very rough and should properly be tackled in a jeep. Entrance to this final stretch is restricted in order to protect the local environment, and to avoid disappointment you should apply for permission at least a week in advance by ringing the Capitania del Puerto (☎82/6-31-10) and paying the $10 fee. On the other hand there's very little reward for so much effort and other than a few pleasant beaches, none better than María La Gorda, there's only a lonely old lighthouse. There are plans to improve the road surface and build a marina at Las Tumbas – the country's far western extremity – but the foreign investment needed to fund the project hasn't yet been forthcoming.

Travel details

VÍAZUL BUSES
Pinar del Río to: Havana (3 weekly; 3hr); Viñales (3 weekly; 40min).
Viñales to: Havana (3 weekly; 4hr 30min); Pinar del Río (3 weekly; 40min).

ASTRO BUSES

Pinar del Río to: Cortés – for Boca de Galafre and Playa Bailén (daily; 2hr 30min); Havana (3 daily; 3hr 30min); Viñales (daily; 40min).

Viñales to: Havana (daily; 5hr); Pinar del Río (daily; 40min).

TRAINS

Pinar del Río to: Havana (daily; 5hr); Boca de Galafre (daily; 1hr 30min); Playa Bailén (daily; 1hr 45min); San Cristóbal (daily; 3hr).

Chapter 3

Varadero and Matanzas

V aradero is Cuban tourism at its most developed: a world apart from most of Cuba, but for its thousands of foreign visitors, the familiar face of the Caribbean. The **Península de Hicacos**, on which Varadero makes its home, reaches out from the northern coastline of the western **province of Matanzas** into the warm currents of the Atlantic as the ocean merges with the Gulf of Mexico. A fingertip of land in the second largest province in the country, its 25-kilometre stretch of fine white sand beaches and turquoise waters, within ten minutes' walk wherever you are on the peninsula, is enough to fulfil even the most jaded sunworshipper's expectations. The beach is undoubtedly of international standard, but the same can't be said of the nightlife, which has some way to go before it can rival the peninsula's natural attributes.

Roughly 25km along the coastline from the peninsula is the provincial capital, also named **Matanzas**, and a little closer but in the other direction the bayside town of **Cárdenas**. These once grand colonial towns now live largely in Varadero's shadow, and have lost some of their character since their relegation to day-trip destinations for Varadero holidaymakers. For anyone determined to dig deeper, however, there is more to be found and neither town is without charm, but the story is mostly one of unfulfilled potential. This is particularly true of Matanzas, where many of the historical buildings are in a disappointingly bad state of repair. These days, the true delights of the area around Varadero lie just outside Matanzas in the paradisical **Valley of Yumurí** and the cave network of the **Cuevas de Bellamar**.

The centre of the province is a bit of a void from the visitor's point of view, no more than a through-route on the Carretera Central or further south on the *autopista*. Endless acres of sugarcane fields and citrus orchards dominate the landscape hereabouts, Matanzas being Cuba's largest producer of agricultural products and traditionally the thumping heart of the country's sugar industry, which has been central to the economy since colonial times. The few places worth pausing at are all along or within a short drive of the

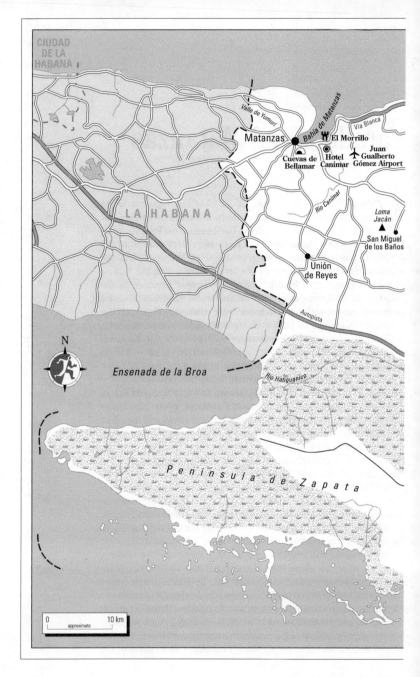

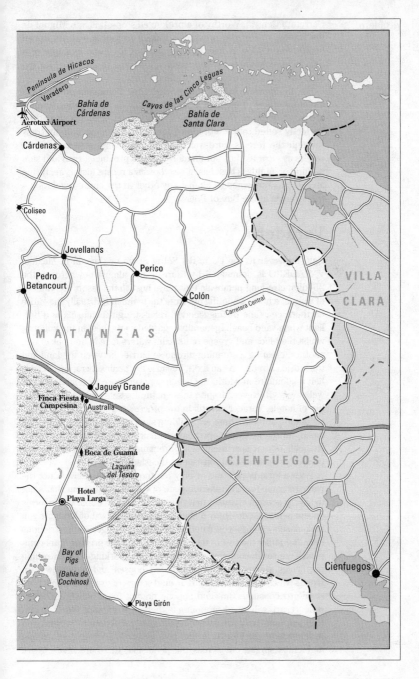

Carretera Central. Worthy of a prolonged stop-off is **San Miguel de los Baños**, one of the province's hidden treasures with its ruined health spa. **Colón** is less picturesque but a classic example of a provincial colonial town and worth a look just to get a feel for the lifestyle of the average town-dwelling Cuban.

On the opposite side of the province, the **Península de Zapata**'s sweeping tracts of unspoilt coastal marshlands and wooded interior are easy to explore, thanks to an efficiently run tourist infrastructure. Perfectly suited to a multitude of activities, including walking trails through the forests, bird-watching on the rivers, scuba diving in waters as clear as those of its more famous provincial rival and sunbathing on faultless beaches, it also boasts a recent history featuring an event as renowned as almost any other in the entire revolution – the invasion at the **Bay of Pigs**.

Varadero

Cuba's answer to the Costa del Sol in Spain or Cancún in Mexico, **VARADERO** is dominated by tourism and almost nowhere on the 25-kilometre-long peninsula that plays host to the resort are you out of sight of a hotel. Shooting out from the mainland, virtually the entire northern coastline of this slender, ruler-straight peninsula is a brilliant white sand beach, generally regarded as the best in the country, whilst the blues and greens of its calm waters fade in and out of one another, creating a stunning turquoise barrier between the land and the Florida Straits. To cap it off, because the peninsula rarely exceeds half a kilometre in width, the beach is never more than a ten-minute walk away. However, despite these natural assets and its large number of hotels, Varadero is still in the process of recovering its former reputation abroad. There are building sites all over the place, though mostly in the less developed eastern half, whilst some of the older, shabbier tourist apartment blocks remain as symbols of the barren period for international tourism on the island.

With a local population of only ten thousand, Varadero is not the place to come for an authentic taste of Cuban culture, but that's not to say, as is often claimed, that this isn't the "real" Cuba. While locals on the peninsula do enjoy a slightly higher standard of living, if you look closely enough, you'll notice the same shortages and restrictions here that afflict the rest of the country. Behind the pristine hotel complexes are residential neighbourhoods full of barking dogs patrolling the drives and porches of flat-roofed houses and bungalows, on streets which occasionally skirt around scraps of grassland. This is no shrine to consumerism, and anyone hoping for a polished Disney-style resort will be disappointed: there are enough faded, paint-chipped walls and patchwork-repaired house-fronts to remind you which side of the Florida Straits you are on. With hotels, shops and nightclubs spread out across the peninsula, there are areas where

Varadero: tourist apartheid?

All over Cuba people talk of Varadero with nostalgia as the place where they once spent their holidays but from which they are now banished, and if you've spent any time amongst Cubans in the rest of the island you might arrive expecting to find not a single local in sight. The notion that Cubans are banned from Varadero has arisen not without good reason, but officially nationals have as much right to use the beaches as foreign visitors. Apart from local people, there are Cuban visitors on the beaches and in some of the cheaper hotels, though they are not permitted in most of the upmarket complexes. However, though the party line is that there are no private or exclusive beaches in Cuba, the reality is that Cubans are often obliged by the police to move on. Unsurprisingly this is done so discreetly that you are unlikely to notice it. More obviously, Cubans entering the resort on one of the local buses from nearby Cárdenas are likely to have their bag checked before being allowed over the bridge connecting this holiday paradise to the mainland. Rules and regulations aside, all prices in Varadero are in dollars and it's this fact that is the single biggest impediment to peso-earning holidaymakers.

activity is more concentrated, but nowhere is there the buzz you might expect from the major holiday resort on the largest Caribbean island.

None of this detracts from what most people come here for: the beach, a seemingly endless runway of uninterrupted blinding white sand along the length of this narrow corridor of land. This is also the best place in Cuba for watersports, with three marinas on the peninsula, and two diving clubs. As well as offering scuba diving, each marina runs its own programme of fishing trips (see box on p.193) and boat trips (see p.194). There are over thirty rewarding **dive sites** around Varadero, predominantly amongst the islets scattered a few kilometres northeast of the peninsula, an hour or so away by boat. Furthest from the mainland is a forty-metre-long boat sunk during World War II providing shelter for an array of different fish including eels, butterflyfish and angelfish. In the opposite direction, heading southwest along the Matanzas coastline, about 5km from Varadero, a two-kilometre stretch of coral reef has a bountiful variety of different corals inhabited by a busy population of parrotfish, trumpetfish and basslets amongst many others.

A series of clampdowns in recent years means that the level of hassle from *jineteros* in Varadero is lower than you might expect, especially if you've come from Havana. Inevitably you will be approached by cigar-merchants on the beach or offered a room at some point, but on the whole tourists blend into the local surroundings with greater ease than in most places in Cuba.

Arrival

All international and most national flights arrive at the **Juan Gualberto Gómez Airport** (☎5/61-30-16), 25km west of Varadero. The single terminal of this modern but modest airport has a bureau de change and credit card withdrawal facilities, an information centre and several **car**

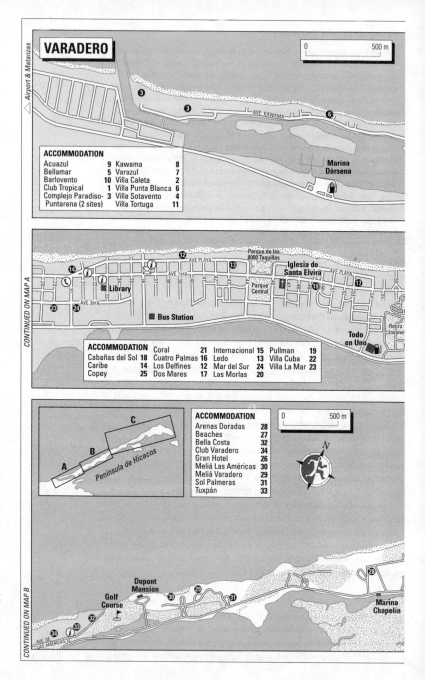

VARADERO

0   500 m

◁ Airport & Matanzas

AVE KAWAMA

Marina
Dársena

ACCOMMODATION

Acuazul	**9**	Kawama	**8**
Bellamar	**5**	Varazul	**7**
Barlovento	**10**	Villa Caleta	**2**
Club Tropical	**1**	Villa Punta Blanca	**6**
Complejo Paradiso-	**3**	Villa Sotavento	**4**
Puntarena (2 sites)		Villa Tortuga	**11**

CONTINUED ON MAP A

Parque de las
8000 Taquillas

AVE PLAYA

Iglesia de
Santa Elvira

AVE PLAYA

Library

AVE 3era

Parque
Central

Bus Station

Todo
en Uno

Retiro
Josone

ACCOMMODATION

		Coral	**21**	Internacional	**15**	Pullman	**19**
Cabañas del Sol	**18**	Cuatro Palmas	**16**	Ledo	**13**	Villa Cuba	**22**
Caribe	**14**	Los Delfines	**12**	Mar del Sur	**24**	Villa La Mar	**23**
Copey	**25**	Dos Mares	**17**	Las Morlas	**20**		

ACCOMMODATION

Arenas Doradas	**28**
Beaches	**27**
Bella Costa	**32**
Club Varadero	**34**
Gran Hotel	**26**
Meliá Las Américas	**30**
Meliá Varadero	**29**
Sol Palmeras	**31**
Tuxpán	**33**

0   500 m

C
B
A

Península de Hicacos

N

CONTINUED ON MAP B

Dupont
Mansion

Golf
Course

Marina
Chapelín

AVE DE
LAS AMÉRICAS

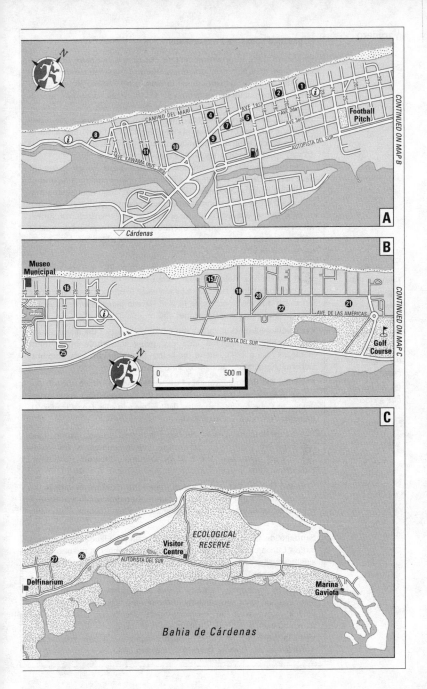

Football
Pitch

CONTINUED ON MAP B

AVE 1era
AVE 2da
AVE 3era

CAMINO DEL MAR

AVE KAWAMA (AVE 1EI)

AUTOPISTA DEL SUR

▽ Cárdenas

A

Museo
Municipal

B

CONTINUED ON MAP C

AVE. DE LAS AMÉRICAS

AUTOPISTA DEL SUR

Golf
Course

0   500 m

C

ECOLOGICAL
RESERVE

Visitor
Centre

AUTOPISTA DEL SUR

Delfinarium

Marina
Gaviota

Bahía de Cárdenas

Varadero

The easiest places to visit independently from Varadero are Havana and Trinidad, both linked directly to the beach resort by the Viazul bus service.

Organized tours and excursions

Varadero's three information centres can all sell you more or less the same excursions at very similar prices. Many of these can also be booked from the *buros de turismo* found in most hotel lobbies. As well as the three travel agencies mentioned on p.185, tours can be booked through Fantástico at Calle 24 y Playa, between the beach and Ave. 1era (daily 9am–7pm; ☎5/66-70-59 or 66-70-61), and Gaviota Tours in the hotels *Coral* and *Caracol* or by phone at either ☎5/66-78-64 or 61-24-75. There is also a Rumbos-run travel agency and information centre at Ave. 1era e/ 26 y 27 specifically for trips to the Península de Zapata.

The most popular excursions leave on a daily basis though during off-peak periods this can change and will depend upon a minimum number of people booking the excursion. With some of the less frequently requested tours there is a minimum number requirement regardless of the time of year. Below is a list of the most worthwhile excursions, the format which they generally follow, the operators that offer them and the kind of price you should expect to pay per person. Tours which last for a whole day usually include lunch at a restaurant.

Havana A packed tour of the capital lasting a whole day and concentrated mostly in Habana Vieja. Includes visits to most of the major sites (see Chapter 1), and there's actually a bit too much to take in in one day. Tiring but worth it if you're not going to visit Havana independently. Rumbos, Cubatur, Fantástico and Havanatur; $50.

Península de Zapata A varied and interesting tour of the major attractions within the national park occupying the whole of southern Matanzas (see p.223). One of the better excursions for kids. Rumbos, Cubatur, Havanatur, Fantástico; $50.

Pinar del Río Fly to the capital of the westernmost province, the tobacco capital of Cuba, and then travel by bus to the unforgettable Viñales Valley, unique in Cuba for its distinctive flat-top *mogote* hills (see Chapter 2). Rumbos, Fantástico, Cubatur; $105.

Cuevas de Bellamar One of the easier-going excursions, lasting about half a day, centring on the network of underground caves just ouside the city of Matanzas (see p.213). Rumbos, Cubatur, Havanatur, Fantástico; $20.

Trinidad This one-day tour of one of Cuba's first cities leaves early in the morning to allow just enough time to take in the stunning concentration of colonial architecture and other highlights. Rumbos, Cubatur, Havanatur; $70.

Santiago de Cuba A 1600-kilometre day-trip by plane to the second largest Cuban city. There are visits to a decent number of the historically significant sites and a chance to amble a little around the characterful city streets. Rumbos, Fantástico, Cubatur; $130.

Yumurí by helicopter Fantastic views of Varadero itself, the city of Matanzas and most spectacularly of the fantastically lush Yumurí Valley hidden away beyond the provincial capital. The twenty-minute journey there and back is the most thrilling aspect of this excursion, but the time spent in the valley, including horseback riding and a farm visit, is also worth savouring. Gaviota Tours; $75, children $64.

rental offices outside in the car park. There is no public bus service although many hotels have buses waiting to pick up guests with reservations, and it may be worth talking to the driver or tour guide to see if there are any spare seats. There are always plenty of taxis about which will take you to the centre of Varadero for $25 ($85 to Havana).

Driving to Varadero from the airport or Havana, the road you need to take is the Vía Blanca, 6km north of the airport, which will take you right up to the bridge providing the only road link between the peninsula and the mainland. There's a $2 charge at the Matanzas-Varadero toll gate a few kilometres before the bridge.

All interprovincial **buses**, whether Víazul (☎5/61-48-86) or Astro (☎5/61-26-26), arrive at the small **Terminal de Omnibus** on Calle 36 and Autopista Sur. There are many hotels within easy walking distance, some less than five minutes away, though most are just beyond the sweat barrier for travellers with heavy baggage. There are often two or three **taxis** waiting out the front but, if not, your best bet is to ring Cuba Taxi on ☎5/61-93-61 or 61-95-60. At least half of central Varadero's hotels are within a $5 ride.

Information

There are plenty of **information** outlets in Varadero with the three most prominent national tourist travel and information agencies represented in the lobby of most hotels, whilst they each also have their own offices. All offer very similar services, including excursions, hotel bookings and information on almost anything in Varadero. The Rumbos **Centro de Información Turística** at Ave. 1era esq. Calle 23 (daily 8am–8pm; ☎5/61-23-84 or 66-76-30) tends to be the best place for picking up written information. At Calle 33 esq. 1era, Cubatur (daily 8.30am–8.30pm; ☎5/66-74-01 or 66-72-17) are also helpful, whilst the travel agent for Havanatur, Tour y Travel, has the largest number of outlets on the peninsula, with the most central office at Calle 31 e/ 1era y Ave. Playa (daily 9am–6pm; ☎5/66-71-54 or 6-31-74).

Orientation and getting around

Varadero is divided into three distinct sections, though all are united by the same stretch of beach. The bridge from the mainland takes you into the main town area, where all the Cubans live. This is where nightlife, eating and entertainment are most densely concentrated and if your hotel is here you may never find cause to go anywhere else. The streets here are in blocks, with calles numbering 1 to 65 running the width of the peninsula; dissecting them all is Avenida Primera, the only street running the five-kilometre length of the whole town.

Avenida Primera appears in addresses and on street signs as Ave. 1era.

Most of the more upmarket accommodation is located on either side of the centre. The two-kilometre section of the peninsula west of the town, separated from the mainland by the Laguna de Paso Malo, is the **Reparto Kawama**, the narrowest section of the peninsula and the least worth visiting: the beach is generally disappointing and, besides three or four restaurants, there's very little which isn't the exclusive domain of hotel guests. Though technically still Avenida Primera, the street running the length of this section is also known as Avenida Kawama.

The majority of the all-inclusive luxury hotels lie **east** of the town on a part of the peninsula wholly dedicated to tourism. From the town Ave. de las Américas runs along a kind of hotel village, while beyond the Varadero golf course, and the Dupont Mansion which overlooks it, you enter the part of the peninsula that's undergoing the most changes, with new hotels constantly appearing along its relatively undeveloped coastline. Linked to the town by the **Autopista del Sur**, the highway running the length of the southern shore of the peninsula, the hotels and the one or two places worth visiting are far more widely dispersed than in the town, and there remain stretches of unspoilt countryside in this half of the peninsula, which you'll need to rent a car or a scooter to explore.

Public transport is even more scarce here than elsewhere in Cuba, though if you can catch bus #47 anywhere along Avenida Primera it'll take you as far as Calle 64 for less than a peso. Far more dependable is the **Omnibus Viaven**, a tourist bus service operating daily between 9am and midnight. From the *Hotel Oasis*, the only Varadero hotel on the mainland, 3km along the Vía Blanca from the bridge, it runs all the way up to the *Gran Hotel*, in the far eastern section of the peninsula, stopping at most of the major hotels and principal attractions en route, for a flat fare of $1. Most people, however, get around in **taxis**; there's a constant stream of them along Avenida Primera, and a taxi rank between calles 54 and 55, next to the Cubana office. Alternatively ring Turistaxi on ☎5/61-44-44 or 61-33-77, Taxis OK on ☎5/66-70-89 or Cuba Taxi on ☎5/61-93-61 or 61-95-60. For a **tour** of the town or beyond you can pick up a **horse and carriage** outside Parque Josone, amongst other places. Charges are $10 for the "whole city", which usually means as far as the *Meliá Varadero* hotel, or $5 for "half the city", usually restricted to the town area.

Accommodation

As Cuba's tourism capital Varadero has no shortage of **places to stay**, but there isn't the variety you might expect, except at the more expensive end of the market. A high percentage of hotel accommodation is in large, indistinguishable apartment block-style buildings, most of which churn out nonstop entertainment throughout the day. Whilst there are differences in price, comfort and facilities, the most significant disparity is location. An overwhelming proportion of the hotels east of the town are all-inclusives, and the further east you stay the more restricted you become to your hotel grounds, as places become increasingly isolated. The distance from the hotel to the

---

Accommodation price codes

All accommodation listed in this guide has been graded according to the following price categories.

① peso hotel equivalent to $5 or less   ④ $30–50   ⑦ $100–150
② $5–20   ⑤ $50–70   ⑧ $150–200
③ $20–30   ⑥ $70–100   ⑨ $200 and above

Rates are for the cheapest available double or twin room during high season, usually May–September and the last two weeks of December. During low season some hotels lower their prices by roughly ten percent. The price given for all-inclusive hotels covers all meals and drinks, entrance to any on-site nightclubs and usually water-sports facilities, but there are extra charges for optional excursions.

---

beach wherever you stay shouldn't be a make-or-breaker as none is further than a ten-minute walk away, though those set back in the town tend to be the least expensive. One or two hotels, such as *Los Delfines*, have exclusive contracts with foreign tour operators and are therefore out of bounds to most travellers.

There are no licensed **casas particulares** in Varadero following the government decision to ban them, eliminating the threat they posed to state control of the market. Locals continue to rent rooms illegally, though, and business is booming, with prices at around $20–30 per room. Touts offering to take you to one are never far away, though the bus station is as good a place as anywhere to find them. **Camping** on the peninsula is no longer possible as the resort's one and only campsite has now been cleared for hotel development.

Reparto Kawama

Complejo Paradiso-Puntarena, Ave. Kawama y Final ☎5/66-71-25; fax 66-70-72. At the western tip of the peninsula, a long walk from all the action, this all-inclusive features two identical high-rise accommodation blocks, an exclusive diving club and two swimming pools. On one of the largest and most private sections of the beach. ⑨.

Kawama, Calle 0 y Ave. Kawama ☎5/66-71-56; fax 66-73-34. Large landscaped all-inclusive complex, bordered by 300m of beach, which loses its character away from the stylish neo-colonial terraced main building founded in 1930 as a gentlemen's club. Choose from private or shared houses or modern homely apartments, all tastefully furnished. There's a fantastically chic restaurant and cosy basement cabaret. ⑨.

Villa Punta Blanca, Ave. Kawama ☎5/66-80-50; fax 66-70-04. This complex stretches for over 1.5km along the narrowest part of the peninsula, on a steeply sloping section of beach; its showpiece is *La Casa de Al*, a refined stone mansion and the former bootlegging headquarters of the Varadero branch of Al Capone's empire, now a restaurant. Well-equipped beachside villas, divided into smaller apartments with communal living rooms. ⑥.

Villa Tortuga, Calle 7 y Ave. Kawama ☎5/61-47-47; fax 66-74-85. The most attractively laid-out complex in Reparto Kawama, with pastel-coloured modern villas and two-storey apartment blocks, all set on a good patch of beach. Pool, tennis court, gymnasium and volleyball. ⑥.

The Town

Acuazul, Ave. 1era y 13 ☎5/66-71-32; fax 66-72-29. An overpriced and characterless apartment block with a poky pool area out the back in one of the more happening parts of town. The spacious and inoffensive rooms, all with small balconies, bely the ugly exterior. Serves as the reception building for neighbouring *Villa Sotavento* and *Aparthotel Varazul*, which are run by the same Horizontes chain. ⑥.

Barlovento, Ave. 1era e/ 10 y 12 ☎5/66-71-40; fax 66-72-18. Stylish and sophisticated complex with over 200 double rooms yet retaining a harmonious atmosphere. Superb atmospheric lobby with a fountain and a captivating pool area enveloped by palm trees and other plant-life. Tennis and basketball courts. ⑥.

Bellamar, Calle 17 e/ Ave. 1era y 2da ☎5/66-74-90; fax 66-72-47. Faded pink and white eight-floor blocks popular with backpackers. Apart from some recently refurbished sections it's fairly run-down, but there is a sizeable pool and reasonable facilities. One of the cheaper options, although still expensive for what it is. ④.

Caribe, Ave. Playa y 30 ☎5/66-74-87; fax 66-74-88. Bland beige accommodation blocks flank a cosy pool area that leads directly onto the beach. Fair-sized rooms with enough space on the square balconies for a chair or two. Restaurant overlooking the shoreline. ⑥.

Club Tropical, Ave. 1era e/ 21 y 22 ☎5/66-71-45; fax 66-72-27. Modern hotel on the beach with a marine sports club and all the necessary facilities but nothing much in the way of character. ⑨.

Copey, Ave. 3era y 60 ☎5/66-75-05; fax 66-75-09. With its back to the Autopista del Sur and the main building resembling a multi-storey car park the *Copey* is not the most picturesque hotel in Varadero. Having said that, the best has been made of a bad design and there are enough trees spread about to breathe some life into the mostly concrete complex. Two tennis courts, a large pool, a disco and mopeds available for rental. All-inclusive. ⑦.

Cuatro Palmas, Ave. 1era e/ 60 y 62 ☎5/66-70-40; fax 66-75-83. A well-balanced artistically designed complex featuring a variety of accommodation buildings and slightly cheaper rooms overlooking the Parque Josone. There's a good choice of eating possibilities, a nice pool and watersports facilities. On the beach in the heart of Varadero's shopping centre. ⑦.

Dos Mares, Calle 53 y Ave. 1era ☎ & fax 5/61-27-02. Untypical of Varadero, this agreeable little hotel is of the kind more often found in provincial colonial towns. Makes up for its lack of facilities with bags of character and a pleasant intimacy. ⑤.

Ledo, Ave. Playa y 43 ☎5/61-32-06. A diminutive two-floor hotel with a down-to-earth vibe in a basic but endearing building over the road from the beach. Neat and compact. ⑤.

Mar del Sur, Ave. 3era y 30 ☎5/66-74-82 or 66-22-46; fax 66-74-81. Large pink complex running along both sides of the road and which, were it not for the colour, would resemble a hospital. Basic rooms in various shapes and sizes contained in box-like buildings spread out over what is best described as a campus. Comprehensive facilities include a kids' playground and a large pool, but nothing looks new and the location is unexotic. ⑤.

Pullman, Ave. 1era e/ 49 y 50 ☎5/66-71-61; fax 66-74-95. One of the smallest and most adorable hotels in Varadero, whose main building is based around a castle-like turret. Very relaxing atmosphere and ideal if you want to avoid the hullabaloo laid on as entertainment at most of the other hotels on the peninsula. ⑤.

Varazul, Ave. 1era e/ 14 y 15 ☎5/66-71-32; fax 66-72-29. Soulless but roomy apartments featuring kitchen, living room, bathroom and bedrooms with unsubtle and outdated furniture. Self-catering with a grocery shop on the ground floor. Exterior is in same uninspired vein as its neighbour and partner *Acuazul*, whose pool, restaurants and reception it shares. ⑥.

Villa Caleta, Calle 19 y Ave. 1era ☎5/66-70-80. Small and friendly site with a three-storey building on the road side, five villas facing the beach and a tiny pool in the centre. Modest but tastefully furnished rooms. ⑤.

Villa La Mar, Ave. 3era e/ 29 y 30 ☎5/61-22-48 or 61-25-08. One of the few hotels accepting both tourists and Cubans, this concrete complex is sociable but unsophisticated. There's no swimming pool and it's located on the wrong side of the peninsula but these compromises are justified by some of the cheapest rooms in Varadero. ④.

Villa Sotavento, Ave. 1era y 13 ☎5/66-71-32; fax 66-72-29. Blending in with the neighbourhood, the 25 one- to eight-room houses in modern, colonial and fairy-tale cottage designs are mostly charming and compact. Good if you want the benefits of a hotel without feeling too cut off from the real world. Reception desk is in *Acuazul*, whose facilities are also available to guests. ⑥.

Avenida de las Américas

Bella Costa, Ave. de las Américas ☎5/66-72-10; fax 66-83-34. The architecture of the main building is a little heavy-handed whilst the villas wouldn't look out of place at a ski resort in the Alps. Pegged to the beach and very close to two of Varadero's best nightclubs, it's one of the best located all-inclusives. Its barbecue grill under a thatched *bohío* roof offers uninterrupted views of the sea and attracts an encouraging number of non-guests. Swimming pool, three restaurants, four bars, watersports centre and hairdressers. ⑧.

Club Varadero, Ave. de las Américas ☎5/66-70-30; fax 66-70-05. Hidden from the road behind a thick rampart of trees and shrubs, this very private all-inclusive luxury resort is for couples and singles aged over 16. Set in thirty acres of landscaped gardens and on the beach it's classy, if a little pretentious, and well equipped for watersports. An impressively comprehensive set of facilities includes a large swimming pool, five bars and four floodlit tennis courts. ⑧.

Coral, Ave. de las Américas e/ H y K ☎5/66-72-40 to 42; fax 66-71-94. A busy complex featuring the largest landscaped swimming pool in Varadero. Thankfully, the imposing architecture is balanced with plenty of trees and plants outside and in. Swimming pool, tennis court, pool room, beauty parlour and watersports. Currently the best bargain amongst the all-inclusives. ⑥.

Internacional, Ave. de las Américas ☎5/66-70-38; fax 66-72-46. One of the original luxury hotels in Varadero now looks decidedly dated next to the super-complexes just down the road, its renowned *Cabaret Continental* in keeping with the 1950s kitsch. Resembling a political conference centre, the oblong four-floor building is painted in two ghastly tones of pink, its lack of grace to some extent compensated for by its location on one of the best stretches of beach. ⑥.

Las Morlas, Ave. de las Américas ☎5/66-72-30 to 34; fax 66-70-07. Deceivingly characterless from the roadside, this is the most compact of the all-inclusive options and considerably more subdued than some of its counterparts. Some of the rooms are quite dark but they're well equipped and most look down onto the leafy pool area. There's a tennis court and gym. ⑨.

Tuxpán, Ave. de las Américas ☎5/66-75-60; fax 66-75-61. One of the smallest complexes on this strip, making it difficult to escape the nonstop entertainment programme. Highlights include one of the few Mexican restaurants in Varadero and free entrance to *La Bamba*, one of the biggest and best discos on the peninsula. Rooms are comfortable but simple. ⑨.

Villa Cuba, Ave. de las Américas ☎5/66-82-80; fax 66-82-82. The main building features an exciting multi-level layout with staircases and gangways zigzagging through a network of different floors and platforms. Spread out around the open-plan complex, which stretches down to the beach, there are various smaller residences, some with their own swimming pool. This impressive all-inclusive includes a sauna, gym, barber shop and beauty parlour, a disco, diving initiation courses and a large swimming pool. ⑧.

East of the Dupont Mansion

Arenas Doradas, Autopista del Sur ☎5/66-81-50; fax 66-81-59. Artistically designed with an oriental flavour. A series of fountains and artificial streams leads to the distinctive Japanese-style villas, but the sense of enchantment is partly lost to the usual nonstop amplified entertainment broadcast from the centre. There are separate pools for adults and children, an open-air jacuzzi, tennis courts, car and scooter rental. ⑦.

Beaches Varadero, Carretera Las Morlas, off Autopista Sur ☎5/66-84-70; fax 66-85-44. A pastel-coloured five-storey main block stands at the top of the spacious grounds of this tastefully designed hotel. The emphasis is on sophisticated comfort, with soft-cushion seats around the lobby bar, a relaxing lounge area and an airy piano bar. ⑦.

Gran Hotel, Autopista del Sur ☎5/66-82-02; fax 66-82-43. This huge complex lacks subtlety and is impressive only for the amount of space it fills up. Facilities, however, are excellent, which is just as well as this is one of the furthest hotels from the town. The all-inclusive package is optional but is only $25 per person more than the standard price for a room. ⑦.

Meliá Las Américas, Autopista del Sur km 7 ☎5/66-76-00; fax 66-76-25. Next door to the Dupont Mansion this is undoubtedly the most stunningly designed complex on the peninsula, like an adventure playground for grown-ups, with paths weaving their way down through the intricately landscaped grounds to a secluded part of the beach. Even the pool drops down a level whilst it twists itself around the pathways and pond. Its rooms are tastefully furnished. ⑧.

Meliá Varadero, Autopista del Sur km 7 ☎5/66-70-13; fax 66-70-12. Highly sophisticated star-shaped deluxe hotel whose seven tentacles meet spectacularly in the centre around an indoor rainforest where ivy cascades down the circular walls from high above. There's a swimming pool with a bar in the centre, and the small collection of contrastingly styled restaurants and bars includes a large thatched-roof hall looking over the sea from a low cliff. Well equipped for business travellers with a series of convention halls and meeting rooms. ⑧.

Sol Club Palmeras, Autopista del Sur ☎5/66-70-09; fax 66-70-08. Enormous luxury resort spread out over tree-swept grounds. Aimed at families, it includes a basketball court, kids' playground, two floodlit tennis courts, a volleyball court, mini-golf, six bars and five restaurants. The cool interior of the hotel, rich in plant life, echoes with the soothing sound of a fountain. ⑦.

The Town

Varadero is low on sites of cultural or historic interest, and those that do exist are quickly exhausted. Central Varadero, specifically the area between Calles 56 and 64, has the highest proportion of things to see, as well as the greatest concentration of shops and restaurants. Don't expect to see any classic works of architecture on the peninsula, other than some of the more luxurious hotels. For pre-twentieth-century churches and monuments you'll have to go to the nearby towns of Cárdenas and Matanzas (see p.216 and p.203); the immaculate but modest **Iglesia de Santa Elvira**, built in 1938, on the corner of Avenida Primera and Calle 47, is about as close as buildings get to being historic this side of the Varadero bridge.

Museo Municipal

Detailing the history of Varadero, with rooms on sport and wildlife thrown in as well, the **Museo Municipal** (daily 10am–5pm; $1), at the beach end of Calle 57, contains a small collection of disparately connected exhibits of varying degrees of interest. Downstairs, the history collection includes some remains from an Amerindian burial site discovered in the province, while displays on more recognizable aspects of local history include photos of the first hotel built on the peninsula, the Hotel Torres. Eye-catching photographs of Fidel Castro, Che Guevara and their colleague Camilo Cienfuegos living it up in Varadero's hotels during the 1960s make a refreshing contrast with the more common images of Cuba's revolutionary heroes. Upstairs, a poorly presented set of stuffed animals, representing a small cross-section of Cuba's fauna, share the tatty brown carpet in one of the rooms. Next door to this are photographs and memorabilia of some of Cuba's sporting greats and some photographs taken during the earlier part of the twentieth century of the straight-faced aristocratic members of the local sailing club, El Club Náutico de Varadero.

Parque Josone

Over the road from the grounds of the Museo Municipal is the entrance to **Parque Josone**, sometimes referred to as Retiro Josone (daily noon–midnight; $1), a landscaped park and the most tranquil and picturesque spot in central Varadero. The design is simple, with no intricately designed gardens, just sweeping well-kept lawns dotted with trees, and a small lake with its own palm tree-studded island. There are three restaurants (see pp.196–97) plus a cafeteria to help you prolong what would otherwise be a short visit. In the cafeteria building, towards the back of the park, there is pool and ten pin bowling. Official tourist literature claims the park to be a reserve for the protection of the local flora and fauna but the only animals being preserved here are a few stone flamingoes, a stone snake and a handful of common-or-garden ducks and geese.

Varadero

East of the town

A visit to the relatively secluded and distant-feeling eastern reaches of the peninsula should ideally focus on one of the few tangible attractions in this area, as wandering about is not really an option, with the landscape dominated by exclusive luxury hotels or covered in inaccessible scrub. The Autopista del Sur, the only road along this stretch, skirts alongside the man-moulded scenery of the giant hotel complexes and the unruffled green of the Varadero golf course and leads to a scrub-covered, dusty landscape which has never made it into the town planners' sketch books and feels quite deserted in places.

The nearest attraction, about 2km from central Varadero, is the **Dupont Mansion** (daily noon–midnight; $3), next door to the *Meliá Las Américas* hotel. Built in 1926 by the American millionaire Irenée Dupont at a cost of over $700,000, it has hardly changed since Dupont and his family fled the island in 1959, and stands testament to the wealth and decadence of the pre-revolutionary years in Varadero. It's not a museum as such, and wandering freely through the immaculately maintained, spendidly furnished rooms, it almost feels like you're trespassing in someone's home. All the hallmarks of opulence are there, from chandeliers to polished marbled floors, and although a significant part of the mansion can't be explored – some of it is now occupied by an excellent restaurant – there's enough on show to get a real flavour of the place. The entrance charge includes a cocktail in the dignified bar at the top of the house from where there are views along the surrounding coastline and of the golf course on the other side.

Two and a half kilometres beyond the mansion, near the Marina Chapelin, is a **dolphinarium** (☎5/66-80-31) with several shows daily ($5). The natural setting of the Laguna Los Taínos makes a novel change and for a bargain $10 you can swim with the dolphins after the show. If you don't have your own car, the best way to go is to book at one of the information centres, where they'll charge you $6, including transport.

Just down the road from the dolphinarium, at the eastern extreme of the peninsula, over three square kilometres of land that have managed to remain outside of the bulldozers' paths were declared in 1997 the **Varahicacos Ecological Reserve**. Billed by its founders as "the other Varadero", it's the only part of the peninsula where you can experience relatively unspoilt if undramatic landscapes, with a chance of viewing up close the flora and fauna, as well as some of the area's history. The reserve's visitor centre (daily 8am–5pm) is by the side of the road, about a kilometre past the *Gran Hotel*. From there you can arrange to follow any one of three routes, each designed to include one or other of the area's ecological or archeological features. Shortest is the half-hour-long visit to the **Cueva de Ambrosio**, where a large number of Ciboney cave paintings have

For reviews of the Dupont Mansion's restaurant and bar, see p.197.

been discovered. Some of the pictographs are easily deciphered but there are plenty more obscure images to exercise the imagination. A smaller cave, the **Cueva Musulmanes**, where human bones over 2500 years old have been discovered, is included on a trail which also offers insights into the local wildlife and plantlife. The third and longest route takes in an impressive 500-year-old cactus plant, then circles round the **Laguna de Mangón** and finishes at the ruins of a colonial salt storehouse and site of the first salt mine in Latin America. On any of the three routes you will be accompanied by a specialist guide, which you can pay for at the visitor centre, but to guarantee an English-speaking one you should arrange to go with a tour group through one of the information centres or *buros de turismo*. For individuals, the charge for being guided around any of the three set routes is $2.50–3.50 per person, but you can also arrange tailor-made excursions to suit your preferences.

Fishing trips

Tailor-made excursions and diving or fishing packages are available through negotiation at any of the marinas, and the *buros de turismo* in most hotel lobbies can usually also help with arrangements. Marina Chapelin and Marina Gaviota are the best equipped but all three will supply any necessary equipment on fishing expeditions. For information on excursions see the box on p.184 and for scuba diving see the box on p.200.

Marina Dársena, Vía Blanca, 1km from the Varadero bridge ☎5/66-80-63; fax 66-74-56. Run by Puertosol and sometimes referred to as Marina Acua because of its link to the Acua Diving Club on the other side of the Laguna de Paso Malo. Has the least impressive selection of boat trips but fishing trips around northern Varadero can work out at comparatively good value with prices per boat for a four-, six- or eight-hour trip at $200, $250 and $300 respectively; boats take up to four passengers.

Marina Chapelin, Autopista Sur Km12 ☎5/66-75-50 or 66-78-00; fax 66-70-93. Operated by Marlin, who also run Club Barracuda and Capitaine Duval Cruises. The most exclusive offer available at this marina is Jungle Tour, a two-hour excursion on two-person ski-bikes which stops off at a cay where crocodiles, iguanas and other creatures are waiting to be observed. There are departures every hour between 9am and 4pm and the cost is $35 per person. A day-trip with four hours of fishing costs $240 for one to four people and $30 for each extra person, including an on-board open bar. There's an information kiosk specifically for the Marina Chapelin at Ave. 1era y 59.

Marina Gaviota, at the end of Autopista Sur, Punta Hicacos ☎5/66-77-55 or 56. The most remote of the three marinas, and run by the Gaviota Group who also operate a number of hotels on the peninsula. The marina features a restaurant, *El Galeon*, where you can choose your main seafood dish whilst it's still alive. Fishing trips are usually from 9am to 3pm with four hours of fishing at a total cost of $250 for up to four people, and $25 per extra person. There's a choice of two smart motorized yachts and an open bar on board along with a welcome cocktail. For another $15 they'll include a lobster lunch and an extra hour and a half's fishing.

Varadero

Boat trips

There are a whole host of different boat trips leaving from the jetties and marinas around Varadero. If you're daunted at the thought of scuba diving, then an easy way to see what you're missing is to take a trip on one of the glass-bottomed boats. Almost all prebooked excursions include transfer from your hotel to the point of departure in the price.

Capitaine Duval Cruises is the most upmarket and stylish glass-bottomed boat in Varadero, operated by Marlin, the organization that runs the Marina Chapelin. Excursions last three hours and cost $30 per person. It leaves from the small jetty on the Laguna de Paso Malo outside the *Complejo Paradiso Puntarena*. Book at any of the information centres or *buros de turismo*.

Caribbean Cruise (Marina Gaviota) is the flattering name given to the seven- to eight-hour excursion to Cayo Blanco. It includes a snack, welcome cocktail, time at the beach and lunch at Cayo Blanco as well as snorkelling (gear supplied). There's a minimum requirement of six people and a cost of $55 per person. Book at the marina, through the *Coral* or *Caracol* hotels or Gaviota Tours (see box on p.184).

Jolly Roger Catamaran Cruises (Marina Chapelin) are half-day, whole-day or sunset excursions on elegant twin-hull sailing boats. Most trips incorporate the Bay of Cárdenas as well as the waters around Varadero itself. There are beach stops and the usual snorkelling opportunities. Drinks are available on all cruises and lunch is supplied on full-day excursions. The cost is $70 per person.

Nautilus, another glass-bottomed boat, leaves from the Marina Gaviota and explores the coral reef around Cayo Blanco. It's the most comprehensive of the three similar trips around Varadero and the five-hour excursion includes the dolphin show at Rancho Cangrejo, all for $30 per person. Contact any of the hotels in the Gaviota Group, such as the *Coral*, *Villa Caleta* or the *Caracol*, to book for the *Nautilus*, or ring the marina direct.

Seafari (Marina Dársena) runs the northern length of the peninsula up to Cayo Piedras where you can snorkel, followed by a stop for lunch at the beach at Cayo Libertad. There's an open bar and the choice of doing the trip in a yacht or motor boat. Daily trips run from 9am to 5pm, at a cost of $65 per person.

Seafari a Cayo Blanco (Marina Chapelin) departs on a daily basis and costs $65 per person but can also be booked for exclusively private parties at a minimum cost of $280 in total. Most of the day is spent on a sailing yacht with a lobster lunch at Cayo Blanco. There's an open bar plus musical entertainment and snorkelling opportunities.

Seafari Crucero del Sol (Marina Gaviota) is the Gaviota Group's catamaran cruise. This is one of the newest and best offers available at the Marina Gaviota and combines all of the best aspects of the other two cruises but on a fantastic catamaran. The cost is $70 per person.

Seafari Exclusivo Especial (Marina Gaviota) is a similar excursion to Caribbean Cruise with the same minimum number requirement but with the added bonus of a dolphin show at Rancho Cangrejo. It's $65 per person or $75 with an open bar.

Varasub is a glass-bottomed boat which also leaves from the Laguna de Paso Malo. You're given between thirty and forty minutes actual viewing time on the coral reef near Boca de Guamarioca to the west of Varadero, parallel with the Vía Blanca. The whole trip costs $25 for adults, $20 for children. Book through any of the information centres.

The beach

Almost from one end of Varadero to the other, facing the Florida Straits, runs a golden carpet of fine sand bathed by placid emerald-green waters, nothing short of a place of worship for sun-lovers and beach bums alike. The whole strip is considered the same beach, though it breaks into smaller pieces at the eastern end of the peninsula, where it effectively becomes the exclusive domain of the all-inclusive hotels. From the Dupont Mansion to the western tip of Varadero the beach is accessible to anyone, whether a hotel guest or not, and there is very little to differentiate any one section of this ten-kilometre highway of sand. There tends to be a livelier atmosphere and more people about on the stretch between Calles 57 and 61 where the *Albacora* restaurant looks over the beach and one of the watersports centres is located. South of Calle 39 there is a concentration of beachfront hotels whose entertainment programmes can ruin the peace, whilst other local buildings create a concrete border which some may find a little intrusive. Snorkelling is poor wherever you go, and you may have a long walk to rent out pedalos and other equipment if you don't aim specifically for one of the watersports clubs (see box, p.200).

Eating

For such a large international holiday resort the quality and variety of food in Varadero's **restaurants** is remarkably mediocre. Most places play safe with almost identical *comida criolla* menus, whilst foreign-food restaurants often leave you questioning the chef's geography. Nevertheless the choice is wider than anywhere else outside Havana, and you should, if you choose wisely, be able to eat out every night for a week before déjà vu of the palate sets in. It's well worth trying some of the restaurants in the deluxe hotels where the quality of food is often higher, thanks to their more direct access to foreign markets, and even the all-inclusives usually open their doors to non-guests. Like *casas particulares*, *paladares* are forbidden by law in Varadero.

Reparto Kawama

La Casa de Al, in the grounds of *Villa Punta Blanca*, Ave. Kawama. Better-than-average Spanish food in one of the most impressive restaurant buildings in Varadero (see p.187).

Kawama Buffet Restaurant, *Hotel Kawama* ☎5/66-71-56. Fantastically atmospheric restaurant (see p.187) with a terrace overlooking the beach. The international menu changes on a regular basis and can include anything from pizza to rumpsteak.

Kiki's Club, Ave. Kawama y 5. A large selection of basic spaghetti dishes and some of the best pizzas in town. The outdoor terrace, despite its tacky tables and chairs, is more pleasant than the packed interior.

La Sangría, Ave. Kawama e/ 7 y 8. One of the cheapest places for lobster in Varadero also offers a mixture of half-hearted and good-quality meals including a small selection of pizzas and pastas, as well as several meat dishes and the recommended Lobster in a Cuban Sauce.

Varadero

The Town

Albacora, Calle 59 at the beach. A great place to enjoy pricey lobster and shrimp from the almost exclusively seafood menu, under a protective canopy of low twisting branches on a large terrace over the beach. Very laid-back when there's not a group playing over-loud music on the built-in stage.

El Aljibe, Ave. 1era y 36. This reasonably priced restaurant specializes in chicken and offers an unlimited buffet of *comida criolla* with chicken *al aljibe* for $12. Tables are set on a wide open veranda under a thatched roof, bordered by a dense selection of plants and small trees which do a pretty good job of blocking out the view of the road, if not the noise.

Antiguedades, Ave. 1era e/ 58 y 59. The menu consists of only three or four expensive but exquisite seafood dishes, though the atmosphere more than makes up for the limited choice. From pictures of jazz greats and bygone Hollywood stars to a wall of old clocks and even a rocking chair hanging from the ceiling, some-how nothing in this Aladdin's cave of a restaurant looks out of place.

Arrecife, Camino del Mar y 13. This quiet street-corner restaurant offers a good variety of moderately priced seafood. A tastefully furnished little room leads onto a compact veranda.

La Barbacoa, Ave. 1era y 64. Steakhouse and barbecue grill tucked into the top corner of town with outdoor seating and shielded from the road by a screen of trees. Topping the menu are the expensive sirloin, T-bone and club steaks, whilst there are also chicken, pork and fish dishes.

La Cabanita, Camino del Mar y 10. The inexpensive seafood served in this beachfront bungalow and brick columned patio isn't as popular as you might expect, probably because it's located in a distant part of town.

La Campana, Parque Josone. Mostly pork-based set meals for above-average prices in this cosy alpine cabin with a large stone fireplace, dark wooden rafters and goats' heads mounted on the walls.

Castel Nuovo, Ave 1era no. 503 (on the first corner as you enter the town from the Varadero bridge). Reasonable Italian cuisine and a good selection of seafood. Popular despite being low on charm, though the fantastic resident musicians will play almost any request and not just the usual corny traditional numbers.

Chong Kwok, Ave. 1era y 55. Cheap semi-authentic Cantonese cuisine and the only restaurant of its kind on the peninsula. Low tables and cushions for seats make for a welcome break from the Varadero norm.

La Fondue, Ave, 1era y 62. French-Swiss food, mostly cheese fondue-based dishes, some much better than others, as well as tasty tortillas and an impres-sive selection of international wines in a quaint homely decor.

Lai Lai, Ave. 1era y 18 ☎5/66-77-93. Westerners may be disappointed by the complete absence of chow mein or chop suey dishes at this oriental restaurant though there is a good selection of seafood and some familiar Chinese dishes. Less exclusive than its grand exterior suggests and suffers from the lacklustre attempt at Chinese ornamental-style decor. It's worth booking one of the two private, cosier rooms upstairs if you're in a group of four or more.

Mallorca, Ave. 1era y 62. One of the few Spanish restaurants in Varadero, specializing in paella. Portions are large but a little heavy. Choose between the sombre and smart interior or the terrace snack bar.

Pizzería Capri, Ave. Playa y 43 ☎5/61-21-17. Unusually, locals outnumber tourists in this pizzeria. Pizzas have more base than toppings and can be paid for in either dollars or pesos but you'll need to get in line and make a reservation if you opt for the latter. Popular and unpretentious.

El Ranchón, Ave. 1era e/ 15 y 16. Views of the sea from a pleasant roadside country ranch serving traditionally prepared fish and meat dishes. The scrappy field which surrounds it detracts slightly from the atmosphere, as does the traffic.

Ristorante Dante, Parque Josone. Acceptable Italian cuisine with placid views across the lake but little in the way of atmosphere.

East of town

Las Américas, Dupont Mansion, Autopista Sur km 7 ☎5/66-77-50. One of the classiest and most expensive restaurants on the peninsula, with seating in the library, out on the terrace and down in the wine cellar. The international menu won't win any awards but is a cut above the average; more outstanding is the selection of cocktails and wines.

El Mesón de Quijote, Ave. de las Américas. They claim to serve "Cuban style Spanish food" but Spanish-style Cuban food better describes the moderately priced lobster, shrimp, chicken and lamb dishes. Rustic interior, with potted plants and vases making up most of the simple decoration.

Bars and cafés

Bar 440, Camino del Mar e/ 14 y 15. A healthy mix of locals and tourists populate this simple little bar set back from the main road. Closes at 10.30pm.

Bar Las Tapas, Camino del Mar e/ 12 y13. A good selection of wines and cocktails is offered in a small cellar-style room with windows opening onto a tiny terrace. Also a good place for a light snack.

Bar Terraza, Complejo Mediterráneo, Ave. 1era esq. Calle 54. Unpolished pseudo-50s style diner bar with about as much local flavour as you can realistically expect in Varadero.

Coffee Shop 25, Ave. 1era esq. 25 One of the only places specializing in hot drinks, albeit a small selection, is this 24-hour café with a shady patio.

Dupont Mansion, Autopista Sur km 7. At the top of this splendid mansion there are views along the coastline and a sophisticated shining bar with an ornate wooden ceiling supported by black pillars.

El Galeón, *Hotel Dos Mares*, Calle 53 y Ave. 1era. One of the most characterful bars in the town, set just below street level with a stylish varnished-wood finish and a slight Mediterranean feel. A good place to come if you want to avoid the trappings of most hotel bars – this is just a straight-up, laid-back place to get a drink.

Fast food and snacks

There are **fast-food** outlets all over town with *El Rápido* best represented whilst the burger chain *Burgui* has a branch at Ave. 1era y 43. Quick-stop open-air **snack bars** line the length of Avenida Primera, selling soft drinks, beers, rum and unadventurous menus of pork, rice, fried chicken and pizza. Most are no more than tables and chairs by the roadside and whilst none stands out for atmosphere there are one or two which do offer something slightly different to the rest. For cheap **ice cream** try *La Casa de la Miel* at Ave. 1era e/ 25 y 26, which also has a private one-room restaurant out the back, or *Coppelia* in the centre of the Parque de las 8000 Taquillas. You can sample raw sugar cane juice for a peso at the *guarapera* on the corner of Ave. 1era and Calle 37.

Papa Fundo, Calle 13 e/ Ave. 1era y Camino del Mar. Lodged inside the *Villa Sotavento* neighbourhood, this simple and slightly cramped snack bar cut into the side of a building serves up *mojitos* for just $1.50.

Piano Bar, Centro Cultural Artex, Calle 60 e/ Ave. 2da y Ave. 3era. A sleek little bar, suited to something more refined than the karaoke that it hosts most nights of the week. Avoid the singing by leaving before 11pm.

Nightlife and entertainment

Note that some clubs do not allow shorts or sleeveless tops to be worn.

Nightlife is almost entirely restricted to the hotels, most of which offer something more akin to a school disco than a fully equipped **nightclub**. The majority are open to non-guests although some of the all-inclusives may restrict entrance to their own clientele. The music policy is more or less the same wherever you go: Latin and Euro-pop and watered-down house and techno. The only factors to take into account are the location and the size of the place: the two biggest clubs are a taxi ride away for most people, at the Dupont Mansion end of Avenida de las Américas. There is also an extraordinary number of venues whose main billing is **karaoke**. These tend to operate as a bar beforehand and a disco afterwards and follow the same format as in the rest of the world.

The most popular alternative to a night sweated out on the dancefloor are the **cabarets**, which again are almost all run by the hotels. There are considerable differences in ambience created by the various settings but the shows themselves are basically the same displays of kitsch glamour, oversentimental crooners and semi-naked dancers wherever you go. There are surprisingly few obvious places to go for **live music** in Varadero and few venues outside of the hotels where live Cuban music is a regular feature. The usually inactive Anfiteatro on the mainland side of the Varadero bridge used to stage concerts by some of Cuba's finest travelling shows and musicians but is now waiting for an injection of life.

There's a **cinema** on Ave. Playa e/ 42 y 43 showing Cuban and foreign films every evening from 6.30pm onwards. Entrance is a single peso.

Clubs, discos and karaoke venues

La Bamba, *Hotel Tuxpán*, Ave. de las Américas. Previously the biggest and most popular club in town but now shares the limelight with *La Rumba* up the road. The entrance charge is $10 but there are reduced rates for anyone staying at any hotel in Varadero. Daily 10.30pm–3.30am.

La Descarga, Ave. Kawama, outside the entrance to *Hotel Kawama*. Intimate and sociable karaoke bar. The $2 at the door entitles you to a free drink. Daily 10pm–5am.

Habana Café, next to the *Sol Club Las Sirenas* hotel, Ave. de las Américas. Like its counterpart in Havana, this touristy venue is littered with 1950s Cuban and American artefacts, from a full-size Oldsmobile parked inside the door to gas pumps, barbers' chairs and Coca-Cola signs. Combines the classic holiday disco with cabaret-style entertainment. Amazingly, entrance is free. Daily 10pm–late.

Havana Club, Calle 62 y Ave. 2da. The biggest nightclub in the town and a popular pick-up joint. Often the last place to close at night. Cover $5. Daily 10pm–late.

El Kastillito, Ave. Playa y 49. In theory this is a disco but the dancefloor often remains empty whilst the punters sit on the beachfront terrace drinking at plastic tables. Understandably free. Daily 11pm–6am.

Palacio de la Rumba, end of Ave. de las Américas just beyond the *Bella Costa*. Often referred to simply as *La Rumba* and as lively a night as anywhere in Varadero. Having paid the $10 to get in, there's an open bar and therefore a guaranteed night of lost inhibitions. Daily 10pm–5am.

La Patana, Laguna de Paso Malo. This floating disco takes place on a boat moored permanently on the far side of the Varadero canal. Open 9pm–5am.

Piano Bar, Centro Cultural Artex, Calle 60 e/ Ave. 2da y Ave. 3era. A compact and classy bar hosting a nightly karaoke from 11.30pm with a short live music show on the tiny stage at weekends. No cover charge.

La Red, Ave. 3era e/ 29 y 30. There's a good mix of Cubans and foreigners at this popular and friendly club which packs out at weekends. Cover $3. Daily 10pm–4am.

Cabarets and live shows

Cabaret Kawama, *Hotel Kawama*. One of the more stylish cabarets in that it's set in a cosy underground jazz-style nightclub. Cover $5 for non-guests. Mon–Sat 11pm–late.

Cabaret Mediterráneo, Complejo Mediterráneo, Calle 54 e/ Ave. 1era y Ave. Playa. By far the cheapest cabaret in Varadero, outdoors in a restaurant courtyard. $2. Open 8pm–3am.

La Comparsita, Centro Cultural Artex, Calle 60 e/ Ave. 2da y Ave. 3era. Shows differ from night to night at this relatively professional stage venue. Most performances are in the cabaret spirit but are not necessarily the full works though live music and dance are a mainstay. Free. Daily 11pm–late.

Continental, *Hotel Internacional*, Ave. de las Américas ☎5/66-70-38. You'll have to pay $25 to see Varadero's best and most famous cabaret. Exceeded in reputation only by the *Tropicana* in Havana, all the exaggerated costumes and heartfelt renditions of cheesy love songs make this classic show, which has travelled internationally. There's a disco afterwards. Tues–Sun 9pm–3.30am.

Cueva del Pirata, Ave. del Sur, next to the entrance to *Club Med* ☎5/66-77-51 or 61-38-29. The show and disco that follows take place in a cave, which makes for a different atmosphere. The performers dress as pirates for a slight twist on the usual dress code. $10. Mon–Sat 9pm–2.30am.

FM17, Ave. 1era esq. 17. A reasonable range of live music, from traditional Cuban music to modern salsa outfits, on a regular basis at this popular but slightly slipshod outdoor cafeteria.

Parque Josone, Ave. 1era e/ 56 y 59. Energetic live Afro-Cuban music and dance shows are staged on the small island on the lake in this landscaped park. The carnival-style performance begins around 9pm and costs $3.

Sport and outdoor pursuits

Most of the luxury hotels have at least one **tennis court** and of course a **swimming pool**, some of which are accessible to non-guests, usually for a few dollars. There are no regular spectator sports in Varadero – the nearest sports stadium is in the city of Matanzas (see p.203) – but there

Scuba diving and watersports

The **diving clubs** on the peninsula can supply you with all the necessary equipment and instruction and also offer excursions to elsewhere in Cuba, commonly to the Bay of Pigs in southern Matanzas. As well as the standard coral reef visits, clubs usually offer night dives and cave dives, often in the Cueva de Saturno to the west of Varadero, not far off the Vía Blanca. Many hotels, especially those on the beach, have their own watersports clubs and often offer beginners' diving classes.

Marina Gaviota, at the end of Autopista Sur, Punta Hicacos ☎5/66-77-55 or 56. Has its own on-site facilities for diving and offers competitive prices as well as complimentary transfers from your hotel to the marina. A single dive costs $35 whilst two dives are offered for just $50. Packages of six and ten dives cost $127 and $200 respectively. They also offer free initiation courses.

Club Barracuda, Ave. 1era e/ 58 y 59 ☎5/61-34-81; fax 66-70-72. Diving and watersports club linked with Marina Chapelin and the best equipped in terms of on-site facilities, including a restaurant, bar and private rooms. Offers the most comprehensive programme of diving including internationally recognized ACUC courses for advanced divers and instructors. The basic packages are $35 for a single-tank dive or $70 with two tanks, though these prices are reduced if you supply your own equipment. Also the best organized for first-time divers, with beginners' classes starting at $70 for a theory class, a lesson in a swimming pool and then a sea dive. Packages on offer include six dives for $150 and ten for $240. The club can also supply equipment for almost any watersport including jet skis ($1 per minute), windsurfing boards ($10 per hour), pedalos ($5 for two people per hour) and snorkelling equipment ($3 per hour).

Acua Diving Centre, Ave. Kawama e/ 2 y 3 ☎5/66-80-64 or 65. Co-ordinates its dives with Marina Dársena and run by the same chain, Puertosol. Offers ACUC and CMAS approved courses. Diving excursions every day, except Thursdays, between 9am and 1pm. Main dive sites located around Cayo Piedras, north of the easternmost point of Varadero, and Boca de Camarioca, about 15km west of the Laguna de Paso Malo. For basic daytime dives it's cheaper than Club Barracuda with a single tank dive for $35 and two tanks for $50.

Acua Sports, Camino del Mar e/ 9 y 10 ☎5/66-71-66 or 61-47-92 (daily 9am–6pm).Watersports club with a good selection of equipment for rent, including jet skis ($1 per minute), surfboards ($4 for 30min), kayaks ($3 for 30min), catamarans ($10 per person for 30min) and good old-fashioned deck chairs ($1 for a day). There's a cafeteria in the club and a few games such as air hockey.

are one or two places for participatory sporting activities. Most notable is the **Varadero Golf Club** (☎5/66-77-88; fax 66-81-80), whose professionally designed eighteen-hole, par 72 golf course was completed in 1998 and occupies over 2km of the peninsula along the Autopista del Sur. The caddy house and golf shop are next to the Dupont Mansion. Green fees are $40 for nine holes or $60 for all eighteen, whilst golf classes are offered at $20 for a 45-minute session. On a smaller scale there's **crazy golf** at El Golfito, Ave. 1era e/ 41 y 42, for just $1.

You can organize your own games of **football** on the pitch running alongside Calle 24 between Ave. 3era and Autopista Sur, where there are full-size goalposts, or take on the locals who usually play in the evening on a patch of grass on the corner of Calle 20 and Ave. 2da. Alternatively challenge the cream of Varadero's budding **tennis** enthusiasts at *La Raqueta Dorada* (daily 9am–noon & 2–6pm) at Ave. 1era e/ 37 y 38. It's an outdoor synthetic surface court which costs nothing to use, but you'll need to supply your own equipment.

Unusually for Cuba, there are two small **leisure complexes** in the town. At Todo en uno, Autopista y 54, there are bumper cars, a small video games arcade (the first on the island), and a four-lane 24-hour bowling alley. Complejo Recreativo Record (daily noon–8am) at Ave. Playa y 46 has a **pool hall**, cafeteria and another bowling alley. For a considerably bigger thrill the Centro Internacional de Paracaidismo offers **parachute drops** for $135, which includes the transfer, a class, and the drop itself. Bookings are taken at any of the information centres.

Shopping, galleries and workshops

Varadero is not the place to plan any big shopping expeditions, although it's still leagues ahead of most Cuban towns for quality and variety. On the whole, shops are few and far between and most are generally worth a quick browse if you happen to be passing anyway, but are unlikely to have you agonizing over whether to break into your emergency travellers' cheques.

For the highest concentration of shops you should head for the top of the town in between Calles 56 and 64, where you'll find two of the three shopping complexes, actually no more than five or six stores clustered together. Of these the **Centro Comercial Copey**, two blocks from Ave. 1era on Calle 62, is missable in the extreme, though the newer **Centro Comercial Caimán**, at Ave. 1era e/ 61 y 62, does at least contain some quality **gift shops** and is a good place for cigars, rum and perfume. Much better than either of these but a bit out of the way for most people is **Plaza América**, in between the hotels *Meliá Las Américas* and *Meliá Varadero*. This collection of small shops is the nearest thing to a mall in Varadero and is where you'll find the largest stock of brand-name clothing and generally the more upmarket merchandise and souvenirs.

Besides Plaza América and the Centro Comercial Caimán, the best places to buy **cigars** are the Casa del Habano on Calle 63 e/ Ave. 1era y Ave. 2da, which stocks a good variety of the best brands; and the Casa de los Tabaqueros at Ave. 1era y 27, where you can also watch cigars being made.

There's a broad selection of **arts and crafts** on sale around the town. The best craft market is the **Plaza de Artesanos** on the corner of Ave. 1era and Calle 12, where artistic Afro-Cuban wood carvings and tacky Che Guevara placemats sit alongside each other. There are smaller selections of arts and crafts in the Artex shops around town (see below). At the **Galería de Arte Sol y Mar** (daily 9am–noon & 1–5pm) at Ave. 1era e/ 34 y 35 there are small but usually pleasing exhibitions of **paintings** and **photographs** by artists from all over Cuba. Everything is for sale and amongst the unimaginative landscapes and unsubtle street scenes there's usually enough soulful stuff to balance things out. In a similar vein is the **Galería de Arte Varadero** (daily 9am–7.30pm), whilst next door at the **Taller de Cerámica** (daily 9am–7.30pm) you can watch **pottery** being made in the busy workshop and then buy a piece in the shop. Both are on Ave. 1era between 59 and 60. There's usually a good selection of arty poster prints amongst the space fillers at Bazar Hicacos on Ave. 1era between 33 and 34.

For **compact discs** and **cassettes**, as well as musical instruments, T-shirts and books, there are a number of Artex shops around Varadero, two of the biggest at Ave. 1era esq. Calle 12, next to the craft market, and in the **Complejo Cultural Artex** on the corner of Calle 60 and Ave. 1era. The widest selection of CDs and tapes is at MaxMusic where you can find the same choice of Cuban music as in the Artex shops but also a number of releases by US and European artists. The shop also stocks books in several different languages including various titles in English, mostly romances. The one place calling itself a **bookshop** is the Librería Hanoí at Ave. 1era e/ 43 y 44, whose limited selection of mostly Cuban political literature and fiction makes up the biggest section of the cramped premises. Mares, specialists in **sports equipment** and clothing, including diving and watersports equipment, is at Ave. 1era e/ 59 y 60, whilst the widest selection of **footwear** is found not far away at Peletería Verona on Calle 63.

There are no big **supermarkets** or food markets on the peninsula. Your best bet for the basics is Grocery Varazul at Calle 15 e/ Ave. 1era y Ave. 2da, where you can buy toiletries, meats, cheese, alcohol, snacks, and canned food, the mini-supermarket in Plaza América or Mini Super Playazul at Calle 13 e/ Ave. 1era and Camino del Mar.

Listings

Airlines Aerotaxi, Ave. 1era y 24 ☎5/61-29-29; Air Canada, Juan Gualberto Gómez Airport ☎5/61-20-10; Air Europe, Juan Gualberto Gómez Airport ☎5/5-36-17; Cubana, Ave. 1era e/ 54 y 55 (Mon–Fri 8am–4pm); LTU, Juan Gualberto Gómez Airport ☎5/5-36-11; Martinair, Juan Gualberto Gómez Airport ☎5/53-62-4.

Airport information ☎5/61-30-16.

Banks and money The Banco Financiero Internacional, Ave. 1era e/ 32 y 33 (Mon–Fri 8.30am–7pm; open at weekends, entrance on Ave. Playa), is the bank most experienced in foreign currency transactions and the best place for wiring money, whilst the Banco de Crédito y Comercio, Ave. 1era e/ 35 y 36 (Mon–Fri 9am–1.30pm & 3–7pm), is the cheapest place to change travellers' cheques. There is a Cadeca *casas de cambio*, for buying pesos, at Ave. Playa e/ 41 y 42.

Bicycle and scooter rental Bikes can be rented from a roadside set-up at Ave. 1era y 58 for $2 per hour. There are scooter rentals at the side of the road every ten blocks or so on Avenida Primera as well as in a number of hotels. Rental points, most of which are run by Rumbos, include Ave. 1era y 17 and Ave. 1era e/ 37 y 38 (☎5/61-31-10), where they also rent bicycles.

Car rental Transautos at Ave. esq. 21 (☎5/66-73-32) and Ave. de las Américas next to *Hotel Las Morlas* (☎5/66-73-36); Havanautos at Ave. 1era y 55 (☎5/66-70-94), Ave. 1era esq. 31 (☎5/61-37-33 or 66-70-29), Ave. Kawama esq. Calle 8 and Ave. 2da y 64; Micar at Calle 20 e/ Ave. 1era y Ave. 2da.

Consulates Canadian Consulate, Casa 223, Villa Tortuga ☎5/66-73-95.

Immigration and legal Immigration office, Calle 39 y Ave. 1era, for visa extensions and passport matters. Tourist cards can also be extended through hotels and information centres. For a more extensive set of services including legal advice and assistance as well as information and help regarding passports, visas and tourist cards, go to the Consultoría Jurídica Internacional at Ave. 1era y 21 (Mon–Fri 9am–noon & 2–5pm; ☎5/66-70-82). Asistur at Calle 31 y Ave. 1era (☎5/66-72-77 or 61-21-64) provide travel and medical insurance services and can deal with lost luggage problems and financial difficulties.

Library Biblioteca José Smith Comas, Calle 33 e/ Ave. 1era y Ave. 3era (Mon–Fri 9am–6pm, Sat 9am–5pm). Small and friendly with a great selection of English literature including a surprisingly good selection of Penguins. You can take books out by leaving your hotel and passport details.

Medical Servimed Clínica Internacional at Ave. 1era y 61 (☎5/66-77-10 or 66-77-11), including the best-stocked pharmacy in Varadero, is open 24 hours. The nearest major hospital is in Matanzas (see p.212). For an ambulance call ☎5/61-29-50.

Petrol stations There are three Servicupet dollar petrol stations at the Todo en uno complex on Calle 54 y Autopista del Sur, Autopista del Sur y 17 and on the Vía Blanca 1km from the Varadero bridge.

Photography Photoservice has branches at Calle 63 y Ave. 2da and Ave. 1era e/ 41 y 42; Photo Express is at Ave. 1era e/ 41 y 42.

Police ☎116. Police station at Calle 39 y Ave. 1era

Post office Branches at Ave. 1era y 36, and Calle 64 e/ Ave. 1era y Ave. 2da (both Mon–Sat 8am–6pm). Many hotels also have their own post office service. DHL have an office at Calle 10 y Camino del Mar ☎5/66-73-30.

Taxis Turistaxi ☎5/61-44-44 or 61-33-77; Taxis OK ☎5/66-70-89; Cuba Taxi ☎5/61-93-61 or 61-95-60; Transgaviota ☎5/61-97-61 or 62.

Telephone The ETECSA Centro de Llamadas and head office is at Ave. 1era y 30 (24hr). There are also ETECSA phone cabins at Ave. 1era y 15 and Ave. 1era e/ 46 y 47.

Travel agents Fantástico, Calle 24 y playa ☎5/66-70-61 or 66-73-78; Gaviota Tours, Ave. 1era e/ 25 y 26 ☎5/66-78-64. Sol y Son, Ave. 1era e/ 25 y 26 (☎5/66-75-93), is the tour operator for Cubana Airlines. Most information offices also double as travel agents.

Matanzas and around

MATANZAS, the biggest city in the province of the same name, is just 25km west along the coast from Varadero, making it one of the closest and most accessible day-trip destinations for anyone staying in the

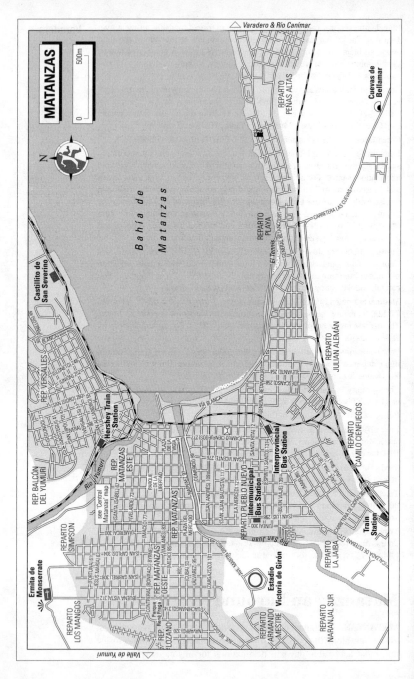

resort. Clustered on the hillsides around a large bay and endowed with a number of small beaches, the city's natural setting is perhaps its greatest asset, though as with much else about the place, this remains largely unexploited and few foreign visitors stay for more than a day.

Having earned the moniker "Athens of Cuba" for the many renowned artists and intellectuals it has produced, particularly during the nineteenth century, today Matanzas lags some way behind its reputation as one of Cuba's **cultural** centres. The birthplace of Cuba's first newspaper as well as the country's national dance, *El Danzón*, and, amongst many others, Augustín Acosta, Cuba's National Poet in 1955, Matanzas has taken a firm back seat to Varadero as far as upkeep and development are concerned. The ample spread of historic buildings are, on the whole, neglected or abandoned. There are, however, still some worth checking out, most located conveniently on or between the two main town plazas, **Parque de la Libertad** and **Plaza de la Vigía**. Beyond the plazas the town centre quickly becomes a series of similar-looking streets plagued by drainage problems. There are, however, reasons to stray away from the centre, and it becomes considerably more pleasant once you get up a little higher. For the best available view of the bay and city head for the Ermita de Monserrate, an abandoned and quaint little church at the top of a hill, from where the **Yumurí Valley**, one of the more picturesque attractions around Matanzas, springs into view. Along with the **Cuevas de Bellamar**, the caves which tunnel into the hillsides on the opposite side of the city, the valley is as good a reason as any to visit this area.

Arrival and information

National network **trains** pull in at the nondescript station on the southern outskirts of the city, from where nothing of any convenience is within walking distance; indeed, if you arrive at night you run a reasonably high risk of being stuck at the station until morning. During the day there are usually private **taxis** waiting outside the station to take you into town for between $2 and $4, depending on how willing you are to negotiate. There is a **local bus service** which leaves from the station at highly irregular intervals and if you're lucky enough to coincide with it, it'll take you to the **Plaza del Mercado**, within a few blocks of the **Parque de la Libertad**, for less than a peso. More likely to be waiting when you arrive are the **coches**, horse-drawn carriages which should charge in pesos to take you at least as far as the market square. The other train service into the city is on the picturesque but leisurely **Hershey** line, running between Matanzas and Havana and carrying the only electric trains in Cuba. The station is in **Versalles**, the neighbourhood north of the Río Yumurí, and within a fifteen-minute walk of the Parque de la Libertad. Interprovincial **buses** arrive at the Estación de Omnibus, over the road from the junction between Calle 272 and Calle 171. There are often private taxis waiting in the car park but there's no other obvious way of getting into the centre, although walking isn't out of the question – you should be able to get to the Plaza de la Libertad within twenty minutes.

There are no information offices in Matanzas but **maps** of the city can be bought from the Artex shop on Calle Medio e/ 288 y 290 and the bookshop at Calle Medio no. 28612 e/ 288 y 282.

Accommodation

The **accommodation** situation in Matanzas is possibly the worst of all comparably sized cities in Cuba. The proximity of Varadero has meant that it has been deemed either unnecessary or simply unprofitable to construct new hotels or rent out private rooms, whilst the government has left two of the three existing state-run **hotels** more or less to their own devices. As a result, the *Velasco* on the Parque de la Libertad is closed indefinitely, whilst the *Yara*, a block away on Calle 79, continues to cater officially to Cubans only. The one ray of light is the neo-colonial *Louvre*, opposite the *Velasco* on the other side of the plaza, currently being renovated and due to accept tourists once it reopens. **Private rooms** do exist but finding them is tricky as there are no signs outside any of the houses. It's worth asking in the reception of the *Louvre* for more details or calling at Calle Medio no. 29415 e/ Dos de Mayo y Manzaneda. Alternatively, if you hang around the Parque de la Libertad it'll only be a matter of time before you'll be approached by a *jinetero* who'll doubtless be able to help. The lack of demand in Matanzas makes it a good place to negotiate, from the visitor's point of view, and you should be able to settle at around $15 a night.

The City

The best place to get your bearings, but also where you are most likely to be pestered by *jineteros*, is the more central of Matanzas' two plazas, the **Parque de la Libertad**. Here you'll find the fantastically well-preserved Museo Farmacéutico Matanzas, which qualifies as one of the few essential places to visit on any tour of the centre. A couple of blocks towards the bay is the Catedral de San Carlos Borromeo, as old as the city itself, and worth a brief look on the way down to the other main square, the **Plaza de la Vigía**. While the plaza itself is less inviting than Libertad, there is more here to occupy your interest, including the historical collection in the Museo Provincial and the stately and still functioning Teatro Sauto.

Parque de la Libertad

A traditional Spanish-style plaza, the **Parque de la Libertad** is a welcome open space amidst the city's claustrophobic streets and provides one of the few central opportunities to sit down and relax outside in pleasant surroundings. The mostly colonial and neo-colonial buildings around the square demand only a passing perusal, such as the

CENTRAL MATANZAS

ACCOMMODATION

Hotel Louvre	3
Hotel Velasco	1
Hotel Yara	2

Río Yumurí

SAN ALEJANDRO 55

Hershey
Train Station

Iglesia de
San Pedro
Apóstol

57

(GÓMEZ) 59

(ISABEL) 63

(AROSTEGUI) 69

VÍA BLANCA

(JAUREGUI) 65

(SANTA ISABEL) 67

(SALAMANCA) 71

(SAN JOSÉ) 65

(SAN BLAS) 67

(SAN ANTONIO)

(ANIMAS) 73

PUENTE
CONCORDIA

(VELARDE) 73

(DAOIZ) 75

(MACEO) 77

ZARAGOZA

SANTA TERESITO 290

282

280

278

276

277

270

N

CONTRERAS (BONIFACIO BYRNE)

Biblioteca Gener y
del Monte

Teatro
Velasco

PARQUE DE
LA LIBERTAD

Museo de
Deporte
Provincial

Museo
Provincial

(MILANÉS) 83

Museo
Farmacéutico
Matanzas

Palacio de
Justicia

Teatro
Sauto

(MEDIO) 85

Catedral de
San Carlos
Borromeo

Galería de Arte

PLAZA
DE LA
VIGÍA

Fire
Station

2 DE MAYO

RÍO

Taller Editorial
Ediciones Vigía

PUENTE
CALIXTO
GARCÍA

SAN SEVERINO 93

NARVAEZ 97

101

PLAZA
DEL
MERCADO

Río San Juan

Las
Ruinas

PUENTE
SÁNCHEZ
FIGUERAS

COMERCIO 99

RECURSO 103

0   100 m

(REFUGIO) 105

(SAN ANDRÉS) 109

Provincial Government headquarters from 1853, which occupies the
entire east side, or the old casino building, founded in 1835, now housing a library. More deserving of your time is the **Museo Farmacéutico
Matanzas**, in the southwestern corner of the square (Tues–Sun
10am–6pm; $1). Founded in 1882 by two doctors, Juan Fermín de
Figueroa and Ernesto Triolet, it functioned as a pharmacy right up
until May 1964, when it was converted into a museum. Claimed to be
the only pharmacy of its kind preserved in its entirety, it represents
one of the most complete historical collections on the island – it's hard
to believe that business has stopped. All the hundreds of French porcelain jars lining the shelves and cabinets, along with the many medicine
bottles, and even the medicines inside them, are originals. Whilst some
of the medicines would have been imported, principally from Spain,
France, Germany and the United States, many were made in the labo-
ratory at the back of the building, using formulae listed in one of the
55 recipe books kept in the compact but comprehensive library. You
can't fail to spot the fabulous old cash till, which looks as though it
should have been driven by a steam engine.

Catedral de San Carlos Borromeo

A block towards the bay from Parque de la Libertad is the **Catedral de San Carlos Borromeo**, whose heavy frame, with its detailed neo-classical exterior, is squeezed in between the two busiest streets in the centre. One of the first buildings of the city, it was founded in 1693 and originally made of wood which, unsurprisingly, didn't last. It was thus rebuilt and finished in its current state in 1755 but despite these reinforcements it has not survived the last two and a half centuries entirely intact. A quick look inside reveals the neglect which so much of the city's historic architecture has suffered in recent years, though there is still much of historic and artistic value, including the original altar. The patchwork interior is a mixture of the chipped and faded original paintwork with sporadic areas of restoration, mostly on the high arches. Slightly at odds with the existing decor are the hung pictures, quite clearly belonging to a different era and in fact painted as recently as 1935.

Opposite the main entrance of the cathedral on Calle 282 is the **Museo de Deporte Provincial** (Mon–Fri 8am–4pm, Sat & Sun 8am–noon; $1). Little more than a glorified trophy cabinet, the one-room museum documents achievements by athletes, past and present, born in the province, including medals won by Joel Isasi, currently one of Cuba's most successful sprinters. There's sometimes a guide available for anyone attempting to master high velocity mumbled Spanish.

Plaza de la Vigía and around

For information call the theatre on ☎52/27-21 or visit one of the Artex shops in Matanzas or Varadero where weekly programmes of local cultural events are sometimes available.

From the cathedral walk two blocks towards the bay along Calle 85 to get to the humble **Plaza de la Vigía**, struggling for space with the heavy traffic running along one side. The plaza itself is little more than a trumped-up road island with a swashbuckling statue of a rebel from the wars of independence in the centre. Opposite, on the other side of Calle 85, facing the ceremonious-looking pink court building known as the **Palacio de Justicia**, founded in 1826, is the august **Teatro Sauto**, holding the easily won position as one of the city's best-preserved historic monuments. Dating from 1863 and considered one of the most prestigious theatre buildings in the country, its Neoclassical architecture has lost none of its grandeur, but the absence of detail and ornamentation on the nevertheless dignified exterior means it falls short of real magnificence. The more decorative interior features a painted ceiling depicting the muses of Greek mythology in the main hall and a three-tier auditorium atmospheric enough to make an attendance at one of its performances a priority whilst in Matanzas. The monthly programmes are usually quite varied as the theatre hosts everything from ballet to comedy acts. It's worth making enquiries a few days in advance, as performance days are

Slavery on the sugar plantations in the nineteenth century

The sugar industry in Cuba and indeed all over the Caribbean was, up until the end of the nineteenth century, inextricably linked to the slave trade and slavery itself. It's been estimated that at least a third of the slaves in Cuba during the nineteenth century worked on sugar plantations, and the fact that slaves were the largest single investment made by all plantation owners is testament to the vital role slave labour played in Cuba's biggest industry. Working conditions were considerably worse on the impersonal sugar estates than for slaves on the smaller tobacco or coffee plantations. Death from over-work was not uncommon as, unlike tobacco and coffee, levels of production were directly linked to the intensity of the labour and plantation owners demanded the maximum possible output from their workforce. The six months of harvest were by far the most gruelling period of the year, when plantation slaves often slept for no more than four hours a day, rising as early as 2am. They were divided into gangs and those sent to cut cane in the fields might be working there for sixteen hours before they could take a significant break. A small proportion would work in the mill grinding the cane and boiling the sugar cane juice. Accidents in the mills were frequent, undoubtedly many the result of sheer exhaustion. Punishments were harsh and most commonly consisted of whippings or the stocks. It was not unknown for slaves to be left in the stocks – which took various forms but usually involved the head, hands and feet locked into the same flat wooden board – for days at a time.

Naturally, it was in the interests of the plantation owner to keep his slaves strong and healthy, and there is evidence that the meals given to slaves on many plantations were quite substantial, usually consisting of about half a pound of meat as well as plantains, yams, sweet potatoes and rice. For similar reasons, each plantation generally had its own small hospital. Slaves were most often housed in communal barrack buildings, which replaced the collections of huts used in the eighteenth century, subdivided into cramped cells, with the men, who made up about two-thirds of the slave workforce, separated off from the women. This was considered a safer way of containing them as there were fewer doors through which it was possible to escape.

as likely to be during the week as at the weekend, and shows often play no more than two or three times.

On the other side of the Teatro Sauto, facing the plaza, the well laid-out, orderly **Museo Provincial** (Tues–Sat 10am–noon & 1–5pm; $2) houses a varied collection charting the political and social history of the province. Its chronological layout, sometimes absent in Cuban history museums, helps to create a succinct overview of the last two hundred years in Matanzas. The first floor features early plans and pictures of the city, including a fantastic, large-scale drawing dating from 1848. Alongside these are a number of displays depicting the living and working conditions of slaves on the sugar plantations and in the mills (see box above). The centrepiece is a large wooden *cepo*, the leg clamps employed in the punishment of slaves. On the second floor, highlights include a 1934 copy of *Bandera Roja*, one of the original newspapers of the Cuban Communist Party, and the mangled remains of a piece of *La Coubre*, a Franco-Belgian ship carrying arms for the revolutionary government and which was blown up in Havana harbour by the United States in March 1960.

On the plaza itself there are a number of simple places worth a brief peek inside. In the corner nearest the river, facing the back of the statue in the middle, is the **Taller Editorial Ediciones Vigía** (Mon–Fri 8.30am–5pm; free). This small, environmentally friendly co-operative-style publisher produces books made entirely from "*materiales rústicos*". There's actually very little to see in the humble workshop besides the small display of endearing hand-made books, all signed by their authors, who range from local poets to nationally known writers. Looking like sophisticated scrapbooks, the delightfully designed covers may tempt you into buying one of these unique publications, especially as prices begin at only $3.

The next door along belongs to the **Galería de Arte** (June–Sept Mon–Sat 10am–5pm; Oct–May Mon–Sat 1–7pm), whose free entry can be explained by the price tags attached to every item on display. All the pieces, ranging from masks and plates to paintings and pottery, are the work of local artists and amongst the more predictable efforts there are some original and interesting pieces. Less ambiguous about its financial aspirations but still in the business of *artesanía* is **La Vigía**, a couple of doors down at the end of the row, whose stock is made up mostly of jewellery and small wooden carvings. The opposite side of the plaza is occupied by a still functioning ornate but austere Neoclassical fire station. It's worth peering inside to see the old fire engine from 1888, which is still in perfect working order.

The Ermita de Monserrate and Parque René Fraga

On the western edge of the city centre is the **Parque René Fraga**, a basic park overendowed with concrete and best visited at dusk after a day of burning sun, when it livens up considerably. Most evenings there are games taking place on the baseball diamond and basketball court whilst joggers circle the park on a sandy running track. There are good views down to the bay but the pillared staircases and trees skirting the edges of this unpicturesque park only create the beginnings of a pleasant atmosphere.

From the park it's a ten-minute walk up Calle 312 through a purely residential neighbourhood to the **Ermita de Monserrate** and some of the best available views of the city and bay on one side plus a fantastic perspective on the magnificent natural arena known as the Yumurí Valley on the other. Perched on a large flat platform at the top of a steep slope, the Ermita is a lonely little abandoned church, built between 1872 and 1875 by colonists from Catalonia and the Balearic Islands. Although it's been completely gutted it has managed to cling on to some of its charm, and its splendid location, away from the claustrophobic centre which it looks down upon, makes this an especially appealing spot.

Versalles

Over the Puente de la Concordia which spans the Río Yumurí is the almost exclusively residential **Versalles** district – though technically the name refers only to the most central of the neighbourhoods on the north side of the river. There's very little of any interest but if you're absolutely determined to see all there is to see, a visit to the once delightful but now abandoned **Iglesia de San Pedro Apóstol**, a short way up the hill at Calles 266 and 57, provides a break in the suburban landscape. The shrubs growing from one of the bell towers are testament to its state of abandonment, the locked gates preventing any closer inspection. It's a pity, as the architecture rivals that of the cathedral, the Islamic-style tower in the centre making it look more prestigious than its location would suggest. Walk a little further up the hill for some good views across the bay and into the city centre.

Eating and drinking

The lack of decent options for **eating** out in Matanzas provides yet more evidence of the lack of investment in the city. Whilst the state-run establishments are almost all either quick-stop fast-food joints for passing tourists or run-down and outdated peso restaurants, the threat of local enterprise steering trade away from these uninspiring eateries has been stamped out by the government's banning of *paladares*. The **state restaurant** most often recommended by locals is *El Paladín del Medio*, a moderately pleasant place serving *comida criolla*. The only other places where you can sit down for something approaching a meal are the 24-hour snack-bar restaurants aimed at day-trippers. *Café Atenas* opposite the Teatro Sauto has a reasonable choice of cheap dishes, ranging from burgers to spaghetti, but prepared with minimum care. In the ruins of a colonial sugar warehouse the *Ruinas de Matasiete*, on the southern side of the Río San Juan next to the busy road to Varadero, has a similar menu and marginally more character. For tasty and filling takeaway *comida criolla* in generous portions you can't go wrong at *La Tarifa*. Popular with locals, it's the nearest thing in town to a *paladar*, but because the food is made to be eaten away from the premises it has managed to avoid the ban on privately run restaurants. The house, which has a small sign outside on its spacious porch, is near the train station on Carretera de Cidra between Ave. 9na and Ave. 7ma.

The majority of the remaining places offer little more than a **sandwich** and a drink in plain surroundings. On the Parque de la Libertad the *Cafetería Velasco*, a 1950s-diner-style bar partitioned off from the *Hotel Velasco* lobby, or *La Viña* next to the Museo Farmacéutico, are your best bet, whilst at *El Jardín del Boulevard* on Medio e/ 288 y 290 you can sit in a leafy courtyard. The clandestine feel of *Cafetería Zaguan*, on the Plaza de la Vigía, makes it the most atmospheric place for a drink.

Nightlife and entertainment

Most of the city's **nightlife** is in the southern part of town but the venues are few and far between and the streets are empty at night unless you're within the vicinity of one of the night spots, most of which don't really justify the walk from the centre. For live Cuban music under the stars *Las Palmas* (Fri–Sun 9pm–1am; $10 per couple), in the Complejo Cultural run by Artex on the corner of General Betancourt and Calle 254, offers the most professionally packaged night out in Matanzas. On Calle 272 e/ 115 y 117 *El Pescadito* (☎52/9-22-58) stages small-scale **cabarets**, whilst *Discoteca Libertad* (Tues–Sun 9pm–2am; 45 pesos), on the Parque de la Libertad, is for couples looking for romance on a budget. Check the noticeboard outside the Casa de la Cultura Provincial on the Parque de la Libertad for details of dance or music **performances**, usually by local artists, which are occasionally hosted there. A few doors away the Teatro Velasco (☎52/37-29) is now a **cinema** showing Cuban and mostly American films. National league **baseball** games are played weekly from October to April at the Estadio Victoria de Girón, twenty minutes' walk from Parque de la Libertad.

Listings

Banks and money For foreign currency and credit card transactions go to Banco Financiero Internacional at Medio esq. 2 de Mayo. For buying pesos the Cadeca *casas de cambio* are behind the cathedral on the edge of the Plaza de la Iglesia.

Bookshop The best one is at Medio no. 28612 e/ 288 y 282. As well as the usual stock of Cuban literature and history books it has maps of the city, dictionaries, travel guides and some stationery.

Left luggage At the interprovincial bus station ($2 per day).

Library Biblioteca Gener y Del Monte, on the Parque de la Libertad, carries few recent titles likely to be of much interest to foreign visitors, including one or two old English-language novels.

Medical The Faustino Pérez on the Carretera Central about 1km from the city is a relatively new and well-equipped hospital. For information, call ☎52/26-29 or 33-20.

Photography Photoservice, Calle 288 e/ Medio y Milanes.

Post office Main branch at Medio e/ 288 y 290. Next door there's a DHL and EMS centre.

Shopping Artex has shops in its Complejo Cultural on General Betancourt and at Medio e/ 288 y 290, selling maps of the city, CDs and various artistic and touristic bits and pieces. The best-stocked supermarket is Mercado San Luis, out from the centre on Calle 298 e/ 119 y 121.

Taxis Transautos can be contacted at the Juan Gualberto Gómez Airport on ☎5/53-62-1

Telephone The ETECSA Centro de Llamadas for national and international calls is on the corner of 288 and Milanés (Mon–Sat 9am–9pm, Sun 9am–8pm; ☎52/31-23). For after-hours calls, there's a payphone in *Cafetería Velasco*, open round the clock.

Travel agents Campismo Popular, Medio e/ 290 y 292 ☎52/39-51.

Around Matanzas

In many repects the places around Matanzas are more appealing than the city itself, making it well worth spending a few days in the area. Getting to any of the sights covered below from the centre of Matanzas shouldn't take more than twenty minutes in a car, while public transport is also a viable option. The comprehensive **Cuevas de Bellamar** make for the most compact day-trip and have become a classic tour for groups visiting the area from Varadero. Not as visitor-friendly but arguably more stunning is the **Yumurí Valley**, a fantastic showcase of Cuban plant life in a sublime and peaceful landscape. Last and probably least is the **Río Canímar**, where you can combine a boat trip with a night or just a meal at the nearby *Hotel Canimao*.

Las Cuevas de Bellamar

In 1897 Samuel Hazard, an American writer and traveller, declared that he who hasn't seen **Las Cuevas de Bellamar** hasn't seen Cuba. Though the cave system to which he referred, just beyond the south-eastern outskirts of Matanzas, does not really live up to such a billing, if you're here for a day or two you should make time for it, even if it means seeing less of the city itself. First happened upon in 1861 – although there seems to be some dispute over whether the discovery should be credited to a slave working in a limestone pit or a shepherd looking for his lost sheep – the caves were not fully revealed until over one thousand tons of rock had been excavated from the pit in which they were discovered. Attracting coachloads of holidaymakers from Varadero, the caves are one of Cuba's longest-standing tourist attractions and certainly as impressive as any other examples you are likely to see in the country. **Guided tours** (daily 9am–5pm; ☎52/61-68-3; $3, extra $2 to take pictures) set off once every hour and it's best to arrive with a tour group (see overleaf) to avoid hanging around. It's possible to simply turn up and join a party but that way there's no guarantee of an English-speaking tour guide.

A small complex, which includes a restaurant serving basic traditional chicken and pork dishes (daily noon–6.45pm), has been built around the entrance to the caves. Working on the tried and tested adage that it's better to save the best until last, the tour would work well in reverse as the first, huge gallery, abundant in stalagmites and stalactites of which the latter are growing at the rate of two centimetres every hundred years, is the most awe-inspiring sight on the whole tour. However, this does nothing to spoil the excitement of descending over 30m along 750m of narrowing and widening underground corridors and caverns lined with crystal formations on the walls and ceiling. Your attention is directed to images which have formed naturally in the rock and you're invited to drink at the unimpressive-looking Fountain of Youth and the Fountain of Love, which are supposed to improve your chances of lasting longer in both. Almost inevitably the tour turns back on itself sooner than expected.

A **private taxi** from either of the two bus stations in Matanzas to the caves shouldn't cost more than $3, and the journey up to the car park offers some nice views of the bay. Alternatively, Rumbos, Cubatur and Havanatur in Varadero all offer a **tour** consisting of a cave visit, including the right to take photos, plus a meal at the restaurant (see p.184).

The Yumurí Valley

Hidden from view directly behind the hills that skirt the northern edges of Matanzas, the **Yumurí Valley** is the provincial capital's giant back garden. Out of sight until you reach the edge of the valley itself, it's one of the most spectacular and yet at the same time most serene landscapes in the country, and it comes as quite a surprise to find it so close to the grimy city streets. A legion of palms crowds the valley but there are thousands of other species and a new scene around every corner, as the landscape changes from rolling pastures to crops of palms, and small forests merge into cultivated fields of banana, maize, tobacco and other crops.

The valley has remained relatively untouched by tourism and the tiny villages here are few and far between; while this is all part of the appeal, it also means that there's no obvious way to explore the valley independently. There are several minor roads allowing you to cut through the centre of the landscape but as good a way to any to explore is to get off at any one of a number of stations on the Hershey line and just wander.

Five trains leave daily from the Hershey line station in Versalles, Matanzas

For a more structured approach, drop in at the only place in the valley offering organized excursions, the *Casa del Valle* (☎52/6-45-84 fax 5-33-00; ④), a reasonably unobtrusive hotel with a pool on the valley floor. The hotel organizes horseback rides which are by far the best way of seeing the surrounding countryside. Excursions usually last for an hour or so and take you to parts of the valley which you would otherwise either have difficulty finding or not be able to visit at all.

If you're **driving** from Matanzas, head for the Parque René Fraga (see p.210), from where the road heading west out of town will take you directly into the valley. To get to the hotel by public transport, take any **train** from the Hershey station and get off at Mena, the first stop on the line and no more than ten minutes from the city. Staying on the same side of the track, follow the road for a kilometre to the hotel.

Río Canímar and around

Snaking its way around fields and woodlands on its journey to the coast the **Río Canímar** meets the Bay of Matanzas 4km east of the city. An impromptu visit will most likely leave you restricted to the shore, but a short stay at the *Hotel Canimao* (☎52/6-10-14, fax 5-31-60; ④) combines well with one of the **boat trips** which leave from the nearby **Centro Turístico Canímar** (☎52/6-15-16).

Located below the bridge which carries the Vía Blanca road over the Canímar, the tourist centre also rents out snorkelling equipment and motor boats. Expect to pay around $20 per person for the one-and-a-half-hour excursion, which usually leaves before midday and includes lunch and musical entertainment. There are various flooded **caves** along the river's borders and the opportunity to swim in one is generally on the itinerary. The **hotel**, which organizes at least one boat trip every week, roosts high above the river, which coils itself halfway around the foot of the steep, tree-lined slopes dropping down from its borders. It's a well-equipped modern complex with views of the river and includes a cabaret building also used for discos at the weekends, when it attracts plenty of young Matanceros. Only twenty minutes by **bus** from Matanzas, it's a convenient alternative to staying in the city itself. Buses #16 and #17 run from the city to the bridge and back, every hour or so on a daily basis. You can pick up either bus outside the cathedral on Calle 83 and you should stay on until the end of the route just over the bridge. The unsophisticated but welcoming *El Marino* **restaurant** (daily noon–10pm; ☎52/6-14-83), at the entrance to the road leading up to the hotel, offers a better choice of food than any of the restaurants in Matanzas, including a range of omelettes and rice dishes and some reasonably priced lobster and chicken meals.

An organized excursion to the river from Varadero can be booked at the Rumbos Centro de Información Turística for $45 per person; see p.185.

Cárdenas, San Miguel de los Baños and Colón

The provincial **interior** of Matanzas, between the two touristic poles of Varadero and the Zapata peninsula, is dominated by agriculture. Islands of banana and vegetable crops break up the seas of sugar cane which flow south into huge citrus orchards and eventually wash up on the edge of the forest and swampland that dominate the southern third of the province. Dotted around this sparsely populated territory is the occasional place offering, at the very least, the chance to set your feet down for an hour or two. The small town of **Cárdenas**, just 10km southeast of Varadero, is ideally placed for a day-trip from the beach resort, and anything more than a day would be pushing it, since what was once one of Cuba's most prestigious towns has, like Matanzas, had little attention paid to its upkeep in recent years.

Heading south from Cárdenas, cutting down first to **Jovellanos**, you can pick up the **Carretera Central**, the main road dissecting the province in two. This takes you into sugar-cane country, huge tracts of land plastered with green forests of reedy grass for pretty much the whole trip all the way down to the Península de Zapata at the other end of the province. Most people cross the Carretera Central and make a beeline for the peninsula, but there are a couple of diversions worth making if you get the exploring itch: the towns of **San**

Cárdenas,
San Miguel
de los
Baños and
Colón

Miguel de los Baños and **Colón**. Closer to Varadero and considerably more picturesque, San Miguel de los Baños was once famous for its *balneario*, which is now in a state of semi-ruin; the real appeal of the place is the natural setting, closely surrounded by forested hills and offering some fantastic views. Colón, on the other hand, makes for an accurate insight into provincial Cuban town life and, with the Carretera Central running through its centre, is a handy stopoff point.

Cárdenas

A ten-kilometre drive from the bridge joining the Península de Hicacos to the mainland, **CÁRDENAS** is the nearest place to Varadero for a glimpse of Cuban life untainted by tourism. Known as the **Ciudad Bandera** (Flag City), it was here in 1850 that what was to become the national flag was first raised by the Venezuelan General Narcisco López and his troops, who had disembarked at Cárdenas in a US-backed attempt to spark a revolt against Spanish rule and thus clear the way for annexation. The attempt failed, but the design of the flag was later adopted by the independence movement. Boasting not just a place in the history books but its own port and cathedral, traditionally the town has been a place of some importance. Today's reality is significantly different and a large portion of the town lies almost dormant, noticeably so during the day, when many of its inhabitants go off to work in Varadero. Its location, hugging the shoreline of the **Bay of Cárdenas**, would be its greatest natural asset, but unfortunately most of the coastal area is an industrial zone. If you've travelled around in Cuba there'll be very little that you haven't seen before and the near perfect grid on which the town plan is based adds a somewhat mundane touch of familiarity. It's far from a waste of time, however, especially if you've only come from up the road, and the cathedral is of greater architectural merit than anything else on the whole of the peninsula.

Arrival, accommodation and orientation

The interprovincial **bus terminal** at Ave. Céspedes esq. Calle 22 (☎5/52-12-14) serves buses arriving from everywhere except Varadero. Travelling to and from Varadero, buses run every hour, theoretically right up to 7pm, from the smaller terminal on Calle 13 esq. Ave. 13 (☎5/52-49-58). From either terminal it's a straighforward ten-minute walk into the centre. In the unlikely event that you arrive by **train** from Colón, you'll pull in at the station on Ave. 8 y Calle 5, a few blocks from *La Dominica* hotel. You can catch the single-carriage train to Colón from here if you get up early enough; it leaves at 6.20am. For further information, call the station on ☎5/52-13-62 or 52-25-62.

There are no tax-paying *casas particulares* in Cárdenas and the only official **accommodation** is run-down *La Dominica* (☎5/52-21-40; ③), the single hotel to have survived the recent years of neglect. The rooms have neither air conditioning nor televisions, the paintwork is grubby and you may need to join two wires together to switch the light on. However, it has retained an endearing character that makes the conditions more amusing than depressing.

Cárdenas revolves around **Avenida Céspedes**, running right down the centre of town towards the port. It's the only street whose modern name the locals are likely to recognize when you ask for directions; the rest have been changed to numbers, though the town's population, as elsewhere in Cuba, have stubbornly stuck with the original street names, few of which are still in evidence. Thankfully, the system is simple. Anything running parallel with Avenida Céspedes is also an avenida, whilst the calles run perpendicular, with Calle 13 crossing Avenida Céspedes in the centre of town. The calles number from 1, at the port, to 27 at the other end of town. Almost all that you are likely to want to see is concentrated within four or five blocks of the crossroads at Calle 13 and Ave. Céspedes.

The Town
The main square, **Parque Colón**, at Ave. Céspedes between Calles 8 and 9, is only just recognizable as a square, dissected down the middle by the main street and conducive to neither a sit-down nor a stroll around. The abandoned and dilapidated *Hotel Europa*, whose construction preceded the current era of tourism, is on the southeastern side. Opposite is the noble but withered **Catedral de la Inmaculada Concepción**, dating from 1846, featuring two stone lighthouse-like columns flanking the entrance, with portholes running the length of the stout building and a straight-edged dome poking its head above the treetops from the rear. Bordered by healthy-looking bushy gardens, it's the best photo opportunity in the city and certainly the grandest building, though it's almost always closed. Further reason to whip out the camera is the elevated statue of a romantic-looking Columbus with a globe at his feet, directly in front of the cathedral. Sculpted in 1862, it's said to be the oldest statue of the explorer in the whole of the Americas.

Three blocks from Parque Colón on Avenida Céspedes, Calle 12 cuts across the main street and two blocks later, between Avenidas 4 and 5, skirts the northeastern border of plain but tranquil **Parque José Antonio Echevarría**, the tranquil town square that Parque Colón fails to be. The real reason to visit, though, is for the museums that comprise two of its borders. Founded in 1900 and one of the oldest museums in the country, the **Museo Oscar María de Rojas** (Tues–Sat 10am–5pm, Sun 8am–noon; $1), on the opposite side of the square, houses an eclectic range of reasonably concise collections, most of them relating to the island's historical, cultural or natural heritage. Of greatest substance are the collections housed in the last two rooms you come to as you're ushered clockwise around the building. The Room of Aboriginal Cuban Culture features human skeletal remains almost 5800 years old; next door, in the Room of American Archeology, are

A history of sugar in Cuba

Despite the old Cuban saying that "sin azúcar no hay país" – without sugar there's no country – the crop is not native to the island. It was first introduced by Diego Velázquez when, in 1511, he led a colonial force of three hundred men in Spain's first settlement of the island. However, though its humid tropical climate and fertile soils make the island ideal for the cultivation of sugar cane, which requires plenty of sun, wind and rain, sugar production in Cuba got off to a slow start. Within a couple of decades of Cuban colonization, Spain turned its attention to the vast quantities of gold and silver found in mainland South America, and the island was relegated to a stepping stone between the mother country and her vast American empire.

Following decades of declining population in Cuba, during which time sugar was produced almost entirely for local consumption, the construction of sugar refineries was in 1595 authorized by Philip II, the king of Spain, as Europe began to develop its sweet tooth. However, while the English and French, elsewhere in the Caribbean, invested heavily and developed new techniques in sugar production, the Spanish failed to take notice and during the next century and a half the industry in Cuba remained relatively stagnant. Whilst water-driven mills were increasing efficiency on islands like Jamaica and Santo Domingo, in Cuba output remained comparatively low as mills were driven by plodding oxen or horses. Furthermore, Spain was slow to stake a claim in the African slave trade which, by the first half of the eighteenth century, was dominated by the English. In the labour-intensive world of sugar production, the lack of a substantial and regular supply of slaves in Cuba was the single most important impediment to the development of the sugar trade up until 1762.

It was in the second half of the eighteenth century that a combination of events coincided to make Cuba one of the world's three biggest producers of sugar. Until 1762 Cuba had been forced to trade only with Spain, which imposed strict and stifling regulations on the export and import of goods to Cuban ports. However, in that year the English took control of Havana and during their short occupation opened up trade channels with the rest of the world, which at the same time opened the industry to the technological advances being made in sugar production, particularly by the English themselves. Subsequently, the number of slaves imported to Cuba almost doubled in the last two decades of the eighteenth century, whilst this expansion was, mostly by luck, met with an increase in the size and value of the marketplace made available to Cuban planters. Prior to 1791, neighbouring Santo Domingo, controlled by the French, had become the dominant force in world sugar, producing an average of over 70,000 tons annually, compared to Cuba's 10,000 tons. Then, in that year, a slave revolt all but wiped out the sugar industry in Santo Domingo, simultaneously causing sugar prices and the demand for Cuban sugar to rise, whilst many French sugar plantation owners relocated to Cuba. At the same time, economic growth and increasing population size in Europe, as well as a newly independent United States after 1783, meant an increase in the global demand for sugar. In the space of a few decades the industry had been turned on its head.

As the nineteenth century got underway, sugar production increased dramatically following the mechanization of the refining process, which included the introduction of steam engines, used to squeeze the juice from the cane, and, in the 1830s, the establishment of the first railways in Latin America and the Caribbean. Advances in technology throughout the century saw Cuba's share of the world market more than double as the crop became the focus of the entire Cuban economy. Cattle ranches and tobacco plantations were converted to cane fields whilst all the largest sugar mills became linked by rail to Havana, thus significantly cutting the cost of transporting cane. It was during this century that sugar profoundly affected Cuban society in general and, to a certain extent, helped shape the islands's modern identity. Hundreds of thousands of slaves were shipped into Cuba as the racial mix on the island came to resemble something like the picture seen today. Equally significant, the economic and structural imbalances between east and west, which were to influence the outbreak of the Ten Years' War in 1868 and its successor in 1895, emerged as a result of the concentration of more and larger sugar mills in the west, closer to Havana. These wars of independence, which ended in 1898 following US intervention in what became the Spanish-American War, were to destroy large parts of the sugar industry in Cuba and, more significantly, weaken it to the point of vulnerability, thus clearing the way for a foreign takeover, which is effectively what happened now that the US had established a stranglehold over the island.

The twentieth century began for Cuba under indirect North American control, with the successful sugar industry a driving force behind the US interest. They further modernized the production process, with huge factories known as *centrales* processing cane for a large number of different plantations. By 1959 there were 161 mills on the island, over half of them under foreign ownership, a fact that had not escaped the notice of Fidel Castro and his nationalist revolutionary followers. It was no surprise then that one of the first acts of the revolutionary government was, in 1960, to nationalize the entire sugar industry, and the *zafra* – sugar harvest – became the measuring stick by which the success of the revolutionary economy was measured. In an attempt to prove just what could be achieved under such a system, Castro declared that in 1970 the nation would harvest ten million tons of sugar. This desperately unrealistic aim was not met, and in the late 1970s the government made the first relatively successful attempt to diversify the economy and move away from the dependency on sugar. With the Russians paying artificially high prices for Cuban sugar, the economy in the 1980s seemed to have shaken off the negative impact of the reliance on sugar production, but when, in 1989, the Soviet Bloc collapsed and along with it over eighty percent of Cuban trade, the economy was exposed, as none of the perceived changes could prevent the country from falling into one of its worst economic crises that century. The government turned to tourism to put the country back on its feet, an industry which, with the revolution, they had vehemently rejected. The development of tourism in the 1990s may at last have brought the country an industry to rival sugar but the crop has already made a lasting mark on the history and future of Cuba.

some fascinating artefacts of **pre-Columbian cultures** elsewhere in Latin America. There's a bizarre shrunken head from southern Ecuador and some stone idols discovered in Mexico, as well as jewellery and various examples of Mayan art. Other highlights include, looming in the entrance hall, a remarkably ornate nineteenth-century funeral carriage, looking appropriately morbid. Other rooms are packed with impressive but essentially dull collections of coins, medals and Cuban banknotes dating back to the middle of the nineteenth century, plus a more eye-catching collection of bugs and butterflies and, as is customary in Cuban museums, a selection of firearms including, more unusually, reproductions of pre-Columbian weapons.

Adjacent is the **Museo José Antonio Echevarría** (Tues–Sat 8am–4pm, Sun 8am–noon; free), birthplace of the anti-Batista student leader, a statue of whom stands casually, with his hand in his pocket, in the square outside. Less engaging than its neighbour but more consistent in its content, the museum's exhibits relate to the nineteenth- and twentieth-century independence and revolutionary struggles with the usual overemphasis on political history and the same undercutting of the social background so characteristic of history museums throughout Cuba. More uniquely, on the first floor there is a space given over to Echevarría himself. Actively involved in the popular struggle against the 1950s dictator Batista and president of the University Student Federation, Echevarría and several of his comrades were shot and killed by Batista's police on March 13, 1957, having attacked the Presidential Palace in Havana.

Eating, drinking and nightlife

In keeping with its role as a quick-stop destination for tourists, there are a disproportionate number of **fast-food** places in Cárdenas, including three branches of hot-dog and pizza pusher *El Rápido*. The nearest thing to a formal **restaurant** is *Café Espriu* on the Parque José Antonio Echevarría, which may lack character but offers the most reliable stock of traditional Cuban dishes. The only peso establishment worth a look is *Las Palmas* at Ave. Céspedes esq. Calle 16. Avoid the gloomy hall and enjoy a quiet **drink** on the shady garden terrace of this half-Japanese, half-Spanish style villa, where food is also occasionally served. Also for a drink try *El Fuerte*, a nineteenth-century fortress-turret offering modest views from the far end of town, in between Calles 26 and 27.

Besides a few of the peso bars playing loud music, **nightlife** in Cárdenas is almost exclusively restricted to *La Cachamba* (Wed–Sun; 3 pesos) in the same grounds as *Las Palmas*, behind the villa. A young crowd pack out the large courtyard at weekends, when they are treated to pure pop and glossy dance routines performed by local talent. Otherwise, you're left with the **cinema** at Ave. Céspedes esq. Calle 14; or you may be able to play some **pool** at the Casa del Educador ($1), a scrappy local hangout on Ave. Céspedes e/ Calle 17 y 18.

San Miguel de los Baños

Off the official tourist track and reachable only by car, **SAN MIGUEL DE LOS BAÑOS** is one of the province's lesser known treats, a cross between an Alpine village and a Wild West ghost town. Twenty-five kilometres southwest of Cárdenas, hidden away in its own cosy valley, it's easy to miss; to get there, head east on the Carretera Central from Matanzas and take a right turn just before entering the small town of Coliseo. Situated 8km from the turn-off, the previously opulent village has lost the greater part of its wealth, the wooden-panelled ranch-style houses and villas on the hillside amongst the few reminders of what it once was. However, these faded signs of success are part of the enchantment of this village, which made its fortune during the first half of the twentieth century through the popularity of its health spa and hotel, the **Balneario San Miguel de los Baños**. Near the centre of the village the palatial mansion-like hotel with its four turrets is now completely derelict, but you can still wander through its entrancingly overgrown gardens. At the rear of the building the large terrace was once part of the hotel's dining area, and down the steps, spread around the garden, the red-brick wells and Romanesque baths built to accommodate the sulphurous springs are still more or less intact. The three wells are only about three metres deep, with inset stone steps which would have allowed guests to descend into them to scoop up the medicinal waters. Each well was supplied with a different source and the healing properties of the waters differed accordingly. However, drinking from the shallow pools slushing around in them now would be more likely to make you vomit than cure you of any ailments. The stone benches encircling the centre of the garden and the wall of shade from the high branches of the old *framboyan* trees make it a pleasant spot for a picnic, the silence broken only by the sound of running water.

Five minutes' walk from the hotel through the centre of the village is a magnificently set public **swimming pool**, raised up on a small mound of land. Even if there's no water in the pool, which is quite possible given the sporadic maintenance it receives, it's worth stopping by for the view of the surrounding fir-covered and palm-dotted hills enclosing the village. There are a few tables and chairs overlooking the pool and a poorly stocked outdoor bar selling mostly rum for pesos, but it's enough to just take a seat and digest the captivating scenery.

If there is water in the pool it's worth waiting before you take a dip and making your way first to the **Loma de Jacán**, the highest peak in the province yet one of the most straightforward to reach, given the large set of concrete steps which lead up to it. At the top is a simple shrine which for years has attracted local pilgrims who leave flowers and coins at its base, though the real attraction is the all-encompassing **view** of the valley and beyond. You should be able to see the route to the foot of the steps from the swimming pool area, a short drive from the northern edge of town up a steep and potholed road. The 448 steps are marked by murals depicting the **Stations of the Cross**, and at the top a concrete dome houses a spooky representation of the Crucifixion, the untouched overgrowth and the airy atmosphere contributing to the appropriate mood of contemplation.

Colón

Back on the Carretera Central, heading east through central Matanzas and its endless miles of sugarcane fields, you'll pass through **Jovellanos**, one of the biggest towns hereabouts but with little to recommend it. After another 30km or so the road cuts straight through the centre of **COLÓN**, a classic colonial town and a better place to stop for something to eat. There's nothing essential to see here, but the town's appeal is that it remains virtually untouched by tourism and a quick wander around the streets, lined almost entirely by modest neo-colonial columned houses, soon gives you a sense of the somewhat subdued pace of Cuban life away from the big cities. The relatively wide streets make Colón feel bigger than it actually is and suggest that there's more to see, but walk down any one of them and you'll find that the town quickly fades away. The only street of any interest besides Máximo Gómez, the Colón strip of the Carretera Central, is Martí, where most of the shops and services are located. Martí leads directly to the town square, the inviting **Parque Colón**, where the flaking and faded paintwork of the big pink building belongs to a **cinema**, still functioning but mostly operating as a *sala de video*. In the centre of the square, guarded by four rather malnourished bronze lions, is a statue of the town's namesake Christopher Columbus (Cristóbal Colón), pointing eastwards to the route out of town.

Practicalities

There are two basic and ugly **hotels** in town, both on Máximo Gómez and within three blocks of one another. The overpriced *Santiago Habana* (☎3-26-75; ③), a four-storey box in need of a paint job, has rooms with air conditioning and puts on a cabaret on Friday, Saturday and Sunday nights. Even more basic but much cheaper, the *Gran Hotel Caridad* (☎3-29-59; ①) still charges in pesos, although this could change any day. It's a similar building to the *Santiago Habana* but the rooms don't have fans or air conditioning. The only place in Colón where you can get a satisfactory **meal** is at *El Faro Amarillo*, a good-quality roof-top *paladar* on Máximo Gómez, where main dishes cost less than a dollar. There's a thankfully underdone nautical theme, restricted to a ship's wheel and three simple portholes in the wall looking out across the neighbouring houses.

Península de Zapata

Forming the whole of the southern section of the province is the
Península de Zapata, also known as the Ciénaga de Zapata, a large,
flat **nature reserve** covered by vast tracts of open swampland and
contrastingly dense forests. The largest but the least populated of all
Cuba's municipalities, the peninsula is predominantly wild and
unspoilt and therefore an ideal location for getting first-hand experience of Cuban animal life, whilst its proximity to the migratory
routes between the Americas make it a birdwatchers' paradise. It's
equally appealing as a more orthodox holiday destination, situated
on the Caribbean side of the island, with over 30km of accessible
coastline and crystal clear waters to rival Varadero.

As one of the most popular day-trips from Havana and Varadero, the
peninsula has built up a set of relatively slick and conveniently packaged diversions. The **Finca Fiesta Campesina** is a somewhat contrived but nonetheless delightful cross between a farm and a small zoo,
with some of the most memorable creatures native to the region kept
in captivity here. Further in, about halfway down to the coast, **Boca de
Guamá** draws the largest number of bus parties with its **crocodile
farm**, restaurants and pottery workshop. This is also the point of
departure for the boat trip to **Guamá**, a convincingly reconstructed
Taíno Indian village on the edge of a huge lake, much of it built over
the water on stilts, and now a hotel resort. The **beaches** at the **Playa
Girón** and **Playa Larga** resorts are less spectacular than those of their
northern counterpart, but there are enough palm trees and white sand
to keep most people happy. There's equal if not greater emphasis on
scuba diving here, most of which takes place relatively close to the
shore. Another dimension to the area is its historical relevance, as it
was on these two beaches that the famous **Bay of Pigs** invasion took
place in 1961, commemorated in a museum at Playa Girón.

Often unfriendly rivals, sun-and-sea holidays and ecotourism exist
comfortably side by side here, with upmarket hotel complexes offering
all the usual beach-based holiday ingredients whilst also providing a base
for treks into muddy forests and bird-spotting river trips. Whilst there
are enough ready-made tourist attractions to fill a week effortlessly,
you'll only make the most of a stay on the peninsula by combining these
with the more active business of bird-watching, diving or trekking. In
order to do this you'll need to be in the company of a **guide**, as entrance
is restricted to most of the protected wildlife zones. Although this does
mean losing a degree of independence, the English-speaking guides,
available through Rumbos (see overleaf) are specialists in the local flora
and fauna, making the whole experience more rewarding.

The *autopista* runs more or less along the northern border of the
peninsula, separating it from the rest of the province. *La Finquita*
marks the turning for the **Carreterra de la Ciénaga**, the only reliable
road leading into the peninsula.

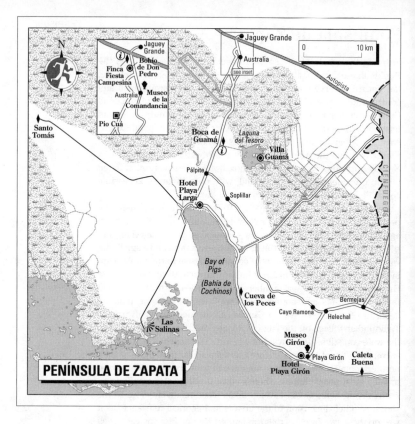

Information and getting around

Rumbos can be contacted in Varadero at the Centro de Información Turística at Ave. 1era esq. Calle 23 (☎5/61-23-84 or 66-76-30) and in Havana at Calle 23 e/ O y P, Vedado (☎7/70-30-75 or 70-04-86).

The travel agent and tour operator **Rumbos** runs most of the attractions and organizes all excursions on the peninsula; the best place to go for **information** on any aspect of a visit is the Rumbos-run *La Finquita* (☎59/32-24), a snack bar-cum-information centre by the side of the *autopista* at the junction with the main road into Zapata. Rumbos also runs *buros de turismo* in the lobbies of the *Hotel Playa Larga* (☎59/72-94) and *Hotel Playa Girón* (☎59/41-10).

Public transport in this area is virtually nonexistent and unless you're content to stick around one of the beach resorts, you're best off renting a car or scooter. Both Havanautos (☎59/41-23) and Transautos (☎59/41-26) rent cars from Playa Girón, whilst scooters are available from either of the two beachfront hotels.. That said, the hotels all run various excursions, and if you take advantage of them then having your own transport becomes less of an issue.

Finca Fiesta Campesina and around

After turning onto the Carretera de la Ciénaga, almost immediately on the right you'll see the **Finca Fiesta Campesina** (daily 9am–6pm; $1). Set up as a showcase of the Cuban countryside, this delightfully laid out little ranch presents an idealized picture of rural life in Cuba but is no less worthwhile for it. It's best approached as a light-hearted introduction to the food, drink and crafts of traditional Cuban life, and there's a good spread of activities and things to see. You can watch **cigars** being made by hand, sample a **Cuban coffee** or take a swig of raw-tasting *guarapo*, pure sugarcane juice. Dotted around the beautifully landscaped gardens are small cages and enclosures containing various species of **local wildlife**, all of which can be found living wild on the peninsula. One of the most fascinating is the *manjuarí*, an eerie-looking stick-like fish which has been around since the Jurassic period. There's an English-speaking guide available and for a dollar you can take a short horse ride or even ride the ranch's own bull. You can admire the whole complex from stone-pillared *El Canelo*, a suitably laid-back patio **restaurant** serving reasonably priced fish, pork, chicken and beef dishes under a low roof in the shade.

The ranch is set up principally to receive large groups of tourists and whilst individuals should have no problems taking a look around and eating at the restaurant, some of the organized activities, such as cock fighting, are unlikely to take place unless you happen to coincide with a group visit. This is most likely during July and August, when coachloads of tourists arrive from Havana and Varadero every two or three hours.

Less than a kilometre beyond the finca is the pocket-sized village of **AUSTRALIA**, where a right turn takes you on into the peninsula. A hundred metres or so past the turning you arrive at **Central Australia** which is not, as you might expect, the heart of the village, but in fact a sugar refinery used by Fidel Castro in 1961 as a base for directing operations during the Bay of Pigs invasion. However, the **Museo de la Comandancia** (Mon–Sat 8am–5pm, Sun 8am–noon; $1), in the building which Castro and his men occupied, is less a tribute to the purpose it served in the famous Cuban victory over the United States and more a survey of the broader history of the whole area. Although the collection is a bit out of date there are some interesting photographs and documentation of life in Australia and nearby Jaguey Grande in the early twentieth century, but it's disappointing to find so little information on the base itself. Natural history is also touched upon with a few stuffed local animals. Outside is an indistinguishable piece of an aircraft which was shot down during the invasion.

Practicalities

Billed as a chance to experience the lifestyle of a typical peasant family, *Bohío de Don Pedro* (no phone, bookings taken through Rumbos on ☎59/32-24; ④), next door to Finca Fiesta Campesina, is thankfully a far cry from the basic, often squalid conditions in which a large number of Cuba's rural population live. That aside, this immaculately kept little **cabin complex** is the best bargain on the whole of the peninsula. Consisting of ten homely and spacious wooden cabins joined by stone pathways running through closely cropped lawns, it nevertheless sacrifices none of the comforts you might expect. There's a **restaurant** on the site but it only opens when there are large groups staying. However, reasonable meals are served within walking distance at *La Finquita*; or, if you have a car, you can try *Pio Cuá* (daily noon–11.45pm; ☎59/33-43 or 23-77), a roadside restaurant serving traditional Cuban food 10km down the peninsula road. Opposite the turning for the Carretera de la Ciénaga is the road leading in a few hundred metres to **Jaguey Grande**, a small and gracious town with a few **shops** and a post office but no accommodation.

Boca de Guamá and Guamá

Eighteen kilometres down the Carretera de la Ciénaga from the *autopista*, **Boca de Guamá** is a heavily visited roadside stop. Most people make straight for the headline attraction, the crocodile farm, but there is also a pottery workshop and, a short boat ride away, a replica Taíno village. Busloads of day-trippers spend an hour or two at this most touristy of the peninsula's attractions, to eat at one of the restaurants, make the brief tour of the complex and purchase mementoes from the ample supply of souvenir shops. Though it can seem rather fake, this efficiently run attraction does make a refreshing change from the half-hearted and underfunded museums and galleries that are all too often the norm in Cuba.

Boca, as it's referred to locally, is most famous for the **Criadero de Cocodrilos** (daily 9am–5pm; $3), a crocodile breeding farm that forms the centrepiece of the complex. The setting is pleasant enough, with a short path leading from the car park, over a pond, to the small swamp where the beasts are fenced in. The stars of the show are left more or less alone and you may even have trouble spotting one on the short circuit around the swamp. However, one or two have usually crawled into conspicuous positions and if you keep your eyes peeled you should be able to catch their sinister glare as they glide through the water. For a more dramatic encounter, it's best to visit at one of the twice weekly feeding times, though unfortunately there is no regular timetable.

Established shortly after the 1959 revolution, the farm was set up as a conservation project in the interests of saving the then endangered Cuban crocodile (*cocodrilo rhombifer*) and American crocodile (*cocodrilo acutus*) from extinction. Since then, these ideals seem to have become a little blurred: before arriving at the edge of the swamp, you are invited to first witness a mock capture of an exhausted-looking baby crocodile and then to eat one. At the *Croco Bar* crocodile meat, a delicacy rare enough for the government to pass laws declaring only tourists may eat it, is served in whole and half portions for $10 and $5 repectively, although chicken and fish also feature on the short menu.

The **Taller de Cerámica Guamá** (no fixed timetable, usually open daily 10am–2pm; free) is Boca's more run-of-the-mill attraction, a kind of pottery warehouse-cum-production line. A walk around the several workshops offers a chance to witness the production process, which includes setting the moulds and baking them in large furnaces, behind the hundreds of pieces of pottery shelved throughout the building. As well as the tacky ornamental pieces there are replicas of Taíno cooking pots and suchlike. Disappointingly, there is nothing to show how the Taínos themselves would have gone about producing their pottery; staff are kept busy churning out five thousand pieces every month, all of which are for sale.

The largest **restaurant** at the complex, *La Boca*, is for pre-booked tour groups only but the *Colibri* (daily noon–4pm) is basically a smaller version of the same and offers a good choice of moderately priced main dishes. If you arrive after 4pm food can be ordered from the bar.

Guamá

Boca serves as the departure point for boats travelling to **Guamá**, the second part of the package usually offered to day-trippers stopping here. Located on the far side of the open expanse of the **Laguna de Tesoro**, Guamá is an inventively designed resort covering a number of small islands and intended to recreate the living conditions of the Taíno, the last of the Amerindian groups to arrive in Cuba, around a thousand years ago. A perfectly straight canal lined by fir trees leads to the Laguna de Tesoro, the largest natural lake in Cuba and named for the treasures which were thrown to the bottom by the local Taínos to prevent the Spanish getting their hands on them. During the crossing the thatched roofs of the *bohío* huts which make up the resort emerge into view. The first of the neatly spaced islets, where you'll be dropped off, is occupied by life-sized Taíno figures in photogenic poses, each representing an aspect of their culture. Cross the footbridge to reach the diminutive **museum** detailing Taíno life and featuring a few genuine artefacts. If the 45 minutes or so allotted by tours isn't enough, you could stay the night in one of the 44 cabins of *Villa Guamá* (☎59/29-79; ④). Dotted around eleven of the twelve islets and joined by a network of bridges and paths, the resort combines the Taíno theme with a disco and swimming pool, neither of which are up to much, as well as a restaurant in the largest of the huts. If you do stay, bear in mind that entertainment is limited, as are trips back to the mainland, and besides taking small boats out on the lake ($2 per hour) there's a good chance you'll end up spending a lot of your time watching TV and swatting mosquitoes.

Passenger **boats** seating 35 people leave Boca for the village at 10am and noon every day; alternatively you can cross in a five- or six-seat motor boat any time between 9am and 6.30pm. In either case an English-speaking guide is available and the round trip costs $10 per person.

Playa Larga and the Cueva de los Peces

At the point where the Carretera de Ciénaga reaches the Bay of Pigs, the road splits. The right turn leads through a tiny village to **Las Salinas** and **Santo Tomás** (see opposite), two of the best areas for birdwatching and both in the heart of the most untouched part of the peninsula. You'll need a guide to get beyond the checkpoint at the entrance to this part of Zapata, and without one your only option is to stay on the main road and make your way down the east side of the bay, where all the diving points, beaches and the rest of the peninsula's attractions are. This way, you'll arrive almost immediately at **Playa Larga**, a resort area right on the beach with nothing more to offer than the facilities of the complex itself. The *Hotel Playa Larga* (☎59/72-25 or 72-94; ④), however, is a reasonably comprehensive resort with comfortable, well-equipped bungalows stretching for at least a quarter of a mile along the coastline and featuring three restaurants, a swimming pool, tennis court and even a small soccer pitch. The beach itself, nestling in the arc of the bay, is about a hundred metres long with traces of seaweed on the shore and the grass encroaching onto the sand from behind. Nearby diving points can be explored by arrangement with the hotel or one of the *buros de turismo* in its lobby.

In between Playa Larga and Playa Girón, another of the area's roadside stopoffs, **Cueva de los Peces** (daily 9am–4pm; $1, free if you eat at the restaurant), beckons you to leave your car and investigate. At the bottom of a short track, a glassy-smooth **natural saltwater pool** emerges, oasis-like, against the backdrop of almost inpenetrable woodlands. Enclosed by the scrub and no bigger than a family-sized swimming pool, it's the kind of place you wish you'd discovered by yourself and kept secret from the rest of the world. Despite its proximity to the road it's perfectly tranquil and you're free to dive in and swim with the numerous species of fish living in the pool, many of which have been introduced since the natural population died out. The pool is actually the face of a flooded cave, more than 70m deep and ideal for **scuba diving**. Its labyrinth of underwater halls and corridors form a complex system of tectonic caves, much of which remains unexplored. There's a **restaurant** which is split in two with a section right by the pool's edge and a more formal section set further back.

Diving can be booked through Hotel Playa Larga, Hotel Playa Girón or Rumbos. A single dive costs $20 and a short initiation class is $8.

Playa Girón and around

Following the coastal road, it's a drive of around 15km from the Cueva de los Peces to **Playa Girón**, where the course of Cuba's destiny was battled out over 72 hours in April 1961 (see box on p.236). Aside from the hotel and beach, the reason for stopping here is the **Museo Girón** (daily 9am–noon & 1–5pm; $2), a two-room museum documenting the events prior to and during the US-backed invasion.

Nature trails and birdwatching

Besides managing most of the attractions on the peninsula Rumbos also organize less touristy trips into the heart of the nature reserve, offering tailor-
made packages which can be spread over a number of days or weeks, or
ready-made day-trips to specific areas of natural interest. They can supply
specialist guides, some of whom speak English, for fishing, diving and especially birdwatching. The three excursions below are to areas of the peninsula
which can only be visited with a guide and which together provide a varied
experience of what the area has to offer. Trips can be arranged through any
of the *buros de turismo* in the hotels or at *La Finquita*.

The Río Hatiguanico Hidden away in the woods on the northwestern edge
of Zapata is the base camp for boat trips on the widest river on the peninsula, the Hatiguanico. As the slow motorboats make their way down the tree-
lined canal to the river, the abundance of bird life becomes obvious as
Zapata sparrows swoop across the water, Cuban green woodpeckers stare
through the branches and a whole host of other birds, large and small, reign
supreme over the untouched landscape. Before reaching the widest part of
the river, the canal flows into a narrow, twisting corridor of water where
you're brushed by leaning branches as the outboard motor churns up the
river grass. As the river opens out into an Amazonian-style waterscape, it
curves gracefully around the densely packed woodland. Trips last between
one and two hours, cost $15 per person and usually include a short nature
trail into the woods, a packed lunch and a swim in one of the river alcoves.
Fishing is also an option; $50 per person pays for a total of six hours includ-
ing equipment.

Santo Tomás Thirty kilometres from the village just before Playa Larga,
along a dirt road through dense forest, Santo Tomás is at the heart of the
reserve. Beyond the scattered huts which make up the tiny community that
lives here is a small two-metre-wide tributary of the Hatiguanico. In winter
it's dry enough to walk but during the wet season groups of four to six are
punted quietly a few hundred metres down the hidden little waterway,
brushing past the overhanging reeds. This is real swamp land and will suit
the dedicated birdwatcher who doesn't mind getting dirty in the interests of
listening and looking out in the perfect tranquillity for, amongst many others, the three endemic species in this part of the peninsula: the Zapata
wren, Zapata sparrow and the Zapata rail. Trips cost $10 per person.

Las Salinas In stark contrast to the dense woodlands of Santo Tomás are
the open salt-water wetlands around Las Salinas, the best place on the
peninsula for observing migratory and aquatic birds. From the observation
towers dotted along the track that cuts through the shallow waters you can
see huge flocks of flamingos socializing in the distance, solitary blue heron
gliding over the shallow water, whilst blue-wing duck and many other
species pop in and out of view from behind the scattered brackeny islets.
Trips to Las Salinas cost $10 per person.

Outside the building is one of the fighter planes used in the defence
of the island to attack the advancing American ships. Inside, the
atmosphere in which the invasion took place is successfully evoked
through depictions of life prior to the 1959 revolution along with
dramatic photographs of US sabotage and terrorism in Cuba imme-

The Bay of Pigs

The triumph of the Cuban revolution was initially treated with caution rather than hostility by the US government, but tensions between the two countries developed quickly. As reforms became more radical, the US tried harder to thwart the process and particularly refused to accept the terms of the agrarian reform law which dispossessed a number of American landowners. Castro attacked the US in his speeches, became increasingly friendly with the Soviet Union and in the latter half of 1960 expropriated all US property in Cuba. The Americans responded by cancelling Cuba's sugar quota and secretly authorizing the CIA to organize the training of Cuban exiles, who had fled the country following the rebel triumph, for a future invasion of Cuba.

On April 15, 1961, US planes disguised with Cuban markings and piloted by Cuban exiles bombed Cuban air fields but caused more panic than actual damage, although seven people were killed. The intention had been to incapacitate the small Cuban air force so that the invading troops would be free from aerial bombardment, but Castro had cannily moved most of the Cuban bombers away from the airfields and camouflaged them. Two days later Brigade 2506, as the exile invasion force was known, landed at Playa Girón. The brigade had been led to believe that the air attacks had been successful and were not prepared for what was in store. As soon as Castro learned of the precise location of the invasion he moved his base of operations to Central Australia (see p.225) and ordered both his air force and land militias to repel the advancing invaders.

The unexpected aerial attacks caused much damage and confusion; two freighters were destroyed and the rest of the fleet fled, leaving 1300 troops trapped on Playa Larga and Playa Girón. During the night of April 17–18 the Cuban government forces, which had been reinforced with armoured cars and tanks, renewed attacks on the brigade. The battle continued into the next day as the brigade became increasingly outnumbered by the advancing revolutionary army. Several B-26 bombers, two manned by US pilots, flew over to the Bay of Pigs from Nicaragua the next morning in an attempt to weaken the Cuban army and clear the way for the landing of supplies needed by the stranded brigade. Most of the bombers were shot down and the supplies never arrived. Castro's army had won and captured 1180 prisoners who were eventually traded for medical and other supplies from the US. Other ways would have to be found to topple the Cuban leader (see box, opposite).

diately prior to the **Bay of Pigs**. The second room goes on to document the invasion itself, with papers outlining Castro's battle instructions and some incredible photography taken in the heat of battle. Various personal belongings and military equipment are laid out in front of the photographs and most poignantly photographs of each of the Cuban casualties. To bring it all to life it's worth asking the staff if you can watch the museum's ten-minute documentary, filmed at the time of combat.

The *Hotel Playa Girón* (☎59/41-10, fax 41-17; ④), a stone's throw from the museum, is the largest of all the tourist complexes on the peninsula, with most of its family-sized, fully furnished bungalows fac-

American assassination attempts on Fidel Castro

Following the dramatic failure of the military offensive at the Bay of Pigs, the US abandoned the idea of invading Cuba and turned to less overt methods for removing Fidel Castro from power. Fabián Escalante, the former head of Cuban State Security, claims that between 1959 and 1963 over six hundred plots were hatched to kill the Cuban president. The plots became more devious, and ludicrous, as the US grew increasingly desperate to remove the communist leader. In 1960, during a visit which Castro was making to the UN, it was planned that he be given a cigar which would explode in his face. Back in Cuba, in 1963, Rolando Cubela, who had been a commander in the rebel army, was given a syringe disguised as a pen to be used in assassinating Castro. The Mafia also had a stab at killing Castro with their poison pill plot but got no further than their CIA counterparts. Some of the more outlandish plots have included poisoning a diving suit, poisoning a cigar, placing an explosive shell on the beach, spraying LSD in a television studio in the hope of inducing an attack of uncontrollable laughter and perhaps most hilariously putting thallium salts in Castro's shoes to make his beard fall out and thus destroy his power and charisma as Delilah did to Samson.

ing out to sea. There's a diving centre, a pool, tennis court, car rental and all the usual services you'd expect from an international hotel. The beach is more exposed than Playa Larga but it's blessed with the same transparent green waters. Opposite the lobby building is a disco.

Eight kilometres on from Playa Girón, the last stop along this side of the bay is **Caleta Buena**, a rocky but very picturesque stretch of coastline which has been converted into a diving and snorkelling centre. Based around the calm waters of a large sheltered inlet with flat rocky platforms jutting out into the sea, the unspoilt serenity befits the most secluded of Zapata's coastal havens. It's a perfect place for lazing about on the beach, with red-tile-roof shelters on wooden stilts providing protection from the midday sun. The most suitable way of expending energy here is to go **snorkelling** or **diving** and take advantage of the fact that you needn't go further than 150m out from the beach to enjoy a coral-coated sea bed. A single dive costs $20 and renting snorkelling equipment a mere $3. Diving initiation courses are available for $8 and should be arranged in advance through Rumbos. There is also a volleyball net and row boats for rent ($3 per hour). Of the two modest eateries here, *Rancho Benito* (daily 9am–4pm; ☎59/32-24), a rustic open-air **grill** tucked away in the corner of the complex, looks over a crystal-clear pool full of lively fish. The speciality is "Stimulant Shellfish". Lobster, shrimp, frogs' legs and fish cocktail are on the menu at the cramped restaurant set further back from the shore.

If you rent any equipment or eat at either the grill or restaurant, **entrance** to Caleta Buena is free, but if all you intend to do is swim or sunbathe then you'll be charged a dollar for the privilege. There's generally nothing happening here in the evenings – arrive after 5pm and you're likely to find the place deserted.

Travel details

ASTRO BUSES

Cárdenas to: Jaguey Grande (1 daily; 2hr); Jovellanos (1 daily; 1hr); Matanzas (1 daily; 1hr 15min); Santa Clara (1 daily; 3hr).

Matanzas to: Camaguey (3 weekly; 9hr); Havana (3 daily; 2hr 10min); Santa Clara (1 daily; 4hr); Santiago (3 weekly; 16hr 45min).

Varadero to: Havana (daily; 2hr 40min); Santa Clara (1 daily; 4hr).

VÍAZUL BUSES

Varadero to: Havana (2 daily; 2hr 45min); Trinidad (3 weekly; 5hr 50min).

TRAINS

Cárdenas to: Colón (1 daily; 1hr 30min); Jovellanos (runs according to availability of fuel; 1hr).

Colón to: Cárdenas (1 daily; 1hr 30min); Havana (3 daily; 3hr); Holguin (1 daily; 12hr); Matanzas (1 daily; 1hr 30min); Sancti Spíritus (1 daily; 4hr).

Matanzas to: Colón (1 daily; 1hr 30min); Havana (1–3 daily; 2hr); Holguin (3 weekly); Jovellanos (1 daily; 50min); Sancti Spíritus (3 weekly; 6hr); Santiago (1 daily; 12hr).

Hershey trains to Havana (5 daily; 2hr 40min to 3hr 30min, depending on departure time).

Chapter 4

Trinidad and the central provinces

As the most perfectly preserved colonial city in the country, Trinidad, in the southwestern corner of the province of Sancti Spíritus, is the essential destination in central Cuba. Only a short drive away from the beach, and with the mountains almost as close, Trinidad is justifiably the single most visited location in this part of the country. This fantastically preserved and restored sixteenth-century town has a time-frozen quality rivalled only by Habana Vieja, and while it has yet to be overtaken completely by tourism, it's fairly well set up to receive visitors, with numerous *casas particulares* and places to eat. The flashier hotels are a fifteen-kilometre drive away on the **Península de Ancón**, host to the best beach on this part of the southern coast. In the opposite direction is **Topes de Collantes**, a mountain resort that makes an excellent base for exploring the lavishly forested steep slopes of the **Sierra del Escambray**. West of Trinidad, the provincial capital of **Sancti Spíritus** attracts few visitors but is not without appeal. Best treated as a one-night stop-off, the city is as much a time capsule of the last ten years as it is of the last four centuries.

Though slowly attracting tourists in their own right, the neighbouring provinces to the north and west currently offer a taste of undiluted Cuban life, albeit at the subdued pace which characterizes so much of the country away from Havana. Here, for once, travel is relatively uncomplicated as the two main cities are linked to Trinidad by the efficient Víazul bus service (see p.292). The most westerly of these, capital of the eponymous province, **Cienfuegos** is one of Cuba's more attractive big cities, situated alongside a large enclosed bay, within easy day-trip distance of the province's other destinations. The nearby beach at **Rancho Luna** is a pleasant enough base if you're staying longer, though the most memorable of Cienfuegos' attractions is the **botanical gardens**, roughly a fifteen-kilometre drive from the city.

Villa Clara, north of Trinidad, has been targeted by the government as one of the next provinces to be developed for international

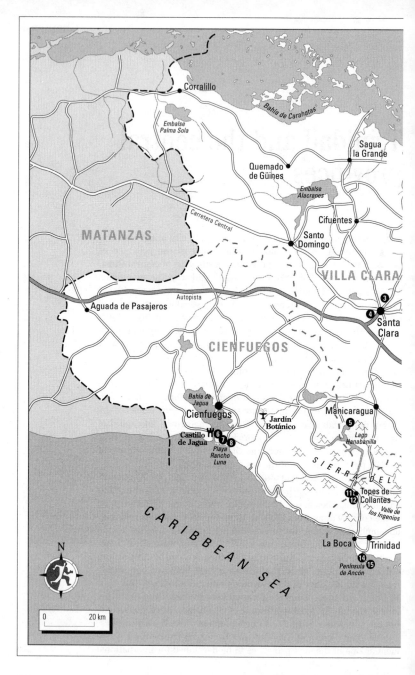

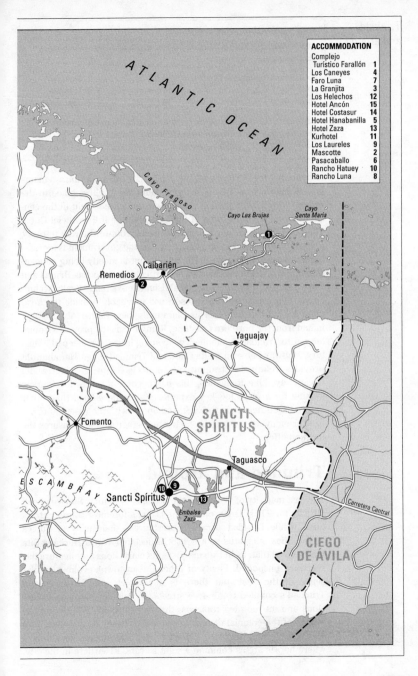

Accommodation price codes

All accommodation listed in this guide has been graded according to the following
price categories.

① peso hotel equivalent to $5 or less ④ $30–50 ⑦ $100–150
② $5–20 ⑤ $50–70 ⑧ $150–200
③ $20–30 ⑥ $70–100 ⑨ $200 and above

Rates are for the cheapest available double or twin room during high season, usually
May–September and the last two weeks of December. During low season some hotels
lower their prices by roughly ten percent.

tourism, but for the moment, the capital city of **Santa Clara** remains
largely unaffected. This is without doubt the liveliest place in the
region: with a large student population and a hotel right in the centre of town, it offers some of the best nightlife in provincial Cuba.
The rest of the province is characterized by out-of-the-way retreats,
poised to move into the limelight now that the government is increasing investment in the area. The investment is mostly being concentrated in the virgin northern cays, particularly **Cayo Las Brujas** and
Cayo Santa María, where the establishment of a fantastically secluded yet fully equipped beach resort will inevitably provide the focal
point for most visitors to Villa Clara in the near future. About 10km
inland from the northern coastline, **Remedios** is the province's quiet
answer to Trinidad, a subdued, welcoming little town steeped in history. Halfway between Santa Clara and Trinidad, **Lago Hanabanilla**
provides relatively straightforward access into the Sierra del
Escambray. Like Remedios, this has become a target for tourists
looking for a more low-key experience: less developed than other
nature-based resorts in Cuba, it's equipped with the essential facilities for enjoying the fishing, hiking and other simple pleasures the
location offers.

Trinidad and around

The vast majority of visitors to the province of **Sancti Spíritus** head
directly for **TRINIDAD**, one of the island's foremost tourist attractions. While Trinidad attracts more tourists than many of Cuba's
larger cities, its status as a UNESCO-declared World Heritage Site
has ensured that, as in Habana Vieja, its marvellous architecture has
remained unspoiled. Plenty of other Cuban towns evoke a similar
sense of the past, but there is a completeness about central
Trinidad's cobbled traffic-free streets, its jumble of colonial mansions and its red-tiled rooftops, that sets it apart. Wandering the
streets of the colonial district in particular, there is something of a
village feel about the place – albeit a large and prosperous village –
where horses are as common a sight as cars. Elsewhere in the city,

there are fewer specific sights, but a wander into the more recently constructed neighbourhoods is a good way of tapping into local life.

For many visitors Trinidad offers an unparalled insight into the close-knit community spirit that pervades so much of Cuba. This isn't a big place and local activity is concentrated in much the same areas as the *casas particulares* visitors tend to stay in, most of which straddle the border between the colonial centre and the untouristed periphery of town. With an unusually high proportion of locals directly involved in tourism – renting out rooms, driving private taxis, working in restaurants or as museum attendants – chances are that after a few days you'll start to recognize the same faces.

From Trinidad, most of the province's highlights are within easy reach. In fact, the city's proximity to the **Valle de los Ingenios**, site of most of the sugar estates on which the city built its fortune, the **Península de Ancón** and its Caribbean beaches, and the lush mountain slopes around the **Topes de Collantes** hiking resort, make it one of the best bases on the island for discovering the different facets of Cuba's landscape.

Some history

Though the chronicles of one of the seamen who sailed with Columbus suggest that the coast around Trinidad was first seen by European eyes in 1494, it wasn't until December 1513 that a Spanish settlement was established here, as part of the conquest of the island by Diego Velázquez and his men. By 1518 there were some sixty or seventy Spanish families living here, alongside the native population, making their living from gold mining, small-scale agriculture or cattle farming. Then, in that year, the gold ran out and interest in the area began to wane, particularly as news spread of the riches to be found on the mainland in Mexico. A steady flow of emigration left the town all but empty by 1544. By this time, however, the indigenous population had adjusted to the ways of life brought by the settlers and it was they who kept the economy alive, farming the land and raising cattle, so that when Spanish interest in the area was reawakened in the 1580s the colonialists simply took over the reigns from the Amerindians.

In 1585 Trinidad was declared a city and embarked on an era which was to become characterized by pirate attacks and smuggling. The late sixteenth and the seventeenth centuries saw the Spanish crown impose strict trading regulations and a monopoly on production. Manoeuvring around these debilitating restrictions, Trinitarios built up illicit trading links with nearby Jamaica and with English, Dutch and French traders sailing the Caribbean. The export of meats, hides and tobacco, in exchange for manufactured products and clothing, saw the wealth of the territory increase enough to attract French, British and Dutch pirates, who ransacked the city three times during the seventeenth century. Despite these setbacks, by the 1750s the region possessed over a hundred tobacco plantations, at least as many farms, 56 cattle and sheep ranches and 25 sugar mills, as well as a number of textile workshops. The population had grown to just under six thousand.

The mid-eighteenth century marked the start of the **sugar boom** (see pp.218–19), a period of around a hundred years that saw Trinidad become one of the most prosperous cities in the country, acquiring a host of splendid colonial mansions, many of which are still standing today. The region now had over forty sugar mills, but land continued to be cleared for planting cane, by far the most profitable crop.

Despite the technological advances gained through contact with Jamaica and therefore Britain, sugar production remained a labour-intensive activity and thousands of **African slaves** were imported to cope with the increasing demands of the local industry. Population ranks were also swelled by an influx of **European** immigrants, attracted by the affluence of the city, thus enhancing Trinidad's standing as one of Cuba's most cosmopolitan nineteenth-century cities. As much as anything, it was the huge wealth of the local elite that graced the city with its artistic flavour. Furniture and jewellery as well as luxury foods were imported from Europe and the United States by sugar barons like Brunet, Iznaga and Borrell, who built elegant mansions both in the town and on their nearby estates.

Trinidad's prosperity reached its peak in the 1830s and 1840s, when the economic tide began to turn. Slave revolts in 1838 and 1839 on the sugar plantations were just the beginning of a series of disruptions to the industry on which the region had come to depend. All the cultivable land had been exhausted by the middle of the century, leading to futile attempts to grow sugarcane on the infertile soils of the coastal areas. Moreover, the clearing of the forests in order to plant sugar meant that one of the region's principal sources of fuel had also been exhausted and wood now had to be imported at increased cost. At the same time, Trinidad's economic foundations were being eroded by outside forces, with European sugar beet production challenging the dominance of Caribbean cane. The downward spiral accelerated with the wars of independence, beginning in 1868 (see Contexts, p.465). A large number of sugar plantations around Trinidad were destroyed, coffee and cattle farming became obsolete, whilst more than half of the local tobacco plantations also disappeared as the rebels fought the Spanish for control of the city and the surrounding land, gaining the upper hand by 1897 but only after the backbone of the local economy had been broken.

The second war of independence ended in 1898, by which time the US had become involved. As the twentieth century got under way US dominance of the economy in Trinidad meant the vast majority of local land falling into foreign hands and the concentration of all

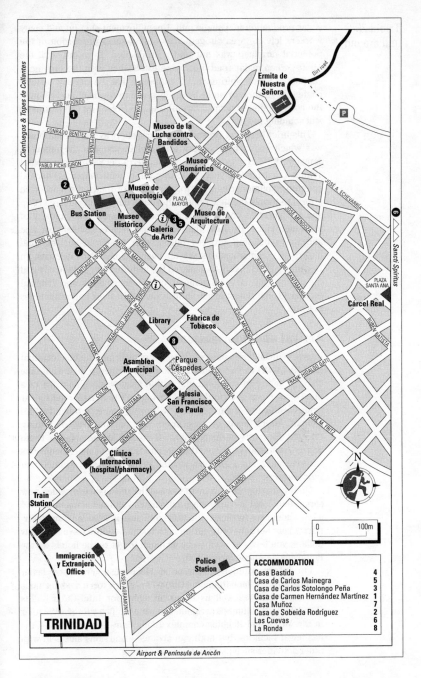

TRINIDAD

Museo de la
Lucha contra
Bandidos

Ermita de
Nuestra
Señora

Museo
Romántico

Museo de
Arqueología

PLAZA
MAYOR

Museo de
Arquitectura

Bus Station

Museo
Histórico

Galería
de Arte

Library

Fábrica de
Tobacos

Asamblea
Municipal

Parque
Céspedes

Iglesia
San Francisco
de Paula

Clínica
Internacional
(hospital/pharmacy)

Train
Station

Immigración
y Extranjera
Office

Police
Station

Cárcel Real

PLAZA
SANTA ANA

Cienfuegos & Topes de Collantes

Sancti Spíritus

Dirt road

Airport & Península de Ancón

N

0   100m

ACCOMMODATION

Casa Bastida	4
Casa de Carlos Mainegra	5
Casa de Carlos Sotolongo Peña	3
Casa de Carmen Hernández Martínez	1
Casa Muñoz	7
Casa de Sobeida Rodríguez	2
Las Cuevas	6
La Ronda	8

Street names: CIRO REDONDO, CONRADO BENÍTEZ, PABLO PICHS GIRON, PIRO GUINART, FIDEL CLARO, VICENTE SUYAMA, INDEPENDENCIA, RUBÉN MARTÍNEZ, SANTIAGO ESCOBAR, SIMÓN BOLÍVAR, ANTONIO MACEO, IZQUIERDO, JUAN MANUEL MÁRQUEZ, LINO PÉREZ, FRANCISCO JAVIER ZERQUERA, JOSÉ MARTÍ, FRANK PAÍS, COLÓN, ANTONIO GUITERAS, GENERAL LINO PÉREZ, ANASTASIO CÁRDENAS, PEDRO ZERQUERA, PASEO AGRAMONTE, JULIO CUEVA DÍAZ, MANUEL FAJARDO, JESÚS BETANCOURT, CAMILO CIENFUEGOS, FRANCISCO CODAHÍA, JESÚS MENÉNDEZ, COLÓN, JULIO A. MELLA, ABEL SANTAMARÍA, FRANK HIDALGO GATO, JOSÉ M. FRITZ, RUBÉN BATISTA, JOSÉ MENDOZA, JOSÉ A. ECHEVARRÍA, SIMÓN BOLÍVAR sugar production in a single mill. Unemployment shot up and many workers left the area altogether as only a small proportion of the potential farmland was put under production. It wasn't until the 1950s, when major road links were established with the provincial capitals of Sancti Spíritus and Cienfuegos, that the city saw a slight change in fortune brought by an increase in tourism, encouraging the construction of a small airport and the *Hotel Las Cuevas*, both still standing today.

This brief period of prosperity was cut short by the revolutionary war which ended with victory for Fidel Castro and the rebels in January 1959. However, it was in the Sierra del Escambray around Trinidad that for five years following the rebel triumph, US-backed counter-revolutionaries were to base some of their most concerted efforts to topple the new regime. Revolutionary militias were set up and the guerrilla conflict that ensued saw significant numbers of local men killed. By 1965 the region had been completely pacified and the rebuilding process began with hospitals, schools and improved communications set up over the next two decades. In December 1988 UNESCO declared the historic centre of the city and the nearby Valle de los Ingenios World Heritage Sites, and Trinidad embarked on its latest incarnation as one of the most important cities in Cuba.

Arrival and information

Interprovincial buses navigate their way slowly into the **bus terminal** (☎419/44-48) at Piro Guinart e/ Maceo e Izquierdo, just inside the colonial centre of the town and within easy walking distance of a number of *casas particulares*. Arriving on the coastal road by **car** from Cienfuegos or further west will bring you into town on Piro Guinart, which leads directly up to the two main roads cutting through the centre of the city, José Martí and Antonio Maceo. From Sancti Spíritus and the east, the Circuito Sur takes cars closer to *Las Cuevas* hotel, but a left turn at Lino Pérez will take you into *casa particular* territory.

On the southwestern edge of town is the **train station**, which now serves only local destinations, including El Valle de los Ingenios, and a few kilometres further in the same direction is Trinidad's small **airport**. From here the only option is to take a taxi into town for a few dollars; you'll pay at least twice as much to get to the hotels on the Península de Ancón (see p.250).

For **information**, try Cubatur at Maceo esq. Francisco Javier Serquera (daily 9am–9pm; ☎419/63-14), which has a desk for taxis and car rental, as well as being an agent for Inter-Cuba flights (☎419/62-12). Rumbos at Simón Bolívar e/ Muñoz y Rubén Martínez in the Mesón del Regidor complex (daily 8am–8pm; ☎419/44-14) has fewer facilities, but both can arrange excursions and help with other activities such as diving or horse-riding.

Orientation and getting around

The historic centre of the city is Trinidad's main attraction, and it's here that you'll spend most of your time. In general, if you're walking on cobbled stones you're in the UNESCO-protected part of the city, often referred to as the "old town". More specifically defined as the area marked off by Antonio Maceo, usually known simply as Maceo, Lino Pérez, José Mendoza and the northern tip of the city, the borderlines have been clearly defined by UNESCO but are slightly more blurred for the visitor. Though most of the official tourist spots are in the old town, beyond these streets there are a number of less feted but equally historic buildings. Walking around the **northern** limits of Trinidad in particular, the absence of motor vehicles, the basic living conditions and the buzz of human activity lend the muddy streets a strong sense of the past, albeit a less pristinely packaged version than the one seen in the old town.

The only way to get about is **on foot**, and as the old town is built on a fairly steep incline this can be quite tiring. The logical place to get your bearings is the **Plaza Mayor**, a five-minute walk from all the best sights and numerous restaurants. Most visitors are unlikely to want or need to walk beyond the area enclosed by **Parque Céspedes**, two blocks south of the historic centre, and **José Martí** to the west. To the north, the city merges into the surrounding hills, offering easily manageable walks with captivating views across the rooftops and down to the coast.

The confusion arising from old and new **street names** encountered in many Cuban towns is particularly acute in Trinidad. Most names were changed after the revolution but new maps and tourist literature are reverting to the old names in the interests of the town's historical heritage. However, street signs still carry the revolutionary names, and the addresses appearing in this book follow suit.

Accommodation

Trinidad has one of the best selections of **casas particulares** in the country, but despite the town's popularity competition remains fierce and prices are still relatively low. They're spread throughout the city, with a particular concentration on and around Maceo and José Martí. Surprisingly, the government has chosen not to build any hotels in the centre of town, preferring instead to renovate one which already existed prior to the 1990s tourism explosion.

Casa Bastida, Maceo no. 587 e/ Simón Bolívar y Piro Guinart ☎419/21-51. One very spacious triple with streetside balcony and one cramped double, both next to a pleasant outdoor terrace and with access to the roof. This was once also a *paladar*, and the meals are of excellent quality. ②.

Casa de Carlos Mainegra, Rubén Martínez no. 21 e/ Simón Bolívar y Francisco Javier Serquera; no phone. Right on the Plaza Mayor with one double bedroom to rent in a modest house with a pleasant but narrow plant-lined courtyard. This is a better place than some to negotiate a cheaper price. ②.

Casa de Carlos Sotolongo Pena, Rubén Martínez no. 33 e/ Simón Bolívar y Francisco Javier Serquera ☎419/41-69. Next door to the Galería de Arte on Plaza Mayor, there's room for four people in the one room for rent in this spacious 1825-built house occupied by sixth-generation Trinitarios. It has an en-suite bathroom and looks onto a large courtyard. ③.

Casa de Carmen Hernández Martínez, Maceo no. 718 e/ Conrado Benítez y Ciro Redondo; no phone. The whole of this basic two-bedroom bungalow is for rent – ideal if you prefer to be self-sufficient. As it's in a more run-down part of town, away from the action, staying here makes for a realistic experience of average Cuban living conditions. ②.

Casa Munoz, José Martí no. 401 e/ Fidel Claro y Stgo Escobar ☎419/36-73. One of the most fantastically furnished and best-equipped colonial residences in Trinidad, this house is a museum piece in itself. Crammed with its original nineteenth-century furniture, it also features two spanking new bathrooms, three large bedrooms, a fantastic rooftop terrace, space to park three cars and to cap it all the owners speak English. Expect to pay about $5 more than average prices. ②.

Casa de Sobeida Rodríguez, Maceo no. 619 e/ Piro Guinart y Pablo Pichs Girón ☎419/41-62. There are three bedrooms in this comfortable house right near the bus station. One of the more modern of the *casas particulares*. ②.

Las Cuevas, Finca Santa Ana ☎419/40-13 to 19, fax 61-33. A twenty- to thirty-minute walk from the Plaza Mayor, this large cabin complex is nonetheless superbly located on a hillside overlooking the town and the coast. There's access to the cave network over which the site was built, a music-based show every night, a tennis court and the only pool in town. ⑤.

La Ronda, José Martí e/ Colón y Lino Pérez ☎419/22-48 or 40-11. The only hotel in central Trinidad, this is an excellent-value, easy-going place near Parque Céspedes, with unremarkable but pleasing little rooms, a patio as well as a rooftop bar and an agreeable restaurant. More character than comfort but no worse off for it. ③.

The Town

Trinidad boasts the highest number of museums per capita in the country, and with most of them within a few blocks of one another you can cram a day full of sightseeing without breaking a sweat. However, simply wandering around the narrow streets in the shadows of the colonial houses whose shuttered porticoes form a patchwork of blues, greens, reds and yellows is one of the highlights of any tour of Trinidad, and it's worth conserving enough time and energy to do just that, even if it means missing out some of the museums. Three of these are on the central **Plaza Mayor**, including the memorable **Museo Romántico**, with another two no more than a few minutes' walk away. If you're prepared to walk a little further, north of the Plaza Mayor, there are wide-reaching views from the hillside which overlooks Trinidad, marked at its base by the ruined **Ermita de Nuestra Señora** church.

Heading downhill from Plaza Mayor will lead south out of the historic centre towards **Parque Céspedes**, the hub of local activity, where people come to while away the afternoons, chatting under the shade of the square's canopied walkway or meeting up at weekends for a street party. To the east, in a more subdued section of town, where visitors are more conspicuous, is Trinidad's main commercial centre and the **El Alfarero** ceramics factory.

Plaza Mayor

At the heart of the UNESCO-protected colonial section of Trinidad is the beautiful **Plaza Mayor**. The steeply sloping streets of Simón Bolívar and Francisco Javier Serquera form its northeastern and southwestern borders, joined at the top and bottom by Echerrí and Rubén Martínez Villena respectively. Though it's populated principally by camera-wielding tourists, there is something quite captivating about this compact and trim little plaza. Comprising four simple fenced-in gardens, each with a palm tree or two shooting out from one of the corners and dotted with various statuettes and other ornamental touches, this is the focal point of the old town, surrounded by colourfully painted colonial mansions adorned with arches, balconies and terraces, and which now house museums and art galleries.

Overlooking the plaza on the corner of Echerrí and Simón Bolívar is the fabulous **Museo Romántico** (Tues–Sun 9am–5pm; $2), an essential part of the journey-in-time experience of visiting Trinidad. With one of the country's finest and most valuable collections of **furniture** packed into its fourteen rooms, there is no better place to go for a picture of aristocratic lifestyle and tastes in colonial times. Dating from 1808, the house itself is a magnificent example of elegant yet unadorned nineteenth-century domestic Cuban architecture, built for the Brunet family, one of the wealthiest in Trinidad during the sugar-boom years. Though the contents have been gathered together from various buildings all over town, there is a wonderful consistency and completeness to the collection, befitting of the perfectly preserved and restored rooms. Not a single piece looks out of place, from the precious eighteenth-century Viennese bureau, intricately decorated with pictures from Greek mythology, to the one-and-a-quarter-ton plain marble bathtub. Though all the rooms are fantastically furnished, two of the richest are the exquisite dining room with its Italian marble floor and the master bedroom with its four-poster bed and French wardrobe, miraculously constructed without nails or screws.

On the other side of Simón Bolívar, occupying the other half of the square's highest border, is the **Iglesia de la Santísima Trinidad**, also known as the Parroquial Mayor, the main city church and the obvious exception to the otherwise exclusively domestic architecture around the plaza. Though there has been a church on this site since 1620, the original building was destroyed in a storm which swept through town in 1812. The structure now standing was officially founded in 1892, the first brick having been laid as long before as 1817, but much of what you'll see inside dates from the twentieth century. Beyond its unremarkable facade, there's plenty to look at within the church's three naves. Amongst the pictures and paintings, it's the disproportionate number of **altars** that grabs most people's attention. The majority were created by Amadeo Fiogere, a Dominican friar named as priest of the church in 1912, who set about livening up the interior, drawing on his own personal fortune to donate many of the images on display today. There's a distinct mix of elaborate artificiality and genuinely impressive craftsmanship about the eleven wooden altars which, whatever your final judgement, won't fail to make you stop and stare. This is especially true of the main one in thecentral nave, a mass of pointed spires and detailed etchings, like a miniature facade of a gothic cathedral. The best **time** to visit is from Monday to Saturday between 11am and 12.30pm, when there is no Mass (a service reserved exclusively for locals).

Working your way clockwise around the square from Echerrí, following the church is the **Museo de Arquitectura** (Mon–Sat 9am–5pm; $1), a sky-blue and white building with a courtyard vibrantly bedecked with plants. The central theme is the development of domestic architecture in Trinidad during the eighteenth and nineteenth centuries, providing a little of the theory behind one of the main attractions of Trinidad itself. However, though the maps, models, pictures, and examples of various fixtures such as doors and railings are worth taking some time over, the best *museo de arquitectura* is outside rather than inside the museum doors. Similarly, it won't take long to look round the **Galería de Arte** (Mon–Sun 8am–5pm), at the bottom end of the square, whose displays comprise a mixture of soulless paintings and temporary exhibitions with a more original slant. Upstairs, lacework, ceramics and sculpture are on show and through the open shutters a perfectly framed view of the plaza.

On the corner of Simón Bolívar and Rubén Martínez, on the plaza's northwestern side, is the so-called **Museo de Arqueología** (Mon–Sat 9am–5pm; $1), currently caught in some kind of an identity crisis. By far the meatiest single exhibit is the original and fully intact nineteenth-century kitchen, the last of the rooms and the only one relating to the house itself. There are plenty of equally un-archeological findings, such as stuffed Cuban animals, sharing glass cases with pre-Columbian tools. Apart from some attempts to explain aboriginal Cuba and one or two more substantial exhibits, notably skeletal remains dating back around a thousand years, the collection of bricks and bones, bottles and bullets does little to illuminate the past – for the most part the museum isn't much more than a collection of old broken things.

Museo Histórico and Museo de la Lucha Contra Bandidos

A few blocks from the Plaza Mayor lie the other highlights of the colonial centre. On Simón Bolívar, a block below the plaza, is the **Museo Histórico** (Mon–Fri & Sun 9am–5pm; $2), another converted colonial residence. The first part of the museum follows the same format as the Museo Romántico, with various examples of choice nineteenth-century furniture brought under the same roof to recreate the everyday surroundings and living conditions of a wealthy family in colonial Trinidad, in this case the Canteros. Born in the town in 1815, Justo German Cantero, like so many Trinitarios, made his fortune in the sugar industry, more specifically as owner of the Buena Vista sugar mill and numerous other properties around Trinidad. His portrait, along with that of his wife, hangs in the study. The first three rooms make up the most well-rounded part of the museum; from here on the collection moves abruptly into a rundown of the area's history. Though there are some interesting objects scattered about, the exhibits never really build a coherent picture of any of the various stages into which it is broken down. Don't leave, however, without making your way upstairs to the next floor, from where a spiral staircase leads up into a tower providing some great views, including a classic snapshot image of the plaza.

A block north of Plaza Mayor, where Echerrí meets Piro Guinart, the building housing the **Museo de la Lucha Contra Bandidos** (Tues–Sun 9am–5pm; $1) is the owner of the dome-topped yellow and white trimmed bell tower that's become the trademark image of Trinidad. The tower is part of the eighteenth-century church and convent, known respectively as the Iglesia and Convento de San Francisco de Asís, which previously stood on this site. Even if the museum's contents don't appeal to you, it's well worth paying the entrance fee to climb the tower by way of its rickety wooden staircase. From the top, there's a panoramic view over the city and across to the hills and coastline. Down in the museum, displays concentrate on the counter-revolutionary groups – the **bandidos**, or bandits – which formed during the years immediately following Castro's seizure of power in 1959. The most striking exhibit is in the central courtyard, where a military truck and a motorboat mounted with machine guns stand as examples of the hardware employed by and against the *bandidos* in their struggle to overthrow the revolutionary government. There's no shortage of detail when it comes to charting the conflict between the two sides, much of which took place in the nearby Sierra del Escambray, but the maps, military equipment and endless mug shots become a little repetitive. It's better to spend more time in the first few rooms, containing dramatic and compelling photographs of the rebel war and the student struggle between 1952 and 1959.

Ermita de Nuestra Señora

As it heads up and away from Plaza Mayor, Simon Bolívar leads out of Trinidad's historic centre and through a less pristine part of town; soon the road becomes a dirt track leading steeply up to the **Ermita de Nuestra Señora**, a dilapidated church marking the last line of buildings before the town dissolves into the countryside. There's nothing to see of the church but a ruined framework, but it's worth making the easy fifteen-minute walk up the hill for the views alone. At the summit the lush landscape on the other side of the hill is revealed, as well as the views back across the town and down to the coast. Just beyond the ruined church you can easily cut across to the *Las Cuevas* complex, on the adjoining hillside, where non-guests can use the hillside swimming pool ($1) and other facilities.

Parque Céspedes and around

Plaza Mayor may be the city centre for sightseers, but as far as the town's population are concerned, **Parque Céspedes** is Trinidad's main square. South of the cobbled streets that define the protected part of the town, a ten-minute walk from Plaza Mayor down Simon Bolívar and left onto Martí, Parque Céspedes may not have the enchanting surroundings of the Plaza Mayor but it's markedly more lively, particularly in the evenings. Schoolchildren run out onto the square in the afternoon whilst older locals head here at the end of the day to chat on the benches lining the three walkways. Local hustlers hang around outside the cigar shop on Lino Pérez, on the southeastern side, whilst town councillors to and fro past the stately yellow-columned entrance of the Asamblea Municipal building, which occupies the entire northwestern side of the square. In the square's centre a distinctive dome-shaped leafy canopy provides plenty of shade, whilst flower-frilled bushes encase the simple gardens around the centre, marked in each corner by a handsome royal palm. Set back from the southwestern edge of the square, next to the school, are a cinema and a modest tiled-roof church.

A few blocks north of Parque Céspedes, on the corner of Maceo and Colón, is the **Fábrica de Tabacos**, Trinidad's tiny cigar factory. There's no entrance fee, as visitors are allowed no further than the first small room. However, from here most of the activity is just about visible: workers sitting at desks sorting leaves or hand-rolling cigars, including the well-known Romeo y Julieta brand. Despite the inevitable brevity of a visit, this window on one of the country's oldest industries is fascinating. There are no fixed opening hours, but it's advisable to turn up before 4pm and to leave a tip.

East of the historic centre

From Parque Céspedes, a ten-minute walk along Lino Pérez brings you to the only other tangible tourist attraction outside of the colonial centre, **Plaza Santa Ana**. The plaza itself is little more than an open space, its neglected status exemplified by the derelict shell of a church, the Iglesia Santa Ana, which stands on one side. It's the shops, bar and restaurant around the courtyard of the converted **Cárcel Real**, the old Royal Prison, that coachloads of tour groups stop here for. Disappointingly, the small **commercial centre** housed here, the most comprehensive of its kind in Trinidad, is the main draw and very little is made of the 1844 building's history as a military jail. Clustered around a large cobbled courtyard, the **shops** stock *artesanía*, books, a few cigars and various other bits and bobs. Also here is the Taller de Alfarería, a small **pottery workshop** with some tasteful and reasonably priced pieces, including masks and vases, whilst behind the old prison railings on one side is a **restaurant** whose speciality, *Bistec Santa Ana* – pork filled with ham and cheese and coated in breadcrumbs – is for some reason heavily touted in the local tourist literature. Above the entrance is a nicely furnished **bar** looking down onto the plaza outside.

Well beyond the historic centre of town, five blocks along Rubén Batista from Plaza Santa Ana, **El Alfarero** on Andrés Berro is a time-worn little **ceramics factory**, decidedly off the beaten track – a fact to which it owes much of its appeal. No provision has been made for receiving visitors, but no one will object to you wandering in and taking a look around during working hours (usually Mon–Fri 7am–4pm). The warehouse-style workshop, in existence since 1892, is filled with shelves of pots of differing shapes and sizes destined for shops, hotels and workplaces all over the country. The workshop turns out an average of around 1500 pieces a day, and the production process is on full display with potter's wheels in amongst the mess and the brick kilns out the back. Characteristic of the Cuban workplace, the scrawled slogans all over the walls encourage workers to keep going in the face of adversity. Ask someone to take you to the small shop down the road if you want a souvenir.

Eating

With so many of the colonial mansions converted into restaurants, eating out is one of the easiest ways to soak up Trinidad's gracefully dignified interiors. Though the choice of food is almost exclusively restricted to *comida criolla*, the quality is, as a rule, far higher than in most of Cuba's larger cities. Breakfasts aren't easy to come by in Trinidad but *Hotel La Ronda* is usually willing to serve up some eggs, bread, fruit and coffee for around $4.

Las Begonias, Maceo esq. Simón Bolívar. Simple snacks delivered relatively quickly in a convenient central location that has become a traditional first stop for recently arrived backpackers.

La Coruna, José Martí no. 430 e/ Piro Guinart y Stgo Escobar. Family-run *paladar* with tables squeezed into a sociably small backyard patio. The selection of *comida criolla* is limited but tasty.

Don Antonio, Izquierdo e/ Simón Bolívar y Piro Guinart. Open for lunches only, there's a fair selection here, from meat dishes to salmon or lighter meals such as tuna salad or vegetable omelette. With an elegant but unintimidating atmosphere, the canopied courtyard and comfortable interior are equally appealing.

Estela, Simón Bolívar no. 557 e/ Juan Manuel Marquez y José Mendoza. Though there are only three (meat-based) main courses on offer at this peaceful backyard *paladar*, a feast of extras are laid on, and the two-tier patio within high walls and under tree tops make this one of the most relaxing spots in town.

El Jigue, Rubén Martínez Villena esq. Piro Guinart. Friendly place in a colonial residence, specializing in chicken dishes. Portions are on the small side, but reasonably priced and of a high quality.

El Mesón del Regidor, Simón Bolívar no. 418 e/ Muñoz y Rubén Martínez. Standard value-for-money *comida criolla*, where the lobster works out particularly cheaply but overall the menu lacks variety. The unpolished decoration features a brick and terracotta tiled floor with pastel pink and blue walls.

Paladar Daniel, Camilo Cienfuegos no. 20. Limited to two pork and two chicken dishes, this spacious backyard *paladar*, well away from the centre, is popular with locals. There's an out-of-town feel to the bare surroundings, though the two trees sealing it all in prevent the atmosphere from escaping completely. You can also eat breakfast here.

Plaza Mayor, Francisco Javier Serquera e/ Rubén Martínez y Muñoz. Large, slickly restored colonial mansion suffering from the stilted feel of a place aimed at tour groups. Choose from the menu or opt for the modest buffet offering some rarely seen though unremarkable alternatives – such as pastas and salads – to the usual Cuban cuisine found in Trinidad.

Sol y Son, Simón Bolívar no. 283 e/ Frank País y José Martí. Choose from a number of spaghetti dishes, an array of fish dishes and plenty of chicken and pork plates. Everything is carefully prepared and full of flavour, served in a romantically lit courtyard brimming with plantlife. The best place to eat in the city.

Trinidad Colonial, Gutiérrez esq. Colón. Miserly portions of chicken, pork, fish, shrimps or lobster are justified by the very reasonable prices in this authentically restored nineteenth-century mansion with chandeliers and antique dressers.

Nightlife and drinking

Bizarrely, given the number of visitors this small town receives, nightlife in Trinidad is decidedly subdued, with townsfolk and tourists alike preferring to stay in after dark. The business of finding somewhere to dance or enjoy music usually throws up more misses than hits and many of the city's night venues regularly close early, especially during the winter. By far the liveliest place is Parque Céspedes. An **open-air disco** is held here every weekend, the modern salsa and pop music geared very much to the large crowd of young locals who provide the atmosphere and numbers so lacking in the tourist-oriented venues elsewhere in the town.

There are one or two other pockets of activity, some open during the week as well, though none has a regular schedule of events but instead depend on word of mouth to draw a crowd. One of the more reliable venues for **live music** is *Casa Fischer*, an old colonial mansion on Lino Pérez e/ Gracia y José Martí (daily 9pm–1am; $1), where folkloric nights are a mainstay and there are sometimes Cuban dance performances. Live music is also the basis for nights at the *Casa de la Música* at Juan Manuel Marquez e/ Simón Bolívar y Jesús Menéndez. Free unless a group is playing, when the cover is $1, this large courtyard surrounded by high stone walls and iron grills plays host to traditional Cuban bands as well as more modern salsa outfits, but don't expect anything other than local groups. The music, if there is any, usually starts at around 10pm, whilst by that time on non-music nights the place is usually empty. Marginally more atmospheric, predominantly because it tends to attract a few people whether or not there is live music, is the *Ruinas de Segarte* on Jesús Menéndez e/ Galdos y Juan Manuel Márquez.

There's only one **nightclub** in town, *La Ayala* (daily 10.30pm–3am; $10, including unlimited drinks), run by the *Las Cuevas* hotel, where the fantastic location in a hillside cave network makes up for a frequent lack of guests. In the *Las Cuevas* complex itself hour-long **live shows** covering different aspects of Cuban music and dance are staged for free on a nightly basis. The themes, from Afro-Cuban to acoustic-guitar based campesino music, can come across as a little contrived but are performed with enough energy to get you involved. A final option for entertainment is the **cinema** on Antonio Guiteras at Parque Céspedes, open Tuesday to Sunday.

For **drinking**, you're best off in the restaurants listed above, many of which have separate bars. *Don Antonio* is as pleasant as anywhere whilst on the same street *Ruinas de Lleoncio* is open later and has an upstairs balcony bar. *La Canchánchara*, in a corner of the old town, on Rubén Martínez Villena, contains souvenir shops and a bar which gives onto a long, thin shady courtyard with easy chairs and a very relaxed atmosphere. The *Casa de la Música* also has a neat little bar.

Listings

Banks and exchange The only bank set up to handle foreign currency transactions is the Banco de Crédito y Comercio (Mon–Fri 7.30am–3pm) at José Martí no. 264 e/ Colón y Francisco Javier Serquera. The Cadeca Casa de Cambio (Mon–Sat 8.30am–5.50pm, Sun 8.30am–12.30pm) is at José Martí no. 166 e/ Lino Pérez y Camilo Cienfuegos.

Car rental Havanautos in the Centro Comercial Trinidad on the edge of town on the road to the airport (☎419/63-01), or Transautos in the Cubatur office on Maceo (☎419/53-14).

Immigration and legal For tourist cards go to Cubatur at Antonio Maceo esq. Rosario. More complicated matters may have to be dealt with at the Inmigración y Extranjera office (Tues & Thurs 8am–noon; ☎419/35-95), in the southern outskirts. To get there follow Paseo Agramonte, turn right onto the dust road, cross the train tracks and look for the white building on the right.

Library Biblioteca Gustavo Izquierdo, José Martí no. 265 e/ Colón y Francisco Javier Serquera (Mon–Fri 8am–10pm, Sat 8am–5pm). Tourists are not permitted to remove books from the building.

Medical Clínica Internacional at Lino Pérez no. 103 esq. Anastasio Cárdenas (☎419/33-91 or 62-40), which has a 24-hour pharmacy, should cover most medical needs. In more extreme cases you may be referred to the Clínico Quirúrgico Camilo Cienfuegos (☎41/2-40-17), the provincial hospital in Sancti Spíritus.

Photography Photoservice, José Martí no. 194 e/ Lino Pérez y Camilo Cienfuegos, and Photoclub, Lino Pérez no. 366 e/ Maceo y Francisco Codania, develop film and sell very basic equipment.

Police Call ☎116.

Post office The only branch providing international services is at Maceo no. 416 e/ Colón y Francisco Javier Serquera (Mon–Sat 9am–6pm).

Scooter rental At *Las Begonias* on Maceo and from *Las Cuevas* (see p.242).

Shopping Casa del Tobaco y el Ron, Maceo esq. Francisco Javier Serquera, and the Casa del Tobaco, Lino Pérez esq. José Martí, have the best selection of rum and cigars. Bazar Trinidad sells poster prints, T-shirts and humdrum *artesanía*. Tienda de Arte Amelia Pelaez (Fondo de Bienes Culturales), Simón Bolívar esq. Muñoz, has the largest selection of handmade crafts. There are three or four grocery shops, with one of the best on Francisco Javier Serquera.

Taxis Transtur ☎419/53-14.

Telephones International calls at the Centro de Comunicaciones ETECSA, Lino Pérez at Parque Céspedes e/ José Martí y Miguel Calzada (Mon–Fri 8am–noon & 1–5pm, Sat 8am–noon).

Around Trinidad

From Trinidad some of the province's foremost attractions are within easy reach, whether you're driving or using public transport. Probably the least energetic option is the twenty-minute drive down to the coast to the **Península de Ancón**, one of the biggest beach resorts on the south coast, though still tiny by international standards, having recently upgraded from a two- to a three-hotel resort. A half-hour train ride from Trinidad is the **Valle de los Ingenios**, home to the sugar estates that made Trinidad's elite so wealthy. At Manaca-Iznaga, one such estate has been partially restored to house a restaurant in the main building. Heading west out of the city for 4km, and a right turn takes you onto the mountain road into the **Sierra del Escambray**, whose borders creep down to the outskirts of Trinidad. Here, 14km from the turnoff, is the **Topes de Collantes**, a rather run-down resort that offers some excellent hikes in the surrounding national park. There are plenty of **private taxis** near the bus station on Piro Guinart in Trinidad looking for tourists travelling to any of these destinations. A day-trip to the mountains can be negotiated for $20–30 depending on the car and the driver you pick, whilst a trip to the beach should only cost half as much; the train is by far the most enjoyable way to get to the valley.

Península de Ancón

A narrow five-kilometre finger of land curling like a twisted root out into the placid waters of the Caribbean, against a backdrop of rugged green mountains, the **Península de Ancón** enjoys a truly fantastic setting. Covered predominantly in scrub, the peninsula itself is not terribly impressive but does boast at least 1500m of sandy **beach** and an idyllic stretch of mostly undisturbed coastline. There's an encouragingly natural feel to the beach, with shrubs and trees creeping down to the shoreline, whilst there is more than enough fine-grained golden-beige sand, the best of it around the three hotels, to keep a small army of holidaymakers happy. In fact, other than hotel staff, holidaymakers are usually the only people on the peninsula, where the hotel resorts exist very much in isolation, and you need only wander a few hundred metres from their grounds to find yourself completely undisturbed.

To **get there** from Trinidad, follow Paseo Agramonte out of town and head due south for 4km to the uneventful village of Casilda. Continue for another 4km, west along the northern edge of the Ensenada de Casilda, the bay clasped between the mainland and the peninsula, and you will hit the only road leading into Ancón. Whether staying in Trinidad and visiting the peninsula as a day-trip or vice versa, the taxi fare is around $10 one-way, but every afternoon, the *Trinibus* from the *Hotel Las Cuevas* makes a round trip every hour or so for just $2 each way.

The beaches

There's little point in spending time anywhere except Playa Ancón, the beach at the far end of the peninsula that has put the area on the tourist map. The newest hotel, the 240-room María Aguilar has made finding a private patch of sand more difficult than it used to be, but you're still unlikely to be disappointed with the boomerang-shaped beach here, the longest stretch on the peninsula. Approaching the tip of the peninsula you reach the much older *Hotel Ancón* (☎419/40-11 or 31-55, fax 61-21; ⑦), right on the seafront. Principally a family orientated all-inclusive, this is where most activity on the peninsula is focused. There are a number of bars and places to eat around the lobby and on the beachfront, as well as a large swimming pool, two tennis courts, a basketball hoop, volleyball net and pool tables. On the beach, the Nautical Sports Centre (daily 9am–5pm) rents out pedalos, kayaks, surfboards and various other bits and pieces. Opposite the hotel, on the other side of the peninsula, Marina Trinidad (☎419/62-05) offers a selection of boat trips, including diving and fishing trips, for $10–50 per person. One of the most popular excursions is to Cayo Blanco, a narrow islet 8km from the peninsula with its own coral reef. Trips cost from $30 per person and usually include a lobster lunch.

A couple of kilometres closer to the mainland is the *Hotel Costasur* (☎419/61-74, fax 61-73; ⑤), the only other hotel on the peninsula, with its own more private but smaller section of beach featuring simple but attractive seafront bungalows. Away from the hotels, the signs of package tourism die out almost immediately, leaving the rest of the peninsula and the adjoining coastline almost

*The Hotel
Ancón rents
bicycles for $7
per day; they
also have a
number of
scooters
available to
rent at $10 an
hour, with
reduced rates
for longer
periods.*

unaffected by the nearby developments. The relatively quiet coastal road along the mostly rocky shore between the hotels and **La Boca**, a waterfront village about 10km along the coast from Playa Ancón, due west of Trinidad, makes a pleasant bicycle or scooter ride, with the Sierra del Escambray never out of sight and the turquoise blue of the Caribbean just a few metres away.

Around halfway is a pleasant stop-off point, the *Grill Caribe*, an outdoor restaurant on a platform above a tiny strip of beach; it's the only place on the peninsula, outside of the hotels, where you can eat. The freshly caught seafood is served up until 10pm, and ideally, you should aim to stop by at sunset when the atmosphere becomes tantalizingly calm. **LA BOCA** itself has remained almost untouched by the hordes of tourists settling upon the main attractions nearby, though there are now a few *casas particulares*, most of them on or within sight of the road to the peninsula and clearly signed.

El Valle de los Ingenios

*The train
usually passes
back through
Manaca-Iznaga
on the return
journey about
45 minutes
after it stops
on the
outgoing
journey.*

A two-carriage train leaves Trinidad four times daily for the **Valle de los Ingenios**, a large valley that was once one of the most productive agricultural areas in the whole country, home to dozens of the sugar refineries on which Trinidad built its wealth during the eighteenth and nineteenth centuries. Today just one remains, but the draw here is not the refinery but the buildings of one of the old colonial estates, at Manaca-Iznaga, the seventh stop, half an hour from Trinidad (50¢).

The journey on the crowded train, through a lush landscape with the ruffled peaks of the Sierra del Escambray visible to the north, brings you to the tiny station platform, two minutes' walk from the old house and tower, the main attractions here. Most people can't resist heading straight for the 45-metre tower, vaguely resembling a concrete rocket-ship with its pointed, spired roof and slender body. The huge bell that once hung in the tower and was used to ring out the start and finish of the working day and designed so as to be audible to slaves working in the fields, sits near the front of the house where there are also some nineteenth-century, rusty old sugar cauldrons and a few stalls with small wooden sculptures, homemade clothing and other arts and crafts for sale. A dollar fee lets you climb the precarious wooden staircase to the top of the tower for views of the entire valley, a sea of sugarcane interrupted by the odd crop of houses.

Next to the tower is the **Casa Hacienda**, the colonial mansion where the Iznaga family would have stayed, though they spent more of their time at their residence in Trinidad or in Sancti Spíritus (see p.259). A museum is planned but, despite one or two touches of the original decoration, for now the building's sole function is as a restaurant, where pork and chicken dishes are served up on the terrace, overlooking a small garden. Though you cannot visit them yet, over the road are the scattered dwellings of the old slave barracks.

Topes de Collantes

Rising up to the northwest of Trinidad are the steep, pine-coated slopes of the Guamuhaya mountain range, more popularly known as the **Sierra del Escambray**. These make for some of the most spectacularly scenic – and dangerous – drives in Cuba, whether you're cutting through between Trinidad and Santa Clara, or over to Cienfuegos, where most of the range, including its highest peak, the 1140-metre Pico San Juan, lies. Three kilometres from central Trinidad along the Trinidad–Cienfuegos coast road, a right-hand turn takes you the 15km or so into the mountains to the scattered houses of **Vegas Grandes** village; immediately beyond here is the resort of **Topes de Collantes**. The resort is a kind of hotel village with roads linking its heavy-handed box-like buildings together. Don't expect too much in the way of eating, entertainment or nightlife, but as a base for **hiking**, this is the only obvious starting point for visiting the much larger area encompassed by the officially declared 175 square kilometre Topes de Collantes **national park**.

The best way to take advantage of what's on offer is to follow one of the designated **trails**, which you can do as an organized excursion from Trinidad or independently. Though the worn-out resort is unlikely to lure you into staying the night, if you want to make the most of the trails it may prove necessary. Conditions, however, are not at all bad, with the one hotel reserved for international tourists as comfortable and well equipped as you could realistically hope, given the obvious lack of investment in this once popular resort.

Unless you book a tour in Trinidad, the place to get advice and maps, both absolutely essential as some of the trails are almost completely unmarked, is the Carpeta Central (daily 8am–5pm; ☎42/4-02-19), the park's **information centre**, a few minutes' walk from most of the hotels. The English-speaking guides can arrange excursions from a basic choice of four trails and you should be prepared to pay at least $4 per person for each hike. Excursions, if booked directly through the Carpeta Central, as opposed to booking an organized excursion from Trinidad, cost between $16 and $25 per person and will usually include a lunch; there is normally a minimum of eight people required. Unless it's pouring with rain, trainers should prove adequate footwear for all of the hikes, typically along shaded trails through dense woodlands, smothered in every kind of vegetation, from needle-straight conifers to bushy fern and grassy matted floors, opening out here and there for breathtaking views of the landscape. Also bear in mind that the air is a few degrees cooler than in the city or on the beach, and you may need more than just a T-shirt outside summer.

The trails

The most popular target for hikers is the **Salto del Caburní**, a fantastically situated **waterfall** surrounded by pines and eucalyptus trees at the end of one of the more challenging trails. This 2.5-kilometre trek begins at the nothernmost point of the resort complex and takes you on one of the more clearly marked trails, down steep inclines through the dense forest to the rocky falls. In the shadow of an impressive expanse of red rock, the 62-metre waterfall only crashes down vertically for a few metres, changing gear as it cascades more gently around a corner of chiselled rock and pours into the small pool at the bottom. You can take a swim in the pool before summoning up the energy to make the fairly strenuous uphill return journey. The round trip should take around three hours, though you should add on at least half an hour's swimming time.

Twelve kilometres north of the resort, at the end of a three-kilometre dirt track, the **Casa de la Gallega**, a simple cabin **restaurant**, is the lunch stop and starting point for one of the most scenic of the hiking routes. This gentler hike follows a river for a couple of kilometres up to the **Rocío** waterfall and incorporates some memorable views along the way of Pico San Juan.

About 6km east of the resort **Hacienda Codina** and **La Batata**, within 500m of each another, are the focal points for the remaining hikes. Hacienda Codina is an old Spanish coffee-growing ranch where you can stop for a drink. From here there are easily manageable walks, some no more than a kilometre, into the forest, alive with a stunning variety of different plant species; these can be combined with circuits around a bamboo garden and an orchid farm. La Batata is a subterranean river at the foot of a lush green valley where you can bathe in the cool waters of the cave. If you fancy more of a challenge you can approach the cave via a poorly marked three-kilometre hike from the lowest section of the hotel complex, on its southern edge.

Resort practicalities

There are four **hotels** within the resort, two of which are permitted to rent rooms to non-Cubans. Best is the dated-looking *Los Helechos* (☎42/4-01-80 to 89 ext. 2244; ④), whose rooms with balconies are surprisingly light and airy. There's a disco and a restaurant in a separate, marginally more run-down building, as well as a bowling alley and a large indoor pool. The only reason to opt instead for the massive *Kurhotel* (☎42/22-66 or 4-02-88; ④) is to make use of its programmes of **therapeutic treatments**. Hotel guests, the majority of them Cuban, are kitted out with identical tracksuits, and wandering around this monstrous building, which resembles a huge inner-city institution, feels a bit like stumbling on the secret hideout of a religious cult. Programmes of treatment, which can include anything from massage to hydrotherapy, start at around $80 per day. In addition to the hotel itself, many of the treatments are administered in the Complejo de Cultura Física (Mon–Fri 10am–4pm, Sat & Sun 9am–5pm), a fitness and therapy centre behind the hotel and open to non-guests also. Facilities, which include outdoor squash and tennis courts, an indoor swimming pool and a gymnasium, aren't exactly top-notch, but neither are the prices.

The only place to **eat** outside of the hotels is in the restaurant at Parque La Represa, a neat little patch of landscaped lawn tucked away in a corner of the complex and overlooking a stream. Away from the dominating presence of the hotel architecture, this is one of the most picturesque parts of the resort and though the restaurant has a very limited choice of platters, the interior, with its wooden rafted ceiling, is nicely in tune with the surrounding countryside.

Sancti Spíritus and around

Beyond Trinidad and its immediate environs, the **province of Sancti Spíritus** offers only one or two interesting destinations. The provincial capital, also called **Sancti Spíritus**, is most often viewed as a transit town, but as one of the original seven *villas* of Cuba, founded by Diego Velázquez in the early 1500s, it offers ample reasons to stop for a day or two. A ten-kilometre drive southeast of the city is the huge **Zaza Reservoir**, ideal for fishing and hunting with some appealing aspects for the non-specialist also.

SANCTI SPÍRITUS is, for the visitor, characterized largely by the Carretera Central that runs right through it. This is a quick-stop town, where the central attractions are more like a sideshow for visitors passing through on their way to more exciting destinations. There are, however, two or three places of more compelling interest and, situated in the dead centre of the island, it's an appropriate place to stop for the night if you're making the journey between Havana and Santiago. Though Sancti Spíritus has kept pace with similarly sized cities in the country in commercial terms, and boasts a relatively high standard of hotels and *casas particulares*, as well as a reasonable selection of shops in the centre, culturally speaking the city lags some way behind its provincial neighbours, particularly Santa Clara and Trinidad. Keep it short and sweet in Sancti Spíritus and you'll leave satisfied.

Arrival and city transport

Arriving by **car**, whether from Trinidad, Santa Clara, the west or the east, you'll enter Sancti Spíritus on the Carretera Central, one of Cuba's principal roads, which cuts along the eastern edge of the city, becoming Bartolomé Masó as it enters Sancti Spíritus proper. To get to the centre, turn southwest off Bartolomé Masó onto Avenida de los Mártires, an attractive boulevard leading directly to the Plaza Serafín Sánchez.

If you arrive by **bus** you'll be dropped at the Terminal Provincial de Omnibus (☎ 41/2-41-42), at the crossroads where the Carretera Central intersects with Circunvalación, the outer ringroad. The only reliable way of getting to the centre from here is by **taxi**, which should cost around $2. The arrival of a Víazul bus usually prompts a

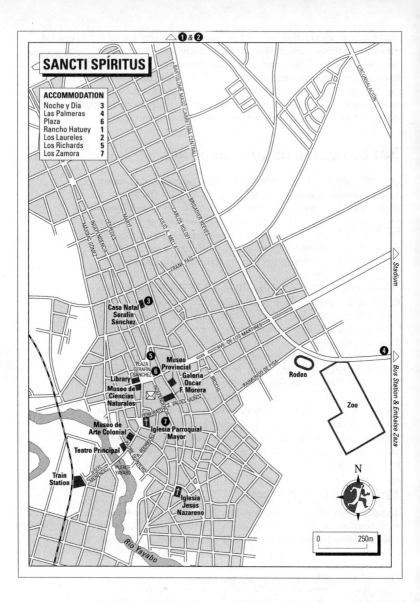

SANCTI SPÍRITUS

ACCOMMODATION
Noche y Día	3
Las Palmeras	4
Plaza	6
Rancho Hatuey	1
Los Laureles	2
Los Richards	5
Los Zamora	7

few private taxi drivers to come looking for business, but there is no taxi rank as such; ringing one of the hotels for a state taxi is usually the safest option.

It's possible to walk to the plaza from the **train station** (☎41/2-47-90), on Ave. Jesús Menéndez, over the river from the city centre, should you arrive from Cienfuegos, Havana or Santa Clara, the only cities linked directly to Sancti Spíritus by rail, but if you opt for a taxi you'll need to phone for one as few drivers ever bother to look for fares here. The city's tiny national **airport** (☎41/2-75-84) is in the northern reaches of Sancti Spíritus, conveniently close to the two best places to stay on the Carretera Central, *Rancho Hatuey* and *Los Laureles*. Otherwise, it's a $3–4 taxi ride to the centre. Although there is a local bus system and a number of horse-drawn carriages operating up and down Bartolomé Masó, it's unlikely you'll find a need to use them – there's no particular reason to venture beyond a very small central section of the city, marked by the Río Yayabo to the south, Plaza Serafín Sánchez to the north, Céspedes to the east and Máximo Gómez to the west. For taxis, see p.262.

Accommodation

Sancti Spíritus is a transit town, and unsurprisingly, there are several places to stay along Bartolomé Masó, the main through-road. Three of them, however – *Nueva Generación*, *Las Villas* and the *Deportivo* – are for Cubans only, or in such dreadful condition that they should only be considered as last resorts. In the centre, the best options are on or within a few blocks of Plaza Serafín Sánchez, including a surprisingly good selection of *casas particulares*. The *Perla del Sur*, on the northern edge of the plaza, was under renovation at the time of writing, but may have reopened.

Los Laureles, Carretera Central km 383 ☎41/2-39-13. A sociable little complex of concrete bungalows by the side of the road with a relatively comprehensive programme of entertainment including an open-air cabaret and karaoke. Rooms are modest but cheery and there are views of the swimming pool from the simple restaurant. ③.

Noche y Día, Martí no. 111 e/ Comandante Fajardo y Frank País. This relaxed, friendly and roomy colonial house has a pleasant open patio around which five different guest rooms are based. All have en suite bathroom and three have a/c. ②.

Las Palmeras, Bartolomé Masó no. 161 e/ Cuba y Cuartel ☎41/2-21-69. A five-minute walk from the bus station, this modest 1950s-style house is identifiable by the small crop of low palms out the front. There's only one room, but it can accommodate up to three people, and there's a spacious if somewhat bare backyard. ②.

Plaza, Independencia esq. Ave de los Mártires ☎41/2-71-02. A characterful and compact city hotel on Plaza Serafín Sánchez, with reasonably equipped but slightly poky rooms – ask for one of the four larger ones. There's a pleasant terrace bar and a shady central patio. ③.

Rancho Hatuey, Carretera Central km 384 ☎41/2-83-15; fax 2-83-50. The most upmarket option in the city, this complex, set back some 400m from the road, is predominantly the domain of tour groups stopping over for a night or two. The grassy site is larger than it needs to be, leaving the box-like villas a little stranded, but there's a nice pool area and facilities are relatively good. ⑤.

Los Richards, Independencia no. 28, Plaza Serafín Sánchez; neighbour's phone ☎41/2-68-05. The three rooms for rent in this ideally located, slightly shabby, family-run apartment have a small balcony looking out onto the plaza, as well as a/c and a small private bathroom. There's also access to a spacious roof terrace which provides good views of the city. ②.

Los Zamora, Independencia no. 56 e/ Honorato y Agramonte ☎ 41/2-48-30 or 2-30-46. Large, well-equipped apartment with two rooms for rent, both with private bathroom and a/c. One of the more professionally run *casas particulares*, whose relatively young landlord is a good source of information on local nightlife. ②.

The Town

The logical place to begin exploring Sancti Spíritus is the central square, **Plaza Serafín Sánchez**, one of the city's few communal spaces with a sense of purpose. All the best sights are south of here, with the **Museo de Arte Colonial** by far the most absorbing. It's worth taking your time over the impressively well-furnished rooms as none of the other museums will keep you longer than ten or fifteen minutes. Best are the modest **Museo Provincial** and the mixture of paintings at the **Galería Oscar F. Morera**, both on Céspedes. If you stay for the evening there are one or two nightspots around the town, but expect a quiet drink, or if you're lucky some live music, rather than a five-course meal and a raucous night on the dancefloor.

Plaza Serafín Sánchez and around

Though certainly one of the more pleasant and lively spaces in the centre of town, the **Plaza Serafín Sánchez** lacks the laid-back, sociable feel characteristic of other town squares. Nevertheless it does attract an enthusuastic young crowd on weekend nights and though it's disturbed by the traffic passing through on all sides during the day, there are plenty of rickety metal seats around the simple bandstand for a sit down in the shade. It's symbolic of Sancti Spíritus that two of the most striking and best-maintained buildings around the square, standing out amongst the otherwise vacant-looking two- and three-storey colonial buildings, are a bank and a fast-food joint. The third is the majestic **Biblioteca Provincial Rubén Martínez Villena**, on the corner of Máximo Gómez and Solano. Built between 1927 and 1929, this provincial library was renovated in 1999 and looks more like a colonial theatre building with its balustraded balconies, Corinthian columns and arched entrance.

Right next to the library, on the other side of Solano, is the **Museo de Ciencias Naturales** (Tues–Fri 8.30am–5pm, Sat 2–9pm, Sun 8.30am–12.30pm; 50¢). Though there are some attractively displayed birds, this small, poorly stocked museum could do with a makeover and is unlikely to hold your attention for more than a few minutes. It's much more fun to visit, or at least look in the window of, **El Canonazo,** within a block of the plaza at Independencia no. 6 e/ Plaza Sánchez y Honorato (Mon–Sun 8am–3pm). Known as a *casa* *de comisiones*, the Cuban equivalent to a **pawnshop**, this is an absolute treasure trove of retro style, packed with miscellaneous bric-a-brac including 1950s pocket watches, 1970s radios, clothes, furniture, jewellery, crockery, old cameras and anything else you can pin a price tag on. Everything is priced in pesos and although you should expect to pay at least a few hundred for anything decent, most items work out relatively cheap.

From the Iglesia Parroquial Mayor to the river

From the plaza it's a short walk on Máximo Gómez to Sancti Spíritus's main church and its oldest building, the **Iglesia Parroquial Mayor**. Were it not so close to the city's finest museum it wouldn't necessarily warrant a visit, the chipped and faded yellow exterior an accurate reflection of what to expect inside. Nevertheless, if you pass by during **opening hours** (Tues–Sat 9–11am & 2–5pm) you might as well take a peek inside. With the dramatic exception of an unusual blue and gold arch spanning the top section of the nave, the interior is simple and slightly bedraggled.

The best museum in Sancti Spíritus is unquestionably the **Museo de Arte Colonial** (Tues–Fri 8.30am–4.30pm, Sat 1–7.30pm, Sun 8am–noon; $2, $1 extra to take photos) at Plácido no. 74 esq. Jesús Menéndez, one block towards the river from the church. Built for the wealthy Valle-Iznaga family, who spent most of their time in and around Trinidad, where they made their fortune as sugar plantation owners, this colonial mansion was used as a short-stop home.

The museum has been restored to resemble a typical home of the nineteenth-century Cuban bourgeoisie, and over half its pieces were already in the house, with many others donated or bought from local families. There's a great selection of precious furniture and household objects, many of them imported from Europe. As eye-catching as anything in the museum and amongst the oldest pieces on display are the opulent French baroque mirrors in the front room, which date back to the eighteenth century. The collection achieves a high level of authenticity, and from the three bedrooms to the music and dining rooms, little seems to be missing. The mood becomes more functional at the back, where you'll find the kitchen, with its built-in cooking surface, and the courtyard – the living and working area for the slaves and servants.

You can visit the residential headquarters of the Valle-Iznaga family's sugar estate in the Valle de los Ingenios, near Trinidad. See p.252.

On the other side of Jesús Menéndez, an area of cobbled streets extends down to the river. Surprisingly, this clearly historic part of the city has been relegated to ignored backstreets and local neighbourhood activity. This does, however, create a sense of stumbling on something undiscovered, and a quick wander around can be fascinating. Walk down to the river from here down A. Rodríguez for a good view of the **Puente Yayabo**, the humpbacked bridge over the river, built in 1825 and said to be amongst the oldest of its kind in Cuba.

Along Céspedes

Running a block east of Plaza Serafín Sánchez is **Céspedes**, where you'll find the rest of Sancti Spíritus's worthwhile sights. The easily manageable **Museo Provincial** (Tues–Sun 8.30am–noon & 1–5pm; $1), at Céspedes no. 11 e/ Ave. de los Mártires y E. Valdes Muñoz, showcases a hotchpotch of historical objects dating mostly from the nineteenth and the pre-revolutionary twentieth centuries. Refreshingly, the temptation to tie as much as possible in with the revolution has been avoided here, and there are even displays from the 1950s unrelated to the dictatorship which Castro and his followers overthrew. Amongst the shackles, clamps and chains, look out for the book which reveals as much about how African slaves were treated as the devices of torture and restraint themselves. Published in 1864 in New York but written in Spanish, the title translates as *Negroes in their Diverse States and Conditions: How They Are, How They Are Presumed To Be and How They Should Be*. Lastly, don't miss the colonial dining room at the back of the house, with a colourfully tiled floor and fully furnished with pieces original to the house.

Over the road at Céspedes no. 26 is the **Galería Oscar F. Morera** (Tues–Sat 8am–noon & 1–5pm, Sun 8am–noon; free), with another entrance on Independencia. The museum is housed in the former residence of the city's first well-known painter, who died in 1946, and the number and variety of works on display here make for an appealing wander around. As well as the purely representational art of Morera – which occupies several of the rooms and includes portraits, landscapes, still lifes and paintings of Sancti Spíritus – there are reproductions of internationally famous paintings as well as two rooms dedicated to temporary exhibitions, usually displaying the work of local artists.

Three blocks north on Céspedes, at no. 112 e/ Comandante Fajardo y Frank País, the **Casa Natal Serafín Sánchez** (Tues–Sat 8.30am–noon & 1–5pm, Sun 8.30am–12.30pm; 50¢) commemorates one of the city's heroes of the two wars of independence, killed in combat on November 18, 1896. Consisting mostly of Sánchez's personal effects and photographs of him and his family, along with a colourful portrait of the man on his horse, it's a bit bare and of specialist interest only.

Eating and drinking

Eating out in Sancti Spíritus is something of a game of chance. There are a number of **paladares** in and around the centre, but none keeps regular opening times, and a lack of dollar-paying customers means that staying in business is a trickier task than in other cities. They can also be difficult to find, with very few openly advertising themselves. However, if you're willing to ask around and knock on doors, you shouldn't have too many problems. A good place to start is on Eduardo Chibas, across the river, where there are two, each within a block of Avenida Jesús Menéndez on either side. To the east of town, *El Rosario*, at F.E. Broche no. 111

e/ Raimundo de Pisa y Adolfo del Castillo, is a local neighbourhood *paladar* set up with the minimum of resources but serving large, inexpensive chicken- and pork-based meals.

Of the state-run options the **restaurants** in the dollar hotels offer by far the best quality and variety, whilst the six or seven clapped-out peso restaurants scattered around the city are hardly worth bothering with. In the centre, only the fast food of *El Rápido*, open 24 hours on the south side of the main square, and the restaurant in the *Hotel Plaza* are passable. The most reliable option in town is *Rancho Hatuey*, where dinner consists of a modest *comida criolla* buffet served in a comfortable canteen-style room. It's a pleasant walk from the centre along Avenida de los Mártires to *Islas Canarias*, a faded but dignified peso restaurant on the twelfth floor of a residential apartment building between Cuartel and Circunvalación. The beef and pork dishes are basic, but there's a **bar** with an outdoor roof terrace and fantastic views of the city. The *Casa de la Trova* has a pleasant patio and is by far the most pleasant place for a **drink** in the city centre. In a quiet corner of town, on Carlos Roloff near Raimundo de Pisa, there's a Rumbos-owned cafeteria and bar.

Nightlife and entertainment

Weekend **nightlife** for locals consists mainly of hanging out around the Plaza Serafín Sánchez. Some find their way into *Café Artex*, in between the bank and *El Rápido*, for the straightforward karaoke and **disco**, where the up-for-it crowd makes this simple venue good for a giggle. On the same side of the plaza, on the corner with Máximo Gómez, the *Casa de la Cultura* hosts occasional *boleros* and live music in its dinky courtyard; the only regular event is the rock night on Saturdays. Round the corner at Máximo Gómez Sur no. 26 e/ Solano y Honorato are the more cultured surroundings of the *Casa de la Trova* which has a busier, more reliable schedule predominantly of traditional **live music shows** from around 9pm onwards each Friday, Saturday and Sunday night; entrance is free and there's a bar. There's plenty of local flavour at *Café Central*, on Independencia just off the plaza, where the music and singing flow with the rum. Beyond the centre there's the outdoor and often empty dancefloor at the small Rumbos complex on Carlos Roloff near Raimundo de Pisa, as well as the inconsistently popular disco in *Los Laureles* hotel.

To while away the evenings, there are two **cinemas** on the Plaza Serafín Sánchez and a *sala de video* in the basement of the library building. The city's venue for **theatre** and **dance** as well as musical concerts is the diminutive Teatro Principal (☎41/2-57-55) at Jesús Menendez esq. Padre Quintero near the Puente Yayabo. The main local event to draw in the crowds is the **rodeo**, held once or twice a month at the weekend, in the Feria Agropecuaria on Bartolomé Masó; entrance is one peso. National league **baseball** games are played at the Estadio José A. Huelga just beyond Circunvalación on Ave. de los Martires.

Listings

Banks and exchange The best bank for foreign currency transactions is the Banco Financiero Internacional, Independencia no. 2 e/ Plaza Serafín Sánchez y Honorato (Mon–Fri 8am–3pm). The Cadeca Casa de Cambio is at Independencia no. 31 e/ Ave. de los Martires (Plaza Serafín Sánchez) y E. Valdes Muñoz (Mon–Sat 8.30am–6pm, Sun 8.30am–noon).

Car rental Transautos has desks in the *Plaza* (☎41/2-71-02) and *Los Laureles* (☎41/2-85-33) hotels.

Library Biblioteca Provincial Rubén Martínez Villena, on the Plaza Serafín Sánchez.

Medical The main hospital is the Clínico Quirurgíco Camilo Cienfuegos (☎41/2-40-17) halfway down Bartolomé Masó.

Pharmacy There's a peso pharmacy at Comandante Fajardo no. 53 e/ Céspedes y Martí.

Photography Photoservice, Independencia no. 50a e/ Laborí y Comandante Fajardo.

Police Emergency number ☎116. There is a small police station on the corner of Independencia and the small square, opposite the crumbling Iglesia de Jesús Nazareno in the south of the city.

Post office Independencia no. 8 e/ Plaza Serafín Sánchez y Honorato (Mon–Sat 8am–6pm).

Scooter rental Try Cubasol (☎41/2-83-14; daily 8.30am–5pm) in the lodge at the turning for *Rancho Hatuey* hotel.

Telephones There is an ETECSA phone cabin on Bartolomé Masó e/ Coronel Legón y Mirto.

Taxis Call reception at either the *Plaza* (☎41/2-71-02) or *Rancho Hatuey* (☎41/2-83-15).

Around Sancti Spíritus: the Zaza Reservoir

Ten kilometres or so from the city is Cuba's largest artificial lake, the **Zaza Reservoir**, a hunting and fishing centre and another option for a night's stopover on a journey across the island. Most activity on the reservoir revolves around the **hotel**, sited on the network of inlets at the lake's northern edge. The *Zaza* (☎41/2-85-12, fax 2-84-01; ④) has become popular with Italian **hunting** enthusiasts who come here to hunt duck, quail, pigeon and other bird species; they have exclusive rights to the hotel's hunting facilities and packages, booked through an Italian tour operator. This, however, does not detract from the utter tranquillity of the location, and taking it easy is the main alternative to hunting. Five kilometres from the main road and with the Sierra del Escambray coating the western horizon, there's a sense of complete serenity disturbed only by the goings-on at the hotel itself.

Unless you rent a boat, your activities will be limited to the hotel and its grounds, from where the reservoir looks bleak and unimpressive, its vastness impossible to gauge. You can combine a bit of boating with a **fishing** session, though these are usually included as part of a package which includes full board at the hotel for between $75 and $90 a night. The hotel is an adapted 1970s Soviet-style building, and though the conversion has mostly been a successful one, the rooms still look a little tired. Nevertheless a green and white paint job coupled with an infusion of flowers and plants in and around the building has lifted the spirit of the place whilst the grounds, which feature a reasonably sized **swimming pool**, spread right down to the water's edge.

Cienfuegos and around

Cienfuegos, sandwiched in between Matanzas, to the west, and Sancti Spíritus and Villa Clara to the east, is one of Cuba's more recently established provinces, having formed, along with Villa Clara and Ciego de Ávila, part of the now nonexistent Las Villas province prior to 1975. This is one of the country's most industrialized zones, with clusters of chimney stacks and factories, including a nuclear power plant, gathered around the **Bahía de Jagua**. Also known as the Bay of Cienfuegos, this rock-steady mass of water, whose calm waters make it appear more like a large lake, is big enough to provide waterfront havens unaffected by the industrial activity elsewhere on its shores. The province's seventy kilometres of **coastline** in all, bathed by the warm currents of the Caribbean Sea and scattered with small beaches and rocky inlets, are all that most people see of the region. Though a large proportion of the Sierra del Escambray nestles within its borders, these forested peaks form no more than a backdrop for most people, who visit them instead from Trinidad or Santa Clara.

In fact, you are unlikely to stray more than 25km from the provincial capital, **CIENFUEGOS**, an attractive easy-going city, noticeably cleaner than most provincial capitals and deserving of its given label as the "Pearl of the South". There's nothing particularly arresting about the place other than its bayside location, and despite a relatively comprehensive tourist infrastructure, you'll find two or three days here more than enough. As a base for seeing what the rest of the province has to offer, however, Cienfuegos is ideal, with several easy day-trip destinations – beaches, botanical gardens and an old Spanish fortress – within a 25-kilometre radius.

Arrival and information

All **buses** pull in at the Terminal de Omnibus on Calle 49 e/ Ave. 56 y Ave. 58, whilst **trains** stop at the station over the road. From here you can walk into the town centre where there are a number of *casas particulares*; if you're staying at the *Jagua* hotel, you'll need to take a **taxi**,which shouldn't cost you more than $4 (☎432/30-21 to 25). The few domestic **flights** into Cienfuegos

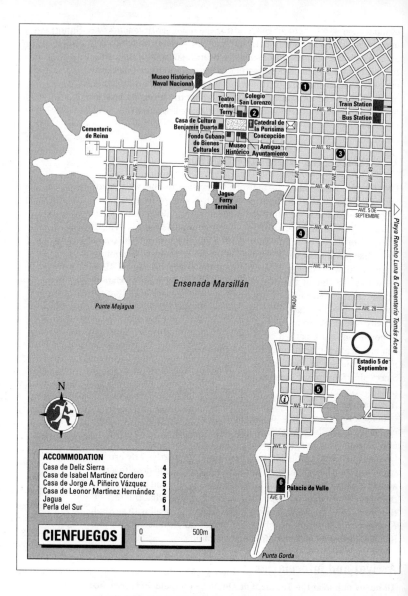

Museo Histórico
Naval Nacional

Teatro
Tomás
Terry

Colegio
San Lorenzo

Casa de Cultura
Benjamín Duarte

Catedral de
la Purísima
Concepción

Fondo Cubano
de Bienes
Culturales

Museo
Histórico

Antiguo
Ayuntamiento

Cementerio
de Reina

AVE. 64

AVE. 58

AVE. 52

AVE. 46

Train Station

Bus Station

❶

❷

❸

AVE. 19

AVE. 25

AVE. 46

AVE. 31

AVE. 37

AVE. 43

AVE. 49

Jagua
Ferry
Terminal

AVE. 5 DE
SEPTIEMBRE

Playa Rancho Luna & Cementerio Tomás Acea

AVE. 40

❹

AVE. 34

Ensenada Marsillán

Punta Majagua

PRADO

AVE. 28

Estadio 5 de
Septiembre

AVE. 18

❺

ⓘ AVE. 12

AVE. 6

❻ Palacio de Valle

AVE. 0

N

ACCOMMODATION

Casa de Deliz Sierra	4
Casa de Isabel Martínez Cordero	3
Casa de Jorge A. Piñeiro Vázquez	5
Casa de Leonor Martínez Hernández	2
Jagua	6
Perla del Sur	1

CIENFUEGOS

0   500m

Punta Gorda

touch down at the **Jaime González Airport**, several kilometres to
the east of the city. In the unlikely event that you arrive by plane
you'll have little choice but to call for a taxi to get into the city.
Arriving by **car** from Trinidad, you'll enter the city on Ave. 5 de
Septiembre which connects up with the city grid four blocks from

Prado, the main street and the road on which you'll arrive if you've driven from Havana or Varadero.

For **information**, head for the Palacio de Turismo on Calle 37 e/ 12 y 14 where, within the same building, you can book excursions into the mountains and to other attractions both within the province and beyond. Havanatur also organizes trips and can be located either in the lobby of the *Jagua* or at Ave. 40 no. 4101 esq. 41 (Mon–Fri 8.30am–noon & 1.30–5pm, Sat 8.30am–noon; ☎432/55-73).

Orientation and city transport

Finding your way around Cienfuegos couldn't be easier, as the entire city is mapped out on a spacious grid system. You'll rarely need to stray more than four or five blocks from the **Prado**, the main road through town, officially known as the Paseo del Prado or Calle 37. Almost everything of interest is either within eight blocks west of the Prado, in **Pueblo Nuevo**, the town area, or in **Punta Gorda**, the southern section of the city, jutting out towards the coast. If you stick to the area between the Prado and the **Parque José Martí**, then you can conceivably get around exclusively on foot. However, there are **buses** and **horse-drawn carriages** operating up and down the Prado all day, as far as the turning for the Marina Jagua. You shouldn't have to wait long for the latter which are supposed to take you anywhere along the line for a peso, but are as likely to ask for a dollar. Apart from the occasional bus down to the beach, travelling further afield, even within the city, means calling for a **taxi**. Turistaxi (☎432/45-11-72) and Panataxi have cars hanging around the *Hotel Jagua* car park.

Accommodation

Unusually for a provincial town in Cuba, Cienfuegos has a four-star **hotel** right in the city centre that's aimed exclusively at the international market. Other state-run options, such as the *Ciervo de Oro*, are mostly run-down, peso-only establishments and only one accepts tourists on an official basis. The options are far from limited, though, thanks to a profusion of *casas particulares*, predominantly in between the bus station and Parque José Martí and along the length of the Prado, with some particularly comfortable options as you get down into Punta Gorda.

Casa de Deliz Sierra, Prado no. 3806 e/ 38 y 40 ☎432/66-38. Modest rooms with a/c in a well-located house on the border between Punta Gorda and the town; good views of the bay. ②.

Casa de Isabel Martínez Cordero, Ave. 52 no. 4318 e/ 43 y 45 ☎432/82-76. Five blocks from the bus station towards the centre of town, there are three large bedrooms for rent in this adequately furnished neo-colonial house. There's a communicating door between two of the rooms and all three share the same bathroom. ②.

Casa de Jorge A. Pineiro Vázquez, Calle 41 no. 1402, Punta Gorda ☎432/38-08. Luxurious by Cuban standards, this airy bungalow is one of the most comfortable and spacious *casas particulares* in Cienfuegos. The three available bedrooms, all with a/c, each have their own private bathroom; there's a pleasant patio where meals are eaten; and an attractive garden. The above average pricing is thoroughly justified. ③.

Casa de Leonor Martínez Hernández, Ave. 56 no. 2927 e/ 29 y 31 ☎432/61-43. Just off the Parque José Martí, this is one of the most centrally located houses with rooms for rent. Conditions are adequate and the friendly, academic owners speak English. ②.

Jagua, Paseo del Prado no. 1 e/ 0 y 2, Punta Gorda ☎432/30-21 to 25; fax 45-12-45. As the only hotel in town aimed at the international market, this has all the attributes you'd expect: the best facilities, including two restaurants, a shop, and a games room, the most comfort and the most picturesque location, at the foot of Punta Gorda with views into town and across the bay. There's a swimming pool in the neat but small grounds. ⑤.

Perla del Sur, Ave. 62 no. 3704 e/ 37 (Prado) y 39 ☎432/2-15-31. The only hotel in the centre of town accessible to tourists, on a lively – and rather noisy – street. Rooms are basic and quite dark and only a few are equipped with a TV and fridge, though all have a/c. This is the cheapest option in town but not without reason. ②.

The City

Sightseeing in Cienfuegos focuses on the picturesque **Parque José Martí**, the main square in the more built-up northern section of the city, Pueblo Nuevo. The illustrious interior of the **Teatro Tomás Terry**, a nineteenth-century theatre, is usually the first place on the square to lure visitors inside, followed by the more modest **cathedral**. Elsewhere on the square, the pleasant but scanty **Museo Histórico** consists mostly of paintings and old furniture, whilst the **Fondo Cubano de Bienes Culturales** and the **Casa de Cultura Benjamín Duarte** offer insights into the contemporary art scene in the city. West of the square the muddled displays in the **Museo Histórico Naval Nacional** make up the largest historical collection in the city whilst in the isolated, westernmost suburb, Reina, the **Cementerio de Reina**, a moody little cemetery, is strictly for people with time on their hands. Going back the other way, eastwards, linking Parque José Martí with the boulevard section of Prado, is the main shopping area, Avenida 54 between Calle 29 and Calle 37, a sociable pedestrianized section of the street with a mixture of poor-quality peso shops and restaurants as well as several jack-of-all-trades tourist shops. Wandering south on Prado takes you down past the city's marina to the **Palacio de Valle**. This is the most architecturally striking building in Punta Gorda, offering pleasing views back across the city from its garden-patio-style rooftop bar. It's also here that the town comes out to play at weekends, large crowds gathering along the bay wall and music blaring out from the open-air dancefloor opposite. Out of walking distance, on the western outskirts of Cienfuegos, is the **Cementerio Tomás Acea**, an attractively landscaped cemetery.

Parque José Martí

Though lacking in good bars and restaurants, this colourful and sometimes lively town square is stamped with definite heart-of-the-city status by the concentration of attractive and strikingly grand buildings around the **Parque José Martí**. With the trademark statue of the square's namesake at the midway point of the central promenade, the traditional bandstand and the neatly kept, tree-swept patches of lawn, the square enhances the city's generally graceful and tidy appearance.

On the northern edge of the square, the **Teatro Tomás Terry** has stood proudly since its foundation in 1890. Dance and theatre productions are still staged here, but not on a regular basis, and the principal attraction for visitors is the building itself. The exterior, though handsome, is in much the same Spanish colonial style as the surrounding buildings. The interior, however, is glorious, and captivating enough to override the dim lighting. The lobby sets the tone with intricately painted flowers on the walls and a ceiling fresco by Camilo Salaya, a Filipino from Madrid. There is also a statue of Terry – a millionaire patron of the city, whose family funded a large part of the construction of the theatre – by the Neapolitan sculptor Tomaso Solari, which was shipped over from Italy. Fashioned on a traditional Italian design, with a semicircular auditorium and three tiers of balconies, the Tomás Terry is one of only three such theatres in Cuba. Almost everything dates back to the original construction of the theatre: the predominantly wooden 950-seat auditorium, which was restored in the mid-1960s; the golden framed stage sloping towards the front row to allow the audience an improved view; and even the ticket booths. In the centre of the ceiling, a dreamy baroque-style fresco incorporates an ensemble of angelic figures representing Dawn (Aurora), surrounded by paintings of flowers and birds. **Guided tours** (daily 9am–6pm; $1) of the theatre are available, unless rehearsals are taking place, and can be arranged through the adjoining shop.

For details of performances check the blackboards at the entrance or ring ☎ 432/33-61. Entrance usually costs between $3 and $5; shorts and sleeveless tops are not permitted.

Next door to the theatre is the **Colegio San Lorenzo**, the most classically Greco-Roman structure on the square, now host to a high school. On the same corner of the square, across from the school, the stained glass and various fetching altars of the **Catedral de la Purísima Concepción** merit a look inside (daily 7am–noon; Mass daily 7.30–8am, Sun also 10–11am). Founded in 1833 as a church, the bell tower was added thirteen years later, and in 1903 cathedral status was granted. It retains much of its original spirit as a local church and receives as many resident visitors as it does tourists, not something that can be said of all Cuban cathedrals. The only sign of ostentation is at the main altar, where a statue of the Virgin Mary, with snakes at her feet, shelters under an ornately decorated blue and gold half-dome.

Opposite the Colegio San Lorenzo is some of the square's most recent architecture, in the form of the provincial government headquarters. Though you won't get further than the lobby, this is nonetheless one of the few buildings in the city that's made it on to the front of a postcard. Next door is the understocked **Museo Histórico** (Tues–Sun 9am–5pm; $1), housed in a building founded in 1894 as a Spanish casino. Following cyclone damage the upstairs has been closed whilst downstairs the exhibits are strictly limited in range and scope. The most coherent displays consist of nineteenth- and early twentieth-century furniture and artefacts from colonial households in Trinidad and Cienfuegos. In the gallery room, look out for the portrait of Tomás Terry.

To see more work by local artists visit the Galería de Cienfuegos on Ave. 54 e/ 33 y 35.

Also on this southern side of the square, between Calles 27 and 25, the **Fondo Cubano de Bienes Culturales** (Mon–Sat 8.30am–7pm, Sun 8.30am–1pm) sells some fetching paintings, carvings and a good set of poster prints; even if you don't intend to buy anything, this is the place to see local arts and crafts. More absorbing than the artwork are the two rooms of antiques from houses in and around the city: most of the items date from the early part of the twentieth century, and everything is for sale. This makes for an enthrallingly motley collection, encompassing old cameras, lamps, ornaments, china sets, clocks and various other personal artefacts.

There are musical and theatrical performances in the evenings at the Casa de Cultura; see p.272.

On the corner of the square where Avenida 54 crosses Calle 25, the **Casa de Cultura Benjamín Duarte** (daily 10am–7pm; 50¢) feels a bit lifeless for a cultural centre but may seem a tad more interesting after a guided tour, led by the multilingual Carlos Quintana. The tour sheds light on the history of the building itself and on Duarte, an artist, writer and political activist born in Cienfuegos in 1900. The highpoint, both literally and figuratively, is at the top of the winding staircase in the attractive six-columned watchtower on the roof. From here you can survey the bay and the harbour, as well as getting a fantastic perspective on the square and Punta Gorda.

Museo Histórico Naval Nacional and Cementerio de Reina

A few blocks northwest of Parque José Martí, on the edge of Pueblo Nuevo, the **Museo Histórico Naval Nacional** (Tues–Fri 9am–5pm, Sat & Sun 9am–1pm; $1) contains a more eclectic mix of exhibits than its name suggests. The first section is devoted to the uprising staged against the government in September 1957, known as the Levantamiento de 5 de Septiembre, in which local rebels joined forces with Fidel Castro's M-26-7 Movement in a revolt which instigated an insurrectionary coup at the naval barracks, now the museum's buildings and grounds. The revolutionaries took control of the city for only a few hours, whereupon the dictator General Batista sent in some two thousand soldiers and crushed the rebellion, ending with a shootout at the Colegio San Lorenzo. As well as various humdrum military possessions, the displays include the bloodstained shirt of one of the rebel marines and a neat little model of the naval base. Rather than the comprehensive rundown of Cuba's nautical past that you might expect, the rest of the museum is a sketchy collection of items related to sea travel, dispersed throughout various displays pertaining to a more general picture of life on the island since pre-Columbian times. These include a small section on natural history and a cabinet full of some fantastic old compasses.

Six blocks south of the museum, following Avenida 48 westwards to its conclusion then walking a block to the right – a twenty-minute walk in total – is the Cementerio Municipal del Paseo de la Reina de Cienfuegos, better known simply as the **Cementerio de Reina**. Crossing the railway tracks on the way, you enter a distinctly residential section of town with a more rural feel, making for a somewhat surreal atmosphere as you step through the heavy gates. Established in 1839 as the first cemetery in the city, the site is stuffed full of marble statues and gravestones – even the walls are lined with tombs. The ruined ramparts at the back are the remains of what was once a covered tomb, where the first priest of Cienfuegos was buried in 1862.

Punta Gorda and the Palacio de Valle

The southern part of the city, **Punta Gorda**, has a distinctly different flavour to the rest of Cienfuegos and it's here that the relatively recent founding of the city is most keenly felt. Open streets and colourful bungalow housing – unmistakably influenced by the United States of the 1940s and 50s – project an image of affluence and suburban harmony. This image would have been more accurately representative of the neighbourhood prior to the revolution than it is now, but nevertheless there are still some very comfortable homes, many of them renting rooms to visitors. Though there are no museums and few historic monuments in this part of town, Punta Gorda is as good an area as any in the city to spend time outside, whether for an evening stroll down the Prado, or a drink sitting on the wall of the malecón – the bayside promenade – or at one of the open-air fast-food joints.

The one sight worth checking out is the **Palacio de Valle**. Equally striking from the outside with its two dissimilar turrets, its chiselled arches and carved windows, it looks something like a cross between a medieval fortress, an Indian temple and a Moorish palace. Tiled mosaic floors, lavishly decorated walls and ceiling, the marble staircase, and the painstakingly detailed arches and adornments throughout the interior are as captivating as the place as a whole is intriguing. Built as a home between 1913 and 1917, the decidedly Islamic-influenced interior appears as a curiosity in a city founded by Frenchmen. An Italian architect, Alfredo Collí, was responsible for the overall design, but structural contributions were made by a team of artesans, who included Frenchmen, Cubans, Italians and Arabs.

Nowadays it functions principally as a restaurant, but if you're not eating there's nothing to stop you wandering up the stairs to the **rooftop bar**, the best spot for a drink in Cienfuegos. The views are better than you might anticipate given the unremarkable height of the building.

Beyond the Palacio del Valle, the land narrows to a two-hundred-metre peninsula, where the most opulent residential architecture in the city, some of it now converted for administrative use, is to be found. Wooden and concrete mansions and maisonettes lead the way down to La Punta, where there is a pretty little **park** right at the water's edge, which makes a great place to chill out.

Cementerio Tomás Acea

A five-minute taxi ride from the centre, on the Avenida 5 de Septiembre, is the much larger, more picturesque of the city's two cemeteries, the **Cementerio Tomás Acea** (daily 7am–6pm; $1). Completed in 1926, the overly grand Parthenon-styled entrance building leads into the gentle slopes of the cemetery grounds, where a wander round won't take very long. There are some interesting tombs to look out for, the most striking being the monument to the Martyrs of September 5, 1957, local rebels who were killed in the uprising commemorated by the Museo Histórico Naval Nacional (see p.268).

Eating

In theory, there are plenty of options when it comes to eating out in Cienfuegos, and wandering around the city centre you will inevitably notice state-run **restaurants** dotted about the place. The reality, however, is that the vast majority are severely limited in what they can offer, and will appeal only if you're on a strict budget or want a hands-on taste of Cuban life. A small number of the state restaurants are aimed at tourists, the best of them located around the *Jagua*. There is only one fixed and easy-to-find **paladar** in Cienfuegos, but it's worth asking around for other *paladares*: the chances are you'll need to be escorted to them and therefore incur the inevitable commission charge.

The most reliable fast-food place in Cienfuegos is El Rápido on Ave. 54 esq. 35; there's also a pool table.

1819, Calle 37 e/ 56 y 58. A reasonable selection for a peso restaurant: no-frills chicken, pork and fish dishes which work out extremely cheaply even though you'll be asked to pay in dollars. Set in the front room of a colonial mansion, whose modest nineteenth-century architecture does little to imprint a sense of history on the bare interior.

El Cochinito, Prado e/ 4 y 6, Punta Gorda. Escalope of pork and fried chicken make up the entire menu, but the food is better quality than at any of the state-run restaurants in the town centre, and cheaper than any of its classier counterparts down in Punta Gorda. Set in a dimly lit, rustic, lord-of-the-manor type hall featuring dark brick walls and a fireplace, it's at its most atmospheric in the evenings.

Covadonga, Prado e/ 0 y 2, Punta Gorda ☎ 432/82-38 or 69-49. Paella is the speciality but there are also a couple of other seafood and chicken dishes. Reasonably priced and nicely located on the edge of the bay – ask to be seated at the back under the tiled roof where the windows on all sides allow the view to perk up the otherwise neutral decor. Erratic opening times.

El Criollito, Calle 33 no. 5603 e/ 56 y 58. Expensive for a *paladar*, the chicken, pork and fish dishes are nevertheless as tasty and well prepared as any in town, whilst the feeble attempts to create some kind of ambience, namely a few posters and some music, are partially made up for by its in-demand atmosphere.

La Cueva del Camarón, Prado e/ 0 y 2, Punta Gorda. Slightly pricey seafood and some exceedingly simple pasta dishes in this tasteful green and white villa on the water's edge. Choose from the graceful indoor rooms or the terrace balcony, which has views of the Sierra del Escambray across the bay.

Giuventud, Prado e/ 52 y 54. Basic pizzas and pasta served on an equally basic open-air patio terrace, but less dingy than most and laughably cheap.

Palacio del Valle, Prado esq. Ave. 0, next door to the *Hotel Jagua*. A wide choice of seafood in various styles, such as Mexican-style shrimps or lobster, with chicken or beef dishes as alternatives, on the most comprehensive menu in town. The pianist and elegant arched interior provide a sense of occasion, though there are not always enough guests to create a buzz.

Drinking, nightlife and entertainment

There are several non-tourist **bars** in the town with cheap rum and plenty of undiluted local flavour. Two of the best are tiny, neon-lit *La Fernandina* at Prado no. 5202 esq. 52, and *El Polinesio* on Parque José Martí, equally dimly lit with a slightly bizarre bohemian vibe. Also on the square is *El Palatino*, a classic old wooden bar serving principally as a watering hole for coach parties. Ideal for a good quality coffee or rum during the afternoon accompanied by the aroma of tobacco is *El Embajador*, at Ave. 54 esq. 33. This cigar shop has a stylishly simple but inviting little bar at the back and a more comfortable upstairs gallery, with easy chairs around a coffee table. In Punta Gorda, the view from the *Palacio del Valle* makes it the best place, hands down, for a drink.

During the week, **nightlife** is restricted almost exclusively to two venues: the *Hotel Jagua*, where there's a cabaret most nights of the week with a $17 entrance charge, and *Discoteca El Benny*, Ave. 54 e/ 29 y 31. Unusually slick and polished for a Cuban nightclub, especially one in the provinces, this operates as a bar until 7pm, and then as a disco between 9pm and 3am, but don't expect any action before 11. The cover charge is $3, and the music predictably dominated by pop and salsa. Outside bets are the *Centro Cultural Artex*, at Ave. 16 no. 3510 e/ 35 y 37, occasionally host to live traditional Cuban music followed by a disco, or the seedier but more popular *La Caribeña*, Calle 35 e/ 20 y 22, under a leafy canopy on a terraced garden patio with a dancefloor and bar. The same spots are more reliably busy at weekends, but a large number of the city's younger residents seem happy hanging around what is little more than an outdoor dancefloor on a patch of open land next to a branch of the El Rápido fast-food chain at the malecón end of the Prado.

More sedate night-time entertainment can be enjoyed on and around the Parque José Martí, with excellent-value musical and theatrical shows occasionally put on at the Casa de la Cultura and the Teatro Tomás Terry. On Saturdays, from around 8pm, some brilliant local musicians grace the bandstand, attracting an older but buoyant and sociable crowd. Also on the main square is the semi-open-air Sala de Video Tomás Gutierrez Alea, which shows films every night except Saturdays and has a basic bar. Films are also shown at the Teatro Luisa, Prado esq. Ave. 50, and Cine Prado, Prado esq. 54. For national league baseball check out the Estadio 5 de Septiembre, Ave. 20 y 47 (☎432/36-44); game days are Tuesday to Thursday, Saturday and Sunday.

Listings

Banks and exchange The bank best prepared to deal with foreign currency is the Banco Financiero Internacional, Ave. 54 esq. 29 (Mon–Fri 8am–3pm). Banco Popular de Ahorro, Ave. 54 no. 3115 esq. 33 (Mon–Fri 8am–5pm), can deal with credit card transactions and travellers' cheques. The only bank open on a Saturday is the Banco de Credito y Comercio, Ave. 56 e/ 29 y 31 (Mon–Fri 8am–2pm, Sat 8am–noon). To buy pesos, head for the Cadeca Casa de Cambio at Ave. 56 no. 3316 e/ 33 y 35 (Mon–Sat 7.30am–6.30pm, Sun 7.30am–1pm).

Car rental Havanautos, Calle 39 esq. 18 (☎432/45-12-11), or Transautos in the lobby of the *Hotel Jagua*.

Immigration and legal Consultoría Jurídica Internacional at Calle 54 no. 2904 e/ 29 y 31 (Mon–Fri 8.30am–noon & 1.30–5.30pm; ☎432/37-32) offer legal advice and assistance. In cases of theft or money problems go to Asistur in the Palacio de Turismo at Prado e/ 12 y 14, Punta Gorda.

Medical Tourists are referred to the Clinica Internacional, Prado no. 202 e/ 2 y 4, where there is a 24-hour pharmacy. This is also the place to call for an ambulance (☎432/70-08). In serious or specialist cases patients are sent to the Dr. Gustavo Aldereguia Lima provincial hospital, Ave. 5 de Septiembre y 53 (☎432/30-11 or 39-11).

Photography Photoservice has a relatively poorly stocked branch in the town centre at Ave. 54 no. 3118 e/ 31 y 33 and a marginally better one in Punta Gorda on the Prado opposite the *Hotel Jagua*.

Police Call ☎116.

Post office The main branch is at Calle 35 esq. Ave. 56.

Shopping The best supermarket for stocking up on your own food supplies is the Mercado Habana, Ave. 58 esq. 31. El Embajador, Ave. 54 esq. 33, has a good selection of cigars.

Taxis Turistaxi ☎432/45-11-72 or 2-79-82.

Telephones International phone card calls can be made at the ETECSA Centro de Llamadas Internacionales at Ave. 54 e/ 35 y 37.

Around Cienfuegos

From Cienfuegos there are several manageable day- or half-day trips, offering the chance to enjoy some satisfyingly uncontrived, tourist-friendly diversions. Fifteen kilometres or so from the city are the exuberant grounds of the **Jardín Botánico**, whose compact size allows you to fit a tour easily into a couple of hours, whilst the huge variety of different species can keep you there for a day if you prefer.

Next to the mouth of the bay, a 45-minute drive from Cienfuegos, is **Playa Rancho Luna**, a pleasant beach, though second rate by Cuban standards, and the most obvious alternative to the city for a longer stay in the province. On the other side of the narrow channel linking the bay to the sea, only two minutes' away by ferry, the **Castillo de Jagua** stands guard over the entrance to the bay. A plain but atmospheric eighteenth-century Spanish fortress, today it contains a small history collection. Though conveniently close to Playa Rancho Luna, it's well worth taking the boat to the fortress from the city and enjoying the full serenity of the bay.

Jardín Botánico de Cienfuegos

About 15km east of the city limits, the **Jardín Botánico de Cienfuegos** (daily 8am–12.30pm & 1–4pm; $2.50) has one of the most complete collections of tropical plant species in the country. The one-square-kilometre site is home to over two thousand different species, divided up into various different collections, most of them merging seamlessly into one another so that in places this feels more like a natural forest than an artificially created garden. A road runs around the outside of the park and cuts into it in places, but the best way to explore is on foot. **Guides** are available, at no extra cost, and are invaluable if you want to know what you're looking at; ask at the lodge at the end of the main road along the northern border of the enclosure. There's a definite appeal to just wandering around on your own, though, following the roughly marked tracks through the varied terrain and past a series of pools and waterways. The most defined sections of the park include the cactus and fern houses, and the palm collection, the most popular amongst visitors with some 325 different species of palm from five continents. If you don't have your own transport the only way to get to the gardens, other than on an organized excursion, is by taxi. Twenty minutes' drive from the centre of Cienfuegos, the round trip should cost around $20.

Organized excursions to the Jardín Botánico can be arranged through either Havanatur or Rumbos in Cienfuegos; see p.265. Trips last 2–4 hours and cost around $10.

Playa Rancho Luna and around

Less than 20km south of the city is the province's most developed section of coastline, an unspoilt but relatively unimpressive stretch of beach called **Playa Rancho Luna**. Three hotels provide the focus for the area, spread out along 4km of mostly rocky, tree-lined shores which reach round to the mouth of the Bay of Jagua. Though there is no reliable timetable, **buses** leave the main station several times a day for the beach and will save you the $7 taxi fare, if you have the patience to wait around for them.

There are only a few hundred metres of actual **beach** in all, and the *Rancho Luna* hotel (☎43/4-81-20 to 23, fax 4-81-31; ⑤) has by far the best of it, a wide curve of soft beige sand, falling under the occasional shadow of a bushy tree, and sinking into the warm, slightly murky waters. With an unobtrusive *bohio*-style **bar** on this part of the beach, and watersports facilities available through the hotel, a hundred or so metres back from the shore, this is the best target for a day-trip to the area. Facilities include a tennis court, a decent size swimming pool and a large cafeteria-style restaurant.

To escape from this more populated section of the beach, you'll have to sacrifice some quality and walk the five minutes or so west along the shore to the scrappier section near the *Faro Luna* (☎43/4-81-62 or 65 or 68, fax 33-50-59; ⑤). Smaller and considerably more subdued than its neighbour, the hotel's modest but neatly kept grounds roost just above the rocky water's edge, with views spreading out to the horizon.

*Costs of
equipment
rental at the
centre include
$1 a day each
for flippers,
snorkel and
mask and $5 a
day for a wet
suit. Diving
times are
usually from
9am to 11am.*

This is also the best place to stay if you're planning to do any **scuba diving**, which is handled by the nearby Faro Luna Diving Centre. Offers include single dives for $25, packages of ten dives for $220, as well as courses starting at $60. All dives take place within a couple of hundred metres of the shore, where a varied stretch of coral is punctuated by a number of wrecked ships, and there are pretty good chances of coming across some big fish, such as nurse sharks, barracuda and tarpon.

About 5km up the road, perched above the channel linking the bay to the Caribbean, is the clumsy 1970s *Pasacaballo* (☎43/9-60-13 or 9-62-12; ②). In light of its better equipped, better kept neighbours, the hotel has little to recommend it besides the cost of its rooms and the views across the bay. Beyond the hotel, at the end of the road, *La Casa del Pescador* has some tasty, nicely prepared fresh seafood dishes and makes a good spot for an informal **lunch**, on the veranda of a small ranch-style building. At the foot of the slopes leading up to the *Pasacaballo* you can catch a **ferry** to the other side of the channel and visit the Castillo de Jagua, but it's much more of an event to take the ferry all the way from the city; alternatively, you could take the ferry all the way back from the castillo.

Castillo de Jagua

*The official
timetable for
ferries to the
fortress is
Mon–Sat at
6am, 8am,
11am, 1pm,
3pm &
5.30pm, Sun
no 6am
service. The
return times
are daily at
7am, 10am,
1pm, 3pm &
4.30pm.*

Half the fun of a visit to the seventeenth-century Spanish fortress at the mouth of the Bay of Jagua, known as the **Castillo de Jagua** (daily 8am–4pm; $1), is getting there. A local passenger **ferry** leaves Cienfuegos six times a day, approximately every two hours between 6am and 5.30pm, from a wharf next to the junction between Calle 25 and Avenida 46, where it'll cost you 50¢ in pesos to climb on board.

A rusty old vessel looking vaguely like a tug-boat, the ferry chugs across the placid waters at a pace slow enough to allow a relaxed contemplation of the bay, including the tiny, barely inhabited cays where the ferry makes a brief call to pick up passengers. The deck is lined with benches but the metal roof is the best place to sit, allowing unobscured views in all directions. After a little less than an hour, the ferry docks just below the fortress, on the opposite side of the channel to Playa Rancho Luna, from where a dusty track leads up to the cannon guarding the castle drawbridge. Overlooking a rustic little collection of bayfront shacks and patched-up villas, the fortress isn't particularly engaging once you get inside. It contains a small museum detailing the history of the fort, originally built to defend against pirate attacks; a couple of tables in a sunken courtyard where you can get something to eat and drink; and steps winding up to the top of the single turret from where there are modest views. Before heading back, take a peek at the cramped and dingy prison cell and the chapel on the courtyard level.

Villa Clara

The government's latest target for investment in Cuba's booming tourism industry, it won't be long before the province of **Villa Clara** makes its appearance in the holiday brochures. The vibrant provincial capital, **Santa Clara**, is one of the most culturally active Cuban cities and yet, unlike Havana and Santiago, has so far remained out of the tourist spotlight. That said, it has long been a place of pilgrimage for **Che Guevara** worshippers, as home to the hero's ashes and the scene of his most famous victory during the revolutionary conflict.

Forty kilometres or so northeast of Santa Clara, the town of **Remedios** is soon to be plugged as Cuban tourism's latest attraction. One of the country's virtually undiscovered historical treats, it has a splendid church and a couple of engaging museums to offer, but perhaps more appealing is the sense that, for the moment, this is a place where history continues to evolve undisturbed by commercialism and hordes of tourists. It remains to be seen whether this will change with the increased number of visitors staying at the newly built resort only 50km away on the northern cays.

Much of the investment in the province is being directed towards the network of dozens of small cays, which begins about 30km offshore. On **Cayo Las Brujas** there is already an attractive cabin complex, next to an empty virgin beach, whilst on larger **Cayo Santa María** the first of a planned four-hotel complex has recently been completed.

One of the few mountain resorts in this region, on the other side of the province, man-made **Lago Hanabanilla**, one of the largest of its kind on the island, attracts Cubans and foreigners alike, tucked into the screaming-green slopes of the Sierra del Escambray and offering good fishing and other excursions, arranged through its solitary hotel.

Santa Clara

One of the largest and most happening cities in Cuba, **SANTA CLARA** thoroughly deserves the increased attention it's receiving from a government determined to make the most of its assets. Home to the country's third biggest university, Santa Clara owes nothing of

Cienfuegos
and around

*From the
fortress a ferry
shuttles to the
opposite side
of the Bay
of Jagua
channel,
where, from
the Hotel
Pasacaballo,
you can take a
taxi to Playa
Rancho Luna
(see p.273).*

its vitality to tourism, and nowhere is the local spirit more apparent than in the main square, **Parque Vidal**, as sociable a plaza as you'll find in Cuba. The square ranks as one of Santa Clara's highlights, but there are plenty of other places worth visiting. Some, like the **Museo de Artes Decorativas**, with its accurate reconstructions of colonial aristocratic living conditions, are on the square itself, whilst within walking distance is one of the city's most famous national memorial sites, **Monumento a la Toma del Tren Blindado**. A derailed train here marks one of the most dramatic events of the Battle of Santa Clara, a decisive event in the revolutionary war of the late 1950s. Linking this with Santa Clara's other most visited attraction, the **Plaza de la Revolución** and the **Memorial al Che**, is the city's adopted native son, **Ernesto Che Guevara**.

Arrival, information and city transport

Astro and Víazul **buses** drop off passengers at the Terminal de Omnibus Nacionales, on the corner of Carretera Central and Oquendo, in the western limits of the city, from where a taxi to the Parque Vidal will cost around $2. The Terminal de Omnibus Intermunicipal (☎422/34-70) on the Carretera Central e/ Pichardo y Amparo is used by buses serving provincial destinations, such as Remedios. Private taxi drivers are scarce at the **train station** (☎422/2-28-95), on the Parque de los Mártires, although walking to the Parque Vidal from here shouldn't take more than ten minutes. Arriving by **car** from the west or east, the Carretera Central takes you right into the heart of town, where it becomes a street called Marta Abreu.

For journeys beyond the city limits, go to the Terminal de Autos de Alquiler, opposite the Terminal de Omnibus Intermunicipal, where private taxis collect passengers travelling within the province.

The only source of tourist **information** in Santa Clara is the Rumbos travel agency desk in *Europa*, the cafeteria on Independencia e/ Luis Estevez y Lorda (Mon–Fri 8am–5pm; ☎422/46-43). It's relatively poorly equipped but can supply basic regional information and excursions to Lago Hanabanilla, Remedios or the northern cays, as well as dealing with visa and tourist card extensions.

From the Parque Vidal to the out-of-the-centre hotels, a **taxi** will be necessary but for the longer distances within the town, principally between the Plaza de la Revolución and the main square, there are a large number of **bicitaxis** and **horse-drawn carriages**. There's a *bicitaxi* rank on Marta Abreu e/ Villuendas y J.B. Zayas, whilst the horse-drawn and motorcycle-carriages operate one way on Marta Abreu (towards the bus terminal) and Rafael Tristá (towards Parque Vidal) as well as running on Cuba (away from Parque Vidal) and Colón (towards Parque Vidal) and up and down Independencia. Though it's less widespread here than in some cities, there are some streets in Santa Clara with both pre- and post-revolutionary names; where applicable, the old names have been given in brackets.

For details of taxi and car rental firms, see pp.286–87.

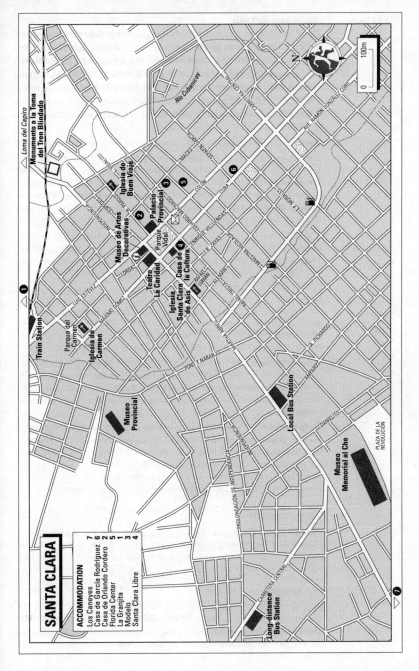

SANTA CLARA

ACCOMMODATION

Los Caneyes	7
Casa de García Rodríguez	6
Casa de Orlando Cordero	2
Florida Center	5
La Granjita	1
Modelo	3
Santa Clara Libre	4

Loma del Capiro

Monumento a la Toma del Tren Blindado

Río Cubanica V

Train Station

Parque del Carmen

Iglesia de Carmen

Iglesia de Buen Viaje

Museo de Artes Decorativas

Palacio Provincial

Parque Vidal

Teatro La Caridad

Casa de la Cultura

Iglesia Santa Clara de Asís

Museo Provincial

Local Bus Station

Museo Memorial al Che

PLAZA DE LA REVOLUCIÓN

Long-distance Bus Station

0   100m

Accommodation

There's a reasonable variety of accommodation in Santa Clara, including a number of **casas particulares**, though few advertise themselves as such, particularly in the centre where it is illegal to do so. Easier to find are the two centrally located **hotels**, which, unusually, accept tourists. For the greatest comfort and the best facilities, *Los Caneyes* and *La Granjita*, beyond the town's outskirts, win hands down, but are only convenient if you've got a car or are prepared to take taxis.

Hotels

Los Caneyes, Ave. de los Eucaliptos y Circunvalación ☎ & fax 422/2-81-40. Tucked away in the low grassy hills just beyond the southwestern outskirts of the city, about 1km from the Plaza de la Revolución and a $2–3 taxi ride from Parque Vidal, this neatly laid out complex on the edge of a small wood features Cuban Amerindian-style accommodation huts, thoughtfully furnished and with good facilities. There's a restaurant, small pool and a jacuzzi, plus scooter and car rental. ⑤.

Florida Center, Candelaria (Maestra Nicolasa) no. 56 e/ Colón y Maceo. Based around a fantastic, jungle-like courtyard, this authentic colonial residence has two relatively distinguished rooms for rent, both of them air-conditioned and with their own sink. ②.

La Granjita, Carretera de Maleza km 2 ☎422/2-81-90 or 91, fax 2-81-92. Sizeable and simply furnished rooms in concrete huts, scattered throughout a spacious site with its own woodlands and a stream. With plenty of palms and pines, the site looks more natural than landscaped and is slightly less contrived than *Los Caneyes*, though the facilities are not as comprehensive. ⑤.

Modelo, Maceo no. 210 e/ San Cristóbal (Eduardo Machado) y Candelaria (Maestra Nicolasa) ☎422/2-75-81. Aimed at Cubans but with a few rooms for tourists. A nondescript building with basic facilities and conditions, this is the cheapest state option and the less impersonal of the town's two tourist hotels. ②.

Santa Clara Libre, Parque Vidal no. 6 e/ Tristá y Padre Chao ☎422/2-75-48 to 50. Lime green, eleven-storey tower block with superb views and an unbeatable location, this cramped but lively hotel attracts a refreshing mixture of Cuban and foreign guests. Some rooms are a little dim and cramped, but all are sufficiently equipped, with closed-circuit video service instead of cable. There's a reasonable restaurant, a basement disco and rooftop cabaret shows. ③.

Casa particulares

Casa de García Rodríguez, Cuba no. 209, apartment 1 e/ Serafín García (Nazareno) y E.P. Morales (Síndico) ☎422/2-23-29. There are two spacious bedrooms available in this well looked after apartment, one double and one triple, both with a/c. Though a little low on natural light, the rooms have en-suite bathrooms, and the owners are extremely helpful – they even have a stash of leaflets on local services. ②.

Casa de Orlando Cordero, Buenviaje no. 16 e/ Parque Vidal y Maceo ☎422/46-22. Two large and well-maintained bedrooms, both with a/c and one with a fridge, in an unremarkable but very clean house, run by a friendly couple. Perfectly situated, less than a block from the main square. ②.

Parque Leoncio Vidal

Parque Vidal is the geographical, social and commercial nucleus of
Santa Clara. A traditional, pedestrianized town square, its enjoyable
atmosphere is due to the fact that it's permanently full of people, night
and day. Weekends are particularly animated, with live music performances on the central bandstand in the evenings, and on the porch of
the ornate Casa de la Cultura each Sunday at 4pm.

The square's attractive core, a paved circular **promenade** laced
with its own diverse plantlife, from towering palms to small, shrub-
peppered lawns, is traversed by shoppers and workers throughout
the day and, in the evenings, fills up with young and old alike, as
kids hide behind trees and race around the promenade, whilst their
elders stick to the benches, and the park hums with chatter. The
scene is elegantly framed by a mixture of predominantly colonial
and neo-colonial buildings, the more modern *Santa Clara Libre*
hotel being the most obvious exception. The grandest of the lot is
the **Palacio Provincial**, now home to the **Biblioteca José Martí**
(Mon–Fri 8am–10pm, Sat 8am–4pm), on the northeastern face of
the square. Built between 1904 and 1912, the wide facade of the
building, with its two bold porticoes, stands out as the square's
most classically Greek architecture. Once the home of the provincial government, the building's exuberant exterior is likely to draw
you in sooner than its neighbours, but a tour of the inside is not
particularly easy to arrange and you'll probably have to make do
with the rooms given over to public use as part of the library.

More receptive to visitors is the **Teatro La Caridad** (☎ 422/55-48
for information), on the adjacent, northwestern face of the square,
with a fabulous, ornate interior, sold short by the relatively sober
exterior of the building. Founded on September 8, 1885, it was built
with money donated by Marta Abreu Estevez, a civic-minded nineteenth-century native of Santa Clara with an inherited fortune of
more than four million pesos. As part of her wider quest to help the
city's poor and contribute to the city's civil, cultural and academic
institutions, a portion of the box office receipts were to be used to
improve living conditions for the impoverished, thus spawning the
theatre's name ("Charity"). Restored for a second time in the early
1980s, the theatre is in fantastic condition, with a semicircular three-
tiered balcony enveloping the central seating area and a stunning
painted **ceiling**. Three central angelic figures, representing Genius,
History and Fame, are stationed in the clouds above a map of Cuba,
whilst around the outside are painted portraits of eight Spanish play-
wrights. The creation of Camilo Salaya, who was also responsible for
the interior decoration of the Teatro Tomás Terry in Cienfuegos (see
p.267), this huge fresco is the theatre's crowning glory. You can get
closer to the painting on a twenty-minute **guided tour** in English,
which takes you up into the balcony (Tues–Sun 8am–5pm; $1, $1
extra to take photos).

*There are
occasional live
musical
performances
in the fabulous
concert room
of the Palacio
Provincial –
check the
board at the
entrance for
details.*

*Performance
nights are
Wednesday,
Friday and
Saturday,
starting at
8.30pm;
Sunday
starting at
5pm. Entrance
costs vary.*

A few doors down on the same side of the square, the **Museo de Artes Decorativas** (Mon & Thurs 9am–noon & 1–6pm, Wed 1–6pm, Fri & Sat 1–10pm, Sun 6–10pm; $2) is the only other old building on Parque Vidal set up for visits. Featuring furniture, objets d'art and artwork spanning four centuries, but dominated by the nineteenth, most of the exhibits have been collected from houses around Santa Clara. Each room is opulently furnished, as it might have been when the building, older than most of its neighbours but of no particular architectural merit, was home to a string of aristocratic families during the colonial period. As well as the front room, with a marvellous crystal chandelier, a dining room with a fully laid table, and a bedroom with an ostentatiously designed wardrobe, there is a room furnished almost entirely in wicker. Though the rooms are impressively well preserved, it can be quite frustrating having to view almost everything from behind a rope at the doorway.

Monumento a la Toma del Tren Blindado

A block behind the Museo de Artes Decorativas, Luis Estévez meets Independencia, Santa Clara's main shopping street, where a right turn and a five-minute walk leads to a memorial to one of the city's most significant and renowned events, the **Monumento a la Toma del Tren Blindado**. The derailed carriages of an armoured train which make up most of the site have lain here since they were toppled from the tracks to the north during the Battle of Santa Clara, in 1958. This clash, between the dictator Batista's forces and a branch of the rebel army, led by Che Guevara, was to be one of the last military encounters of the revolutionary war. In December 1958, over ten thousand government troops had been sent by Batista to Santa Clara to prevent the rebels from advancing further west towards Havana, and one of the principal components of this defensive manoeuvre was an armoured train. However, Guevara, with only three hundred or so men, took the upper hand when, using tractors to raise the rails, they crashed the armoured train and ambushed the 350 soldiers within, who soon surrendered, and the train became a base for further attacks.

Few visitors leave Santa Clara without a snapshot of the derailed train, but don't expect to be occupied for more than a few minutes. Though the Cuban historians responsible for churning out government-approved books and texts on the revolution never tire of telling the tale of the against-the-odds military victory which the monument commemorates, there is surprisingly little fuss made of the story here. The five derailed carriages lie strewn at the side of the road, in between the river and the train track, with plenty of local traffic passing by, giving the sense that they're as much a part of the local landscape as the trees and the buildings around them. Rather more drama is evoked by the large concrete monoliths shooting out from the wreck, while the bulldozer which helped do the damage sits atop a large concrete star looking over the scene. You can step inside the carriages (Mon–Sat 8am–6pm, Sun

8am–noon; free), where there are exhibits relating to the event and some dramatic photos of the scene just after the derailment.

Northwest of Parque Vidal

Less than a five-minute walk from Parque Vidal along Máximo Gómez is the pleasant little park housing the **Iglesia de Carmen**, a simple church with an altar almost as large as the back wall it sits up against. Unless you have a particular interest in the history of the city, the church, which served as a prison for women during the 1868–78 First War of Independence, doesn't really warrant a visit for its own sake but is one of the obvious targets for a stroll away from the main square. In the northwestern corner of the park stands a bizarre-looking monument commemorating the first Mass held by the Spanish founders of Santa Clara on July 15, 1689. A circular concrete girder, held aloft by a set of concrete columns, encloses a tree in the centre.

From the park follow Padre Tudury westwards and turn right on Pons y Naranjo to get to the **Museo Provincial** (Mon–Fri 9am–6pm, Sat 9am–1pm; 1 peso), situated on a hill at the top of a piece of scrap land. Despite its large size and the fact that there are plenty of exhibits, attempts to convey a sense of history are lost to the revolutionary overkill and muddled layout. Look out for a few interesting photos, including some of the Battle of Santa Clara. There are natural history displays downstairs, supposedly representing Cuba's fauna, but featuring a distinctly foreign zebra, baboon and anteater.

Other local churches of note are the Iglesia Santa Clara de Asis (open in the mornings) on Marta Abreu e/ Rafael Lubián y Alemán and the older and more run-down Iglesia de Buen Viaje on Pedro Estevez esq. Rolando Pardo.

Museo Memorial Che and Plaza de la Revolución

In the southwestern outskirts of the city, about fifteen blocks along Rafael Tristá from Parque Vidal, Santa Clara pays tribute to its adopted son and hero, **Ernesto Che Guevara**. The monument commemorating the man and the vital part he played in the armed struggle against General Batista's dictatorship is in classic Cuban revolutionary style: simple, bold and made of concrete. On a thick, table-top base stand four concrete slabs; towering down from the tallest one is a burly-looking statue of Che Guevara, on the move and dressed in his usual military garb, rifle in hand. Inscribed on the concrete podium are the words "Hasta La Victoria Siempre" ("Ever onwards to victory"), one of the catchphrases of the revolution. The slab next to the statue depicts, in a huge, somewhat jumbled mural, Guevara's march from the Sierra Maestra to Santa Clara and the decisive victory over Batista's troops.

Spreading out before the monument, the **Plaza de la Revolución**, like its counterpart in Havana, is little more than an open space. The statue of Che and the mural are classic photo opportunities but the best place to spend time here is in the **Museo Memorial al Che**, underneath the monument (Tues–Sat 8am–9pm, Sun 8am–6pm; free). You'll be ushered first through a door marked "Memorial", which leads into a softly lit chamber where the mood of reverence and respect is quite affecting. Resembling a kind of tomb, this is a

Ernesto "Che" Guevara

No one embodies the romanticism of the Cuban revolution more than Ernesto "Che" Guevara, the handsome, brave and principled guerrilla who fought alongside Fidel Castro in the Sierra Maestra during the revolutionary war of 1956–59, and who has become the most recognizable face of the rebel victory and the revolution itself. He was born in Rosario in Argentina on June 14, 1928, to middle-class parents, his father a politically active anti-Peronist who, along with his wife, held strong left-wing views. The young Ernesto Guevara – later to be nicknamed "Che", a popular term of affectionate address in Argentina – suffered from severe asthma attacks as a child. Despite this life-long affliction, he became a keen soccer and rugby player whilst at the University of Buenos Aires, where, in 1948, he began studying medicine.

By the time he graduated in 1953, finishing a six-year course in half the time, he had made an epic journey around South America on a motorbike, with his doctor friend Alberto Granado. These travels, which he continued after graduation, were instrumental in the formation of Guevara's political character, instilling in him a strong sense of Latin American identity and opening his eyes to the widespread suffering and social injustice throughout the continent. He was in Guatemala in 1954 when the government was overthrown by a US-backed right-wing military coup, and had to escape to Mexico.

It was in Mexico, in November 1955, that Guevara met the exiled Fidel Castro and, learning of his intentions to return to Cuba and ignite a popular revolution, decided to join Castro's small rebel army, the M-26-7 Movement. The Argentinian was among the 82 who set sail for Cuba in the yacht *Granma* on November 24, 1956, and, following the disastrous landing (see box, p.423), one of the few who made it safely into the Sierra Maestra mountains. As a guerrilla and as a doctor Guevara played a vital

dedication to the Peruvians, Bolivians and Cubans who died with Che in Bolivia, each of whom is commemorated by a simple stone portrait set into the wall. The mood lightens in the museum opposite the memorial door, where Che's life is succinctly told through neatly presented photos, maps, quotes and other paraphernalia, including his beret, jacket and camera. There are some memorable photographs, and it's these that hold the interest in the face of the usual technical information and array of weapons. There are some refreshingly lighthearted pictures of Che before he became a revolutionary, showing that he was recognizable even at two or three years of age. Besides those of his early childhood,there are pictures of him alongside his rugby team mates, on his contraption of a motorbike about to set off on a tour of his native Argentina in January 1950, and on a raft on the Amazon. Some of the now classic photographs taken during the Sierra Maestra campaign, depicting Guevara, Castro and their rebel companions in the thick forests of the eastern mountains, are also here. Near the end, you will find the most famous photograph of them all, taken on March 5, 1960, at the burial of a group of sabotage victims; this portrait of Guevara, complete with beret, staring role for the rebels as they set about drumming up support for their cause amongst the local peasants whilst fighting Batista's troops. His most prominent role in the conflict, however, came later, when in 1958 he led a rebel column westwards to the then province of Las Villas, where he was to cut all means of communication between the two ends of the island and thus cement Castro's control over the east. This he did in great style, exemplified in his manoeuvres during the Battle of Santa Clara (see p.280).

Unlike Castro, Guevara endured the same harsh conditions as the other rebels and refused to grant himself any comforts that his higher status might have allowed. It was this spirit of sacrifice and brotherhood that he brought to the philosophies which he developed and instituted after the triumph of the revolution in 1959, during his role as Minister for Industry. The cornerstone of his theories was the concept of El Hombre Nuevo – the New Man – and this became his most enduring contribution to Cuban communist theory. Guevara believed that in order to build communism a new man must be created, and the key to this was to alter people's consciousness. The emphasis was on motivation: new attitudes would have to be instilled in people, devoid of selfish sentiment and with a goal of moral rather than material reward, gained through the pursuit of the aims of the revolution.

Despite these theories Guevara remained, at heart, a man of action, and having served four years as ambassador for Cuba, he left for Africa to play a more direct role in the spread of communism, becoming involved in a revolutionary conflict in the Congo. In 1966 he travelled to Bolivia where he once again fought as a guerrilla against the Bolivian army. There, on October 8, 1967, Guevara was captured and shot. Referred to in Cuba today simply as "El Che", he is probably the most universally liked and respected of the revolution's heroes, his early death allowing him to remain untarnished by the souring of attitudes over time and his willingness to fight so energetically for his principles viewed as evidence of his

sternly beyond the camera, is perhaps one of the most iconic images of the twentieth century.

From the monument, head down towards the Carretera Central for the **shop** on the edge of the road junction for a selection of memorabilia and books on Che, as well as more general books, CDs, T-shirts and postcards. The shop, and the small café next door, are open daily from 9am to 5.30pm.

Loma del Capiro

On the northeastern side of the city, a couple of kilometres from the centre, is the surprisingly inconspicuous **Loma del Capiro**, a large mound of a hill rising abruptly from the comparatively flat surroundings, and providing splendid views over the city and the flatlands to the north and east. This is a peaceful, unspoilt spot for a picnic, where you're more likely to encounter a few kids flying kites than other tourists. There's a small car park near the summit from where a concrete staircase climbs gently up 150m to the top and a steel monument commemorating the taking of the hill by Che Guevara in 1958, during the Battle of Santa Clara.

Villa Clara

To get to the hill, a good half-hour's walk from Parque Vidal, follow Independencia past the Monumento a la Toma del Tren Blindado, turn right onto Ana Pegudo, then left onto Felix Huergo, which you should follow to its conclusion and then turn right for the car park. Alternatively, you can take a taxi there for around $2 .

Eating

One of the few places where you can get a cooked breakfast, served between 7am and 10am, is La Cima in the Hotel Santa Clara Libre.

There are a number of **paladares** in the city, with a cluster on Cuba and Colón, but if you go out after dark you'll need to look pretty hard to spot them. Recent laws in Santa Clara have decreed that any new *paladares* are forbidden to provide their customers with tables and chairs, and can only offer a limited range of food and drink, excluding alcohol, seafood and dairy products. As a result, there are several standing-only *paladares* around the city, whilst those opened prior to 1999 have been allowed to continue to operate outside of the new restrictions. On the whole, the state restaurants fail to combine good food with an agreeable atmosphere and usually lack either one or the other – thankfully, there are some exceptions.

1878, Máximo Gómez e/ Parque Vidal e Independencia. The best peso restaurant in town serving standard *comida criolla*. Though the finish is decidedly unpolished, it lends the place a certain authenticity, combined with its considerable colonial style. Reservations must be made in person between 8am and 9am on the same day. Closed Mon.

Bodeguita del Centro, Villuendas 264 e/ San Miguel y Názareno ☎ 422/43-56. With an extensive selection of meals, the owners of this atmospheric *paladar* have made the most of what the law has left them with. The many nicely presented main courses include liver, ham, pork chop and chicken dishes, with eggs making up the several non-meat alternatives. Photos of the city and scribbled autographs and writing decorate the walls – an idea borrowed from the *Bodeguita del Medio* in Havana.

El Castillo, San Miguel no. 9 e/ Cuba y Villuendas. If you don't mind standing up at a bar whilst you eat your food, you won't get better value for money than at this *paladar* in a neo-colonial fort-like residence. Decent helpings of reliable pork, chicken or liver dishes for around a dollar each.

La Concha, Carretera Central esq. Danielito. The jack-of-all-trades, master-of-none menu of this roadside restaurant includes seafood, chicken, beef, pork, spaghetti and pizza at reasonable prices. The mural of a Cuban landscape on the wall isn't enough by itself to create an atmosphere but this is one of the few places where you can eat late at night.

El Marino, Carretera Central esq. Comandante González Coro ☎ 422/55-94. Authentic seafood specialist operating in both dollars and pesos with a sky-blue haze of tablecloths and curtains that make for a somewhat dizzying atmosphere. Reservations are usually necessary if you intend to pay with pesos.

El Sótano, *Santa Clara Libre*, Parque Vidal no. 6. Cheap sandwiches and fried chicken in a dark basement cafeteria where you expect Huggy Bear to appear at any moment. Open in the daytime only.

La Terraza, Serafín Sánchez no. 5 e/ Cuba y Colón. The usual chicken, pork and fish in *criolla* style, served on a simple indoor rooftop terrace that suits eating in the daytime, when you can look out over the surrounding neighbourhood.

Los Tainos, *Los Caneyes*, Ave. de los Eucaliptos y Circunvalación ☎ 422/2-
81-40. Some of the best-quality restaurant food in the city, including the
speciality, pork, as well as other meat dishes, seafood and pizzas, served up
in a faithfully designed if slightly contrived Taino-style circular lodge, with
bamboo-lined walls and hanging wicker lamps.

Drinking, nightlife and entertainment

The most atmospheric places for a drink are the saloon-style bar in
1878 (see opposite), or *Salón Topper* in the *Hotel Santa Clara
Libre*, a dark, intimate bar with great views. The 24-hour *Europa* at
Independencia esq. Luis Estévez redeems its otherwise soulless character by its location on a sociable corner of the pedestrianized boulevard, whilst *La Marquesina* on Parque Vidal esq. Máximo Gómez, in
the corner of the theatre building, has rum, coffee, a couple of cocktails and a lot of flies but is one of the best bars for hanging out with
the locals – you should be charged in pesos.

Nightlife focuses on the lively Parque Vidal, with plenty of people,
both young and old, buzzing around until the early hours of the
morning at weekends. Around the square's borders, in a large
derelict building at Rafael Tristá esq. Cuba, the *Discoteca Villa
Clara* (10.30pm–late; 2 pesos) has the strongest party vibe in the
city, a very basic peso bar, and rocks with locals at weekends.
Slightly more sophisticated but with less spirit, *El Sótano*, the basement disco in the *Santa Clara Libre*, gets going between 11pm and
midnight (Thurs–Sun; $1). At the opposite end of the hotel, on the
cramped U-shaped roof terrace, there's an unglamorous small-scale
cabaret ($1 per couple), probably best approached as a chance to
hear some live musicians with views of the city as a backdrop. For a
more full-on cabaret experience, check out *Cabaret Cacique* near
Hotel Los Caneyes at Carretera de los Eucaliptos y Circunvalación
(Thurs–Sun; ☎ 422/45-12). The most varied programme of live
shows, dances and music is at *El Mejunje*, Marta Abreu no. 12 e/ J.B.
Zayas y Rafael Lubián (2–5 pesos). Staged in an Arcadian open-air
courtyard, the entertainment ranges from rock nights to live jazz and
salsa, whilst on Saturdays, there's either a disco or a transvestite
show. Check for notices on the door or a board just inside for details
of the week's programme.

Films are screened at the Cine Cubanacan, at Independencia no.
60 e/ Villuendas y J.B. Zayas, and the Cine Camilo Cienfuegos
(☎ 422/30-05), in the *Santa Clara Libre*. The noticeboard outside
the latter has details of films showing at *salas de video* at these two
cinemas and around the city.

Santa Clara's busy cultural calendar, the fullest in the region,
includes a seven-day theatre **festival** at *El Mejunje* which takes place
between mid-January and mid-March, and a city-wide **film festival** for
about five days towards the end of November. Other cultural events
take place at the Teatro La Caridad and the Casa de la Cultura, both on
Parque Vidal. As well as **plays**, the Teatro La Caridad hosts **orchestral**

performances and ballet and though it doesn't follow a strict programme of events, show nights are generally Wednesday, Friday and Saturday from 8.30pm onwards and on Sunday from 5pm. Theatre tickets vary in price but should rarely exceed $10. At the Casa de la Cultura, on Friday and Saturday nights you can attend a live music performance, starting around 9 or 10pm, for just a peso.

Liga Nacional **baseball** games are held at the Estadio Sandino, entrance on Calle 2 (☎422/2-64-61 or 38-38), on Tuesdays, Wednesdays, Thursdays, Saturdays and Sundays during the season; as at all live sport venues in Cuba, it'll cost you a peso to get in.

Listings

Banks and exchange The best bank for foreign currency transactions is the Banco Financiero Internacional, Cuba e/ Rafael Tristá y Eduardo Machado (Mon–Fri 8am–3pm). Credit card withdrawals and travellers' cheques are handled at the Banco de Crédito y Comercio, Rafael Tristá e/ J.B. Zayas y Alemán (Mon–Fri 8am–2pm, Sat 8–11am), and the Banco Popular de Ahorro, Cuba esq. Candelaria (Maestra Nicolasa) (Mon–Fri 8am–5pm). For changing dollars to pesos, go to the CADECA Casa de Cambio, Rafael Tristá esq. Cuba (Mon–Sat 8.30am–6pm, Sun 8.30am–12.30pm).

Bookshop Librería Vietnam, Independencia e/ Luis Estévez y Plácido, sells maps and predominantly Cuban books.

Car rental Transautos and Havanautos (☎422/58-95) operate from the *Santa Clara Libre* and *Los Caneyes* hotels respectively, the latter also renting out scooters and bicycles.

Immigration and legal To extend the duration of your tourist card go to the Rumbos desk (Mon–Fri 8am–5pm; ☎422/46-43) in *Europa*, the cafeteria on Independencia e/ Luis Estevez y Lorda. For all other legal matters visit the Consultoría Jurídica Internacional at Rafael Tristá no. 5 e/ Villuendas y Cuba (Mon–Fri 8.30am–noon & 1.30–5.30pm).

Laundry The only functioning launderette is at Lavatin Astral at Lorda no. 67 e/ Martí e Independencia.

Medical The Clínico Quirurgico Arnaldo Milián Castro is the most comprehensively equipped hospital in the area. For information call ☎422/7-12-34 or 7-12-56. Call ☎422/2-22-59 or 39-65 for an ambulance.

Pharmacy There are no dollar pharmacies: of the peso pharmacies the one at Luis Estévez y Boulevard is as good as any.

Photography Photoservice has a branch at Independencia no. 55 e/ Villuendas y J.B. Zayas.

Police In an emergency call ☎116. The central police station is at Colón no. 222 ☎422/2-69-77.

Post office Main branch is at Colón no. 10 e/ Parque Vidal y Eduardo Machado (Mon–Sat 8am–6pm, Sun 8am–noon); DHL and EMS services are available. Faxes can be sent and received in the small branch at Cuba no. 7 e/ Rafael Tristá y San Cristóbal (Eduardo Machado).

Shopping The best place for groceries is the Supermercado Siboney, Independencia esq. Villuendas. Rum and a small selection of cigars are sold at La Isla, Colón no. 6 e/ Parque Vidal ySan Cristóbal (Eduardo Machado). For tapes and CDs, try Video Centro, Parque Vidal esq. Leoncio Vidal.

Taxis Cubataxi, Carretera Central e/ J.B. Zayas y Alemán ☎ 422/2-26-91 or 2-69-03; Taxi OK ☎ 422/39-99 or 2-81-39; and Transtur ☎ 422/41-00.

Telephones You can make international calls with a prepaid phone card in the ETECSA Cabina de Llamadas at San Cristóbal (Eduardo Machado) esq. Cuba (daily 8am–6pm).

Remedios

Just over 40km northeast of Santa Clara and less than 10km from the coast, the town of **REMEDIOS** sits unobtrusively in between the provincial capital and the developing resort area on the northern cays. One of the earliest Spanish towns in Cuba, founded shortly after the establishment of the seven *villas* (see p.460), Remedios has a history longer than Santa Clara's, going back as far as the 1520s. Today's provincial capital was, in fact, founded by citizens of Remedios who, following a series of pirate attacks towards the end of the sixteenth century, transplanted the settlement further inland. However, the local populace were far from united in their desire to desert Remedios and in an attempt to force the issue, those who wanted to leave burnt the town to the ground. Rebuilt from the ashes, by 1696 the town had its own civic council and went on to produce not only one of Cuba's most renowned composers, Alejandro García Caturla, but also a Spanish president, Dámaso Berenguer Fuste, who governed Spain in the 1930s.

With a history rivalling that of Trinidad, Remedios remains relatively unexploited in comparison, albeit less elegant. The faded paintwork and tiled roofs of the generally modest, still-lived-in colonial homes and the noticeable absence of motorized transport around the centre reflect a town whose lifestyle seems to have been undisturbed by the advent of tourism and the market economy. Though the modest number of visitable buildings and museums in Remedios will provide no more than half a day of sightseeing, its superb and reasonably priced hotel, the *Mascotte*, and the town's tranquil atmosphere make it well worth stopping over for a night.

If you **arrive** at the **bus station** on the outskirts of the more urbanized centre of the town, there are no straightforward alternatives other than to walk the eight blocks north along Independencia which lead directly to Plaza Martí.

The Town

Easily manageable on foot, Remedios is an inviting place to stroll around without having to think too much about what you choose to visit. All the museums are either on or within shouting distance of the central **Plaza Martí**, the unremarkable main square. It's well worth calling in at the *Mascotte*, on a corner of the square, before you begin any sightseeing, as one of the staff, most of whom speak English, may be willing to act as a **guide**.

By far the most stunning sight in Remedios is the main altar of the **Iglesia de San Juan Bautista**, the town's principal church, occupying the southern face of the Plaza Martí, with more to offer than the similar-looking Iglesia de Buen Viaje, set back from the plaza on the opposite side. Entry is usually via the back door but don't let the fact that you may have to knock deter you, as the friendly staff are well used to receiving foreign visitors. Once inside, the magnificence of the main altar seems all the more shocking in comparison to the attractive but simple and rather withered exterior. Made from gilded precious wood, not a single square inch of the surface has escaped the illustriously detailed design of this impressively large shrine. It was commissioned by a Cuban millionaire named Eutimio Falla Bonet, who funded the restoration of the whole church between 1944 and 1954 following his discovery that he had family roots in Remedios. Though the building now standing dates back only as far as the late eighteenth century, a church has stood on this site since the sixteenth century. However, it was only after Bonet's revamping of the interior that the church acquired its most notable features, such as the splendid timber ceiling and the set of golden altars lining the walls, collected from around Cuba and beyond, which have transformed the place into a kind of religious trophy cabinet.

The museum has a small concert room where you can sometimes catch live musical performances in the afternoon or evening.

Also on the Plaza Martí, the simple **Museo de la Música Alejandro García Caturla** (Mon–Sat 9am–noon & 1–5pm, Sun 9am–1pm; free) is dedicated to the town's most successful musician, who lived and worked in the building for the last twenty years of his life. Managing to combine his profession as a lawyer with his passion for music, especially the piano and violin, he reached the lofty heights of performing with the Havana Philharmonic Orchestra as well as laying some of the foundations of modern Cuban music with his boundary-breaking combinations of traditional symphonic styles and African rhythms. He was murdered in December 1940 by a man whom he was due to prosecute the following day. His study has been preserved and still contains all its original furniture and books, whilst photographs charting the various stages of his life, including some of his many trips overseas, go some way to redressing the balance upset by the overwhelming number of documents and photocopies on display.

One and a half blocks north of the *Mascotte* on Máximo Gómez, the **Museo de las Parrandas Remedianas** (Tues–Sat 9am–noon & 1–5pm, Sun 9am–1pm; $1) is the nearest you'll get to experiencing *las parrandas*, the annual event for which Remedios is renowned throughout Cuba – unless, that is, you happen to be here on December 24. Though the event itself lasts only one night, the townsfolk spend several months preparing for it. The town divides into two halves, north and south, and most of the preparations revolve around the creation of two large floats, known as *trabajos de plaza*, built to represent their respective half of the town. The floats are wheeled out into Plaza Martí on December 24 to be judged on looks and originality. The festivities go on into the night with a lantern parade and fireworks as the entire town celebrates this 200-year-old tradition. Downstairs in the museum there are photographs of some of the spectacular floats which have graced the event, as well as examples of the torches and instruments which form such an integral part of the raucous celebrations. The displays upstairs feature scale models of the *trabajos de plaza*, the centrepieces of *las parrandas*, alongside colourful costumes, flags and more photographs.

Slightly deeper into the local neighbourhood, a few minutes' walk away from the Plaza Martí, at Maceo no. 56, the **Museo de Historia Local** (Tues–Sat 8am–5pm, Sun 8am–noon; $1) charts the history of the town and surrounding region from aboriginal times to the revolution. There are some fine examples of nineteenth-century Cuban baroque furniture, easier to appreciate than some of the other displays in the museum, which skim the surface of a whole host of different aspects of society and politics. This all changes however, if you're treated to a tour of the museum, when everything is placed in its historical context.

Practicalities

To get to Remedios from Santa Clara, you'll have to catch an inter-municipal **bus** from the terminal on the Carretera Central e/ Pichardo y Amparo. Alternatively, you can make the ninety-minute journey in a private **taxi**, which you can find opposite the bus terminal. The *Mascotte* (☎42/39-51-44 or 39-54-67; ④), on the Máximo Gómez side of Plaza Martí, is not just the only **hotel** in Remedios but doubles up as an **information** centre, supplier of tour guides and home to the best restaurant in town. It has a charming down-to-earth character, an elegant yet unostentatious interior, and there are few better-value hotels in the whole country. There are only ten, well-furnished rooms, most of them located around an open-air balcony overlooking the delightful patio bar. The **restaurant**, *Las Arcadas*, is the only place worth considering for a meal, serving reasonably priced seafood and meat dishes. Choosing where to **drink** is equally straightforward, as, other than the bar in the hotel, *El Louvre*, on the same side of the plaza, has twice as much choice and style as the one or two basic alternatives.

Nightlife in Remedios takes place almost exclusively at weekends. The Casa de la Cultura, facing the plaza on the same side as the Iglesia de San Juan Bautista, usually hosts live bands on Friday, Saturday and Sunday nights at about 9pm. The other focus for musical and social activity is the Parque de la Trova, an extension of the Plaza Martí where outdoor discos are held. One of the liveliest times to be here is in the first week of March, when **La Semana de la Cultura** (Culture Week) sees concerts and cultural activities taking place day and night.

The northern cays

From Remedios it's about 10km to the run-down port town of **Caibarién**, where in the *Cafetería Villa Blanca*, eight blocks from the seafront, you can arrange a taxi to the **cays**. Even if you have your own transport you should stop by here to pay $5 for the receipt you'll need to pass the checkpoint on the 48-kilometre-long causeway that links the mainland to the outcrop of miniature islands. The drive out there is quite spectacular, the dark deeper waters nearer the land giving way to shallow turquoise around the cays.

Virtually untouched prior to Cuba's 1990s tourism explosion, the emerging resort on this cluster of cays is typical of the current moves to develop the country's wealth of untapped resources. There are few places in the country that combine the same level of comfort and escapism that can be found on the two cays distinguished for their remoteness, that have been chosen for the first stage of the development.

Turning left on arriving at the first of the two cays, **Cayo Las Brujas**, a road skirts around the edge of the small airport and cuts through the green brush which covers most of the cay. At the end of the road is a small car park from where a short wooden gangway leads up to the carefully hidden away **beach** and the *Complejo Turístico Farallón* (book through Rumbos in Santa Clara ☎422/46-43; ④), the base for any visit. The complex is simple, picturesque and peaceful, with a line of wooden cabins facing out across the water, raised just above sea level on a natural platform along the rocky shore. Marking the beginning of the beach, sitting snugly on the corner section of this craggy platform, *Restaurant El Farallón*, serving a few moderately priced meat and seafood dishes, has been appropriately designed and fitted with wooden furniture, floors and walls, in keeping with the overall natural feel. A spiral staircase leads up to the look-out tower and a modest view of the ocean on one side and a sea of green scrub on the other. Dividing the two is the narrow, curving sandy beach which arches round enough to form an open bay of usually placid bluey-green waters.

Cayo Santa María, at the end of the causeway, around 15km beyond Cayo Las Brujas, is set to be the focal point for the resort area covering this section of Villa Clara's cays. With a twenty-kilometre-long beach, which Fidel Castro is said to have described as superior to Varadero, the 300-room hotel, unfinished at the time of writing, is sure to be only the first step in a much larger project which includes plans to link the cay with Cayo Guillermo in Ciego de Avila, almost 30km away.

Lago Hanabanilla

Closer to Trinidad but easier to access from the Santa Clara side, a fifty-kilometre drive away, **Lago Hanabanilla** twists, turns and stretches around the hills on the northern edges of the Sierra del

Escambray. Tucked away behind the steep slopes which effectively mark the border between the countryside south of Santa Clara and the more mountainous terrain it merges into, the elongated 36-square-kilometre lake, technically a reservoir, looks more like a wide river that has spilled its banks. Views of the lake reveal no more than a small section as it slinks out of sight behind the steep, hilly slopes which come right down to the water's edge, but the valley in which it rests provides a beautiful backdrop unlikely to disappoint from any angle.

Almost all visits to the lake are channelled through the *Hanabanilla* hotel (☎ 42/8-69-32 or 4-91-25; ③). Thankfully the dull, unimaginative architecture of the hotel, which stands right on the edge of the lake, near the northern tip, takes a back seat to the location. A day-trip to the hotel is a viable option, with the rowing boats for rent, most of which come with an outboard motor, offering a great way to get out on the water. The boats are usually rented as part of a **fishing** session which includes a guide and one to four hours of fishing, for $20, though no equipment is supplied. The hotel has attracted a large number of Canadian tourists as a result of the lake's abundance of trout and largemouth bass, whilst most other guests are Cuban.

On the whole, the banks of the lake are difficult to access but they are well worth exploring, in places covered in thick forest, in others idyllic grassy hillocks peppered with palms. The best and easiest way around this, and the most rewarding way to spend your time here, is to take advantage of one of the four or five boat excursions offered by the hotel. Each costing between $15 and $30 for two people, they all last two or three hours and feature a **meal** at the *Río Negro Restaurant*, an excursion in itself and, if you're here for the day only, probably the best single option. It's $15 if you rent your own two-person motor boat, or $3, excluding the cost of the food, if you can join a group trip on one of the larger boats, usually taking place daily. The outdoor restaurant, perched on one of the forested slopes at the top of a stone staircase, is an assemblage of tiled platforms under matted *bohío* roofs and feels a little like an elaborate Tarzan camp. It's set up to cater specifically for excursion groups, so there's usually no choice: you take what they've got, which will invariably be roast pork or fish accompanied by vegetables, rice and *viandas*.

Of the other two worthwhile excursion destinations there is the **Casa del Campesino**, a *guajiro* family house in a clearing in the woods where you can sample and buy the locally grown coffee, honey or cigars manufactured here. There are various animals scuttling about and whilst clearly tourism has had its influence there's a genuine authenticity. Other than that you can visit a waterfall, a short walk from where the boat will leave you, with opportunities for bathing.

To get to the lake from Santa Clara, take a right turn at the crossroads in the centre of the small town of Manicaragua and take the left turn marked by the faded sign for the lake about 15km beyond this.

Prebooked excursions to the lake can be arranged through Rumbos in Santa Clara and Trinidad and are likely to cost upwards of $30 per person depending on demand.

Travel details

ASTRO AND INTERMUNICIPAL BUSES

Cienfuegos to: Havana (5 daily; 4hr 30min); Sancti Spíritus (3 weekly; 3hr 30min); Santa Clara (2 daily; 1hr 40min); Santiago de Cuba (3 weekly; 14hr); Trinidad (2 daily; 2hr).

Sancti Spíritus to: Camaguey (3 weekly; 3hr 30min); Cienfuegos (1 daily; 2hr 15min); Havana (3 weekly; 5hr); Santa Clara (2 daily; 1hr 45min); Trinidad (1 daily; 1hr 45min).

Santa Clara to: Caibarien (3 daily; 2hr); Cienfuegos (2 daily; 1hr 15min); Havana (2 daily; 4hr 30min); Sancti Spíritus (2 daily; 1hr 50min); Trinidad (1 daily; 3hr); Varadero (1 daily; 4hr); Remedios (4 daily; 1hr 40min).

Trinidad to: Cienfuegos (2 daily; 2hr); Havana (3 weekly; 5hr 30min); Sancti Spíritus (6 daily; 2hr); Santa Clara (1 daily; 3hr 20min).

VÍAZUL BUSES

Cienfuegos to: Havana (1 daily; 3hr 45min); Trinidad (1 daily; 1hr 30min).

Sancti Spíritus to: Havana (2 weekly; 6hr); Santa Clara (5 weekly; 1hr 30min); Trinidad (3 weekly; 1hr 30min); Varadero (3 weekly; 4hr 45min).

Santa Clara to: Havana (2 weekly; 4hr 30min); Sancti Spíritus (5 weekly; 1hr 30min); Trinidad (3 weekly; 3hr); Varadero (3 weekly; 3hr 15min).

Trinidad to: Havana (1 daily; 5hr 30min); Cienfuegos (1 daily; 1hr 30min); Sancti Spíritus (3 weekly; 1hr 30min); Santa Clara (3 weekly; 3hr); Varadero (3 weekly; 6hr 30min).

TRAINS

Cienfuegos to: Havana (3 weekly; 12hr); Sancti Spíritus (1 daily; 6hr); Santa Clara (2 daily; 2hr 30min).

Sancti Spíritus to: Cienfuegos (3 weekly; 6hr); Havana (3 weekly; 8hr); Santa Clara (3 weekly; 2hr).

Santa Clara to: Caibarien (1 daily; 2hr); Cienfuegos (2 daily; 2hr 30min); Havana (3 daily; 4hr); Sancti Spíritus (3 weekly; 2hr).

Chapter 5

Ciego de Ávila and Camagüey

S panning the trunk of the island some 450km east of Havana, the provinces of **Ciego de Ávila** and **Camagüey** form the farming heart of Cuba, their handsome lowland plains given over to swathes of sugarcane, fruit trees and cattle pasture. The westernmost of the two, sleepy **Ciego de Ávila** is sparsely populated, with only two medium-sized towns often bypassed by visitors keen to reach the province's star attraction: the ridge of breakaway cays stretching west from **Cayo Guillermo** to **Cayo Coco**, home to some of the country's most dazzling white-sand beaches and most flamboyant birdlife, with one of the Caribbean's biggest barrier reefs creating a superb diving zone offshore. Home to a hard-working agricultural community, the low-key provincial capital, **Ciego de Ávila**, doesn't particularly pander to tourists, though its couple of attractive buildings and unaffected air make it an agreeable place for a pit stop. Smaller but more appealing, picturesque **Morón**, further north, is quietly becoming established as a day-trip centre and can easily be incorporated into a visit to the cays – it's also a handy budget alternative to the luxury accommodation there. Also in the town's favour is its proximity to the nearby lakes, **Laguna de la Leche** and **Laguna Redonda**, the nucleus of a hunting and fishing centre popular with enthusiasts from Europe and Canada.

As most of the sights in the province are focused in the north, much of what remains is verdant farmland with comparatively little to offer the visitor. An exception are the gentle hills around Chambas and Florencia in the west, which offer up the chance to explore the surrounding landscape. Heading south, the countryside becomes a generous expanse of cane fields and citrus groves that continue unabated to Camagüey.

Livelier than its neighbour, **Camagüey** province has several sights worthy of a visit, including provincial capital **Camagüey city**, one of the original seven *villas* founded by Diego Velázquez in 1515. Nurtured by

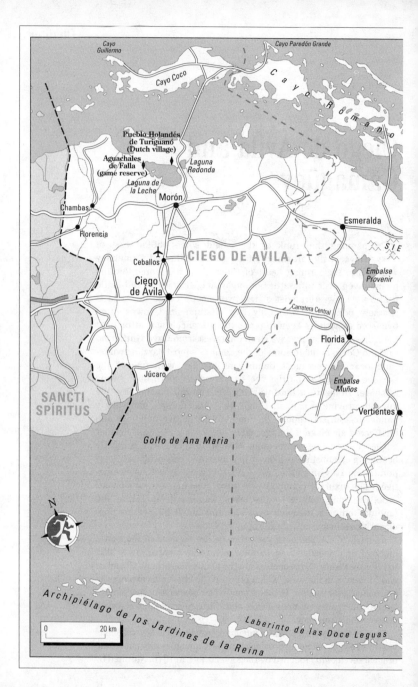

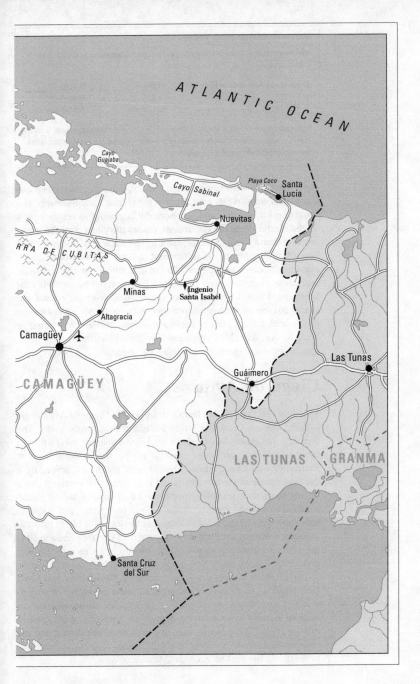

sugar wealth from the late sixteenth century, Camagüey has grown into a large and stalwart city with many of the architectural hallmarks of a Spanish colonial town, and is deservedly beginning to compete as a tourist centre. While the government pushes the plush northern beach resort of **Santa Lucía** as the province's chief attraction, the least spoilt beach in the region is just to the west at **Cayo Sabinal**, Camagüey's easternmost cay, which offers 33km of undisturbed beaches yet to be overrun by big hotels, their peace thus far preserved by a treacherous access road that deters the casual visitor. Away from the capital and tourist attractions, Camagüey province is the country's cattle-farming centre, and it's common to come across lone bullocks wandering or being herded skilfully by *vaqueros* (cowboys) beneath the palm trees, a sight perfectly in keeping with this rural region.

Ciego de Ávila

Spanning less than 100km from north to south, **Ciego de Ávila** is the slender waist of Cuba and forms the island's narrowest point. The territory was granted to Jacomée de Ávila, a Spanish conquistador, by the colonial municipal council in Puerto Príncipe – now Camagüey – as a hacienda in 1538. "Ciego" means flat savannah, a fair description of the low plains and marshland that make up much of this somnolent province, and even the provincial capital to the south, also called **Ciego de Ávila**, causes barely a ripple, its main attraction lying in its remote charm and the insight it offers into traditional provincial living. More attractive than Ciego de Ávila itself is the province's second largest town, **Morón**, with its eye-catching architecture and friendly ambience.

The province's main draw, the paradisial **Cayo Coco** and **Cayo Guillermo** lie to the north and offer the twin pleasures of superb beaches and virgin countryside – perfect for those seeking an escapist holiday in a Caribbean Shangri-la. With one of the longest offshore reefs in the world, the cays offer excellent **diving** and are themselves home to a variety of wildlife, prompting the government to designate the cays an ecological protected zone.

La Trocha Júcaro to Morón

Driving though the province on the road that runs from Júcaro to Morón via Ciego de Ávila, you'll see tumbledown stubby structures along the route which are the remains of a fortification line built under Spanish rule between April 1871 and 1873. Increasingly worried by growing rebellion by the Mambises, the rebel army fighting for independence, and their invasion plans to move west through the island, the Spanish General Blas Villate de la Hera, Count of Balmaseda, devised the idea of a row of fortifications 67km long to block the advance. The forts were made of concrete with solid walls of stone, brick and wood and built at intervals of 3–4km. Each was manned by a single sentry who had to enter by a removable wooden staircase which was then wheeled away, and each had two cannons. It was supposedly an impassable chain of defence, but the ineffectuality of the whole idea was immediately proved in 1874 when the Cuban General Manuel Suárez triumphantly breezed through with his cavalry. Most of the forts today are in a poor state of repair, though the odd one still gives an impression of their original appearance. Plans to restore them are under way.

South of the cays, on the mainland, the **Laguna de la Leche** and **Laguna la Redonda**, bordering the **Isla de Turiguanó** peninsula, are a popular spot for hunting and shooting. Those not bent on destruction can enjoy the natural charms of the area, as well as visiting the curious **Pueblo Holandes**, a reconstructed Dutch village set among swaying palms. In contrast, the caves and cool rivers surrounding the **Boquerón** campsite, on the western edge of the province near the town of Florencia, offer a refreshing and scenic natural alternative, while the far south of the province is given over to farming countryside flecked with one-street towns. The biggest draw of the area are the unspoilt **Jardines de la Reina** cays, 77km off the southern coast and reached from the undistinguished port of Júcaro, which offer several excellent dive sites and virgin cays to explore.

Aside from the blossoming tourist trade, the province makes its money from cattle farming, sugar production and, primarily, as the country's main fruit producer. The pineapple, in particular, is so vital to the economy that it has been used as Ciego de Ávila's town motif since the eighteenth century.

Ciego de Ávila city

CIEGO DE ÁVILA is like the suburb of a larger town. A friendly though pedestrian place set in the plains of the province, it is surprisingly young for a provincial capital, only established in 1849 – and its youth is its sole newsworthy feature. With no immediate tourist attractions, and precious little nightlife, Ciego de Ávila is often bypassed by visitors en route to the northern cays, but the town is not without charm and a stop-off here, on your way to the showier parts of the province, will reveal Cuba at its most modest and unaffected. Encounters with tourists are not everyday occurrences for the locals, but you are generally warmly, if curiously, received;

refreshingly, Ciego de Ávila has much less of a problem with hustlers and *jineteros* than bigger towns like Havana or Santiago de Cuba.

Arrival and information

Domestic **flights** from Havana arrive twice weekly at the Máximo Gómez airport at Ceballos 24km north of town; the waiting metered **taxis** will charge about $5 to take you to the centre, or you can share a *colectivo* (as a foreigner you may be charged a couple of dollars) or, except for when there are petrol shortages, take the **bus**. International flights also arrive from Europe and Canada, but these are almost exclusively for package-tour holidaymakers en route to the cays, in which case onward transport is included.

All **buses** pull into the terminal on the Carretera Central Extremo Oeste, about 3km from the town centre. You can share a horse-drawn carriage into the centre for a handful of pesos or catch a *bicitaxi* for a couple of dollars. The **train station** is six blocks from the centre on Avenida Iriondo; *bicitaxis* can ferry you into town if you're not up to walking.

The Islazul office on Joaquin Agüero no. 85 e/ Maceo y Honorato Castigo (Mon–Fri 8am–noon & 1.30–5pm; ☎33/2-53-14) gives out some tourist information but is essentially a hotel booking centre for Cubans. For information on trips to local sights, head instead to Rumbos, Edificio Girón 1 Micro A (☎33/2-87-38), or the Cubatur desk at the *Hotel Ciego de Ávila*, where you can also buy maps.

Accommodation

The best of the three hotels in Ciego de Ávila is the recently renovated *Hotel Sevilla*, well located in the centre. With little tourist trade to cater for, few *casas particulares* can afford the mandatory registration tax and subsequently operate outside the law. You can find out about them by asking around at the bus terminal, a stamping ground for touts, or chatting to one of the *bicitaxi* men who wait for fares around Parque Martí.

Ciego de Ávila, Carretera a Ceballos km 1.5 ☎33/2-80-13. Spartan 1960s hotel with friendly staff 2km from the centre of town, though *bicitaxis* wait outside to ferry you back and forth. It's best at weekends when the pool is lively with townsfolk, and boasts a passable restaurant, hairdresser, disco, bar and car rental offices. ③.

Santiago-Habana, Calle Honorato Castillo no. 73 esq. Carretera Central ☎33/2-57-03. Although conveniently located for access to the town centre, the *Santiago-Habana* is rather down-at-heel with clean but dingy rooms, some with balconies. The unappetizing restaurant and cafeteria are for guests only. ③.

Sevilla, Independencia no. 57 e/ Maceo y Honorato Castillo ☎33/2-56-03. This recently renovated, 25-room turn-of-the-century hotel is by far the best choice in town, with an airy reception full of squawking caged parakeets and budgerigars, a richly tiled balcony overlooking Parque Martí, and small, well-maintained rooms. The third floor plays host to the *Macarena Cabaret* (nightly 9pm–1am; $2), while the small ground-floor restaurant serves tasty pork and chicken dishes. ④.

The City

With residential streets lined with squat whitewashed modern houses just three blocks from the main square, much of Ciego de Ávila has a close-knit, suburban feel, and on a swift tour round you can see families on their verandas, old men in rocking chairs, mothers feeding babies and entrepreneurs selling corn fritters and fruit juice from peso stalls. The pace of Ávilean life flows slowly, the roads are dominated by bicycles rather than cars, while horse-drawn *coches* weighed down with passengers sweat and strain their way across town.

At the heart of town is the small but pleasant **Parque Martí**, fringed with sturdy trees and with a central 1920s bust of the ubiquitous Jose Martí in reflective pose, in which he appears more poet than warrior (see p.90). In the daytime older folk line the benches, shooting the breeze with the *bicitaxi* men while they wait to pick up fares or watching children playing marbles. The park is bordered by the town's four main streets, and any essentials you are likely to need can be found around here. On the park's south side stands the central **church**, a bland modern structure with a gigantic concrete saint tacked to the outside, next to which is the stately **town hall**. Far prettier is the **Teatro Principal** on the corner of Joaquín Agüero and Honorato del Castillo. It was built between 1924 and 1927, ordered and funded by Angela Hernández Vda de Jiménez, a wealthy society widow, in an attempt to make the town more cosmopolitan. Its decadently regal columned exterior, a riot of clashing Baroque, Renaissance and Imperial styles, gives way to a sumptuous interior, where Adonic marble figures nestle into alcoves and elaborate bronze chandeliers hang from an ornate stucco ceiling. There is no official guide, but you are free to enter and look around in the day-time. On the same side of the square, on Independencia, is the **Galería de Arte Provincial**, with a collection of glossy oil land-scapes painted by local artists.

Walking west on Independencia, past the general stores and peso ice-cream parlours, you reach the **Museo Provincial de Ciego de Ávila** (Tues–Sat 9am–noon & 1–6pm, Sun 8am–noon; $1) by the train tracks on Jose Antonio Echevarría. Housed in an old school building set around a tranquil courtyard, it boasts a sparse collection of pre-Columbian artefacts, a natural history room featuring skele-tons of marine life and some interesting relics from Ciego de Ávila's revolutionary heroes such as the seed necklaces the guerrillas would wear in the early days of the struggle to identify one another. Within view of here, parallel to the tracks on Chicho Valdes and Fernando Callejas, is the **farmer's market** (Tues–Sun 8am–5pm) with fresh produce and a vibrant atmosphere.

The town's **Parque Zoológico** (Sat & Sun 9am–4pm; free) is 3km west of Parque Martí at Independencia Final and Carretera Central. Set in a children's amusement park, it is home to a modest menagerie of local animals and features domestic horses, a reptile house and an aviary. Before the Special Period, the Ciego de Ávila zoo had one of Cuba's better collections of exotic animals, includ-ing a pair of elephants and some zebras, but the onset of shortages meant that many perished through starvation whilst others were rehoused in the Havana zoo.

Eating, drinking and entertainment

Though good state **restaurants** are thin on the ground in Ciego de Ávila, you can snack well at the peso stalls along and around Independencia. The *Hotel Sevilla* has a pleasant restaurant serving tasty chicken and pork, as well as a small **cabaret bar** on the third floor, but your best bet for a full meal is to ask a taxi driver for the whereabouts of the town *paladares*. In a small town like Ciego de Ávila these are unlicensed and therefore can't advertise; although as a visitor you will be charged in dollars, the bill will be considerably less than in the bigger towns.

Batanga Disco, Carretera a Ceballos km 1.5. Ciego de Ávila's teenage trendies and older swingers converge nightly on the *Hotel Ciego de Ávila* disco, where, despite the age differences, everyone has a laugh together dancing to salsa and Euro-pop in near-total darkness. Nightly 9.30pm–2.30am; $2.

Casa de la Trova, Libertad no. 130 e/ Maceo y Simon Reyes. The best bet for a night out – the bar sometimes serves locally brewed beer and always has good Cuban rum, while local music groups play traditional *boleros*, *son* and *guarachas* to an older crowd when there's a full house.

Colonial, Independencia no. 102 e/ Maceo y Simon Reyes. A Spanish theme restaurant hung with bullfight posters, with some outdoor seating in a dainty courtyard complete with a well. The menu includes pottage, *fabada* (bean stew) and tortilla, making a change from the usual Cuban fare. A meal with drinks costs about $10.

Doce Rumbos, Bajo Edificios Doce Plantas Honorato del Castillo e/ Libertad y Independencia. Café-bar serving pizza and fried chicken, with live music sometimes played on a dodgy Hammond organ. Daily 24hr.

Don Pepe, Independencia no. 303 e/ Maceo y Simon Reyes. An atmospheric little eatery serving good pork dishes with rice and peas and the unique Don Pepe cocktail, a house speciality made from rum and orange with a sprig of mint and a slice of orange, with live music and dancing most nights. Along the walls are caricatures of local characters, some of whom regularly prop up the bar.

Yisan, Carretera Central e/ Calle 8 y 13 de Marzo. Salty fried rice and pork chow mein, adapted to use local vegetables, are served in a pleasant restaurant decorated in faded chinoiserie. Closed Tues.

Listings

Airline The Cubana office is on Carretera Central ☎33/2-53-16.

Airport Information ☎33/3-25-25.

Banks You can change travellers' cheques and get cash advances on credit cards at Cadeca, Independencia no. 118 e/ Maceo y Simon Reyes (Mon–Sat 8.30am–6pm, Sun 8.30am–12.30pm), or the Banco Financiero Internacional Honorato del Castillo, at the edge of the square (Mon–Fri 8am–3pm, last working day of month 8am–noon).

Car rental Cubacar has a desk in the *Hotel Ciego de Ávila* (☎33/2-80-13) and at the *Hotel Morón* (☎33/5-39-01).

Medical Try the 24-hour surgery on República no. 52 esq. A. Delgado ☎33/2-26-11.

Pharmacy There is a 24-hour pharmacy at Independencia no. 163.

Post office You can buy peso stamps and send telegrams at the main 24-hour post office on Máximo Gómez esq. Carretera Central.

Taxis Turitaxis ☎33/2-29-97.

Telephones There's an international call centre opposite the square in the Doce Planta building, where you can buy phonecards (Mon–Thurs 7am–11pm, Fri & Sat 7am–3pm).

Morón and around

Lying 36km north of Ciego de Ávila on the road to the cays, surrounded by flat farming countryside replete with glistening palm trees, banks of sugarcane and citrus trees, picturesque **MORÓN** is fast becoming an essential stop on the tourist itinerary. Fanning out from a cosy downtown nucleus, its few gaily painted colonial buildings and proximity to Cayo Guillermo and Cayo Coco have recently made it quite popular with day-trippers from the cays, and it's certainly the best place to stay if you want to visit the cays but can't afford to stay in a luxury hotel there. For now, though, the area's main tourist revenue comes from hunting and fishing, as enthusiasts from around the world converge on **Laguna de la Leche** and **Laguna de Redonda** 15km north of town, where several species of fish and flocks of migrating ducks are sitting targets.

Morón makes a great base for exploring the sights en route to the cays, most of which can be squeezed into a day-trip. Chief among them is the peninsula **Isla de Turiguanó**, whose peak, Loma de Turiguanó, you can see throughout the flatlands, and the **Pueblo Holandés**, an incongruous mock Dutch village built in the 1960s. On the western edge of the province, between the two small farming villages of Florencia and Chambas, the **Boquerón campsite**, beside a clearwater river overhung with deep-grooved cliffs pocked with caves, is a rustic retreat that's a perfect alternative to the beaches.

Arrival and information

The daily **train** from Ciego de Ávila to Camagüey releases its passengers at the elegant station in the hub of the town; this also serves as the drop-off and collection point for *colectivos*, *camiones* and **buses**. Although all the sights and accommodation are within walking distance, the private **taxis** waiting under the trees in front of the station are useful for forays into the countryside. There is no tourist office in Morón, but the *Hotel Morón* has some **information** about local excursions and sells maps, as does the *Jardín del Apolo*. The main street, Martí, boasts most of the town's services, including the post office and telecommunications centre, next door to each other in the blue-and-white 1920s period building, *Colonial Española*.

Accommodation

Most visitors are en route to the cays and stay at the concrete-block *Hotel Morón* lurking on the edge of town. Due to basic shortages the peso hotel *Perla del Norte* on Avenida de Tarafa doesn't accept tourists, but the helpful staff can often steer you towards a good *casa particular*, of which there are several although few as yet registered. Otherwise your best choice is the small, amicable *La Casona de Morón*.

La Casona de Morón organizes boat and gun rental for Laguna de la Leche as well as tours around Laguna la Redonda (see p.306).

La Casona de Morón, Cristóbal Colón no. 41 ☎335/45-63. Pretty, friendly sunshine-yellow villa with bags more personality than the region's bigger hotels, hidden behind a mass of trees east of the train station. It has seven rooms, all with marble floors and high ceilings, and usually caters to the hunting and fishing crowd from the big lakes, offering organized tours and gun, boat and tackle rental. You can cook your spoils yourself on the open grill by the tiny swimming pool. Reservations are advisable. ④.

Juan C. Peréz Oquendo Belgica Silva, Castillo no. 189 e/ San José y Serafin Sánchez ☎335/38-23. Juan is one *casa particular* proprietor whose prices are not open to negotiation, probably because he has to meet high tax bills every month, but he offers comfortable, if dark, a/c rooms with hot and cold water. ②.

Morón, Ave. Tarafa s/n ☎335/30-76 or 39-01 to 39-04; fax 30-76. As the only big hotel in the region, the *Morón* draws the crowds of visitors heading to and from the cays, despite being rather run-down, ugly and anonymous. Rooms are spacious though colourless, but the hotel's saving grace is the swimming pool which is large, warm and clean. ③–④.

The Town

The first thing to strike you about clean, compact Morón is the shining **bronze cockerel**, symbolizing the town's turbulent Spanish heritage (see box below), perched at the foot of a clock tower on an oval green in front of the *Hotel Morón* just inside the town. The big bird sets the tone for this charming, slightly quirky town sliced in two by train tracks that aren't separated from the road by any barriers – it is quite usual to see trains impatiently honking horns as bicycles bearing two or three passengers lazily roll over the rails – and slice through the town's main street, **Martí** (its southern reaches also known as Avenida Tarafa). At the mouth of the tracks is the **train station** with elegant archways and fine wrought-iron awnings. Built in the 1920s, it remains largely unchanged and inside you can still buy tickets at original ticket booths and check destinations on a hand-painted blackboard, while high above the rows of worn wooden benches and the original stained-glass *vitrales* birds nest under the eaves.

The cock of Morón

Named by Spanish settlers after their home town, Morón de la Frontera in Andalucía, the Cuban town has also appropriated one of its founders' legends. In the sixteenth century, the townsfolk of Spanish Morón found themselves the victims of a corrupt judiciary which continually levied high taxes and appropriated their land without explanation. Having suffered these oppressive conditions for several years, the collected townsfolk set upon and expelled the main offender, an official nicknamed "the cock of Morón". The gamble paid off, as the remaining officials, fearing a more serious rebellion, promptly lessened the taxes. The incident was quickly immortalized in an Andalucían ballad which proclaimed that "the cock of the walk has been left plucked and crowing", a saying still used throughout Cuba today to mean that somebody has had their plans scuppered, and has ensured Morón's slim slice of fame in the annals of Cuban history. The first rooster monument was erected in the 1950s, under Batista's rule, but was torn down after the revolution by officials who saw it as a symbol of the previous regime. Fond of their town mascot, locals complained and in 1981 the present bronze statue was erected at the foot of the clock tower. With a stroke of genius the clock tower was fitted with a crackling amplifier, enabling everyone to hear the mechanical cock manfully crowing twice daily at 6am and 6pm.

Ciego de Ávila

From the station, a five-minute walk along Martí will take you to the **Museo Municipal**, Martí no. 374 (Tues–Sat 9am–5pm, Sun 9am–noon; $1), newly opened in one of the town's eye-catching colonial buildings fronted by simple columns and wide steps. It houses an assortment of small pre-Columbian Cuban artefacts, mainly fragments of clay bowls and shards of bone necklace. By far the most impressive exhibit is the *Idolillo de Barro*, a clay idol shaped into a fierce snarling head, found outside the city in 1947. Further north along Martí is the **Galería del Arte** at no. 151 (Tues–Sat 8am–noon & 1–5.30pm, Sun 8am–noon), exhibiting and selling an array of locally painted landscapes, colourful abstracts, lovingly executed sculptures of female nudes and mawkish religious figures. If you're planning to buy a sculpture, this is the place to do it as they're a lot cheaper here than at the resorts.

Eating, drinking and entertainment

Morón is a town of modest means where the locals' idea of a good night's entertainment is to cluster round a neighbour's television, or even peer through their window, to catch up with the latest soap opera. Your tame options are to enjoy a gentle promenade around the star-lit streets or, if you are driving, heading out early evening to one of the lakeside restaurants (see pp.305–6).

Alondra, Martí no. 298, e/ Serafin Sánchez y Callejas. Slick, shiny glass and tile ice-cream parlour, charging around $1.50 for a very kitsch candy-coated sundae complete with spangly cocktail stick. Daily 10am–10pm.

Casa de la Trova, Libertad e/ Narciso López y Martí. A small but pleasantly unassuming local watering hole where the town's minstrels serenade drinkers with traditional *guajiras* and *son* amid basic decor that's remained unchanged for years. An authentic Cuban experience. Closed Mon.

Dona Neli, Serafin Sánchez no. 86 e/ Narciso López y Martí. A bakery serving an excellent selection of fresh breads, flaky pastries and cakes elaborately coated in meringue. Arrive early in the morning to avoid being stuck with the bullet-like bread rolls. Daily 8am–8pm.

Florida, in front of Parque Martí. A peso restaurant where the usual Cuban cuisine is served slowly.

Jardín del Apolo, Martí e/ Carlos Manuel de Céspedes y Resedad. Fried chicken and beer served in a courtyard to the accompaniment of charmless soft rock music. You can also buy maps of the city. Open 24hr.

Around Morón

Set in lush countryside dappled by lakes and low hills, the area around Morón offers a welcome contrast to the unrelentingly flat land of the south, and holds a few surprises well worth venturing beyond the town limits to explore. Ten kilometres north of town, the large **Laguna de la Leche** is fringed by reeds and woodland that hide the **Aguachales de Falla** game reserve, while 7km further northeast the tranquil **Laguna la Redonda** is an idyllic spot for drifting about in a boat. Together the lakes form a wide trench creating the peninsula **La Isla de Turiguanó**, home to the mock-Dutch village **Pueblo Holandés**, its faux-timbered, red-roofed houses anomalous beneath tropical palms. Towards the east, rising from the plains like the hump of a tortoise, is the gently rounded 364-metre **Cunagua Hill**, its dense tangle of woodland home to bright parakeets and parrots, and a favourite spot for day-trekkers and birdwatchers. To the west of the province, straddled by the tiny villages of Chambas and Florencia, are the **Boquerón caves** and **campsite**, its riding, river swimming and rock climbing opportunities an irresistible draw for nature enthusiasts.

Laguna de la Leche

With a circumference of 66km, **Laguna de la Leche**, or Milk Lake, 10km north of Morón, is the largest lake in Cuba and, decked out with palm trees and a pint-sized lighthouse, looks like a tiny seafront. The opacity comes from gypsum and limestone deposits beneath the surface but despite the evocative name it looks nothing like Cleopatra's bath: rather, the lake fans out from a cloudy centre to disperse into smudgy pools of green and blue around the edges. Despite its murky appearance there are always a few local children splashing in the shallows and anglers regularly plumb its depths for the wealth of bass, tilapia and carp within. The wooded north and west sides of the lake, soupy with rushes and overhung branches, are great for exploring but accessible only by boat. Boat rental should be pre-arranged through *La Casona de Morón* in Morón (☎335/45-63; see p.302). This peaceful spot is only mildly disturbed by the distant reports issuing from the guns of eager sportsmen at the **Aguachales de Falla hunting reserve** on the west side of the lake as they fire at the hapless ducks, white-crowned pigeons and doves that swoop through the area. The government's promotion of blood sports here may seem at odds with the ecotourism touted on the northern cays just a few kilometres north (see p.307), but firearms are entrenched in Cuban culture and familiarity with them is seen as an essential skill in a country still intermittently defending its sovereignty. As the popular motto goes, "Every Cuban should know how to shoot and shoot well."

Set back slightly from the southern edge of the lake is *La Cueva de la Laguna de la Leche* (daily 8am–7pm), an open-air bar and restaurant shaded with palms which serves fresh catches from the water. Round the back of the bar is a gloomy manmade cave with a dimly lit dancefloor where, on Fridays and Saturdays (9am–2am), there's a free cabaret featuring scantily clad women lip-synching and dancing as professionally as their elaborate fruit turbans will allow.

No buses go to the lake, but a private taxi from Morón should cost no more than $5. If driving, take Martí north out of town, hang a left and head for the cays until the signposted turning.

Ciego de Ávila

If you are not driving, the only way to get around Morón is to negotiate a day rate with one of the Morónero taxi drivers (see p.302). The bigger your group the more they'll want to charge you, but for two people you should count on around $15.

Laguna la Redonda

The smaller of the region's two lakes, measuring only 3km at its widest point, **Laguna la Redonda** or Circle Lake is 7km further north, reached by a canalside turning off the main road to the cays. Quieter and altogether more intimate, it's perfect for an idle afternoon's boating, fishing for trout or just drifting over to the uncharted territory on the far side of the lake and wandering through the bush of undergrowth. The serene *La Redonda* **restaurant** (9am–8pm) which overhangs the lake serves standard *comida criolla* and rents out a boat ($12 each for a maximum of 6 people), while *San Fernando*, Carretera Ciego de Ávila Rotonda, is a pleasant villa off the lakeside road, converted into an upmarket restaurant serving good Cuban cuisine and dire spaghetti for around $7 to $10 a head. It has an attractive outside bar which should be avoided on Saturday nights when a tawdry cabaret show takes over. Tours to the lake and boat rental are organized by *La Casona de Morón* in Morón (☎335/45-63; see p.302).

Pueblo Holandés de Turiguanó

Sitting in the middle of a frill of palms and purple bougainvillea, 6km north of the Laguna la Redonda and 26km from Morón, at the foot of the causeway to the cays, the Dutch-timbered houses of the **Pueblo Holandés de Turiguanó** are nothing if not anomalous. Before the revolution, this was a US-owned cattle farm, virtually inaccessible because of widespread marshland; in the early 1960s, with the Americans fled, the land was expropriated and drained and the present mock-European village built to house the Cuban cattle hands who had previously lived here under poor conditions. The Dutch styling was the whim of Celia Sánchez, a core revolutionary, secretary and special friend of Fidel Castro, who had developed a penchant for Dutch architecture while spending time in Holland in the 1950s. Still serving its original function, the village raises Santa Gertrudis cattle, one of the island's best breeds, much of whose meat goes to feed the tourists in the cays. Ducks waddle around the village green and across the neat lawns that separate the whitewashed gabled houses. The red-tiled roofs are actually painted corrugated iron, but this discovery doesn't really spoil the illusion. The hamlet has now been twinned with the Dutch and plans are afoot to renovate some of the shabbier houses and open a Casa de Cultura telling the history of the area. No buses come here but a taxi from Morón will cost between $5 and $8.

Florencia and around

The undulating terrain around the tiny towns of **Florencia** and **Chambas**, 30km west of Morón, is prime farming country, pocketed with dazzling sugar fields, corrals of slow-moving cattle and tobacco meadows. Dotted around the area are several sugar mills and villages, which, despite their unassuming appearance as clusters of concrete houses, bear witness to the changes that revolution brought to rural Cuba. Before 1959 these areas were crippled by grinding poverty, illiteracy, unemployment and inadequate health care. Work in the privately owned fields was seasonal and there was no welfare structure to tide people over from one year to the next.

The glorious countryside can be explored on a guided **horse trek**, run daily by Rumbos in Ciego de Ávila (☎33/2-87-38), through the coconut groves and banana fields. The guide takes you past local farms on to a rodeo show where local cowboys wow the crowd with demonstrations of their animal-handling prowess before the day finally culminates in a pig roast. During the **tobacco** harvest the tour includes a trip, by bus, to a tobacco-curing house near Florencia.

In this area, keep a look out for the majestic ceiba tree, believed in Santería, the Afro-Cuban religion, to have magical powers.

There's no better place to stay in the area than the superb **Campismo Boquerón** (bookings through Islazul on ☎33/2-53-14; ②), 5km west of Florencia. Tucked away down a series of twisted lanes which at times becomes waterlogged dirt tracks, it's not the easiest place to reach independently, but is really worth the hassle. Veiled behind the folds of the Jatibonico Sierra hills, the rugged tail of the Sierra de Meneses chain stealing into the province from Sancti Spíritus, and framed by a halo of royal palms, the campsite occupies a hidden paradise of banana groves, fruit trees and flitting hummingbirds. It offers an area to pitch tents, as well as triangular **huts**, each lined with four clean but basic single bunks for which you should take your own sheets. The Jatibonico river twists through the hills and makes an excellent spot for shady **swimming**, while a phalanx of skinny horses wait to take you **cross-country trekking**, and the cavernous crags jutting out above the site are ripe for **mountaineering**. The campsite promises **food**, but you're better off taking your own provisions and cooking on the communal barbecue. An alternative place to stay if you are touring around the area is *Agua Azul*, Carretera Circuito Norte, Santa Clarita Chambas (☎6/7-32-36; ①), a modest peso hotel with worn but serviceable rooms and a lobby bar set amid mango and lime trees.

Trips to the area can be arranged through Islazul in Ciego de Ávila (☎33/2-53-14), while Chambas and Florencia are served by a daily **train** from Morón.

The northern cays

Christened "The King's Garden" by Diego Velázquez in 1514 in honour of King Ferdinand of Spain, the **northern cays**, lying 30km off Ciego de Ávila's coast and hemmed in by 400km of coral reef, are indisputably the dazzling jewels in the province's crown – a rich tangle of mangroves, mahogany trees and lagoons iced by sugar sands and thick with pink flamingoes, and a top **diving** location with an infrastructure to match.

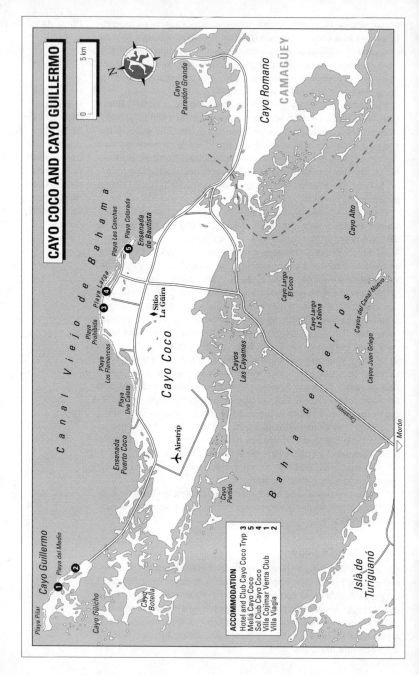

CAYO COCO AND CAYO GUILLERMO

0 5 km

Cayo Guillermo
Playa Pilar
Playa del Medio
Cayo Güicho
Cayo Botella

C a n a l   V i e j o   d e   B a h a m a

Cayo Paredón Grande

Cayo Romano

CAMAGÜEY

Ensenada Puerto Coco

Playa Prohibida
Playa Los Flamencos
Playa Uva Caleta
Playa Larga
Playa Las Conchas
Playa Colorada
Ensenada de Bautista

✈ Airstrip

Cayo Coco

Sitio La Güira

Cayo Partido

Cayos Las Cayanas

B a h í a   d e   P e r r o s

Cayo Largo El Coco
Cayo Largo La Salina
Cayos del Canal Nuevo
Cayos Juan Griego

Cayo Alto

Causeway

Morón

Islá de Turiguanó

ACCOMMODATION
Hotel and Club Cayo Coco Tryp 3
Meliá Cayo Coco 5
Sol Club Cayo Coco 4
Villa Cojímar Venta Club 1
Villa Viagia 2

Despite being lauded so highly in the sixteenth century, the numerous islets spanning the coastline from Ciego de Ávila to Camagüey remained uninhabited and relatively unexplored until as recently as the late 1980s, visited only by colonial-era pirates and corsairs seeking a bolthole to stash their spoils; Ernest Hemingway, who sailed around them in the 1930s and 40s; and former dictator Fulgencio Batista, who had a secret hideaway on tiny Cayo Media Luna, a mere pinprick on the map and now deserted.

Their exclusivity was only eased in 1988 by the construction of a 29-kilometre stone **causeway** or *pedraplén* across the Bahía de los Perros, connecting the Isla de Turiguanó peninsula to Cayo Coco. The narrow road, barely raised above water-level and offering untrammelled views over the tranquil Caribbean Sea, was built by Cuban workmen and panegyrized in several state publications as a revolutionary triumph over the hardships of the Special Period, exemplary of the Cuban people's selfless devotion to the common good. The delighted state began to create a tourist haven destined to be as sumptuous as Varadero (p.180), and so far two of the islands – **Cayo Coco**, very popular with European holidaymakers (particularly Italians), and smaller **Cayo Guillermo** – have been primed for luxury tourism, with all-inclusive hotels sprouting up along their northern shores. Ironically, Cubans are today banned from visiting the cays, except on allocated holidays and honeymoons, casual access being prohibited by the state in a bid to prevent an influx of *jineteros*. The building of the causeway has also had a negative impact on the cays themselves, disrupting the natural flow of water and impoverishing conditions for local wildlife.

The two cays are connected by a causeway, with an offshoot running to the breakaway **Cayo Paredón Grande** in the east, uninhabited but another option for beaches should you exhaust those on the main cays.

Arrival, information and getting around

Because of the ban on Cubans, getting to the cays without the umbrella of a tour guide, state taxi or rental car can be a bit of a mission. Don't try to go in a private taxi, as your driver will just have monumental hassle with the authorities before being routed back home, leaving you dumped at the barrier. One or two independent travellers generally sneak onto one of the worker buses that leave from the bronze cockerel in Morón at 7am, but many more are turned away. Alternatively, you can hitch a lift with the **tour bus** that leaves from the *Hotel Morón* (see p.303) if there's space.

All **road traffic** enters the cays along the causeway – where passports are checked and rental cars looked over to make sure they're not harbouring nationals – and then takes the fork either for Coco or Guillermo. **Flights** from Havana arrive three times weekly at the airstrip on the west of Cayo Coco, from where hotel representatives whisk passengers off to their accommodation. Tour buses drop off at the hotels.

BOAT TRIPS, DIVING AND EXCURSIONS

Whilst many head to the cays to bask in the Caribbean sun, there's a wide variety for those who are up for more energetic pastimes. Diving is a prime activity as is exploring on foot or on horseback through the lush interior that spreads south through Cayo Coco.

DIVING

Encrusted in the waters of the Atlantic Ocean is one of the world's longest coral reefs, with shoals of angelfish, nurse sharks and surgeonfish weaving through forests of colourful sponges and alarmingly large barracudas bucking below the waterline. There are at least five excellent **dive sites** spread between Cayo Paredón and Cayo La Jaula, where you can reach depths of 35m, and all the hotels organize dive trips and give free induction classes to guests, while the international Italian/Cuban-run **diving school**, Coco Diving Centre (☎33/30-13-23), on the **Marina Aguas Tranquilas** at the edge of Playa Colorada on Cayo Coco's northeastern peninsula, offers dives for $35, including all equipment, transport to the dive site and a free initiation course. It also offers **"seafari"** trips around the coast in a pleasure yacht or catamaran for off-shore swimming and snorkelling.

FISHING AND BOAT TRIPS

The marina also runs **fishing expeditions** around Cayo Media Luna, where the plentiful billfish, snapper and bass make rich pickings. The ecotourism group Ecotur Eza, at the *Hotel and Club Cayo Coco Tryp* (see opposite), offers a boat tour to see the coral reefs and along the coast (3–4hr; $20–30 inclusive of food and drink).

EXCURSIONS

Though you can strike off on your own – ask at the hotels' public relations desks about hiring horses or arranging horse-drawn carriage tours – **Rumbos** (information on ☎33/3-87-38 or from the hotels) organizes **horse-treks** to various locations throughout the cays and day-trips to Morón.

Cubatur (☎7/33-41-35) offers day-trips from Havana to Cayo Coco for $104, departing Havana at 5.30am and Cayo Coco at 4.30pm, including flight and all-inclusive entrance to the Sol Club Cayo Coco Hotel. It also organizes longer stays.

Once on the cays, the best way to **get around** is by moped. Transautos rents mopeds, jeeps and sand buggies from its office at the *Sol Club Cayo Coco*. **Maps** of the cays are available from all the hotels and give a good impression of the islands but are distinctly lacking in specifics. There's no tourist office, but each hotel has a public relations officer who can provide general information.

Cayo Coco

With 22km of creamy white sands and cerulean waters, **Cayo Coco** easily fulfils its tourist blurb claim of offering a holiday in paradise. The islet is 32km wide from east to west, with a hill like a camel's hump rising from the middle, with the best beaches clustered on the north coast, dominated by the all-inclusive hotels (all built since 1992) whose tendrils are gradually spreading along the rest of the northern coastline. **Playa Colorada** and **Playa Larga** are boisterous

beaches with activities laid on by the hotels, but if you'd rather have
peace and quiet than volleyball and beach aerobics, you'll still find a
few pockets of tranquillity, like **Playa Los Flamencos**. Away from
the beach strip, dirt roads threaded through the island – perfect for
mopeds – allow easy access into the lush wooded interior where hidden delights include hummingbirds, pelicans, some gorgeous
lagoons and **Sitio La Güira**, a recreation of an old Cuban peasant village. Heading toward the extreme south, the land becomes marshier
but still explorable on foot and is a haven for herons and the white
ibis or *coco* that gives the cay its name. A number of animals live here
too, and it's not uncommon to see wild boars scooting out of the
undergrowth and wild bulls lumbering across the road. Also keep an
eye out for the colony of **iguanas** that originally floated here on
coconut husks from other islands.

Accommodation

With no towns or villages to offer *casas particulares*, accommodation
on Cayo Coco is almost totally limited to a few plush **all-inclusives**
grouped together on the main beach strips. The only alternative is right
at the other end of the scale, bedding down at the **beach hut** on Playa
Los Flamencos (ask at the *Flamenco* bar). Otherwise your best bet, if
your budget's not up to the luxury hotels, is to head back to Morón and
seek out the cheaper options there (see p.302).

Hotel and Club Cayo Coco Tryp, Playa Larga ☎33/30-13-11; fax 30-13-86.
The oldest and best hotel on the strip is actually two hotels combined into
one, built to look like a colonial village with accommodation in two-storey
cobalt-blue and yellow buildings shaded by healthy palms. Although reminiscent of a theme park, and equipped with all the usual mod cons including
baby club, nursery and beach activities, it feels more Cuban than the other
four-stars on the strip. ⑤–⑦.

Meliá Cayo Coco, Playa Colorada ☎33/30-12-80; fax 30-12-95. Opulent hotel
with deluxe chalet-style accommodation, a large pool, children's area and a full
range of activities, including sauna, gym and watersports. The theme nights
and organized games make it feel like a holiday camp, albeit a very upmarket
one. ⑦.

Sol Club Cayo Coco, Playa Colorada ☎33/30-12-80; fax 30-12-85. Palatial
but anonymous glass-fronted hotel with three international-quality restaurants, sauna, gym, mini-club for kids and a multitude of sports, including free
preliminary dive classes in the pool. ⑦.

The beaches

The big three beaches, home to the all-inclusives, hog the narrow
easternmost peninsula jutting out of the cay's north coast. Spanning
the tip and home to the *Sol Club Cayo Coco*, **Playa Colorada**,
though filled with crowds of beach chairs, is exceptionally picturesque, with fine sand and calm shallow waters. It's a good place
for watersports, busy with cruising **catamarans and pedalos** – a $50
all-inclusive day-pass, which includes all meals and drinks, will let

---

Cock fighting

Cock fighting has been the sport of Cuban farmers since the eighteenth
century, with sizeable sums of money changing hands on bets, and thefts
of prized specimens and allegations of rooster nobbling common crimes.
Since the ban on gambling introduced by the revolution, the practice has
been pushed underground although the sport itself is still legal. Nowadays
cock fighting is a clandestine affair, taking place on smallholdings deep in
the country at the break of dawn when the fowl are in vicious ill-humour
and at their fighting best. Unlike the shows laid on for tourists, where the
cocks are eventually separated, the spurred cocks here will slug it out to
the death. There is a particular breed of rooster indigenous to Cuba which
exercises considerable cunning in defeating its opponent, parrying attacks
and throwing false moves, and the bloodlines of these birds are protected
and nurtured as carefully as those of any racehorse.

---

you join in. Three kilometres west, **Playa Larga** and **Playa Las
Conchas**, divided by name only, are a continuous strip of pure sand
beach. With shallow crystal waters lapping silvery beaches, they are
arguably the best beaches on the island, although very crowded during the organized activities laid on by the *Hotel and Club Cayo Coco
Tryp*. Non-guests are welcome to use the beaches during the day –
access is through the hotel – though to use any facilities you must
pay $40 for an all-inclusive day-pass; access is restricted at night.

For solitude, head west along the main dirt road to **Playa Los
Flamencos**, demarcated by a stout stucco flamingo, which has 3km
of clean golden sands and clear waters where tangerine-coloured
starfish float through the shallows and there is good **snorkelling** out
to sea. It gets busy in the daytime but wandering down the beach
away from the lively, expensive **bar** should guarantee some privacy.
For a night beneath the stars, a few **beach shacks** (ask at the bar; ③)
offer basic shelter, though you should watch out for the mosquitoes.

Finally, hidden behind a sand dune 1km east off the same road is
Playa Prohibida. Although parts of the beach are narrower than Los
Flamencos and strewn with seaweed, a high dune seeded with wild
grasses makes a pleasing backdrop to this often deserted beach.
There's a tiny **beach bar** serving tasty barbecue chicken, fish and
soft drinks.

Sitio La Güira

In the centre of the cay, 6km from the north coast, is **Sitio La Güira**,
a mocked-up turn-of-the-century peasant community built in 1994 to
give some idea of traditional Cuban farming culture to visitors who
might not venture further than the beach. Though it's something of
a novelty theme park, a number of interesting exhibits rescues it
from tackiness, and if you don't feel like venturing to Morón for some
more authentic sights this is a reasonable substitute. The main features are a typical country cottage made entirely from palms with a
thatched roof, a ranch where charcoal is made, and a *bohío*, a trian-

gular palm hut in which tobacco leaves are dried; the star attraction, however, is a **cock fighting pit** where virile Cuban roosters goad one another in a flurry of iridescent feathers. If you want to see the fights, you'll need to go on, or at least coincide with, a tour (times are available from any of the hotels), but otherwise it's more peaceful to make your own way round.

Surrounded by lush greenery, Sitio La Güira also offers **walking and riding tours** ($5 an hour for the horse; rates for a guide are negotiable) through the mangrove outback filled with woodpeckers and nightingales and onto the lakes in the interior which are nesting sites for waterfowl and wild ducks. The ranch also has a **restaurant** (see below).

Eating, drinking and entertainment
With all food and drinks included in your hotel bill you probably won't need to look elsewhere for meals if you're staying on the cays, although there are a few places that cater for day-trippers. If you've paid for a day pass at one of the hotels, you can dine there and go on to the hotel disco afterwards. *Hotel Sol Club Cayo Coco* has a central disco with live salsa and tacky floorshows, but the one at *Hotel and Club Cayo Coco Tryp* is better, with a raucous palmwood bar overlooking the sea at the end of a pier, and a house DJ alternating *salsa* with Europop.

Cueva del Jabalí This natural cave 5km inland from the hotel strip takes its name from the formerly resident wild boar evicted to make way for the restaurant, which serves moderately priced tasty roast pork and grilled meats. It's best during the day when you can peacefully admire the surrounding countryside, but more animated in the evening with a glittery, loud cabaret. Tues–Sat noon–midnight.

Playa Flamenco Bar A friendly, though pricey, beach-bar with ample trestle tables under a palm wattle roof, serving Cuban cuisine and occasionally lobster to the strains of a Mariachi band.

Playa Prohibida Bar A tiny beach bar serving tasty barbecued chicken and fish.

Sitio la Güira A ranch restaurant in the midst of the theme park, specializing in *escabeche* – meats and fish prepared in a pickle made from oil, vinegar, peppercorn and herbs – and holding a *Guateque*, "a farm party with animation activities and lessons on typical dances". Daily 9am–10pm.

Cayo Paredón Grande
Connected to Cayo Coco by a small causeway starting around 6km west of Playa Colorada, **Cayo Paredón Grande** is a thumbnail of a cay 12km northeast. With a couple of clean, pleasant beaches, it makes an ideal retreat if you can get there, particularly as the view over the sea as you cross the causeway is glorious. The islet's focal point is the elegant nineteenth-century **lighthouse** (no entry) on the rocky headland of the northern tip, built by Chinese immigrant workers to guide ships through the coral-filled waters. If spending a day on the island, take

provisions as there are no facilities. The causeway leads through the uninhabited **Cayo Romano**, which is technically in Camagüey province though usually treated as an extension of the major cays.

Cayo Guillermo

Bordered by pearl-white sand melting into opal waters, **Cayo Guillermo**, the somnambulant cay west of Cayo Coco, to which it's joined by a fifteen-kilometre causeway, is a quieter, more serene retreat than its neighbour, a place to fish, dive and simply relax. It is here that the cays' colony of twelve thousand **flamingos** (celebrated in all Cuban tourist literature) gathers, and although they are wary of the noise of passing traffic, as you cross the causeway you can glimpse them swaying in the shallows and feeding on the sand banks. As the presence of the birds testifies, there is a wealth of fish, notably marlin, in the waters and the cay's marina offers a range of deep-sea fishing expeditions.

At only thirteen square kilometres the cay is tiny, but its 4km of deserted beaches seem infinite. It's quite a trek from the mainland if you are not staying overnight, but arriving early and spending a day lounging on the heavenly beaches and exploring the beautiful off-shore coral reef definitely merits the effort.

All the hotels and beaches are strung along the north coast, apart from gorgeous **Playa Pilar** on the western tip of the cay, named after Ernest Hemingway's yacht *The Pilar*, and the author's favourite

---

Ernest Hemingway's hunt for submarines

Ernest Hemingway's affection for Cuba sprang from his love of fishing, and numerous photographs of him brandishing dripping marlin and swordfish testify to his success around the clear waters of the northern cays. He came to know the waters well and when in 1942 the United States entered World War II Hemingway, already well-versed in war technique, having fought in World War I and the Spanish Civil War, was more than ready to do his bit. With the full support of the then US ambassador to Cuba, Ambassador Spruille Braden, he began to spy on Nazi sympathizers living in Cuba, calling his organization – colleagues from the Spanish Civil War and staff from the US Embassy – the "Crook Factory". He gathered enough information to proceed to the next stage of his war effort, which was having his twelve-metre fishing boat *The Pilar* commissioned and equipped by the Chief of Naval Intelligence for Central America as a kind of Q-ship (an armed and disguised merchant ship used as a decoy or to destroy submarines); the crew, all men devoted to Hemingway, were even armed with grenades for lobbing down the periscope towers. His search-and-destroy mission for Nazi submarines off the cays continued until 1944 and he was commended by the ambassador, although according to some critics, notably his then wife Martha Gellhorn, it was mainly a ruse for Hemingway to obtain rationed petrol for his fishing trips. Although he never engaged in combat with submarines, Hemingway's boy's-own fantasies found their way into print in the novel *Islands in the Stream*, where the protagonist did just that.

---

hideaway in Cuba. Every year as the swordfish swarmed to cross the coral reef in the gulf stream Hemingway would set sail from Cojímar to pursue them off the coasts of Cayo Guillermo. So enchanted was he by the cay that he immortalized it in his novel *Islands in the Stream* in which his protagonist Thomas Hudson eulogizes, "See how green she is and full of promise?" (see box opposite). With limpid clear shallows and squeaky-clean beaches, Playa Pilar is without doubt the top beach choice on Guillermo if not in the entire cays, with no facilities other than a small beach bar.

The two other main beaches on Guillermo are **Playa El Medio** and **Playa El Paso** on the north coast, serving the *Villa Viagía* and *Villa Cojímar* respectively. Popular with package-tour holidaymakers, both are suitably idyllic with shallow swimming areas and lengthy beaches, though El Medio also has towering sand dunes celebrated as the highest in the Caribbean, and in low tides sandbars allow you to wade out to sea.

Practicalities

Accommodation on Cayo Guillermo is restricted to two slick all-inclusives largely patronized by Italians. Shamelessly milking the Hemingway connection, *Riu Villa Viagía*, which backs onto Playa El Medio (☎33/30-17-60, fax 30-17-48; ⑧), is named after the author's Havana farm. It's a good-quality all-inclusive with sports, tennis courts, two restaurants, a snack bar, Transauto and Havanauto desks, and pleasant, spacious rooms, some with a sea view. *Villa Cojímar Venta Club* on Playa El Medio (☎03/10-21; ⑨) also offers all the four-star services, with snazzy rooms, a large free-form pool, two restaurants, ample sports facilities and car rental services. Day-passes for either (inclusive of meals and drinks) will set you back $40, but you can use *Riu Villa Viagía*'s stretch of beach for free. Outside of the hotel restaurants you are limited to a floating bar and a beach restaurant on Playa Pilar, a simple wooden lean-to where you can eat excellent but pricey barbecued fish and lobster as skinny cats twirl around your ankles. Opening times fluctuate depending on the whims of the chef but you are usually guaranteed service around lunchtime. The Marina Cayo Guillermo, at the entrance to the cay near the *Villa Cojímar Venta Club*, runs deep-sea fishing excursions, dive trips to the best sites around Cayo Media Luna, the tiny crescent cay off Playa Pilar, and yacht "seafaris" with time set aside for off-shore swimming and snorkelling.

Moped and jeep rental is available from Transautos and Havanautos, both based at Hotel Riu Villa Viagía.

Southern Ciego de Ávila

Back on the mainland, the area below Ciego de Ávila is made up of agricultural farming areas and small one-street towns like **Venezuela** and **Silveira**, each a clutch of humble concrete houses (built since the revolution to house workers who previously lived in shacks), a central *bodega* and a doctor. Even in the smallest community, however, you can see electricity lines, one of the achievements of the revolution, and despite severe shortages rural households have electricity for at least part of the day.

As you journey south on the road to the coast you will pass the remnants of an old Spanish garrison which at one time divided the province from north to south. The countryside is snaked with narrow rail tracks which indicate the extensive infrastructure that serves the sugar industry, conveying the crop from the fields to the towns and ports; part of the railways are still in use, with working stations at Morón and Ciego de Ávila.

Thirty-two kilometres south of Ciego de Ávila is the barren fishing village of **JÚCARO**, a miserable collection of wooden shacks and half-finished cement constructions set around a derelict-looking Parque Martí, a malodorous fishing port and a fly-blown soft-drinks stand. There's absolutely no reason to venture down here, unless you plan to visit the tiny virgin cays of the **Archipiélago de los Jardines de la Reina**, which boast seven fantastic **dive sites** and endless **fishing** possibilities. Although most of the islets are scrubby and piled with driftwood, **Cayo Las Caguamas**, 120km offshore from Júcaro, has a reasonable beach where members of the fearless iguana community will eat from your hand. Staying until nightfall will reward you with the sight of **turtles** venturing out onto the sand in the moonlight. Mercifully, if you want to sleep over, you don't have to bed down in town; instead you can be ferried from Júcaro port to *La Tortuga* (no phone; ④), an air-conditioned eight-berth floating hotel moored offshore. Information on the hotel and diving opportunities is available from **Júcaro Marina**, whose office is on the seafront opposite the square (☎33/9-81-26), or from Franco at the *Hotel Morón* in Morón (☎335/39-01).

See p.330 for more on the Archipiélago de los Jardines de la Reina.

Camagüey

Sandwiched between Ciego de Ávila to the west and Las Tunas to the east, **Camagüey** is Cuba's largest province, a half-moon of sweeping savannah, with a central ripple of high land, curving into the Caribbean Sea. Most of the province is given over to cattle farming and what little tourism there is tends to be low-key: perfect if you fancy exploring a pocket of Cuba largely unswamped by crowds. Most visitors head straight for the **beaches** rimming the northern cays, bypassing completely the centre of the province and the colonial charms of **Camagüey city**. One of the seven original settlements founded by Diego Velázquez in 1514–15, birthplace of one of the country's most renowned poets, Nicolas Guillén, and former home of the celebrated revolutionary Ignacio Agramonte, this one-time pirate haunt is brimming with history, its handful of sights, museums and buildings – particularly its enigmatically decaying churches – infused with legend. North of the city, tourism is now starting to blossom along the cay-fringed coast, with lively **Santa Lucía**, famous for its well-kept golden beaches, the region's main resort. For real desert-island appeal, head for the sands of **Cayo Sabinal**, at the northernmost point of the province, where empty beaches and rustic accommodation make the perfect retreat for solitude-seekers.

South of the provincial capital, much of the land is dominated by large tracts of panoramic pasture and while there is little to tempt you this far, offshore the **Archipiélago de los Jardines de la Reina**, near virgin coral cays, better accessed through Júcaro in Ciego de Ávila (see opposite and p.330), offer several excellent dive sites.

Camagüey city

Nestled in the heart of the province **CAMAGÜEY**, 30km from the north coast, is aptly named the city of legends, its winding streets and wizened buildings weaving an atmosphere of intrigue. On first view it is a bewildering city to negotiate, with a seemingly incomprehensible labyrinth of roads that were deliberately laid out on an irregular scheme in a futile attempt to confuse marauding pirates (see p.319). So long as you're not in a hurry to get anywhere this needn't matter too much, and an aimless wander along the narrow cobbled streets overhung by delicate balustrades and Rococo balconies is the best way to explore, as you round corners onto handsome parks and happen upon crumbling churches which have, since the Pope John Paul II's visit on his tour of Cuba in January 1998, begun to attract larger congregations. Several museums and fine buildings offer further sightseeing.

Despite its quaint appearance Camagüey is by no means a sleepy colonial town. Every Saturday, people cram onto Independencia for the weekly "Camagüeyan night" shindig (see "Entertainment", p.328), and pull out all the stops for the annual June **carnival**, the highlight of the Camagüeyan calendar.

Some history

One of the seven original settlements in Cuba, Camagüey was established between 1514 and 1515 on the site of a sizeable Amerindian village, and although the original inhabitants were swiftly eradicated, traces of burial sites and ceramics have been found in the area. Now the only legacy of the indigenous people remains in the city's name, thought to originate from the word *Camagua*, a wild shrub common to the lowlands and believed to have magical properties.

Initially known as **Santa María del Puerto del Príncipe**, the fledgling city started life as a port town on the north coast where modern-day Nuevitas lies. Just a year later, when agriculturists from Seville arrived in 1516, it was moved to the fertile lands of modern-day Caonao on the northwestern edge of the province, until, according to some sources, a rebel band of Amerindians forced the settlers out, and the town moved once more, to its pre-

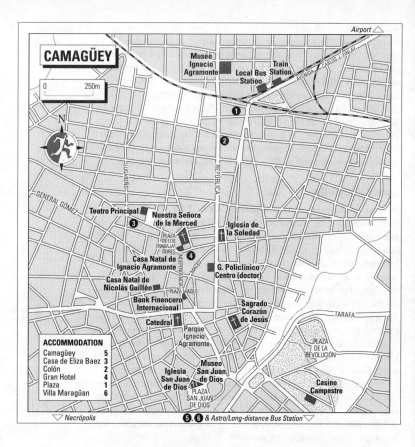

CAMAGÜEY

0   250m

N

Airport

Museo Ignacio Agramonte

Local Bus Station

Train Station

AVENIDA CARLOS J. FINLAY

❶

❷

LUGAREÑO

GENERAL GÓMEZ

REPÚBLICA

Teatro Principal ❸

Nuestra Señora de la Merced

Iglesia de la Soledad

PLAZA DE LOS TRABAJADORES

Casa Natal de Ignacio Agramonte

❹

MACEO

INDEPENDENCIA

G. Policlinico Centro (doctor)

Casa Natal de Nicolás Guillén

PLAZA MACEO

Bank Finencero Internacional

Sagrado Corazón de Jesús

TARAFA

Catedral

Parque Ignacio Agramonte

PLAZA DE LA REVOLUCIÓN

ACCOMMODATION

Camagüey	5
Casa de Eliza Baez	3
Colón	2
Gran Hotel	4
Plaza	1
Villa Maragüan	6

Iglesia San Juan de Dios

Museo San Juan de Dios

PLAZA SAN JUAN DE DIOS

Casino Campestre

▽ Necrópolis

❺,❻ & Astro/Long-distance Bus Station ▽

sent site, in 1528. Straddling the two rivers Tínima and Hatibonico, so as to be in the middle of the trade route between Sancti Spíritus and Bayamo, the newly settled town began to consolidate itself. During the 1600s its economy developed around sugar plantations and cattle farms, generating enough income to build the distinguished churches and civil buildings the following century. Despite intermittent ransacking by pirates, Puerto Príncipe grew into a sophisticated and elegant city, one its townsfolk fought hard to win from the Spanish during the wars of independence. Eventually in 1903, following the end of Spanish rule, the city dropped its lengthy moniker and adopted the name by which it is now known.

Arrival and information

Flights arrive at the Ignacio Agramonte **airport**, 7km north of the city, from where you can catch a bus or unmetered taxi ($4) into town. Two daily **buses** from Havana pull in at the Astro bus station

Pirates in Camagüey

Although not the only city to suffer constant attack from **pirates**, irresistibly wealthy Camagüey was one of those consistently plagued, and buccaneers regularly rampaged through the city before retiring to the northern cays or the Isla de la Juventud to hide their spoils. Beset from its inception by attack, instead of following the usual plan of a colonial city with roads laid out in a regular grid pattern, the heart of the city was built as a web of narrow and twisted streets designed to confound pirates, though to little avail.

The first to arrive was the singularly unpleasant Frenchman Jacques de Sores in 1555, who roamed the farms on the north coast stealing cows, cheeses and women. These last he would abandon violated in Cayo Coco to the mercy of the elements. In 1668 the terror of the Caribbean seas, English buccaneer Henry Morgan, arrived and managed to occupy the city with his men for several days before making off with a hefty booty of gold and jewels belonging to the Spanish bourgeoisie. With a dashing show of irreverence, he is also reputed to have locked the town elders into the Catedral de Santa Iglesia to starve them into revealing the whereabouts of their riches. Struggling to reassert itself eleven years later, in 1679 the city fell prey to the wiles of another Frenchman, François de Granmont. Nicknamed *El Caballero* (the gentleman), he sacked the city and captured fourteen women. After nearly a month of occupying the town he marched to the coast and released all the women unharmed, thus earning his nickname.

on the Carretera Central, 3km north of the town centre, from where you can catch an unmetered taxi or horse-drawn carriage in for around $2–4. **Trains** from Havana and the neighbouring provinces arrive at the frenetic train station on the northern edge of town. A ride to the centre in a *bicitaxi* should cost no more than fifteen pesos, an unmetered taxi $1. If you feel up to negotiating the imbroglio of town planning, it's a fifteen-minute walk along Van Horne to Republica, the straight road leading directly into the centre.

Essentially a booking office for its chain of hotels, the unhelpful Islazul **tourism bureau**, at no. 448 Ignacio Agramonte e/ López Recio y Independencia (Mon–Fri 8am–noon & 1–4.30pm, Sat 8–11.30am; ☎322/9-25-50), has little information, although it occasionally stocks **maps**. You can get much better **information** at the Rumbos office at no. 108 López Recio e/ Santa Rita y Santo Esteban (Mon–Fri 8am–5pm; ☎322/9-72-29), which also has plans for expansion.

Accommodation

In comparison to the towns in Ciego de Ávila, Camagüey has a variety of reasonably priced **hotels**, most of them charming hideaways rather than fancy tourist palaces. Centrally located *casas particulares* are also springing up around town; though few have organized all their official paperwork yet, they are still a viable option.

Camagüey, Carretera Central Este, km 4.5, Reparto Jayamá ☎322/7-20-15. Modern block-style hotel on the outskirts of town with serviceable, clean but rather dark rooms. A bit far from the centre but a good option if you are driving and need somewhere to park. A good-sized pool, charging $3 to non-guests. ④.

Casa de Eliza Baez, Astillero no. 24 e/ San Ramón y Lugareño ☎322/9-69-69. Two double rooms and huge tasty home-cooked meals in a comfortable, clean and very friendly *casa particular* close to the centre. Call to make a reservation. ②.

Colón, Calle República no. 274 ☎322/8-33-80. Beautiful but crumbling small hotel in the heart of the city that's almost a museum piece, with corridors bathed in greenish light, a cracked marble staircase and exquisite tiling. It mainly caters for locals, with foreign visitors sometimes told it's full even if it's not, but it's worth asking as it's a good cheap option. ②.

Gran Hotel, Maceo no. 67 e/ Ignacio Agramonte y General Gómez ☎322/9-20-93. Graciously faded eighteenth-century building that became a hotel in the 1930s, with well-maintained rooms, some with balconies overlooking the busy street below, a small pool and a dark and sultry piano bar. Star feature, though, is the elegant marble dining room on the fifth floor: its mottled mirrors, dulled bronzed figurines and panoramic views over the spires of the city, mean you can almost forgive the snail's pace service. ③.

Plaza, Van Horne no. 1 e/ República y Avellaneda ☎322/8-24-35. Basic accommodation at a reasonable rate, in a shabby but friendly hotel that feels more like a youth hostel. ③.

Villa Maragüan, Camino de Guanamaquila, Circunvalación Este ☎322/7-20-17; fax 36-52-47. Very spacious, Spanish-style villa complex set in leafy palm- and cactus-filled gardens about 6km east of town. The excellent rooms are large and clean, and the good pool, basketball court and peaceful surroundings make this a good chill-out spot from which to venture into the town. ⑤.

The Town

Sprinkled with churches and colonial squares, Camagüey will take a couple of days to fully explore, although those breezing through can do the main sights in a half day or so. Since the pope's visit in January 1998 during his three-day trip to Cuba, church attendance in the city has risen, as it has throughout Cuba, and money is accordingly being poured into repairing the romantically crumbling facades and maintaining church interiors.

Although the city's irregular town plan makes it difficult to get your bearings, most of the main sights are clustered together in easy walking distance of the main shopping drag, **Calle Maceo**, including **La Iglesia de la Soledad**, one of the city's oldest churches. Very close to hand is the **Plaza de los Trabajadores**, a prosaic little square much enhanced by the **Iglesia Nuestra Senora de la Merced**, the most impressive of Camagüey's churches, and the **Casa Natal de Ignacio Agramonte**, birthplace of the city's most revered son, a martyr of the struggle for independence. A couple of streets away the **Gran Teatro Principal** makes a minor diversion while the nearby **Casa Natal de Nicolás Guillén** honours the life and times of one of Cuba's premier poets. Heading south of here, past the **Plaza de Antonio Maceo**, a useful landmark at the southern end of Maceo, takes you to the congenial **Parque Agramonte**, the city's main park and a popular gathering spot for locals, home to the important but rather dull **Catedral de Santa Iglesia**, while a few blocks east is the more picturesque **Sagrado**

Corazón de Jesús. Further south is the Plaza de San Juan de Dios which, blessed with the Iglesia San Juan de Dios and Museo de San Juan de Dios, is Camagüey's most attractive colonial square. Further afield, to the southwest in the city's oldest quarter, is the Necrópolis cemetery where several of the city's most lauded figures repose beneath munificent marble tributes, while roughly equidistant to the southeast is Casino Campestre, an expansive town park with several amusements famed as the largest of its kind in Cuba.

Although the northern end of town has fewer sights, it's still worth venturing up for a breeze around the Museo Ignacio Agramonte, the provincial museum which has several interesting exhibits and a quietly impressive collection of paintings.

La Iglesia de la Soledad

The hub of town centres around the two streets of Maceo and República, where the most picturesque hotels are clustered, dollar shops and peso markets are strung along the roads, and the streets are thronged with window-shoppers and gaggles of people all queuing to buy the same single pair of trainers, voluptuous Barbie-style dolls – their big thighs and generous smiles a good indication of the female ideal in Cuba – threadbare towels or secondhand books. Presiding over the intersection of the two streets is La Iglesia de la Soledad (daily 8am–noon), tiered like a wedding cake and with a lofty tower that can be seen from all over the city. There has been a church on this site since 1697, the original built from wood and guano, the present structure dating from 1758; although the exterior is in disrepair, the interior, its domed roof painted with Baroque frescoes, merits a look. Like others in the town, the church has its very own creation myth. Apparently one rainy morning an animal carrier became stuck in the mud in the road in front of the site now occupied by the church. Everyone gathered around to push the wagon free and in the process a box bounced off the back and smashed open to reveal a statue of the Virgin. As the cart-driver could lay no claim to it, it was taken as a sign that the Virgin wanted a chapel built on this spot.

It was in La Iglesia de la Soledad that Ignacio Agramonte was baptized and married.

La Iglesia Nuestra Señora de la Merced

One block west of Maceo is the Plaza de los Trabajadores, a disappointingly modern polygon of tarmac beautified by a border of attractive colonial buildings and La Iglesia Nuestra Señora de la Merced (daily 9am–4pm), Camagüey's most impressive building. Its current state of disrepair, the creamy plasterwork flaking off to expose the brickwork underneath, only adds to the romance of its whispered origins. The story goes that one day in the seventeenth century, when the plaza was still allegedly submerged beneath a lake, the townsfolk heard shouts and screams from the thickets on the banks. Terrified to approach, they kept watch from a distance over

Plaza de los Trabajadores comes alive at carnival when a temporary stage turns it into a pulsating dance area complete with jugglers, parades and cabarets.

several days until, to their amazement, a shimmering white church emerged from the water. Beckoning from the portal was a priest with a cross clasped in his hand: the Merced church had arrived. A more prosaic history tells that the church was established in 1747 as a convent, and the rooms to the left of the chapel, set around a central patio, still serve as such today. Inside the grounds, shadows of mango leaves dapple the patio and large well-kept *tinajones* (see p.325) perch on the cloisters. Art Deco frescoes swirl across the corridor ceiling in muted shades of grey and yellow, while doors open onto classrooms, reading rooms and an ample library where you can browse through weighty religious works.

The adjoining church is a confection of styles. Built on the side of the seventeenth-century chapel, the first church was constructed in 1748, rebuilt a hundred years later, and again between 1906 and 1909 following a fire that destroyed the altar. Now it boasts a richly ornate neo-Gothic wood and gilt altar imported from Spain, a contrast to the delicate eighteenth-century Baroque balconies swooping above. The most intriguing item, however, is the **Santo Sepulcro**, an ornate silver coffin, thickly coated with intertwined hand-beaten bells and flowers, made in 1762 from 25,000 molten silver coins by Mexican silversmith Juan de Benítez, and commissioned by an ill-fated merchant (see box below).

Hidden beneath the church, accessible by a tiny flight of stairs behind the main altar, is a fascinatingly macabre little crypt. Formerly an underground cemetery that ran all the way to López Resco, 500m away, much of it was bricked up following the fire and only a claustrophobic sliver remains. Among the musty relics several life-sized statues gleam in the half-light, while embedded in the

---

The story of El Santo Sepulcro

In eighteenth-century Puerto Príncipe (as Camagüey was then known), a wealthy merchant, Manuel de Agüero, and his family employed a widowed housekeeper, one Señora Moya. Master and servant each had a son of the same age, and it seemed natural for the boys to play and grow up together. Agüero paid for both to go to Havana to study at the university, and they seemed assured of bright futures. However, disaster struck when both young men met and fell in love with the same woman, and in a fit of pique Moya challenged Agüero to a duel and killed him. Distraught, Agüero Senior promptly banished the murderous boy and his mother from his sight, lest his remaining sons avenge their brother's death, making sure they had enough money to live on. However, his woes were not over, as his wife, sick with a broken heart, wasted away and died soon after. Torn apart by grief, Agüero decided to enter the church and become a friar, and with his remaining sons' approval poured their inheritance into jewels and treasures for the church. The most splendid of all his tributes was the Santo Sepulcro, the silver coffin which he commissioned in readiness of his own death. Long seen as a hero who rose above personal disaster to overcome bitterness, his is a puzzling tale of uneasy blame and colonial values.

walls are the skeletal remains of a woman and her child: look carefully and you will see that live cockroaches play across their surfaces. For a guided tour of the church and convent, ask at the convent (daily 9am–4pm).

Casa Natal de Ignacio Agramonte

Facing the church and convent, on the other side of Plaza de los Trabajadores, is the **Casa Natal de Ignacio Agramonte** (Mon & Wed–Sat 1–6pm, Sun 8am–noon; $2), an attractive colonial house with dark wood balustrades and a fine heavy wooden door, birthplace of the local hero of the first war of independence. All Agramonte's possessions were confiscated when he took up arms against the colonial powers and, although never returned to him while he was alive, now form part of the museum's collection. After his death the Spanish authorities converted his home into a market and then later, to add insult to injury, a bar. It opened as a museum in 1973, and has recently been refurbished. The standard of life enjoyed by wealthy sugar plantation owners like the Agramontes is well highlighted in their impressive furniture displayed, including a well-crafted piano and oversized *tinajones* out in the central patio. Rather more mundane are the personal papers, pocket watch and other ephemera belonging to Agramonte himself.

Teatro Principal

Tucked two blocks northeast of Plaza de los Trabajadores along San Ramón is Camagüey's **Teatro Principal**. Its splendour dulled with a thick matt coat of ochre paint, the theatre is not the jewel that many townsfolk enthusiastically claim it to be, but instead is quietly stylish, with yellow and red *vitrales*. Inside, a marble staircase sweeps up to the spacious first floor where a central oval balcony gazes down on a splendid chandelier. Now the home of the Camagüey

---

Ignacio Agramonte – daredevil of the wars of independence

Ignacio Agramonte (1841–73), the son of wealthy Camagüeyan cattle farmers, studied law in Havana and then in Spain before returning in 1868 to become a revolutionary leader in the first war of independence against Spain. Back in his homeland, he incited the men of Camagüey to take up arms against the Spanish, taking the town at the end of that year and forming a small unorthodox republic with some of the local farm owners. He was known as the **daredevil of the wars of independence** for his often misguided valour – on one occasion when one of his fighters was captured by the Spanish, he dashed off to rescue his unfortunate compatriot from the 120-strong enemy column armed only with a machete and 34 of his most trusted men and lived to tell the tale. Killed aged 32 on the battlefields of Jimaguayú, his youth as well as his passion for his province guaranteed him a revered place as one of Camagüey's martyrs amongst those who lost their lives in the wars of independence.

Ballet, the theatre keeps erratic opening hours, but there's usually someone around to let you in; if there's no one in the main hall, take the alleyway on the left-hand side to the back and ask for an impromptu tour.

Casa Natal de Nicolás Guillén

One block south of Plaza de los Trabajadores is the **Casa Natal de Nicolás Guillén** (Mon–Fri 9am–3pm; $1). An Afro-Cuban born in 1902, Guillén was one of Cuba's foremost poets and is renowned throughout Latin America, particularly for his eloquent pieces on the condition of black people in Cuba, whose profile he raised and cause he championed in his writing. A founding member of the National Union of Writers and Artists (UNEAC), an organization responsible for much of the promotion of the arts in Cuba, and recipient of the Lenin Peace Prize, he died in 1989 after a lifetime of achievement. The small house has relics of his life but despite a half-hearted attempt at a reconstruction of his kitchen nothing really gives you much of an insight into his days there. There are, however, many of his poems in poster form on the walls, and a good selection of photographs to peruse. In an adjoining building is the Centro Nicolás Guillén, a socio-cultural study centre.

Parque Agramonte and the Catedral de Santa Iglesia

A few blocks south of the Casa Natal de Nicolas Guillén is the bijou **Plaza de Antonio Maceo**, from where it's one block south through narrow streets to **Parque Agramonte**, the town's social centre. The small square is filled with shady tamarind trees, *tinajones* (see box opposite) and marble benches, where parents watch their offspring whizz about on makeshift skateboards and clamber all over the central statue to Ignacio Agramonte.

Each corner of the square is pegged by a royal palm to symbolize the deaths of four independence fighters – leader Joaquín Agüero, Tomás Betancourt y Zayas, Fernando de Zayas and Miguel Benavides – shot for treason here by the Spanish in the early struggles of independence. The men were immediately hailed as martyrs and the townsfolk planted the four palms as a secret tribute, the Spanish authorities ignorant of their significance. Local women also sheared off their long hair, claiming that it was unseemly to be beautiful in times of hardship. By such subversive means they kept the memories of the heroes alive; now, in front of each palm, is an explanatory plaque.

Dominating the parque's south side is the **Catedral de Santa Iglesia** (daily 9am–noon), built in the seventeenth century to be the largest church in the Puerto Príncipe parish. It was rebuilt in the nineteenth century when it took its present form, but despite its auspicious heritage it is one of Camagüey's least impressive churches with a large though empty interior and a jaded exterior.

Tinajones

Tucked beneath the trees in Parque Agramonte are the large bulbous clay jars known as **tinajones**. Seen throughout Camagüey, they were originally storage jars used to transport wine, oil and grain and introduced by the Spanish as the solution to the city's water shortage, placed beneath gutters so that they could fill with water. Slightly tapered at one end, they were half-buried in earth, keeping the water cool and fresh. They soon came to be produced in the town and every house had one outside; inevitably, they became a status symbol, and a family's wealth could be assessed by the style and quantity of their *tinajones*. They also came in handy during the wars of independence when soldiers escaping the Spanish would hide in them. Indeed so proud are the Camagüeyans of their *tinajones* that a local saying has it that all who drink the water from one fall in love and never leave town.

La Iglesia de Sagrado Corazón de Jesús

A ten-minute walk east from Parque Agramonte along Luaces is one of the city's only twentieth-century churches, **La Iglesia de Sagrado Corazón de Jesús** on Plaza de la Juventud (daily 9am–noon). Built in 1920, it is quaint rather than awesome, but nevertheless worth a look if you are passing. Through the forbidding mahogany doorway is a neo-Gothic crossed roof, while lining the walls are four wooden altars skilfully painted in a *trompe l'oeil* to look like marble, typical of the era. Birds nest behind the real-marble main altar, while light trickling through cracked stained glass give this rather faded church a pleasing air of serenity.

Plaza de San Juan de Dios

Head six blocks west of the Sagrado Corazón to reach the eighteenth-century **Plaza de San Juan de Dios**, the city's most photogenic square. A neat cobbled plaza with red-tiled pavements and little traffic, it's bordered with well-kept lemon-yellow and dusty pink buildings, their windows hemmed with twists of sky-blue balustrades.

On the northern corner sits **La Iglesia San Juan de Dios** (daily 8am–noon), built in 1728. A single squat bell tower rises like a turret from a simple symmetrical facade saved from austerity by soft hues of green and cream. The dark interior is richly Baroque, typical of Cuban colonial style, with rows of chocolatey wood pews and a gilded altar. Notice the original brick floor, the only one remaining in any church in Camagüey.

Fitted snugly to the side of the building is the old **Hospital de San Juan de Dios**. It was to this hospital that the body of Ignacio Agramonte was brought after he was slain on the battlefield (see p.323); the Spanish hid his body from the Cubans without allowing them to pay their last respects and burned him as an example to other would-be dissidents. It now houses the **Museo de San Juan de Dios** (Mon–Fri 8am–5pm; $1 including Spanish-speaking guide)

A good place to relax and enjoy the peace of the square is La Campana de Toledo restaurant (see p.327).

with some early maps and photographs of the town in bygone years. The display only takes up a small corner of the hospital, and the real pleasure lies in looking around the well-preserved building, admiring the original heavy wood staircase, cracked *vitrales*, courtyard filled with *tinajones* and palms and the view over the church tower from the second floor.

Necrópolis

Southwest of Plaza San Juan de Dios is the older part of town, but although the streets are narrower and the curled iron grilles framing the windows more eroded, there's not much to distinguish it from the rest of colonial Camagüey. It's home to the **Necrópolis** (daily 6am–6pm; free) next to the nondescript Iglesia Santo Cristo del Bien Viaje. Buried here are Camagüeyan martyrs Fernando Zayas y Cisneros and Tomás Betancourt y Zayas, assassinated by the Spanish (see p.324). Lime-green lizards skitter over the extravagant Gothic mausoleums, signs of early largess, and marble Christ figures gleam in the sunlight. More modern graves are brightly tiled and quietly tended by mourners, while at the back of the cemetery the tombs are tightly packed into cupboard-style rows like a morgue to make the most of remaining space. Although the Necrópolis is in constant use, you are free to wander quietly around.

Casino Campestre and around

Continuing southeast from Plaza San Juan de Dios will eventually bring you to the main road through the town, Avenida Tarafa, which runs parallel to the murky Río Hatibonico. On the other side of this is the vast **Casino Campestre**, the biggest city park in Cuba. Spliced by the Hatibonico and Juan del Toro rivers and dappled by royal palms, it has a beer tent, children's area and a bandstand, whilst amongst the shady trees are monuments to local martyr Salvador Cisneros Betancourt and former mayor Manuel Ramón Silva.

To the west of the park is the huge concrete **Rafael Fortún Chacón Sports Centre** (daily 6am–9pm; ☎ 332/9-47-93), the biggest of its kind in any provincial town. Named after Camagüey's 100-metre athletics champion of the 1950s, it boasts a swimming pool and large arena with activities as varied as tae kwan do, basketball and trampolining, as well as a beauty centre offering mud wraps, honey treatments and the chance to bake in the sauna for a nominal fee. Amateur sports competitions, including judo and basketball, and salsa concerts are often held here; ask for details at reception.

Museo Ignacio Agramonte

Whilst the north end of town has less to see, you should still make the effort to check out the **Museo Ignacio Agramonte**, on Avenida Martires at the top end of República (Tues, Thurs & Sat 9am–5pm,

Wed & Fri 1–9pm; $1). Also known as the Museo Provincial, it's an elegant Art Deco exterior, its unassuming white facade masking its sleek lines and geometric lettering. Whilst there's nothing within to suggest a connection with its namesake, the museum's engaging array of exhibits include some quality nineteenth-century furniture, most notably a *tinajero* washstand with a stone basin inset and some fine Sèvres china. Most impressive is the fine art collection, which includes a Victor Manuel García original, *Muchacha*, and a good example of the Cuban vanguard movement. You may wish to avoid the dusty cages of stuffed birds and beasts in the natural history room and head instead for the garden where original *tinajones* sit at the base of the breadfruit trees.

Eating

As a provincial capital Camagüey has a good selection of **restaurants**, and a couple of **local specialities** that will come as a welcome break after the gastronomic wastelands of other parts of the island. At carnival time steaming pots of meat and vegetable broth called *ajiaco* scent the air, cooked in the street over wood fires. All the neighbours pile out of the houses and chuck in their own ingredients while an elected chef, often a hapless child, stirs the concoction to perfection. You can occasionally sample this delicacy in local eateries throughout the year; it's particularly delicious washed down with the locally brewed Tiníma, a thirst-quenching malty beer. Apart from the restaurants listed below, there's a small, no-name *paladar* – head two blocks down on Cisneros past the cathedral, then take a right – serving massive portions of rice with beans and marinated pork for around $5.

La Campana de Toledo, Plaza San Juan de Dios. Set in a leafy courtyard, a pretty blue and yellow building with a red-brick roof and a quaint tradition of tolling the bell when anyone enters or leaves. It serves the usual quasi-international and Cuban cuisine, but the tranquil setting makes it top choice for a mellow, moderately priced meal.

Rancho Luna, Plaza Maceo. For an authentic Cuban experience, join the queue outside this basic peso restaurant and wait to be seated and bossed about by gloriously irreverent waitresses. Daily noon–10pm.

La Tinajita, Cristo no. 77 e/ Santa Catalina y Benbeta. A pleasant, friendly saloon-style restaurant with a small bar, serving inexpensive Cuban cuisine in an airy setting. Daily noon–8pm.

Vicaria Principena, República no. 222 esq. Callejon del Castellano. Chinese, Italian and Cuban cuisine in a rather soulless setting redeemed by a central location and reasonable quality. Daily 11am–10pm.

La Volante, Parque Agramonte. An old colonial house with tall windows overlooking the park, serving basic food that bears little relation to what's on the menu. The appetizing *Vieja Ropa* (meat stew) and lamb dishes are the best bets. It caters mainly for Cubans and you may get away with paying in pesos. Daily noon–9pm.

Drinking, nightlife and entertainment

An excellent weekend **nightlife** makes Camagüey a lively town. Every Saturday night, revellers stream onto Maceo for the free weekly knees-up **"Camagüeyan night"**, when salsa queens get down to the sound of live groups while shyer souls, usually tourists, pin themselves to the walls and watch wistfully. Although some Camagüeyans consider the event rowdy and lowbrow, for the visitor it's lively and friendly and an excellent opportunity to meet locals, although you should keep an eye out for pickpockets. During the rest of the week, Camagüey has a quiet, understated nightlife based around a handful of central **rum bars**.

Camagüey is particularly lively during its week-long **carnival** in late June. An exuberant parade takes place on the main streets and musicians dressed in multicoloured, frilled costumes twirl huge batons adorned with silver glitz and shaped like prisms or bang drums and clap cymbals whilst others dance, swig beer and quarrel with the parade officials. Floats with disco lights, bouncing speakers and unsmiling girls in home-made costumes dancing energetically bring up the rear, while running in between the different trucks are *diablitos*, men disguised head to foot in raffia, who dart into the crowd with the sole purpose of terrorizing the assembled children. Stages are set up at various points around the town centre, and local *salsa* singers, acrobats and other performers entertain the gathered throngs while stalls selling gut-rot beer in vast paper cups (hang on to your empties – supplies often run out) and roast suckling pig provide refreshment.

The local **cinema**, *Cine Casablanca* on Ignacio Agramonte e/ República y López Recio, shows a selection of Cuban, Spanish and North American films and charges 60 centavos entry. The Teatro Principal (☎322/9-30-48) has regular theatre and ballet performances, usually thoroughly entertaining.

Bar Siboney, San Rafael esq. Lugareño. Much cleaner, lighter and friendlier than most – and less intimidating for lone women – this excellent rum bar sells a couple of local specialities, and has the added benefit of peso prices.

El Cambio, Parque Agramonte. A friendly 24-hour rum bar opening onto the park, with an old-fashioned though silent jukebox. A great place to slowly sip an afternoon away.

Casa de la Trova, Salvador Cisneros no. 171 e/ Martí y Cristo. Though fairly staid during the week, the town's Casa de la Trova is a good place to catch live music all day long. In the evening, bands, steadfastly oblivious to any attempts you may be making at conversation, croon traditional ballads at your table.

Gran Hotel, Maceo no. 67 e/ Ignacio Agramonte y General Gómez. Though all the big hotels have their own bars, the only one worth lingering in is this dark, atmospheric piano bar, which sometimes has live music.

Shopping

Although most of what's on offer in Camagüey is a collection of home-grown cosmetics and Cuba T-shirts, a few gems make **shopping** here a worthwhile pursuit. Chief among them is a nameless little emporium, tucked away at Cisneros no. 208 e/ Hermanos Agüeros y Martí, selling a fast-moving collection of original screen-printed Cuban film posters – sadly for Cuban film buffs, the poster of the classic cartoon *Los Vampiros de la Habana* vanished long ago. **Wooden carvings** are thick on the ground, worth considering if you have room in your luggage for a weighty piece of mahogany; the best bet is to buy direct from one of the town's best sculptors, Julaín Besu Ruiz, at Avenida Betancourt no. 2, Reparto Puerto Príncipe. Funerama on Ignacio Agramonte has a good selection of CDs, tapes and maps, along with kitsch souvenirs along the lines of jolly Cuban crocodiles waving cigars. On Cisneros, the town **art gallery** (Mon–Fri 10am–6pm, Sat 10am–2pm) has a good selection of visual arts by local notables.

Listings

Airlines Cubana, República no. 440 esq. Correa ☎322/9-13-38.

Airport Aeropuerto Ignacio Agramonte ☎322/6-15-25.

Banks and money You can draw cash advances on Visa or Mastercard and change travellers' cheques at the *casa de cambio* at República no. 353 e/ San Esteban y Santa Rita, or El Banco Financero Internacional, Independencia no. 221 Plaza Maceo, where there's usually less of a queue. Unofficial money-changers work outside the dollar stores in Maceo and offer reasonable rates.

Car rental Both Havanautos (☎322/7-20-15) and Transautos (☎322/7-24-28) have a desk at the *Hotel Camagüey*.

Medical The 24-hour Policlínico Centro, República no. 211 e/ Grl. Gomez y Catellano (☎322/95-70-06), has fifty doctors. At the other end of town try Consultario, Domingo Puente no. 20 e/ Avenida la Libertad y San Joaquín (Mon–Fri 8am–noon; ☎ 322/9-88-49).

Pharmacy Ave. la Libertad no. 207 e/ Pancho Agramonte y Domingo Puente (daily 8am–10pm).

Photography The Photo Service is on General Gómez e/ Maceo y Independencia.

Police Call ☎332/9-30-28, or 9-91-92 in an emergency.

Post office The main post office is at Ignacio Agramonte no. 461.

Telephones The ETECSA booth on the corner of Ignacio Agramonte sells phonecards.

Around Camagüey

Although it's the country's largest province, aside from its capital and northern beaches (see p.331) there isn't that much to see in Camagüey. The small villages dotted around the city are quiet and rural, more concerned with the day-to-day management of their cattle and sugar farms than entertaining tourists. If you have your own transport you can roam around the essentially flat countryside east and west of the provincial capital, admiring the swathes of shimmering sugarcane and breezing through some of the larger one-horse towns. A possible diversion is tiny **GUÁIMARO**, 65km east of Camagüey, almost on the border with Las Tunas province.

It centres around a careworn town square with a statue commemorating the town's moment of fame: it was here that the first Cuban constitution was drafted in April 1869 by such luminary revolutionaries as Ignacio Agramonte (see p.323) and Carlos Manuel de Céspedes (see p.419).

North of Camagüey, the flat scenery begins to bulge gently into the low hills of the Sierra de Cubitas, although the near-straight road to the coast, off which lie a couple of minor sights, is as even as anywhere else in the province. The musically minded might like to stop off in **MINAS**, about 40km from Camagüey, for a breeze around Cuba's only string instrument factory, the **Fabrica de Instrumentos Musicales** (Mon–Sat 9am–5pm; $2), to view a selection of violins, cellos and guitars being lovingly hand-crafted. Also worth a look is the **Ingenio Santa Isabel**, just east off the road roughly 17km from Minas. An intriguing tumbledown tower, standing alone by the side of the Río Saramaguacán, this is all that remains of an early sugar mill built at the end of the eighteenth century by local merchant Francisco de Quesada y Agüero and named after his daughter.

The most important town in the area is **NUEVITAS**, 77km northeast of Camagüey. Despite being an industrial centre with several factories and a thermoelectric plant, with its sea view and wooden pastel-coloured houses it still retains an air of an out-of-the-way provincial village. Despite the clouds of smoke and electrical wires crisscrossing the sky, you can still see vestiges of a colonial past in the colonnades outside the older buildings. There's not much to see and nothing to do but it's an agreeable enough spot to stop and refuel at one of the food stands in the main street.

Made up of low-lying farmland dappled with a few rural villages, the area south of Camagüey holds little of interest; offshore, however, the waters around the virgin cays of the **Archipiélago de los Jardines de la Reina** offer magnificent diving and fishing opportunities. Access from Camagüey's south coast is very limited: you could try heading to the tiny fishing town of Santa Cruz del Sur, where you may find an opportunist fisherman willing to take you the 40km out to sea, but the only reliable way is from Júcaro in Ciego de Ávila (see p.316) or through the Camagüey Rumbos office (☎322/9-72-29), who run daytrips by light aircraft to Cayo Caguama.

Practicalities

Although you're unlikely to want to make an overnight stop in the region, should you need a **bed** for the night your best option is the rather run-down *Hotel Caonaba* (☎32/4-21-56; ②) in Nuevitas, while should you find yourself stranded in Guáimaro, head for the passable *Hotel Guáimaro* (☎32/8-21-02; ②). You can get snacks and cold drinks at the *Parador de Carretera Santa Isabel*, just beside the Ingenio Santa Isabel.

Cut off from the mainland by the Bahía de Nuevitas, 10km north of
Nuevitas town, are Camagüey's north coast **beaches**. Defined by
their remoteness, the resort of **Santa Lucía**, and Cayo Sabinal to
the west, both make perfect retreats for those seeking sun and sea
holidays. While Santa Lucía derives an infrastructure of sorts from
the knot of all-inclusive hotels arrayed along the beach front, **Cayo
Sabinal** is castaway country. With only the most basic accommodation, it virtually guarantees solitude. Those wishing to explore
completely virgin territory should head for **Cayo Romano** in the far
western reaches of the province.

Santa Lucía and around

Hemmed in by salt flats on the northern coast, 128km from
Camagüey, **SANTA LUCÍA** is one of Cuba's most recently developed
beach resorts. It's perfect if you want to park yourself on the sand for
a fortnight, soak up some rays and indulge in a few watersports, but
those looking for a more rounded destination may find it lacking. The
resort, such as it is, consists of little more than a beach strip lined by
a few hotels, set well back from the coastal road and heavily guarded, while the surrounding vicinity is restricted by marshland.
Meeting townsfolk is near impossible as they are refused entrance to
the hotels and the beaches, and any visitors who look a bit Cuban and
don't display an all-inclusive armband are likely to be treated with
suspicion. The town, which you pass en route to the hotel strip, has
nothing to offer tourists, and you quickly get the impression that you
are out in the middle of nowhere with nothing to see or do away from
the sun and sea.

Diving at Santa Lucía

Blessed with five good sites, Santa Lucía offers some excellent **diving** possibilities, although most will suit skilled divers more than complete beginners. All sites are accessible by boat and have sharp drop-offs. Highlights
include the stingrays, eagle rays and mantas at **Valentinal**; the iridescent
orange sponges and black coral at El Canyon; and the **Spanish wreck**
Mortera, sunk in 1896, coated with soft corals, gorgonian corals and
sponges, and home to myriad snooks, snappers and bull sharks – arguably
the most fascinating site of all, though beware of the strong currents.
Iridescent tropical fishes clustering around the coral-covered canyons at
El Canyon 2 include snappers, silverside fish and brightly coloured whips,
while the inquisitive tarpon and groupers at **Poseidon 2** are perfect subjects for underwater photography.

The optimistically named **Shark's Friend Diving Centre** (☎32/36-52-
94), on the stretch of beach nearest to *Hotel Cuatro Vientos*, runs two
dive trips daily at 9am and 1pm ($30–70), rents out equipment ($17 a day)
and offers ACUC (American Canadian Underwater Certification) registered courses (around $385). It also runs trips to Cayo Sabinal.

However, the **beaches** themselves are wide expanses of soft, fine sand bordered by turquoise waters, if a little sullied by seaweed drifting in from the barrier reef. There are five excellent **dive sites** catered to by a competent dive centre. As with many nascent resorts in Cuba, the scene revolves around the all-inclusive hotels, most of them set in attractive properties and all with friendly staff.

Practicalities

With no public transport to Santa Lucía, your best option, if not driving, is to take an unmetered **taxi** ($25) from outside the train station in Camagüey. There is no independent information bureau, but each hotel has a public relation officer who will be able to give general information. The resort revolves around its four excellent all-inclusive **hotels**, which between them carve up the entire beach strip. Residency at one entitles you to use the beaches, though not the facilities, of the others. All hotels offer a range of watersports, including windsurfing, snorkelling and catamarans. All meals are taken in the hotel **restaurants** with little in the way of independent **eating** and **drinking** in the area, although the main road behind the beach strip has a couple of Rumbos cafés selling chicken and fries. Similarly you are limited to the hotels for evening **entertainment**, an endless diet of jovial staff roping drunken guests into bawdy Benny Hill-type pantomimes.

Amigo Mayanabo ☎32/36-51-68; fax 36-51-76. The shabbiest and oldest hotel on the strip, with old-style breeze block architecture but helpful, friendly staff and facilities that include a gym, tennis courts and a large pool. ⑤.

Club Santa Lucía, ☎32/36-51-46. This part-Italian-owned complex, geared to Italian guests, enjoys a spacious layout of bungalows and two-storey apartment blocks, with palatial rooms, ample shops, a good pool, gym, two restaurants and a pier-end bar that's perfect for sunset-watching. ⑥.

Club Vita Club Caracol ☎32/36-51-58; fax 32/36-51-59. The cabin-style layout of this hotel gives it a more personalized and less institutional feel than the others. The emphasis is on activity, with archery, horse riding, mountain biking and tennis offered. It caters primarily for Italians, with Italian-speaking staff and literature. ⑥.

Cuatro Vientos ☎32/36-51-20; fax 36-51-42. A friendly and unpretentious hotel with excellent rooms, a pool with a swim-up bar, and activities ranging from watersports to jolly participatory games. ⑥.

Playa Coco

Offering a change of scene 8km west from the main beach drag is **Playa Coco**. The local claim that it's a beach to rival the best in Cuba is stretching it a bit, but it certainly makes a welcome change to Santa Lucía, as it's open to Cubans and has a less touristy feel. On the way there you pass salt flats swarming with the flamingos and egrets (*cocos*) that give the beach its name. There are few facilities other than the unappetizing pasta and fried chicken on offer at the overpriced **snack bar**. A minibus picks up from the Santa Lucía hotels at 10am and drops you back at 3pm.

Cayo Sabinal and Cayo Romano

Twenty-five kilometres west along the north coast from Santa Lucía, **Cayo Sabinal** could not be more different – a deserted white-sand beach cay that's an almost-eerie paradise. The reason it's yet to be discovered by the masses is its geographical isolation, hidden away at the end of a stretch of bumpy dirt-track road, part of which forms a causeway across the bay, flanked by foaming salt marshes – no public transport, and very little general traffic, makes it this far. It's a resort for tourists only, with passports examined and Cubans allowed no further than the entry checkpoint, something to bear in mind if travelling in an unmetered taxi. All the beaches are on the north side, accessible by signposted turnings off the single main road, bordered by thick vegetation, in the centre of the cay.

The longest beach is pearl-white **Playa Los Pinos**, where the sea is a clear, calm turquoise and wild deer and horses roam through the woodland that backs onto the sand. Occasionally a group of holiday-makers arrive by boat from Santa Lucía, but otherwise it's a top choice for a couple of days' total tranquillity. Just 2km further west, smaller **Playa Brava** has similar soft white sands, but a break in the coral reef that spans the coast means rougher waves, hence the name, which means that swimming here can be a bit hairy. The beaches' sole **accommodation** option is a simple hut with a palm-rush roof and cold running water on Playa Los Pinos; you can turn up on spec but you're better off making a booking through Rumbos in Nuevitas (☎32/4-22-01). There is also a **restaurant** serving fresh fish here, and a **snack bar** on Playa Los Pinos.

On the west side of the coastline, **Cayo Romano**, a ninety-kilometre long mass of fragmented cays covered with marshes and woodland, has yet to be developed. With no accommodation or restaurants it is an archetypal untamed wilderness worth discovering if you have the time and your own transport. A causeway runs from Playa Jigüey on the north coast into the centre of the cay, although you can also reach the western tip from Cayo Coco.

Travel details

BUSES

Camagüey to: Ciego de Ávila (3 daily; 1hr 40min); Havana (2 daily; 8hr); Las Tunas (1 daily; 2hr); Manzanillo (3 weekly; 5hr); Matanzas (1 daily; 7hr); Minas (2 daily; 40min); Nuevitas (2 daily 1hr 20min); Santa Lucía (2 daily; 2hr 30min).

Ciego de Ávila to: Camagüey (3 daily; 2hr); Cienfuegos (1 daily; 4hr 30min); Havana (1 daily; 6hr); Holguín (1 daily; 6hr); Las Tunas (1 daily; 4hr); Matanzas (1 daily; 7hr 30min); Morón (2 daily; 1hr); Santa Clara (1 daily; 3hr).

Morón to: Ciego de Ávila (6 daily; 1hr).

**Travel
details**

TRAINS

Camagüey to: Bayamo (1 daily; 7hr); Ciego de Ávila (2 daily; 1hr); Havana (1 daily 9hr); Holguín (1 daily; 4hr 30 min); Matanzas (1 daily; 6hr); Nuevitas (1 daily; 2hr); Las Tunas (1 daily; 2hr).

Ciego de Ávila to: Havana (3 daily; 7hr); Holguín (1 daily; 5hr); Matanzas (1 daily; 5hr); Morón (3 daily; 4hr).

Morón to: Camagüey (1 daily; 3hr); Ciego de Ávila (3 daily; 4hr); Júcaro (1 daily; 40min); Nuevitas (1 daily; 3hr); Santa Clara (1 daily; 4hr).

DOMESTIC FLIGHTS

Camagüey to: Havana (9 weekly; 1hr 35min).

Cayo Coco to: Havana (3 weekly; 2hr).

Ciego de Ávila to: Havana (2 weekly; 1hr 25min).

Chapter 6

Northern Oriente

T raditionally, the whole of the country east of Camagüey is known simply as the "Oriente", a region that in many ways represents the essence of Cuba, awash with historic sites and political feeling. Running the length of the north coast, the three provinces that make up the **northern Oriente** – Las Tunas, Holguín and Guantánamo – form a landscape of panoramic mountains fringed by flatlands, with some of the country's most breathtaking peaks and stunning white-sand beaches.

The smallest and most westerly of the three provinces is **Las Tunas**, a band of land given over mainly to farming. Possibly the quietest and least dynamic province in Cuba, it is often overlooked by visitors journeying across the country, though the unassuming provincial capital, **Victoria de las Tunas**, is not without charm, its friendly atmosphere and unaffected lifestyle chief among its low-key attractions. Nearby, the picturesque coastal town of **Puerto Padre** is another of the province's modest highlights, with a couple of congenial beaches not too far distant.

By contrast, larger and livelier **Holguín** province has a variety of attractions. It was here that Christopher Columbus first came ashore, and the stunning countryside and white-sand beaches prompted his famous utterance that "the island is the most beautiful eyes have ever seen". Chequered with parks and filled with people, busy **San Isidoro de Holguín**, the provincial capital, manages to be modern and cosmopolitan while retaining the feel of its colonial past, with several handsome old buildings, museums and antique churches.

The once-powerful nineteenth-century port of **Gibara**, presiding over the north coast, also has vestiges of its former glory visible in a few fine buildings and an old fort, while the gently undulating hills that surround it are the perfect place to explore independently. Holguín's biggest attraction is the **Guardalavaca** resort, where dazzling white beaches and a lively atmosphere draw scores of holidaymakers. Nearby, the province's ancient face can be seen in the remnants of pre-Columbian Taíno culture in and around the little village

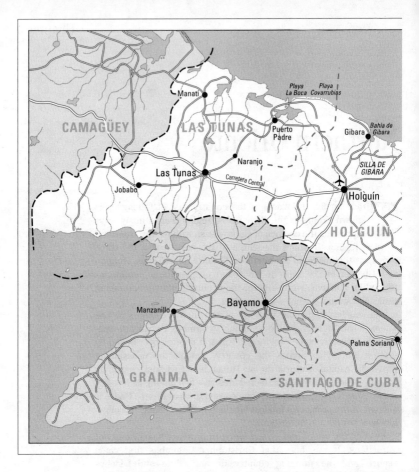

of **Banes**. Further east, the exclusive beach resort of **Cayo Saetía** is a well-guarded paradise of white sands and glistening seas, with exotic animals to be seen in its lush woodland – an altogether idyllic place to relax.

Inland, where rugged terrain dominates the landscape, the cool pine forests, waterfalls and lakes of **Mayarí** are unmatched for isolated serenity. Further south, buried in the heart of sugar farm country, Fidel Castro's prosaic birthplace at **Biran** fascinates many on the revolutionary pilgrimage across Cuba.

Of the three provinces it is undoubtedly **Guantánamo**, with the notorious US naval base at **Caimanera**, that is best known. Although the town of Guantánamo is largely unspectacular, it forms a useful jumping-off point for the seaside settlement of **Baracoa**, one of Cuba's most enjoyable destinations. Sealed off from the rest of the

island by a truly awe-inspiring range of rainforested mountains – fantastic for trekking – Baracoa's small-town charm is immensely welcoming and a visit here is the highlight of many trips.

Las Tunas

Not blessed with bright lights, glistening beaches or beautiful colonial buildings, little **Las Tunas** is often side-stepped by visitors heading off to more glamorous regions. But while it's not somewhere you're likely to want to linger, the province is pleasant and attractive, studded with the flat-leafed prickly pear *tunas* cactus that gives it its name, and has enough modest attractions to merit a brief detour.

With a refreshing absence of hustlers, amiable **Victoria de las Tunas** – or, more usually, just Las Tunas – feels more like a village than a provincial capital. On the north coast, near the old colonial town of **Puerto Padre**, the small resort at **Playa Covarrubias** and the undeveloped beach at **Playa La Boca** are worth visiting for their pretty pale sands. Elsewhere the province is mostly agricultural, the main industry being **sugar** production, as the fields of emerald green cane bear witness.

Victoria de Las Tunas

VICTORIA DE LAS TUNAS seems to have been built to a traditional Cuban recipe for a quiet town; take one central plaza and a small main hotel, a revolution square and a thriving market, add a pinch of culture and bake in the sun for two hundred years. The result is a pleasant but slow-moving rural town where the pace of life elsewhere in the world seems like a rumour.

The hub of town is **Parque Vicente García**, a small but comfortable central plaza hemmed by trees. It's an appealing spot to watch the town's comings and goings, with horse-and-cart taxis clip-clopping through the streets and fleets of kerbside manicurists sharpening their files for a day's business. On the east side of the park, the **Museo Provincial Mayor General Vicente García** (Tues–Sat 1–9pm, Sun 8am–noon; $1) is housed in a distinguished ice-blue and white colonial building adorned with an elegant clock face. The city history detailed within includes a worthy though brief record of slavery, featuring some horrific chains and shackles, while upstairs a natural history room displays a motley collection of stuffed sea creatures. On the southern corner of the park is the **Plaza Martiana de Las Tunas**, a modern art monument to José Martí made up of six white man-sized spikes, one of which is embossed with a bust of Martí. The whole sculpture forms an ingenious gigantic sundial which illuminates the bust annually on May 19 to commemorate the hero's death on the battlefield.

If you have time you could breeze round the **Museo Memorial Vicente García** (Mon–Sat 11am–7pm; $1), five minutes' walk west of the square. The museum is built on the birthplace of one Major

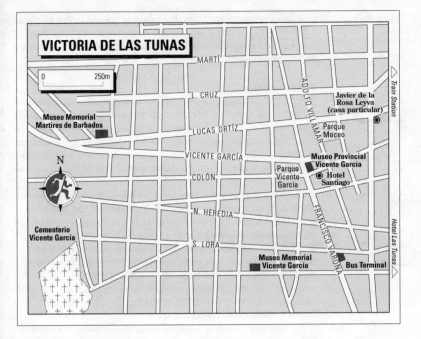

VICTORIA DE LAS TUNAS

0   250m

MARTÍ

L. CRUZ

ADOLFO VILLAMAR

Train Station

Javier de la
Rosa Leyva
(casa particular)

Museo Memorial
Martires de Barbados

LUCAS ORTÍZ

Parque
Maceo

VICENTE GARCÍA

N

COLÓN

Parque
Vicente
García

Museo Provincial
Vicente García

Hotel
Santiago

Cementerio
Vicente García

N. HEREDIA

S. LORA

FRANCISCO VARONA

Hotel Las Tunas

Museo Memorial
Vicente García

Bus Terminal

General Vicente García, who led Las Tunas into battle against the Spanish in September 1876. In the face of the town's imminent recapture, in 1897, he rashly declared that Las Tunas would rather be burnt to the ground than become slave to the Spanish, and promptly torched the city. Consisting of a few antique ceremonial swords and photographs of the hero and his family, the museum is set around an attractive central courtyard filled with spiky *tunas* cacti.

The most arresting museum in Las Tunas is the small but poignant **Museo Memorial Martires de Barbados**, at Lucas Ortíz no. 344, roughly 500m further west (Mon–Fri 11am–7pm; free), which commemorates the national junior fencing team wiped out in a plane crash in 1976. Within minutes of taking off from Barbados, en route to Cuba, there was a massive double explosion and the plane plunged into the sea; all 73 passengers, including the team, were instantly killed. When it was revealed several months later that the bomb had been planted by four terrorists working for the CIA, the incident was popularly seen as a direct attack on Cuban youth and achievement.

The museum is in the tiny former home of one of the three team members from Las Tunas, and is an evocative tribute. Unsmiling photographs of the victims and of weeping crowds in Havana, old fencing gear and trophies, and a script of the pilot's final pleas for help skilfully tug at the heartstrings. Outside in the grounds, a part-time fencing school for local students was opened in the 1980s as a tribute. On the other side of the road, the lively local **market** (closed Mon 6am–6pm) sells fresh milkshakes, fruit, vegetables and assorted ephemera.

Practicalities

Interprovincial **buses** pull in at the terminal just under 1km south of the centre on Francisco Varona, from where you can get a *bicitaxi* into town. The **train station** is about 2.5km northeast of town on Avenida Cienfuegos, with the provincial bus station in an adjacent building. Again, *bicitaxis* and horse-drawn carriages wait to whisk you into the centre, or you can hire unmetered **taxis** for excursions around the province.

There's no real reason to stay here, but there are several **accommodation** options should you find yourself so inclined, the best of them being the friendly *Casa de Javier de la Rosa Leyva*, Lucas Ortíz no. 109 Alto e/ Gonzalo de Quesado y Coronel Fonseca (☎031/4-26-57; ②), the only authorized *casa particular* among several along this road. Otherwise, the very basic peso *Hotel Santiago*, Angel Guardia no. 112 e/ Francisco Varona y Adolfo Villamar (☎031/4-33-96; ①), sometimes accepts foreigners and is more central than the standard, rather grim, tourist choice, *Hotel Las Tunas*, Ave. 2 de Diciembre esq. Carlos J. Finlay (☎031/4-50-14; ③).

The best place to **eat** is *Taberna Don Juan*, Francisco Varona no. 225, near Parque Vicente García, where you can enjoy decent Cuban food and excellent local beer in pesos. The dollar option is the twee, 24-hour *La Boguedita*, Francisco Varona no. 296, part of the Rumbos chain, selling fried chicken to masses of holidaying Miami Cubans. *Doña Neli*, opposite the bus terminal on Francisco Varona, does pastries and cakes, and has a small pizzeria to one side.

There's not much nightlife or entertainment to speak of except in summer, when the **El Cucalambé music festival** is held annually over three days in June or July. Based in the grounds of the otherwise unremarkable *Hotel El Cornito* (☎031/4-50-15), the festival features live folk and *salsa* in a lively atmosphere awash with beer and food stalls.

All the main dollar **shops** are strung along Vicente García and Francisco Varona, and it's around this area that you'll find the **bank**, **telephone centre** (daily 7am–11pm) and main **post office**.

Puerto Padre and the north coast

Although Las Tunas has just 70km of coastline, a small stretch compared to neighbouring provinces, there are still some pleasant spots. The attractive little seaside town of **PUERTO PADRE**, 56km north of Las Tunas, is a pleasant diversion on the coastal road through the province. A clutch of colonial buildings, including a church with a handsome spire, spreads along a spacious boulevard that heads down to a *malecón* seafront. Chief attraction is a small and crumbling stone **fort**, built by the Spanish at the turn of the nineteenth century and quietly impressive, with a circular tower on two of its four corners linking its once-solid walls. Best viewed from the outside, within it is a mass of overgrown weeds and graffiti.

Buses from Las Tunas (Avenida Cienfuegos terminal) arrive in town twice daily, except when there are severe fuel shortages. The *Hotel Villa Azul*, General Rabí no. 27 e/ S. Cisnero y Playa Girón (☎110/5-20-17; ②), has an open-air restaurant and is nice enough if you find yourself stranded for a night.

Playa La Boca
Playa La Boca, 19km east of Puerto Padre, is a wide sweep of clean golden sand spread around a clear blue-green bay, backed by palms and shrubs and dotted at intervals by mushroom-shaped concrete shades. Despite its obvious charms, it's often fairly deserted – no public transport comes this far, making it one of the few beaches in northern Oriente not overrun with sun-worshippers, windsurfers, snorkellers and the like.

The hotel nearby is strictly Cuban-only, but try *Villa Ileana María*, Calle 4 no. 16 (☎31/5-71-80; ②), a self-contained *casa particular* with a sea view and use of a kitchen. The only place to **eat** on the beach is a peso stall selling pizza and lukewarm soft drinks.

Playa Covarrubias
Playa Covarrubias, 30km west along the coastal road from Puerto Padre, is a small, white-sand beach with shallow, crystal-clear waters, wide sand banks and an offshore coral reef, all in the lee of a large, perplexingly located all-inclusive hotel. It's a pleasant beach, though by no means spectacular, and a long haul for a day-trip.

Buses from Las Tunas run as far as Manatí, 13km short of the coast, so you're better off taking one of the unmetered taxis ($25) from outside Las Tunas train station. The only **place to stay** is the deluxe, all-inclusive *Hotel Villas Las Covarrubias* (☎31/4-62-30; ⑥), which offers comfortable rooms with all mod-cons, a large pool and nightly entertainment.

Holguín

Wedged between Las Tunas to the west, Granma and Santiago de Cuba to the south and Guantánamo to the east, **Holguín** is among Cuba's most varied provinces, with low-lying lush farmland, sublime mountains, historical sites and appealing rural towns, as well as the dazzling beaches that are the main attraction for many visitors.

In the centre of the province, the capital, **San Isidoro de Holguín**, is a well-ordered town and a developing tourist destination. Known throughout Cuba as the "City of Parks", it has an almost European feel and enjoys a quirky fame as the country's sole manufacturer of mechanical organs – their music can be heard around the town. Close by, the secluded coastal fishing village of **Gibara** boasts a wealth of history and is one of the most captivating corners of the province.

On the coast further east, the dazzling beaches at **Guardalavaca** and **Esmeralda** form the third-largest resort in the country, a lively destination for throngs of dedicated fun-seekers. However, those in search of solitude and natural beauty are equally likely to find what they are looking for just inland, in the cool, pine-forested mountains around **Mayarí**, dotted with lakes, caves and waterfalls. Of all the provinces in Cuba, Holguín has the largest number of Taíno sites, particularly near **Banes**, where a museum pays tribute to the region's pre-Columbian heritage. The province's industrial core is betrayed by the nickel mines and factories that taint the air around **Moa**, in the far east, and **Nicaro**, on the coast near Mayarí; ugly as they are, they provide valuable revenue.

San Isidoro de Holguín

Nestling in a valley surrounded by hills, 72km from Las Tunas, **SAN ISIDORO DE HOLGUÍN** – or Holguín for short – is a thriving industrial town balancing quieter back streets with a busy centre of handsome colonial buildings, bicycles and horn-blasting cars. Despite having the bustling air of a large metropolis, Holguín's centre is compact enough to explore on foot and has a couple of fine eighteenth-century **churches** and some small-scale **museums** which will keep you quietly absorbed for a day or so. Meanwhile the city is spotted with numerous elegant **plazas**; these open spaces, ideal spots to watch the street life, are central to the Holguín lifestyle and in the evenings it seems that the whole city turns out to sit, chat and watch their children play in one or other of them.

On the northwest edge of town, a hearty climb up to the summit of **La Loma de la Cruz** affords a panoramic view over the city. Named for the cross that sits at the top, this hill is the site of the fervent **Romería de Mayo** pilgrimage held every May 3, when a Mass at the summit is followed by a three-day celebration down in town.

Some history

The area around Holguín was once densely populated by indigenous Taíno, but by 1545 they had been wiped out by the Spanish, after Captain García Holguín, early colonizer and veteran of the conquest of Mexico, established his cattle ranch around La Loma de la Cruz. Although a small settlement remained after his death, a town wasn't fully established here for two centuries, and it was only officially named on April 4, 1720 – San Isidoro's Day – with a commemorative Mass held in the cathedral.

As an inland town with no port Holguín was never destined to exert great influence in the country, overshadowed in provincial

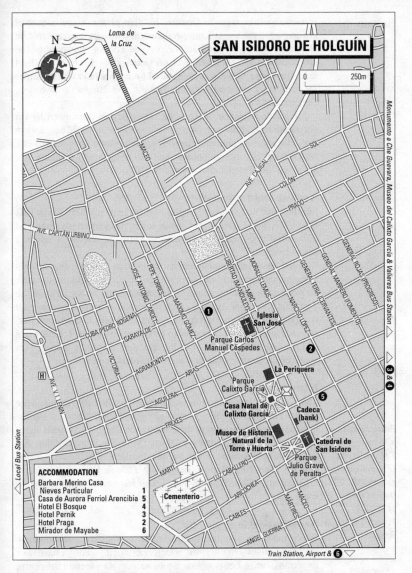

SAN ISIDORO DE HOLGUÍN

Loma de la Cruz

N

0   250m

Monumento a Che Guevara, Museo del Calixto García & Valleres Bus Station

1 Parque Carlos Manuel Céspedes

Iglesia San José

2

La Periquera

Parque Calixto García

5

Casa Natal de Calixto García

Cadeca (bank)

Museo de Historia Natural de la Torre y Huerta

Catedral de San Isidoro

Parque Julio Grave de Peralta

Local Bus Station

Cementerio

ACCOMMODATION

Barbara Merino Casa Nieves Particular	**1**
Casa de Aurora Ferriol Arencibia	**5**
Hotel El Bosque	**4**
Hotel Pernik	**3**
Hotel Praga	**2**
Mirador de Mayabe	**6**

Train Station, Airport & **6**

importance by coastal Gibara (see p.351). In spite of its rather grand layout, laid out in accordance with Spanish colonial city planning laws, it developed slowly. However, by the nineteenth century the economy had established itself in sugar production and fruit-growing, as well as a little tobacco cultivation, and the town grew accordingly.

Holguín

As with other areas in Oriente, Holguín province saw plenty of action during the wars of independence, and the city was captured by Mambises led by General Julio Grave de Peralta shortly after the inception of the Ten Years' War on October 30, 1868. It was held until December 6, but was recaptured four years later on December 19, 1872, by General Máximo Gómez and Holguín's own son, General Calixto García.

After independence, the province was largely dominated by US corporations and Holguín chugged along much the same as it always had. Since the revolution, however, it has become an industrial city with several factories and plants, and was designated provincial capital when the province was created in 1975.

Arrival and information

International and domestic **flights** land at the Aeropuerto Frank País (☎24/43-93-40), about 4km out of town, from where metered and unmetered taxis will run you to the centre for about $7 and $12 respectively.

Local buses and interprovincial **colectivos** pull into the Valiares Terminal de Omnibus in front of the Calixto García stadium car park on Avenida de los Liberatadores. **Interprovincial buses** arrive at the Astro Estación José María, Carretera Central e/ Independencia y 20 de Mayo, about 1km west from the centre where horse-drawn carriages, *bicitaxis* and taxis wait to ferry you into town. **Trains** arrive at Terminal de Ferrocaril Vidal Pita no. 3 e/ Libertad y Maceo, 1km south of the town centre, and served by taxis and *bicitaxis*.

Information

There's no real centre for tourist information, although at a pinch the *Islazul* reservations office, Libertad no. 199 esq. Martí, by Parque Calixto García, may be of limited assistance. The Pedro Rojena shop, Frexes no. 193 e/ Frexes y Martí (Mon–Fri 9am–5.30pm, Sat 9am–3pm), sells **maps**, which become harder to find the further east you go. The central **post office**, by Parque Calixto García, at Libertad no. 183 e/ Frexes y Martí, also has decent maps and postcards.

Pedro Rojena also sells T-shirts, tapes, CDs, postcards and socialist-themed books in English, French and Spanish.

Accommodation

Whilst the three state hotels catering for tourists are sound options, they're all slightly out of town, which is a drag if you don't have your own transport. A better option if you want to stay around the centre are the *casas particulares* which are just beginning to open up in Holguín, although as yet few of these are authorized. The proprietors of the two listed may be able to suggest other places, and the *bicitaxi* drivers who congregate around Parque Calixto García are good people to ask, though the latter are likely to charge a $5 daily commission that will be added to your bill.

Hotels

El Bosque, Ave. Jorge Dimitrov Reparto Pedro Díaz Coello ☎024/48-10-12. The best dollar hotel in Holguín, on the outskirts of town, 2km east of the centre. Although not modern, the individual self-contained blocks, with two or three rooms apiece, are well-maintained and set in leafy grounds. Some rooms have refrigerators and all are super-clean, with spotless bathrooms and hibiscus flowers on the bed. Two restaurants, a bar and a pool flesh out the package. ③–④.

Mirador de Mayabe, Alturas de Mayabe ☎024/42-21-60. Panoramic views over the valley and plenty of giant butterflies making the most of the open space make this the most picturesque of Holguín's hotels, although it's 8km south out of town. Rooms are decent though dark and the pool is invitingly large. ③–④.

Hotel Pernik, Ave. Jorge Dimitrov ☎024/42-47-18 or 42-41-17. A bulky, imposing hotel located near the Plaza de la Revolución, a good half-hour's walk from the town centre, although taxis wait outside to ferry you in. It's a bit grim and the service is half-hearted but there are usually rooms available and these are good-sized, with satellite television. Although there's no hot water in the bathrooms there's often a complimentary lizard. ③.

Hotel Praga, Narcisco Lopez no. 143 e/ Frexes y Aguilara ☎024/42-26-65. An airy peso hotel four blocks northeast from the centre, and hidden at the top of a flight of stairs. Rooms are reasonable, staff are friendly and there's an attractive lobby paved with black and white marble. The bathrooms, all cracked tiles and leaky showers, are rather grimy but overall this place offers good value for money. ①.

Casas particulares

Casa de Aurora Ferriol Arencibia, Martí no. 102, e/ Morales Lemus y Narciso Lopez ☎024/46-11-91. An a/c room near the centre, with its own bathroom and lurid girlie picture above the bed. ②.

Casa de Bárbara Merino Nieves, Martires no. 31 e/ Agramonte y Garayalde ☎024/42-38-05. One excellent, cavernous double room with its own bathroom. The separate front door allows for privacy whilst you still have the option of hanging out with the friendly owners next door. ②.

The Town

The centre is easy to negotiate and most of the sights spread out from the central **Parque Calixto García**, an oval expanse of ornamental pink marble and Cuban jade-green marble. In the centre, a square marble column is topped by the statue of war hero Calixto García, leaning upon his sword. While there are no grassed areas, a bushy rim of trees lines the park's outer edge and the benches beneath are packed with old men relaxing in the shade, the more garrulous of whom will gladly fill you in on the entire history of the province.

It was part of the original Spanish plans for colonial towns to build a square, presided over by a church, every four blocks and an overview of the city shows that in Holguín this was well executed. The squares were used for public meetings, markets and fairs, and to allow the church authorities to keep a beady eye on all parishioners.

The Mirador de Mayabe hotel's celebrity is Pancho, a beleaguered donkey whose star turn is consuming vast quantities of Mayabe beer bought for him by well-meaning guests. Rumour has it that the original donkey died some years ago and his successor is a pale imitation who can't hold his drink and has been seen staggering after one too many.

Holguín's several **churches** are all handsome enough to warrant closer inspection. **Iglesia San José**, north of Parque Calixto García, is hands down the most picturesque while the grand **La Catedral de San Isidoro de Holguín**, two blocks south of Parque Calixto García, is austere but quietly splendid.

Of the town's museums, the **Museo Provincial de Holguín**, which fronts Parque Calixto García, houses a worthy collection of artefacts spanning pre-Columbian times to the revolution, though the building's own history is easily as interesting as anything within. Round the corner, the **Museo de Historia Natural de la Torre y Huerta** is worth a peek if only for the building it is housed in, while the modest **Casa Natal de Calixto García**, two blocks east of the parque, has a small collection of exhibits honouring the city hero.

In the outskirts of town, you might want to head for the **Museo del Estadio Calixto García**, with a tiny but engaging exhibition of sporting trophies and photographs, and the sombre but impressive **Monumento al Guerrillero Heróico Ernesto Che Guevara**, commemorating the national hero. Finally, a climb up **La Loma de la Cruz** is a literally breathtaking way to admire the city from on high.

Museo Provincial de Holguín

Presiding over the northwestern side of Parque Calixto García is the **Museo Provincial de Holguín** (Mon–Fri 9am–5pm, Sat 9am–1pm; $1), where a number of worthwhile exhibits are displayed in one of the town's most impressive buildings. The handsome ochre edifice, lined with simple columns, delicate iron balconies and an elegant rooftop balustrade, was built between 1860 and 1868 as both the private house and business premises of Francisco Roldán y Rodríguez, a wealthy Spanish merchant. He devoted much time and effort to the project, even ferrying the head carpenter and mason over from Spain, but never managed to move in. While the great house awaited the finishing touches, the first war of independence broke out and, with Rodríguez's blessing, the Spanish army in Holguín hastily holed up there, capitalizing on its fortress-like proportions. The measure paid off and throughout the siege of the city (see p.344), the Mambises, unable to capture the building, had to content themselves with yelling "Parrots, parrots climb out of your cage" at the yellow-and-red-clad Spanish soldiers as they peeked from the windows. The house subsequently became known as **La Periquera** or the parrot cage, a nickname popular with locals to this day.

The building's indomitability – proved once more in a further attack by Mambises in 1872 – earned it a long life of public service, and it functioned variously as governor's residence and town hall until its conversion into a museum in 1978. It retains some beautiful features, most noticeably the iron door-knocker cast in the form of a woman's head, representing the spirit of friendship and the symbol of the city, along with an attractive central courtyard.

Occupying the ground floor, the museum's collection of historical flotsam and jetsam is rather sparse, with independence fighter Jose Martí's sword in prime position in a glass case, while the modern revolutionaries are represented by a grisly selection of bloodstained shirts accompanied by solemn staring photographs of their unfortunate owners. The best section is the small set of pre-Columbian artefacts found in and around Holguín, including bone fragments of necklaces and pieces of clay pots. Most impressive is a polished, olive-coloured peridot Taíno axe, known as the Axe of Holguín, which was discovered in 1860 in the hills surrounding the city. Carved with a grimacing male figure crowned with a diadem, it was used in religious ceremonies.

Museo de Historia Natural and Casa Natal de Calixto García

A block south of the plaza, at Maceo no. 129, is the Museo de Historia Natural de la Torre y Huerta (Tues–Sat 8am–noon & 1–5pm, Sun 8am–noon; $1). The building itself is the real reason to come here, a fanciful nineteenth-century confection with a pillared portico and an entrance portal exquisitely tiled in bright ceramic squares of lacquered aqua and rose, complementing the richly patterned floor inside. Added to the light raining down through the stained-glass windows, the décor completely outshines the lacklustre collection of *polimitas* snail shells, stuffed animals and dead fish that form the museum exhibits.

Also disappointing is the austere, faded white and blue Casa Natal de Calixto García, a block east of the plaza at Miró no. 147 (Mon–Fri 9am–5pm, Sat 9am–1pm; $1), where General Calixto García was born on August 4, 1839. Although he won several battles during the Ten Years' War, the general is not a particularly significant figure in the history of Cuba and is highly honoured in Holguín mainly because he was born here. Inside, the bland glass cabinets filled with disjointed trivia and the dry histories related on placards tell little of the man himself and you are left feeling that his rust-spotted swords, his mother's black lace mantilla, and his wire-rimmed spectacles would be better off incorporated into a larger collection elsewhere.

Iglesia San José

Three blocks north of the Casa Natal de Calixto García, fronting the shady, cobbled Plaza Carlos Manuel de Céspedes, is the Iglesia San José. With its single weatherbeaten clock tower rising above regular stone arches and topped with a domed turret, the church is easily the most attractive spot in town. On Saturdays at 8pm a mechanical organ player fills the park with romantic tunes. There's been a church on this site since 1815, though various overhauls over the years have rendered the original building unrecognizable. The present Neoclassical tower, added in 1841, was the town's tallest structure for a while and was used as a lookout point by the Mambises during the siege of the city in 1868.

Holguín

The church's opening hours are irregular, but mornings are usually a safe bet.

Vibrant and welcoming, contrasting with many Cuban churches, the ornate Baroque interior has sturdy central pillars appealingly decorated in pink and white candy-like spirals above a faded black and white marble-flagged floor. The rest of the church leans towards more traditional Catholic decor, with life-sized effigies of saints huddled above altars and sentimental paintings of the life of Christ on the walls.

Catedral de San Isidoro

The **Catedral de San Isidoro de Holguín** (daily 8am–noon & 4–6pm; free), named for the patron saint of the city, lords it over the stately Parque Julio Grave de Peralta (also known as Parque de los Flores and originally called the Parque San Isidoro). Surrounded by a walled patio, the stalwart but simple cathedral, with two turrets and a red-tiled roof, glows in the Caribbean sun. A recent slick of magnolia paint has somewhat diminished its crumbling romanticism, but has added a debonair austerity.

The original church on this site, completed in 1720, was one of the first buildings in Holguín; a humble affair built from palm trees, it lasted ten years until a sturdier structure with a tiled roof and stone floor was erected in 1730. When this started to deteriorate, in the late 1790s, the church elders exerted gentle pressure on the wealthier Holguíneros, and the current building was erected in 1815. The small Jesús de Nazareth chapel to the back of the building, now an office-cum-inner sanctum for church officials, was added in 1862, and the twin towers in 1900–10. Built as a parish church, and also used as the city crypt, it was only elevated to cathedral status in 1979, which accounts for its straightforward design and small size.

A spicy, warm smell of wood drifts through the simple interior, where graceful high ceilings lined with unadorned wooden rafters, balustrades over the windows and celestial blue altars add to the church's dignified air. On your way out, have a look at the heavy, wooden main door, pockmarked by bullets in the battles of the wars of independence.

Museo Calixto García and Monumento al Ernesto Che Guevara

Away from the sights clustered around the centre are two attractions worth visiting. Housed in the Calixto García stadium, 1km east of town, the minute **Museo del Estadio Calixto García** (Mon–Fri 9am–noon & 1–5pm; $1) is entertaining enough, although essentially a space-filler for the stadium foyer. It combines trophies and medals from various local sports stars with some quaint photographs of such revolutionaries as Camilio Cienfuegos and Raúl Castro playing baseball. Check out the one of a youthful and lithe Fidel Castro, baseball bat poised, and another of Che Guevara enjoying a more sedentary game of chess.

From here you can stroll further east for roughly 1km along Avenida de los Libertadores for a look at the **Monumento al Guerrillero Heróico Ernesto Che Guevara**, an impressive three-part sculpture with panels showing a silhouette of Guevara approaching, striding forward, and receding. Executed in sombre stone, it's an eye-catching and accomplished piece of work, said to allude to his revolutionary influence, presence and lasting legacy.

La Loma de la Cruz

Rising above Holguín, **La Loma de la Cruz**, or Hill of the Cross, is the largest of the hills that form a natural border to the north of the city. It's a steep walk up 458 steps, starting from the northern end of Maceo, to the summit, where you'll find the hefty wooden cross erected on May 3, 1790, by Friar Antonio de Algerías, following the Spanish tradition of the *Romería de la Cruz* (Pilgrimage of the Cross). This custom commemorates St Elena, mother of Constantine the Great, who, according to legend, rediscovered the original cross of Christ's crucifixion on that day. Every May 3, a Mass is held for the faithful – who until the construction of the staircase in 1950 had to toil up the hill the long way round – along with a low-key week-long festival in Holguín, where locals gather nightly around beer stalls and food stands set up around the centre.

The hill was also used by the Spanish as a look-out during the wars of independence, and a bijou **fort** on the plateau set back from the cross remains as evidence. You can appreciate why the Spanish chose this point when you gaze down at the town's rigid grid below and the panorama of lush green land on one side and dry countryside on the other, with parched and dusty hillocks visible in the distance. The fort now houses a small gallery, with a selection of local artwork and original gifts like handmade notebooks for sale. Also taking advantage of the magnificent views is a **restaurant**, the *Mirador de Holguín* (see p.350), strategically placed at the summit.

If you don't fancy the climb, a metered taxi will run you up to the summit for around $5–6.

Eating and drinking

In common with other areas, Holguín has lost several of its *paladares* to high taxes, although those that remain are still the best choice for somewhere to eat, offering tasty, good-value meals in convivial surroundings. There are also a couple of good-quality state restaurants, while peso snack stalls are plentiful around the central streets and, further out, in the car park of the Calixto García stadium. **Bars** are thin on the ground and if you're looking for somewhere to drink you are better off in one of the restaurants or cafés listed below.

La Begonia, Maceo s/n e/ Martí y Frexes. A pretty 24-hour open-air café beneath a canopy of begonias overlooking Parque Calixto García, popular with *jineteros*. The greasy fried chicken, fries and pizza mean it's a better place to drink than eat.

Holguín

La Boguedita de Holguín, Aguilera no. 249 esq. Martires. A pleasant restaurant specializing in grilled pork and occasionally beef, with seating beneath grapevines and a bar area where *trovadores* play in the evenings.

Cafetería Cristal, Martí s/n esq. Libertad. A clean and shiny 24-hour ice cream parlour with a/c overlooking Parque Calixto García. Flavours include guava and almond as well as the ubiquitous strawberry and chocolate. It also does some tasty, uncomplicated snacks like chicken sandwiches and fries.

Cremería Guamá, Luz Caballero y Libertad. Join the queue for the best peso ice cream in Holguín. Standard flavours on offer are strawberry and chocolate.

La Granjita, Máximo Gómez no. 264 e/ Frexes y Aguilera. No-frills peso restaurant doling out basic, inexpensive Cuban meals.

Mirador de Holguín, La Loma de la Cruz. Good-value peso restaurant at the top of the hill, with chargrilled dishes and superb views over the city. Friendly and unpretentious.

El Mirador de Riveron, Martires no. 7 e/ Cuba y Garayalde. With a view over the hills this friendly *paladar* is the best place to watch the sunset, and enjoy a variety of inventively cooked pork, chicken and lamb dishes, all accompanied by rice and beans with salad.

Paladar Dos Palmas, Cable no. 99 esq. Libertad. Standard *paladar* serving up generous portions of pork or chicken with rice and beans, and simple salads.

Taberna Pancho, Ave. Jorge Dimitrov. A short drive or a long walk east out of town, this ugly restaurant specializes in foamy beer and fat, if lukewarm, sausages.

Entertainment and nightlife

You can brush up on your bolero and salsa technique at the Casa de la Trova (☎24/42-21-71), which offers dance classes and prebooked conferences ($50) on Cuban music and folklore.

Whilst Holguín doesn't boast masses of **nightlife**, there are a couple of places that offer a cheap and lively night out and the entrance fee shouldn't exceed $5. It you're feeling brave check out *Disco Alba* on Martires e/ Frexes y Aguilera, where partygoers queue to squeeze through a gap in the wall of a roofless, crumbling building converted into an unofficial disco. It feels a bit edgy but is safe enough. Another spot popular with the younger crowd is *Cabinete Caligari*, Martí esq. Maceo, an open-air rooftop disco. Music is limited to whatever tapes the clientele brings along but it's a merry place, where the drink of choice is an unnamed, lethal blend of neat rum and Day-Glo mint cordial. More conventional is the *Casa de la Trova*, Maceo no. 174 e/ Frexes y Martí (Thurs–Sun), where a mixed crowd of cross-generational visitors and Cubans fill the big wooden dancefloor for exuberant *salsa* and traditional *trova* sessions, with live bands playing from Thursday to Saturday. The *Pico Cristal*, on the third floor of the *Cristal* building on Libertad esq. Martí, is a brash disco whose sole virtue is that it stays open later than the rest.

The small and intimate *Cine Martí*, beside Parque Calixto García, shows Cuban and international **films**, as does the *Cine Baría*, four blocks east on Libertad. The *Teatro Eddy Suñol*, on the north side of Parque Calixto García, puts on **plays** and musical entertainment. There are **baseball** games between November and April during the national series and occasional games throughout the year: the Estadio Calixto García is at Avenida 20 Aniversario esq. Avenida de los Libertadores (☎24/42-49-24).

Listings

Airlines Cubana, Edificio Pico de Cristal, Libertad esq. Martí ☎24/42-57-07.

Banks and exchange CADECA, Libertad no. 205 e/ Martí y Luz Caballero (Mon–Sat 8.30am–6pm, Sun 8am–1pm), can change travellers' cheques and give cash advances on Visa and Mastercard.

Immigration and legal The immigration office, where you can renew standard tourist visas, is at Fromento s/n esq. Peralejos Repto Peralta (Mon–Fri 8am–noon & 2–4pm). Arrive early to avoid long queues.

Medical The *Hotel Pernik* and the *Hotel El Bosque* both have medical services, while the main hospital, Hospital Lenin, is on Avenida Lenin (☎24/42-53-02). Call ☎24/42-27-48 for a state ambulance.

Photography Photo Services, Libertad no. 132 e/ Frexes y Aquilera.

Post office The main post office is at Libertad no. 183 e/ Frexes y Martí (Mon–Fri 10am–6pm, Sat 10am–noon), with a DHL service and phones for international calls.

Taxis Turistaxi can be reached on ☎24/42-41-87.

Telephones The ETECSA international call centre is on Republica 9 Rastro esq. Frexes (Mon–Fri 7am–10pm, Sat & Sun 7am–9pm), with dollar phone cards sold for international calls.

Gibara

After travelling 35km north from Holguín, through a buxom set of mountains that locals compare to a woman's breasts, you reach the pleasingly somnolent fishing port of **GIBARA**, spreading from a calm and sparkling bay and seeping into the surrounding rugged hillside. This little-visited gem is just the place to spend a few hours – or even days – enjoying the tranquil views, away-from-it-all atmosphere and lush scenery, and seeking out the traces of history glimpsed in the attractive colonial buildings.

Some history

Founded in 1827, Gibara became the main north-coast port in Oriente, due to its wide, natural bay, and during the nineteenth century the town enjoyed valuable trade links with Spain, the rest of Europe and, later, the United States. It was considered important enough to reinforce with a small fortification, built on the Los Caneyes hilltop, the ruins of which remain. Though small, Gibara was a fashionable and wealthy town, home to several aristocratic families and famed for its elegant edifices. Its beauty prompted several pseudonyms – "Encanto Eden" (Enchanted Eden), "Perla del Oriente" (Pearl of the Orient), and, from sailors approaching the bay and dazzled by its whitewashed houses, "La Villa Blanca".

The glory days were not to last, however, and Gibara's importance began to slip away with the introduction of the railway, which could more easily transport freight around the country. The decrease in trade left the town floundering, and during the 1920s and 1930s many townsfolk moved elsewhere in search of work, leaving Gibara

About 20km
east of Gibara,
in the Bahía
de Bariay,
Playa Don
Lino was the
site of
Christopher
Columbus's
first landing
in Cuba, on
October 28,
1492. A small
monument
marks the
spot.

to shrink into today's pleasant village where farming and fishing make up the main industry. Vestiges of the town's halcyon era are still evident, though, in the ornate tiles adorning several buildings and the elegant sweep of the municipal buildings.

The name "Gibara" comes from the word *giba*, or hump, and refers to the **Silla de Gibara**, a hill which, seen from the sea, looks like a horse's saddle. Gibarans swear this is the one Christopher Columbus mentioned in his log when approaching Cuban shores, but although he did first land in Holguín province the hill is generally taken to be El Yunque in Baracoa, Guantánamo province (see p.373).

The Town

An enjoyable place for a wander, Gibara's streets fan out from the dainty Plaza de la Iglesia. Rimmed with large *Inbondeiro* African oak trees imported from Angola in the 1970s, the plaza is dominated by the Iglesia de San Fulgencio, a late nineteenth-century church built in a medley of styles. In the centre of the square is the marble **Statue of Liberty**, erected to commemorate the rebel army's triumphant entrance into town on July 25, 1898, during the second war of independence. Sculpted in Italy, the statue is smaller and less austere than her North American counterpart and bears the winsome face of Aurora Peréz Desdín, a local woman who was considered so captivating that the town supplied the sculptor with her photograph so that he might preserve her beauty forever.

Even the smallest Cuban town has a motheaten collection of stuffed animals, and Gibara is no exception, though at least this one, the **Museo Historia Natural** (Tues–Sat 8am–noon & 1–5pm, Sun 8am–noon; $1), bordering the park, is worth a peek, not least for its *piéce de résistance* of Cuban grotesque: a long-dead hermaphrodite chicken which was once both rooster and hen. The rest of the exhibits include a collection of *polimitas* shells and a sad old humpback whale killed by mistake in 1978.

The best museum in town is the **Museo del Arte Colonial** (Tues–Sat 8am–noon & 1–5pm, Sun 8am–noon; $1), one block away at Independencia no. 19. The sumptuous building, beautifully lined with yellow and blue tiles, was built in the nineteenth century as the private residence of José Beola, a wealthy local merchant. Its interior is quietly splendid, with a narrow, sweeping staircase leading upstairs to the fine, though small, collection of paintings. This includes a meticulous depiction of the town in its glory days, with ships approaching a wide sweep of harbour, and majestic houses crowding the hillside beyond. Amongst the collection of colonial furniture is a spectacular bedroom suite, with a huge mirror studded with pineapples – a showy display of the family's wealth. The delicately coloured stained-glass windows, set with pale segments of pink and blue arrayed into a half circle of colour, are original to the house and the biggest in the province.

Next door, at no. 20, the **Museo Municipal** (Tues–Sat 8am–noon & 1–5pm, Sun 8am–noon; $1) is not as captivating but still worth a glance. Along with some general colonial ephemera are odds and ends from Cubans who fought and died in Angola during the 1970s. A torn flag and discarded asthma inhaler are poignant reminders of the war.

Gibara is at its prettiest along the seafront, where **Playacita Ballado** and **Playa La Concha** are both tiny but scenic scoops of yellow sand enjoyed by local kids and are good places for a dip after a meander through the town. Finally, one sight not to be missed is the old naval **fort** overlooking the town up on Los Caneyes hill – a forty-minute walk from sea level. Although the small fort is little more than a broken-down shell, the view over the bay and town below easily compensates.

Practicalities

Buses to Gibara leave the Valiares depot in Holguín around 7am daily and reach Gibara around 9.30am, or you can catch a private *camión* truck from the same place. An unmetered taxi will take you there and back for around $15.

There's only one place to **stay** here, but it's well above average. *Villa Miguel*, no. 61 J. Peralta e/ J. Morra y Mariana Grajales (☎24/34-2-11; ②), a *casa particular* with a view over Playa La Concha, has two excellent, clean and spacious rooms with private bathroom and off-road parking. The telephone number given is the next-door neighbour's – ask for Miguel. For one of the best **meals** in the province, head to *La Negra*, Máximo Gómez, no. 5 e/ Cuba y J. Aguero, for mouthwatering but inexpensive seafood.

Guardalavaca and around

Despite being the province's main tourist resort, **GUARDALAVACA**, on the north coast 112km from Holguín, retains a charmingly home-spun air. Surrounded by hilly countryside and shining fields of sugar-cane, it combines small-scale intimacy with the vibrancy lent by a youthful clientele. Four hotels are centred around the lively **Playa Guardalavaca**, and there's a more exclusive satellite resort at **Playa Esmeralda**, about 5km away. Guardalavaca town, which backs onto the resort, is little more than a clutch of houses, though the surrounding area has enough excellent sights to keep you busy for a few days should you tire of sunning yourself on the beaches.

All the hotels arrange excursions to the fascinating **Taíno burial ground** uncovered about 3km away in the Maniabon hills, which incorporates the Museo de Chorro de Maita and a recreation of a Taíno village that really brings the lost culture to life. Close to Playa Esmeralda, at the Bahía de Naranjo, an offshore **aquarium** offers an entertaining day out, also arranged via the hotels. Alternatively one of the most rewarding pastimes is to rent a bicycle or moped and head

The name Guardalavaca means "keep the cow safe", thought to refer to the need to protect livestock and valuables from marauding pirates who used the area as a refuge point.

Holguín

Excursions from Guardalavaca

There are several excursions centred around the province, as well as others that are more wide ranging. While you can get to most sites independently, it may be easier to go on a tour. All are organized by Cubatur (☎27/3-01-71), which has a representative in each hotel.

Banes Although Banes itself is a bit of a backwater, this half-day trip takes you to the Museo Indocubano with its small but worthy collection of pre-Columbian artefacts. $25. See p.358.

Cayo Saetía, Holguín Province. A day-trip to one of the most unusual resorts in the country. Enjoy the charms of the white sand beach and take a safari through the surrounding woodland and savannahs to see zebras, ostriches and the like roaming freely. $60. See p.359.

Havana You are flown to Havana for a whistle-stop tour of Habana Vieja and Vedado, with some free time for shopping. Lunch at one of the better Havanan restaurants is included. $100.

Holguín A half-day trip to the provincial capital, offering a visit to a cigar factory where you can see cigars being handmade in the classic Cuban way, a trip up the Loma de la Cruz hill and free time to explore the town centre. Although you could just rent a car to get to Holguín, the only way to visit the cigar factory is as part of an organized tour. $45. See p.341.

Santiago de Cuba A full day-trip to Cuba's second biggest city. The bus ride there and back takes you through some of the regions' most scenic countryside, while Santiago itself is a handsome colonial city bursting with historical sites. The trip includes visits to the Museo de Ambiente Histórico Cubano, the Santa Ifigenia cemetery and the Moncada barracks. $70. See p.377.

off into the dazzling countryside to enjoy stunning views over hills and sea; you can also make the trip on horseback with a guide (see p.354).

Arrival, information and transport

Flights for visitors on package holidays land at Holguín's Aeropuerto Frank País (see p.344) and are ferried to the resort by special buses. Each hotel has their own **excursions** officers who arrange trips to the local sights (see box above) and can supply some information in the absence of formal tourist offices.

In theory, **local buses** run from Holguín's Valiares bus terminal once a day, leaving at 7am and pulling up in front of the hotels at around 9.30am, though these are subject to petrol shortages. **Colectivo** shared taxis also run this route and leave throughout the day until about 5pm.

All the hotels have **car rental** desks. Alternatively, you can visit the central offices of Cubacar, Playa Guardalavaca (☎24/3-02-43), or Havanautos, at the Cupet Cimex garage, Playa Guardalavaca (☎24/3-01-07). **Mopeds** can be rented from a roadside stand opposite *Delta Las Brisas Club Resort* ($10 for the first hour, $7 for the second, $5 for the third). All the hotels rent **bicycles**, an excellent way to get around. **Taxis** usually loiter outside hotels, or you can call Taxi-OK (☎24/3-02-43) for taxis or Transgaviota (☎24/3-01-66), which offers cars and minibuses.

Accommodation

As a prime resort, Guardalavaca's **accommodation** consists of all-inclusive hotels at the top end of the price range, and whilst most deliver the standards you would expect for the price-tag, a couple are slightly lacking. As the region has grown up with the tourist industry, there are no peso hotels nor any registered *casas particulares*, although you might be able to find unregistered accommodation in the houses near the beach.

The three hotels around Playa Guardalavaca are interconnected, with guests at each entitled to vouchers that allow them to eat in the restaurants of the others; *Delta Las Brisas Club Resort* is based on Playa Las Brisas, 1500m east. All four offer free **watersports** including kayaks, catamarans and diving classes in the hotel pools (open water dives cost extra), although you have to pay for activities that use gas, namely jetskis and rides on the inflatable yellow banana.

The two hotels at Playa Esmeralda are decidedly fabulous, facing the low peaks of the Cerro de Maita mountains and with a full complement of facilities.

Playa Guardalavaca and Playa Las Brisas

Atlántico ☎24/3-01-80; fax 3-02-00. A relatively aged hotel, though a recent, costly makeover has almost brought it into line with its more modern neighbours, and with big, airy rooms it's a reasonable choice. Twinned with *Atlántico Bungalow*, and guests are free to use the facilities there too. ⑥–⑦.

Atlántico Bungalow ☎24/3-01-95; fax 3-02-00. With spacious, well-appointed rooms laid out in "bungalow" blocks, a generously proportioned pool and good international food, this hotel makes for a comfortable stay, though it's a short walk from the beach. There's a full complement of free facilities, including the use of a large pool, non-motorized watersports, bars and restaurants and a children's club. Those after peace and quiet might not appreciate the friendly staff's relentless encouragement to join in the rumbunctious fun and games. ⑥.

Club Amigo Guardalavaca ☎24/3-01-21. As the oldest on the strip, this hotel is something of a poor relation, with slightly shabby rooms and lacklustre service – it's telling that this is the only hotel on the strip open to ordinary Cubans. That said, the staff are friendly and what they lack in competence they make up for in enthusiasm. ⑦.

Delta Las Brisas Club Resort, Calle 2 no. 1 ☎24/3-02-18; fax 3-00-18. The plushest hotel on the strip, with four restaurants, three snack bars, a beauty salon, massage parlour, kids' camp and watersports, as well as mercifully restrained variety show-style entertainment. There's a choice between rooms and suites within the hotel block or more privacy in newer bungalow-style rooms, although all are equally luxurious (suites have jacuzzis). Non-guests can wallow in luxury for $25 a day. ⑦–⑧.

Playa Esmeralda

Sol Club Río de Luna ☎24/3-00-30. The posher of Playa Esmeralda's two hotels has an attractive lobby area full of tall leafy plants beneath a wooden roof. The well-appointed rooms are spacious and light and come equipped with cable television and security boxes, plus many have a sea view. The hotel also

There's a souvenir shop (Mon–Sat 9am–9pm) behind the Atlántico hotel, towards the beach.

You can cash travellers' cheques at most of the hotels and get advances on Visa and Mastercard at Delta Las Brisas Club Resort.

boasts extra activities including tennis, sauna, gym, sailing school and excursions into the surrounding countryside. ⑧–⑨.

Sol Río de Mares ☎24/3-00-60. A well-designed hotel similar to the *Sol Club Río de Luna*, with an attractive entrance filled with a mass of greenery home to several tame birds. Large comfortable rooms overlook a central swimming pool, and the hotel offers a range of facilities including two restaurants, three bars, extensive watersports and a pool table. ⑦.

Playa Guardalavaca and Playa Las Brisas

A 1500-metre-long stretch of sugar-white sand dappled with light streaming through abundant foliage, **Playa Guardalavaca** is a delight. A shady boulevard of palms, tamarind and sea grape trees runs along the centre of the beach, the branches strung with hammocks and T-shirts for sale. One of the most refreshing aspects of Playa Guardalavaca is that, unlike many resort beaches, it's open to Cubans as well as tourists, which gives it a certain vitality. Groups of friends hang out chatting or resting in the shade while children play in the water. Locals mingle with tourists but with a marked lack of hustle. Those seeking solitude should head to the eastern end, where the beach breaks out of its leafy cover and is usually fairly deserted. Midway along, a **restaurant** serves simple snacks and drinks, and there are stands renting out **snorkelling equipment** so you can explore the coral reef offshore.

A chain of large natural boulders divides the public beach from **Playa Las Brisas**, which lies to the east of Playa Guardalavaca and is the private property of the *Delta Las Brisas Club Resort*. Guests of the other hotels may use the beach, though locals can't.

Playa Esmeralda

A five-kilometre trip from Guardalavaca west along the Holguín road, picture-perfect **Playa Esmeralda** – also known as Estero Ciego – boasts clear blue water, a smooth swathe of powdery sand speckled with thatched sunshades, and two luxury hotels hidden from view by thoughtfully planted bushes and shrubs. If you want unashamed hassle-free luxury where the intrusion of local culture is kept to a bare minimum, this is the place for you. The beach is owned by the hotels but open to non-guests, although to go on the beach you'll have to pay for a day pass (around $40) for facilities, meals and drinks.

Also in the resort is a **horse-riding centre**, opposite the hotels, with negotiable rates for treks into the countryside depending on group size and excursion length, and *Hotel Sol Club Río de Luna*'s **dive centre**, Easy Sport (☎24/3-01-02), offering dives for $30 and courses for between $35 and $500.

Museo de Chorro de Maita and the Aldea Taína

The fascinating **Museo de Chorro de Maita** (Tues–Sat 9am–5pm, Sun 9am–1pm; $2), 6km east of the hotel strip in a somewhat isolated spot in the Maniabon hills, is a must for anyone interested in pre-Columbian history. In a shallow pit in the middle of the museum are 108 Taíno skeletons that were buried on this site between the 1490s and the 1540s, and uncovered in 1986. Although some of the original skeletons were removed to other museums, reproductions have replaced them and you can walk around the viewing gallery above the pit to inspect them, still folded into the traditional foetal position in which they were buried. Tests have revealed that all the deaths were natural, although perplexingly, fifty percent of the group were children.

The most interesting aspect is that one of the skeletons was found to be a young male European buried in a Christian position with his arms folded across his chest. Whilst no records exist, it's thought that the European had been living in harmony with the Taíno community, possibly as a friar, and other evidence, like the fragments of ceramics influenced by Spanish design also on display in the museum, points to European contact. Interestingly, some of the later skeletons are also buried in a Christian manner, suggesting that the mystery European managed to convert at least some members of the community.

In cabinets around the walls of the museum are fragments of earthenware pots along with shell and ceramic jewellery, while arrows positioned in the grave indicate where these were found. The area around the museum has more indigenous remains than any other part of Cuba and villagers still unearth artefacts and remnants of jewellery today.

Aldea Taína

Just across the road is the **Aldea Taína** (Tues–Sat 9am–5pm, Sun 9am–1pm; $2), an excellent and evocative reconstruction of a Taíno village, offering an insight into an extinguished culture and bringing to life many of the artefacts seen in museums around the country. Pains have been taken to authenticate the enterprise and the little settlement features houses made from royal palm trees like those the Taínos used to construct, populated by groups of life-sized models of Taínos posed cooking and preparing food or attending to community rituals. Of particular note is the group inside one of the houses watching the medicine man attempt to cure a patient, and another group outside depicted in a ceremonial dance. Details like the colourful *eanáhuas* skirts that each woman began to wear after her first menstruation have been carefully reproduced and decorated with shells, and life-like model dogs – the Taínos trained them never to bark – add to the atmosphere.

The **restaurant** in the village, decorated with designs found on the wall of Taíno caves, continues the theme, serving Taíno foods including herb teas, sweet potato and cassava bread. The recommended dish is the *ajiaco*, a tasty potato, maize and meat stew.

*All access to
the Acuario
Cayo Naranjo
is by boat.*

Acuario Cayo Naranjo

The main reason to visit the **Bahía de Naranjo**, 6km west of Guardalavaca beach, is the **Acuario Cayo Naranjo** (daily 7am–4pm; marine show noon–1pm; see box below for prices), a complex built on stilts in the shallows of the bay about 250m offshore. Although calling itself an aquarium it's really more of a tourist centre-cum-marine zoo, its smattering of sea creatures in tanks overshadowed by giddier attractions: yacht and speedboat "seafari" excursions around the bay, a saccharine sea-lion show and, most thrillingly, the chance to swim with a few frisky dolphins. Though undoubtedly more commercial than educational, it's a pleasant enough day out, and there's a good **restaurant** on site dishing up lobster dinners while hosting an interesting but rather incongruous Afro-Cuban dance and music show.

Aquarium prices

The aquarium has a range of offers, of which the cheapest is a simple boat passage, with entrance fee and sea-lion show ($15). It currently costs $20 extra to swim with the dolphins, but you should check this price as it seems to rise every few months. The above deal with a "seafari" trip around the bay will cost you an additional $35 in a yacht and an additional $40 in a catamaran, while the same offer plus a lobster dinner and Afro-Cuban musical show is $45. All local hotels offer these deals and can arrange transport.

Banes

There are two reasons to stop off at the sleepy town of **BANES**, made up of a clutch of characterful wooden houses and rather more anonymous concrete houses, 31km east of Guardalavaca. The first is to gawp at the **Iglesia de Nuestra Señora de la Caridad**, on the edge of a central park with a neat domed bandstand, where on October 10, 1948, **Fidel Castro** married his first wife, Mirta Diaz-Balart, sister of a university friend and daughter of the mayor of Banes. The couple divorced in 1954, the bride's conservative family allegedly disapproving of the young Castro, already known as a firebrand at the university.

The second, rather more substantial attraction is the **Museo Indocubano**, on Avenida General Marreo no. 305 (Tues–Sat 9am–5pm, Sun 8am–noon; $1), the only museum in Cuba exclusively devoted to pre-Columbian Cuban history. Whilst many of the fragments of ceramic pots and utensils and the representational sketches of indigenous communities are similar to exhibits in larger museums in the country, there is a unique and absorbing gathering of jewellery gleaned from the Holguín region, its centrepiece a tiny but stunning gold idol.

If you have time, take a look at the **Casa de la Cultura** on the opposite side of General Marreo, at no. 327 (daily 9am–5pm). With a black-and-white marble tiled floor, pale pink and gold walls and a sunny courtyard at the back, this elegant building is one of the town's most outstanding. As the town's theatre and music hall it has regular performances, and players are generally unfazed if you pass by to admire the building and catch snippets of their rehearsals during the daytime.

Practicalities

You can see Banes in a couple of hours, but should you decide to **stay**, check out *Casa de Bruno Meriño*, no. 3401A e/ Delfin Pupo y Jose Maria Heredia (no phone; ②), an attractive *casa particular*. The best place to **eat** is *Las Delicias*, a *paladar* at Augusto Blanca no. 1107 e/ Bruno Meriño y Bayamo Reparto Cardenes (knock on the door if it looks shut), where a friendly family cooks up portions of roast pork for about $5 a head.

Eastern Holguín

Towards the east the province becomes at once astonishingly beautiful and increasingly industrial, with several open-cast nickel mines and their processing plants scarring the hillsides. Cuba is one of the world's largest producers of nickel and it's in this region that all the mining action takes place.

Among the most significant features for visitors is **Cayo Saetía**, a magnificent island near the crescent-shaped **Bahía de Nipe**, the largest bay in the country. Once the exclusive resort of state officials, it is now a holiday resort combining a safari park of imported wildlife, with a fabulous white-sand beach and excellent diving. Its beauty, oddly, is not diminished by the pale orange smog drifting across the bay from grimy **Nicaro**, a distinctly uneventful town wreathed in plumes of factory smoke and set in the mineral-rich red earth of the region. From here, the ground swells and erupts into livid green mountains, with the peaceful **Pinares de Mayarí** a perfect base for exploring the waterfalls, lakes and ancient caves hidden throughout this clear, cool highland region.

Much of the lowland countryside ripples with sugarcane, and there's a particularly notable plantation near **Biran**, though it's famous as the birthplace of Fidel Castro rather than for its produce – an interesting diversion for the obsessive. The far eastern corner of the province ends in the small manufacturing town of **Moa**, a useful jumping-off point for Baracoa in Guantánamo province.

Cayo Saetía

Hidden away on the east side of the Bahía de Nipe near the village of Felton, and connected to the mainland by a narrow strip of land, picture-postcard, isolated **Cayo Saetía** is the most bizarre – and exclusive – resort in the country, a one-time private game reserve and paradisical beach catering to government party officials. Although it opened to the public during the 1990s, it retains its air of exclusivity. It's run by Gaviota, the tourist group owned by the army, which may explain the vaguely military aura, present in the ranks of Soviet helicopters waiting to ferry guests to and from the resort.

The perfect place to escape from the outside world, Cayo Saetía has two quite distinct faces. On the one hand are the scoops of practically deserted soft white **beach** along its northern coast, hemmed in by buttery yellow rockface and sliding into the bay's sparkling turquoise waters. Close to shore, the island's shelf makes for perfect **snorkelling**, with a wealth of brightly coloured sea life to explore, while further out to sea a coral reef offers good rather than spectacular **diving** possibilities.

Inland, Cayo Saetía's 42 square kilometres of woodland and meadows are home to the most exotic collection of animals in the country – a menagerie of imported zebras and antelopes, deer, wild boars and even ostriches, all freely galloping about. It's as close as Cuba gets to a **safari park** and guests are presented – totally without irony – with the choice of taking a jeep safari through the lush grounds, to admire and photograph the creatures, or blasting the hell out of them with rifles rented out at the central lodge house.

Practicalities

Most guests arrive at Cayo Saetía by **helicopter** from Nicaro airport (call Gaviota for details ☎ 7/33-97-80), rather than chancing the ten-kilometre-long bumpy dirt track from the coast. There's no way to visit without staying, and you're better off checking availability rather than turning up on spec as **accommodation** is limited to a central lodge house with five comfortable double cabins and one suite (☎ 24/42-53-50; ⑤), catered to by a **restaurant** well-stocked with exotic meats like antelope. You are not encouraged to roam about on your own – in case someone takes a pot shot at you. Instead, **jeep safari tours** ($9) take you through the grounds, and the lodge house also provides transport ($2) to the beach, 8km away. The hotel also offers horse riding, snorkelling expeditions and day-trips around the cay by speedboat.

The Pinares de Mayarí

High in the mountains of the Sierra de Nipe, 45km south of Cayo Saetía, the isolated and beautiful **Pinares de Mayarí** pine forest, based around the *Villa Pinares de Mayari*, is a great place to trek through or just chill out in. The forest is reached from the nondescript little town of **Mayarí**, 18km north via a steep hill road from which there are crisp views over the Bahía de Nipe and the terracotta open-cast nickle mines to the east, near Nicaro. This lofty region is also Cuba's main producer of **coffee**, with stretches of coffee plants visible along the way.

On your way up the hill, look out for a turning on the left that leads to **La Planca**, a scenic little flower garden with a bench overlooking the placid La Presa lake. At the top of the hill the sharp incline evens out into a plateau, where the lush green grass, low hills and cool air form a scene that's more alpine than Caribbean. Perched up here, the alpine-themed *Villa Pinares de Mayari* hotel

To get to the hotel from Mayarí, head for the Carretera Pinares and take the right-hand track where the road forks, past tiny Las Coloradas.

(☎24/5-33-08; ④), comprising two chalet-style villas with quaint rooms richly inlaid with wood, makes a perfect base for exploration and is decidedly picturesque in itself, with a small pool and a central dining hall like a giant cabin. It's next to wide and tranquil **La Presa lake**, though there's more exhilarating swimming at the majestic **Saltón de Guayabo waterfall**, hidden in woodland a short walk away. Also nearby are the intriguing **Farallones de Seboruco caves**, tucked away through a tangle of countryside roughly 2km away, with faint but still perceptible traces of pre-Columbian line sketches on the walls – bring a torch. The wide-mouthed caves, overhung by gnarled cliffs and spattered with delicately ringed snails' shells, have an aura of mystery helped along by the rumour that this deserted spot is the sight of illegal cow killings by black-market profiteers – many locals refuse to come here after dark.

Biran and the Finca Las Manacas

The whole swathe of land beneath the Bahía de Nipe is given over to sugar: a vast area of swaying cane and working plantations. There's nothing here for the casual visitor, though the truly devoted may wish to make a pilgrimage to the tiny community of **BIRAN**, 44km southwest of Mayarí, near which, at the **Finca Las Manacas** plantation, **Fidel Castro** was born on August 13, 1926. He spent part of his youth here, until sent to school in Santiago, and still owns the farm, which he visits regularly. Not promoted as a tourist attraction, it's a challenge to find: follow the road to Mayarí then turn west onto the road to Marcané; take a left at the sign to Biran and carry on. You are not allowed inside without permission from the Communist Party HQ in Holguín, but from outside the fence you can see a tidy and well-maintained farm with red-roofed buildings. In the foreground are the well-tended graves of Castro's father Angel Castro and mother Lina Ruz.

Moa

On the northern coast, close to the border with Guantánamo province and dominated by the nickel-smelting plant on the east side of town, is desolate, industrial **MOA**. The town is bereft of attractions but makes a handy jumping-off point for Baracoa in Guantánamo province, linked along the coastal road (though there are no buses), and has an airport servicing three weekly flights to and from Havana (tickets are sold at the Cubana office on Avenida del Puerto Rolo Monterrey; ☎24/6-76-78). A morning **bus** to Holguín leaves from the Terminal de Omnibus, near the town centre, which is also served by *colectivo* shared taxis. In the unlikely event that you'll want to **stay**, head for the *Miraflores* hotel, Avenida Amistad, on the hilltop west of the city (☎24/6-61-03; ③).

Holguín

The hotel offers guided walking trips to the Saltón de Guayabo waterfall and treks to the Farallones de Seboruco caves.

Nicknamed "the sacred cow", all cattle in Cuba come under the jurisdiction of the state and their private slaughter is strictly prohibited, part of the state drive to maximize milk yields in the face of shortages and to control profit from the sale of beef and dairy products.

Guantánamo

Synonymous with the beleaguered history of the US naval base, **Guantánamo** is an enduring legacy of the struggle between the US and Cuba. In name at least, it's one of the best-known places in Cuba: many a Cuban and a fair few visitors can sing the first bars of the immortal song *Guantanamera* – written by Joseito Fernández in the 1940s as a tribute to the women of Guantánamo. Made internationally famous by North American folk singer Pete Seeger during the 1970s, it has become something of a Cuban anthem and a firm – if somewhat hackneyed – favourite of tourist bar troubadours the country over, a fitting fate for the song which includes words from José Martí's most famous work, *Versos Sencillos*.

For many visitors, the **base** is the main reason to come to Cuba's easternmost province, and it's undeniably a fascinating piece of the Cuban-American relations jigsaw, although you cannot actually enter from Cuban territory. But Guantánamo province has a lot more to offer than its most notorious attraction, with a sweeping, deeply varied landscape of desert and thick rainforest and a uniquely mixed population. Many Cubans living in this region are of Haitian and Jamaican origin – the result of late nineteenth- and early twentieth-century immigration – while an indigenous heritage is still visible in the far east.

The provincial capital, small and quiet **Guantánamo**, is a very ordinary place, for all the fanfare, but it makes a useful starting-point for excursions into the fine surrounding countryside, as well as to **Mirador Malones** and **Caimanera**, from where you get a reasonable – albeit long distance – view of the naval base. The real charms of the province lie to the east, where **Baracoa**, one of the most enchanting towns in the country, clings to the north coast in splendid isolation, the last tip of the island as it trails off into the mixed waters of the Atlantic Ocean and the Caribbean Sea.

Guantánamo town and around

GUANTÁNAMO town is only on the tourist map because of the proximity of the US Guantánamo naval station, 22km southeast, but the base plays a very small part in the everyday life of the town itself. For the most part, this is a slow-paced provincial capital marked by a few ornate buildings, attractive but largely featureless streets and an easy-going populace. Most visitors bypass it altogether, and those who don't tend to use it simply as a stepping stone to the naval base and attractions further afield.

The small town fans out around the central **Parque Martí**, a small concrete square neatly bordered by intricately trimmed evergreens with hooped gateways. On its north side is the **Parroquía Santa Catalina de Riccis**, a pretty ochre church built in 1863 and given a facelift in 1960. Running parallel to the park is Pedro A.

Pérez, where the town's most beautiful building towers over the road: built between 1918 and 1920, though looking older than its years, the **Palacio de Salcines** is an eclectic neo-Rococo building with shuttered windows, cherubs over the door and, on its high spire, an outstretched figure with bugle in hand which has become the symbol of the city. It now houses an **art museum** of local works (Mon–Fri 8am–noon & 1–6pm, Sat 8am–noon; free).

Two blocks behind the park, at Martí no. 804, is the humble **Museo Provincial** (Mon 2–6pm, Tues–Sat 8am–noon & 2–6pm; $1). The site of an old prison, it displays the remains of some fearsome padlocks and bolts, though more interesting are the photos of US antics at the naval base, including one of a delinquent marine baring his bottom at the Cuban guards. Finally, one of the most intriguing buildings in town is the quite fantastical **agricultural marketplace**, on Moncada, three blocks from the park, with a big pink dome and a crown-like roof bearing statues of regal long-necked geese at each corner. Amid an atmosphere of intense activity, housewives scrutinize the piles of fresh fruit and vegetables, farmers hawk their wares and scavenging dogs slink underfoot.

Practicalities

Buses from Santiago, Bayamo, Havana and Holguín arrive at the Astro Terminal de Omnibus, Carretera Santiago, 2.5km out of town. Daily trains from Santiago, Havana and Las Tunas pull in at the central **train station**, housed in a squat Art Deco folly on Pedro A. Pérez.

The main **hotel**, *Guantánamo*, Ahogados esq. 13 Norte, Reparto Caribe (☎21/38-10-15; ③), is a hulking, fading monolith 5km from the centre, a typical old-style Cuban hotel. Much nicer is the intimate *Casa de los Sueños*, a further 500m along the street, at Ahogados esq. 15 Norte (☎21/38-16-01; ③), with three double rooms. *Casa de Elsye Castillo Osoria*, Calixto García no. 766 e/ Prado y Jesús del Sol (②), is a friendly *casa particular* with a sunny courtyard.

There are several **restaurants** in the centre, though few that are well-stocked with food. *El Colonial* and *La Cubanita*, two neighbouring *paladares* on Martí esq. Crombet, both serve adequate portions of pork or chicken with rice and beans for around $5, while the *Guantánamo* hotel restaurant, *Guaso*, boasts a more interesting menu than most, with a house speciality of chicken "Gordon Blue" – stuffed with ham. The tastiest food, including fritters, milkshakes and hot rolls, comes from the street stands clustered at the south end of Pedro A. Pérez, while *Coppelia*, at Pedro A. Pérez esq. Varona, does bargain bowls of ice cream for a couple of pesos.

Guantánamo's bank and main shops are all close to Parque Martí.

Around Guantánamo

Many visitors come to see the US base, and although you can get to the two lookout points, **Mirador Malones** and **Caimanera**, with a little groundwork, there really isn't a lot to see and you cannot enter the base itself. Venturing into the **countryside** is more rewarding, with bizarre contrasts between lush valleys and the weird desert scenery of sun-bleached barren trees. Just north of town is the off-beat **Zoológico de Piedras**, a zoo entirely populated by sculpted stone animals.

Mirador Malones

The closer to Guantánamo of the two naval base lookouts, **Mirador Malones** is 32km from town, on the east of the bay, near Boquerón. At the top of a steep hill of dusty cacti and grey scrubs, a purpose-built platform is equipped with a restaurant and high-powered binoculars. At a distance of 6km and at 320m above sea level the view of the base is rather indistinct, but you can make out a few buildings and see the odd car whizzing past, and its lights blaze through the night. The real wonder is the view of the whole bay area: dramatically barren countryside, luminous sea and unforgiving desert mottled with hovering vultures. You can arrange a trip with a guide through the *Guantánamo* hotel in town (see p.363; $6 per person plus roughly $15 for an unmetered taxi), or *Villa Gaviota* in Santiago (☎226/4-13-68; around $40).

The US naval base at Guantánamo

Described by Fidel Castro as the dagger in the side of Cuban sovereignty, the naval base is approximately 118 square kilometres of North American territory defiantly planted on the southeast coast of Cuban soil. Seemingly ever poised for attack, with more than 3000 permanent military personnel, two airstrips and anchorage for 42 ships (enough for an entire war fleet, as Cubans often point out), it seems ludicrously over-equipped for its official functions as a refuelling stop in the Caribbean and a training base for US marines. Its real role is nothing less than a permanent thumbing of the nose to the Cuban authorities and at an estimated annual cost of $40 million it is an expensive – and oppressive – gesture.

The history of the naval base begins when Cuba emerged as the nominal victor of the wars of independence with Spain, whereupon the US government immediately began to erode Cuba's autonomy. Under the terms of the 1901 Platt Amendment, the US ordered Cuba to sell or lease to the US land necessary for a naval station, declaring without irony that it was "to enable the United States to maintain the independence of Cuba". An annual rent was set at 2000 gold coins (which today works out at $4085, or less than a cent per square metre of land) and the base was born. A 99-year lease drawn up in 1934 formalized the agreement and now Cuba is in the thankless position of waiting out their unwelcome tenants' stay until 2033. Famously, Fidel Castro has not cashed a single rent cheque from the US government, preferring to preserve them for posterity in a locked desk drawer.

Although the US quickly broke off all relations with the Cuban government after the revolution, they were less speedy to give up their territory. Communications broke down badly between base and host country, and acts of provocation ensued on both sides. Troops taunted one another across the formidable barricades and US marines took random pot-shots – in at least

---

Caimanera

Bordered by salt flats that score the ground with deep cracks and lend a haunting wildness, **CAIMANERA**, 23km south of Guantánamo, takes its name from the giant caiman lizards that used to roam here, although today it's far more notable as the last point in Cuba before you reach the US naval base. The village is a restricted area, with the ground between here and the base one of the most heavily mined areas in the world, although this hasn't stopped many dissolute Cubans from braving it in the hope of reaching foreign soil and escaping to America. Until 1995, many Cubans who chanced it, along with those who were brought to the base after being rescued from makeshift rafts in the Florida Straits, were allowed into the US on humanitarian grounds, but illegal Cuban immigrants are now returned to Cuban territory. The village is entered via a **checkpoint** at which guards scrutinize your passport before waving you through. The lookout is within the grounds of the *Hotel Caimanera* (☎9/94-14-16; ④), which has a view over the bay and mountains to the base – though even with binoculars ($1), you only see a sliver of it. You can use the lookout without being a guest of the hotel but you must phone ahead to let them

---

one case fatal – at Cuban soldiers. In an attempt to isolate the base, Cuba cut off the fresh water supply, prompting the installation of a desalinization plant. The whole area bristles with animosity, and the base is now surrounded by a dense minefield and rimmed with sentry posts brandishing the Cuban star-and-stripes flag, an atmosphere that prompted one writer to describe the perimeter of the base as "the cactus curtain".

Inside, the base is like an American theme park where stateside cars zoom along perfectly paved roads bordered by shops and drive-in movie theatres. There are softball and soccer fields, even a *McDonalds*, all imported to cater for the 7000 or so personnel and their attendant families. From the 1970s until the mid-1990s, such material riches gave the base an El Dorado lustre that lured many a dissident Cuban to brave the heavily mined base perimeter or chance the choppy waters surrounding the base to reach this ersatz chunk of North America. Some received the dubious reward of US citizenship as political asylum-seekers but the events of August 1994, which filled the base with 32,000 *balsero* Cubans who had been scooped out of the Florida Straits by US coast guards, changed attitudes. Although many were allowed into the US, an act passed in 1995 decreed that all Cuban emigrants similarly picked up in future would be returned to their home country, a fate already enjoyed by several thousand would-be emigrants from Haiti, for whom the base serves as a holding pen.

There's no way you can visit the base from within Cuba, but the Cuban authorities have seized on the commercial potential of the base with admirable aplomb. Two viewpoints have been created as tourist attractions from which visitors can content themselves with peering at this exemplary slice of US absurdity through binoculars.

---

know you are coming: staff then alert the checkpoint of your imminent arrival. A taxi from town costs $15–20, and you will need a guide, which you can arrange through the *Guantánamo* hotel (see p.363). On the seafront is a small **museum** ($1), with a history of the base and photos of US marines mooning at cameras and waving their weapons at the Cuban soldiers.

Prior to the revolution the town was the site of debauched carousing between the naval base officers and the townswomen, its main streets lined with bars, and prostitution, gambling and drugs – all anathema to the present regime – the norm. Little evidence of that remains today, however, and modern Caimanera is a sleepy and parochial town.

Zoológico de Piedras

Roughly 20km north of Guantánamo, in the foothills of the Sierra Cristal, is an altogether more whimsical attraction. Set in a private coffee farm, the slightly surreal sculpture park known as the **Zoológico de Piedras** (daily 9am–6pm; $1) was created in 1977 by local artist Angel Iñigo Blanco, who carved the stone in situ. Cool and fresh, dotted here and there with lime and breadfruit trees, hanging vines and coffee plants, the park centres on a path that weaves around the mountainside, with stone animals peeking out from the undergrowth at every turn. Slightly cartoonish in form, the creatures bear little relationship to their real-life counterparts: a giant tortoise towers over a hippo the size of a modest guinea pig. You can wander round on your own or take a guided tour with the sculptor's father, who absentmindedly pats his favourite pets. Needless to say it's a hit with children. Before you leave, venture up the path on the right-hand side of the car park for a superb view over the lopsided farmland of Guantánamo.

Baracoa

In the eyes of many who visit, **BARACOA** is quite simply the most beautiful place in Cuba. Set on the coast on Cuba's southeast tip and protected by a deep curve of mountains, its isolation has so far managed to protect it from some of the more pernicious effects of tourism creeping into other areas of the island. Self-contained and secluded, the tiny town vibrates with an energy surprising for such a small place.

On a spot christened Porto Santo by Christopher Columbus, who arrived here in 1492 and, as legend has it, planted a cross in the soil, Baracoa was the first town to be established in Cuba, founded by Diego de Velázquez in 1511. The early conquistadors never quite succeeded in exterminating the indigenous population and direct descendants of the Taíno population are alive today, with Baracoa the only place in Cuba where they survive. Their legacy is also present in several myths and legends that are habitually told to visitors.

Surrounded by awe-inspiring countryside – whose abundance of cacao trees makes it the nation's **chocolate** manufacturer, with local brand *Peter's* widely available – Baracoa is fast becoming an absolute must on the travellers' circuit. Although many will be happy to wander through the town, enjoying its easy charm, there are several tangible attractions. Baracoa's most notable exhibit is **La Cruz de la Parra**, the celebrated cross reputed to have been erected by Christopher Columbus himself. It is housed in the picturesque **Catedral de Nuestra Señora de la Asunción**, on the edge of leafy **Parque Independencia**, a local gathering point. On the east side of town you'll find the **Fuerte Matachín**, one of a trio of forts built to protect colonial Baracoa, and now the site of the town **museum**. Further east is the town's main beach, **Playa Boca de Miel**, shingled in jade, grey and deep crimson stones, and a lively summer-time hangout. Converted from the second of the town's fortifications, which overlook the town from the northern hills, the **Hotel El Castillo** is a beautiful and peaceful retreat, and an appealing place for a refreshing cocktail. On the western side of town, the third fort, **Fuerte La Punta**, is now a restaurant and overlooks the smaller of the two town beaches, **Playa La Punta** – the better bet for solitude seekers.

Arrival, information and transport

If you're **driving**, half the fun of a visit to Baracoa is getting there. Before the revolution, the town was only accessible by sea, but the opening of **La Farola**, a road through the mountains that provides a direct link with Guantánamo 120km away, changed all that and a flood of cars poured into the previously unseen town. Considered to be one of the triumphs of the revolution, the road was actually started by Batista's regime but temporarily abandoned when he refused to pay a fair wage to the workers, and work was only resumed in the 1960s. Today, it makes for an amazing trip through the knife-sharp peaks of the Cuchillas de Baracoa mountains.

The **airport**, Aeropuerto Gustavo Rizo (☎4/2-52-80), is near the *Porto Santo* hotel, on the west side of the bay 4km from the centre; taxis wait to take you into town for $2–3. **Buses** pull up at the Astro bus terminal, west on the Malecón; it's a short walk down Maceo to the centre, or you can take a *bicitaxi* for ten pesos. The private peso trucks that arrive from over the mountains via La Farola drop off on Maceo.

There's no official **information** bureau in town, but the staff at the *El Castillo* hotel are extremely helpful. The best way to **get around** is on foot as most of the places you'll want to see are within easy reach of the centre. If you're travelling further afield, catch a *bicitaxi* or unmetered taxi from outside the tobacco factory at Calle Martí no. 214. There's little point relying on public transport – buses are scarce and always jam-packed.

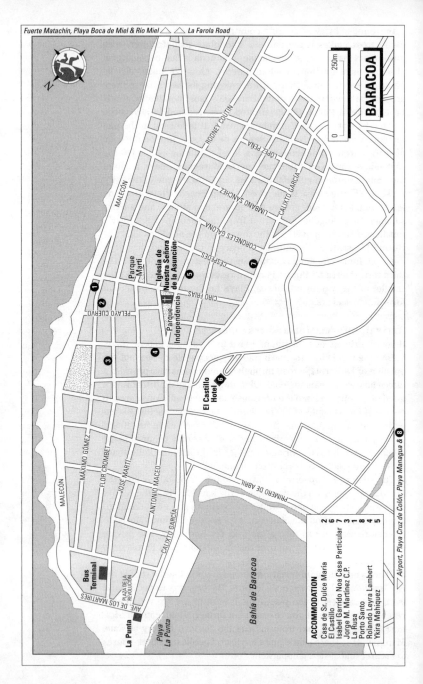

BARACOA

0 — 250m

MALECÓN

RODNEY COUTIN

LÓPEZ PEÑA

CALIXTO GARCÍA

LIMBANO SÁNCHEZ

CORONELES GALANO

CÉSPEDES

Parque Martí

Iglesia de Nuestra Señora de la Asunción

CIRO FRÍAS

PELAYO CUERVO

Parque Independencia

MÁXIMO GÓMEZ

FLOR CROMBET

JOSÉ MARTÍ

ANTONIO MACEO

CALIXTO GARCÍA

PRIMERO DE ABRIL

MALECÓN

AVE. DE LOS MÁRTIRES

PLAZA DE LA REVOLUCIÓN

Bus Terminal

La Punta

Playa La Punta

Bahía de Baracoa

El Castillo Hotel

▽ Airport, Playa Cruz de Colón, Playa Manglaro & 8

ACCOMMODATION

Casa de Sr. Dulce María	2
El Castillo	6
Isabel Garrido Noa Casa Particular	7
Jorge M. Martínez C.P.	3
La Rusa	1
Porto Santo	8
Rolando Leyra Lambert	4
Ykira Mahiquez	5

Accommodation

In *El Castillo*, Baracoa has one of the most characterful **hotels** on the island, though the sheer volume of visitors means that this and the two other hotels are often full at peak times. Until new hotels are built – plans are afoot for two on Maguana beach – the taxes on private accommodation remain low, and you'll find a number of superb **casas particulares**, all within a few streets of one another.

Hotels

El Castillo, Calixto García ☎ 4/21-25. Perched high on a hill overlooking the town, this former military post, one of a trio of forts built to protect Baracoa, was built between 1739 and 1742 and is now an intimate, comfortable and very welcoming hotel. Glossy tiles and wood finishes give the rooms a unique charm, while the handsome pool patio ($2 for non-guests) is the best place in town to sip *mojitos*. Very popular and often fully booked, making reservations essential. ④–⑤.

Porto Santo, Carretera Aeroporto ☎ 4/35-90 or 4/35-46. Set on diminutive Cruz de Colón beach, where Columbus is said to have planted the first cross in Cuba, this old-style hotel on the outskirts of town is convenient for the airport but not much else. The rooms are well-maintained but dark. ④.

La Rusa, Máximo Gómez no. 161 ☎ 4/30-11. Named after its much-esteemed Russian former owner Magdelana Robiskiai, who settled in Baracoa before the revolution, small and squat *La Rusa* sits on the Malecón. The charming rooms are modest but cosy and complemented by a friendly atmosphere. ③.

Casas particulares

Casa de Sr Dulce Maria, Máximo Gómez no. 140 e/ Pelayo Cuervo y Ciro Frias ☎ 4/22-14 (after 5pm). A charismatic little room with one double bed and one single, as well as a private bathroom and a kitchen with fridge. Good for a longer stay. ②.

Isabel Garrido Noa, Calixto García no. 164A e/ Cornel Galano y Céspedes ☎ 4/35-15. Handsome blue house with a flight of stairs leading up one side to two large rooms which open onto a rooftop patio. Each room can accommodate at least three people and there's an al fresco dining area for communal meals. ②.

Jorge M. Martinez, Flor Crombet, no. 105 e/ Maraví y Frank País ☎ 4/23-76. A range of rooms all with private bathrooms, a/c and warm water, run by an enterprising man who also serves food and runs excursions. ②.

Rolando Leyva Lambert, Frank País no. 19 e/ Martí y Maceo ☎ 4/36-34. This ample, central property has pleasant wood-panelled rooms, a single shared bathroom and a small covered courtyard out back. ②.

Ykira Mahiquez, Maceo 168A e/ Céspedes y Ciro Frías; ☎ 4/24-66. Casual accommodation on a friendly street one block from the main square. The owner knows almost everyone in town with a room to let, so if her place is full she'll be able to point you elsewhere. ②.

The Town

Just walking around Baracoa is one of the town's greatest pleasures. Its quaint and friendly central streets are lined with tiny, pastel-coloured colonial houses with wedding-cake trim, and modern development is confined to the outskirts, where new apartment blocks were built after

---

Hatuey, the first Cuban rebel

The last chief of the Taíno, Hatuey fled the Spanish conquest of Hispaniola, arriving in Cuba with four hundred men determined to rouse the Cuban Taínos against the invaders. After a bloody, three-month struggle fought from the heights surrounding Baracoa, he was finally betrayed by one of his own people, and captured at his mountain headquarters by leading conquistador Diego Velázquez (see p.460). In 1512 he was taken to Yara, in Granma province, where he was sentenced to be burnt at the stake. Just before he died, a priest made a final attempt to persuade him to be baptized, thereby saving his soul and guaranteeing himself a place in heaven. Hatuey is supposed to have asked if this was where Christian Spaniards would go, and on being told it was, to have defiantly declared, "I would rather go to hell and avoid the lot of you." Today his effigy sits in uneasy proximity to the church that doomed him, and his name is immortalized in the excellent Cuban beer.

---

the revolution. All the sites of interest are within easy walking distance of one another, radiating out from the Parque Independencia, on Antonio Maceo, where under the shade of the wide laurel trees, generations of Baracoans gather around rickety tables to play chess and dominoes.

On the plaza's east side, opposite a bust of Taíno hero Hatuey (see box above), stands the **Catedral Nuestra Señora de la Asunción** (daily 8am–noon), built in 1805 on the site of a sixteenth-century church. This unobtrusive structure houses one of the most important religious relics in the whole of Latin America, the antique **La Cruz de la Parra**, supposedly the antique cross brought from Spain and planted in the sands of the harbour beach by Christopher Columbus. It's undeniably of the period, having been carbon-dated at 500 years old, but as the wood is from the *Cocoloba Disversifolia* tree, indigenous to Cuba, the truth of the legend is doubtful. It was in front of this cross that the celebrated defender of the Indians, Fray Bartolomé de Las Casas, gave his first Mass in 1510. Originally two metres tall, the cross was gradually worn down by time and souvenir hunters to its present modest height of one metre, at which point it was encased in silver for its protection. The cross now stands in a glass case to the left of the altar, on an ornate silver base donated by a French marquis at the beginning of the twentieth century. When Pope John Paul II arrived on his Cuban visit in 1998, it was the first thing he asked to see.

Parque Martí and Fuerte Matachín

A block north of Parque Independencia towards the sea, **Parque Martí**, more a collection of benches and trees than a park, is the town's busiest square, crowded with shops and stalls selling snacks and drinks, notably *Prú*, the local speciality (see opposite).

East of here, along Martí past the shops and the triangular Parque Maceo – complete with bust – is the **Fuerte Matachín** (daily 8am–noon & 2–6pm; $1), one of a trio of forts that protected Baracoa from marauding pirates in the nineteenth century. Built in 1802, the fort is well preserved to this day, and you can see the original cannons ranged along the fort walls. Its cool interior now hous-es the town **museum**, with a good collection of delicately striped *polimitas* snail shells, some Amerindian relics and a history of the town's most celebrated characters.

The Malecón and Playa Boca de Miel

A walk along the **Malecón**, a ragged collection of the backsides of hous-es and ugly apartment blocks, is something of a disappointment. To the west is the town's **Plaza de la Revolución**, surely the smallest in Cuba, decorated with a couple of revolutionary posters. On its westernmost point, the Malecón is sealed by the third of the town's forts, **La Punta**, built in 1803 and now converted into an elegant restaurant (see p.372). A door built into the western wall leads down a flight of stairs to the tiny **Playa La Punta**, a good spot for a quiet dip (daily 9am–5pm).

At the eastern end of the Malecón, accessed by the stone stairs to the right of an imposing stone statue of Christopher Columbus, is the main town beach, **Playa Boca de Miel**, a boisterous hangout mobbed in summer by vacationing schoolchildren. People walk their dogs along the multicoloured shingles near town, but the brilliant stones fade into sand a little further along, and you can swim. The best spot for a pad-dle, however, lies beyond the clump of trees at the far eastern end of the beach, in the gentle **Río Miel**, which has its own legend. Many years ago, a Taíno maiden with honey-coloured hair used to bathe daily in the waters. One day a young sailor steered his ship down the river and spotted her. Captivated by her beauty, he instantly fell in love and for a while the happy couple frolicked daily in the river. However, as the day of the sailor's departure approached, the young girl became increasingly depressed and would sit in the river crying until her tears swelled its banks. Impressed by this demonstration of her love, the sailor decided to stay in Baracoa and marry her, from which grew the saying that if you swim in the Río Miel, you will never leave Baracoa, or that if you do you will always return.

Across the bay are the Sleeping Beauty mountains, so called because they look uncannily like a generously endowed woman lying on her back.

Eating and drinking

After the monotonous cuisine in much of the rest of Cuba, **food** in Baracoa is ambrosial, drawing on a rich local heritage and the region's plentiful supply of coconuts. Tuna, red snapper and swordfish fried in coconut oil are all favourite dishes, and there is an abundance of clan-destine lobster, as well as a few vegetarian specials. Look out for *cucu-rucho*, a deceptively filling concoction of coconut, orange, guava and lots of sugar sold in a palm-leaf wrap. Other treats for the sweet-toothed include the locally produced *Peter's* chocolate and the soft drink *Prú*, widely available from *ofreta* stands, a fermented blend of sugar and secret spices that's something of an acquired taste.

Caracol, halfway down the Malecón. A peso restaurant serving cheap, filling fried pork with rice and beans and occasionally fresh fish. Check beforehand as they've been known to charge visitors in dollars.

Casa del Chocolate, Maceo no. 121. The barren little chocolate café, furnished with just the minimum of chairs and tables, sells hot and cold drinking chocolate subject to availability. You can also buy the local brand *Peter's* chocolate, served on a plate with a knife and fork.

Casa Tropical, Martí no. 175 e/ Céspedes y Ciro Frias. A very central *casa particular* with a cool interior and a friendly atmosphere that offers food to non-guests. Excellent swordfish and generous helpings of shellfish, when available, are served in a courtyard beside an ailing papaya tree.

El Castillo, Calixto García ☎4/21-25. The weekly buffet night at this hotel restaurant offers the best meal you will have in town – a feast of Baracoan dishes featuring coconut, maize, local vegetables and herbs, all for $10–15.

La Colonial, Martí no. 123 e/ Maravi y Frank País ☎4/31-61. A homely place offering standard, though very well prepared Cuban dishes. It gets very busy, so reservations are recommended – as is early arrival to get the day's speciality before the rush. Daily 10am–midnight; $6–8 per person.

La Punta, Ave. de los Martires, at the west end of the Malecón. An elegant 24-hour restaurant in the grounds of La Punta fort, serving traditional Cuban and Baracoan food, some spaghetti dishes and the house speciality, *bacan*, a delicious baked dish with meat, green bananas and coconut milk. There's a cabaret show on from 9pm to midnight, so arrive early if you want a peaceful meal.

Walter's, Rupert López no. 47 e/ Céspedes y Coroneles Galano. Conspicuous by its lurid Barbie-pink paint job, this open-air restaurant offers an excellent view over the bay, perfect for watching the sun set over *El Castillo*, and serves satisfying portions of rice and beans with pork, goat or the catch of the day.

Entertainment and nightlife

Baracoa has quite an active nightlife, perhaps surprisingly so for such a small town, though it's essentially centred on two small but boisterous venues near Parque Independencia, and things are much quieter further afield. The most sophisticated option is twilight cocktails at the *Hotel El Castillo* rooftop bar. Baracoa's small cinema, Cine-Teatro Encanto, Maceo no. 148, screens Cuban and North American films every evening.

Casa de la Cultura, Maceo e/ Frank País y Maraví. A haven of jaded charm, with live music and dancing on the patio nightly. Tends to get going around 9–10pm.

Casa de la Trova, Victorino Rodríguez no. 149B e/ Ciro Frias y Pelillo Cuevo. Concerts take place in a tiny room opposite Parque Independencia, after which the chairs are pushed back to the wall and exuberant dancers spill onto the pavement. Mon–Fri 9pm–midnight, Sat 9pm–1am.

Circulo Social Industrias Locales, Maceo no. 125. A sweat-box disco with a faltering sound system. Dark and dingy but popular with Baracoan teenies. Entry is $2 per person, or $3 per pair. Tues–Fri 8pm–midnight, Sat & Sun 8pm–1am.

485 Aniversario de la Fundación de la Ciudad, Maceo 141, in front of Parque Independencia. Known by all as "el cuatro ocho cinco", this is *the* place to hang out in town. In a room reminiscent of a village hall *salsa* bands play for a mixed crowd of Cubans and visitors, while across the courtyard, a fire escape leads to a precarious roof-top disco where you've every chance of taking a dive over the edge. Downstairs 9pm–3.30am; upstairs 9pm until they decide to close.

Listings

Airlines Cubana, Martí no. 181 ☎4/21-71 (daily 8am–noon & 2–6pm).

Car rental Transautos at *La Punta* restaurant; Havanautos at the *Hotel El Castillo* (☎4/21-25) and *Hotel Porto Santo* (☎4/35-90).

Medical The 24-hour *policlinico* is on Martí no. 427 (☎4/21-62). Call ☎115 for a public ambulance. The most central pharmacy is at Maceo no. 132 (☎4/22-71), open 24 hours.

Photography For film and batteries, Photoservice is at Martí no. 204 (daily 8am–10pm).

Police The police station is on Martí towards the Malecón (☎4/24-79).

Post office Maceo no. 286 (daily 8am–6pm).

Shopping The picturesque Yumurí Convenience Store, Maceo no. 149 (Mon–Sat 8.30am–5.30pm, Sun 8.30am–noon), is an old-style general store with a small bakery. Identifiable by the swarms of people outside, La Primada dollar store is on Martí opposite the park, selling food, clothes and electrical goods. Baracoa has a strong tradition of local art, with reasonably priced originals sold at La Casa Yara, Maceo no. 120 (Mon–Fri 8am–noon & 1–6pm, Sat & Sun 8am–noon), along with coconut-wood jewellery, hand-made boxes and other trinkets. Art work is also available from the Casa de la Cultura, on Maceo no. 124 – look out for paintings by Luís Eliades Rodríguez.

Telephones Next door to the post office is an ETECSA phone booth, where you can buy phonecards. You can also make international calls at *El Castillo* hotel.

Tours Excursions to the surrounding countryside can be arranged through the *El Castillo* and *Porto Santo* hotels. For a less official trek pay a visit to Castro at the Fuerte Matachín museum (☎4/21-22), a knowledgeable town character who will be happy to negotiate a tailor-made trip for you.

Around Baracoa

Cradled by verdant mountains smothered in palm and cacao trees, and threaded with swimmable rivers, the Baracoan countryside has much to offer. **El Yunque**, the hallmark of Baracoa's landscape, can easily be climbed in a day, while if you have a car and a little time to spare you could take a drive along the coast and seek out some quintessentially Cuban fishing villages, including **Boca de Yumurí**. Alternatively, just head for the **beach** – there are a couple of good options northwest of town.

El Yunque

As square as a slab of butter, **El Yunque**, 10km west of Baracoa, is an easy climb. At 575m, streaked in mist, it seems to float above the other mountains in the Grupo Sagua Baracoa range. Christopher Columbus noted its conspicuousness: his journal entry of November 27, 1492, mentions a "high square mountain which seemed to be an island" seen on his approach to shore – no other mountain fits the description as well. El Yunque is the remnant of a huge plateau that dominated the region in its primordial past. Isolated for millions of years, its square summit has evolved unique species of ferns and palms, and much of the forest is still virgin, a haven for rare plants including orchids and bright red epiphytes.

The energetic, though not unduly strenuous, hike to the summit should take you about two hours, starting near *Campismo El Yunque*, 3km off the Moa road. If you don't fancy the climb, you can drive to the summit, though you should be sure to choose a sturdy rental car or taxi: follow the Moa road heading west from town and take the first turning on the left for El Yunque. Guided excursions are a good way to see the mountain and can be arranged through *El Castillo*, *Porto Santo* or Castro at the Fuerte Matachín museum.

Playa Maguana and Playa Nava

The two main **beaches** near Baracoa are close to each other on the right-hand side of the Moa road, 25km northwest of town. Partly lined with the spindly though leafy *Coco Thrinas* palm indigenous to the area, **Playa Maguana** is an attractive narrow beach with golden sand, plenty of shade and a reef for snorkelling. It's also near an archeological zone where fragments of Taíno ceramics have been found. Popular with locals as well as visitors, the beach is less exclusive than many in Cuba, although plans to build new hotels close by may change this. Along the beach fishermen hang freshly caught iridescent fish from the trees, which they will offer to cook with rice and banana, washed down with coconut milk. At the far end of the beach is the *Maguana* (no phone; ⑤), a secluded **hotel** with comfortable rooms and plenty of privacy; book through any Islazul office, or at *La Rusa* in Baracoa (see p.369).

Six kilometres further on is tiny **Playa Nava**. There are no facilities and the yellow sand is often smothered in seaweed and sea debris, but it's almost always deserted, making it one of the few places in Cuba that's virtually guaranteed to be a complete retreat.

Boca de Yumurí

Thirty kilometres east of Baracoa, past the Bahía de Mata – a tranquil bay with a slim, shingled beach and a splendid view of the mountains – is the little fishing village of **BOCA DE YUMURÍ**, standing at the

---

Polimitas snail

Along the beach you may spot the brightly coloured shell of the **polimitas snail**. According to local Amerindian legend, there was once a man who wanted to give his beloved a gift. As he had nothing of his own to give, he set out to capture the colours of the universe: he took the green of the mountains, the pink of the flowers, the white of the foam of the sea and the yellow of the sun. When he went to claim the blue from the sky it vanished as the sun went down and he had to content himself with the black of the night. He then set all the colours into the shells of the snails and presented them to his love. Each snail is unique, ornately decorated in delicate stripes and consequently quite sought after – the Duchess of Windsor in the 1950s, for instance, had a pair encrusted with gold studs and made into earrings. Such caprices have severely depleted the snails' numbers, and although locals still sell them, buying them is not recommended. With luck and a little searching, however, you may find an empty shell or two lying on the beach.

---

mouth of the eponymous river. Known as a place to find the highly prized *polimitas* snails (see box on opposite), the rather bland, brown-sand beach is also lined with houses whose owners will offer to cook you inexpensive and wholesome **meals** of fish, rice and bananas: a particularly good bet is Neris Acosta Cardesuñer's wooden house, about halfway down the beach – locals will point it out to you. At the end of the beach is a wooden jetty from where you can catch a **raft taxi** ($1) further upstream, where the river is clearer and better for swimming, or across the river.

Travel details

As with everywhere in Cuba public transport is a haphazard affair prey to last-minute cancellations and delays. You should always check to see if buses and trains are still running the route required before setting off.

TRAINS

Guantánamo to: Havana (1 every other day; 18hr); Las Tunas (1 every other day; 8hr); Matanzas (1 every other day; 17hr); Santa Clara (1 every other day; 12hr).

Holguín to: Guantánamo (3–4 weekly; 5hr); Las Tunas (1 daily; 2hr 30min); Santiago (1 daily; 3hr 30min).

Las Tunas to: Camagüey (2 daily; 12hr); Ciego de Ávila (2 daily; 8hr); Guantánamo (1 daily; 4hr); Havana (2 daily; 12hr); Holguín (1 daily; 3hr); Santiago (1 daily; 8hr).

BUSES

Baracoa to: Santiago (10–11 weekly; 6hr); Guantánamo (10–11 weekly; 4hr); Havana (1 every other day; 20 hr).

Guantánamo to: Baracoa (3 weekly; 6hr); Bayamo (3–4 weekly; 4hr); Havana (1 daily; 17 hr); Holguín (3–4 weekly; 5hr); Las Tunas (3–4 weekly; 7hr).

Holguín to: Banes (3 daily; 4hr); Gibara (3 daily; 2hr); Guantánamo (1 every 8 days; 5hr); Guardalavaca (1 daily; 3hr); Havana (10–11 weekly; 12hr); Mayarí (3 daily; 4hr 40min); Moa (1 every other day; 4hr).

Las Tunas to: Bayamo (1 daily; 2hr); Havana (1 daily; 11hr); Puerto Padre (2 daily; 1hr 40min); Santiago (1 daily; 4hr).

DOMESTIC FLIGHTS

Baracoa to: Havana (3 weekly; 2hr 30min).

Guantánamo to: Havana (1 daily; 2hr 45min).

Holguín to: Havana (2 weekly; 1hr 15min).

Las Tunas to: Havana (4 weekly; 1hr).

Moa to: Havana (3 weekly; 2hr 30min).

Chapter 7

Santiago de Cuba and Granma

The southern part of Oriente – the island's easternmost third – is defined by the **Sierra Maestra**, Cuba's largest mountain range, which binds together the provinces of **Santiago de Cuba** and **Granma**. Rising directly from the shores of the Caribbean along the southern coast, the mountains make much of the region largely inaccessible, a quality appreciated by the rebels who spent years waging war here.

At the eastern end of the sierra, the roiling, romantic **city of Santiago de Cuba**, capital of the eponymous province, draws visitors mainly for its **music**. Brewed from the legions of bands that have grown up here, the regional scene is always strong, but it boils over in July when **carnival** drenches the town in *rumba* beats, fabulous costumes, excitement and song. This talent for making merry has placed Cuba's second city firmly on the tourist map, but there's much more to the place than carnival. Briefly the island's first capital, Santiago has a rich colonial heritage, evident throughout its historical core and in the splendid coastal fortification of **El Morro**. The city played an equally distinguished role in more recent history, as recorded in the **Moncada barracks** museum, where Fidel Castro and his small band of rebels fired the opening shots of the revolution, and the **Museo de la Lucha Clandestina**, in the old police station burnt to the ground during the troubles.

Spread along the coastline **around Santiago**, the visitor attractions of the **Gran Parque Natural Baconao** – and especially its **beaches**, of which **Playa Siboney** is the outstanding favourite – form the perfect antidote to the hectic pace of city life. A day-trip to the east offers gentle **trekking** into the **Sierra de la Gran Pierda**, where one of the highest points in the province, Gran Pierda itself, offers far-reaching vistas. In the lush, cool mountains to the north of the city, magisterial **El Cobre**, west of Santiago, is the one of the most important churches in the country, housing the much-revered relic of the Virgen de la Caridad del Cobre. Still further west, bordering Granma province, the heights of the **Sierra Maestra** vanish into awe-inspiring cloudforests, and although access to the **Parque Nacional Turquino** – around Pico Turquino, Cuba's highest peak – is often restricted, you can still admire from afar.

Unlike Santiago de Cuba, which revolves around its main city, the province of **Granma** has no definite focus and is much more low-key than its neighbour. The small black-sand beach resort at **Marea del Portillo** gives Granma some sort of tourist centre, but the highlight of the province, missed out on by many, is the **Parque Nacional Desembarco del Granma**. Lying in wooded countryside at the foot of the Sierra Maestra, the park can be explored easily from the beach of **Las Coloradas**. Further north, along the coast of the Gulf of Guacanayabo, the museum at **La Demajagua**, formerly the sugar estate and home of Carlos Manuel de Céspedes, celebrates the war of independence amidst tranquil, park-like grounds.

Granma's two main towns are underrated and often ignored, but the fantastical Moorish architecture in **Manzanillo** is reason enough to drop by, while **Bayamo**, the provincial capital, with its quiet atmosphere and pleasant scenery, appeals to discerning visitors looking for a low-key spot to stay.

Santiago de Cuba city

Beautiful, heady **SANTIAGO DE CUBA** is the crown jewel of Oriente. Nowhere outside of Havana is there a city with such definite character or such determination to have a good time. Spanning out from the base of a deep-water bay and cradled by mountains, the city is credited with being the most Caribbean part of Cuba, a claim borne out by the laid-back lifestyle and rich mix of inhabitants. It was here that the first slaves arrived from West Africa and today Santiago boasts a larger percentage of black people than anywhere else in Cuba. Afro-Cuban **culture**, with its music, myths and rituals, formed its roots here, with later additions brought by the French coffee-planters fleeing revolution in Haiti in the eighteenth century. Santiago's proximity to Jamaica has encouraged a natural crossover of ideas, and it is one of the few places

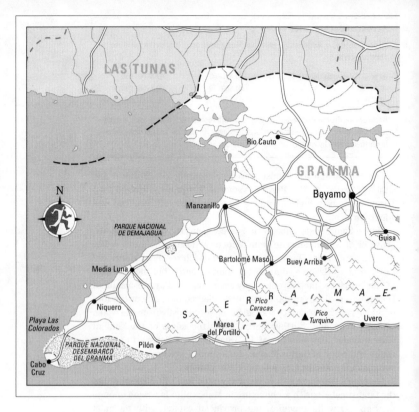

in Cuba to have a strong Rastafari following, albeit a hybrid one –
devout Jamaican Rastas are teetotal vegetarians who don't wolf down
huge plates of fried pork with lashings of beer.

The leisurely pace of life doesn't make for a quiet city, however,
and the higgledy-piggledy net of narrow streets around the colonial
quarter rings night and day with the beat of drums and the toot of
horns. **Music** is a vital element of Santiagero life, oozing from the
most famous **Casa de la Trova** in the country and various other
venues around the city, not to mention numerous impromptu gath-
erings. These fiestas reach a crescendo around **carnival** in July,
attended by rucksacked visitors seeking *rumba* and rum.

Although music and carnival are good enough reasons to visit, the
city offers a host of more concrete attractions too. Diego Velázquez's
sixteenth-century merchant house and the elegant governor's residence, both around **Parque Céspedes** in the colonial heart of town,
and the commanding **El Morro** castle at the entrance to the bay,
exemplify the city's prominent role in Cuban history. Added to this,

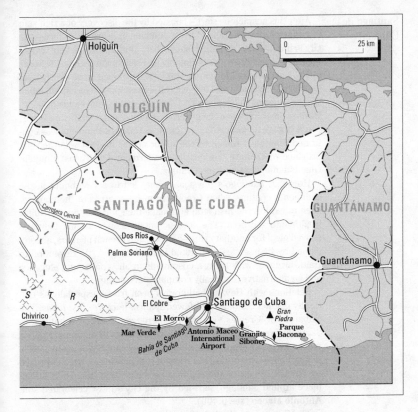

the part played by townsfolk in the **revolutionary struggle**, detailed
in several fascinating museums, makes Santiago an important stop-
off on the revolution trail, while the legions of single men who visit
the city armed with pretty frocks and fat wallets have an altogether
different agenda, involving the local *jineteras*.

Some history
Established by **Diego Velázquez de Cuéllar** in 1515 and moved to
its present location from its original site on the banks of the Río
Paradas the following year, the port of Santiago de Cuba was one of
the original seven *villas* founded in Cuba. Pleased to find so excellent a natural port near to reported sources of **gold** – which were
quickly exhausted – and satisfied by its proximity to Jamaica,
Española and Castilla del Oro, Velázquez established a settlement
close by and named the port Santiago (St James) after the patron
saint of Spain. With the establishment of the central trading house
shortly afterwards, it became the island's capital.

Santiago de Cuba city

After this auspicious start – boosted by the discovery of a rich vein of **copper** in the foothills of the mountains in nearby El Cobre – the city's importance dwindled somewhat. Buffeted by severe earthquakes and **pirate attacks** – notably by Frenchman Jacques de Sores in 1554 and Henry Morgan in 1662 – it developed more slowly than its western rival and in 1553 was effectively ousted as capital when the governor of Cuba, Gonzalo Pérez de Angulo, moved his office to Havana. In 1558, when the governor decreed that only Havana's port could engage in commerce, its future as Cuba's second city was confirmed, though it remained the major centre in what was then the province of **Oriente**, comprising modern-day Las Tunas, Holguín, Guantánamo, Santiago and Granma.

However, Santiago's physical bounty led to a new boom in the eighteenth century, when Creoles from other areas of the country, keen to exploit the lush land and make their fortune, poured **sugar** wealth into the area. The cool mountain slopes around Santiago proved ideal for another crop – **coffee** – and French planters, accompanied by their slaves, emigrated here after the 1791 revolution in Haiti, bringing with them a cosmopolitan air, continental elegance and an alternative, culturally complex slave culture.

Relations with Havana had always been frosty, especially as culturally distinct Santiago had fewer Spanish-born *Península res*. The Cuban-born Creoles, of whom there were larger numbers in Santiago, were not keen to cede their fortunes to Spain, and minor power struggles erupted sporadically between the two centres. This rivalry boiled over during the **wars of independence**, which were led by Oriente, much of the fighting between 1868 and 1898 taking place around Santiago, part-led by the city's most celebrated son, **Antonio Maceo** (see p.400).

The Cuban army had almost gained control of Santiago when in 1898 the United States, which had until then been shouting instructions from the sidelines, intervened. Eager to gain control of the imminent republic, they usurped victory from the Cubans by securing Santiago and subsequently forcing Spanish surrender after a dramatic battle on **Loma de San Juan**, a hill in the east of the city, between Roosevelt's army of six thousand "Rough Riders" and the Spanish army of seven hundred. The Cubans were not even signatories to the resultant Paris peace settlement between the North Americans and the Spanish, and all residents of the province of Santiago were made subject to the protection and authority of the United States. As an added insult, the rebel army that had fought for independence for thirty years was not even allowed to enter Santiago city.

Over the following decades, this betrayal nourished local anger and resentment, and by the 1950s Santiago's citizens were playing a prime role in the civil uprisings against the US-backed president Fulgencio Batista. Assured of general support, **Fidel Castro** chose

> **Racism and harassment**
>
> It's often said that Cuba is not a racist country, although it might be near-
> er to the truth to say that it's a country where institutional racism is less
> widespread – or overt – than in some of its neighbours. Recent social prob-
> lems, specifically the poverty of the Special Period and consequent rise in
> crime and prostitution, have caused a resurgence of the **racial discrimi-
> nation** that existed before the revolution. Cubans from Havana and the
> west tend to blame easterners for the rise in crime and cast them as the
> perpetrators of *jineterismo*, but they are essentially, possibly uncon-
> sciously, talking about black people.
>
> An unpleasant side effect is that hotels and shops have a tendency to
> discriminate against black people regardless of whether you are Cuban (or
> criminal) or not. Unless accompanied by white friends, **black visitors** to
> Santiago can expect to encounter some level of **harassment**, whether it's
> being asked to produce a passport, questioned about why they want to
> enter a hotel or bar or just looked up and down – especially if dressed casu-
> ally. You can sometimes circumvent this by talking audibly in a non-
> Spanish language, or just brandishing your passport at the first sign of
> trouble. Whilst causing a scene is obviously to be avoided, asking why you
> have been singled out may mean that next time you are left alone –
> although it doesn't help Cubans much.

Santiago for his debut battle in 1953, when he and a small band of
rebels attacked the **Moncada barracks**. Further support for their
rebel army was later given by the M26-7 underground movement
spearheaded in Santiago by **Frank and Josue País**. It was in
Santiago's courtrooms that Fidel Castro and the other rebels were
subsequently tried and imprisoned.

When the victorious Castro swept down from the mountains, it
was in Santiago he chose to deliver his maiden speech, on the night
of January 1. The city, which now carries the title "Hero City of the
Republic of Cuba", is still seen – especially in Havana – as home to
the most zealous revolutionaries, and support for the revolution is
certainly stronger here than in the west. The rift between east and
west still manifests itself today in various prejudices, with
Habaneros viewing their eastern neighbours as troublemaking criminals, and considered by Santiagueros as solipsistic and unfriendly
in return.

Arrival, information and city transport

International and domestic **flights** arrive at the **Aeropuerto
Internacional Antonio Maceo** (☎226/9-10-14), near the southern
coast, 8km from the city. Metered and unmetered **taxis** wait outside
and charge around $10–15 to take you to the centre, while there is
sometimes a **bus** that meets flights from Havana, charging around 5
pesos for the same journey. You can arrange **car rental** at the
Havanautos desk at the airport (☎226/91-87-3) or at agencies in
town (see p.406).

Santiago de Cuba city

Interprovincial **buses** pull in at the **Astro bus terminal** on Avenida de los Libertadores (☎226/2-30-50), 2km from the town centre. Next door, tourist buses arrive at the **Víazul bus depot** (☎226/12-84-84). A taxi to the centre from either terminal is $3–4. Provincial buses pull in at the **Terminal de Omnibus Intermunicipal**, on Paseo de Martí, north of Parque Céspedes (☎226/24-32-5).

Arriving by **train**, you'll alight at the attractive new station near the port, on Paseo de Martí esq. Jesús Menéndez (☎226/2-28-36), from where horse-drawn buggies and **bicitaxis** can take you to the centre for around $3, while a taxi will cost around $5.

Information

Santiago boasts an excellent **tourist information bureau** on the Plaza de Marte, at no. 5 Perez Carbo (Mon–Sat 8am–5pm; ☎226/23-30-2), with a wealth of information on the city's music scene, plus weekly events bulletins and cinema listings. You can also buy **maps** here, as well as from the Tienda Rialto shop below the cathedral, at no. 654 Santo Tomás, and the shop in the basement of the *Hotel Casa Granda*. Some general information is also available from the *Hotel Santiago* (see p.384).

Santiago's weekly newspaper, the *Sierra Maestra* (20 centavos), is available from street vendors and occasionally from the bigger hotels, and has a brief **listings** section detailing cinema, theatre and other cultural activities.

City transport

Although a large city, Santiago is easy to negotiate, as much of what you'll want to see is compactly fitted into the historic core around Parque Céspedes. Even the furthest sights are no more than approximately 4km from Parque Céspedes, making it an excellent city for exploring on foot. Taxis are the best way to reach outlying sights as the buses are overcrowded and irregular.

Metered taxis wait on the cathedral side of Parque Céspedes or around Plaza Marte and charge between forty and eighty cents per kilometre with a $1.50 surcharge, while the **unmetered taxis** parked up on San Pedro negotiate a rate for the whole journey – expect to pay about $3–4 to cross town. Touts skulk around the main streets but you will strike a slightly cheaper deal if you negotiate with drivers themselves. For state-registered taxis try Taxi-OK, *Hotel Santiago de Cuba* (☎226/86-66-6); Transautos, *Hotel Casa Granda* (☎226/86-10-7); or Turistaxi, *Hotel Las Américas* (☎226/42-01-1).

A good option for the brave – or foolhardy – are the **motorbike taxis** that hare round town as fast as their two-cylinder engines can carry them. These congregate at the corner of San Pedro and Aguilera, by the Casa de Cultura, and all rides within the city cost 10 pesos.

SANTIAGO'S STREET NAMES

Many streets in Santiago have two names, one from before the revolution and one from after. Theoretically street signs show the post-revolutionary name but as these signs are few and far between, and locals tend to use the original name in conversation, we follow suit in the text. Cuban maps, however, usually show both names, with the original in brackets; in our maps we've followed their example. The most important roads are listed below.

OLD NAME	NEW NAME
Calvario	Porfirio Valiente
Carnicería	Pio Rosado
Clarín	Padre Quiroga
Enramada	José A. Saco
Máximo Gómez	San Germán
Reloj	Mayía Rodríguez
Sagarra	San Francisco
San Félix	Hartmann
San Gerónimo	Echevarría
San Pedro	General Lacret

Renting a car can be handy for out-of-the-way places, and the city itself is easy to negotiate. There are Havanautos **car rental** offices at the airport, in the basement of *Hotel Casa Granda* (☎226/3-93-28) and at *Hotel Las Américas* (☎226/41-38-8). Cubacar has a desk at *Hotel Santiago de Cuba* (☎226/42-61-2) and another on Avenida de los Defiles (☎226/54-56-8).

In the *Hotel Casa Granda* you'll also find Havanatur (Mon–Sat 8am–5pm; ☎226/86-1-52), one of the two agencies in Santiago offering **city tours**. Its rival, Agencia de Viajes Rumbos (daily 8am–5pm; ☎226/2-22-22), opposite the hotel, is friendlier and can also make bookings at state hotels elsewhere in the country. Both agencies offer similarly priced **excursions** throughout the province.

Accommodation

Accommodation in Santiago is plentiful and varied, and further development is planned over the next few years. Except during carnival in July, when rooms are snapped up well in advance, you can usually turn up on spec, though making a reservation will save you the possibility of having to trudge around the city looking, especially as accommodation is spread over a wide area. There are a handful of **state hotels**, from the luxurious *Hotel Santiago de Cuba* through the characterful smaller city hotels, like *Casa Granda*, to various places set in suburban greenery. **Casas particulares** are abundant, many conveniently central and most offering reduced rates for stays longer than a couple of nights. Look out for the state-issued stickers – a blue triangle on a white background – which let you know they are open for business. Touts for these are everywhere; avoid them – and their $5 a night surcharge – by booking directly.

Hotels

Casa Granda, Heredia no. 201 e/ San Pedro y San Félix ☎226/86-6-00; fax 86-0-35. A tourist attraction in itself, the beautiful *Casa Granda* is a recently restored 1920s hotel overlooking Parque Céspedes. From the elegant, airy lobby to its two atmospheric bars, it has a stately, colonial air matched in its tasteful rooms. ⑥.

Gran Hotel, Enramada esq. San Félix ☎226/20-4-72. A very central hotel operating in dollars for visitors and pesos for Cubans. Whilst it no longer merits the "grand" of its title, the vaguely colonial exterior and faded charm of the rooms is very appealing if you don't mind roughing it a bit – there's no hot water in the somewhat grubby bathrooms. Singles, doubles and triples all come with a/c and many with a tiny balcony overlooking the busy shopping street. ③–④.

Las Américas, Ave. de Las Américas y General Cebreco ☎226/42-69-5; fax 86-07-5. Whilst not the ritziest in town, this pleasant low-key hotel combines a comfortable, friendly atmosphere and good facilities – including a taxi rank, car rental office and pool – with clean, bright and functional rooms equipped with cable TV and refrigerator. A short taxi ride from the main sights. ⑤.

Santiago de Cuba, Ave. de las Américas y Calle M ☎226/42-63-4; fax 86-17-0. Santiago's biggest, brashest hotel caters for business types and luxury-seekers. The blocky red, white and blue exterior is ultra-modern and fits well with the shiny green marble interior, while facilities include a beauty parlour, boutiques, a gym, conference rooms and the best pool in town ($3 for non-guests), as well as bars and restaurants galore (see p.402). The rooms are tastefully decorated, some with original paintings by local artists, and fully equipped with all mod-cons. ⑦.

Villa San Juan, Carretera de Siboney, km 1 ☎226/4-24-78; fax 8-61-37. Close to historic Loma de San Juan (see p.400), *Villa San Juan* has the most congenial setting of all the Santiago hotels, set amid tropical trees and lush plants. The hotel itself is tasteful though a bit bland, with smart, attractive rooms and clean communal areas. An inviting pool area and friendly staff complete the pleasant atmosphere. Roughly 4km from the centre, this is a good choice if you're driving. ⑤.

Casas particulares

Casa de Eumelia Marisy, Calle Clarín no. 3 e/ Aguilera y Heredia ☎226/2-05-09. Two light and fairly spacious rooms – one with two beds and both with a/c – in a comfortable house with a rooftop patio, a communal refrigerator and a laundry area. A good choice for self-catering accommodation. ②.

Casa de Giovanni Villalón, Heredia no. 353 e/ Reloj y Calavario ☎226/5-19-72. This centrally located colonial house offers two rooms and a shared cold-water bathroom (though the owners will heat saucepans of water as required). Gracefully shabby premises likely to suit backpackers, hence the budget price. ②.

Casa de Idania Lardoeyt Creach, Heredia no. 104 e/ Corona y Félix Peña ☎226/2-68-79. This very central, rough-and-ready two-bedroom apartment will not suit all, but it's self-contained and the cooker and fridge make it a good self-catering option. ②.

Casa de Leonard Rodríguez Calleja, Clarín no. 9 e/ Aguilera y Heredia ☎226/2-35-74. Two smallish, rather dark a/c rooms (with a shared, hot-water bathroom) in a wonderful eighteenth-century house with period ironwork, wooden walls, high ceilings and red and blue stained-glass windows. Out back is a serene courtyard filled with leafy palm trees and vibrant flowers. ②.

Casa de Mabel Martínez Torrez, Corona no. 753 e/ Santa Rita y Santa Lucía; no phone. An independent house with two rooms sharing a bathroom and a kitchen. Excellent for security, as it's self-contained, and perfect for a self-catering group. ③.

Mujeres de Arena, Félix Peña no. 554 Altos e/ Enramadas y Heredia ☎226/2-00-76. A/c rooms in a top-floor apartment smack in the town centre. The darkish rooms aren't the prettiest, but the location makes this a popular choice. ②.

Casa de Nolvis Rivaflecha, San Basilio no. 122 e/ Padre Pico y Teniente Rey ☎226/2-25-38. Two clean a/c rooms each with its own hot-water bathroom, in a friendly household with a lively communal area. Close to the Padre Pico steps, in a quiet area of town with off-road parking, this is a good choice for those driving. Call before 9pm to make reservations as the phone belongs to a neighbour – ask for Nolvis. ②.

Casa de Raimundo Ocana y Bertha Pena, Heredia no. 308 e/ Pío Rosado y Porfirio Valiente ☎226/2-40-97. A charming, very central household with an attractive sunny patio bedevilled by noisy passing traffic. Two rooms, one with a/c, share a bathroom with hot water. ③.

The City

While many of the city sights are gathered in the colonial quarter to the west side of town – and you will need at least a day to do this area justice – you'll also want to take a half-day or so to explore the newer suburbs out to the east and north. The other sights are dotted randomly on the outskirts and can be squeezed into the tail end of a visit to other areas.

The colonial district's must-see sights are clustered around the picturesque **Parque Céspedes**, among them three of the most eye-catching buildings in the city – the **Cathedral**, the sixteenth-century governor's house (now the **Ayuntamiento**, or town hall) and the **Museo de Ambiente Cubano**, once the home of Diego Velázquez and the first grand house built in Cuba. Close by, the **Balcón de Velázquez**, site of an early fortification, offers a splendid view west over the red rooftops and beyond to the bay.

A couple of blocks southwest of Parque Céspedes, in the **El Tivolí** district, is the **Museo de la Lucha Clandestina**, which details Santiago's pre-revolutionary underground movement. It adjoins the celebrated **Padre Pico escalinata** on Calle Padre Pico, a staircase built to straddle one of Santiago's steepest hills.

Heading east from Parque Céspedes lands you on the liveliest section of **Calle Heredia** with its craft stalls, music venues and museums, amongst them the quirky **Museo de Carnaval**. In the street parallel to Heredia, the suberb **Museo Emilio Bacardí** houses one of the prime collections of fine art, artefacts and absorbing curios in the country and even has an Egyptology room.

Scattered north through the lattice of streets and beyond are a few secondary sights, some of which are worth going out of your way to see, most notably the **Casa Natal Mayor General Antonio Maceo**, the great general's humble birthplace, and, out on the city limits, the **Cementerio Santa Ifigenia**, burial site of José Martí.

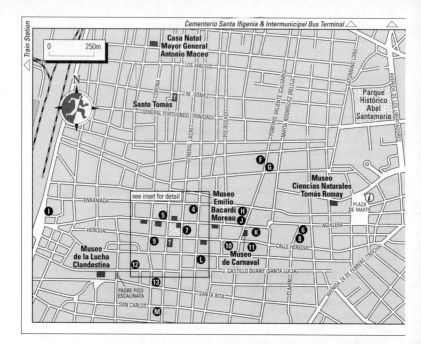

Despite what many Cubans say (see box on p.381), street hustle – begging, bag snatching and being propositioned – is no more of a problem in Santiago than in other tourist areas, although that's not to say that it doesn't happen.

East of the historic centre, Avenida de los Libertadores, the town's main artery, holds the **Moncada barracks** where Santiago's much-touted **Museo Histórico 26 de Julio** fills you in on Fidel Castro's celebrated – though futile – attack. At its north end, a massive, modernist **monument to Antonio Maceo** presides over the Plaza de la Revolución – much more memorable than the rather feeble museum to him beneath the plaza. Further east still, the once-wealthy suburb of **Reparto Vista Alegre** shows off some of the city's finest and most fantastical mansions, particularly along **Avenida Manduley** where several have been converted into restaurants. South of here, on the edge of the city, is the **Loma de San Juan**, the hill where Teddy Roosevelt and his Rough Riders swept to victory during the Spanish-American War in 1898.

Eight kilometres outside the city, presiding over the bay, is Santiago's most magnificent sight, the **Castillo del Morro San Pedro de la Roca**, a statuesque seventeenth-century fortress built by the Spanish. Just a kilometre from here, tiny **Cayo Granma** with its handful of houses and restaurants makes a good venue for a leisurely meal.

Parque Céspedes

The spiritual centre of Santiago is without a doubt charismatic **Parque Céspedes**. Originally the Plaza de Armas, the first square laid out in the town by the conquistadors, it is more of a plaza than a park, its plants

SANTIAGO DE CUBA

Cuartel Morcado

Museo de la Imagen

Balcón de Velázquez

Ayuntamiento

Casa de Cultura

Museo de Ambiente Cubano

Parque Céspedes

Casa Granda Hotel

Casa Natal de José María Heredia

Catedral de Nuestra Señora de la Asunción

Loma de San Juan & Parque Zoológico

RESTAURANTS

Coppelia	E
La Corona	M
Don Antonio	J
Doña Nelly	G
Las Gallegas	F
La Maison	D
Matamoros	H
Pizza Nova	A
El Rápido	I
Santiago 1900	L
Sodería Alondra	C
La Teressina	K
El Zunzun	B

ACCOMMODATION

Casa de Eumelia Marisy	8
Casa de Giovanni Villalón	11
Casa de Idania Lardoeyt Creach	9
Casa de Leonard Rodríguez Calleja	6
Casa de Mabel Martínez Torrez	13
Casa de Nolvis Rivaflecha	12
Casa de Raimundo Ocaña y Bertha Peña	10
Casa Granda Hotel	7
Gran Hotel	4
Las Américas	2
Mujeres de Arena	5
Santiago de Cuba	1
Villa San Juan	3

and shrubs neatly hemmed into small flowerbeds, its wrought-iron benches neatly spaced along smart red and grey flagstones. There's a gentle ebb and flow of activity as sightseers wander through between museums, and old folk sit enjoying the expansive shade of the weeping fig trees and watching the hustlers size up the tourists. There's often a brass and percussion band playing, which draws a crowd irrespective of the time of day. The engaging nineteenth-century tradition of the evening promenade, which saw gentlemen perambulating the park in one direction, ladies in the other, coquettishly flirting as they passed, has been replaced in recent years by a less attractive influx of Western men on the prowl for *jineteras*. The park is known as a favourite pick-up point, although new legislation (see p.56) has seen this trade pushed underground for the time being.

On the south side of the park a small **monument** celebrates **Carlos Manuel de Céspedes**, one of the first Cubans to take up arms against the Spanish, issuing the *Grito de Yara* (cry of Yara) and urging his slaves and his comrades to arm themselves (see p.419). Splendid buildings surround the plaza, as described below. On the east side, the balcony bar of the picturesque **Hotel Casa Granda** is the best place to people-watch over a tall glass of fresh lemonade, while next door, the **Casa de Cultura** (daily; 9am–6pm) is housed in an exquisite nineteenth-century building that begs a visit if only to admire the romantic decay inside.

The Casa Granda's second equally excellent bar is on the rooftop – a good place to watch the sun set behind the mountains.

On the north side is the brilliant-white **Ayuntamiento**, or town hall. During colonial times, the building on this site was the Casa del Gobierno, the governor's house, though the first two structures were reduced to rubble by earthquakes and the present building, erected in the 1940s, is a copy of a copy. It's not open to the public, but you can still admire the front cloister covered in shiny red tiles and fronted by crisply precise arches, with snowflake-shaped peepholes cut into the gleaming walls and shell-shaped ornamentation below the windows. The balcony overlooking the park was the site of Fidel Castro's triumphant speech on New Year's Day 1959 (see p.381).

Museo de Ambiente Cubano

Built in 1515 for Diego Velázquez, one of the first conquistadors of Cuba, the magnificent stone edifice on the west side of the park is the oldest residential building in Cuba. It now houses the **Museo de Ambiente Cubano** (Mon–Sat 9am–5pm, Sun 9am–1pm; $2, $1 extra for each photo taken), a wonderful collection of early- and late-colonial furniture, curios, weapons and fripperies which offers one of the country's best insights into colonial lifestyles, and is so large that it spills over into the house next door.

Start your tour on the first floor, in the family's living quarters, where you'll find some unusual **sixteenth-century** pieces. All the windows have heavy wooden lattice balconies and shutters – intended to hide the women, keep the sun out and protect against attack – which lend the house a surprising coolness, as well as the look of an indomitable fortress. The original ceilings, now restored, are lavishly timbered in heavy cedar wood and detailed with crests, while the hallway walls are chased with magnificent Moorish swirls and blocks of muted primary colour in place of wallpaper.

The house was strategically built facing west so that the first-floor windows looked out over the bay, and a cannon is still trained out of the bedroom window. The low daybed in the corner of the same room, spread with rich fabrics, sits incongruously with the heavy artillery but would have been where the gentlewomen of the household spent their days sewing on silken cushions.

The next two adjoining rooms represent the mid- and late **seventeenth century**. In the first is a chunky, carved mahogany chest, a wooden plaque painted with a portrait of Velázquez and a delicate Spanish ceramic inkwell which has survived intact through three centuries. Reflecting the refinement and European cultural influence that had infiltrated Cuban society by the end of the seventeenth century, the second room houses an exquisite, Spanish secretaire, its twelve mahogany drawers inlaid with bone mythological figures.

The final rooms on this floor take you into the **eighteenth century**, and the furnishings seem incongruously grand, set against the plain white walls and cool tiled floors of the house. Note the luxurious Cuban mahogany four-poster bed, the cedar wardrobe inlaid

with large pansies, the English desk and the profusion of dainty
French porcelain. Also in this room, cut into the inner wall, there's a
very peculiar feature in the bizarrely named **Pollo de la Ventana**
(Window Chicken), a tightly latticed spy window overlooking the
hallway which allowed inhabitants to check on the movements of
other people in the house.

Out in the cool, dark-wood upstairs **hallway** you can fully appreciate the cleverness of the design in the stark contrast with the dazzling
sunny central courtyard visible below, where there's an elegant central
fountain and a huge *tinajón* water jar (see p.325) from Camagüey.
Before you venture downstairs, walk to the end of the hallway to see
the remains of the stone **furnace** that Velázquez built into the corner
of the house so that he could smelt his own gold.

The rooms on the **ground floor**, where Velázquez had his offices,
are now laid out with more extravagant eighteenth-century furniture
and artefacts – among them a particularly curvaceous French chest
of drawers and a beautiful French clock representing the world's first
air-balloon journey. More impressive, perhaps, are the details of the
house itself, such as the wide entrance made to accommodate a carriage and the expansive trading rooms with a stone central arch,
marble flagged floor and window seats.

The collection overflows into the house next door, which has a
similar decor but dates from the nineteenth century. Again, much of
what's on display is imported from Europe and shows off the good
life enjoyed by the bourgeoisie, but the most interesting items are
native to Cuba. These include the *pajilla* chair with latticework back
and seat, invented in Cuba to combat the heat, the tobacco-drying
machine in the kitchen, and the *Tinajero* water stand which was
filled up at night to filter drinking water through porous rock into an
earthenware jar beneath, ready for the morning. Possibly the most
quintessentially Cuban item on display is the reclining *pajilla* smoking chair with an ornate ashtray attached to the arm, made for the
proper enjoyment of a fine cigar.

Catedral de Nuestra Señora de la Asunción

On the south side of the square is the handsome **Catedral de Nuestra
Señora de la Asunción** (daily except Tues 8am–noon; Mass daily at
6.30pm, plus Sun 9.30am). Painted white and primrose-yellow, it is
ornate without being extravagant and has a pleasing symmetry that
blends well with the other buildings in the square. The first cathedral
in Cuba was built on this site in 1522, but repeated run-ins with earth-
quakes and pirates – in 1662 English privateer Christopher Mygns
even snaffled the church bells after blowing the roof off – made their
mark, and Santiagueros started work on a second cathedral on the
site in 1670. They finished in 1675, only to see the building demolished by an earthquake just three years later. Reconstruction began
again, and in 1680 another cathedral was up and running, this one

holding out for over a hundred years, though debilitated by earth-quakes in 1766 and 1800, before being finally damaged beyond repair by a tremor in 1803.

The present cathedral, completed in 1818, has fared better, having been built with a fortified roof and walls in order to withstand natural disasters. Raised above ground level, it's reached by flights of stairs on its east and west fronts, with the cavernous space below, once the cathedral crypt, now housing dollar shops. A Baroque-style edifice, its twin towers gleam in the sunshine and its doorway is topped by an imposing herald angel, statues of **Christopher Columbus** and **Bartolomé de las Casas**, defender of the Indians, erected in the 1920s, and four Neoclassical columns.

The cathedral interior is no less ornate, with an arched Rococo ceiling rising above the first rows of pews into a celestial blue dome painted with a cloud of cherubs. Cherubs and angels are something of a theme, in fact, being strewn across the ceiling and up the walls. Facing the congregation is a modest marble altar framed by rich dark-wood choir stalls, while to the right a more ornate altar honours the Virgen de la Caridad, patron saint of Cuba. Since the visit of Pope John Paul II in January 1998, the state has relaxed its hitherto censorial stance on the Catholic Church, once seen to be in league with capitalism, and the cathedral, like other churches throughout Cuba, now has a daily procession of devotees supplicating the Virgen de la Caridad for favours, as well as a few *jineteros* keen to take advantage of the tourists. The prize piece of the cathedral, though almost hidden on the left-hand side, is the tremendous **organ**, now disused but still replete with tall gilded pipes. Lining the wall is a noteworthy frieze detailing the history of St James, patron saint of Santiago.

The best view of the cathedral is from the rooftop bar at the Hotel Casa Granda.

In a small upstairs room round the cathedral's east side is a tiny **museum** (Mon–Sat 9am–5pm; $1) exhibiting a small collection of beautifully penned calligraphic correspondence between various cardinals and bishops, portraits of all the past bishops of the cathedral and not much else. It's the only museum of its kind in Cuba and worth checking out if you're into that sort of thing.

Balcón de Velázquez

From the cathedral, make a detour to the fortification known as the **Balcón de Velázquez** (daily 7am–8pm; free), on Heredia esq. Corona. Built between 1539 and 1550, it was a lookout point for incoming ships, and originally equipped with a semicircle of cannons facing out over the bay. When it fell into disrepair a house was built on the site, and it wasn't until 1950 that the city council decided to rebuild it in honour of Velázquez. It was completed in 1953, sadly without its most intriguing feature, a tunnel entered from beneath the circular platform in the centre of the patio and running for less than a kilometre down to the seafront. This was presumably used by the early townsfolk for making a swift exit when under siege. The

modern covered entrance is lined with a history of Santiago (in
Spanish) and honorary plaques to influential dignitaries. Despite
these worthy efforts, however, by far the best part of the fortification
is its view over the ramshackle, red-tiled rooftops down towards the
bay and the ring of mountains beyond.

El Tivolí

In the hills about four blocks south of the Balcón de Velázquez is the
El Tivolí neighbourhood, named by the French plantation owners
who settled there after fleeing the Haitian slave revolution at the end
of the eighteenth century. With no real boundaries – it lies loosely
between Avenida Trocha to the south and Calle Padre Pico in the
north – there's not much to distinguish it from the rest of the old
quarter, save for its intensely hilly narrow streets writhing down
towards the bay. The immigrant French made this the most fashionable area of town, and for a while its bars and music venues made it
the place for well-to-do Santiagueros to be seen. While the *Casa de
la las Tradiciones* (see p.404) is still good for a knees-up, the area
has lost its former glory and the main attractions now are the **Museo
de la Lucha Clandestina** and the **Padre Pico escalinata**, a towering
staircase of over five hundred steps, built to accommodate the
almost sheer hill that rises from the lower end of Calle Padre Pico.

Museo de la Lucha Clandestina

Just west of Padre Pico, perched on the Loma del Intendente, the
Museo de la Lucha Clandestina (Mon–Sat 9am–5pm; $1; English,
Italian and Spanish guides available; no photographs) is a tribute to
the pre-revolutionary struggle. Spread over two floors, the museum
comprises a photographic and journalistic history of the final years
of the Batista regime and is a must for anyone struggling to understand the intricacies of the events leading up to the revolution.

The immaculate building is a reproduction of an eighteenth-century
house built on the site to be the residence of the quartermaster general under Spanish rule. In the 1950s it was being used as the Santiago
police headquarters until burnt to the ground during an assault
orchestrated by schoolteacher-cum-underground leader **Frank País**
on November 30, 1956. The three-pronged attack also took in the
customs house and the harbour headquarters in an attempt to divert
the authorities' attention from the arrival of Fidel Castro and other
dissidents at Las Coloradas beach on the southwest coast (see p.423).
The attack is well documented and part of the museum focuses on the
lives of Frank País and his brother and co-collaborator Josue, both
subsequently murdered by Batista's henchmen in 1957. However, as
in so many museums in Cuba, there's little discrimination in the
exhibits, so that photographs of Frank's massively attended funeral
procession share space with a red jumper he once wore, making the
experience by turns moving and slightly comical.

The best exhibits are those that give an idea of the turbulent climate of fear, unrest and excitement that existed in the 1950s in the lead-up to the revolution. During this period, the M-26-7 group instigated general strikes and civil disorder to disrupt the Batista regime, even burning the sugar crop. Most memorable is a clutch of **Molotov cocktails** made from old-fashioned Pepsi Cola bottles, a hysterical newspaper cutting announcing Fidel Castro's death and another published by the rebels themselves refuting the claim. Also noteworthy are the evocative images of a young Castro and comrades in Mexico, Castro's revolution manifesto written in exile, and a photograph of the triumphant gang on the town hall balcony on the day of Castro's victory speech.

Calle Heredia

A couple of blocks east of Parque Céspedes is the lively patch of **Calle Heredia** where the cat-calls and suggestive comments of the street vendors hawking hand-carved necklaces, polished wood sculptures, shell hair-clasps and gimcrack souvenirs combine with the drums emanating from the *Casa de la Trova* music hall to create one of the hippest, friendliest areas in the city. Santiagueros often comment that you haven't really been to the city until you've been to Calle Heredia, and you can spend hours checking out the sights, namely the mildly interesting **Casa Natal de José María Heredia** and the excellent **Museo de Carnaval**, and just drinking in the atmosphere.

Don't miss the tiny second-hand bookshop on the corner of Pio Rosado where a trovador trio plays requests all day long.

Casa Natal de José María Heredia

The handsome colonial house at Heredia no. 1260 is the **Casa Natal de José María Heredia** (Tues–Sat 9am–9pm, Sun 9am–1pm & 4–8pm; $1), the birthplace of one of the greatest Latin American poets. Whilst not the most dynamic museum in the world, it's worth a quick breeze through the spartan rooms to see the luxurious French *bateau* bed, the family photos and the various first editions.

Although Heredia only lived in the house for two and a half years before his family moved to the US in 1806 (returning to Cuba for a brief spell in 1810 before leaving again for Venezuela and later Mexico), he is considered a son of Santiago and honoured accordingly, with the street itself named after him. After the death of his father in 1820 he returned to Cuba, settling in Matanzas. He practised law there until denounced as a supporter of independence by colleagues at the prestigious law firm where he worked, whereupon he went into exile in the United States in 1824. His poetry was a combination of romanticism and nationalism, and forbidden in Cuba until the end of Spanish rule. His best-remembered work is *Himno del Desterrado* (Hymn of the Outcast), which he wrote when he sailed close to Matanzas en route to Mexico from New York. He died in 1839.

Local poets meet for discussions and recitals on the sunny patio at the back of the Casa Natal (Tues & Thurs 5–9pm; free).

Museo del Carnaval

Santiago de
Cuba city

*See box over-
leaf for more
on Santiago's
carnival*

Much more enjoyable is the **Museo del Carnaval**, at no. 301 Heredia
(Tues–Sun 9am–5pm; $1, plus $1 per photo taken, $5 for camcorder),
a must if you can't make it for the real thing in July. Thoughtfully laid
out on the ground floor of a dimly lit colonial house, the museum is a
bright and colourful collection of psychedelic costumes, atmospheric
photographs and carnival memorabilia.

Beginning with scene-setting **photographs** of Santiago in the early
twentieth century, showing roads laced with tram tracks and well-
dressed people promenading through the parks, the exhibition
moves on to photographs, newspaper cuttings and **costumes** belonging to the pre-revolutionary carnivals of the 1940s and 1950s.
Pictures of extravagant floats – including one bearing the logo of
now-exiled sponsors Bacardí – are jumbled together with minutely
embroidered satin capes garlanded with flowers, harlequin outfits
and giant, papier-mâché, head-shaped masks.

In a separate room are photographs of some of the musicians
who have played at carnival accompanied by their **instruments**,
displayed in glass cases. A final room shows off costumes made for
post-revolution carnivals, often rather less glamorous than their
predecessors. The most recent prize-winning costume is kept in the
centre of the room, along with some of the immensely intricate pro-
totypes of floats that are constructed in miniature months before
the final models are made.

When the museum closes the flamboyant carnival atmosphere
continues with a free, hour-long **dance recital** (Tues–Sat 5–6pm,
Sun 11am–noon), the Tardes de Folklórico (folklore afternoon),
which is given outside, on a patio to the back of the museum (see
p.405).

Museo Emilio Bacardí Moreau and around

If you only go to one museum in Santiago, make it the stately **Museo
Emilio Bacardí Moreau**, on the corner of Aguilera and Pío Rosado,
the street parallel to Heredia (Tues–Sat 9am–6pm, Sun 9am–1pm;
$2, $1 extra for each photograph). Its colonial antiquities, excellent
collection of Cuban fine art and archeological curios – including an
Egyptian mummy – make it one of the most comprehensive hoards
in the country.

Styled along the lines of a traditional European city museum, it was
founded in 1899 by Emilio Bacardí Moreau, then mayor of Santiago
and patriarch of the Bacardi rum dynasty, to house his vast private
collection of artefacts, amassed over the previous decades. The original museum occupied a more modest venue on Enramada, but
Bacardí felt that the tremendous collection deserved better and the
present structure was purpose-built to his instructions. Photographs
on the first floor recall the man, his project and his wife Elvira Cape,
who saw the building through to fruition when Bacardí died.

Santiago de Cuba city

The three-day extravaganza that is Santiago's carnival has its origins in the festival of Santiago (St James), the patron saint of Spain, which is held annually on July 25. While the Spanish colonists venerated the saint, patron of the city, their African slaves used the day to celebrate and practise their own religions, predominantly Yoruba, as this was one of their only free days in the year. A religious procession would wind its way around the town towards the cathedral, with the pious Spanish taking the lead and reveller slaves bringing up the rear. Once the Spanish had entered the cathedral the slaves took their own celebration onto the streets, with dancers, singers and musicians creating a ritual that had little to do with the solemn religion of the Spanish – the frenzied gaiety of the festival even earned it the rather derisive name Los Mamarrachos (The Mad Ones).

Music was a key element right from the start, and slaves of similar ethnic groups would form *comparsas* (carnival bands) to make music with home-made bells, drums and chants. Often accompanying the *comparsas* on the procession were *diablitos* (little devils) – male dancers masked from head to toe in raffia costumes. This tradition is still upheld today and you can see the rather unnerving, jester-like figures running through the crowds and scaring children. In the seventeenth century the festival was gradually extended to cover July 24, the festival of Santa Cristina, and July 26, Santa Ana's day.

When the French colonials arrived with their African slaves, following the 1791 slave revolution in Haiti, they brought significant contributions to Los Mamarrachos. The *comparsas* began to incorporate elements of French dance genres, most notably the *contredanse*, with its highly choreographed, ballroom-style steps, and as a result the parades became more stylized and structured. Although the festival was still essentially a black celebration, it was watched by bourgeois Cubans from their windows and balconies, from where they would often throw money at the feet of performers as they passed through the streets.

The exhibits are arranged over three floors. The ground floor is devoted to the **Sala de Conquista y Colonización**, full of elaborate weaponry like the sixteenth-century helmets, cannons and spurs, and a heavy mace like a twist of silver candy, although copper cooking pots and the like add a suggestion of social history. Much more sinister are the whips, heavy iron chains and *Palo Mata Negro* (or Kill-the-Black stick) used to whip and beat slaves into submission. The chopping board on display was used to slice off insubordinate slaves' arms, hands or feet, a punishment which took place in public, on Calle Carnicería ("Carnage Street"). Also on display are drums, a crown and a chair used as a throne by the Congo Juan de Góngora *cabildo*, one of the secret slave chapters that used to practise their own religion in defiance of colonial Catholicism.

From here the theme turns to the history of the fight for **independence**, exhibiting the printing press where the independence manifesto newspaper *El Cubano Libre*, edited by Carlos Manuel de Céspedes, was produced. Representing the wars is an assortment of

The festival underwent its biggest change in 1902 with the birth of the new republic, when politics and advertising began to muscle in on the action. It was during this era that the festival's name was changed to the more conventional "*carnaval*", as the middle classes sought to distance the celebrations from their Afro-Cuban roots. With the introduction of the annually selected *Reina de Carnaval* (Carnival Queen) – usually a white, middle-class girl – and carnival floats sponsored by big-name companies like Hatuey beer and Bacardí rum, the celebration underwent a transformation from marginal black community event to populist extravaganza. With sponsorship deals abundant, the *carrozas* (floats) flourished, using extravagant and grandiose designs.

After the revolution the new regime poured money into all areas of carnival entertainment, which in the absence of big-name sponsors became reliant on public funding. Following the hiatus of the Special Period, which saw carnival cancelled for several years in the 1990s, the festival regained its egalitarianism and every neighbourhood now has its own *comparsa* made up of adults and children, all wearing home-made costumes. Bands practise extensively, often rehearsing in the parks and local streets in the run-up to main parade. Everything and anything is used to make music, including metal tyre rims and frying pans for percussion, as well as the more conventional trumpets and drums. An essential part of the Santiago carnival sound is formed by the *corneta china* (Chinese horn), a double-reeded horn with a plaintive, wailing sound that was introduced by Chinese indentured labourers in the late nineteenth century.

Perhaps the most distinctive element of modern-day carnival in Santiago is the conga parade that takes place in each neighbourhood on the first day of the celebrations. Led by the *comparsas*, seemingly the entire neighbourhood, many still dressed in hair curlers and house slippers, leave their houses as the performers lead them around the streets in a vigorous parade. Children join in with home-made rattles and drums while the adults dance in what has become the unofficial signal of the start of carnival.

the Mambises' ingenious bullet belts, cups, sandals and trousers, all hand-made from natural products in the face of shortages whilst on the warpath. The generals' gallery is less exciting, with an unenlightening array of artefacts from the key players, like Antonio Maceo's drinking cup, top hat and saddle, and José Martí's fountain pen. Better, although unrelated, is the armaments gallery over to one side, with more pistols, machetes, daggers and engraved Samurai swords than you can shake a stick at.

The museum really comes into its own on the second floor, with an excellent display of **paintings** and **sculpture**, including some fascinating nineteenth-century portraits of colonial Cubans, amongst them Frederico Martínez Matos's insightful society studies and Manuel Vicens's 1864 family portrait, *Interior de la Casa de Juan Bautista Sagarra*, which depicts a nineteenth-century household. A surprise is the delicately executed series of watercolours – including a rather camp cavalryman and an enigmatic picador – by the multi-talented Emilio Bacardí himself.

There is also a strong collection of **contemporary** painting and sculpture, with several of the country's most prominent artists represented. Highlights include the iridescent *Paisaje* by Víctor Manuel García, who died in the late 1960s, and Fauvist Adigio Benitez's captivating *Punto de Control*, in which a steely yet sensual daughter of the revolution operates machinery. The simple but powerful *Maternidad*, by Pedro Arrate, is a perfect composition, with a young mother kneeling on a bare wooden floor nursing her newborn child. *Formas*, on the other hand, is a rather disappointing mass of brown by Wilfredo Lam.

A separate room, round the side of the museum, houses the **Sala de Arqueología**, where a substantial selection of Egyptian artefacts includes some fine jade and blue-stone eagle-head idols, and the only **Egyptian mummy** in Cuba, thought to be a young woman from the Thebes dynasty and brought over from Luxor by Bacardí himself; her well-preserved casket is on display nearby, covered in hieroglyphics and pictures. Other relics include two Peruvian mummies from the Paracas culture, believed to be over a thousand years old, and artefacts from the Tsantsa people of the Amazon region, including an arm shield, a bow decorated with clumps of hair from victims' scalps, and some small but perfectly formed shrunken heads. There is little here from Cuba, other than a few tenth- and eleventh-century stone and quartz idols from Oriente, depicting pregnant women with hollowed-out eyes and gaping mouths.

Museo Ciencias Naturales Tomás Romay and Plaza Marté

At the east end of Enramada, about a ten-minute walk east from the Museo Emilio Bacardí Moreau, taxidermy enthusiasts will thrill to the motheaten stuffed animals at the **Museo Ciencias Naturales Tomás Romay** (Tues–Sat 9am–5pm, Sun 9am–1pm; $1), but everyone else can head up to the lively **Plaza Marté**, where gaggles of game-playing schoolchildren, loudspeakers transmitting radio broadcasts and plenty of benches beneath shady trees make this an enjoyable place to sit down or have your photo taken by the aged photographer and his Box Brownie. The tall column, a **monument** to local veterans of the wars of independence, has a particular significance as the plaza was formerly the execution ground for prisoners held by the Spanish. The Smurf-like cap at its summit is the *gorro frigio*, given to slaves in ancient Rome when they were granted their freedom, and is a symbol of Cuban independence.

The Cuartel Moncada and Parque Abel Santamaría

East of Aguilera, and just off the Avenida de los Libertadores, the **Cuartel Moncada**, futilely stormed by Fidel Castro and his band of revolutionaries on July 26, 1953, is a must-see, if only for the place it has in Cuban history. With a commanding view over the mountains, the ochre and white building, topped with a fat row of castellations, is peppered with bullet holes from the attack. These were plastered over on Fulgencio Batista's orders, only to be hollowed out again rather obsessively by Fidel Castro when he came to power, with photographs used to make sure the positions were as authentic as possible.

Castro closed the barracks altogether in 1960, turning part of the building into a school, while the one-time parade grounds outside are now occasionally used for state speeches. Also inside is the **Museo 26 de Julio** (Mon–Sat 9am–5pm, Sun 9am–1pm; $1, $1 extra for each photograph), which is not without flashes of brilliance when it comes to telling the story of the attack, but is otherwise rather dry.

English-, Spanish- and Italian-speaking guides will take you round the museum at no extra charge.

After learning that it was built by the Spanish in 1850, occupied by the North American army in 1898 during the wars of independence, accidentally burnt down in 1937 and rebuilt in 1938, you can bypass the pedantic history of the garrison. The museum properly gets underway with its coverage of the 1953 attack. A meticulous **scale model** details the barracks, the hospital – now demolished – and the Palacio de Justicia, and gives the events a welcome clarity – it's even marked with the positions where rebel bullets landed. The museum pulls no punches on the subject of the **atrocities** visited upon the captured rebels by the Regimental Intelligence Service, Batista's henchmen: a huge collage, blotted with crimson paint, has been created from photographs of the dead rebels lying in their own gore. There are short biographies of some of the unfortunates, along with gruesome blood-stained uniforms and some sobering sketches of the type of weapons used.

Thankfully the last room has a less oppressive theme, with photographs of the surviving rebels leaving the Isla de Pinos (now Isla de la Juventud), where they had been imprisoned following the attack (see p.398), and in exile in Mexico, as well as a scale-model of the celebrated yacht *Granma* that carried them back to Cuba. If you can tear yourself away from the lovingly preserved burgundy jumper and US-issue backpack that Castro wore in the Sierra Maestra, have a look at the **guns** used in the war, in particular the one in the middle of the display, carved with the national flag and the inscription "*Vale más morir de pies a vivir de rodillas*" (It's better to die on your feet than to live on your knees).

Exhibits peter out after this and you're left with a cluster of cuttings from early editions of revolution newspapers, full of promises about the forthcoming utopia, some of which have been fulfilled; a dinner jacket belonging to José Martí; and an incomprehensible diagram showing how the different levels of assemblies, committees and local bodies mesh together to form the Cuban government. The museum ends with a big mural lauding Santiago's achievements in health, education and culture.

Parque Histórico Abel Santamaría

A couple of blocks west of the barracks, just over Avenida de los Libertadores, on the site of the Civil Hospital which Santamaría captured during the Moncada attack, **Parque Histórico Abel**

The attack on the Moncada Barracks

Summing up his goals with the words "a small engine is needed to help start the big engine", Fidel Castro decided to make an attack not only to acquire the weapons his guerilla organization would need but also with the hope that the attack would spark a national uprising against the Batista regime and lead to a general strike. The Moncada barracks seemed perfect: not only was it the second largest in the country, with some thousand-odd troops, but it was also based in Oriente, where support for the clandestine movement against the government was already strongest.

The attack was organized from Havana in such secrecy that only two members of the group, besides Castro himself, knew of the plan – some of the supporters thought they were being taken to Santiago carnival as a reward for hard work. Castro shrewdly chose July 26, reckoning that many soldiers would be unfit to fight in the early hours of the morning after carousing at carnival the night before. He rented a farm at Siboney, about 14km from the city, and the attackers mustered here. With limited funds and only a few secondhand weapons, it was always going to be an ambitious military debut for the small cell of 135 men and 2 women who would stage the attack.

A three-pronged assault was planned, with the main body of men, led by Fidel Castro, attacking the barracks themselves while Raúl Castro, Fidel's brother, would attack the nearby Palace of Justice, overlooking the barracks, with ten men to form a covering cross-fire. Abel Santamaría, Castro's second-in-command, was to take the civil hospital opposite the Palace of Justice with 22 men; the two women, his sister Haydee Santamaría and his girlfriend, Melba Hernández, were to treat the wounded.

The attack was an unqualified fiasco. At 5.30am on July 26, a motorcade of 26 cars set off from Siboney headed for Santiago. Somewhere between the farm and the city limits, several cars headed off in the wrong direction and never made it to the barracks. The remaining cars reached the barracks, calling on the sentries to make way for the general, a ruse which allowed the attackers to seize the sentries' weapons and force their way into the barracks.

Outside things were going less well. Castro, who was in the second car, stopped after an unexpected encounter with patrolling soldiers and the subsequent gunfire alerted the troops throughout the barracks. Following their previous orders, once they saw that Castro's car had stopped, the men in the other cars streamed out to attack other buildings

Santamaría is less of a park and more like a small field of concrete centred on a monument to Abel Santamaría. Set above a gushing fountain, a gigantic cube of concrete is carved with the faces of Santamaría and fellow martyr José Martí and the epigram "*Morir por la patria es vivir*" (To die for your country is to live). Seemingly buoyed up by the jet of water, the floating cube is rather impressive and worth a look whilst you're in the area.

Reparto Vista Alegre and Loma de San Juan

East of town, residential **Reparto Vista Alegre** grew up at the beginning of the twentieth century as an exclusive neighbourhood for Santiago's middle classes. Today its lingering air of wealth is confined in the barracks before Castro had a chance to re-evaluate the situation. The men inside the first building found themselves cut off amid the general confusion and as free-for-all gunfire ensued, the attackers were reduced to fleeing and cowering behind cars. Castro gave the order to withdraw, leaving behind two dead and one wounded.

By contrast, the unprotected Palace of Justice had been captured successfully, although Raúl Castro's group were also forced to withdraw once their role was rendered useless. Similarly, the attack on the hospital had also been successful, although the attackers did not receive the order to retreat and had to hide in the hospital itself, disguised as patients.

The real bloodshed was yet to come, however, as within 48 hours of the attack somewhere between 55 and 70 of the original rebels had been captured, tortured and executed by Batista's officers, who had rooted out the rebels in an extensive operation in which thousands were detained. The casualties included Abel Santamaría, whose eyes were gouged out, while his sister, Haydee, was forced to watch. Her boyfriend, Boris Santa Coloma, was castrated and other prisoners were beaten with rifle butts before being shot. The soldiers attempted to pass the bodies off as casualties of the attack two days before.

Thirty-two rebels survived to be brought to trial, including Fidel Castro himself who managed to hide in the mountains around the city before his capture several days later. Others managed to escape altogether and returned to Havana. Although a disaster in military terms, the attack was a political triumph: the army's brutality towards the rebels sent many previously indifferent people into the arms of the clandestine movement and elevated Fidel Castro – previously seen as just a maverick young lawyer – to hero status throughout Cuba.

The rebels were tried in October and despite efforts to prevent Castro appearing in court – an attempt was apparently made to poison him – he gave an erudite and impassioned speech in his own defence. Speaking for five hours, he charted the plight of Cuban people using an arsenal of statistics to assault the regime and charging Batista with being the worst dictator in Cuban history. A reprisal of the speech was later published as a manifesto for revolution, known as "history will absolve me". Although the declamation did little to help Castro at the time – he was sentenced to fifteen years' imprisonment – the whole episode set him on the path to the leadership of the revolution.

---

to a few top-notch **restaurants** dotted around wide and regal Avenida Manduley, which are most people's reason for visiting (see p.403). Some of the handsome Neoclassical buildings lining the main road – best seen in springtime under a cloud of pink blossom – are still private residences, while others are government offices. Although most are a bit worn around the edges they make for pleasant sightseeing, especially the madly ornate peach palace – one-time Bacardí family residence – that's now the headquarters of the children's *Pionero* youth movement.

Well worth checking out should you be in the area is the small and quirky **Museo de la Imagen**, Calle 8 no. 106 (Mon–Sat 9am–5pm; $1), a brief history of photography told through antique Leicas,

Polaroids and Kodaks, and some brilliant one-off photographs including Fidel Castro, in Native American feathered headdress, accepting a peace pipe from the leader of the White Bird tribe. Also worth remembering is the **Casa del Caribe**, on Calle 13 no. 154, which has music and dance shows daily.

Loma de San Juan

The **Loma de San Juan**, the hill where Teddy Roosevelt rode his army to victory against the Spanish, is about 250m from Avenida Manduley, which runs through the centre of Reparto Vista Alegre. The neatly mowed lawns framing a bijou fountain, the sweeping vista of mountain peaks and the dainty flowerbeds make it look more suited to a tea party than a battle, but the numerous plaques and monuments erected by the North Americans to honour their soldiers are evidence enough. Squeezed into a spare corner, the sole monument to the Cuban sacrifice was erected in 1934 by Emilio Bacardí to the unknown Mambí soldier, a tribute to all liberation soldiers whose deaths went unrecorded. The park would be a peaceful retreat were it not for the persistent attentions of the crowd of hustlers.

On Avenida Raúl Pujol, 250m west of Loma de San Juan, is Santiago's **Parque Zoológico** (Tues–Sun 10am–5pm; $1). Covering 19 hectares, it is larger than most zoos in Cuba, but still a rather miserable place where a menagerie of mournful creatures lie, for the most part, cramped and listless in rather squalid cages. The most celebrated animals include a chimpanzee who smokes cigarettes – given the chance – a pair of lions who cower when approached, and some apathetic hyenas. With more space to move about, the numerous species of birds – including parrots, flamingos and Cuba's national bird, the Tocorro – fare slightly better, with the exception of the ill-fated white ducks which are bred exclusively to feed the torpid pythons caged nearby. The wide range of animals also includes horses which you can ride ($2 an hour), but it's really not the place for animal lovers.

North of the centre

At the bottom of Avenida de los Américas, by the busy junction with Avenida de los Libertadores, is the **Plaza de la Revolución**, an empty space backed by a park in which stands the gargantuan **Monumento Antonio Maceo**. The sixteen-metre steel effigy, on a wide plateau at the top of a jade marble staircase, shows the "Bronze Titan" – so named because he was of mixed race – on his rearing horse, backed by a forest of gigantic steel machetes representing his rebellion and courage. On the other side of the marble plateau, wide steps lead down behind an eternal flame dedicated to the general, to the **Museo Antonio Maceo** (Tues–Sat 9am–5pm; $1), housed in the plateau basement, where you'll find a somewhat lifeless collection of sketches representing key events and some fuzzy holograms showing Maceo's watch, ring and pen in three-dimensional detail.

Cementerio Santa Ifigenia

Most visitors who trek out to the **Cementerio Santa Ifigenia** (daily
7am–6pm; $1), about 3km west of Parque Céspedes, do so to visit
José Martí's mausoleum, a grandiose affair of heavy white stone with
the inevitable statue. It's located near the cemetery entrance at the
end of a private walkway, and once you've paid your respects, you can
escape the hordes and wander undisturbed through the palm trees,
admiring the magnificent tombs and trying to ignore the smell of
sewage wafting over from the town plant. Although you'll find Carlos
Manuel de Céspedes' tomb here, as well as that of Antonio Maceo's
widow, it's the lesser-known structures, like the Naser family's
mosque-like domed tomb, and the replica of El Morro fort honouring
Spanish and Cuban war veterans, that are the most eye-catching.

Out from the city

Just 8km south of the city is one of Santiago's most dramatic – and
popular – sights, the **Castillo del Morro San Pedro de la Roca**, a
fortress poised on the high cliffs that flank the entrance to the Bahía
de Santiago to Cuba. A half-day trip out here by taxi can easily take
in the diminutive **Cayo Granma**, 2km away, where a peaceful village
in a rural setting offers an excellent spot for a meal.

El Castillo del Morro San Pedro de la Roca

Undeniably one of the most unmissable sights in Santiago, **El
Castillo del Morro San Pedro de la Roca** (Mon–Fri 9am–5pm, Sat &
Sun 8am–4pm; $3, $1 extra for a camera, $5 for a camcorder) is a
giant stone fortress designed by the Italian military engineer Juan
Bautista Antonelli, who was also responsible for the similar fortification in Havana (see p.113). Named after the governor of Santiago at
the time, though usually shortened to "El Morro", it was built
between 1633 and 1639 to ward off pirates. However, despite
appearing to be indomitable – with a heavy drawbridge spanning a
deep moat, thick stone walls angled sharply to one another and,
inside, expansive parade grounds stippled with cannons trained out
to sea – it was nothing of the sort, and in 1662 the English pirate
Christopher Myngs, finding to his surprise that the fort had been left
unguarded, made a successful rearguard attack.

Ramps and steps cut precise angles through the heart of the
fortress, which is spread over three levels, and it's only as you wander deeper into the labyrinth of rooms that you get a sense of how
awesomely huge it is. Even when it is completely overrun by busloads of visitors, you can move through the prison cells, chapel and
dormitories – with accommodation for the 150 soldiers once billeted
there – without feeling too packed in. The small, square *tinajones*
water carriers and the twisted, blue balustrades in front of the windows add a note of distinction, while the room stacked with cannon-
balls and fitted with the heavy shaft that would roll them to the can-

non illustrates the seriousness of the castle's business. The feeblest feature is the exhibition room on the second level, which has a largely forgettable pictorial display of warships, although a pirate exhibition, amongst others, is planned for the future.

Cayo Granma

Take the turn-off by El Morro and head down the road for 2km to reach the ferry point for tiny **Cayo Granma**, a grassy, beachless dune just offshore, with red-tiled homes and a scattering of eating places clustered round the coast. There's no sign for the ferry point, but it's roughly opposite the cay and there are usually a few people queuing. Have 20 centavos ready for the ten- to fifteen-minute crossing. The ferry crosses back and forth continuously from 7am to 9pm, and the longest you'll have to wait is around 25 minutes.

You can work up an appetite walking round the cay – it only takes twenty minutes – and taking in the near-panoramic view of the mountains from the top of its one hill before relaxing at one of the restaurants. *Restaurant El Cayo* does fancy seafood, including lobster, paella and shrimp, while *Restaurant Paraíso* does basic peso meals very cheaply. You can also ask around for a *paladar*.

Eating

Avoid drinking unsterilized or unboiled water, especially during the summer months, when reports of parasites in Santiago's water supply are common.

As with most other regions in the country, the majority of restaurants fall back on the old favourites of pork or chicken accompanied by rice and beans, although there are a few original dishes and most state restaurants, especially the ones at the top end, usually have a tasty seafood dish. You won't be stuck for places to try, with plenty of restaurants and cafés around the **centre** all serving decent meals at affordable prices.

The best area for daytime **snacks** is by the bus station on Avenida de los Américas, where there's an abundance of maize fritters and fried pork sandwiches, with a few more stands dotted around closer to the centre. Around Avenida Manduley, in **Reparto Vista Alegre**, the restaurants are more upmarket and it's here that you can dine out in some style. Away from the state arena choice is very limited as high taxes and tight controls on what food can be served have pushed most of the **paladares** in town out of business, but some *casas particulares* make tasty meals for their guests.

Casa Granda, Heredia 201 e/ San Pedro y San Félix. This hotel restaurant is the best place for breakfast, with an extensive hot and cold, Continental, English and Caribbean buffet. Also scores highly for lunch and dinner, with lemon roast chicken, steak and lobster as well as some drinkable wines. Prices start from $6.

Coppelia, Ave. de los Libertadores esq. Garzón. Freshly made ice cream at unbeatable peso prices in an outdoor café that looks like a crazy-golf course. Very popular locally, so arrive early before the best flavours sell out. Tues–Sun 9am–11pm.

La Corona, Félix Pena no. 807 esq. San Carlos. Excellent bakery with an indoor café, serving up a wide variety of breads, sweets and pastries filled with custard or smothered in super-sticky meringue.

Don Antonio, Esq. Aguilera y Calvario. Pleasant, mid-range Rumbos café-bar with a view of the port. Dishes up the standard fried chicken and spaghetti.

Doña Nelly, Carnicería no. 412 e/ San Francisco y San Gerónimo. Al fresco eating in this friendly *paladar*, with tasty roast chicken, fillet of pork or lamb accompanied by generous portions of salad and fried green banana.

Las Gallegas, Carnicería e/ San Gerónimo y San Francisco. Excellent *paladar* close to the centre with a range of typical, well-prepared Cuban food. There's a tiny balcony that's perfect for a pre-dinner drink.

La Maison, Ave. Manduley esq. 1 no. 52, Reparto Vista Alegre ☎226/4-11-17. A swanky restaurant in the La Maison fashion house complex, serving good steaks, red snapper and seafood specialities including paella and surf 'n' turf grill. Prices start at $8.

Matamoros, Calvario e/ Aguilera y Enramadas. This agreeable restaurant has more variety than most, with beef casserole and roast pigeon supplementing the standard Cuban food. It's reasonably priced and a musical trio plays while you eat.

Pizza Nova, *Hotel Santiago de Cuba*, Ave. de las Américas y Calle M. This outdoor café is the only place offering superb thin-crust pizza with a range of toppings, and great spaghetti at sensible prices. There's also a takeaway service.

El Rápido, Ave. Alameda Jesús Menéndez esq. Aguilera. Cheap branch of the national fast-food chain doling out hot dogs, chicken and fries. A local favourite.

Santiago 1900, San Bacilio no. 354 e/ Carnicería y San Félix. Elegant restaurant in a colonial house serving simple Cuban meals on the cheap.

Sodería Alondra, Garzón esq. Calle C. It's a bit of a trek to this ice-cream parlour but worth it for the excellent ice cream and the thick frozen yoghurt, all served neat or under a layer of sugar sprinkles for $1–2.

La Teressina, Aguilera e/ Reloj y Calvario Plaza Delores. Light, airy Rumbos café with the usual cheap pizza and spaghetti, plus pricier seafood and other Cuban dishes.

El Zunzun, Ave. Manduley no. 159 e/ Ave. 5ta y 7pta ☎226/41-36-9. Arguably the classiest restaurant in town, with a series of private dining rooms for an intimate dinner. Choose from a varied menu including aromatic chicken, garlic shrimps, mixed grill and shellfish. Prices start at $7.

Drinking and nightlife

As much of the action in Santiago revolves around music, there are few places that cater specifically for **drinkers**, although the *Hotel Casa Granda* has two excellent bars (see p.404). **Musical** entertainment in Santiago is hard to beat, with several excellent live *trova* venues – all a giddy whirl of rum and high spirits with soulful *boleros* and *son* banged out by wizened old men who share the tunes and the talent of the likes of Ibrahim Ferrer and Compay Segundo, if not their fame. Oriente is the birthplace of the *trova* (or ballad) and it really does seem as though every second resident of Santiago can whip out a guitar and sing like a nightingale. Keep an eye out for the superb Estudiantina Invasora *trova* group, who often play at the Casa de la

Trova. You don't have to exert too much effort to enjoy the best of it; the music often spills onto the streets at weekends and around carnival time (see pp.394–95) when bands set up just about everywhere. Sometimes the best way to organize your night out is to follow the beat you like the most. The best nights are often the cheapest, and it's rare to find a venue charging more than $5.

Music played in **discos** tends to be as loud as the sound system will permit, sometimes louder, and anything goes, from Cuban and import *salsa*, through reggae and rock to very cheesy handbag house. They tend to draw a young, sometimes edgy and high-spirited crowd, including many of the *jinetero* and *jinetera* types who hang out in Parque Céspedes trying to win your attention. Both male and female visitors should be prepared for lots more of this behaviour, and taken in the right vein it can be amusing and even make you some friends, but it's a situation that attracts a lot of police interest, and trouble-spots are often closed without warning in a bid to stem the flesh trade. At those discos that are open, you can expect to pay between $1 and $5 entrance.

*Cuban music
is covered in
detail in
Contexts; see
p.480.*

Bar Claqueta, Santo Tomás e/ San Basilio y Heredia. Small but perfectly formed open-air club with excellent live music from the resident *salsa* group, Tierra Caliente. Closed Mon.

Barra Ron Caney, Ave. Jesus Menéndez s/n (near the train station). Friendly staff and a wicked, silky-smooth 15-year-old rum make this bar a top choice.

Casa de la Cultura, San Pedro, opposite Parque Céspedes. Formerly a high-society club, this gracefully decaying venue is perfect for classic sounds. There's usually a band playing on Saturdays, a fairly regular rumba night, occasional classical music, and once a month, on the Noche Tradiciónal (traditional music night), a *trova* group.

Casa de las Tradiciones, Rabí no. 154 e/ Princesa y San Fernando. A different *trova* band plays into the small hours every night, in a tiny, atmospheric house with walls lined with photographs and album sleeves.

Casa de la Trova, Heredia no. 208. A visit to the famous *Casa de la Trova* is the highlight of a trip to Santiago, with musicians playing day and night to an audience packed into the tiny room or hanging in through the window. Although a recent refit has tidied up some of its ramshackle charisma, nothing short of demolition could completely ruin it.

Club 300, Aguilera no. 300 e/ San Pedro y San Felix. Slick and sultry, this dark little hideaway with leather seats is open till 5am, with cheap cocktails, quality rum and single malt whiskies. It's busier when bands play – ask inside for details.

Discoteca La Irís, Aguilera no. 617 e/ Barnada y Plácido. Pitch-black and packed, this club plays a hotch-potch of *merengue*, soul, reggae, rock and *salsa*, all of it at top volume.

Hotel Casa Granda, Heredia no. 201 e/ San Pedro y San Félix. Benefiting from a cool breeze, the hotel's balcony bar is the best central spot to soak up the local atmosphere, and somewhere to linger given the comfortable seating and the troubadour trio that sometimes plays. Later on you should retire to the open-air rooftop bar, which has views over the bay and the surrounding countryside and is the best place from which to watch the sun slide down behind the mountains. Both bars are open all day.

Museo del Carnaval, Heredia no. 301. An ebullient, open-air *folklórico* floor-show, with its roots in Santería, in which the dances and music of various *orishas* (deities) are performed. Tues–Sat 5–6pm, Sun 11am–noon.

Pico Real, *Hotel Santiago de Cuba*, Ave. de las Américas y Calle M. Rooftop bar and a good setting for a panoramic soak, though expect livelier evenings with a nightly fashion show (around $25) followed by a small-scale *salsa* disco.

Pista Bailable, Teatro Heredia, Ave. de las Américas s/n ☎226/4-31-90. Pumped-up *salsa*, *son*, *bolero* and *merengue* all get the crowd dancing at this unpretentious local club, with live music some nights.

Theatres, cabaret and cinemas

Santiago's obsession with music means that there's not much in the way of straight **theatre**. Teatro Heredia, beside the Plaza de la Revolución (☎226/4-31-90), is the only large venue for plays, musicals and children's drama. Also in the complex is the *Café Cantante*. It's pot luck as to what you see at this Cuban variety show evening (Fri–Sun) which pulls acts from a mixed bag of musicians, magicians, poets and comedians.

Cabaret fares better, with twice-weekly open-air spectaculars of bespangled dancers and variety acts at the Santiago Tropicana (☎226/4-10-31), just over 1km northeast of the centre on the *autopista*, and tamer versions of the same thing at *Cabaret San Pedro del Mar*, near El Castillo del Morro (☎226/9-10-11). Shows at both venues will set you back around $40–50.

Of the several **cinemas** in town, Cine Rialto, near the cathedral, is the most central, while the one in the Teatro Heredia complex is usually guaranteed to show the latest Cuban releases. There's also a **video room** at Santo Tomás no. 755 which screens mainly US imports.

Shopping and galleries

Whilst Santiago is no shoppers' paradise, there are several places you can go to sniff out an authentic bargain or curiosity, whilst the several galleries in town occasionally have some worthy paintings and sculptures. The peso shops in **Enramada**, one street north of Parque Céspedes, still bedecked with original, though now non-functioning neon signs, hold some surprising treasures if you're prepared to root. Not to be missed is the peso department store near the corner of San Pedro, with two floors of goodies ranging from small tropical fish in plastic bags to cotton dresses. Also on Enramada are several dollar shops, supermarkets and, at no. 309, an Artex **music** store with an excellent selection of CDs, including a large selection of *son*, *bolero*, *salsa* and more by Santiago musicians. Also good for CDs is the Tienda Rialto shop at Santo Tomás no. 654, in the former crypt of the cathedral, which has a decent selection of history and natural history books too. At Tienda la Catedral, round the corner, it's worth trawling through the tacky handmade dolls, woven boxes and woodcuts for occasional finds like handmade leather belts and sandals.

Nearby, Heredia boasts a wealth of little trinket shops – including Artex, at no. 304, with papier-mâché masks and elephants – as well as a thriving **street market** (daily 9am–6pm) selling bone and shell jewellery, bootleg tapes, maracas and drums, as well as general souvenirs. Another great place for high-quality souvenirs is Fondo Cubano de Bienes Culturales, on Heredia esq. San Pedro, with a diverse selection of paintings by local artists, cloth wall-hangings, trinket boxes, leather bags and silver jewellery set with semi-precious local stones, as well as some big and beautiful – though not very portable – sculptures made from ebony, lignum vitae and other precious woods.

Of several commercial **galleries** dotted around the centre, the best are Galería Oriente, at San Pedro no. 163 (daily 8am–8pm), with some excellent revolutionary and carnival posters and some colourful surrealist oil paintings by local artists, and the small but notable Galería El Zaguan, Heredia e/ San Félix y San Pedro (Mon–Sat 9am–6pm), which sells a real mixture of paintings, from delicate landscape miniatures to thick oil portraits and rather ugly abstracts.

Listings

Airlines Cubana, Enramada e/ Santo Tomás y San Pedro ☎226/5-15-77.

Banks and exchange There are several banks near Parque Céspedes, including Banco Financiero International, at Santo Tomás no. 565; Cash Banco Nacional de Cuba at Santa Isabel esq. Aguilera; and Cash Cadeca at Aguilera no. 508. *Hotel Santiago de Cuba* gives cash advances ($100 minimum).

Car rental Havanautos at *Hotel Las Américas* (☎226/4-13-88) and at the airport (☎226/91-87-3); Cubacar at *Hotel Santiago de Cuba* (☎226/4-26-12) and Avenida de los Defiles (☎226/5-45-68).

Immigration and legal The tourist support group Asistur (☎226/33-80-87) offers 24-hour assistance in emergency situations. The headquarters (daily 8am–5.30pm; ☎226/8-61-28) are in the offices beneath the *Hotel Casa Granda*, though service can be a bit flustered due to staff shortages. You can renew visas at the immigration office, Ave. Raúl Pujol no. 10 (☎226/4-19-83).

Medical Call ☎185 for a public ambulance or ☎226/26-57-1 to 9 for a private one. State hospitals include the Hospital Provincial Clinico Quirúgico Docente, Ave. de los Libertadores (☎226/26-57-1/9), the most central; and for foreigners, the Clinica International is on Calle 13 esq. 14, Vista Alegre (☎226/4-25-89). Policlinico Camilio Torres is a 24-hour doctor's surgery at Heredia no. 358 e/ Reloj y Calvario. There are pharmacies at Enramada no. 402 and at the Clinica International. The latter also has a dental surgery.

Newspapers Some US publications and Italian and Spanish newspapers can be found at the gift shop in the *Hotel Santiago de Cuba*.

Police The main station is at Corona y San Gerónimo. In an emergency call ☎116.

Post office The main post office is at Aguilera y Clarín and has a DHL service. Stamps can also be bought from the *Hotel Casa Granda* and *Hotel Santiago de Cuba*.

Sports Domestic baseball games are played at the Guillermon Moncado Estadio (☎226/4-10-78) from December to April.

Taxis The state-operated metered taxis include Taxi-OK, *Hotel Santiago de Cuba* (☎226/8-66-66); Transautos, *Hotel Casa Granda* (☎226/8-61-07) and Turistaxi, *Hotel Las Américas* (☎226/4-20-11).

Telephones The Centro de Llamadas Internationales (daily 24hr) sells phone cards and allows international calls. Phone cards are also available from the *Hotel Casa Granda* and the *Hotel Santiago de Cuba*, which both have international pay phones.

Santiago de Cuba province

The urbanity and sheer personality of the capital city dominate the otherwise rural province of **Santiago de Cuba**, but to see only the city would be to miss out on much of the region's character. The **mountains**, with their rich wildlife, beg to be explored and you can make it to the **Sierra de la Gran Piedra** in an easy day-trip, as well as taking in the rare blooms at the nearby **Jardín Botánico Sevilla** and the old coffee plantation at **La Isabelica**.

For information on treks in the Sierra Maestra, see box on pp.416–17.

Along the coast, the **Gran Parque Natural de Baconao** is most often visited for its **beaches**, notably Playa Siboney and Playa Cazonal. West of the city, the **Iglesia de la Caridad del Cobre**, or "El Cobre" for short, is one of the country's most revered churches and worth a visit. Frankly, even a drive along the magnificent **coastal road**, with the clear sea on one side and the sensual mountain curves on the other, comes highly recommended.

East of Santiago

Many of the attractions you'll want to see outside Santiago lie to the east and you'll need at least a couple of days to see it all properly. Cool and fresh, the accessible mountains of the **Sierra de la Gran Piedra** make an excellent break from the harsh city heat, and the giant Gran Piedra itself is a fine lookout point. Nearby is the atmospheric, little-visited **Museo Isabelica**, set on one of several colonial coffee plantations in the mountains, and the often-overlooked **Jardín Botánico**, with an excellent display of tropical flowers.

Spanning the east coast is the **Gran Parque Natural Baconao**, not so much a park as a vast collection of beaches and other tourist attractions, among them a vintage **car collection** and the **Comunidad Artística Verraco**, home, gallery and workplace of several local artists. Although none of the province's **beaches** is spectacular, all are attractive and well-served by hotels.

If you've got your own **transport**, head east out of the city towards the Loma de San Juan, then turn off down Avenida Raúl Pujol, from where the road runs straight towards the coast and the turn-off for the Sierra de la Gran Piedra.

Sierra de la Gran Piedra

Just east of Santiago, the **Sierra de la Gran Piedra** is one of the most easily accessed ranges in the country. Twenty-six kilometres from town, a purpose-built staircase leads up from the road to the mountains' highest peak, **La Gran Piedra** (daily 9am–6pm; $1, evenings free), or "The Big Rock", sculpted by ancient geological movement from surrounding bedrock and now forming a convenient viewing plateau 1234m above the city. It's an easy though invigorating climb to the top, through woodland rich in animal and plant life, including over two hundred species of fern. When the thick fug of cloud that often hangs over the area melts away there's a panoramic view over the province and beyond to the sea. Locals say you can even see the lights of Haiti should you venture up at night. Although there's no public transport to get you there, an unmetered taxi from Parque Céspedes will charge you $10–15 to take you to the foot of the staircase.

Museo Isabelica

A kilometre or so further along the same mountain road, a left turn leads to the **Museo Isabelica** (Tues–Sat 9am–5pm, Sun 9am–1pm; $1), set in the grounds of the Cafetal Isabelica, a coffee plantation established by an immigrant French grower who fled the Haitian slave revolution of 1791. Spread over the two storeys of a small estate house covered in red lichen and surrounded by ferns, the museum's collection is fairly dull, with axes, picks and bits of old machinery downstairs and the owner's living quarters above, furnished with a collection of nineteenth-century pieces. One of the main reasons for coming is the atmosphere, with the unearthly hush of the mountains broken only by birdcall and the tapping of sheep crossing the stone coffee-bean drying area. Low mist drifts down through the trees and across the pathways. You can explore the overgrown paths leading off round the house into the derelict plantation and inspect what is left of the disused mill – now just a stone wheel and a few wooden poles.

Jardín Botánico

About 2km before the Gran Piedra steps, the **Jardín Botánico** ($1) is more of a nursery than a botanical garden, as it grows flowers for weddings and other ceremonies. The tidy beds of heavy-scented white gardenias and Cuban forget-me-nots share space with orange and pine trees and the flame-coloured rainfire bush. Several types of fruit grow here, including apples, which can grow only here in the coller mountains. The prize of the collection is the blue and orange bird of paradise flower, each bloom resembling a bunch of spiky fireworks.

Gran Parque Natural Baconao

An area of attractive countryside interspersed with several tourist attractions and some of the province's best beaches, the **Gran Parque Natural Baconao**, 25km southeast of Santiago, makes for a good day out but is hardly the rugged wilderness suggested by its name. With no public transport serving the area, your best bet – unless you're driving – is to take a taxi, which will cost upwards of $25. A cheaper way to get there is with one of the moterbike taxis that congregate around Parque Céspedes, though not all will go this far out of town.

To Playa Siboney

The first diversion en route to the coast is the **Prado de las Esculturas** (daily 9am–5pm; $1), a drive-through sculpture park that you can explore in just a couple of minutes. Most of the twenty exhibits, all by international artists, are rather ugly hulks of metal, though Japanese artist Issei Amemiya's temple-like, wooden *Meditation II* is quietly impressive.

About 2km further on is the **Granjita Siboney** (daily 9am–5pm; $1), the farm which Fidel Castro and his rebel group used as their base for the Moncada attack (see pp.398–99). The pretty little red-and-white house, pock-marked by original bullet holes, now holds a museum that largely reproduces information found in bigger museums in the city, with the usual round of newspaper cuttings, guns and bloodstained uniforms, presented in glass cabinets.

From here it's a kilometre and a half to **Playa Siboney**, 19km from Santiago. This is the nearest and biggest beach to the city and the best if you want to join in with the beach crowd culture rather than bask in solitude. The brown sands, overlooked by a towering cliff, are lively with crowds of Cubans and visitors, while the small but ebullient seaside is dappled with palm trees and jaunty wooden houses. There is a **restaurant**, *La Rueda Carretera Siboney*, offering inexpensive fried chicken, tasty fish and good lobster, as well as sandwiches and pizza. The only place to stay is the excellent *Casa de Ovidio González Sabaldo* (②), a *casa particular* with a sea view on Avenida Serrano Alto de Farmacia.

To Playa Daiquirí

A further 4km east on the main road, **El Oasis Rodeo** (Wed & Sun 9am & 2pm; $5) is tailor-made for the tourist industry, a chance to see Cuban cowboys ride, lasso, and generally show off their impressive acrobatic skills with a series of long-suffering bulls. The rodeo also offers **horse riding** in the surrounding countryside (daily 9am–5pm; $5 for the first hour, $3 per hour thereafter).

Along the same road, 4km from the Rodeo, is one of Baconao's biggest attractions, the **Museo Nacional de Transporte Terrestre por Carretera** (daily 9am–5pm; $1, $1 extra to take photos), which has an excellent collection of vintage cars and a formidable display of 2500 toy cars. Outside in the car park sit the 1929 Ford Roadster belonging to Alina Ruz, Fidel Castro's mother; Benny Moré's ostentatious golden Cadillac; and the 1951 Chevrolet that Raúl Castro drove to the attack on the Moncada barracks (see pp.398–99). Whilst you can see many similar models still limping around the country, it's quite heart-warming to see those here looking scrubbed up and shiny.

More or less opposite the museum is the turning for **Playa Daiquirí** (daily; $2), the beach where the US army landed when they intervened in the war of independence in 1898. The beach itself has good recreational facilities – including watersports, a dive shop and horse-riding from the nearby *Hotel Daiquirí* – but is a rather unappealing scraggy stretch of grey. A better beach, the golden-sand **Playa Bacajagua**, lies just ten minutes to the east, although you'll have to make do with the facilities at Playa Daiquirí.

To Playa Cazonal

Back on the main road, 10km from the turning for Playa Daiquirí in an attractive clearing beneath tall trees, is the unique **Comunidad Artística Verraco** (daily 9am–6pm; free), a small artists' community that's home to nine sculptors, painters and potters. At the far end of the clearing, a central gallery sells a selection of the artists' works – particularly good are the wildly psychedelic musicians by local painter Renilde. However, you get a better sense of the place by wandering around the houses-cum-workshops, where you can check out pieces in progress and buy additional exhibits, whilst sculptors quietly shape wood, painters ponder their next brush stroke and people strum guitars.

Continuing east for 8km you'll come to the **Acuario Baconao** (Tues–Sat 9am–5pm; $3), an aquarium with a selection of marine animals, including turtles and sharks, housed in rather small tanks. Faring a little better, with a reasonably sized pool, are the dolphins – the big stars – performing their party pieces three times a day (shows at 10.15am, 11.30am & 2.45pm); there's also the chance to hop into the pool with them yourself ($20).

Playa Cazonal, less than a kilometre from Acuario Baconao, is the best beach east of Santiago. Backed by the congenial all-inclusive *Hotel Los Corales* (☎226/35-61-22; ⑤), a wide curve of cream-coloured sand nestles against a dazzling green hillside from which the palms spill onto the beach's edge. Pretty as it is, it's no secluded paradise, awash with windsurfers, Western sun-worshippers and snorkellers exploring the nearby rocky coastline. Non-guests are charged $15 for use of the beach, although this includes a buffet meal and drinks.

The last attraction to the east, roughly 3km from Playa Cazonal, **Laguna Baconao** is a serene spot from which to enjoy the unaffected beauty of the surrounding mountains. There's little wildlife, but you can hire a boat ($2) to row on the lake. Unless you're driving, however, there's no point heading out this far as there's no public transport nor any facilities.

West of Santiago

Although there are fewer sights to see west of Santiago, those that exist are interesting enough to warrant a visit if you've a spare day. The **Iglesia de la Caridad del Cobre**, presiding over the town of El Cobre in the hills to the west, houses the icon of Nuestra Señora de la Caridad, Cuba's patron, and is one of most important – and most visited – churches in the country. The **beaches** west of the city are smaller than those on the eastern side, and correspondingly less developed and more intimate, the playgrounds of Cubans rather than visitors. In contrast, the resort of **Chivirico** is dedicated to international tourism, with two palatial hotels dominating its fine-sand beach.

Iglesia de la Caridad del Cobre

The imposing and lovely **Iglesia de la Caridad del Cobre** (daily 6.30am–6pm), 18km east of Santiago, is one of the holiest sanctuaries in the country, home to the statue of the Virgen de la Caridad. In 1606 the icon was found floating in the Bahía de Nipe, off the northern coast of the province, by three sailors from El Cobre town on the point of shipwreck. They claimed that not only was the icon – a mother and child figurine – completely dry when drawn from the water but that the sea was instantly becalmed. Inscribed with the words "I am the Virgin of Charity", the icon became the most important image in Cuban Catholicism, gaining significance by becoming intertwined and twinned with Ochún, the Santería goddess of love, whose colour, yellow, mirrors the virgin's golden robe. In 1916 the Virgen de la Caridad became the patron saint of Cuba, following a decree by Pope Benedict XV.

Mass takes place in the mornings from Tuesday to Saturday (8am), with additional Masses on Thursday (8pm) and Sunday (10am & 4.30pm).

Pleasingly symmetrical, its three towers capped in red domes, the present church was constructed in 1927, on the site of a previous shrine to the icon. Inside, coloured light rains down from the portholes of stained glass set into the ceiling, and a huge, ornate altar throws the surprisingly plain walls into relief. The icon has pride of place high up in the altar and during Mass looks down over the congregation; at other times she is rotated to face the other way, into an inner sanctum reached by stairs at the back of the church, where she faces another altar always liberally garlanded with floral tributes left by worshippers.

Soon after her discovery, local mythology endowed the virgin with the power to grant wishes and heal the sick, and a steady flow of believers visit the church to solicit her help. A downstairs chamber holds an eclectic display of the many relics left by grateful recipients of the virgin's benevolence, including a rosette and team shirt from Ana Fidelia Quirot Moret, the Olympic 800m gold medalist, college diplomas, countless photographs and, most bizarrely, an asthmatic's ventilator. The most famous relic is the small, golden guerrilla figure pledged by Lina Ruz, the mother of Fidel, in return for her son's safe deliverance from the fighting in the Sierra Maestra. The other cele-brated exhibit, the Nobel prize medal won in 1954 by Ernest Hemingway for his novel *The Old Man and the Sea*, can no longer be seen after being stolen by a visitor in 1986. Although later recovered, the medal is now kept safe in a vault.

The western beaches and Chivirico

The drive along the coast west towards Chivirico, with the seemingly endless curve of vivid mountains on one side and a ribbon of sparkling shallow sea on the other, is one of the most fantastic in the country. Don't be put off by **Playa Mar Verde**, a small, rather grubby hoop of roadside shingle-sand about 15km from the city, but carry on along the coastal road for 2km or so to **Playa Bueycabón**. An almost orderly lawn of grass dotted with short palms stretches almost to the sea, and with its calm, shallow waters and narrow belt of sand, it is altogether an excellent little spot to pass the day.

Sixty-eight kilometres from Santiago, **CHIVIRICO** is a quiet coastal village and an interchange point for buses and trucks running between Pilón and Santiago. Other than that, the main action, such as it is, centres around a micro-resort of three hotels capitalizing on good brown-sand beaches and impressive mountain views. This is a better place to stay rather than visit on a day-trip as the best beaches are now the domain of two large all-inclusive resort hotels which charge non-guests for the privilege of using them.

Access to **Playa Sevilla** (daily 9am–5pm; $30 per day, inclusive of meals and drinks) is controlled by the palatial beachfront *Super Club Sierra Mar* (☎226/2-64-36; ⑦), which has a full complement of water sports, five bars and several restaurants. It's almost worth the price tag to spend a luxurious day in the beautiful setting, with its wide, soft sands and superb mountain views, though you'll be jostling with crowds of holidaymakers from the expansive hotel.

The central beach, **Playa Virginia**, is narrower but free to enter. Tiny mangrove-coated cays lie not far offshore, though there can be dangerous undertow currents. It's here you'll find the rather appealing *Motel Guáma* (no phone; ②), the strip's budget accommodation option, though the only café is often closed.

Finally, **Playa Chivirico** is the preserve of the attractive hilltop *Hotel Los Galeones* (☎226/2-61-60; ⑦), which boasts magnificent views over the rolling mountains and the sea. The small swathe of brown sand is speckled with palms and couples from the hotel.

Granma and the Sierra Maestra

Protruding west from the main body of Cuba, cupping the Bahía de Guacanayabo, **Granma** is a tranquil, slow-paced province, with **Bayamo**, its appealingly low-key capital and birthplace of the father of Cuban independence, Carlos Manuel de Céspedes, probably the closest things get to bustling. Granma is nonetheless growing in popularity: the peaceful black-sand resort on the southern coast at **Marea del Portillo** is already a firm favourite with Canadian retirees, and you could do worse than spend a couple of days here, sampling some of the day **excursions** into the surrounding mountains of the Sierra Maestra or the numerous **diving** opportunities. A visit to the small and simple rural town of **Pilón**, just a few kilometres away, brings a new dimension to the all-inclusive world.

On the southwestern tip of Granma's coastline, **Las Coloradas**, where Fidel Castro and his revolutionaries came ashore on the *Granma*, is the highlight of any revolution pilgrimage, while nearby, the **Parque Nacional Desembarco del Granma** has several excellent guided nature trails, including **El Guafe** with its three pre-Columbian petroglyphs. Along the coast, sleepy **Manzanillo**, though not somewhere you're likely to spend a lot of time, is worth visiting for the flashes of brilliant Moorish architecture that light up the town centre. There is little to draw you to the Llanura del Cauto Guacanayabo plains north of Manzanillo, characterized by swampland and a few one-street towns.

The **Sierra Maestra**, Cuba's highest and most extensive mountain range, stretches along the southern coast of the island, running the length of both Santiago and Granma provinces. The unruly beauty of the landscape – a vision of churning seas, undulating green-gold mountains and remote sugar fields – will take your breath away. That said, once you've admired the countryside there's not an awful lot you can do: national park status notwithstanding, much of the Sierra Maestra is periodically declared out of bounds by the authorities, who sometimes give the reason of an epidemic in the coffee crops but more often give no reason at all. Should you get the opportunity to go **trekking** here, seize it.

There are some excellent trails, most notably through the stunning cloud forest of the **Parque Nacional Turquino** to the island's highest point, Pico Turquino, at 1974m. Although a considerable part of the Sierra Maestra falls in Santiago province, Parque Nacional Turquino included, the best chance you have to do any trekking is to base yourself in Bayamo, where you can arrange a guide and suitable transport.

Bayamo

On the edge of the mountains in the centre of Granma, provincial capital **BAYAMO** is one of the most peaceful towns in Cuba. Its spotless town centre is based around a pleasant park filled with playing children; there are near-zero levels of hassle on the streets; and, with the centre pedestrianized, even the cars are silenced.

Although a fire destroyed most of the town's colonial buildings in 1869, it left the heart of town untouched, and the splendid **Iglesia de Santísimo Salvador** still presides over the cobbled **Plaza del Himno**. Elsewhere, neat rows of modern candy-coloured houses, dotted with pretty tree-lined parks, stand testament to a well-maintained town. There are a couple of engaging museums, notably the **Casa Natal de**

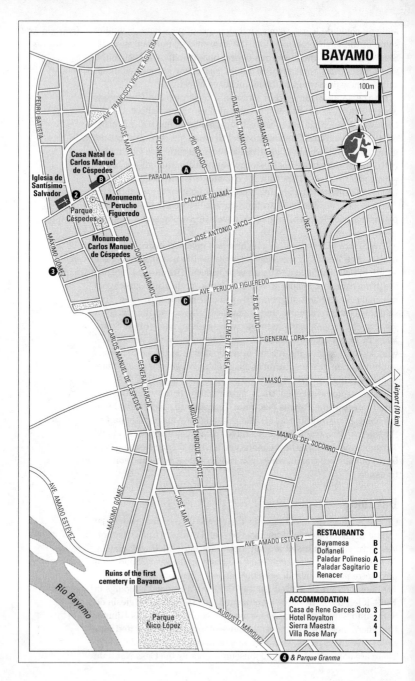

BAYAMO

0   100m

N

Casa Natal de
Carlos Manuel
de Céspedes

Iglesia de
Santísimo
Salvador

Parque
Céspedes

Monumento
Perucho
Figueredo

Monumento
Carlos Manuel
de Céspedes

Ruins of the first
cemetery in Bayamo

Río Bayamo

Parque
Nico López

Airport (10 km)

& Parque Granma

RESTAURANTS

Bayamesa	**B**
Doñaneli	**C**
Paladar Polinesio	**A**
Paladar Sagitario	**E**
Renacer	**D**

ACCOMMODATION

Casa de Rene Garces Soto	**3**
Hotel Royalton	**2**
Sierra Maestra	**4**
Villa Rose Mary	**1**

Street names: AVE. FRANCISCO VICENTE AGUILERA · PEDRO BATISTA · JOSÉ MARTÍ · CISNERO · PIO ROSADO · IDALBERTO TAMAYO · HERMANOS LOTTY · PARADA · CACIQUE GUAMÁ · LINEA · MÁXIMO GÓMEZ · JOSÉ ANTONIO SACO · DONATO MÁRMOL · AVE. PERUCHO FIGUEREDO · 26 DE JULIO · JUAN CLEMENTE ZENEA · GENERAL LORA · CARLOS MANUEL DE CÉSPEDES · MASÓ · GENERAL GARCÍA · MIGUEL ENRIQUE CAPOTE · MANUEL DEL SOCORRO · MÁXIMO GÓMEZ · JOSÉ MARTÍ · AVE. AMADO ESTÉVEZ · AVE. AMADO ESTÉVEZ · AUGUSTO MÁRQUEZ

Carlos Manuel de Céspedes, which celebrates the town's most famous son, a key figure in the wars of independence. Bayamo is smaller than you'd expect a provincial capital to be, and you could cram its few sights into one day, but if you've no agenda, it's better to do some gentle sightseeing, eat well and match the unhurried pace.

Some history

The second of the original seven towns or *villas* founded by Diego Velázquez de Cuéllar in November 1513, Bayamo flourished during the seventeenth and eighteenth centuries when, along with its neighbour Manzanillo, it was heavily involved in dealing in contraband goods. Here European smugglers exchanged slaves, leather, precious woods and luxurious goods like the Dutch ceramic tiles still visible on the roof of the town's Iglesia de Santísimo Salvador. It became one of the most prosperous towns in the country and by the nineteenth century had capitalized on the fertile plains to the west of the city, becoming an important sugar-growing and cattle-rearing area.

Bayamo's cosmopolitan and literary-minded sons were often educated abroad, and they returned home with progressive views. Influential figures like wealthy landowner Francisco Vicente Aguilera and Pedro Figueredo, a composer, established a revolutionary cell here in 1868 to promote their call for independence. They were joined by Carlos Manuel de Céspedes, another wealthy local plantation owner, who freed his slaves and set off to war. By the end of October 1868, his modest army of 147 had swelled to 12,000 and he had captured Bayamo and Holguín. His forces managed to hold out for three months before victory began to slip and the rebel troops were overwhelmed by the Spanish. Rather than relinquish the town, the rebels set fire to it on January 12, 1869, and watched the elegant buildings and plazas burn to the ground. Bayamo's glory days were over.

Bayamo moved into the twentieth century without fanfare, continuing to support itself by producing sugar and farming cattle. The town's last memorable moment was the unsuccessful attack on the army barracks on July 26, 1953 (see p.420), timed to coincide with the attack in Santiago orchestrated by Fidel Castro, and though this happened the best part of fifty years ago it still keeps several old-timers gossiping today.

Arrival and information

Domestic flights arrive from Havana at the Aeropuerto Carlos M. de Céspedes (☎23/42-36-95), 10km northeast of the centre on the Holguín road, where unmetered taxis wait to bring you into town for around $3–5. The towm is well served by three main roads from Las Tunas, Holguín and Santiago de Cuba; interprovincial buses pull in at the Astro terminal in the western outskirts of town, on the Carretera Central towards Santiago de Cuba. From here horse-drawn coaches will take you into the centre for about five pesos. Colectivos also use

THE SIERRA MAESTRA

Despite their tantalizing beauty and seemingly ideal conditions for trekking, it is actually quite difficult, and sometimes impossible, to visit the mountains of the Sierra Maestra. Visitors are not permitted to go trekking without a guide but even having one will not guarantee entrance as the routes are often closed. Reasons, if given, range from reports of epidemics in the coffee plantations, to trails being in disrepair and even closure due to visiting dignitaries. The only place to get guaranteed information on access to the Sierra Maestra, including the areas in Santiago province, is at the **Agéncia de Reservaciónes de Campísmo**, General García no. 115 e/ Lora y Maco (☎23/42-42-00). Permission to **access** the high mountains can sometimes be arranged here; otherwise, **permits** ($10) and **guides** ($5 per person) can be arranged at the *Villa Santo Domingo* or *Campismo La Sierrita* (see below). Just heading into the mountains on your own, you risk landing yourself in serious trouble with the authorities.

The best **place to stay** in the mountain area is at the *Villa Santo Domingo*, about 75km southwest of Bayamo (no phone; ③). Set on the banks of the Río Yara, in the foothills of the mountains, the picturesque cabins make an ideal spot to relax even if access to the mountains is denied. Similarly rural and idyllic is the *Campismo La Sierrita* (no phone; ③), beside the Río Yara, 50km southeast of Bayamo, which has 27 cabins with self-contained bathrooms. Call in at the Agéncia de Reservaciónes de Campísmo in Bayamo (☎23/42-42-00) to book and make sure they are open.

The main trails begin at the look-out point of **Alto del Naranjo**, 5km southeast of *Villa Santo Domingo*, which marks the start of the mountains proper. When the mountains are off-limit this is as far as many people get, but at 950m above sea level, the panoramic views over the surrounding mountains are awe-inspiring. Most people, especially those planning to trek further into the mountains, make the journey up the immense-

the Astro terminal as their unofficial base. The **train** station is on Calle Linea e/ Prada y Figueredo (☎23/42-49-55), 1km from the centre, and from here you can catch a horse-drawn coach into the centre.

While there are no official tourist offices, the Artex shop at General García no. 9 sells **maps** of the town and province, while the Agéncia de Reservaciónes de Campísmo, General García no. 115 e/ Lora y Maco (☎23/42-42-00), has information on **campsites** and **excursions** into the mountains. You can also get general information about excursions at the tourist bureau in the *Hotel Sierra Maestra* (☎23/48-10-13).

Accommodation

Unless you're driving, you'll want **to stay** in the centre at the *Hotel Royalton*, the most picturesque hotel in town. Bayamo isn't likely to fill up, so you're more or less guaranteed a room if you turn up on spec. With little passing tourist trade, *casas particulares* are yet to make their mark and to date there are only two registered in the whole town, though both are excellent.

ly steep ascent road in a sturdy vehicle. There's no public transport but trips can be arranged through the Agéncia de Reservaciónes de Campísmo.

PICO TURQUINO TRAIL

At 1974m above sea level, Pico Turquino stands proud as the highest point in Cuba. From Alto de Naranjo it's approximately 12km to the summit and while it's possible to ascend and return in a day, you are better off arranging with your guide to stay overnight at the very rudimentary *campamento de Joaquín* mountain hut (no phone; ②) and stretching the trek over a day and a half. This is not a trek for the faint-hearted: the final kilometre is a very steep slog, though not dangerous. Take something warm to wear as temperatures plummet after nightfall and even the days are cool in the high cloud forest.

The trail is overhung with plants and ancient tree ferns, the forest air exudes an earthy dampness and the ground oozes with thick red mud. Through the breaks in the thick foliage you can occasionally see blue-green mountain peaks and birds circling lazily above the gullies. Just before the final ascent, a short ladder to the left of the path gives a panoramic view over the surrounding landscape; it's worth grabbing the opportunity as the summit itself is often shrouded in thick cloud.

LA PLATA TRAIL

A less taxing trek is to La Plata, 3km west of Alto de Naranjo, where Fidel Castro based his rebel headquarters during the revolution. The trail is well marked and you can complete the reasonably strenuous climb in around two hours. Set in a clearing in the forest, the wooden huts were covered with branches to protect them from enemy air strikes. The base is preserved as a museum and you can see Castro's small quarters, consisting of a rudimentary bedroom with a simple camp bed and a kitchen.

Casa de Rene Garces Soto, Máximo Gómez no. 42 e/ Saco y Leon. Two excellent, very central double rooms in a *casa particular* with shared bathroom and use of the kitchen. The landlord will sometimes rent out his spare bicycle to careful riders. ②.

Hotel Royalton, Maceo no. 53 ☎23/42-22-24. The pretty sky-blue and white exterior blends into its elegant surroundings right on Parque Céspedes. Recently renovated, with decent rooms, this is hands down the best choice in town. ③.

Sierra Maestra, Carretera Central (vía Santiago de Cuba) ☎23/48-10-13; fax 48-17-98. Hulking great hotel on the fringes of town, within walking distance of the bus terminal. Bog-standard rooms (cold water only) well served by two restaurants and a large swimming pool. ④.

Villa Bayamo, Carretera Central (vía Manzanillo) km 5.5 ☎23/42-31-02. This hotel, on the outskirts of town in a quiet, flower-filled area, has a good selection of well-appointed singles, doubles and cabin-style suites which sleep up to four. With a large and busy swimming pool, and restaurant and bars on the grounds, this is the best choice for larger groups with their own transport. ③–④.

Villa Rose Mary, Pío Rosado no. 22 e/ Ramírez y Avenida Aguilera ☎ 23/42-39-84. This chatty household offers one attractive, self-contained double room with a large terrace overlooking the street. ②.

The Town

Most of the sights in Bayamo are within view or easy walking distance of the central **Parque Céspedes** – also known as Plaza de la Revolución – a shiny expanse of marble fringed with palm trees where children play outside their *Pioneros* club house or queue for rides in the goat-pulled pony cart. At opposite ends of the plaza are two monuments honouring the town's most famous sons. At the northern end is a small three-panel tribute to **Perucho Figueredo**, a local independence fighter principally remembered for writing the patriotic poem *La Bayamesa* in 1868, which later became the Cuban national anthem, still sung today. The elegant black and white marble monument features a solemn bust of the hero accompanied on one side by the words of his poem and by the musical score, finely detailed in gold, on the other. The monument to **Carlos Manuel de Céspedes** (see opposite), at the southern end of the plaza, is rather more grandiose: a statue of the man himself, dignified and sombre in tailcoat, on top of a podium with four bas-relief panels depicting his struggle for independence, including the shooting of his son, Oscar.

La Iglesia de Santísimo Salvador, survivor of the great fire of 1869, is a good landmark, situated just west of the park. The **Casa Natal de Carlos Manuel de Céspedes**, next door to the *Hotel Royalton* on the north side of the plaza, is stuffed full of exhibits, some more relevant than others. A short walk south along General García, the main shopping street, are the old barracks, site of the July 26, attack, now named the **Parque Nico López** in honour of one of the men involved.

The only sight that you'll need transport for is pleasant **Parque Granma**, out on the Carretera Central towards Santiago. Rambling over two square kilometres and with a central lake, it's a great place to relax.

La Iglesia de Santísimo Salvador

The showpiece of Bayamo architecture, the sixteenth-century **La Iglesia de Santísimo Salvador** (daily 9am–noon & 3–5pm) was one of the few buildings to survive the great fire of 1869. Although further damaged over subsequent decades, it is slowly being restored to its former glory, its freshly painted biscuit-brown exterior rising to an elegant domed pinnacle. Inside, the impressive mural over the main altar depicts an incident on November 8, 1868, when Diego José Baptista, the parish priest, blessed the rebel army's newly created flag before a mixed congregation of Cuban rebels including Vicente Aguilera, an early Bayamo independence fighter, and Perucho Figueredo (see above). Hovering above the congregation is an image of the Virgen de la Caridad painted in 1919 by the

Dominican artist Luis Desangles. It's unique in Latin America as an ecclesiastical painting with political content – the imagery indicates that the new republic received the approbation of the Church. Oval portraits of the stations of the cross line the walls, while winged cherubs swoop across the celestial blue ceiling.

Granma and the Sierra Maestra

See p.411 for more on the Virgen de la Caridad.

Casa Natal de Carlos Manuel de Céspedes

The **Casa Natal de Carlos Manuel de Céspedes** (Tues & Wed 9am–5pm, Fri 3–10pm, Sat 9am–1pm & 8–10pm, Sun 9am–1pm; $1) is another survivor of the fire of 1869, and contains a hotchpotch of exhibits relating to the nineteenth century in general and the life of Carlos Manuel de Céspedes, born here in 1819, in particular.

The walls of the ground floor are plastered with fulsome quotes about the man, many relating to the death of his son, Oscar (see box below), while various cabinets on the ground floor hold some staid personal effects, among them his ceremonial sword, as well as more individual pieces like his second wife's jewellery box and an ingenious table bell in the shape of a nodding tortoise.

Upstairs, efforts have been made to furnish the rooms in an authentic nineteenth-century manner, and the stuffy tapestry chairs, marble floors and European and North American china and furniture all create an image of sterile opulence. In the bedroom is the *pièce de résistance*: a magnificent bronze bed with ornate oval panels, inlaid with mother-of-pearl and depicting a fantastical coastline, at the foot.

Carlos Manuel de Céspedes

A key figure in the war of independence, Carlos Manuel de Céspedes is much lauded in Cuba as a liberator. A wealthy plantation owner, he freed his slaves on October 10, 1868, and called for the abolition of slavery – albeit in terms least likely to alienate the wealthy landowners upon whose support he depended. Giving forth his battle cry, the *"Grito de Yara"*, summoning Cubans whether slaves or Creoles to take arms and fight for a future free of Spain, he marched in support of the independence movement. Céspedes summed up the dissatisfaction that many Cubans felt in a long declaration which became known as the October 10th manifesto, nationally credited as the inception of Cuban independence because it was the first time that Cubans had been talked about in terms of a nation of people.

The newly formed army set out with the intention of capturing the nearby town of Yara, but were overtaken by a column of the Spanish army and utterly trounced, reduced to a fragment of the original 150-strong force. Undefeated, Céspedes proclaimed, "there are still twelve of us left, and we are enough to achieve the independence of Cuba".

Céspedes is most remembered for the death of his son, Oscar, captured by the Spanish and subsequently shot when Céspedes refused to negotiate for peace under Spanish conditions. This act earned him the title "Padre de la Patria" (Father of the Homeland): as he famously replied to the letter requesting his surrender, "Oscar is not my only son. I am father to all the Cubans who have died to liberate their homeland."

Parque Ñico López

Bayamo's spacious walled garden, **Parque Ñico López**, landscaped
with swaying palms and intersected with layers of marble steps, was
arranged in the grounds of the Bayamo barracks – rebuilt in 1973 after
the original had crumbled away – as a tribute to Ñico López, one of the
28 men who tried to storm and capture the building on July 26, 1953.

The attack was synchronized with the assault on the Moncada barracks in Santiago, partly to raise weapons for the rebel cause but primarily to prevent more of General Batista's troops being drafted in
from Bayamo to Santiago. The attempt failed when the whinnying of
the cavalry horses, alarmed at the sound of the rebels scrambling
over the wall, aroused the sleeping soldiers, and though López
escaped, later meeting up with fellow rebels in exile in Mexico, several other men died in the attempt. López returned to Cuba aboard
the yacht *Granma* in 1958, only to be killed a few days later in an
early skirmish. The garden honours both his contribution to the
cause, and, more crucially, his status as the man who introduced Che
Guevara to Fidel Castro in 1955.

Inside the barracks is a rather poor **museum** (Tues–Sat 8am–4pm,
Sun 8am–noon; $1) giving a scanty account of events accompanied
by photographs of the men involved and a cutting from the following
day's newspaper. You'd be better off giving it a miss and instead
striking up a conversation with the old men who sometimes sit in the
park, many of whom remember the attack. López himself is commemorated by a sculpture in the grounds.

Parque Granma

Parque Granma (daily 9am–5pm; free), south of the centre, past the
Hotel Sierra Maestra, is one of Bayamo's highlights, purely for its
serene setting around a lake complete with a tumbledown pagoda
reached by a boardwalk, in a great expanse of countryside. Wild cotton and tamarind trees loom out of the long grasses, and it's one of
the few places in the town where you can enjoy an unrestricted view
of the mountains. At the southern end of the park is a children's fun
park, filled with rickety swings and roundabouts reminiscent of tin
clockwork toys, while close by is a **microzoo** (daily 9am–4pm; 20
centavos) housing a set of rather pedestrian animals, including a
herd of bulls and a caged and disgruntled tabby cat. To reach Parque
Granma, head out of town on the Carretera Central (vía Santiago)
and take the first right after the Cupet garage.

Eating

Surprisingly for a small town, Bayamo boasts several restaurants,
although many of them are peso-only establishments, cheap but
rather run-down – the better ones are listed opposite. Around the
park end of General García are several stalls selling snacks, some of
them, like the corn pretzel-style cracker, unique to Bayamo.

Bayamesa, Parque Céspedes, esq. General García. Large portions of chicken, pork, duck or turkey with rice, salad and fried green banana at rock-bottom prices. Excellent value but rather grubby, it's a good option if you are completely penniless.

Donaneli, Capotico esq. Figueredo. A small café dishing up pizza and spaghetti for a couple of dollars.

Hotel Royalton, Maceo no. 53. Decent Cuban cuisine served on the veranda overlooking the park; the most handsome venue in town.

Paladar Polinesio, Parada no. 125 e/ Pío Rosado y Capotico. Unpretentious place – basically four tables in a living room – serving good food at reasonable prices.

Paladar Sagitario, Marmol no. 107 e/ Ave. Castro y Maceo. Long-established *paladar* serving well-priced, generous portions of pork and chicken in a pleasant open-air eating area equipped with a lively pair of *trovadores*.

Renacer, General García e/ Lora y Figueredo. Basic, decent Cuban peso food.

Tropicrema, Figueredo e/ Libertad y Céspedes. Pleasant, open-air peso ice-cream parlour, sometimes serving up cake too. Tables are shared with the next person in the queue and everyone waits for everyone else to finish before leaving the table. Oddly, if they run out of ice cream, they'll occasionally substitute Spam rolls.

Drinking and nightlife
Bayamo is a relaxed place to go out – the choice isn't huge, but what there is is good value and most places are within a couple of streets of each other. The best place to sink a few **cocktails** is the outdoor bar-cum-restaurant on the veranda of the *Hotel Royalton*, while for something a bit livelier head to the peso bar *La Bodega* on Plaza del Himno, where there's beer and dancing until 3am in an intimate courtyard overlooking the Río Bayamo.

Everyone in town who can sing or play the guitar does so at the *Casa de la Trova*, Maceo no. 111 (Mon–Fri 9am–5pm, Sat & Sun 9am–5pm & 8pm–1am), easily Bayamo's best **live music** venue, while the Casa de la Cultura, on General García (☎42-59-17), promises **theatre** and **dance** in the early evenings. On the western fringes of town, outside the *Sierra Maestra*, on the Carretera Central, a raucous informal **disco** draws hordes of local youths at weekends.

Listings
Airlines Cubana, Martí no. 52 esq. Parada ☎23/42-39-16.

Banks and exchange Cadeca has a branch on Saco e/ General García y Marmol where they change travellers' cheques and give cash advances on Visa and Mastercard.

Car rental Havanautos is based at the Cupet Cimex service station on the Carretera Central (vía Santiago) ☎23/42-26-28.

Medical Call ☎185 for a public ambulance. Bayamo's general hospital is Carlos Manuel de Céspedes, Carretera Central (vía Santiago) ☎23/42-50-12 or 42-65-98. The most central 24-hour *policlinico* doctors' surgery is on Pío Rosado, and there's a 24-hour pharmacy, *Piloto*, at General García no. 53.

Police In an emergency, call ☎115.

Post office The post office on Parque Céspedes has a DHL service and sells phone cards.

Taxis Cubataxi, Martí no. 480 e/ Armando Estévez y Coronel Montero ☎42-43-13.

Telephones The ETECSA office (daily 7am–11pm) is next door to the post office on Parque Céspedes.

Marea del Portillo and around

*Transport
links to and
from Marea
del Portillo are
diabolical – if
you can rent a
car before you
arrive, do so.*

Backed by a sweeping wave of mountains smack in the middle of Granma's southern coast is the resort of **Marea del Portillo**. Accessible from Granma's west coast and 150km from Bayamo, the resort is set on a black sand beach which looks impressive from a distance, but like a muddy field close up. It won't be most people's first choice for a beach holiday, although the white sands of tiny **Cayo Blanco** just offshore go some way to making up for this.

Appealing largely to older Canadians and Germans, as well as a few families, it doesn't have the universal appeal of some resorts, especially as there is little infrastructure – just two hotels on the beach and another nearby, and a dive shop. The surrounding countryside is beautiful, however, including the picturesque **El Salton waterfall**, and there are eighteen **dive sites**, including the *El Real* Spanish galleon sunk in 1846, to keep keen divers busy.

Practicalities

*Make sure you
have sufficient
cash before
you arrive as
the only banks
in the
province are
in Bayamo.*

The newer and better of Marea del Portillo's two beach **hotels** is the all-inclusive *Hotel Farallón del Caribe* (☎23/59-40-81; ⑥), with two restaurants, five bars, a handsome pool area and a resident iguana, while next door the rather down-at-heel *Hotel Mara del Portillo* ☎23/59-70-08; ⑤) offers a similar package though in less congenial grounds. Away from the all-inclusive resorts, the best place to stay, and **eat**, is the *Motel Mirador de Pilón* (☎23/59-43-65; ②) on the road towards Pilón (see below), with four cabins high up on the hillside overlooking the sea. A further 2km along the same road, *Villa Punta Piedra* (☎23/59-44-21; ③) has basic rooms, including triples, and a restaurant.

The resort's Albacora **dive centre** (☎23/59-70-34) rents out equipment and offers dives from $25, as well as deep-sea fishing and trips to Cayo Blanco. Land-based **excursions** from the resort include horse-riding to the El Salton waterfall ($29 for a four-hour trip), organized by Rumbos at the *Hotel Farallón del Caribe*, and hiking along the El Guafe nature trail to see the pre-Columbian petroglyphs ($35; see p.424).

Pilón

Tiny sugar town **PILÓN**, 8km west of Marea del Portillo, is a step back in time, with open-backed carts laden with sugarcane zigzagging across the roads and the smell of boiling molasses enveloping the town in its thick scent. There's little to do, but the two beaches, **Playa**

The *Granma*

Under constant surveillance and threat from the Batista regime following his release from prison, Fidel Castro left Havana for exile in Mexico in the summer of 1955. Along with other exiled Cubans sympathetic to his ideas, he formed the 26 July Movement in exile – the Cuban counterpart was run by Frank País – and began to gather weapons and funds to facilitate the return to Cuba. It was during his time in Mexico that many of the significant players of the revolution were drawn together, most notably Ernesto "Che" Guevara, who was introduced to Castro in November 1955 by Ñico López, veteran of the attack of the Bayamo army barracks.

Castro was anxious to return to Cuba as soon as possible. Leaks within the organization had already resulted in the confiscation of arms by the Mexican government and there was an ever-present threat of assassination by Batista's contacts in Mexico. By October the following year Castro had gathered enough support and money and declared himself ready to return. He bought a 58-foot yacht with the winsome name of *Granma* from a North American couple for $15,000, and hatched a plan to sail it from Tuxpan, on the east coast of Veracruz in Mexico, to Oriente, following the tracks of José Martí who had made a similar journey sixty years before. A cache of weapons was found by the Mexican police following a tipoff, and escalating events led the rebels to leave sooner than they planned. On November 21 the Mexican authorities gave Castro three days to leave Mexico City and the rebels left from Veracruz so quickly that several received no military training.

At around 1.30am, on November 25, 1956, with 82 men crammed into the eight-berth yacht, the *Granma* set off for Cuba. Due to the stormy weather all shipping was kept in port and the yacht had to slip past the Mexican coastguard to escape. Foul weather, cramped conditions and a malfunctioning engine meant that the journey that was supposed to take five days took eight. The plan had been to come ashore at Niquero, where Celia Sánchez, a key revolutionary, was waiting to ferry them to safety, but on December 2 they ran out of petrol 35m from the coast, and at 6am the *Granma* capsized. As Che later commented: "It wasn't a landing, it was a shipwreck."

Exhausted, sick and hungry, the 82 young men waded ashore only to find themselves faced with a kilometre of virtually impenetrable mangroves and sharp saw grass. They eventually made camp at Alegría de Pío, a sugarcane zone near the coast, with the intention of resting for a few hours. It was to be their baptism by fire as Batista troops, who had been tipped off about their arrival and had been strafing the area for several hours, came across the men and attacked. Completely unprepared for attack, the rebels ran for their lives, scattering in all directions. Thanks to the efforts of Celia Sánchez, who went through the area leaving messages detailing a meeting point in the mountains at the houses of peasants sympathetic to the rebels' cause, the rebels were able to regroup two weeks later. It was hardly a glorious beginning, but the opening shots of the revolution had been fired.

Media Luna, with beautiful views over the Sierra Maestra and a rocky coastline good for snorkelling, and the narrow white-sand **Playa Punta**, have an unruliness that's refreshingly different from the smart resort beaches. The small but engaging **Casa Museo Ceila Sánchez Manduley** (Mon–Sat 9am–5pm, Sun 9am–1pm; $1), erstwhile home

of revolutionary Ceila Sánchez, offers a rag-bag of exhibits, from
Taino ceramics through shrapnel from the wars of independence to a
photographic history of the town.

There's nowhere to stay or eat, though the local service station on
the Marea de Portillo road sells sweets, snacks and cold drinks.

Parque Nacional Desembarco del Granma

West of Pilón, the province's southwestern tip is commandeered by the
Parque Nacional Desembarco del Granma, which starts at the tranquil holiday haven of **Las Coloradas**, 47km from Pilón, and stretches
some 20km west to the tiny fishing village of **Cabo Cruz**. The forested
interior of the park is littered with trails, but the most famous feature is
the **Playa Las Coloradas**, on the western coastline, where the *Granma*
yacht deposited Fidel Castro on December 2, 1956, see p.423.

Named after the red colour that the mangrove jungle gives to the
water, the beach is completely hidden and you can't see or even
hear the sea from the start of the path that leads down to the
Monumento Portada de la Libertad (Mon–Fri 8am–5pm, Sat &
Sun 8am–2pm; $1, including guide), which marks the spot of the
landing. Flanked on either side by mangrove forest hedged with
jagged saw grass, the kilometre-long path presents a pleasant walk
even for those indifferent to the revolution, although even the most
jaded cynics will find the enthusiasm and respect the guide has for
his subject hard to resist and his compelling narrative (in Spanish)
brings to life the rebels' journey through murky undergrowth and
razor-sharp thicket.

The tour also takes in a life-size replica of the **yacht**, which the
guide can sometimes be persuaded to let you clamber aboard, and a
rather spartan **museum** with photographs, maps and an emotive
quotation from Castro on the eve of the crossing that neatly sums up
his determination to succeed: "*Si salimos, llegamos. Si llegamos,
entramos, y si entramos triumfamos*" (If we leave, we'll get there.
If we get there we'll get in, and if we get in we will win).

El Guafe

The interior of the park is made up of idyllic woodland that skirts the
Sierra Maestra. From Las Coloradas you can walk to the start of **El
Guafe** (Mon–Fri 8am–5pm, Sat & Sun 8am–2pm; $3, including guide),
one of the four trails in the park, celebrated for the intriguing stone
petroglyphs found in the vicinity, the remnants of Indian culture. It's
an easy and reasonably well-signposted walk – roughly a 3km circuit –
which you can do on your own, although the guides have extensive
knowledge of both the history of the area and the cornucopia of birds
and butterflies, trees and plants you'll see along the way. Look out for
the ancient cactus nicknamed "Viejo Testigo" (the Old Witness),
thought to be 500 years old and now so thick and twisted it has formed
a thick, tree-like trunk.

The small, humaniform **petroglyphs**, sculpted with haunting, hollowed-out eyes, are in a low-roofed cave musty with the smell of bats, believed to have been used as a crypt by the aboriginal Indians, who carved the idols as guardians. Fragments of ceramics and a large clay jar decorated with allegorical characters were also found, sup

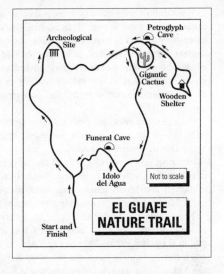

porting the theory. A second cave close to the exit of the trail houses another petroglyph known as the **Idolo del Agua** (the water idol), thought to have been carved into the rock to bless and protect the sweet water of the cave – a rarity in the area.

The **other trails** are along the southern coastline twenty to thirty kilometres east of El Guafe. Highlights include the Agua Fina cave, roughly 20km from El Guafe, and, some 7km further east, the Morlotte and El Furstete caves and Las Terrazas, a natural coastline shelf sculpted by geographic formations to look like man-made terraces. To visit any of these places you'll need to contact **Cubamar** (see below).

The only **place to stay** in the park, *Villa Las Coloradas*, on Playa Las Coloradas, has excellent simple, clean chalets with air conditioning and hot water, along with a **restaurant** and **bar**. Bookings should be made via **Cubamar** (☎7/66-25-23; ②) and are essential at weekends, when this is a favourite target for Cubans. Cubamar can also arrange **group excursions** (for ten or more) to visit the other trails.

Look out for the tiny, iridescent green, red and blue Cartacuba bird, which looks like a pom-pom and has a gruff call like a grunting pig.

Manzanillo and around

Though run-down and ramshackle, **MANZANILLO**, 75km up the coast from Playa Las Coloradas, is not completely devoid of charm. Now a fairly pedestrian coastal fishing village, it was established around the harbour at the end of the eighteenth century and enjoyed a brisk trade in contraband goods. Sugar trade replaced smuggling in the nineteenth century, but the town's heyday had passed and it never grew much bigger.

Manzanillo's sole attraction these days is its fantastical **Moorish
architecture**, built in the 1910s and 1920s. The sensual buildings,
all crescents, curves and brilliant tiles, are best seen in the town's
central **Parque Céspedes**. Most eye-catching is the richly decorated gazebo presiding over the park, giving an air of bohemian elegance well suited to the sphinx statues in each corner and the
melée of benches, palm trees, and faux-nineteenth-century street
lamps.

Opposite the park, the pink **Edificio Quirch** is no less splendid,
although its crescent arches and tight lattice design are rather
wasted on the couple of dollar shops it houses. If you have time, it's
fascinating just to wander around the surrounding streets looking
at the various spires, domes and peaks. Don't miss the roof of an
unnamed apartment block, one block east of Parque Céspedes,
coated in brown and cream tiles like discs of milk chocolate.

Trains from Bayamo arrives at the train station on the eastern edge
of town, around 1km from the centre. **Buses** from Bayamo and Pilón
pull in at the bus station 2km east of town, but the service is irregular
and if coming from Bayamo you're better off catching one of the *colectivo* **taxis**. There's no real reason to **stay** in Manzanillo but should you
need to, the rather grim *Hotel Guacanayabo*, on Avenida Camilio
Cienfuegos (☎5/40-12; ③), is your only option. It also has a mediocre
restaurant.

Parque Nacional de Demajagua

Twenty kilometres south of Manzanillo, the **Parque Nacional de
Demajagua** (Mon–Sat 8am–5pm, Sun 8am–noon; $1, $1 extra for a
camera, $5 for a camcorder) is a pleasant place to while away an
hour or two. It was from here that Carlos Manuel de Céspedes set out
to win Cuban independence from Spain (see box on p.419), and with
splendid views over the bay and the cane fields, the one-time sugar
plantation is a picture of serenity. The small building housing the
museum was built in 1968, the centenary of the uprising, the original plantation having been completely destroyed by shells from a
Spanish gunboat on 17 October, 1868.

The museum is depressingly sparse, with a brief history of the
plantation detailing its ownership by Céspedes' older brother forming the main part. Glass cases display various metal keys and broken
fragments of plate, as well as a motheaten square of red, white and
blue cloth, the highlight of the museum, which turns out to be the
first Cuban flag ever made, hand sewn by Céspedes' mistress. The
grounds, while not extensive, are a pleasant place to relax for half an
hour or so – look out for the two big tubs just beyond the museum's
entrance, which were originally used to boil the sugarcane. The most
significant sight, however, is the Demajagua bell, built into a dry-
stone wall on the far side of the lawn, with which Céspedes sum-
moned his slaves to freedom.

Travel details

DOMESTIC FLIGHTS
Bayamo to: Havana (3 weekly; 2hr).

Manzanillo to: Havana (3 weekly; 2hr 30min).

Santiago de Cuba to: Havana (17 weekly; 2hr 15min).

TRAINS
Bayamo to: Camagüey (1 daily; 6hr); Havana (10 weekly; 12hr); Manzanillo (4 daily; 1hr 55min); Santiago de Cuba (10 weekly; 4hr 20min).

Manzanillo to: Bayamo (10 weekly; 1hr 55min); Havana (10 weekly; 14hr); Santiago de Cuba (10 weekly; 6hr).

Santiago de Cuba to: Bayamo (10 weekly; 4hr 20min); Havana (10 weekly; 14 hr); Manzanillo (10 weekly; 6hr).

BUSES
Note that problems relating to petrol shortages are particularly severe in this region.

Bayamo to: Manzanillo (4 daily; 2hr); Niquero (1 daily; 4hr); Pilón (3 weekly; 4hr); Santiago de Cuba (4 daily; 2hr 30min).

Manzanillo to: Bayamo (4 daily; 2hr); Havana (1 daily; 12hr); Pilón (6 weekly; 2hr 30min).

Pilón to: Bayamo (3 weekly; 4hr); Chivirico (3 weekly; 4hr); Manzanillo (6 weekly; 2hr 30min).

Santiago de Cuba to: Bayamo (4 daily; 2hr 30min); Chivirico (2 daily; 2hr 40min); Mar Verde (5 daily; 40min).

Chapter 8

Isla de la Juventud and Cayo Largo

S outh of the mainland, the little-visited **Isla de la Juventud** (Island of Youth) is the largest of over three hundred scattered emerald islets that make up the **Archipiélago de los Canarreos**. Most visitors to the archipelago, however, are destined for its comparatively tiny neighbour **Cayo Largo**, arguably Cuba's most exclusive holiday resort.

Extending from the personable island capital of Nueva Gerona, in the north, to the superb diving region of Punta Francés, 70km to the southwest, the comma-shaped **Isla de la Juventud** is bisected by a military checkpoint designed to limit access to ecologically vulnerable areas. The northern part is mostly farmland, characterized by citrus orchards and mango groves, while the southern swampland is rich in wildlife. Although it has an air of timeless somnolence, the island was once a pirate haunt, dominated for three centuries by French and English buccaneers and adventurers. Development has been unhurried, and even today there are as many horse-drawn coaches on the roads as there are cars or trucks.

The island probably won't be your first choice for a beach holiday, although it's a good place to unwind once you've visited the more flamboyant – and hectic – sights in the rest of Cuba. With little tourist trade, its charm is anchored on its unaffected pace of life and pleasant beaches, and the lack of traffic and predominantly flat terrain make cycling an excellent way to explore. The island capital, **Nueva Gerona**, has few of the architectural crowd-pullers that exist in colonial towns, and so is a refreshingly low-key and relaxing place to visit, easily discovered in a weekend. For those keen to explore further, there are some intriguing pre-Columbian **cave paintings** in the south and, close to the capital, the museum at the abandoned **Presidio Modelo**, whose most famous inmate was Fidel Castro. With a couple more small but worthy museums, some of the country's best offshore **dive sites** and one beautiful white-sand beach, Isla de la Juventud is one of Cuba's best-kept secrets.

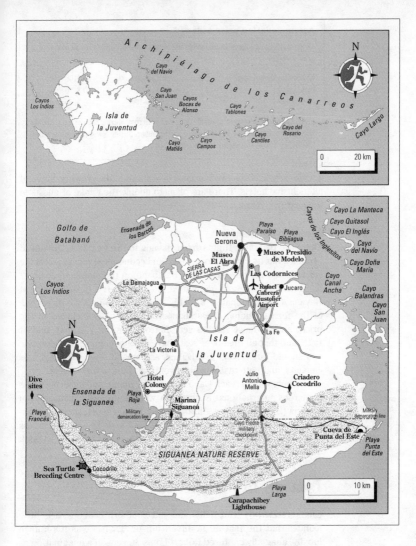

A necklace of islets streaming 150km east, the Archipiélago de los Canarreos is a fantasy paradise of pearl-white sand and translucent, coral-lined shallows. Whilst most are still desert cays too small to sustain a complex tourist structure, **Cayo Largo**, the second largest landmass after La Isla, is beaten only by Varadero in terms of package tourist pulling power. Capitalizing on a flawless, 22-kilometre ribbon of white sand, the resort was created in 1977 to serve the sun-worshipping Canadians and Europeans who flock here in high season,

and already features two marinas, dive shops and a growing clique of
all-inclusive hotels. There are plans to double the intake of guests in
the next five years.

Getting to the islands

There are two daily **flights** from Havana to the **Isla de la Juventud**
(40min), but by far the most scenic and economical way to reach the
island is to take the **ferry** from Batabanó on the mainland coast (2
daily; 2hr). Buying a combined bus and ferry ticket ($11) at
Havana's bus terminal is probably the best option, as the direct bus
to the ferry terminal at Batabanó (2hr 40min) is included in the
price, and as most visitors set off from Havana you may find at
Batabanó that all the dollar seats have already been sold. If possible
you should buy tickets in advance, as demand often outstrips seat
capacity, and note that you need your passport to buy tickets.

The only way to reach **Cayo Largo** is by **plane**, and its airport sees
numerous international arrivals, as well as domestic planes from
Havana (2 daily; 40min). Although only 140km apart, short of swimming, there is no way to get here from the Isla de la Juventud unless
you're sailing your own yacht. Note that you'll be required to book
accommodation along with your flight.

Isla de la Juventud

Characterized by fruit fields and soft southern beaches, it is little
wonder that the **Isla de la Juventud**, or "La Isla", as it's known
locally, allegedly captured Robert Louis Stevenson's imagination as
the original desert island of *Treasure Island*. Although
Christopher Columbus chanced upon the island in 1494, on his
second trip to the Americas, the Spanish had scant interest in it
until the nineteenth century, mostly because the shallow, coral-
lined waters surrounding the island had repeatedly scuppered their
ships (see p.432). Instead it was left to swarms of pirates to discover the lush, pine-forested land, hidden caves and impenetrable
swampy interior in the south. They soon realized that not only was

its proximity to the mainland convenient for Havana – the most lucrative port in the Caribbean – but also it was ideally placed for attacks on the trade routes; a conspicuous lack of governors cemented its appeal.

Development of the island unfolded at an unhurried pace and even today the quiet, underpopulated countryside and placid towns have an air of a land waiting to awaken. The nucleus of the island is in the **north**, where you'll find many of the sights and most of the population. Nestling with its back to the Sierra de la Casa, mined for its rich vein of marble, **Nueva Gerona**, the island capital, is small and satisfyingly self-contained, ambling along a couple of decades behind developments on the mainland. Spread around it is a wide skirt of low-lying fields, lined with orderly citrus orchards and fruit farms and peppered with most of the island's modest tourist attractions. It is a testament to the island's longstanding underpopulation and relative isolation that chief among these are two former prison buildings: **El Abra**, a hacienda converted in 1869 into a holding pen for the Cuban independence suffragist José Martí pending his exile to Spain, and the **Presidio Modelo**, set up in 1926 to contain more than six thousand criminals, most famously Fidel Castro, who was sent there following the failed attack on the Moncada barracks in Santiago. Deserted, but still a dominating presence on the island's landscape, the formidable prison and its museum make for a fascinating excursion. There are also a couple of brown-sand beaches, **Playa Bibijagua** and **Playa Paraíso**, within easy reach of Nueva Gerona.

South from the capital are several sights that can be explored in easy day-trips. Beyond the island's second biggest town, rather mundane La Fe, is a **crocodile farm** offering an excellent opportunity to study the creatures at close range. Just beyond here is the military checkpoint at Cayo Piedra, in place to conserve the marshy region to the southeast which forms the **Siguanea Nature Reserve**, much of which is off-limits to visitors.

South of the checkpoint on the east coast you'll find one of the island's most impressive sights, the **pre-Columbian paintings** in the caves of Punta del Este, which are believed to date back some 1100 years. On the west coast is the tiny hamlet of **Cocodrilo**, set on a picturesque curve of coastline and an ideal spot for swimming, while close to hand is the island's picture-perfect white-sand beach, **Playa El Francés**, from where you can enjoy the island's celebrated dive sites, including underwater caves and a wall of black coral.

Some history

The earliest known inhabitants of the island were the **Ciboney** people who, some 1100 years ago, sailed in dugout canoes from island to island through the Caribbean, settling in the most favourable places. Living a simple life, they stayed close to the shores where they could

Other than one hotel on the southwest coast (see p.451), Nueva Gerona is the only place you'll find accommodation on the island.

Though it's not strictly policed you do need to obtain a pass to cross the checkpoint (see box on p.446).

fish and hunt, eschewing the pine forested interior. Tools and utensils made from conch shell and bone have been found at Punta del Este, suggesting that the Ciboney based themselves around the eastern caves, although some remains at Caleta Grande, in the north, indicate the presence of another, smaller group.

By the time **Christopher Columbus** landed here in June 1494, on his second trip to the Americas, and stayed twelve days gathering firewood and water, there were no longer Indians living on the island. According to a chronicler on board the ship, one crew member out on his own saw 33 clothed men, paused long enough to take an accurate head count and then turned tail and fled screaming back to the ship. As early as 1827 historians were ridiculing this account, however, speculating that the crewman had been fooled by a flock of large birds, probably storks.

Although Columbus named the island "Juan La Evangelista" and claimed it for Spain – suspected Indian occupation not withstanding – the Spanish Crown had little interest in the island over the next four centuries. Neither the northern coastline, webbed with mangroves, nor the excessively shallow southern bays afforded a natural harbour to match the likes of Havana, and the Golfo de Batabanó, separating the island from mainland Cuba, was too shallow to navigate on the overblown Spanish galleons. These failings effectively killed off investigation from all but the most dedicated pioneers and although the territory was given to the Spanish nobleman Jerónimo de Rojas y Avellaneda in 1576, he and subsequent owners were little more than absentee landowners. The island remained largely unexplored with a micro-population of untitled cattle farmers and labourers – mainly from Galicia and Mallorca – settled near the coast.

Left outside the bounds of Spanish law enforcement, the island attracted scores of **pirates** between the sixteenth and eighteenth centuries, most famously the Frenchman Latrobe, John Hawkins, Henry Morgan and John Rackham, better known as Calico Jack. A choice refuge, it was close to the trade routes used by Spanish flotillas returning to Europe, and pirates would skulk in the island's shallows before following unprotected ships into the high seas and pouncing upon the gold, spices and indigo the traders had gathered throughout the Americas. It was known as **La Isla de Pinos** – after the pine trees that flourished so readily, ideal for making masts and repairing ships – and, informally, as the Isla de las Cotorras, after the endemic green parrot population. Lurid stories of a Bacchanalian commune fuelled by wine, women and warmongering were enough to keep all but the most determined settlers away from the island, and the pirates ruled the roost for nigh on three hundred years. Their success was in part due to a barter system set up with the incipient cattle-farming community with whom they would exchange their booty of bolts of cloth, alcohol and African slaves for leather, sugar and other basic commodities.

The pirates' glory days drew to a close in the early nineteenth century when Spanish interest was renewed in the island. Visiting priests expressed dismay at the pirates' moral laxity and the conspicuous absence of a church, and in 1821 the United States, which had been slowly growing in influence in the region since its independence, established an anti-pirate naval squadron. Supported by Spain and England, who were eager to protect their own commercial interests, trouncing the enemy proved a relatively simple task, and many of the pirates even proved compliant. Key figures such as **Henry Morgan**, **Francis Drake** and **William Dampier** renounced piracy and leapt at the chance to become pillars of the community, accepting prestigious governor positions and knighthoods, or retiring with their wealth.

Rather belatedly, the Spanish set about staking their claim and in 1827 Colonel Clemente Delgado y España was despatched, along with **Dr José Labadía**, by the Capitán General of Cuba to assess the island's potential. On the basis of Labadía's report, it was decided that the island should be fortified against illegal trading, and in 1830 it was rechristened "Colonia de la Reina Amalia", though it continued to be known as Isla de Pinos. Delgado y España named its newly appropriated township Nueva Gerona in honour of the Capitán General of Cuba's victorious battle in Gerona in Spain – an act of sheer obsequiousness which shortly paid off when he was put in military command of the island.

Despite a massive push by royal decree for whites to populate the island there was comparatively little response, and even by the turn of the twentieth century, the population still stood at under four thousand. The Spanish authorities capitalized on the island's isolation, using it as a convenient **offshore prison** during the wars of independence, but they still failed to exploit its full potential. By the early twentieth century, they were rueing their indifference, as much of the property had fallen into the hands of shrewd North American businessmen and farmers who had waited in the wings during the troubled years.

When Cuba won its independence from Spain in 1901, the island's small population allowed the North Americans to muscle in and start development unimpeded, and by the time the Spanish deigned – in 1926 – to ratify the 1902 treaty ensuring the Isla de Pinos was Cuban territory, a US-funded infrastructure of banks, hotels and even prisons – namely the vast Model Prison – was already in place, and by the time of the revolution it had become a popular North American holiday resort.

The North Americans promptly departed following the revolution, and the history of the island took another turn when the state's drive to create arable land established it as one of the country's major producers of fruit for export. In 1966 it became a centre for experimental agriculture to which a flood of students, the particularly dedicated as young as twelve, came to work the fields and study. In

1976 the government extended this free education to **foreign students** from countries with a socialist overview, and until the Special Period curtailed the flow, thousands of students arrived from countries including Angola, Nicaragua and South Yemen. When the island hosted the eleventh World Youth and Student Festival in 1978, the government changed its name from Isle of Pines to **Isle of Youth**, shedding the final trace of the island's rebellious past, although islanders still refer to themselves – and their national league baseball team – as Pineros.

Nueva Gerona

The island's only sizeable town, **NUEVA GERONA** lies in the lee of the Sierra de la Casa, on the bank of the Río Las Casas. Whether you are coming by plane or boat, this is where you will arrive and where you're likely to be based. According to a census of 1819, the population stood at just under two hundred and it boasted just "four guano huts and a church of the same". While the town has certainly moved on since, it's still a small and quirky place, with a cosiness more suited to a village than an island capital, and a peacefulness bordering on sleepiness well offset by the hub of action around the central streets. Half a day here breeds a sense of familiarity, and much of the town's attraction lies in wandering the streets, chatting with locals, a few of whom speak English, and visiting the low-key museums.

Architecturally, Nueva Gerona floats in a no-man's-land between old-style colonial buildings and modern urbanity. When the town was brought under Spanish control in the 1830s there were only thirty-odd private houses, and life centred around the military garrison, the commander's house and a prison galley (since removed) by the dock. Today, it's a pretty town, with many of its concrete, one-storey buildings painted into cubes of pastel colour, and its few older buildings all stately colonnades and red-tiled roofs, adding a colonial touch. The scattering of apartment blocks on the town fringe is impressively smart, and there are no sprawling suburbs and few decaying buildings.

You'll find most of the town's attractions on and just off the main street, cheerful **Calle Martí**, starting at the **Museo de los Deportes**, with its somewhat scanty display of sporting trophies and medals. From here, Martí runs south past the **Fondo de Bienes Culturales**, which offers souvenirs, some locally produced, and the **Galería de Arte Gerona**, which has a regularly changing display of local artwork. A block further south, the handsome **Iglesia Nuestra Senora de los Delores y San Nicolas de Barí** brightens up the rather bland **Parque Julio Antonio Mella**, while opposite, the **Museo Provincial** shows off the island's heirlooms. One block east of Martí, the **Taller de Cerámica Artistica** makes a passable enough diversion for those interested in the production of ceramics, while three blocks west, the fascinating **Museo de la Lucha Clandestina**, the town's best museum, displays memorabilia relating to the underground revolutionary

Zoológico de Piedras, Guantánamo

Holguín

Baracoa, Oriente

Santa Lucía, Camagüey

Antonio Maceo monument, Santiago de Cuba

Guemillere - fiesta of orishas

Baracoa, Oriente

Fiesta of Fire, Santiago de Cuba

Sierra Maestra

Cutting sugarcane by hand

Museo de Presidio Modelo, Isla de la Juventud

movement of the 1950s. The town's most far-flung attraction, the rather sparse **Museo Historia Natural y Planetario**, stands ten minutes' walk southwest of the centre; it boasts a large rock collection and a full-size reproduction of the pre-Columbian cave paintings to be found in the south of the island.

Arrival and information

Flights from Havana arrive at Rafael Cabrera Mustelier airport (☎61/2-26-90 or 2-21-84), 10km from the town centre. Have some pesos ready for the buses that meet the planes and run to the town centre, or take a taxi for about $7. The **ferry** from Batabanó docks at the terminal in Nueva Gerona (6am–4pm; ☎61/2-44-06), a ten-minute walk from the centre. A **hydrofoil** sometimes replaces the ferry at random, and although it is about twenty minutes faster, it makes for a less scenic trip as there's no outside deck.

It's best to pick up a map of the island from the Infotur office on Obispo in Habana Vieja before you go.

With no tourist board and few places selling maps, the *Villa Gaviota* hotel on the town outskirts (see p.436) is your best bet for information, especially on diving activities, or you could ring the *Hotel Colony*, on the southwest coast of the island (see p.451).

Transport

Renting a car or jeep is the best way to explore the island, since the bus network is skeletal and often suspended anyway due to petrol shortages. Havanautos **car rental** office, Calle 23 esq. 29 (☎61/2-44-32), is also the only place you can buy a **permit** to cross the military checkpoint to reach the south of the island. **Taxis** are an alternative option but you'll find fewer unmetered taxis than in other towns; a good place to look is outside the dollar supermarket on Calle 32 e/ 35 y 37, or ask in a *casa particular*. A state taxi company, Turistaxi, is based at the *Hotel Colony* (see p.451), though they can pick you up by arrangement (☎61/9-82-81). The best way to see the north end of the island is by **bike**; there are no rental outlets, but *casas particulares* are often willing to loan you the family bicycle for a few dollars a day.

Accommodation

Unless you've come for the diving, in which case you'll be based in the western Ensenada de la Siguanea (see p.451), Nueva Gerona is the only base for a stay on the island. The state hotels on the town outskirts have the advantage of cool swimming pools and pretty countryside, but to really enjoy the centre of town you're probably best off in one of the excellent *casas particulares*. To stem what was in reality only ever a minor, though as everywhere, a politically sensitive *jinetera* problem, *casas particulares* on Isla de la Juventud cannot be self-contained and the landlord must sleep on the premises. In the unlikely event that all are fully booked you can try the state *Hotel La Cubana* (①), next to the Cubana office, which occasionally accepts foreigners.

Hotels

Los Codorinces, Carretera Aeropuerto km 4.5 ☎61/2-49-25. Above-average rooms in a chalet-like hotel with good views over the surrounding country-side, though rather inconvenient for everything but the airport. Take the right fork after the bridge on the airport road then turn right at the open-air peso café. ③.

Villa Gaviota, Autopista La Fe km 1.5 ☎61/32-56; fax 24-54-25. Rather plain state hotel on the outskirts of town, whose highlight is a small pool with sun terrace. Decent single, double and triple rooms, all with bathrooms. ③.

Casas particulares

Casa de la Alegría, Calle 43 no. 3602 e/ 36 y 38; no phone. One large, plainly furnished double room with a/c. This friendly house is close to the centre and also does laundry. ②.

Casa de la Amistad, Calle 24 e/ 53 y 55 ☎61/2-44-37. Small but pretty rooms in a pleasant private house with a big living room and eye-catching red and white floor tiles. Meals are available. ②.

Casa de Joel Diaz Prout, Calle 49 no. 2214 e/ 22 y 24; no phone. One room in an extremely friendly *casa particular* about eight blocks from the cen-tre. An airy balcony, tasty meals and informative hosts make this a sound choice. ②.

Casa de Nieve Corbello, Calle 24 no. 5108 e/ 51 y 53 ☎61/2-44-37. This pleasant, second-storey *casa particular*, accessed by a white spiral staircase, has two air-conditioned double rooms and a fresh, bright sitting room com-plete with rocking chairs. ②.

Villa Hilda, Martí no. 3212 e/ 32 y 34 ☎61/2-24-73. One block west of Parque Julio Antonio Mella, this *casa particular* has two rather old-fashioned, air-conditioned rooms set around a pleasant patio and garden. ②.

Villa Marizol, Calle 24 no. 5107 e/ 51 y 53 ☎61/2-44-75. Airy, homely *casa particular* with two air-conditioned rooms and frilly costume dolls on each bed. Six blocks from the centre on a quiet, pretty street with hill views. ②.

Villa Ninita, Calle 32 no. 4110 e/ 41 y 43; no phone. Two fridge-equipped rooms and a shared hot-water bathroom in a light, spacious upstairs *casa par-ticular* with an attractive tiled floor and gorgeous hill views from the front and back terraces. ②.

Villa Pena, Calle 10 no. 3710 e/ 37 y 39 ☎61/2-23-45. Big, friendly household offering two rooms and a shared bathroom with electric hot-water shower. There's food available and use of a kitchen. Around 400m out of town but a good choice. ②.

The Town

The place to start any walking tour is on Calle Martí, the hub of the town, where you'll find the main shops as well as the town gallery and a local museum. At the southern end, set around the plaza, you'll find the Iglesia Nuestra Señora de los Delores and the provincial museum, while the streets west of Martí hold further attractions. Beyond the centre, the only attraction is the Museo Historia Natural y Planeterio.

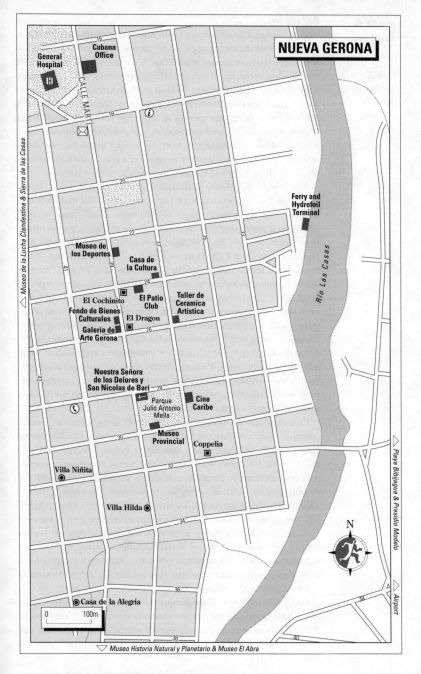

NUEVA GERONA

General Hospital
Cubana Office
CALLE MARTÍ
Ferry and Hydrofoil Terminal
Museo de los Deportes
Casa de la Cultura
El Cochinito
Fondo de Bienes Culturales
El Patio Club
Taller de Ceramica Artistica
El Dragon
Galería de Arte Gerona
Nuestra Señora de los Delores y San Nicolas de Barí
Parque Julio Antonio Mella
Cine Caribe
Villa Niñita
Museo Provincial
Coppelia
Villa Hilda
Casa de la Alegría

Rio Las Casas

0   100m

△ Museo de la Lucha Clandestina & Sierra de las Casas

▷ Playa Bibijagua & Presidio Modelo

▷ Airport

▽ Museo Historia Natural y Planetario & Museo El Abra

N

Calle Martí

Nueva Gerona's heart lies on **Calle Martí**, the central street which
gives the town its defining character and where you'll find most of
the shops, restaurants and attractions. It's a good-looking strip, with

the running verandas of the low buildings offering welcome respite
from the sun. At the northern end is a small and rather ordinary park.
At no. 2223, the tiny **Museo de los Deportes** (Mon–Fri 8am–noon &
1–5pm, Sat 1–5pm; free) serves as a modest tribute to local sports
heroes who have gained national recognition. The tiny one-room
museum displays sweatshirts worn by record breakers, photos of
athletes and baseball players in action and a time-worn collection of
trophies, all proudly laid out as if in a grandmother's parlour.

The **Fondo de Bienes Culturales**, a little further down, at no.
2418, on the opposite side of the street (Mon–Sat 9am–noon &
1–5pm), has an eclectic range of souvenirs, from finely detailed
ornamental plates and Che Guevara lighters to guinea pigs sculpted
from hairy coconuts. More thought-provoking is the **Galería de Arte
Gerona**, close by at Calle Martí esq. 26 no. 2424 (daily 10am–5pm),
which has a small collection of local art, some of it for sale. The regularly changing selection of ceramics, for which the island enjoys a
quiet fame, big splashy abstracts, obscure watercolour collages and
even underwater photography merits a quick stop. At the end of the
road, past the pedestrianized centre lined with kiosks selling everything from soap to frilly knickers, is the **Parque Julio Antonio Mella**.
Although unspectacular in itself – it's basically a wide slab of plaza
sweltering in the sun – it's bordered by some picturesque buildings.
On the western side, for example, is a handsome, pastel yellow villa,
now converted into a school, with elegant, unadorned arches and
wonderful stained-glass windows.

Presiding over the plaza's northern corner is the grandiose, ochre-
coloured church of **Nuestra Señora de los Delores y San Nicolas de
Barí** (Mon–Fri 8.30am–noon), boasting a curvaceous red-tiled roof
and a sturdy bell tower with two delicate rounded balconies painted
with snail-shell rings. The stalwart design is intended to ensure that the
church does not suffer the same fate as its predecessor which, built in
1853, collapsed in the face of a hurricane in 1926. The present building was completed in 1929 and though reminiscent of a colonial
Mexican church, is actually a copy of the San Lorenzo de Lucina
church in Rome. The interior is disappointing: a sparsely decorated
sky-blue shell houses a huddle of pews. It's only worth entering for a
swift glance at the altar to the Virgen de la Caridad, the patron saint of
Cuba, backed by the national flag.

On the opposite side of the parque is the **Museo Provincial**, closed
at the time of writing but due to reopen at some unspecified point in
2000. It has an impressive collection of artefacts relating to the history of the island, notably the Ciboney and the pirate era.

Museo de la Lucha Clandestina

Three blocks behind the park, on Calle 24 e/ 43 y 45, the **Museo de la Lucha Clandestina** (Tues–Sat 9am–5pm, Sun 8am–noon; free) packs into a modest wooden house a surprising number of items relating to the islanders' part in the revolutionary struggle. While Cuba is stuffed with such museums, there are a couple of exhibits that make this one special.

Even if your Spanish is up to it, you probably won't want to linger too long on the anthology of letters sent from the Presidio Modelo by the Moncada rebels, including Fidel Castro, or the rather staid personal effects of underground member Montané Orapesa, who opened his house, at great personal risk, to family and friends who came to visit the rebels during their imprisonment. Instead, head for the second room, where you can see an original copy of *Sierra Maestra*, the official organ of the M-26-7 movement, published in Miami and smuggled back to Cuba by the core cell of revolutionaries in exile in Mexico. With progress reports on the revolutionary struggle, this exemplary piece of propaganda has an unstudied feel, particularly in the arresting shot of Castro, flanked by rebels, reclining on a grassy verge in trainee beard and full camouflage regalia.

Other exhibits include the black and red M-26-7 armbands worn by supporters to show allegiance and a copy of the commemorative photo album compiled following the revolution to celebrate the original band which arrived on the yacht *Granma*. Each page of the album features photographs of two revolutionaries, most of them still in their twenties, framed by a dramatic line-drawing depicting their struggles, making them look like comic-book heroes. Also noteworthy are the 1960s photos of crowds of excited people outside banks and factories as they celebrate nationalization, and, best of all, an ingenious fake cigar used to smuggle messages.

Taller de Ceramica Artistica

Lined with trestle tables at which potters and ceramicists silently work on surreal plates, some featuring disembodied eyes and breasts, and over-elaborate ornaments, the **Taller de Ceramica Artistica**, Calle 26 esq. 37 (Mon–Fri 8am–noon & 1–4pm; $2), four blocks east of the Museo de la Lucha Clandestina, is a rather transparent attempt to cash in on passing tourist trade, and despite the eye-catching red-brick entrance, built to resemble a giant chimney, there's not a lot to do inside; even wandering the aisles feels intrusive, like spying on artists at work. The island's rich red earth – mounds of which are crushed in a vast tub on the premises, with demonstrations freely available – is ideally suited to ceramics, and the workshop supplies many of the country's tourist shops as well as selling pieces on the premises. Plans are apparently afoot to develop this into a full-blown working museum with a hands-on area for visitors to satisfy their own artistic ambitions.

Isla de la Juventud

Although you must, in theory, have a group of six or more to visit the planetarium, a small donation to the guard should ensure access.

Museo Historia Natural y Planetario

Fifteen minutes' walk southwest of the town centre, on Calle 41 esq. 52, the **Museo Historia Natural y Planetario** (Tues–Sat 8am–5pm, Sun 9am–1pm; $2) essentially consists of a motley menagerie of stuffed animals, a rock collection, and a scaled-down model of the pre-Columbian cave paintings in the south of the island that doesn't do them justice. Despite the inclusion of a grotesque but strangely compelling deformed and pickled pig, the museum is a bit of a sorry affair, and Cuba boasts far superior collections of stuffed animals. Somewhat better is the small domed **planetarium** (Tues–Sat 8am–5pm, Sun 9am–1pm), housed in a separate building next door, which is whimsically decorated with zodiac symbols on the outside and the constellations of the stars within. There is a telescope for public use.

Eating

Though Nueva Gerona is hardly a gastronomic capital, and many **restaurants** rely on the tried-and-tested formula of pork with rice and beans, you can always find homely establishments dishing up cheap and filling meals. Higher taxes have squeezed out the majority of *paladares*, but several of the *casa particulares* have a licence to prepare food – it's always worth asking. For **snacks**, stock up at the dollar supermarket on Calle 32 e/ 35 y 37 (Mon–Sat 9am–6pm, Sun 9am–1pm) or buy filled rolls at one of the roast-pork stands in the centre of Calle Martí. Prú, the ginger beer-like spicy soft drink common to Oriente, can also be bought here, and is a better choice than a peso *refresco* for a cold drink, as the water in it has been boiled – the **water supply** on the island can be affected by parasites when there has been little rain. Whether you apply the same logic and avoid the delicious ice creams on sale at *Coppelia* and the home-made ones from a stall on Calle 24 is up to you.

El Abra, Carretera Ciboney km 1 ☎61/4-9-27. A backdrop of mountains, a lake and a field scattered with large stone abstract sculptures carved by local artists make this a better than average setting for standard though inexpensive Cuban cuisine of turkey, pork and tortilla. Closed Mon.

El Cochinito, Calle Martí. Dig into ample portions of sautéed pork with yucca, rice and beans at this standard peso-dollar restaurant. To eat al fresco pass through the dingy restaurant to the patio at the back.

Coppelia, Calle 32 esq. 37. Excellent ice cream up to the usual *Coppelia* standard, sometimes served with sauces and wafers. Particularly good sprinkled with a handful of the warm roasted peanuts sold by numerous street vendors.

El Dragon, Calle Martí esq. 26. Chinese food served with a Cuban twist. Fried rice with chicken, pork and vegetables is the house speciality.

El Marino, Calle Martí s/n e/ 22 y 24. Part bakery, part general store conjuring up flaky chocolate *señorita* pastries and extravagant, foamy meringue cakes.

Tienda Imagen, Calle Martí s/n e/ 24 y 26. Gem of a peso restaurant serving delicious *chorizo* sandwiches, chicken and chips and sticky sweet refrescos. A snack meal will cost just 20 pesos.

Drinking and entertainment

While those with new-found friends among the islanders may be swept away to wild parties, if you're left to your own devices you're more likely to find that much of the entertainment is relaxed and low-key, notable for a refreshing absence of tacky foreigner-only discos. The standard night out is to take some beers or a bottle of rum along to the open-air **street bar** halfway along Calle Martí, where the crowds gather of a night to dance to the booming *salsa* and watch the town's fashion queens prowl past on improbably high platform heels.

For a more active night out, the lively *Casa de la Cultura*, Calle 24 e/ 37 y 39, is well worth a visit, with entertainment most nights ranging from singing troupes and Afro-Cuban **dancing** to burlesque pantomimes and day-time children's shows. Check out Thursday's *trova* night, kicking off at 8.30pm, when accomplished local artists play a selection of classic *boleros* and *son*. Off Calle Martí on Calle 24, *El Patio* (Tues–Sun evenings; $5) hosts a fabulously camp **cabaret** with girls in fluffy bras and fishnets gyrating with lissom young men, and a crooner thrown in for the ladies. *El Dragon*, Calle Martí esq. 26, offers a less elaborate version of the same, with a nightly variety show plus regular singers and occasional guest performances by magicians and comedians.

Cine Caribe, on the east side of Parque Julio Antonio Mella, shows Cuban and international **films**, while a *sala de video* on Calle 39 e/ Calle 39 y Calle 26 offers similar fare on the small screen.

Listings

Airlines Cubana, Calle Martí no. 1415 e/ 16 y 18 ☎61/2-25-31.

Banks and exchange Banco Financero, Calle Martí esq. 20, gives cash advances on Mastercard and Visa, changes travellers' cheques and converts dollars to pesos. There are no ATMs on Isla de la Juventud.

Car rental The Havanautos office is at Calle 32 esq. 29.

Medical The only hospital on the island is the Héroes del Baire, on Calle 41 e/ 16 y 18. For an ambulance, call ☎61/2-27-20 or 2-41-70. The state hotels have medical posts in the grounds, while the most accessible pharmacy is in the hospital grounds, facing the entrance.

Photography Photoservice, Calle Martí e/ 30 y 32 (10am–12.30pm & 1–6.30pm), sells and develops films.

Police Call ☎116 in an emergency; otherwise call ☎61/2-26-52.

Post office The main post office, from where you can send telegrams, is on Calle Martí e/ 18 y 20 (Mon–Sat 8am–6pm).

Taxis For unmetered taxis, see p.435. Turistaxi is based at the *Hotel Colony* (see p.451).

Telephone You can buy phone cards and make international collect calls at the 24-hour ETECSA office on Calle 21 e/ 28 y 28.

Around Nueva Gerona

The hillsides, beaches and museums around Nueva Gerona will easily keep you occupied for a couple of days. West of the centre, the gently undulating **Sierra de las Casas** hills make for a pleasant and energetic climb, with the additional attraction of a lagoon in the caves beneath.

East of Nueva Gerona is the **Presidio Modelo**, where Fidel Castro and his Moncada renegades were incarcerated following the attack in Santiago. Walking through the now disused prison is an eerie experience that's not to be missed. Two kilometres further east are the nearest beaches to town, the small and rather insignificant **Playa Paraíso** and, close by, the larger and more attractive **Playa Bibijagua**.

Southwest of town, the road passes through farmland and orchards irrigated by reservoirs and dappled with small settlements. The picturesque **Museo El Abra** is housed at the farm where José Martí was imprisoned in 1869, and while the exhibits lack flavour, the high bank of mountains behind the farm and the pretty grounds dappled with flowers and shady trees make it worth the trip.

Sierra de las Casas and Cueva del Agua

The crackled salt-and-pepper rock-face that abounds on the hilltop is known as diente de perro *(dog's tooth) for its sharp, fang-like configuration.*

The best way to appreciate Nueva Gerona's diminutive scale is to take the short but exhilarating climb up the hills of the **Sierra de las Casas** range west of town for a bird's-eye view over Nueva Gerona and the surrounding countryside. The best route is to follow Calle 24 west from the town centre, past the swell of banana plants and rustling breadfruit trees peeking out of back gardens; take the first left turn where the road thins to a pathway and carry on along a well-trodden path until you reach the foot of the hill, oddly marked by two lone concrete poles poking out of the ground. It's under an hour's easy climb from the foot of the hill to the summit, beneath which are spread the town's orderly rows of streets, curtailed by the stretch of blue beyond. To the east, below the cliff edge, the flat landscape of the island is occasionally relieved by a sparse sweep of hills; to the south, birds of prey stream past the gleaming quarry which yields the stone for so many of Cuba's marble artefacts.

Before heading back to town, make time to explore the underground **Cueva del Agua**, whose entrance (24hr; free) is at the foot of the hill. The steep, narrow staircase cut from the rock bed can be slippery, so take care descending and bring a torch. Of the numerous caves dotted around the island, the natural lagoon and captivating rock formations make this one well worth a visit. Although locals sometimes swim in the large, rather stagnant lagoon, it's probably better for your health just to wade out a little way. The real treat of the cave lies along a narrow tunnel on the right-hand side just before the mouth of the pool, where intricate, glittery stalactites and stalagmites are slowly growing into elaborate natural sculptures.

Museo El Abra

Two kilometres southwest of town, on the road heading towards *Hotel Colony*, a signposted turning leads to the **Museo El Abra**

(Tues–Sun 9am–5pm; $2), the Spanish-style hacienda where José Martí (see p.90) spent three months in 1869. Although just sixteen years old, Martí had already founded the magazine *La Patria Libre*, and his editorials contesting Spanish rule had him swiftly pegged as a dissident. Arrested after the discovery of a letter he'd written to a friend accusing him of supporting Spain, Martí was sentenced to six years' hard labour in a chain gang working the San Lazaro stone quarry in Havana.

Thanks to the small amount of influence his father, a Havanan policeman, was able to use, the sentence was mitigated and the now ailing teenager was exiled to El Abra, where he was permitted to serve out his sentence under the custody of family friend and farm owner José María Sardá. Martí only spent three months there before the Spanish governor expelled him altogether, but it was long enough for the family to record that he was melancholic and quiet, and would wander through the handsome estate reading poetry. It was here that he wrote the essay *El presidio político en Cuba* ("The Political Prison in Cuba"), which became the seminal text of the independence struggle.

Nestling at the foot of the marble Sierra Los Caballeros, and edged with spiky mother-in-laws' tongue, the whitewashed farmhouse – with Spanish-style red-tiled roof, Caribbean-blue balustrade windows and a charming stone sundial from Barcelona – has rather more style than substance. Inside is a strained collection of inconsequential artefacts from Martí's life, or at least those that could be spared by larger museums in Havana. Letters and documents vie for attention with his old bed and with a replica of the manacles from which Martí was freed on his arrival.

Blessed with panoramic views, the lakeside Restaurant El Abra, 5km further south along the Carretera Siguanea, serves basic comida criolla.

Museo de Presidio Modelo

Overlooked by the mountains of the Sierra de Caballos, the **Museo de Presidio Modelo** (Tues–Sat 8am–4pm, Sun 8am–1pm; free) lies 2km east of Nueva Gerona – turn off the road to Bibijagua at the small housing scheme of Reparto Chachol. Although this massive former prison has housed a fascinating museum for over thirty years and is now one of the most visited sights on the island, its forbidding atmosphere has been preserved. Surrounded by guard towers, the classically proportioned governor's mansion and phalanx of wardens' villas mask the four circular cell buildings which rise like witches' cauldrons from the centre of the complex.

Commissioned by the dictator Machado, the "Model Prison" was built in 1926 by its future inmates as an exact copy of the equally notorious Joliet Prison in Illinois. At one time, it was considered the definitive example of efficient design, as up to six thousand prisoners could be controlled with a minimum of staff, but it soon became infamous for unprecedented levels of corruption and cruelty. The original plan for six wings was amended to four but even so, the capacity in the circular blocks alone was for 3720 men. The last prisoner was released in 1967, since when the buildings have slid into decay, although the magnificent governor's mansion has been converted into an extracurricular centre, run by the Pioneros organization (similar to the Scouts and Guides movement), where children between eight and fifteen years old can develop their academic and vocational skills.

The prison
Unmanned by the museum staff and falling into disrepair, the four huge cylindrical **cell blocks** – which you are free to wander into – still feel as oppressive as they must have been when crammed with inmates. As you wander past row after row of vacant cells, and listen to the eerie echo, it's easy to imagine the desperation and injustice in which the prison's history is steeped. The prisoners, housed two or more to a cell, were afforded no privacy, with every moment of their lives on view through the iron bars. Note the gun slits cut into the grim tower in the dead centre of each block, allowing one guard and his rifle to control nearly a thousand inmates from a position of total safety. To really appreciate the creepy magnitude of the cell blocks you can take the narrow marble staircase to the top floor, although with all the iron bars and railings long since removed, it's not a trip for vertigo sufferers.

The prison museum
Less disturbing than the cell blocks, the **prison museum** (Tues–Sat 8am–4pm, Sun 8am–1pm; $2, photography $3 extra) is located in the hospital block at the back of the grounds. Knowledgeable, Spanish-speaking guides take you round and will expect a small tip. While the exhibits include scores of original blueprints, faded ledgers of prison admissions and other unexceptional artefacts like giant soup pots – painstakingly hoarded for the best part of seventy years – the captivating showpieces like the impressive portfolio of 1930s stills of prisoners breaking rock and the aerial photos of the massive complex more than compensate.

The most impressive part of the museum, however, is the dormitory beyond the courtyard, where **Fidel Castro** and the rebels of the Moncada attack (see pp.398–99) were sequestered on the orders of Batista, for fear of them inflaming the other prisoners with their firebrand ideas. Above each of the 26 beds is the erstwhile occupant's mug shot, with a brief biography, and a piece of black cloth on each sheet symbolizes the rags the men tore from their trouser legs to cover their eyes at night, when lights were shined on them constantly as torture.

On February 13, 1954, Batista made a state visit to the prison. As he and his entourage passed their window, the rebels broke into a revolutionary anthem. As a result, Castro was confined alone in the room that now opens off the main entrance but was at the time next to the morgue, within full view of the corpses. For the early part of his forty-week sentence he was forbidden any light – prompting the wry joke that he now metes out the same to his own people in the form of the frequent blackouts. Despite the prohibition, a crafty homemade lamp – a replica of which is displayed in one corner – enabled Castro to read from his small library and to perfect the speech he had made at his defence, which was later published by the underground press as *La Historia me absolvara* and became the manifesto of the cause. His bed sits in the middle of the room and while there is nothing intrinsically remarkable about it, you can squeeze in an extra thrill by perching on it yourself.

If you have any foreign notes or souvenirs you can leave them for the guards' display cabinet, which is gradually filling up with items from around the world.

The northern beaches

East of the Presidio Modelo, a couple of beaches lie just a bike ride away from town. Take the signposted turning off the main road from the prison, from where it's a pleasant 2km to **Playa Paraíso**. The small hoop of somewhat grubby, seaweed-strewn sand is redeemed by a striking hill behind, whose shadow lengthens over the beach in the afternoon. About 60m out to sea the odd hump of land, **Cayo los Monos**, used to be a monkey zoo but is now deserted.

Rather better is **Playa Bibijagua**, another 4km along the road, which has an attractive and well-maintained grassy approach through the *Hotel Bibijagua* (closed indefinitely for repairs). Billed as a black-sand beach, it's actually a mottled brownish colour, the result of marble deposits in the sand. Although not the prettiest beach on the island, it has a charming view over a curve of coastline enveloped with pine trees, and a lively atmosphere, with local families watching their children play and men fishing patiently on the pier.

The rest of the island

Travelling south along the sole main road, the land is like a tamed and well-run estate, with row upon row of orderly fields and orchards. It is sparsely inhabited, with only a few bunches of neat houses clustered into modest roadside hamlets. The road runs out just west of **La Fe**, the island's tiny second settlement, before dissolving into the pot-holed track that leads south. At the point where the fecund farmland begins to metamorphose into swampland is an open-plan **crocodile farm**, home to several hundred reptiles bred every year for release into the southern marsh, and, just beyond, the military checkpoint at **Cayo Piedra** (see box overleaf).

Rumours abound concerning the purpose of the **military zone**, but the primary function seems to be to conserve the area to the southeast that forms the **Siguanea nature reserve**, parts of which

Isla de la Juventud

Crossing the military border

To cross the military zone you will need to buy a **pass** and engage a **registered guide** before you set off. The only place to organize this is through the Havanautos office at Calle 32 esq. 20, Nueva Gerona. Be aware that the staff in the Havanautos office have been known to overcharge for the service: a car plus guide should come to no more than $59 a day. As you'll have to make the trip in a rental car, it's a good idea to find some other people with whom to split the cost. You shouldn't encounter any difficulties at the checkpoint as long as you avail yourself of the necessary documentation – there's usually only one or two guards there to wave you past the checkpoint hut; however, should you arrive at the checkpoint without a guide and pass you will be unceremoniously turned back.

are closed to the public, as the luxuriant vegetation of the area shelters such **wildlife** as the tocoroco, Cuba's national bird, wild deer and green parrots. However, it has been rumoured that the military are in occupation because rogue parcels of narcotics floating in from other Latin American countries wash up on its southern shores. Another theory claims that since the 1960s it has been seen as an ideal invasion point for counter-revolutionaries based in Miami.

As flat as the north, if not more so, the land south of the checkpoint conforms to the storybook ideal of a desert island, with caves and sinuous beaches fringing a swampy interior of mangroves and thick shrubs teeming with wild deer, gigantic crabs and the green parrots that are endemic to the island. It's also home to one of the most impressive sights on the island: the **pre-Columbian paintings** in the caves of the Punta del Este, which are believed to date back some 1100 years, making them among the oldest in the Caribbean. The white-sand beaches of nearby **Playa Punta del Este** and **Playa Larga**, further along the coast, are clean and soft, though a bit narrow.

Further south near the island's western hook is **Cocodrilo**, a tiny hamlet cupped by the sea that's a pocket of English speakers, with a population largely descended from the Cayman Islanders who came over in the early part of the twentieth century. Its pleasant charms are increased by a rugged granite-rock coastline that forms natural pools and is ideal for snorkelling. An additional attraction here is the Sea Turtle Breeding Centre, which allows you to view several species at close range. Close by, **Playa El Francés**, named after the French pirate Latrobe who spent time there, is easily the island's best white-sand beach and accordingly is often reserved by the cruise ships that dock nearby once a week – check when you apply for your southern permit. The diving off this western point is superb, with over fifty sites to explore, among them two wrecks sunk in the 1970s and a wall of black coral.

La Fe and the Criadero Cocodrilo

The island's one motorway – such as it is – heads south from Nueva Gerona through orchards and pine forests towards the southern marshes. Though it's bypassed by the road, you can take a marked turning to detour through LA FE, or Santa Fe as it's sometimes called by Pineros, the island's second largest town, 27km from Nueva Gerona – although it's not much more than a handful of streets lined with utilitarian housing blocks built after the revolution.

The town lives out a modest existence, with little to attract visitors other than the **Manantial de Santa Rita** (open 24hr; 1 peso), a natural underground spring which surfaces at the northeast end of town. The small but deep red-brick well and nearby bathing area date back to the mid-1880s, when La Fe became quietly popular with well-to-do Creoles who came to bathe and take the waters, which were reputed to cure a multitude of complaints from tuberculosis, laryngitis and kidney complaints to arthritis, epilepsy and even elephantiasis. Although it remained popular in the twentieth century with visiting North Americans, it fell into disrepair in the 1960s, and was gradually submerged by floods and land movement. Work started in mid-1999 to drain the excess water and there are tentative plans to re-develop the site as a tourist attraction. Although work is in process you can still take a dip, but drinking the water is not a good idea no matter what locals may tell you.

Criadero Cocodrilo

A subtle change begins to come over the terrain beyond La Fe, as the road opens up with potholes and the prolific fruit groves gradually become marshy thicket. Just past the settlement of Julio Antonio Mella, 12km south of La Fe, a turning heads left off the road to the **Criadero Cocodrilo** (Mon–Fri 7am–5pm, Sat & Sun 7am–4pm; $3). Looking more like a swampy wilderness than a conventional farm, the crocodile nursery is, on closer inspection, teeming with reptiles. The large white basins near the entrance form the nursery for a seething mass of four-month-old, 25cm-long snappers, surprisingly warm and soft to the touch – ask to pick one up. Nearby, what at first looks like a seed bed reveals itself to be planted with a crop of crocodile eggs which are removed from the female adults once laid, and incubated for around eighty days before hatching.

Take small dollar bills to pay the entrance fee and to tip, as the keepers rarely have change.

The crocodiles are endemic to the area, but were in danger of extinction until the creation of the farm. It keeps five hundred animals at any one time, and periodically releases herds of crocodiles into the southern wilds when they reach seven years of age. The prize of the collection is a 25-year-old monster kept as a showpiece: 3m long and weighing 186kg, the irascible male eats once every three days and conserves his energy by lying motionless most of the time,

---

To visit anywhere beyond the crocodile farm means crossing the military border, for which you'll need a pass and a guide; see box opposite for full details.

---

although the keeper will obligingly throw him a couple of titbits so you can watch his head whip round at an astonishing speed.

Cuevas de Punta del Este

Within walking distance of the coast, 17km down a dirt track leading east from Cayo Piedra, the **Punta del Este** caves, half-buried amid overgrown herbs and greenery, contain significant examples of early pre-Columbian art, pointing to an established culture on the island as early as 900 AD. The paintings are among the few remaining traces of the Ciboney – the first inhabitants of Cuba – who arrived from South America via other Caribbean islands between three and four thousand years ago and are thought to have died out shortly after the paintings were made.

The caves were discovered by accident at the turn of the twentieth century by one Freeman P. Lane, who disembarked on the beach and sought shelter in the cave. The discovery made archeologists reconsider their assumption that Ciboney culture was primitive: the paintings are thought to represent a solar calendar and reveal that they had a sophisticated cosmology. Annually, on March 22, the sun streams through a natural hole in the roof, illuminating the pictographs in a beam of sunlight. Being linked to the vernal equinox, the effect is thought to celebrate fertility and the cycle of life and death. When bones were excavated from the back of the cave in 1939, it became apparent that its function was not only ceremonial, but that it had also been used for habitation and burial.

Of the 230 pictographs, the most prominent are the tight rows of concentric red and black circles overlapping one another on the low ceiling of the largest of the six caves (**Cave One**). Despite creeping erosion by a particularly virulent algae, the fading images are still very visible. Major excavation work got under way in the 1940s, when five more caves were discovered, though the paintings within are in a far worse state of repair and you'll need a keen eye to spot them. Even so, you should take a look at **Cave Two**, 500m away, where more fragments of circles are outshone by the fragile remains of a painted fish.

Further along the path, tufts of undergrowth give way to beach after a surprisingly short distance. The small white-sand strand of **Playa Punta del Este**, sown with sea grass and rimmed by mangroves, is a good spot for a refreshing dip, though it can't compare to the beauty of the beaches to the south.

Playa Larga and the Carapachibey lighthouse

Following the road south from the checkpoint all the way to the coast, you come to the narrow wedge of sand that comprises **Playa Larga**. Though not really the best spot for a swim, it's a popular place with local fishermen from Cocodrilo, to the west, and the pretty pine-backed stretch is littered with golden-pink conch shells emptied of their flesh and discarded by fishermen. The beach was the landing site for several Camagüean *balseros* (rafters) intent on emigrating to the United States, who arrived here in 1994 after a turbulent journey from the mainland, jubilantly believing themselves to be on North American soil, only to discover that they had not left Cuban territory.

About 5km west of Playa Larga you can take a quick detour down the pine-lined drive to the **Carapachibey lighthouse**. Although it looks Art Deco in its straight-lined simplicity, it wasn't built until 1983 and only enjoyed thirteen trouble-free years before being damaged by Hurricane Lili in 1996. It has since been repaired and a wall surrounding the base shows typical Cuban resourcefulness, being made of rubble salvaged from the destruction. While you can't go up the tower it's worth a look in passing.

Cocodrilo and the Sea Turtle Breeding Centre

A few kilometres north of Playa Larga, the main highway from Nueva Gerona branches west to run along the southern coast of the island, petering out just beyond **COCODRILO**. This peaceful haven boasts just a few palm-wood houses and a school, in front of a village green that backs onto the sea. Isolated from the north of the island by poor transport and the military checkpoint, it's a fairly rustic community seemingly unaffected by the developments of the twentieth century, albeit healthy and well educated thanks to the revolution. Originally named Jacksonville, after one of its first families, the hamlet was founded at the beginning of the twentieth century by Cayman Islanders who came to hunt the large numbers of turtles – now depleted – that once populated the waters and nested along the southern beaches.

At the north end of the hamlet, cupped by a semicircle of rocky cliff, the electric-blue water of a natural **rock pool** is an excellent place to spend a few hours. It's about a two-metre drop to the water below, but take care if jumping, as the pool is shallow. If you've brought equipment, it's also worth heading offshore to snorkel among the myriad tiny, darting fish.

You can get a good lunch near the rock pool, where the proprietor of the blue house sometimes serves up tasty plates of lobster and fish for around $5 a head.

The Sea Turtle Breeding Centre

One kilometre west from the village, past breaks in the coastline where spume shoots through gaps in the rocks, is the frequently unstaffed **Experimental Sea Turtle Breeding Centre** (daily 9am–5pm; free). Swimming in rows of tanks, livid-green with algae, the turtles range in size from hand-sized tiddlers to impressively huge adults. The centre is not a tourist attraction but rather an attempt to boost the turtle population, which is depleted every year by hunting. Though the farm is a worthy attempt to redress the problem, some of its pens do seem rather overcrowded and several of the turtles have battered and beaten fins where others have taken a chunk out of them.

Despite the efforts of conservationists, turtle meat is still considered a delicacy in Cuba, and turtleshell products, including mounted heads, are widely available. Legislation is in place to limit turtle hunting and ban it outright during the breeding season, but there are always those who flout the law. Refusing to buy turtle products is one way of helping conservation efforts.

Punta Francés and the Hotel Colony

From Cocodrilo a track heads northwest to the island's most remote upturned hook of land, **Punta Francés**, where you'll find the silver sands and limpid water that make **Playa Francés** the island's top beach. Equally attractive is the excellent **diving** offshore (see box below). Punta Francés is not the easiest place to visit independently, as it is often closed to allow cruise ship passengers to enjoy the

---

Diving off the west coast

There are two places on the island where you can organize diving: the *Hotel Colony* and the Marina Siguanea. A three-day CMAS course with either costs $300 and gives you a training day in the swimming pool, plus four dives. If you already have a diving certificate, a single dive costs $35, two dives in a day $56, and a night dive $40.

There are over fifty sites close to Punta Francés, running from north to south, parallel to the west coast, while Los Indios Wall and the two shipwrecks are all close to Cayos Los Indios, about 30km from the *Hotel Colony*. The best sites are listed here.

El Arco de los Sábalos, 2km northwest of Punta Francés. At a depth of just 13m, this is a straightforward dive for initiates, teeming with inquisitive yellowtail snappers, tarpon and bright sponges.

El Cabezo de la Isabelitas, 5km west of Playa El Francés. This shallow site has plenty of natural light and a cornucopia of fishes, including goatfish, trumpetfish and parrotfish. An uncomplicated dive, ideal for beginners.

Cueva Azul, 2km west of Playa El Francés. Reaching depths of 42m, this site takes its name ("the blue cave") from the intensely coloured water. Although there are several notable types of fish to be seen, the principal thrill of this dive is ducking and twisting through the cave's crevices.

Los Indios Wall, 5km from Cayos Los Indios. A host of stunning corals, including brain, star and fire coral, cling to a sheer wall that drops to the sea bed. At 30m, there's black coral, while you can see stingrays on the bottom, some as long as 2m. At $10 it's cheaper than the other dives in the area, but you need a minimum of five people.

Jibacoa and Sparta, 15km north of Playa El Francés. A small, uninhabited clutch of cays, these two wrecks are shallow enough to be seen by snorkellers. You can arrange transfer from Marina Siguanea ($10) although you must have at least a group of four.

Pared de Coral Negro, 4km northwest of Punta Francés. The black coral that gives this dive its name is found at 35m, while the rest of the wall is alive with colourful sponges and brain corals as well as several species of fish and green moray eels.

Latrobe's treasure

The beach at **Punta Francés** is named after the French pirate Latrobe, who frequented the Ensenada de la Siguanea, on the north side of the land spit. In 1809 he singlehandedly captured two Spanish ships laden with gold and jewels and made swiftly for the southern coast to hide, rightly deducing that the theft was unlikely to pass unavenged. With just time to bury his treasure, Latrobe was captured by North Americans and sent to Kingston, Jamaica, where he was promptly executed for piracy.

The whereabouts of the treasure has haunted bounty hunters ever since. The night before his execution Latrobe is supposed to have written a note to his fellow pirate Jean Lafitte, cryptically hinting that the hoard was buried ninety paces "from the mouth of the boiling spring", but Lafitte never received the note and the treasure is still hidden. Though unlikely to be anything more than romantic fancy, legend has it that the booty is buried somewhere on the coast of the Ensenada de la Siguanea.

beach without the hoi polloi; ask if the beach is open when you buy your permit for the military zone, and bear in mind there are no facilities there whatsoever.

The best way to get to the beach, with guaranteed access, is to take a **diving trip** with the *Hotel Colony* or nearby Marina Siguanea, around the bay from Punta Francés and reachable by road from Nueva Gerona. Built in the 1950s by the Batista regime as a casino hangout for American sophisticates, **Hotel Colony** (☎61/9-81-81; ④) was abandoned just weeks after its opening when Batista fled the revolution. It's now somewhat run-down and old-fashioned, but still the only place to stay with access to Punta Francés. **Turistaxi** is based here and can pick up and drop off in Nueva Gerona by arrangement (☎61/9-82-81). Two kilometres south of the hotel, the **Marina Siguanea** (daily 8am–6pm) offers the same variety of dives and courses as the hotel and has a decompression chamber. Small and strictly functional, the marina is not somewhere to pass time: there are no services other than the dive facilities and a medical post.

Cayo Largo

Separated from the Isla de la Juventud by 140km, **Cayo Largo**, a narrow, low-lying spit of land fringed with powdery beaches, is totally geared to package-holiday makers. The tiny islet, measuring just 20km from tip to beachy tip, caters to the quickening flow of European and Canadian tourists who swarm here to enjoy the excellent watersports, diving and Club Med-style hotels. For a holiday cut adrift from responsibilities and the outside world, this pristine island is as good a choice as any, though some may find it a tad contrived.

Life on the cay began in 1977 when the state, capitalizing on the extensive white sands and offshore coral reefs, built the first of eight hotels that now line the western and southern shores. There

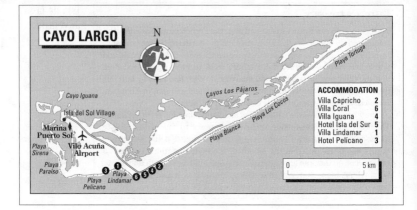

is still ample room for development, however, and whilst plans are underway for more hotels, the cay has a long way to go before it is spoilt; indeed so sparse is the infrastructure away from the hotels that at times hanging out in the resort can seem rather monotonous. The artificiality which works well in the hotels fails somewhat in the small "village" on the west of the island, which has a distinctly spurious air: it's just a sparse collection of a shop, restaurants and a bank and, behind the tourist facade, blocks of workers' accommodation.

Arrival, information and transport

All national and international **flights** arrive at the tiny Vilo Acuña airport, 1km from the main belt of hotels; courtesy buses meet every flight and whisk passengers off to their hotels. All domestic flights are from Havana, on a rickety Russian twenty-seater plane; note that if you come independently, you will need to book accommodation when you arrange your flight. As there is no boat service between the islands, only **yacht** owners – for whom the clear shallow seas, excellent fishing and serviceable marinas make it a favourite destination – can breeze in by water to the main *Marina Puerto Sol* on the village coastline.

Though there is no main **tourist office** on the cay, the reception at the *Villa Iguana* offers general information and also has a Cubatur office running excursions. You can buy **maps** at the main hotel complex shop and there's a **bank** on the corner of the village plaza. Although the cay promotes itself as all-inclusive, diving, motor sports and excursions usually cost extra.

The island is small enough to negotiate easily and courtesy **buses** regularly do the circuit of the hotels, running from early morning to midnight. A free **ferry** leaves from the marina to Playa Sirena and Playa Paraíso twice daily at 9.30am and 11am, returning at 3pm and

5pm. There's also a speedboat service running intermittently, charging $2. The best way to take in the east of the island is to rent a moped from the Havanautos office in front of the *Villa Iguana*. It also rents out dune buggies, bone-shaker bicycles and cars, though there's little point in renting the last of these.

Accommodation

Though the standard is high, **hotels** are not cheap as they tend to be block-booked by overseas package-tour operators at a specially discounted rate. If you're not on a package booked from abroad then you'll have to choose your accommodation when you buy your flight as flights and prebooked accommodation to Cayo Largo are sold as a deal by tour operators. All eight hotels are all-inclusive, between them forming a complex offering a range of shared facilities. The price codes below represent what you'll pay if you book through a Cuban tour operator.

The address of each hotel is: Cayo Largo del Sur Archipiélago de los Canarreos and, with the exception of Hotel Pelícano, they all share a phone and fax number ☎ 61/4-81-11; fax 4-82-01.

Villa Capricho Ideal for couples, with a series of rustic thatched cabins comprising all the accommodation, each with a hammock and sea view. The buffet, bar and curvy pool make this a good choice. ⑦.

Villa Coral Fresh and very user-friendly, this attractive hotel has graceful, pale yellow blocks with red-tiled roofs, divided by neat beds of sea shrubs and palms to ensure a sense of privacy. Rooms have spacious sun terraces and balconies while the pool area is the most attractive on the cay, with smart sun terraces and shaded seating surrounding a circular pool. The lack of an all-inclusive restaurant on site may prove inconvenient, though. ⑦.

Villa Iguana Lacking a focal point of its own, the *Villa Iguana* is very much linked to neighbouring *Isla del Sur* and the two hotels really function as one large though lacklustre establishment. Although the rooms are clean and well appointed, it's still slightly jaded, with a tired little bar and refectory-style canteen. Not the choice if you like your comfort to be matched by style. ⑦.

Isla del Sur Though its reception is sunny and pleasant, this is a slightly dowdy hotel with rooms strung along old-style shadowy corridors. Along with the *Hotel Iguana* next door, it is the cay's least-expensive option. ⑦.

Villa Lindamar Backing onto an ample stretch of beach lined with sun shades and loungers, the spacious thatched cabins perch on stilts and overlook a garden of sea grass and hibiscus bushes. Each stylish cabin feels self-contained and private – a definite plus. ⑧.

Hotel Pelícano ☎ 61/4-83-33; fax 4-80-67. The only hotel to have its own independent reception, the *Hotel Pelícano* is an appealing, buzzy, Caribbean-themed hotel on wide and roomy Playa Pelícano. With smart rooms in stylish white-washed blocks set around palm trees and rather parched lawns, it is the biggest and plushest place on the cay, with a clientele of twenty-something couples, families and retirees all mingling happily. ⑨.

Villa Soledad A poor relation to the other hotels. Although it has comfortable, well-kept rooms, some with a sea view, it's let down by the absence of pool, restaurant and snack bar, which makes it rather odd that it's more expensive than *Villa Iguana* and *Hotel Isla del Sur*. ⑦.

The Cay

Whilst Cayo Largo is undoubtedly the stuff of exotic holiday fantasy, it's not a place to meet the people. There are no born-and-bred locals, and the hotel staff are from Havana, Isla de Juventud or further afield, living on the island in shifts, so whilst people are as easy-going and friendly as elsewhere in Cuba, the atmosphere is more than a little contrived.

Built on the southwestern coast – to optimize the pleasant view over cay-speckled waters – is the artificial **Isla del Sol village**. Among the prettified, red-roofed ochre buildings ranged around the small but attractive Plaza del Pirata you'll find the obligatory tourist trappings: a shop selling cigars, postcards and sunscreen, a bank, restaurant and bar. The main focal point is the **Marina Puerto Sol**, west of the plaza, and when motorboats dock to collect or release the sunbathers, snorkellers and divers en route to and from dive sites and beaches, the area bustles with activity. For the rest of the day the village sinks into a slightly unnerving somnolence, from which the attractions of the **Turtle Farm** (Tues–Sat 9am–4pm; $1), just off the plaza, offer a brief diversion. The farm houses a restless collection of the wild turtles that populate the waters around the archipelago. Although they look healthy enough, their small pens seem a poor exchange for the open sea.

There's rather more activity around the beaches to the south and along the hotel strip, where warm shallow waters lap the narrow ribbon of pale downy sand. Protected from harsh winds and rough waves by the offshore coral reef, and with over 2km of white sands, **Playa Sirena** enjoys a deserved reputation as the most beautiful of all the beaches and is consequently the busiest. There's a road to the beach from the *Pelícano Hotel*, but as it's frequently covered by rifts of sand you're better off catching one of the ferries or speed boats from the marina. There's a café (prices not included in the package) on the beach which serves drinks, sandwiches and snacks. Further south along the same

Rather than struggling through the sand rifts on the beach road that starts near Hotel Pelícano, the best way to get to the west coast beaches is to take the ferry from Marina Puerto Sol.

Diving and boat excursions on Cayo Largo

With over thirty **dive sites** in the clear and shallow waters around the cay, Cayo Largo is deservedly well-known as one of Cuba's best diving areas. Particularly outstanding are the coral gardens to be found in the shallow waters around Cayo Largo, while other highlights of the region include underwater encounters with hawksbill turtles and sea green turtles. The cay boasts two dive centres, one at the Marina Puerto Sol and the other on Playa Sirena, although both are managed by the marina and offer identical packages. Each dive costs $30, including all equipment and transfer to the dive site.

The marina also runs two **snorkelling** expeditions: to the coral gardens (40min; $14) and to the waters around the tiny Cayo Iguana, the nearest cay to Cayo Largo (50min; $12). For a more leisurely trip, you can marvel at the fabulous coral gardens from the safety of a glass-bottomed boat ($54 for the day). The waters around the cays also harbour excellent **fishing** and the marina offers deep-sea expeditions for $220 for four hours inclusive of equipment and $290 for eight hours. Also on offer is a day-trip in a **catamaran** which includes snorkelling and a lobster lunch ($69 for the day).

strand, **Playa Paraíso** is almost as attractive and popular as Sirena, with the added advantage that the shallow waters are ideal for children. Heading east, **Playa Lindamar** is a serviceable 5km curve of sand in front of the *Lindamar, Pelícano, Soledad* and *Villa Coral* hotels and is the only one where you can play volleyball and windsurf.

For real solitude you need to head off up the central road that runs the length of the island to the southeastern beaches. **Playa Blanca** boasts over 7km of deserted, soft beach, backed by sand dunes, and staking out your own patch shouldn't be a problem, though you'll need to bring your own refreshments as there's not an ice cream in sight. Further east still, the lovely **Playa los Cocos** is seemingly endless, and it's the only nudist beach on the cay. The far-flung **Playa Tortuga** is similarly deserted, while the interior is largely a mass of pine trees with not much to see.

Eating, drinking and entertainment

Although the holiday package entitles all visitors to eat in any of the buffet restaurants, only the better ones are listed below, along with the couple of restaurants that operate outside the deal. The food is fairly standard, with all the buffets offering a range of international dishes. The hotel bars tend to have more character, and you can sip from your bottomless glass of free cocktails in something approaching style.

Of the buffet **restaurants**, *Hotel Pelicano* has the largest selection and the cheeriest atmosphere. *Villa Coral* has a pleasant and airy snack bar in a pink-tiled pool area, serving small pizzas, sandwiches and ice cream. Also at the *Villa Coral* is an à la carte restaurant (not included in package), which serves reasonably authentic Italian food. Down in the quiet of the village, the thatched *Taberna del Pirata*, on the plaza overlooking the picturesque harbour, serves pricey lobster, fresh fish and the ubiquitous fillet of pork.

Hotel Pelicano is best for **drinking**, with a friendly lobby bar and a larger one by the pool that's mercifully set back from the stage where an entertainment team puts on nightly cabaret shows with enforced hilarity. The island **disco**, the *Iguana Azul*, on the west of the island, 2km from Isla del Sol village, is packed with sunburned merry-makers dancing to a selection of Latino and mainstream pop tunes.

Travel details

There is little public transport on the Isla de la Juventud – only a few bus routes, which are often cancelled. To journey south of the check-point you'll need to rent a car and guide (see box on p.446). There is no public transport on Cayo Largo.

BUSES

Nueva Gerona to: *Hotel Colony* (1 daily; 4hr); La Fe (2 daily; 2hr 30min); Reparto Chachol (3 daily; 30min).

La Fe to: *Hotel Colony* (1 daily; 4hr); Nueva Gerona (2 daily; 2hr 30min).

Reparto Chachol to: Nueva Gerona (3 daily; 30min).

The Contexts

A brief history of Cuba

The strategic and geographical importance of Cuba to the shifting global powers of the last five centuries has dictated much of this Caribbean island's history. Having served principally as a stepping stone between Spain and its vast American empire for 250 years, Cuba has been struggling to achieve a real and lasting independence ever since, passing from Spanish colony to US satellite and, despite the nationalist revolution of 1959, relying on economic support from the Soviet Union until 1989. At the start of the twenty-first century Cuba is at a crossroads, having finally reached a stage in its history when it can claim genuine self-sufficiency, with the ideals and achievements of one of the world's last remaining communist countries set firmly against survival in a capitalist global economy.

Pre-Columbian Cuba

Unlike Central America with its great Maya civilization, no advanced societies had emerged in Cuba by the time Columbus arrived in 1492. Although ancient cultures – Amerindians who had worked their way up through the Antilles from the South American mainland – had inhabited the island for thousands of years, they lived in simple dwellings and produced comparatively few artefacts and tools for future archeologists to discover. There are thought to have been at least 100,000 Amerindians living in Cuba on the eve of

the European discovery of the Americas, but piecing together the history of the island prior to the arrival of the Spanish relies heavily on guesswork.

The **Guanahatabey** were the first to arrive and were almost certainly living in Cuba by 3000 BC. These primitive hunter-gatherers were based in what is now Pinar del Río, often living in cave systems, such as the one in Viñales. The **Ciboney** arrived later and lived as fishermen and farmers, but it wasn't until the arrival of the **Taíno**, the last of the Amerindian groups to settle in Cuba, that the cultural make-up of the islanders reached a level of significant sophistication. Most historians agree that the Taíno found their way to Cuban shores around 1100 AD and certainly by the time Columbus got there they were the dominant cultural group. Settling predominantly in the eastern and central regions, they lived in small villages of circular thatched-roof huts known as *bohíos*, an architectural style replicated in hotel accommodation throughout the island today; grew tobacco, cassava, yucca and cotton; produced pottery; and practised religion. Though there is some evidence to suggest that the Taíno enslaved some of the Ciboney or drove them from their home territory, they were a mostly peaceful people, largely unprepared for the conflict they were to face once the Spanish arrived.

The conquest

On October 27, 1492, having already touched down in the Bahamas, **Christopher Columbus** landed on the northeastern coast of Cuba, probably in the natural harbour around which the town of Baracoa was later to emerge, though the exact spot where he first weighed anchor is hotly disputed. This first short expedition lasted only seven days, during which time Columbus marvelled at the Cuban landscape, briefly encountered the locals, who fled on sighting the new arrivals, and left a wooden cross now preserved in the Catedral Nuestra Señora de la Asunción in Baracoa.

On their second voyage of discovery in 1494, Columbus and his men worked their way along the southern coast of the island, landing also at the Isla de la Juventud. One of the principal aims of this expedition was to establish whether Cuba was an island or, as Columbus himself suspected, part of the mainland. After a number of weeks spent exploring, he concluded that the width of the coastline meant it was too large to be an island, and made every man in the fleet swear an oath that Cuba was part of the mainland of Cathay, or China. On his later voyages to the Caribbean, Columbus paid little attention to Cuba, but his insistence that he had discovered a western route to Asia left the Spanish unconvinced and by the time King Ferdinand sent an expedition for a more thorough exploration of the island, the myth had been dismissed.

The first colonial expedition did not begin until late 1509 when **Diego Velázquez**, a rich settler from neighbouring Hispaniola, and the man charged with the mission by the Spanish Crown, landed near Guantánamo Bay with three hundred men. By this time the Amerindians were wary of the possibility of an invasion, word having spread via refugees from other already occupied Caribbean islands. The most legendary of these forced immigrants was **Hatuey**, a bold Taíno from Hispaniola who led the most concerted resistance effort against the advancing colonists. The Indians fought fiercely but their initial success was cut short by the Spanish capture of Hatuey. Before burning him at the stake the Spaniards offered him salvation if he would convert to Christianity, an offer met with a flat refusal as Hatuey declared that heaven would be the last place he'd want to spend eternity if it was full of Christians.

The rest of the indigenous population did not last much longer and were either slaughtered or enslaved as the conquistadors worked their way west across the island, driving them eventually into the furthest reaches of Pinar del Río where, on the Península de Guanahacabibes, the last settlements of Cuban Amerindians lived out their final years. Those who were not killed died from either diseases brought over from Europe or the harsh living and working conditions forced upon them through the *encomienda* system (see below), whilst some even committed suicide rather than face enslavement. By the end of the sixteenth century there was almost no trace of the original Cuban population left.

Meanwhile the colonizers had exhausted the small reserves of gold on the island and interest in Cuba quickly died out as Spain expanded its territories in Central and South America, where there was far greater mineral wealth to be found. However, as Spain consolidated its American empire, Cuba gained importance thanks to its location on the main route to and from Europe, with ports like Havana becoming the principal stop-off points for ships carrying vast quantities of gold, silver and other riches across the Atlantic.

Colonization

By 1515 Velázquez had founded the first towns in Cuba, known as the **seven villas**: Baracoa, Santiago de Cuba, Bayamo, Puerto Príncipe (now Camagüey), Sancti Spíritus, Trinidad and San Cristóbal de la Habana. The population grew slowly, consisting mostly of Spanish immigrants, many from the Canary Islands, but also Italians and Portuguese. Numbers were also increased as early as the 1520s by the importation of African **slaves**, brought in to replace the dwindling indigenous population. Still, by the seventeenth century Havana, the largest city, had only a few hundred inhabitants.

Early colonial society was based on the **encomienda** system, whereby land and slaves, both African and Amerindian, were distributed to settlers by the ruling authorities. The conditions of slavery in Cuba during the sixteenth and much of the seventeenth centuries, though dehumanizing, were, in some ways, less oppressive than those experienced elsewhere, in the British colonies of North America, for example. This did not, however, signal that the Spanish colonizers were any more compassionate than their European counterparts, but merely reflected the comparative underdevelopment of the Cuban economy. The more advanced industries on islands such as Saint-Domingue and Jamaica meant not only a higher demand for slaves, but more gruelling living and working conditions for the slaves themselves.

The proportion of slaves in Cuba up until the British occupation of 1762 was lower than almost anywhere else in the Caribbean, the larger number of them working as servants in the cities, and the smaller scale of plantations translating to a less impersonal relationship between slave and master. Spanish law also influenced the conditions of slavery. Whereas the English allowed their colonies to develop their own independent codes of practice, the detailed laws governing slavery in Spain were applied equally to their territories overseas. Though this would not have necessarily meant that the Spanish slave master would have fed his slaves any better or punished them less brutally, it did grant slaves a degree of legal status unheard of in other European colonies. Slaves in the Spanish empire could marry, own property and even buy their freedom. Known as the right of *coartación*, this entitlement to freedom meant that by the eighteenth century there was a higher proportion of **free blacks** in Cuba than in any other major Caribbean island. Slaves would often earn money through extra work in the cities or by way of growing and selling their own produce, made possible by their right to own small plots of land. These rights were, on the other hand, far from guaranteed, with the lawmakers thousands of miles away in Spain, and the priorities of the Spanish Crown lay in the wealth its colonies could create, with the rights of slaves incidental at best. Furthermore, Spanish ordinances did as much to perpetuate slavery as they did to allow individual slaves their freedom. Laws were passed banning slaves from riding horses or from travelling long distances without their masters' permission and preventing women slaves from keeping their children. The life of a slave, particularly in the countryside, was a miserable existence, characterized by constant beatings, chains and shackles, overwork and suicides. The worst was yet to come, however, as the sugar boom of the late eighteenth and nineteenth centuries was to usher in the most intense period of slave importation in Cuban history (see p.462).

Many of the early settlers created huge cattle ranches, trading with the hides and meat, but the economy came to be based heavily on more profitable **agricultural farming**. Cassava, tropical fruits, coffee and increasingly tobacco and sugar were amongst the chief Cuban export products on which the colony's trade with Spain depended. Sugar production got off to a slow start, and sugar was initially produced principally for local consumption. However, as Europe developed its sweet tooth and the Spanish Crown saw the potential selling power of the crop, by the early seventeenth century the sugar industry was given preferential treatment, subsidized and exempted from duties, and an estimated fifty sugar mills were constructed. The commercial value of tobacco, on the other hand, was more immediate and needed no artificial stimulus. In fact, following its increased popularity in Europe

in the late sixteenth century, it became the object of increasing government regulation and taxation as the monarchy in Spain sought to commandeer the large profits being made through the **tobacco trade**. As tobacco farming expanded across the island it served to disperse the population further inland, in part because farmers sought to escape the fiscal grip of the colonial government, whose relatively scarce resources were concentrated in the towns and whose jurisdiction did not, effectively, apply to the Cuban interior.

Despite these developments the economic and political structure of Cuba remained relatively unchanged throughout the late sixteenth and seventeenth centuries. The island continued to be peripheral to the Spanish Empire and life evolved somewhat haphazardly, with contraband an integral part of the economy, removed from the attentions and concerns of the monarchy in Spain.

However, when, at the beginning of the eighteenth century, the Bourbon dynasty took over the throne in Spain, it sought to regain control of Spanish assets overseas, particularly in the Caribbean, and, through improved colonial administration and closer, more direct links between the empire and home, to direct more of the revenue from the colonies into royal purses. This was particularly true of Cuba, which had quietly and slowly become a source of potentially significant wealth. The Bourbons stepped up their monopoly on trade, and in 1717 ordered that all tobacco be sold to commercial agents of the Crown. Resentment from the tobacco farmers, by this time drawn predominantly from the Cuban-born population, increased as these Spanish agents paid them artificially low prices and, in the same year, growers in Havana revolted, surrounding the residence of the colonial governor. The uprising, and two subsequent ones in 1721 and 1723, were easily repressed by the colonial authorities and had no effect on the restrictive measures employed by the ruling elite. In fact these measures became even more institutionalized when in 1740 a trading company, the **Real Compañia de Comercio de la Habana**, was set up by a group of wealthy merchants in Havana. With direct links to Madrid, the Spanish merchants in charge of the company sought to control all trade entering and leaving Cuba, fixing artificially high prices on imported products from Europe and slaves from Africa whilst paying well below the odds for Cuban-produced items. Discontent increased as profits for Cuban producers dropped, and the lines drawn between the *criollos*, those of Spanish descent but born in Cuba, who tended to be small-scale farmers or members of the emerging educated urban class, and the *peninsulares*, those born in Spain who made up the ruling elite, became more pronounced. This situation was aggravated further when the Spanish monarch, King Philip V, reacting to the growing discontent in the colony, introduced dictatorial measures affecting the way in which Cuba was governed. Almost all political power was taken away from the local town authorities, known as *cabildos*, who up until then had worked in conjunction with the governor and shared the responsibility for the leasing of land, enforcement of the law and all general administrative duties. Power was now vested more exclusively in the governnor, enabling him to implement Spanish wishes without opposition. The military presence on the island, already considerable, especially in Havana, was stepped up as Cubans were frozen out of holding positions of any civil or military authority. These divisions between *criollos* and *peninsulares*, in other words between the interests of Spain and Cuba, were to widen during the course of the next century.

The first half of the eighteenth century saw Cuban society become more sophisticated, as wealth on the island slowly increased. Advancements in the **cultural** character of Cuba are particularly notable during this era, partly as a result of encouragement from the Bourbons but also as a consequence of an emerging Cuban identity, unique from that of Spain. By the end of the century the colony had established its first printing press, newspaper, theatre and university.

British occupation of Havana

Economic progress had been severely held back by the restrictive way in which Cuba, and indeed the whole Spanish Empire, was run by the Crown, forcing the colony to trade exclusively with Spain and draining the best part of the wealth away from the island into the hands of the colonial masters. This was to change in 1762 with the **British** seizure of Havana. Engaged in the Seven Years' War against Spain and France, the British sought to weaken the Spanish position by attacking Spain's possessions overseas.

With Spanish attention focused in Europe, the British navy prepared a strike on the Cuban capital, control of which would strengthen their own position in the Caribbean and disrupt trade between Spain and its empire. With a force of 200 ships and 22,000 men, the English landed at Cojímar, just outside the city, and attacked El Morro fortress. Militias from Havana and neighbouring Guanabacoa, made up largely of peasants and less than half the size of the British forces, managed to withstand a siege for two months under the leadership of José Antonio Gómez, better known as **Pepe Antonio**, a councilman from Guanabacoa. Despite this brave effort, on August 12, 1762, the British took control of Havana. They immediately lifted the disabling trade restrictions and opened up new markets in North America and Europe. Within eleven months Cuba was back in Spanish hands, exchanged with the British for Florida, but the impact of their short stay was enormous. A plethora of hitherto unobtainable and rarely seen products, including new sugar machinery as well as consumer goods, flowed into Cuba, brought by traders and merchants from the North American colonies and elsewhere in the Caribbean who were able for the first time to do business on the island. Cubans were able to sell their own produce to a wider market and at a greater profit and, even in such a short space of time, standards of living rose, particularly in the west where much of the increased commercial activity was focused. So much had changed by the time the Spanish regained control that to revert back to the previous system of tight controls would, the Bourbons realized, provoke fierce discontent amongst large and powerful sections of the population. What's more, the new Spanish king, Charles III, was more disposed to progressive reforms than was his predecessor, and the increased output and efficiency of the colony did not pass him by. Free trade was therefore allowed to continue, albeit not completely unchecked, transforming the Cuban economy beyond recognition.

Sugar and slavery

After 1762, with the expansion of trade, the profitability of sugar increased, causing the industry to begin operating on a much larger scale and marking a significant development in Cuban society. In 1776 the newly independent United

States was able to start trading directly with Cuban merchants whilst at the same time the demand for sugar in Europe and the US increased. The plantations and mills grew in number and size, and Cuban landowners began modernizing their means of production, leading to a considerable increase in output. However, none of this would have been possible without stepping up the size of the workforce and as a consequence slaves were imported in unprecedented numbers. The racial make-up of the island changed, shaping itself into something closer to the mix seen on the island today.

In 1791 **revolution in Haiti**, then known as Saint-Domingue, destroyed the sugar industry there and ended French control of one of its most valuable Caribbean possessions. Cuba was now the largest producer of sugar in the region. Fleeing Haiti, thousands of French sugar plantation owners and coffee growers settled in Cuba, bringing with them their superior knowledge of sugar production. The decrease in the world supply of sugar caused by the revolution coincided with a rising demand, principally in Europe and North America, which in turn sent prices up, whilst Cuba gained a greater share of the market. These developments, combined with scientific advances in the sugar industry and improved transportation routes on the island during the first four decades of the nineteenth century, transformed the face of Cuban society. The introduction of steam power to Cuban mills in 1817, the construction of the first Cuban railroad, completed in 1838, and the destruction of forests to clear the way for sugar plantations, all contributed to the sugar boom that has characterized the history of the island. With ever increasing portions of the land being taken over for the planting of sugarcane and the number of mills rising from just over 500 in 1792 to over 1400 in 1850, labour, still the most important component in the production of sugar, was needed on a vast scale. In the 1820s some 60,000 **slaves** were brought to the island and total numbers during the first half of the nineteenth century reached over 350,000.

As the size of the slave population swelled so the conditions of slavery, particularly in the sugar industry, worsened, fuelled by the plantation owners' insatiable appetites for profit. The seemingly endless demand for sugar, increasingly from the United States, and the capacity to meet these demands meant slaves were worked harder than ever before. Those who worked in the cities, as domestic servants, coachmen, gardeners, carpenters and even musicians, were afforded higher status than rural slaves, with greater opportunities to earn extra cash, closer relationships with their white masters, and sexual relations between black and white all features of urban life. The story was quite different in the countryside, where the vast majority of slaves lived and worked. Some worked on coffee and tobacco farms, but most were involved in sugar production, where conditions were at their worst. On the vast sugar estates, the kind of personal relationships between master and slaves found in the towns, cities and the more intimate tobacco and coffee plantations were nonexistent. Where before, in the seventeenth and eighteenth centuries, slaves had lived in collections of small huts and even been allowed to work their own small plots of land, now they were crowded into barrack buildings and all available land was turned over to sugarcane. Floggings, beatings and the use of stocks were common forms of **punishment** for even minor insubordinations and often were used as an incentive to work harder. The whip was in constant use, employed to keep the slaves on the job and to prevent them from falling asleep, most likely during the harvest season when they could be made to work for eighteen hours of every day for months at a time.

Unsurprisingly, such harsh treatment met with resistance and **slave rebellions** became more common in the 1840s, 50s and 60s. A large proportion of the slaves in Cuba during this period were West African Yoruba, a people with a strong military tradition, who enacted frequent and fierce revolts against their oppressors. Uprisings were usually spontaneous, and frequently very violent, often involving the burning and breaking of machinery and the killing of whites. Not all sugar estates experienced rebellion, but those owned by particularly ruthless sugar barons, or run by especially cruel overseers, suffered recurring disturbances. A minority of slave rebellions were highly organized and even involved whites and free blacks. Two such revolts occurred in Matanzas, where sugar production, and therefore slavery, was most intensely concentrated, followed by the other three main sugar provinces, Colón, Santiago de Cuba and Sagua la Grande. In 1825 a slave uprising there resulted in the destruction of 25 sugar estates; another in 1843 at the Triunvirato estate, also in Matanzas, involving several hundred slaves, was afterwards declared to have been part of a conspiracy to overthrow the government. Such scaremongering was commonly used by the colonial authorities as justification for the executions that always followed uprisings and the continued use of brutally repressive measures to prevent similar rebellions in the future.

Reform versus independence

In the final decade of the eighteenth century and the first few decades of the nineteenth, a number of new cultural and political institutions emerged, alongside new scientific developments, all aimed specifically at improving the lives of Cubans. Though most of these changes affected only a small proportion of Cubans they formed the roots of a **national identity**, a conception of Cuba as a country with its own culture, its own people and its own needs, separate from those of the Spanish, who formed a minority of the population but held all the highest political and administrative positions.

In 1791 the **Sociedad Económica de Amigos del País** was established, counting many big *criollo* landowners amongst its founder members. This organization was set up to promote business interests in all areas of industry, agriculture and commerce, acting as an avenue through which scientific, economic and political information could be shared, for the mutual benefit of the island's businesses. As time passed its role expanded and it began actively encouraging educational programmes, opening the first public library in Cuba and providing financial support to schools. The founder of the society, a leading sugar mill owner named **Francisco de Arango y Parreño**, sought to enhance production techniques within the industry whilst favouring the abolition of internal restrictions on trade, such as the tobacco monopoly and restrictions on buying and selling land, which, despite the improvements since the British occupation of Havana, still existed. In the same year as the founding of the Sociedad Económica de Amigos del País, 1791, the *Papel Periódico de la Habana*, Cuba's first **newspaper**, was published, written with solely Cuban interests in mind. There were scientific developments during the 1790s also, including the introduction of the first steam engine for use on sugar plantations and the use of water mills for the first time in Cuba.

The slave rebellions, which tended to increase in number and frequency as each decade of the nineteenth century passed, were symptomatic of an increasingly divided society, one which pitted *criollos* against *peninsulares*, black against white, and the less developed eastern half of the country against the more economically and politically powerful west. However, further lines of division were drawn between each of these opposing groups so that, for example, a wealthy *criollo* sugar baron in the west had closer ties and greater coinciding interests with the Spanish administrators controlling trading laws than with a small-scale *criollo* farmer from the east. The sugar boom had caused Cuban society to become more stratified, creating sharper lines between the landed elite, who had benefited most from the sugar revolution, and the smaller landowners, petit bourgeoisie and free blacks who had become increasingly marginalized by the dominance of large-scale sugar production.

The American Revolution of 1776 proved to be a precursor to the wars of independence that swept across mainland Spanish America during the initial decades of the nineteenth century, prompted by Napoleon's invasion of Spain in 1808 which cut the colonial master off from its subjects, leaving Spain with just Puerto Rico and Cuba by 1826. Though these events inspired ideas of independence and freedom amongst Cuban traders, merchants and farmers who desired greater autonomy and more political power, there were forces against independence not found on the mainland that delayed the arrival of Cuba's own bid for self-rule. Not least of these was the period of economic prosperity, which had come late to Cuba compared to other Spanish colonies and went some way to appeasing sections of the wealthier classes that had, up until the sugar boom, desired self-government as a way to greater profit. Furthermore, most *criollos* identified more closely with the Spanish than with the black slave population, who, by the start of the nineteenth century, formed a larger part of the total population than in any other colony, and *criollo* calls for reform were tempered by a fear of the slaves gaining any influence or power. The economy in Cuba relied more heavily on slavery than any of the South American states, with the livelihood of *criollos* and *peninsulares* alike dependent upon its continued existence.

Nevertheless, a **reformist movement** did emerge, but though there were a number of dissatisfied groups, they were unable to present a united front as their various grievances did not form a compatible set of demands. There were calls, predominantly from big businessmen and well-to-do trade merchants, for fiscal reform within Spanish rule; separatists who wanted total independence; and another group still that formed an **annexationist movement** whose goal was to become part of the United States. As the US was the biggest single market for Cuban sugar, many of the largest plantation owners supported the idea; there was growing support within the US, too, where it was felt that Cuba held tremendous strategic importance, especially since the purchase of Louisiana in 1803, which had made the Mississippi a vital trading route for the central states. Annexation was attempted by force when **Narcisco López** led an invasion at Bahía Honda in 1851, with an army recruited in the US, but failed miserably, in part because López, a former officer in the Spanish army, spoke as little English as his troops spoke Spanish.

With the wealthier *criollos* and the *peninsulares* unwilling to push for all-out independence, the separatist cause was taken up most fervently by *criollos* of modest social origins and free blacks. Their agenda, unaffected by the concerns of their wealthier counterparts, became not just independence but social justice and, most importantly, the abolition of slavery. As the reformist movement became more radical, Spanish fear of revolution intensified and, following the slave rebellions in Matanzas and elsewhere in the country in the early 1840s, the colonial government reacted with a brutal campaign of repression known as **La Escalera** – the ladder – taking its name from a punishment employed by the Spanish which involved tying the victim to a ladder and whipping them. In an atmosphere of hysteria fuelled by the fear that a nationwide slave uprising was imminent, the Spanish authorities killed hundreds of enslaved and free black suspects and arrested thousands more. At the same time, the military presence on the island grew as soldiers were sent over from Spain, and the governor's power was increased to allow repression of even the slightest sign of rebellion. The reform movement and the abolition of slavery became inextricably linked, and this idea was increasingly embraced by reformers themselves. In 1865 the **Reformist Party** was founded by a group of *criollo* planters, providing the most

coherent expression yet of the desire for change. Amongst their demands were a call for Cuban representation in the Spanish parliament and equal legal status for *criollos* and *peninsulares*.

The wars of independence

The life of the Reformist Party proved to be a short one. In 1865 an official review of the demands of the party had been set up by the liberal O'Donnell administration in Spain. However, two years later the Junta de Información, the board that had been elected to carry out the review, was dismissed by a new, reactionary Spanish government. Having failed to obtain a single concession the Reformist Party soon dissolved, whilst the reform movement as a whole took further blows as the new Spanish government issued a wave of repressive measures, including the banning of political meetings and censorship of the press. Meanwhile, pro-independence groups were gaining momentum in the east, where the proportions of *criollos* to *peninsulares* was twice that in the west and where the interests of smaller planters had become increasingly overlooked, isolated by the huge sugar estate owners whose land was concentrated in the west.

Since 1866 a group of landowners, headed by **Carlos Manuel de Céspedes**, had been plotting a revolution; it had got no further than the planning stage when the colonial authorities learned of it and sent troops to arrest the conspirators. Pre-empting his own arrest on October 10, 1868, Céspedes freed the slaves working at his sugar mill, La Demajagua, near Manzanillo, effectively instigating the **Ten Years War**, the first Cuban war of independence. The size of the revolutionary force grew quickly as other landowners freed their slaves, soon numbering around 1500 men. Bayamo was the first city to fall to the rebels and briefly became the headquarters of a revolutionary government. Their manifesto included promises of free trade, universal male suffrage, though this meant whites only, and the "gradual" abolition of slavery. Though there were disturbances elsewhere, the war itself was mostly confined to the east and the rebels initially took the upper hand. Supported by the peasants, they were able to master the local terrain, adopting guerrilla tactics to outmanoeuvre the visiting Spanish troops. During the course of the war Spain sent over to Cuba one hundred thousand soldiers.

Support for the cause spread quickly across eastern and central parts of the country as two of the great heroes of the wars of independence, the mulatto **Antonio Maceo** and the Dominican **Máximo Gómez**, emerged as military leaders. The most revered name of all in Cuban history books, **José Martí** (see p.90), first came to prominence in the west of the country, where a much smaller insurgency movement, concentrated in Havana, had taken its cue from the events in the east, but was soon arrested and exiled. On the whole, however, the landowners in the west of the country remained on the side of the colonial authorities. Attempts were made to pull the western third of Cuba into the war but an invading force from the east, led by Gómez, got only as far as Colón in Matanzas. Then, in 1874, Céspedes was killed in battle and the revolutionary movement began to flounder, losing a number of subsequent leaders either in battle or through exile, and becoming increasingly fragmented as many *criollos* did not trust the peasants and ex-slaves who fought on the same side.

Seizing on this instability, the Spanish offered what appeared to be a compromise, which was accepted by most of the military revolutionary leaders as the best they could hope for given their own loss of momentum. The **Pact of Zanjón** was signed on February 10, 1878, and included a number of concessions on the part of the Spanish, such as increased political representation for the *criollos*. There remained, however, sections of the rebel army, led by Maceo, that refused to accept the Pact of Zanjón, asserting that none of the original demands of the rebels had been met. In 1879 this small group of rebels reignited the conflict in what became known as the **Guerra Chiquita**, the Small War. It petered out by 1880 and Maceo, amongst others, was forced into exile.

Over the course of the next fifteen years reformists, amongst them ex-rebels, became increasingly dismayed by the Spanish government's failure to fulfil the promises made at Zanjón. Though in 1880 the first phase in the **abolition of slavery** seemed to suggest that genuine changes had been achieved, this development proved to be something of a false dawn. Slavery was replaced with the apprentice system whereby ex-slaves were forced to work for their former owners, albeit for a small wage. It was not until 1886 that slavery was entirely abolished,

whilst in 1890, when universal suffrage was declared in Spain, Cuba was excluded.

These years saw the independence movement build strength from outside Cuba, particularly in the US where many of the rebels had moved and where there was already a sizeable Cuban émigré community. No one did more to stimulate support and interest in Cuban independence than **José Martí**. From his base in New York he worked tirelessly, visiting various Latin American countries trying to gain momentum for the idea of an independent Cuba, appealing to notions of Latin American solidarity. In 1892 he founded the **Cuban Revolutionary Party** (PRC), aiming to unite the disjointed exile community and the divided factions on the island in pursuit of a common goal: a free and fully independent Cuba. Martí did more than any single individual to unify the separatist cause and inspire ideas of nationhood. He believed in complete racial equality and wrote passionately on social justice whilst warning of the imperialist intentions of the US. The PRC began to co-ordinate with groups inside Cuba as preparations were laid for a **Second War of Independence**.

On February 24, 1895, small groups, in contact with the PRC, mounted armed insurrections in Havana, Matanzas, Las Villas, Camagüey and Oriente. Then, on April 1, Maceo landed in Oriente, followed a fortnight later by Martí and Gómez, bringing with them a liberation force of around six thousand. The uprisings in the west had been easily dealt with by the Spanish army and the fighting was once again based in the east.

In May of the same year, in his first battle, at Dos Ríos, Martí was killed. The revolutionaries were not deterred and they fought their way across the country until on January 1, 1896, they reached Havana province. Intense fighting took place here, where the Spanish forces were at their strongest. Meanwhile, the newly appointed governor of Cuba, Valeriano Weyler, instituted a measure known as the **reconcentración**, a forced relocation of the country's rural poor to the cities designed to freeze production, remove popular support for the rebels and cut off food supplies. Thousands died but the rebels fought on and by 1897 almost the entire country, besides a few heavily garrisoned towns and cities, was under their control.

Riots in Havana gave the US the excuse they had been waiting for to send in the warship **Maine**, ostensibly to protect US citizens in the

Cuban capital. On February 15, 1898, the *Maine* blew up in Havana harbour, killing 258 people; the US accused the Spanish of sabotage and so began the **Spanish-American War**. To this day the Cuban government remain adamant that the US blew up its own ship in order to justify its intervention in the war, but evidence is inconclusive. Whatever the true cause of the explosion, it was the pretext the US needed to enter the war, though their support was far from welcomed by many Cubans who believed that victory was already within their grasp. Furthermore, they were not oblivious to US intentions and rightfully feared an imperial-style takeover from their powerful neighbour. In an attempt to allay these fears, the US prepared the Teller Amendment, declaring that they did not intend to exercise any political power in Cuba once the war was over, their sole aim being to free the country from the colonial grip of Spain. Yet despite Cuban involvement in battles fought at El Caney and San Juan in Santiago, Cuban troops were either forced into the background or their efforts ignored. When the Spanish surrendered on July 17, 1898, Cuban troops were prevented from entering Santiago where the victory ceremony took place.

The pseudo-republic

On December 10, 1898, the Spanish signed the **Treaty of Paris**, thereby handing control of Cuba, as well as Puerto Rico and the Philippines, to the US. Political power on the island lay in the hands of **General John Brooke**, who maintained a strong military force in Cuba whilst the US government decided what to do with the island they had coveted for so long. The voices of protest in Cuba were loud and numerous enough to convince them that annexation would be a mistake, so they opted for the next best alternative. In 1901 Cuba adopted a new constitution, devised in Washington without any Cuban consultation, which included the **Platt Amendment**, declaring that the US had the right to intervene in Cuban affairs should the independence of the country come under threat – an eventuality open to endless interpretations. The intention to keep Cuba on a short leash was made even clearer when at the same time a US naval base was established at Guantánamo Bay. On May 20, 1902, under these terms, Cuba was declared a **republic** and Tomás Estrada Palma, the first elected Cuban president, headed a long line of US puppets.

With the economy in ruins following the war, **US investors** were able to buy up large stakes of land and business relatively cheaply. Soon three-quarters of the sugar industry was controlled by US interests and few branches of the economy lay exclusively in Cuban hands as the North Americans invested in cigar factories, railroads, the telephone system, electricity, tourism and anything else that made money. Tourism was particularly lucrative: with millions of Americans just over ninety miles away and, during the second decade of the century, the Cuban economy beginning to prosper, conditions were perfect for attracting visitors to this holiday paradise. Places like Havana and Varadero became flooded with casinos, strip-clubs, fancy hotels and exclusive sports clubs, as the island gained a reputation as an anything-goes destination, a reputation enhanced during the years of prohibition in the US.

The Machado era

The first two decades of the pseudo-republic saw four corrupt Cuban presidents come and go and the US intervene on a number of occasions, temporarily installing a governor in 1906 after a rebellion against Palma's government and sending in troops in 1912 following an uprising in protest against racial discrimination under the presidency of José Miguel Gómez. In 1925 **Gerardo Machado** was elected on the back of a series of promises he had made to clean up government. Though initially successful – he was particularly popular for his independent stance in defiance of US involvement in Cuban politics – his refusal to tolerate any opposition wrecked any legitimate efforts he may have made to improve the running of the country. Strikes by sugar mill and railroad workers, led by **Julio Antonio Mella**, founder of the **Cuban Communist Party** in 1925, led to the assassinations of a host of political leaders. In 1928 Machado changed the constitution, extending his term in office to six years and effectively establishing a dictatorship.

The global economic crisis which followed the Wall Street Crash in 1929 caused more widespread discontent, and opposition became increasingly radical. Machado ruthlessly set about trying to wipe out all opposition in a bloody and repressive campaign involving assassinations of anyone deemed to be of any threat, from students to journalists. Fearing a loss of influence, the US sent in an ambassador, Sumner Welles, with instructions to get rid of Machado and prevent a popular uprising. As Welles set about negotiating a withdrawal of the Machado administration, a general strike across the country in late 1933, together with the loss of the army's support, which had long played an active role in informal Cuban politics, convinced the dictator that remaining in power was futile and he fled the country. Amidst the chaos that followed emerged a man who was to profoundly shape the destiny of Cuba over the following decades.

The rise of Fulgencio Batista

A provisional government led by Carlos Manuel de Céspedes y Quesada filled the political vacuum left by Machado but lasted only a few weeks. Meanwhile, a young sergeant, **Fulgencio Batista**, had staged a coup within the army and replaced most of the officers with men loyal to him. Using his powerful military position he installed **Ramón Grau San Martín** as president, who went on to attempt to nationalize electricity, which was run by a US company, and introduce progressive reforms for workers. This was too much for US President Franklin Roosevelt, who accused Grau of being a communist and refused to recognize his regime. Not wanting to antagonize the US, Batista deposed Grau and replaced him in January 1934 with **Carlos Mendieta**. Batista then continued to prop up a series of Cuban presidents until in 1940 he was himself elected.

Demonized more than any other pre-revolutionary leader by the current regime, Batista was not, at least during these early years, the hated man that communist Cuba would have people believe. Some of his policies were met with widespread support and, despite the backing he received from the US, he was no puppet. In 1934 he presided over the dissolution of the Platt Amendment, which was replaced with a new agreement endowing Cuba with an unprecedented degree of real independence. In a move designed to harmonize some of the political groupings in Cuba and appease past opponents, in 1937 Batista released all political prisoners, whilst using the army to institute health and education programmes in the countryside and amongst the urban poor. By the time he lost power in 1944, ironically to Ramón Grau, Cuba was a more independent and socially just country than it had been at any other time during the pseudo-republic.

Grau showed none of the reformist tendencies that he had demonstrated during his previous short term in office and was replaced in 1948 after proving himself no less corrupt than any of his predecessors. **Carlos Prío Socarrás**, under whom very little changed, led the country until 1952 when Batista, who had left the country after his defeat in 1944, returned to fight another election. Two days before the election was to take place, Batista, fearing failure, on March 10 staged a military coup and seized control of the country. He subsequently abolished the constitution and went on to establish a dictatorship bearing little if any resemblance to his previous term as Cuban leader. Fronting a regime characterized principally by violent repression, corruption and self-indulgent decadence, Batista seemed to have lost any zeal he once had for social change and improvement. Organized crime became ingrained in Cuban life, particularly in Havana where Meyer Lansky controlled much of the gambling industry. During these years living conditions for the average Cuban worsened as investment in social welfare decreased.

Fidel Castro and the revolutionary movement

Amongst the candidates for congress in the 1952 election was **Fidel Castro**, a young lawyer who saw his political ambitions dashed when Batista seized power for himself. Effectively frozen out of constitutional politics by Batista's intolerance of organized opposition, Castro sought to challenge the authority of the new regime and make a mark for his own movement, aimed at restoring democracy and implementing social reform. A year after the military coup, on July 26, 1953, Castro and around 125 others attacked an army barracks at **Moncada** in Santiago de Cuba. Castro regarded the attack "as a gesture which will set an example for the people of Cuba". The attack failed miserably and those who weren't shot fled into the mountains where they were soon caught. Castro would certainly have been shot had his captors taken him back to the barracks, but a sympathetic police sergeant kept him in the relative safety of the police jail. A trial followed in which Castro defended himself and gave what has become one of his most famous speeches. In his summing-up he uttered the now immortal words, "Condemn me if you will. History will absolve me." He was sentenced to fifteen years' imprisonment but had served less than three when, under popular pressure, he, along with the other rebels, was released and sent into exile.

Now based in Mexico, Castro set about organizing a revolutionary force to take back to Cuba; amongst his recruits was an Argentinian doctor named **Ernesto "Che" Guevara**. They called themselves the **Movimiento 26 de Julio**, the 26th of July Movement, often shortened to **M-26-7**, after the date of the attack at Moncada. In late November 1956 Castro, Guevara and around eighty other revolutionaries set sail for Cuba in a large yacht called the *Granma*. Landing in the east at Playas Coloradas, in what is today Granma province, they were immediately attacked and suffered massive casualties, but the dozen or so who survived headed directly for the Sierra Maestra, where they wasted no time in building up support for the cause amongst the local peasantry and enlisting new recruits into their army. Waging a war based on guerrilla tactics, the rebels were able to gain the upper hand against Batista's larger and better-equipped forces.

As the war was being fought out in the countryside, an insurrectionary movement in the cities began a campaign of sabotage aimed at disabling the state apparatus, as the base of support for the revolution grew wider and wider. By the end of 1958 the majority of Cubans had sided with the rebels and the ranks of the revolutionary army had swelled. The US, sensing they were backing a lost cause, had withdrawn military support for Batista, and there were revolts within the army – not only had hundreds of troops been killed but large numbers of those captured by the revolutionaries had been humiliatingly returned to Batista, many of them refusing to continue fighting. Realizing that he no longer exercised any authority, on January 1, 1959, Batista escaped on a plane bound for the Dominican Republic. The army almost immediately surrendered to the rebels and Fidel Castro, who had been fighting in the east, began a victory march across the country, arriving in Havana seven days later on January 8, 1959.

On the eve of the revolution Cuba was a prosperous country, the United States' favoured Latin American state. With good relations between the countries, Cuba enjoyed an imported culture through public services and manufactured goods including cars, clothes and electrical equipment – even the telephone system was North American – whilst the US benefited from cheap sugar, the reward for massive investment in the agricultural industry. The flip side of the picture was that the US used Cuba as its playpen and showed scant regard for its citizens, with the Mafia, crime and prostitution all operating behind the scenes, while Cuba's opulent hotels, cabarets and casinos glittered for the world. Meanwhile, outside of the cities the rural population lived in abject poverty, with no running water, electricity, health care, education or even at times enough food. Peasant wages were desperately low and those working on sugar farms would only draw a wage for a few months of seasonal work a year.

The Cuban Revolution: the first decade

Though the revolutionary war ended in 1959, this date marks only the beginning of what in Cuba is referred to as the Revolution. The new government appointed as its president Manuel Urrutia, but there was no doubt that the real power lay in the hands of Fidel Castro, who, within a few months of the revolutionary triumph, took over as prime minister. The **1960s** were both trying and exciting times for Cuba, as the government, with Fidel Castro at its head, and Che Guevara soon in charge of the economy, to a large extent felt its way through the decade. It wasted no time in instituting its programme of social and political transformation, passing more than 1500 laws in its first year.

Early reforms

One of the most radical of the new laws was the first **Agrarian Reform Law** of May 1959, by which the land, much of it foreign-owned until now, was either nationalized or redistributed amongst the rural population. Under the new law, individual ownership could not exceed 400 hectares – just under 1000 acres – and any land in excess of this limit was put under direct state control. Much of it remained in state hands, to be farmed by co-operatives set up for the purpose, but some was given to peasant farmers at a minimum of 27 hectares – almost 70 acres – per individual holding. By 1961 over forty percent of Cuba's farmland had been expropriated and reorganized along these lines. The 1959 law also established the **Agrarian Reform Institute** (INRA),

Education in the revolution

In Cuba, children are educated to believe in the revolution wholeheartedly and no opportunity to debunk the ideals of capitalist society, specifically the United States, is lost, as can be seen by a glance at any Cuban textbook, be it geography, history or Spanish. While the limited political, historical and ideological perspective inhibits independent thinking and analysis, the education system has been innovative in other ways. Following the dictum that education should go beyond academia, in the early years Che Guevara developed schemes to make rural farm work a part of every child's experience, in order to break down the barriers and prejudices dividing rural labourers and white-collar urban workers. Countryside boarding schools were set up where work and study were combined and were considered very successful during the

1970s and 1980s, although the Special Period of the 1990s saw them affected by massive short-ages. Even today schoolchildren annually spend several weeks of their summer at camp, har-vesting crops and learning how to shoot weapons and fight in combat. Further to their formal education, from the age of six to thir-teen, children are expected to be part of the **Pioneros**, the José Martí Pioneers Organization, similar to the Boy Scouts or the Girl Guides, in which socialism replaces reli-gion. As well as sporting, cultural and recre-ational activities children learn the core values of the revolution. Not for nothing is the motto of the Young Cuban Communists (UJC) "Trabajo, Estudio, Fusil" – "Work, Study, Gunmanship"; being ever ready to defend your country is a cornerstone of revolutionary ideology.

which soon became a kind of government for the countryside, administering most of the rural reform programmes, including new health and educational facilities, housing developments and road construction. Also affecting the peasants more than anyone else was the push to eradi-cate **illiteracy**, initiated in 1961, when Fidel Castro sent more than 250,000 teachers, volun-teers and schoolchildren into the countryside to teach reading and writing. The programme was so successful that illiteracy was slashed from 23.6 percent to 3.9 by the end of 1962. Empowering the peasants both financially and intellectually was seen as key to correcting exist-ing inequalities, and by addressing the imbal-ance in the distribution of resources between town and country, the revolutionaries changed the social landscape of Cuba beyond recognition.

Health and **education** in particular became the focus for the reshaping of the country and the conditions in which its citizens lived. Free educa-tion for all was one of the core dicta of revolu-tionary objectives, as private schools were nationalized and education until the sixth grade made compulsory. Universities proliferated, as numbers of teachers and schools multiplied. By 1968 there were almost 60,000 school teachers across the country, compared to just under 20,000 ten years earlier, whilst the number of schools had doubled. Che Guevara once called

youth the "anchor of the revolution" and it is clear that now as in the early days of power the state uses education to put its message across as early as possible (see box above).

Health, too, saw great gains in the early years of the revolution and is an area that continues to elicit praise for Cuba. Although medical care had been well represented prior to the revolution, with a sophisticated, albeit exclusive health ser-vice, staffed by 6300 doctors, there was no national health service and half the doctors worked in Havana. Outside the cities hospitals, where they existed, were badly managed and medicines expensive. New hospitals and health-care centres were built and a new emphasis put on preventive medicine and care in the commu-nity, thus allleviating some of the hospitals' bur-den. There was also investment in medical research in an attempt not just to provide a domestic source of medical products but also to develop medical technologies for export. There was, however, a rise in infant mortality in these early years and, though by the 1990s the rate had dropped to a level comparing favourably with some of the most highly developed coun-tries in the world, in 1967 rates had gone up by ten percent compared to ten years earlier, with just under 45 deaths per 1000 live births.

Sport was another area targeted for reform in the early 1960s, as Cuba laid the foundations of a system that has gone on to produce some of the world's finest athletes and make Cuba one of the most successful sporting nations on the planet. In 1961 the National Institute of Sport, Physical Education and Recreation (INDER) was set up to administer a programme of mass participation in physical activity, which the revolutionaries regarded as a vital proponent of social development. Specialist sport schools were established and exercise routines were introduced into the workplace, ensuring that everybody became engaged in some kind of regular physical activity.

Opposition and emigration

Whilst these very real gains for large sections of the Cuban population ensured continued popular support for the new regime, not everyone was happy and the revolution was not without its victims in these early years. Many of those who had served under Batista, from government officials to army officers, were tried, and – with little regard for their legal rights –convicted for sometimes purely ideological crimes, and sentenced to execution. Moderates and liberals became increasingly isolated from the political process and increasingly disillusioned, both with the nature of revolutionary change and the way in which it was carried out. Under Castro, the government had little sympathy for the constitutional framework in which the liberals felt it must operate and, appealing to what it regarded as the higher ideals of justice and the interests of the collective over the individual, swept much of the legal machinery aside in its drive to eliminate opponents of the revolution and carry out programmes of reform. Amongst those deemed to be too liberal was the president, Manuel Urrutia, who, despite his defence of the government against some of its opponents, was forced out of office in July 1959. As the decade wore on, the regime became more intolerant of dissenting voices, declaring all those who challenged government policy to be counter-revolutionaries, and by the end of the 1960s there are estimated to have been over 20,000 **political prisoners** in Cuban jails.

Those in Cuba who, in material terms, stood to gain least and, especially in the case of landowners or big-business moguls, were actually more likely to lose both money and capital, were the upper-middle and upper classes, amongst them doctors, lawyers and a whole host of other professionals. During the first few years of the revolution, as Cuba–US relations soured (see below) and the revolution seemed to be swinging further to the left, these groups sought refuge overseas, predominantly in the US. Between 1960 and 1962 around 200,000 **emigrants**, most of them white, left Cuba, forming large exile communities, especially in Florida, and setting up powerful anti-Castro organizations, intent on returning to Cuba as soon as possible, even if it meant another war.

Cuban-Soviet-US relations

As huge sectors of Cuban industry were **nationalized** and foreign businesses, most of them US-owned, found themselves dispossessed, the US government retaliated by freezing all purchases of Cuban sugar, restricting exports to the island and then, in 1961, breaking off diplomatic relations. Seeking to overthrow the new regime, the US now backed counter-revolutionary forces within Cuba as well as terrorist campaigns in the cities aimed at sabotaging the state apparatus, but finally, under President Kennedy, opted for all-out invasion. On April 17, 1961, a military force of Cuban exiles, trained and equipped in the US, landed at the **Bay of Pigs** in southern Matanzas (see box, p.230). The revolutionaries were ready for them and the whole operation ended within 72 hours.

In December of that year, in the face of complete economic and political isolation from the US – the country Castro had hoped would support the revolution and which he had visited as early as April 1959, seeking diplomatic ties – the Cuban leader declared himself a **Marxist-Leninist**. The debate continues to this day as to whether this was considered opportunism on the part of Castro or whether, as he himself declared, he had always held these beliefs but chosen up until then not to make them public for fear of scaring off potential support for the revolution. Sincere or not, there was no doubt whose support he coveted at the time of his declaration, and the **Soviet Union** was only too happy to enter a pact with a close neighbour of its Cold War rival.

The benefits for Cuba were immediate as the Soviets agreed to buy Cuban sugar at artificially high prices whilst selling them petroleum at well below its market value. Then, in 1962, on Castro's request, the Soviets installed over forty

Cuban revolutionary ideology

First and foremost, the Cuban revolution was an expression of nationalism. In Fidel Castro's earliest speeches, following the attack on Moncada in 1953, for example, he made numerous references to self-determination, social justice and equality, but there was little indication of the Marxist-Leninist ideologies with which the Cuban state has become associated.

Despite Castro's claims that he had always been a communist, it is more likely, considering the text of his speeches, that his beliefs and those of many of his fellow revolutionaries evolved into the system that now characterizes the revolution. Castro and his followers arrived at what is now established Cuban ideology partly through opportunism and circumstance – specifically the break with the US and the alliance with the Soviet Union – and partly through a need to intellectualize the revolutionary process, thereby providing a theoretical guide to what they hoped and intended to achieve.

A milestone in Cuban revolutionary theory – and now a core text of the official ideological framework on which the Cuban state is based – is Che Guevara's *Man and Socialism in Cuba*, first published in 1965. This immediately became one of the key theoretical bases informing the programmes of development and reform in Cuba. At its essence is the concept of what Guevara called *El Hombre Nuevo* – The New Man – a state of mind to which all Cubans should aspire. Fundamental to achieving an egalitarian and just society, Guevara believed, was not just what people did, but also what they thought. Capitalism, he argued, encouraged the individual to pursue only selfish ends and material gain, and to change that would require an entirely new political culture. The revolution would have to transform the motivations that determine behaviour: people would have to be taught to be motivated by the interests of the collective. This idea – that the values of *El Hombre Nuevo* would not simply be acquired but would have to be taught – effectively legitimized the process of indoctrination through schools, the workplace, the media and sloganeering that still exists today. It was believed that there was a kind of ideological hangover from the previous regime, that market forces had affected the social conscience and that what was required was a kind of rehabilitation of the individual. Once this transformation was complete, there would be no need for material incentives in the workplace, as people would be satisfied by moral rewards and the knowledge that they had served the wider objectives of the revolution.

---

missiles on the island. Angered by this belligerent move, Kennedy declared an embargo on any military weapons entering Cuba. Krushchev ignored it, and Soviet ships loaded with more weapons made their way across the Atlantic. Neither side appeared to be backing down and nuclear weapons were prepared for launch in the US. A six-day stalemate followed, after which a deal was finally struck and the world breathed a collective sigh of relief – the **Cuban Missile Crisis** had passed. Krushchev agreed to withdraw Soviet weapons from Cuba on the condition that the US would not invade the island. This triggered the tightening of the trade embargo by the US.

Economic policy in the 1960s

The government, attempting to diversify the economy and institute massive social change, occasionally allowed revolutionary ideals to outweigh realistic policy and planning. Nowhere was this more apparent than in the new **economic policies**. The basic aim, initially, was to reduce Cuba's dependence on sugar production, through industrialization and expansion in both the output and the variety of agricultural products and consumer goods manufactured. In their enthusiasm for the principles of what they were doing, and spurred on by the knowledge of how much they had already achieved, a number of factors were overlooked.

The mass exodus of professionals during the early years of the decade, though eliminating a large part of the potential opposition, made the transition from an essentially monocultural capitalist economy to a more diverse, industrialized yet highly centralized one extremely problematic. There were simply not enough workers with the kinds of skills and experience necessary to realize such ambitious plans. Furthermore, the impact of the US embargo had been severely underestimated: the Americans had supplied machinery, raw materials and manufactured goods easily, quickly and inexpensively and, despite subsidies from the Soviet Union, the greater distances involved and less sophisticated economy of Cuba's new suppliers could not match up. Agricultural output actually dropped significantly and in 1962 rationing had to be introduced. The revolutionaries had aimed too high and in doing so had placed extra stresses and strains on an economy simply not prepared for such rapid change. After the failure of initial attempts at producing the type of industrial goods and machinery that had been imported until now, and following Castro's visit to the Soviet Union in 1964, during which the Russians promised to purchase 24 million tons of sugar over the next five years, it was decided that the economy should focus once again on **sugar**. Ambitious targets were set for each harvest, none more so than in 1970, when Castro declared that Cuba would produce ten million tons of sugar. This blind optimism was to prove disastrous as not only were the impossible production targets not met, but other areas of the economy suffered from neglect and underinvestment, leaving Cuba even more dependent on sugar than it had been prior to the revolution.

The 1970s and 1980s

The 1960s had been a period of experimentation and discovery for the Cuban revolutionaries. In the following decades, with an established ideological framework and the foundations of genuine social gains for large parts of the population, despite the hardships caused by failed economic policies, the government sought to consolidate its objectives. Having already encouraged and, in cases like that of Bolivia, participated in popular uprisings against what they saw, usually correctly, as oppressive regimes, the Cubans expanded their foreign policy in the 1970s, becoming engaged in a fifteen-year conflict in Angola and a shorter war in Ethiopia, amongst others.

Economic policy and performance

Following the disastrous economic experiments of the 1960s, Cuba began the next decade with a complete reappraisal of economic policy and planning. Much had been learned, and the wild optimism that inspired previous policy was rejected in favour of a more realistic programme. A balance was struck, with the state still in control of heavy industry and the essential components of the economy, whilst the private sector was expanded and given greater freedom. In a clear compromise of revolutionary ideology, **material incentives** were introduced, whilst wage policies were also adjusted to bring them into line with the needs of the economy.

In 1975 the government adopted its first Five Year Plan, setting relatively realistic targets for growth and production, not all of which were met. With rises in the price of sugar on the world market in the first half of the decade and increased Soviet assistance, there were tangible improvements in the country's economic performance. The policy changes were carried on into the next decade as the economy continued to make modest improvements, though the mass exodus of some 125,000 Cubans in the **Mariel boatlift** of 1980 demonstrated that, for many, times were still hard. As more private enterprise was permitted, however, Castro became alarmed at the number of people giving up their state jobs and concluded that he had made a mistake. In 1986 he issued his **Rectification of Errors** and the economy returned to centralization. With increasing sums being ploughed into defence, the economy survived only through heavy Soviet support.

The politics of a one-party state

The government, having declared itself the **Cuban Communist Party** (PCC) in 1965, did not hold its first Congress until 1975. The following year a new constitution was drawn up and approved. Castro's position as head of state became constitutionalized, thus doing away with the last vestiges of democracy and openly declaring his power and authority as unchallengeable. Attempts were made, on the other hand, to decentralize power by introducing an extensive system of **local government**. However, as agents of central government these local assemblies had little or no real independence.

Countless mass **organizations** had, by this time, been established, amongst them the Committees for the Defence of the Revolution (CDR), the Union of Young Communists (UJC) and the Federation of Cuban Women (FMC). In theory, membership of these organizations was the popular expression of support for the revolution and its ideals, but in reality they were – and are – closer to being the watchdogs of the regime, ensuring that at every level people are behaving as good citizens.

The 1990s and beyond

In 1989 the bubble burst. The collapse of the Soviet bloc and subsequently the Soviet Union itself led to a loss of over eighty percent of Cuba's trade. In 1990, as the country stumbled into an era of extreme shortages, the government declared the beginning of the **Special Period** to combat the problems, a euphemism that essentially meant compromise and sacrifice for all Cubans in all areas of life. Public transport deteriorated dramatically as the country lost almost all of its fuel imports, strict rationing of food was introduced, and timed power cuts became frequent as even electricity had to be rationed.

The US government, in 1992, took advantage of Cuba's crisis to tighten up the trade embargo even further as, not for the first time since 1959, thousands of Cubans risked their lives trying to escape the country across the Florida Straits. The Cuban exile community in Miami, by now consisting of a number of well-organized and powerful political groups, obsessed with toppling the regime, rubbed their hands with glee at the prospect of the revolution crumbling, as reports in the US press regularly predicted the fall of Fidel Castro. Forced to make huge ideological readjustments and drastic changes to the way the country was run, the government embarked on one of its most ideologically risky journeys yet, when, in August 1993, the **US dollar** was declared legal tender. With this came other reforms as the Cubans sought to rebuild the economy by opening the flood gates to the worldwide tourist trade. To wrest back control of the economy the state was forced to make all but the most basic products and services charge-

---

Race relations in Cuba

At the onset of the revolution in 1959, Fidel Castro declared that he would erase racial discrimination, establishing the unacceptability of racism as one of the core tenets of the revolution. He carried through his promise with legislation that threw open doors to previously white-only country clubs, beaches, hotels and universities and, more importantly, established equality in the workplace. However, the question of race in Cuba is still a problematic issue. Official statistics put the racial mix at 66 percent white (of Hispanic descent), 12 percent black, 21.9 percent mulatto (mixed race between Hispanic and black) and 0.1 percent Asian. There is, however, an obvious disparity between figures and facts and the claims by some that as much as 70 percent of the population have some trace of black heritage seem to be closer to the truth. Some critics of the official figures suggest that they are a way of downplaying the importance of the black heritage.

Although institutional racism has been considerably lessened, its existence is still apparent in the lack of black people holding the highest positions across the professional spectrum.

Very few top jobs are held by Afro-Cubans outside of sport or entertainment and, especially in the tourist industry, lighter skinned people hold the front-line jobs while black people are more usually employed in menial labour, as cleaners, maids or chauffeurs. Overturning the racism inherent in the colonial structure will take longer than forty years.

Certainly to express overtly racist opinions is taboo and Cuba's citizens are acutely aware of the prescribed view on the subject, but behind closed doors attitudes differ. Various negative racial stereotypes prevail in Cuba: Afro-Cubans are often considered lazier, less intelligent and more likely to commit crime than white people, and marriage between a black man and a white woman is more likely to be frowned upon than between a black woman and white man. A more recent dimension in the race question has arisen from the tourist trade. *Jineteros* and *jineteras* are nationally perceived as exclusively Afro-Cuban, and this in turn has led to the stereotype of wealthy Afro-Cubans as prostitutes, pimps and touts, while white Cubans with money are generally assumed to be supported by relatives in Miami.

---

able in dollars, opening dollar stores, restaurants and hotels, ensuring that the money made its way back into the state coffers. However, until the new tourism industry began to boost the beleaguered economy, people were scrabbling to survive: sugar and water were at times all that some had to live on.

Tales of survival from the era are by turns grotesque, comic and heroic. While stories of vendors replacing cheese with melted condoms on pizzas and CDR meetings called with the express purpose of ordering people to stop dining on the neighbourhood cats and dogs may be urban myth, their very existence highlights the desperate living conditions during those times. Hard-currency black markets prospered as those who could used dollars to buy products that were not available in the empty peso stores. Small-scale **private enterprise** was also legalized as the face of modern-day Cuba began to take shape. Private farmers' markets became the norm, industrious cooks took to selling their culinary creations from the front windows of their houses, and house-owners began renting out their bedrooms to tourists. The risk to both revolutionary ideology and its control of the economy that the government has taken by allowing even this limited degree of capitalism to exist may prove to be the start of the ending for the Cuban revolution.

Into the twenty-first century

While the country may have survived, the Special Period left deep scars on society. Shortages still prevail, particularly of medicines, which has tarnished the state's excellent health record, and for those without dollars life is extremely difficult. The legalization of the dollar and the advent of private enterprise has led to distinct class-based divisions in society. Revolutionary ideology has been severely undermined, with people blatantly pursuing personal rather than collective gain, through all kinds of activity. While the rural community, which has benefited most from improvements in healthcare, housing and education, remains overwhelmingly loyal to the revolution, in the cities, where the influence of capitalist culture is greater, there is a distinct restlessness.

The economic hardships following the collapse of the Soviet bloc and the measures taken by the government to deal with them have made Cuba's lack of social and political **freedoms** more apparent than at any time since the 1960s.

Without the right to demonstrate, organize political opposition or vote for government, widespread feelings of powerlessness and frustration, numbed in the past by economic security, have developed. Equally widespread is recognition of the improvements made since 1959, not just in health and education but in social attitudes, particularly towards women and in terms of racism. Many Cubans, in private, voice the opinion that worthwhile though the gains have been, enough material sacrifice has been made and now it's time for some real change. Cubans speak wistfully of how much better things were "*antes*" – before – and while many foreigners have taken this to mean before the revolution, often people just mean before the Special Period began.

Denouncing anyone who criticizes the revolution publicly, or talks to the foreign press, as an enemy of the state, Fidel Castro has always externalized the country's problems, laying the blame at the feet of capitalist powers and conspirators. Though, since the 1960s and 70s, the regime has witnessed a degree of liberalization in terms of its handling of dissidents, there are still political prisoners in Cuba, and open opposition to the government, the party and even the principles of the revolution remains all but illegal. Whilst right-wing detractors wait to destroy the revolution, Cubans have heard all the complaints before. The feeling is that these are historical issues with little relevance to their daily lives and the issues that affect them.

It has been suggested by the younger generation within the party that the best way to preserve the revolution would be for Fidel Castro to step down and leave the country in the hands of an elected successor, thus silencing the claims from right-wingers that the revolution will end with his leadership. Not only would this usher in new ideas but it would do much to alleviate the political apathy affecting many of Cuba's citizens. However, whether Cuba is the country decried in right-wing discourse as suffering at the hands of a dictator or, as more moderate pundits suggest, a country whose people would elect a similar government were they not denied the privilege, many Cubans continue to support the ideologies of the revolution, even though they feel frustrated by their impotence to change their own lives. So convinced are they that the present situation will last forever that it is not uncommon to hear people surmise that *if* Fidel dies, rather than *when*, things may change.

Wildlife and the environment

Over the last five million years, the island of Cuba has been shaped by a combination of violent volcanic activity, erosion and continental plate movement. Odd-shaped, often flat-topped mountains fall away to swamps, plains and pouch-shaped bays, an unusually varied geography that provides a diversity of habitats and some unique wildlife species. The vast majority of Cuba's animal life is invertebrate: mammals are scarce, and even reptiles and amphibians are few when compared with the Central American region. Bird-life, however, is abundant; marine life is mesmerizing; and there are some spectacular types of insect. While many species are common to southern Florida, Mexico, and neighbouring islands, Cuba is also graced with a large number of specialized local species.

Unfortunately, the predictable consequences of human habitation have driven many of these endemic species to extinction. Over the last two hundred years, uncultivated land cover has dropped from ninety percent to a paltry nineteen percent and it is only in designated national parks, or inhospitable landscapes, that you will come across wildlife. Where they do exist, mangrove forests, pine forests, and tropical rainforests are largely unspoiled with sparse facilities.

Fauna

The main characteristics of Cuban fauna are large numbers of highly localized groups, an unusually high quantity of small-sized animals, and a great deal of interspecies variety. In practice this means that the delicate and strange takes precedence over the massive and magnificent.

Marine life

Running underneath the island is a flat, silty ledge that extends out to a chain of clear, coral-fringed cays. This is one of the most biologically productive ecosystems on earth, although none of the species found here is endemic to Cuba.

On the seabed grow large "fields" of monotonous **turtle grass,** home to myriad molluscs, sea urchins, sea stars, sponges, fish, and even the occasional **manatee**, also known as a **sea-cow**. This implausible creature can be seen grazing on the underwater grass beds with the same inscrutable ease as its land-bound namesake. Although carrying an inflated head of wrinkled grey rubber, these six-foot beasts were once thought to be beautiful mermaids tempting sailors to suicide.

The **hawksbill** and **loggerhead turtles** from which the underground savannah gets its name are all but gone now. A more frequent visitor is the **common octopus**, which subsists on the muscle of the **queen conch**, a huge mollusc that scrapes microscopic algae from the ocean floor. Vicious-looking **barracuda** and the charming **bottle-nosed dolphin** also make appearances, although these fish tend to congregate around outcrops of rock and their consequent forests of coral and sponge. Here many smaller fish, such as **snappers**, **hogfish**, the repulsive **toadfish** and the glorious **parrot fish**, feed on the oasis of microscopic life the rocks provide. The same fish can also be found further out from shore, towards the cays, where wide coral reefs host thousands of species. Taking a boat trip or diving from one of the coastal resorts are the easiest ways to get out to the reefs.

Typically for an island, **freshwater** fauna is sparse. There are some curiosities, like the **Cuban blind fish**, and various species of delicate **shrimp**, but most impressive are the **Cuban garfish** and the **manjuari**, both crocodile-sized species that have been around since the dinosaurs. Few visitors to Cuba who see one of these beasts forget the experience.

Insects, spiders and molluscs

With over 17,000 described species, **insect life** on Cuba is varied and abundant. Amongst the usual bewildering array of tiny oddities, there are some impressively large spiders and scorpions. None is dangerous, although this is hard to believe when you see the **giant Cuban millipede**. Also known as "the dog maimer", these repulsive creatures cause swelling and great discomfort when stepped on. Less commonly found are Cuba's huge-headed **harvester ants**.

Land **snails** are, if anything, what Cuba is famous for, as a look around any of the country's natural history museums will confirm. Amongst species of all sizes and hues, the most extraordinary is the spectacular **painted snail** (*polymita*), some of which are striped with all the colours of the rainbow. Such intense pigmentation would appear to be counter-productive, but being multicoloured they are difficult for predators to fix on. Human beings have no problem, of course, and have reduced their numbers to dangerously low levels.

Cuba is not as magnificently well-endowed with **butterflies** as neighbouring regions, but it is home to the unusual **Cuban clearwing**, distinguished, as the name suggests, by large but completely transparent wings. Some of the most eye-pleasing colours can be found on the **avellaneda**, named after the Cuban poet Gertrude Avellaneda. An inhabitant of the Sierra Maestra, this large yellow and orange insect often finds its way inland.

Mammals

Mammals other than humans and dogs are rarely seen in Cuba. There are now only 32 species of mammal on the island, the majority of which are **bats**. Although some bats live in deserted buildings, most make their homes in the innumerable caves of the limestone regions. Most eat fruit and vegetable matter, although Cuba's largest bat feeds on small fish. The second smallest bat in the world, the **butterfly bat** is native to Cuba, though it is unlikely to be seen as it lives in caves and hunts by night in woody areas. The **Cuban hot caves bat** is a little more sociable, feeding as it does from the pollen of the ubiquitous royal palm.

The largest indigenous land mammals are the gentle **tree rats** (*jutías*), of which there are three species. More like a beaver than a rat, the timid, vegetarian *jutías* are rarely seen. Even more difficult to spot is the dishevelled **almiquí**, the only insectivore common exclusively to Cuba. This odd nocturnal rat-like creature, another of Cuba's "living fossils", faces an uncertain future as its habitat, the Bayamo region, continues to be developed for human use.

Reptiles and amphibians

The **Cuban boa** is the largest snake in the Greater Antilles. Brown, with flashes of iridescent green, this ground dweller feeds mainly on birds. Some eat bats and rats, but unfortunately many have a particular taste for poultry, and have thus been largely exterminated by irate peasants. Even more highly endangered is the **Cuban crocodile**, now restricted to the Península de Zapata and Lanier swamps, where food is becoming more difficult to come by.

The inoffensive but disconcertingly fast **jubo** snake may be encountered, as may the long and thin blue **correcosta** lizard, both of which are quite common, and, like other Cuban reptiles, harmless. Of these most widespread are the **anole** family of lizards. The **bearded anole**, a miracle of camouflage, blends impressively with lichen-coloured trees and stones. Its bright cousin, the small **blue anole**, is commonly seen in many of Cuba's parks and gardens. Other common varieties include the pale brown **stream anole** and the large green **knight anole**.

In Cuba's lakes and rivers you might be lucky enough to find a **Cuban turtle**, although numbers are dwindling. More common are various types of frog and toad.

Birds

Over 300 varieties of **bird** can be seen in Cuba, about seventy of which are indigenous. Cuba is a popular resting place for migrating birds, which mingle with the wide range of local teals, sparrows, warblers, owls, hawks, cranes, herons and parrots. Keen bird-watchers usually head for the Baracoan mountains and the Sierra Maestra, where **peregrin falcons**, **blue-winged teals**, **great blue herons** and **mourning doves** can all be spotted. The Península de Guanahacabibes and the Sabana-Camagüey cays are home to a wide range of colourful **spoonbills**, **flamingos** and **black hawks** – all, alas, in danger of extinction.

The three endemic bird species which seem most to have endeared themselves to Cubans are as colourful as the flamingo but at the other end of the spectrum in size. The **tocororo** or Cuban trogon is the national bird, sharing the red, white and blue of the Cuban flag. It is still abundant in forest areas, where it perches in an almost vertical position, nests in holes made by woodpeckers, and feeds on fruits, flowers and insects which it catches in flight. Other features are its distinctively shaped tail and the call that gives it its name.

The *cartacuba* or **Cuban tody** is only 12cm high, with a brilliant green back and a bright red patch under its bill. Though never abundant, it can be found in forested areas throughout Cuba. It feeds on insects for which it is constantly searching among the foliage. It lays its eggs at the end of a tunnel which it digs in a bank or in a tree trunk, and its chicks seem to be the best-fed in the world; it is reckoned that a pair of parents will bring each chick up to 140 insects a day.

Cuba is also home to the smallest bird in the world, the **zunzuncito** or bee hummingbird, 6.5cm in length. The female is slightly larger than the male, but the male boasts more brilliant colours. Like other hummingbirds, the *zunzuncito* hovers on rapidly beating wings to extract the nectar from flowers. It can be found in forested areas such as Cienaga de Zapata and Sierra del Rosario, and in mountainous areas like Escambray and the Sierra Maestra.

Another beautiful bird is the **blue-headed quail dove**. Although its main form of locomotion is walking, the unique clacking of its wings is as close as many get to seeing its fine plumage, as it too is becoming rare. More common and equally fantastic is the fierce-looking light-brown **Cuban pygmy owl**, which emits a fifteen-note piercing shrill. Also frequently seen, and more frequently heard, are the many species of woodpecker that inhabit the island. Most attractive is the **Cuban red-bellied woodpecker** with its elegant yellow headgear and fine red breast, although the **Cuban green woodpecker** is also pretty.

Flora

Cuba, it is said, looks all ways of the world, and nowhere is this more evident than in Cuba's diverse flora, of which over 6000 species, more than any other island in the Antilles, grow even today.

The principal zones of remaining forest are the mountains of Pinar del Rio, the Sierra del Escambray, the Sierra Maestra, and the highlands of Baracoa. Those arboreal species still surviving in the heavily deforested plains are few. One is the dignified silver-stalked **royal palm**. Adorning the country's coat of arms, it is known for its majesty – heights of over 30m are not uncommon – and its utility: from roots to leaves, every portion serves some useful purpose. There are more than thirty other species of palm, including the common **coconut palm**, a rare and ancient species of **cork palm**, and the bulbous **big belly palm**. The oddly shaped, lichen-painted **sabal palm**, now threatened by parrot poaching and charcoal production, is the cornerstone of the Península de Zapata's ecosystem, housing and feeding many species of bird, lizard and small mammal.

Another tree left on the plains is the strange **ceiba** tree. These silk-cotton trees, frequently reaching an immense 45m, are sacred to all Cuban cultures, aboriginal and colonial alike. The most famous in the country can be found at the Plaza de Armas in Havana, marking the spot where the city was founded.

Other commonly found trees include the **sea grape** (*uva caleta*), found along stretches of coast and bearing grape-like fruit; the great **jaguey** fig tree with its peculiar aerial roots; and a far eastern import, the bright red- and orange-flowered **royal poinciana**.

Orchids and cacti are represented by hundreds of varieties. Cuba's national flower, the delicate white **butterfly jasmine**, is common.

Threats to the environment

Columbus remarked on his initial survey of Cuba that he had "never seen anything so beautiful. The country around the river is full of trees, beautiful and green and different from ours, each with flowers and its own kind of fruit. There are many birds of all sizes that sing very sweetly, and there are many palms different from those in Guinea or Spain." Since then, Cuba's natural fortunes have declined tragically.

Cuba lost most of its **primary forests** (which once covered about 95 percent of the territory) in the early years of European occupation.

Calculations suggest that by 1774 the forested area of Cuba had been reduced to 83 percent. The Spanish settlers enthusiastically began clearing virgin forests for sugarcane plantations. This intensive log-farming, along with the introduction of foreign dogs, rats, monkeys and goats, did little for the fortunes of local fauna. Insects thrived of course, and sea-life was yet to be affected, but the giant walking owls, Cuban monkeys, and colossal sloth soon disappeared.

The new arrivals, in their defence, unwittingly brought with them viruses and bacteria against which local wildlife had no defences, and much colonial rapacity was due to simple ignorance. Nevertheless with Cuba's breathtaking wilderness now huddled in a few isolated pockets it is hard not to see conscious human policy as the main environmental threat.

Destruction reached its peak in the **nineteenth century**, with 200 square miles a year being destroyed. By 1900 the forested area had been reduced to 41 percent, by 1926 to 21 percent and by 1958 to just 16 percent. After the 1959 revolution serious attempts at reforestation were made for the first time, but mistakes were made, such as inappropriate selection of species and

inadequate care of plantations, and replanting went side by side with continued deforestation for the construction of dams, roads and further clearing for sugar production. In recent years the tide has turned, with forested areas increasing to 19 percent coverage by 1990. But even today, amongst the vast majority of local people ignorance and economic necessity prevail.

There is hope, however. The 1990s have seen a discernible increase in **ecological awareness** and acknowledgement of the need for urgent measures to conserve animal and plant species. There have been serious attempts to identify and count endemic species, and the work of the National Enterprise for Conservation of Flora and Fauna has included a census of parrots, cranes and parakeets and a conservation programme for the pink flamingo which has led to a significant increase in the population. **Ecotourism** has taken hold, and though it brings its own problems it has provided an added incentive for the conservation of wildlife in general and endangered species in particular. How far these measures are successful in reversing the mortal tide of human activity remains to be seen.

Darren Bills

Cuban music

Cuba is beyond question the most important source of music in Latin America. Its root rhythms – rumba and *son* – created the pan-Latin music of salsa, as developed in New York, Miami and across Latin America, and in their older forms they continue to provide abundant riches, now globally recognized in the success of the *Buena Vista Social Club* projects. But Cuban musical success and influence is by no means new. Its *danzón* groups helped to shape jazz in the early decades of the twentieth century and continued at the forefront of the music through to the 1950s, unleashing *mambo* and *chachachá* crazes throughout Europe and the US, and providing the template for much modern African music, in particular Congolese *soukous*. And even after the non-Latin West backed away from post-revolutionary Cuba, the island continued to produce a wealth of jazz, *salsa* and *son*, as well as the influential *nueva trova* or "new song" (see p.488).

Son and Afro-Cuban music

"¡Qué rico bailo yo!" – "How well I dance!" The title of a classic song by Orquesta Ritmo Oriental epitomizes the confidence and spirit of Cuban music. For this is the island that has given the world the *habanera*, *rumba*, the *mambo*, the *danzón*, the *chachachá* – dance music that has travelled all over the new world, the old world, and gone back to its roots in Africa. And at home it is a music that feels inseparable from Cuba's daily life and history, whether drawing on African rituals, commenting on topical issues, or just celebrating rhythm and sensuality.

African roots

African slaves were imported to Cuba from the 1520s until well into the nineteenth century. Little surprise, then, that Cuban music has deep and evident roots in **African ritual and rhythm**, even when its forms are essentially developments of the European dances brought by the Spanish colonists. By contrast, there is almost no detectable influence from the pre-Hispanic tribes, beyond the use of *maracas* (shakers); Cuba's indigenous culture was effectively obliterated by colonization.

Cuba's slaves were brought mostly from the West African coast – Nigeria, Ghana, Togo, Cameroon, Benin and Congo – and by the 1840s they constituted nearly half of the population. They preserved their identity in mutual aid associations called *cabildos*, from which emerged the four main Afro-Cuban religions of Lucumi, Abakua, Congo and Arara, and their cults, each of which developed its own music, rhythms and rituals. **Santería**, the dominant Afro-Cuban religion, drew on a spread of cults, and revered a panoply of African deities or *orishas*, later paired with Catholic saints.

In Cuba today a fair section of the population maintains a faith based on Santería and you can see dances and music performed in honour of the various **orishas**. Each orisha has its own colour: Changó, the spirit of war and fire (twinned with Santa Barbara), is red and white, while Oshún, the flirtatious goddess of love and water (twinned with the Virgen de la Caridad del Cobre, Cuba's patron saint) has gold. As well as a colour and an element, each deity has its own characteristic set of **toques** – rhythms played by the hourglass-shaped **batá** drums and **chekere** (rattles), which provide the sounds and ambience for religious rituals.

These complex rhythms are the heartbeat of Cuban popular music, working away beneath the Latin layers on top. The batás and chekere of the ceremonies crop up regularly in contemporary bands, and the physical and emotional intensity of Cuban music derives in part from the power of African ritual and its participatory nature. Celina González, for example, Cuba's "Queen of Country Music", pays homage to Changó in her wonderful song "Santa Barbara" (a classic, immortalized by Cuban exile Celia Cruz). The links between Afro-Cuban religions and music-making remain significantly close.

Afro-Cuban rumba

Forget the glitzy ballroom-dancing image of **rumba**. The genuine article is informal and spontaneous – a pure Afro-Cuban music for voices and percussion. Performed in neighbourhood bars, tenement patios or on street corners, it becomes the collective expression of all who take part.

Rumba has roots in Afro-Cuban religion but it consolidated as a form in the docks of Havana and Matanzas, with workers in their spare moments singing and dancing and playing rhythms on cargo boxes. Its modern repertoire divides into three main dances: the *guaguancó*, *yambú* and *columbia*. The **guaguancó** is a dance for a couple in which a symbolic game of sexual flirtation is initiated; at its climax the man executes a pelvic thrust or *vacunao*, which the woman may, through her own dance, accept or reject. The **yambú** is also a couple dance, with slower, more stately steps (and no *vacunao*), popular with older people. In contrast, the **columbia** is a fast, furious and highly acrobatic solo male dance.

The music of rumba consists of percussion and vocal parts. The typical percussion includes one or two *tumbadores* (low-pitched conga drums), a high-pitched conga drum called a *quinto* (which is usually the "lead" drum) and a pair of *palitos* – sticks beaten against the wooden body of one of the drums. The vocal sections involve a leader (solo voice and quinto) and responder (chorus, low congas and palitos). Guaguancó and yambú also include a short defining, vocal introduction called the *diana*.

As interlocking cross-rhythms are created, the *claves* – a pair of sticks struck against one another – join in and establish the pattern called the **clave**, meaning "key", in the sense of a key

to a code, to which all the other rhythms relate. Further percussion might include the *cata* or *guagua* (a wooden tube played with sticks); the *maruga* (an iron shaker); and often a *cajón* (wooden packing-case). For religious occasions, batá drums might be added.

The basic **pattern of rumba** informs much Afro-Cuban music. A long lyrical vocal melody unfolds above the muttering drums, allowing the lead singer an opportunity to express emotions and show mastery of improvisation. Then on a cue from the band leader, the rhythm tightens up, the chorus joins in, and the call-and-response section steams off, the *quinto* improvising wildly under the singer's *inspiraciones*. This section, when the band really gets going and the dancing starts to heat up, is known as the *montuno*. Fused with the rhythms of son, it created **son montuno** – which was in turn transformed into salsa.

Rumba texts deal with a wide variety of concerns – sad, humorous or everyday topics – and are generally sung in Spanish, although the columbia often interjects chants from Santería and other Afro-Cuban cults. Rumbas may be improvised through repetition of just a few phrases.

Roots-style rumba can be heard easily enough around the island. Good events and places to check out in **Havana** are the *Sabados de Rumba* (Rumba Saturdays), organized by the Conjunto Folklórico Nacional, and the Callejon Hamel, in Centro Habana, which painter Salvador González has set up with the spirited young group Claves y Guaguanco. In the town of **Matanzas**, you should visit the local Casa de la Trova where the stunning **Los Muñequitos de Matanzas** (Little Dolls of Matanzas) perform. The group have been going for near on fifty years, their members now embracing three generations.

Danzón, charanga and the chachachá

While the rumba represents the essential Afro-Cuban tradition, *danzón* is the basic musical strain of Cuba's European settlers. Played by an *orquesta típica*, these (mostly) sedate and dignified dances were Cuba's original dance music exports.

The **orquesta típica** developed partly as a recreational version of the military marching band, its sound coming from the lead of violins and brass, with a pair of *timpani* (round-bottomed marching drums) playing melodies descended from European dance traditions. Originally played in the ballrooms of the big colonial houses, these were gradually Africanized as they were adopted by domestic servants and urban Cubans, until they took shape as the *habanera* (of which more below). Their petty-bourgeois flavour is about as "respectable" as Cuban music gets – not that there are any associations of class. Most of today's danzón aficionados are black and creole, and, on the whole, elderly, meeting up in atmospheric dancehalls on a Saturday night.

Cuban band leader **Miguel Failde** is allegedly responsible for the first danzón, when he slowed down the country dance form in the late 1880s, dividing it into sections and adding a provocative pause and syncopated rhythm. The country dance originated in the *contredanse* brought in the 1800s by the French who had fled to the Santiago area from nearby Saint-Domingue (today's Haiti) after the Haitian slave revolution. Listen carefully to danzón and you'll hear those insistent Afro-Cuban percussion rhythms, reminding you where you are.

Other danzón pioneers, who developed the music at a similar time and along a similar course to New Orleans jazz, include **Antonio María Romeu, José Urfe** and **Enrique Jorrín**, all of whom were active in Havana in the early decades of the twentieth century. Later, in the 1930s, a key contribution was made by the orchestra **Arcaño y sus Maravillos**, who introduced a final montuno section to the danzón. They also incorporated *congas*, a new style, close to son, which caught on like wildfire, consolidating the pre-eminence of son over danzón as the leading Cuban dance music.

In the early twentieth century, the orquestas típicas playing danzón had also created an offshoot known as *charanga* or *charanga francesa*, in which brass instruments were replaced with violins, flute, double bass and piano. The "francesa" tag had a double source: the absorption of the classic French trio of flute, piano and violin; and the music's popularity with *las francesas*, the madames who ran the high-class brothels in turn-of-the-century Havana.

The charanga ensemble thrived through the twentieth century, taking many Cuban musical forms and making them a part of its repertoire, particularly in their glory years between the 1930s and 1950s. Great charangas of this age included **Orquesta Aragón, Orquesta Riverside** and **Orquesta América**. The last, founded by the violinist Enrique Jorrín, are acknowledged as the creators of *chachachá*, the most popular ever Cuban dance, which swept across Europe and, above all, the USA in the 1950s. Jorrín apparently composed the first chachachá, "La Engañadora", after watching Americans struggle with the complex Cuban dance rhythms. In New York, chachachá, with its straightforward 1-2-3 footwork, was popularized by top Cuban-led big bands such as those of **Machito, Perez Prado, Tito Puente** and **Tito Rodríguez**, until it was pre-empted by the *mambo*, a development that came more from the tradition of *son conjuntos* (see below).

In Havana, several of the leading charangas are still going, half a century after their creation, often with musicians who played with the founders. The most notable is Orquesta Aragón, who have flourished for years under the guidance of virtuoso flautist **Richard Egües**. Among younger generation charangas, **Candido Fabré y su Banda** and **Charanga Habanera** carry on the tradition of adopting and mutating styles, the latter playing a style forged in the late 1990s called *timba*.

Cuban counterpoint

The thread that links these earlier Cuban styles of danzón and charanga to son and salsa is what music writer Peter Manuel has called the "anticipated bass" – a bass line pattern in which the final note of a bar anticipates the harmony of the following bar. This characteristic evolved from the *habanera*, with its suave, romantic melodies and recurring rhythm, and from its offshoot, the *bolero*. Its persistence underpins the flowing sequence and fertile relationship between dance genres that has developed over the decades in Cuba.

The rhythm works through the omission by the bass of the downbeat of the first bar, with an elision into the second bar, so that the music follows a two-bar pattern. The deliberate avoidance of the downbeat – with the rhythm in effect riding over it, with a multitude of polyrhythms released by other instruments – lends the music its unique flow and momentum, making it ideal for the fluid and supple salsa dance style. The body can choose to follow various rhythms at any one time, with different unstressed-stressed moments playing, yet all the time the maracas and cowbell underlying the strong tempo.

Manuel maintains – and he is almost certainly right – that this Cuban rhythm pattern has influenced the whole basis of modern Latin music, from Colombian *cumbia* to Dominican *merengue*.

The great Cuban folklorist Fernando Ortíz explains the development of the island's music as the interplay between **sugar and tobacco**. Cuba's African slaves were settled on the great sugar estates and created their religious and secular music from African traditions. The Spanish grew tobacco, and they brought with them the tradition of *décima* verse (ten-line verses, with a rhyming scheme established by the first line), and couple dancing. Most popular music forms – and not only in Cuba – have developed from the fusion of these two cultures.

Ortíz wittily calls this "Cuban counterpoint" – and son, which stands at the core of Latin music, is its prime example.

The sound of son

Son is the predominant musical force in Cuba and is regarded almost as a symbol of the island, unifying its European and Black culture. These days it takes many forms, from simple, rustic bands to the brassy arrangements of New York salsa. It has a common form, however, which as in rumba is centred upon a clave rhythm (related to the rumba clave). Bongos, maracas and *guiro* (scraper) add an improvisatory rhythmic counterpoint to the clave, while the bass plucks the "anticipated" movement described above. On top comes what is often referred to as the "Latin" layer of harmonic and melodic elements – notably the Cuban guitar known as the *tres* (so-called for its triple sets of double strings), which, with the vocals, provides the classic sound and texture.

Structurally, or at least lyrically, sones follow either the traditional Spanish décima form or the verso form. Son begins with a set of opening verses, then moves into a section known as the *montuno* in which the improvising *sonero* sings a repeated phrase, accompanied by the melodies of the tres, and is answered by the chorus.

As one of the most famous early soneros, Miguel Matamoros, told it: "No one knows exactly where son is from. It is from the Oriente countryside, the mountains, but not from any one place. They say it is from Baracoa but anywhere in the mountains there someone would bring a

tres guitar and right away a song was created. The old sones were made of nothing more than two or three words, which when I was young old black men could sing repeatedly for the whole night. Like that son which goes "Alligator, alligator, alligator, where is the alligator?"

In the late nineteenth century, **Oriente** had a very mixed population that included thousands of refugees – black and white – from Haiti's revolutionary wars. The francophone immigrants brought new elements to Cuba's African and Spanish mix, lending the extra ingredient to son, which was being forged in the 1880s by black and mulatto musicians. Son reached Havana around 1909, notably via the **Trio Oriental** who during the following decade created the classic sextet format. Renamed the **Sexteto Habanero**, they featured tres, guitar, bongo, string bass and a pair of vocalists (who also played claves and maracas).

Son began spreading in all kinds of directions, gathering Afro-Cuban roots in the bongo players' adoption of rhythmic elements from the cults, and at the same time being brought into the repertoire of the society danzón orchestras. American companies began recording groups like the Sexteto Habanero and **Sexteto Boloña** as early as 1912, but it was the advent of Cuban radio in 1922 and the regular broadcasting of live bands that consolidated son's success. In 1920 the singer and bandleader Miguel Matamoros copyrighted a son for the first time – "El Son de La Loma", one of the most popular ever written.

In the late 1920s, with the addition of a trumpet, the *sexteto* became a **septeto** and the son began to swing. One of the most significant *septetos*, **Septeto Nacional** (another group still going strong) came into being in 1927 under the leadership of the great **Ignacio Piñeiro**. Piñeiro was the composer of the acclaimed and enduring "Echalé salsita" (Throw Some Sauce In It), whose opening theme was adapted by George Gershwin for his Cuban Overture, after he had befriended Piñeiro on a trip to Havana. The song is also thought to be one of the sources for the term "salsa" in Latin music. During a long career, Piñeiro composed *guajira-son, bolero-son* and *guaracha-son*, a fusing of genres typical of Cuban popular music.

Another classic son, "El Manicero" (The Peanut Vendor), emerged in 1928. Written by Moises Simon for **Rita Montaner**, it was a huge hit for her in Paris, breaking Cuban music for the first time in Europe. In 1930 Don Aspiazu's Havana

Soneros, lyrics and boleros

The essential skill of every **sonero** is a total awareness of what every instrument is doing in order to improvise their vocals. The voices of the great soneros differ, but in general a high-pitched, somewhat nasal voice has been favoured.

The most popular themes in son **lyrics** are love and romance. Cuban musicians are besotted with their island and its women, composing romantic serenades to each, often interlinked and metaphorical. The language, usually very witty, often has a double meaning, which can be both chauvinistic and very funny.

The **bolero**, which evolved in the early twentieth century as a popular slow-dance song with lyrics in European *bel canto* style, unashamedly illustrates this sentimental and romantic tradition. It became popular as a voice and guitar idiom throughout much of Latin America from the 1920s. Although heavily influenced by Italian song, the bolero also accommodates subdued Afro-Cuban rhythms.

Orchestra, with their singer **Antonio Machín**, took the song to New York. Machín sang it to a slow rumba rhythm, with dancers performing choreographed rumbas on stage, and it became the top selling record in the US in 1931 – the first Cuban music to chart in America.

Two leading instrumentalists and bandleaders furthered the son sound in the middle years of the century: the blind tres player **Arsenio Rodríguez** and trumpeter **Félix Chappotín**. Rodríguez is considered the father of modern Afro-Cuban sound. His musical roots lay in the Congolese rituals of his family, instilled in him by his grandfather who was a slave, and he brought many of the *toques* used to address deities into son. He was a prodigious composer – his sones remain dominant in the repertoire – and his group, which he expanded with first congas and later an extra trumpet, more percussion and piano, became the most influential of the 1940s. Rodríguez also changed the structure of son, expanding the montuno with a *descarga* section of improvised solos. In 1951 he moved to New York, turning his group over to Chappotín, whose most significant innovation was to add the tight horn arrangements favoured by American swing bands of the period. Buena Vista star Rúben González was just one of the great Cuban musicians who passed through these bands.

A perhaps even more seminal bandleader – and one of Cuba's greatest ever soneros – was **Beny Moré**, the "Barbarian of Rhythm". Moré began his career singing with Miguel Matamoros and then with the highly influential jazz-oriented band of Cuban ex-pat Pérez Prado, in Mexico City. When he returned to Cuba in 1953, he formed a trailblazing band which he led with characteristic showmanship, singing, dancing and conducting. He was a brilliant arranger, too, drawing on a whole spectrum of styles, including son and guaracha rhythms, slower, romantic boleros, and the mambo that he had evolved with Prado. After the revolution, he stayed in Cuba and kept the party going until his death, hastened by alcohol, in 1963. Just 43, he was already a legend: 100,000 Cubans attended his funeral, and he continues to be cited by modern son musicians as the greatest of them all.

Cuban son, in the broader sense, was very much a part of mainstream popular music in the 1940s and 1950s, in North and South America as well as the Caribbean. The big US crazes were for chachachá and up-tempo mambo, while all other variants tended to be termed rumba (or rhumba), which came to be a catch-all for anything Latin. In New York, the mix of mambo with the Latin rhythms of Puerto Rico, Colombia and Dominican Republic – added to an injection of hi-tech instrumentation and rhythm –was eventually to transmute son into **salsa**.

Music and the revolution

It is impossible to understand developments in Cuban music without taking into account the **politics of the island**. Havana, during the 1920s and 1930s, became the favourite nightclub playground for American tourists evading the prohibition laws, and, post-war, developed as a major centre for gambling and prostitution. While this gained Havana Mafia connections and an undesirable reputation as the "whorehouse of the Caribbean", it did mean good money for entertainment and music – even though the population at large remained desperately poor. In addition, the close links with New York gave rise to stylish, inventive and cutting-edge big bands.

After 1959 and the **revolution**, the island's music business was, like everything else, transformed. Radio stations and record companies became state institutions. The mob pulled out with dictator Batista, and US-owned property was appropriated for workers. As hotels and nightclubs remained empty, many musicians joined those Cubans leaving the country for exile in Miami or New York. Among their number were **Celia Cruz** and her band **Sonoro Matancera**, who applied for US residency after securing a series of gigs at the Hollywood Palladium. In the decades since, Cruz has become the unrivalled "Queen of Salsa", while identifying herself strongly with the anti-Castro/Cuban boycott movement.

For Cubans who remained, the US boycott meant a desperate struggle for economic survival amid chronic shortages of basic goods. For musicians, at least until the liberalizing of the economy in the late 1990s, opportunities to record and sell records, or to tour, were severely limited. It is only in the past few years that Cuban music, as played in Cuba, has re-entered the international mainstream.

On the island, the post-revolution music scene soon shifted from the glamour of nightclubs and big orchestras to more local music making centred on **Casas de la Trova** (see box below) and to a system of state-employed musicians. From the 1960s onwards, promising young players were given a Conservatoire training – a university musical education drawing on both classical and popular island traditions. When they graduated, they joined the ranks of full-time musicians categorized as *profesionales*, and could draw a state salary from the Ministry of Culture – which in turn took ninety percent of their earnings.

With few opportunities to travel, musicians were forced to return to their roots, playing continually to local audiences. This was frustrating, especially for younger musicians who found it tough and often impossible to get equipment to form bands or to make their own records. **Egrem**, Cuba's state-owned recording company, had to function in an economy which had higher priorities than importing vinyl. Popular albums sold out

---

Casas de la Trova

The best place to hear music in Cuba is in a **Casa de la Trova**. Most towns have at least one of these clubs, which are essentially a revolution-era update of an old Cuban institution – a place where *trovas* or ballads are sung by *trovadores*. Nowadays the performances are more diverse and often completely spontaneous, with people joining in and getting up to play whenever they feel like it. You can hear anything from a single trovador with a guitar to a traditional Cuban sexteto or septeto.

The casas range from grand old colonial buildings with courtyards and palm trees to small, impromptu performing spaces with a few chairs off the street. In practice they are like informal clubs or bars where musicians gather to play, people gather to listen and everybody exchanges opinions and reminiscences.

The most celebrated Casa de la Trova is in **Santiago**, on Heredia, and there is music here afternoons and evenings, every day of the week. It's just one room with wide windows and doors open onto the street and a small platform at the

end for the performers. Further up Heredia are other venues like the *Peña del Tango* and the *Museo de Carnival*, which often have more organized musical performances. At the weekends there are likely to be bands on the street as well.

In **Havana** there are two Casas de la Trova, the *Cerro* (Panchito Gómez 265 e/ Perfecto Lacoste y Néstor Sardiñas) and the *10 de Octubre* (Calzada de Luyanó e/ Reforma y Guanabacoa). The latter is a little out of the way, in the Lujana area, but worth finding: a small local hall in a line of severely peeling colonial terraces, it possesses all the charm of old Havana, and appropriately enough features regular performances by the historic Sexteto Habanero.

There are other good Casas de la Trova in **Baracoa, Sancti Spiritus, Matanzas, Trinidad, Pinar del Río** and **Guanabacoa**. See the relevant chapters for more information.

Also worth checking out for concerts are the **Casas de Cultura** around the island, another revolutionary Cuban institution.

Son veterans: Buena Vista Social Club

"This is the best thing I was ever involved in," said **Ry Cooder** upon the release of *Buena Vista Social Club*, the album of acoustic Cuban rhythms he recorded in Havana. Since then *Buena Vista* has sold more than two million copies, won a Grammy award and become a live show capable of selling out New York's Carnegie Hall.

Yet Cooder is the first to admit that *Buena Vista* is not really his album at all. He rightly wanted all the glory to go to the legendary Cuban veterans who were rescued from obscurity and retirement and assembled in Havana's Egrem studio to record the album over seven days in March 1996. "These are the greatest musicians alive on the planet today, hot-shot players and classic people," says Cooder. "In my experience Cuban musicians are unique. The organization of the musical group is perfectly understood, there is no ego, no jockeying for position so they have evolved the perfect ensemble concept."

The role of composer and guitarist **Compay Segundo** was central to the project. "As soon as he walked into the studio it all kicked in. He was the leader, the fulcrum, the pivot. He knew the best songs and how to do them because he's been doing them since World War One."

Initially a clarinettist, Segundo invented his own seven-stringed guitar, known as the *armonico*, which gives his music its unique resonance. In the late 1920s he played with **Nico Saquito** before moving to Havana where he formed a duo with Lorenzo Hierrezuelo. In 1950 he formed **Compay Segundo y su Grupo**, yet by the following decade he had virtually retired from music, working as a tobacconist for seventeen years.

Rúben González (born in 1918) is described by Cooder as "the greatest piano soloist I have ever heard in my life, a cross between Theolonius Monk and Felix the Cat." Together with Lili Martínez and Peruchín, González forged the style of modern Cuban piano playing in the 1940s. He played with Enrique Jorrín's orchestra for 25 years, travelling widely through Latin America.

When invited to play on *Buena Vista*, González did not even own a piano. However, since the release of his first solo album, González has toured Europe and recorded a second solo album in London.

Other key members of the Buena Vista club included **Omara Portuondo**, the bolero singer known as "the Cuban Edith Piaf", **Eliades Ochoa**, the singer and guitarist from Santiago who leads Cuarteto Patria, and the sonero **Ibrahim Ferrer**, whose solo album Cooder produced on a return visit to Havana.

Archive footage of Segundo and González can be seen in Wim Wenders' full-length documentary feature **film**, *Buena Vista Social Club*, filmed in Cuba and at the Buena Vista concerts in Amsterdam and New York in 1998.

Nigel Williamson

---

instantly on release and the shortage of vinyl meant no re-pressing.

Artists who managed to tour abroad could record for foreign labels. But life wasn't so easy for them, either, and the defection of Irakere musicians **Arturo Sandoval** and **Paquito D'Rivera**, both at one time ardent supporters of the revolution, brought into sharp focus the pressures on the music industry under Castro's government. And for musicians who didn't make it on to international tours, the US blockade continued to frustrate any direct contact with the Latin fusions developing in places like New York.

The legalization of the dollar and consequent changes in the economy have been welcomed by musicians. These days they are still nominally organized through Institutes of Music but they can work freely inside and outside the country, contract to a recording company, negotiate their own rates, and pay only a small percentage of hard currency earnings to the government. Some musicians are now amongst the highest paid professionals in Cuba.

Egrem, meanwhile, has been licensing its priceless archive to a host of companies around the world and renting out its old studio in Havana to producers and bands from outside Cuba. They have built a new up-to-date recording studio, as have other private investors, among them the musicians Silvio Rodríguez and Pablo Milanés. Many new **venues** for live music have also been opened, for both tourists and the Cuban public.

CONTEXTS

Such changes perhaps reflect a belated recognition of Cuba's musical resources by the government. In the 1980s, it was reported that musicians travelling abroad brought in the economy's largest hard currency earnings after sugar, fruit and tobacco. And that figure must have soared in the last years of the century, spurred by the vastly successful *Buena Vista Social Club* recordings, produced by US guitarist Ry Cooder, Cuban arranger Juan de Marcos González and the London-based World Circuit label (see box on p.486).

The son goes on

With the exception of the "singer-songwriter" *nueva trova* artists (see p.488), all of the best-known contemporary Cuban bands and musicians – both on the island and abroad – have evolved from the son tradition. They include traditionalists, revivalists and a good number of groups re-booting the tradition, or fusing it with other forms.

Among the traditional groups, leaders include **Septeto Nacional**, originally founded by Ignacio Piñeiro and re-established in 1985 to perform classic son, and the the wonderful, unfeasibly long-established **Orquesta Aragón**, with their even more old-fashioned charanga. **Orquesta Ritmo Oriental**, with a traditional flute and violin charanga line-up, play a mix of son, charanga and música campesina (country music), while **Orquesta Original de Manzanillo** have also adapted the charanga sound.

An excellent revival band, following the classic sexteto traditions, is **Sierra Maestra**. They remain firmly Cuban-based but tour frequently in Latin America and Europe. One of their founders was tres player and arranger **Juan de Marcos González**, the mastermind behind Buena Vista Social Club. These projects are, of course, themselves son revivals, bringing together old and new generation players – something Cuba has always been good at. Their "old world" sound, harkening back to the pre-revolutionary era when many of the players made their names, contrasts with the more urgent, streetwise music coming out of Cuba today.

Two important musics that have fed into son are *música campesina* and *changui*, both of them rural. Campesina (country music) is characterized by classic vocal harmonies and upbeat, swingy guitar and percussion. Its top exponent, who has really created her own form with doses of Afro-Cuban rumba and son, is **Celina González** (see box below). The key player in changui, over the past decades, was the late **Elio Revé**, whose **Orquesta Revé** provided opportunities for a string of young players. The potency of Revé's music came from the fusion of its strong regional form with urban son and the use of batá drums from Santería ceremonies. His lyrics were imaginative, too, reflecting popular opinions on social and political issues. A charismatic personality, his death in a car accident in 1997 was a major loss. His sound lives on, in a rather more salsa-driven

---

Celina González and Cuban country music

With its layers of pulsating African percussion, Latin melodies on guitar and tres and Afro-Cuban rhythmic patterns, there's no mistaking Cuban country music for its American namesake. **Música campesina** is a kind of roots salsa and its undisputed queen is **Celina González**. Her music ranges from a sparse combination of voice, percussion and guitar, to more of a big-band sound with punchy brass and strings. But whatever the line-up, her style is rooted in the music of the Cuban countryside.

In the 1970s, after the death of her husband, their son Reutilio Junior joined Celina as her singing partner, and, with the band **Campo Alegre**, helped update the music by incorporating the trumpet, bass, congas and marimba from the urban septetos of Havana. Although this kind of music was looked down on and discriminated against before the revolution, these days every single Cuban radio station has at least one daily programme devoted to música campesina, while Celina has her own daily programme on Radio Taino.

In 1998, her fiftieth anniversary as a performer, Celina recorded a new album of her own as well as another with the classic charanga group, **Orquesta América**, singing witty guarachas in her startlingly bright, swingy tones. She's a huge star in Colombia, Venezuela and beyond, with numerous awards to her name, and her popularity shows no sign of waning.

form, in **Dan Den**, a band formed by his long-time cohort Juan Carlos Alfonso.

An earlier partner in Revé's band – and arguably the most significant figure in late-twentieth-century son – was Juan Formell, who in 1969 formed his own group, **Los Van Van**. At root a very tight charanga band – flute, violin, piano and percussion – Los Van Van invented new changes in rhythm and timbre, with Formell introducing Afro-Cuban elements and, like band leaders before him, duplicating percussion parts to other instruments, notably strings. Adding a trombone, synthesizer and drum, Van Van developed a variant of son called **songo**. They remain at the innovative edge of Cuban dance music, producing infectious hit songs like "Titimani" and "Muevete", whose topical lyrics capture the ironic edge of daily life in the capital.

A more jazz-oriented direction was taken by the group **Irakere**, which was formed in 1973 by composer-pianist Jesús "Chucho" Valdés, Paquito D'Rivera and Arturo Sandoval. Irakere were the first big contemporary Cuban jazz group, combining son and Afro-Cuban music with modern jazz. Their name and their music emphasized their African inheritance – Irakere is Yoruba for "forest" – and their arrival heralded a new age in Cuban and Latin jazz. Irakere's line-up has changed often over the years, with members going on to found their own groups, though its most notable transformation came in the late 1980s when D'Rivera and Sandoval both defected from the island.

In the same period, Adalberto Alvarez and his band **Son 14** took son further, demonstrating a challenging awareness of salsa developments outside the island, and creating a wealth of compositions which have had huge coverage abroad.

As to a new generation, perhaps the future was indicated at the beginning of the 1990s by the band whose name implies just that: **NG La Banda** (New Generation The Band). Founded in 1988 by ex-Van Van and Irakere flautist José Luis Cortés, they set out to "search for the Cuban music of the future", establishing a more aggressive, street-based contact with their public. Their position on the musical map was established with the 1993 hit, "Echale Limon" – literally, "Put a Lemon In It", the Cuban slang for when things go wrong. The lyrics, couched in uncompromising barrio slang, caught the mood of the country.

A decade on, NG remain hugely popular and innovative, mixing in elements of rap and jazz,

along with complex arrangements by *los metales de terror* – the horns of terror. Their lead in bringing rap into son looks set to become a pattern – already Havana has a number of young would-be **rap** stars. One group that looks interesting is **Las Orishas**, who recorded their first album in Paris in 1999, rapping above son and rumba riffs.

Trova and Nueva Trova

Post-revolution Cuba produced one great musical style that stood outside the mainspring of son, and which instead had close links with the pan-Latin American developments of nueva canción.

Nueva trova (new ballad) – like nueva canción – is associated with the 1960s and 1970s, the years of protest throughout Latin America, when Cuba was seen by many as a beacon against the oppression of the continent's dictators. Cuba's new song, like its Chilean and Argentinian counterparts, miraculously instilled politics into achingly beautiful songs of love and loss and personal exploration, and perfectly suited the times.

Although no longer at the forefront of Cuban music, trova remains an active part of the scene, to be heard throughout the island in Csas de la Trova (see p.485). Its key singers – **Silvio Rodríguez** and **Pablo Milanés** – remain hugely respected both on the island and throughout the Spanish-speaking world.

Troubador roots

Cuba's original *trovadores* were true troubadours, who roved the island in the early decades of the twentieth century, accompanying themselves on guitar while singing country songs, sones and boleros. Their songs were typically concerned with love and patriotism, often with Cuba personified as a woman.

One of Cuba's most popular singers of all time was the diminutive **Sindo Garay**, from Santiago de Cuba, the creator of the unforgettable bolero "La Bayamesa" (Girl from Bayamo), written in 1909 and still a part of the trova repertoire. The town of Bayamo was the cradle of the independence movement and the "girl" in question was thus the love of all Cuban patriots. Garay was a leading trova singer during the Machado dictatorship in the 1930s and 40s and was a fixture at the *Bodeguita del Medio*, a bar near the cathedral in Habana Vieja which was to play a key role in the runup to the revolution as a meeting place of intellectuals and critics of Batista.

Another major figure of the early canción world was **Joseíto Fernández**, who wrote the rustic "Guantanamera" (a tribute to the women of Guantánamo, with various versions including lines from Cuba's national poet, José Martí), one of the most covered songs of all time, and regarded as a kind of national hymn. **Nico Saquito** from Santiago de Cuba composed over five hundred songs in the trova tradition (and, incidentally, worked with both the young Celina González and Compay Segundo). **Carlos Puebla**'s quartet sang witty songs of the revolution's achievements, including such classics as "Y en eso llegó Fidel" (And Then Fidel Arrived) and "El son de la alfebetización" (The Son of Literacy).

A regular at the *Bodeguita del Medio*, Carlos Puebla's strength – bolstered by his *cuarteto típico*, the **Tradicionales** – lay in his lilting, poetic subversion of country guajira and guaracha forms, singing in duo with his right-hand man and with key use of the *marimbula*. Nicknamed

"the voice of the revolution", he was Cuba's only notable political singer until the nueva trova movement of the early 1970s. In common with those later singers, however, political songs amounted to only a small portion of his output, and he also performed covers of sones by Matamoros and others.

New ballads

The **nueva trova** movement had clear links with the *nueva canción* (new song) composers appearing in this period throughout Latin America, but its emergence was entirely independent. The form was created by those who were reaching adolescence at the time of the revolution – those for whom Fidel's maxim of "Within the revolution, everything; outside the revolution, nothing" seemed only logical given the experiences of their childhood. Great emphasis was placed on lyrics, replacing the love and nationalism of the old trova with an exploration of personal experience and desires, relating the

---

¡Ojala! – Silvio Rodríguez

¡Ojalá! – Let's hope! – is the name given to the recording studios **Silvio Rodríguez** built in Havana in the mid-1990s, and seems to epitomize a man who is arguably the most significant singer-songwriter of his generation in the world. One of those responsible for creating nueva trova, Rodríguez, like his close friend and fellow singer Pablo Milanés, has been one of the revolution's major supporters and, for a time, one of its major wage earners. As well as building the studios where the Ojalá label records everything from Cuban rap to new, young trovadores, Rodríguez has recently been involved in directing the building of a large complex of state-owned studios in Havana, one of which can accommodate an entire symphony orchestra.

"In the beginning people didn't understand us," Rodríguez recalls. "Our songs were self-critical and there was no tradition of that, but they were songs full of commitment. The 1960s were the hot soup of what was happening – new things – and there was a moment when the nueva trova was in the front line of the ideological fight. Now we see clearly that it was and it is a privilege that before us no other generation of trovadores could be real protagonists."

While his actions have rarely cast a shadow on his steadfast relationship with the state – which he explores in the classics "Te Doy una Canción" (I Offer You A Song) and "Vamos Andar" (Let's Walk) – Rodríguez's undogmatic, metaphoric songs, many with a broad, international perspective, are very far from being a mouthpiece for the revolution. Despite his membership of the Cuban parliament since 1992, he states that "I have never tried to be the voice of the revolution – that is Fidel. It doesn't appeal to me to be something official because there hasn't been anything more anti-official than my songs, which are critical a lot of the time, show contradictions, doubts and reservations. But yes, I am someone who feels for the revolution, who believes in it, who believes in Fidel. I feel it is necessary to have a sense of unity in terms of feelings for the country and the will to overcome all the problems we have. Even though I think it will always be like this, there will always be things to overcome and we are going to be in disagreement with a whole lot of things because that is life. One does things for human reasons not for ideological ones."

DISCOGRAPHY

COMPILATIONS

Cuba, I Am Time (Blue Jackal Entertainment, US). This magnificent 4-CD compilation, released in 1997, features more than fifty artists and includes pretty much the best of each style.

VINTAGE RECORDINGS

Various *Hot Cuban Dance Music 1909–37* (Harlequin, UK) and *The Cuban Danzón – 1906–29* (Arhoolie, US). Surprisingly good recordings of son in its earliest acoustic form – a transition between formal dance tunes and jazz.

Various *The Roots Of Salsa* and *Sextetos Cubanos* (Arhoolie, US). A pair of discs that move the story on to the 1920s and 1930s, and the developed son of the Havana sextetos. Tracks are rough and ready and utterly charming.

Conjunto Chappotín y sus Estrellas *Tres Señores del Son* (Egrem, Cuba). The unfailingly inventive trumpeter Chappotín has a status in Cuban music on a level with Louis Armstrong in American jazz. This fabulous collection showcases some of the great figures of the 1940s and 1950s.

Conjunto Matamoros *Bailaré tu Son* (Tumbao, Spain). An entrancing selection of classic-era son, with hugely enjoyable vocals, performed by a typical old-style combo with congo, bongo, piano and trumpet.

Machito and his Afro-Cubans *Cha Cha Cha at the Palladium* (Tio, US). The powerful riffing and layered textures of big swing jazz bands brought to Cuban dance music to majestic effect.

Beny Moré *La Colección Cubana: Beny Moré* (Nascente, UK). A budget introduction to the master, compiled mainly from RCA recordings of the 1950s.

Orquesta Aragón *Riverside Years* (RCA International, US). The seminal charanga band, featuring the golden voice of Beny Moré and stunning piano solos from Perez Prado.

Arsenio Rodríguez *Dundunbanza* (Tumbao, Spain). This is irresistible Cuban-era Arsenio, featuring tracks recorded in Havana from 1946 to 1951 with a horn section led by Felix Chappotín.

MODERN RECORDINGS

Various *Ahora Sí! Here Comes Changui* (Corason, Mexico). A superb set of changui from Grupo Changui de Guantánamo, Familia Valera Miranda and Grupo Estrellas de Campesinas.

Various *Cuba Caribe* (EMI Hemisphere, UK). A fine 1999 selection of contemporary bands unashamedly oriented around salsa. Hot tracks from Adalberto Alvarez, Juan Formell, Tamayo, and a salsa-rock creation from José Luis Cortés and NG La Banda.

Various *Cuba Classics 2: Dancing with the Enemy* and *Cuba Classics 3: ¡Diablo al Infierno!* (Luaka Bop/Warner, US). Compilations mixing the big names with some truly obscure recordings. *Vol 2* covers the Cuban sound of the 1960s and 70s; *Vol 3* delves into the more eclectic 1980s and 90s.

Various *Cuba Música Campesina* (Auvidis, France). The best campesina anthology – a collection of bands capturing the country style in all its freshness. It even has a decent version of the most popular of Cuban songs, "Guantanamera".

Adalberto Alvarez y Su Son *La Salsa Caliente* (Sonido/Vogue, France). This is a good example of pianist, singer and guiro supremo Alvarez's highly commercial sound – making the odd nod to son – that goes down a storm on his regular festival tours.

Afro-Cuban All Stars *A Todo Cuba Le Gusta* (World Circuit, UK). A second wonderful record from the Buena Vista crew, with irresistible swing, formidable singing, and great arrangements. *Distinto, Diferente* (World Circuit, UK), the combo's 1999 follow-up, has some great moments, too.

Buena Vista Social Club *Buena Vista Social Club* (World Circuit, UK). Big band son of the old style, with historic songs imaginatively and seductively updated.

Cuarteto Patria *A Una Coqueta* (Corason, Mexico). Cuarteto Patria emerged in 1940 in Santiago de Cuba and is still going strong. Recorded in Cuba and Mexico between 1986 and 1993, this is a delightful selection of well-known sones and boleros with a gentle country sound.

Cubanismo *Cubanismo!* (Hannibal/Ryko, UK). Jesús Alemañy has been reworking the classic Cuban trumpet sound over the past few years to stunning effect with his fifteen-piece group, Cubanismo. This was their first album.

Dan Den *Viejo Lazaro y Otros Exitos* (Qbadisc, US). Trombone-heavy dance band Dan Den hit a peak of popularity in the mid-1990s with their funky mix of contemporary Cuban dance grooves.

Estrellas de Areito *Los Heroes* (World Circuit, UK). The "Stars of Areito", a dream band including three generations of musicians, got together for a legendary five-day recording session in 1979. The sound ranges through classic conjunto son, danzón and chachacha into more jazz-oriented *descargas*.

Ibrahim Ferrer *Buena Vista Social Club Presents Ibrahim Ferrer* (World Circuit, UK). Ferrer sings mainly romantic boleros but also shows he can mambo with the best.

Celina González *Fiesta Guajira* (World Circuit, UK). An excellent compilation drawn from Celina's 1980s albums on the Havana-based Egrem label.

Rubén González *Introducing Rubén González* (World Circuit, UK). An utterly wonderful series of son/jazz improvisations, with elegant, restrained backing from the Buena Vista crew.

Irakere and Chucho Valdes *La Colección Cubana* (Nascente, UK). This budget-priced 1998 compilation exhibits the band's tradition of combining virtuoso musicianship and sophisticated improvisation with a profound appreciation of their African roots.

Jóvenes Clásicos del Son *Fruta bomba* (Tumi, UK). A new band, revisiting the son tra-dition with a sensibility drawn from rap, funk, soul, salsa, merengue, pop and jazz.

NG La Banda *En la Calle* (Qbadisc, US). The 1992 debut: a disc of flat-out performances and innovative arrangements.

Orquesta Revé *La Explosión del Momento* (Real World, UK). Afro-Cuban changui-son at its best, played by its creators: quirky, rhythmic and infectious with sassy contemporary lyrics.

Orquesta Ritmo Oriental *Historia de la Ritmo Vol 1* and *Vol 2* (Qbadisc, US). Retains the line-up of a traditional charanga band but the arrangements and style of playing reflect the sharper, more punchy sound of modern Cuban dance music.

Orishas *A Lo Cubano* (EMI, France). An inspired mix of traditional son and rumba riffs and instrumentation, over which rap alternates with the soulful voice of a sonero.

Compay Segundo *Compay Segundo y su Grupo, 1956–57* (Tumbao, Spain). Strong melodies with tight rhythm, perfect harmonies and a killer chorus, this reissue is a winner.

Septeto Nacional *Más Cuba Libres* (World Network, Germany). This celebration of the Septeto's 70th anniversary brought in some very special guests, including Buena Vista star Pío Leyva.

Sierra Maestra *Dundunbanza* (World Circuit, UK). Superb 1994 disc fusing sensual rhythms with witty lyrics and a wonderful, caressing mellowness.

Son 14 *Son 14 with Adalberto Alvarez* (Tumi, UK). An unerring, joyously headlong selection of the very best from the group's eleven albums.

Los Van Van *Los Van Van: La Colección Cubana* (Nascente, UK). A budget-priced, sixty-minute selection of Los Van Van's finest 1980s and 90s tracks.

Vieja Trova Santiaguera *Hotel Asturias* (NubeNegra, Spain). This experienced quintet support rough-voiced harmony vocals with tres, guitar, bass and hand percussion. A uniquely Cuban mixture of passion, sweetness and relaxation.

Continues overleaf

DISCOGRAPHY (CONTINUED)

RUMBA AND AFRO-CUBAN MUSIC

Various *Afro-Cuba: A Musical Anthology* (Rounder, US). A useful selection of field and studio recordings from the main Santería cults.

Various *Tumi Cuba Classics Volume 3: Rumba* (Tumi, UK). Probably the best compilation of rumba available, mostly guaguancó, but with examples of columbia, yambú and others.

Clave y Guaguancó *Dejalá en la Puntica* (Egrem, Cuba). Contemporary street-corner rumba with an edge. Racing drums underpin richly textured coros and dramatic solo singers on this fine record.

Grupo Afrocuba De Matanzas *Rituales Afrocubanos* (Egrem, Cuba). Packed full of ritual music, this recording includes not only the usual songs of praise from the Lucumí religion, but also Arara and Bantu music from alternative African roots.

Los Muñequitos de Matanzas *Rumba Caliente* (Qbadisc, US). One of Cuba's top ensembles plays classic Cuban rumba – rich in African elements, using only percussion and vocals, and brilliantly melodic.

Lazaro Ros *Olorun* (Green Linnet/Xenophile, US). Lázaro Ros is the best known Cuban singer of religious music. Eleven toques for eleven orishas, with beautiful singing from Ros and Grupo Olórun, backed only by drumming.

Yoruba Andabo *El Callejón de los Rumberos* (PM, Spain). Accessible and exciting roots rumba: passionate singing above well-recorded drumming of startling complexity.

NUEVA TROVA

Pablo Milanés *Cancionero* (World Pacific, US). A marvellous 1993 anthology. Recommended.

Carlos Puebla *Carlos Puebla y sus Tradicionales* (Egrem-Artex, Canada). Some of Puebla's great songs – political and otherwise – with his classic quartet of guitar, marimbula, close harmonies and percussion.

Silvio Rodríguez *Cuban Classics 1: Canciones Urgentes* (Luaka Bop/Warner). As the Cuban press has said of his songs: "Here we have the great epic poems of our days." This compilation shows the man at his very best – check the live recording of "Unicornio" in particular.

Carlos Varela *Monedas al Aire* (Qbadisc, US). Varela's revelatory first album, rocking up the familiar guitar with less metaphoric, more direct lyrics than nueva canción.

---

contradictions and anxieties of life from within the context of a revolutionary society.

The new music drew on folk guitar traditions from Cuba and the wider Spanish-speaking world (which in turn were influenced by French *chanson*). Its singers became known as *canto-autores* (singer-songwriters) and while their philosophy and perspective was Cuban, it had something in common with North American and British singer-songwriters, as well as with singers such as Joan Manuel Serrat and Lluis Llach, struggling to maintain their Catalonian identity under Franco's dictatorship, and with the nueva canción singers of Chile and Argentina.

A key development in nueva trova occurred when a group of young musicians came together at Havana's ICAIC film school and recorded basic sessions with Cuba's leading composer and guitarist, **Leo Brouwer**. Among a group which included Vicente Feliú, Noel Nicola and Sara González were **Pablo Milanés** and **Silvio Rodríguez**, arguably the most influential singers of their generation in the Spanish-speaking world.

Both Milanés and Rodríguez have composed a huge body of work, including bitter-sweet love songs which captured a mood absent in other Cuban music. The root ingredients are those of the classic troubadour – vocals and solo acoustic guitar – though both have gone on to lead bands of varying size, their music developing in various directions, easily adapting itself to big arrangements.

Hallmarks of their songs are a sense of metaphysical emotion in joy and loss, an existential questioning (particularly of the vicissitudes of personal relationships), a pervasive use of metaphor and indirect subject, a sense of reflection and vulnerability and a non-gendered approach to the complex and uneven experience of love.

The Cuban experience is pre-eminent in the lyrics of both composers. Indeed, in the early 1990s, after a key tour to celebrate the achievements of the revolution – singing from a huge repertoire of love songs on every aspect of island life – Silvio Rodríguez seemed to have followed in the steps of José Martí and taken on the mantle of national poet in the eyes of his public and the Cuban press. Between 1992 and 1996 he produced a triptych of albums, this time paring down from his big band to solo vocals and guitar. The feel of the records was almost deliberately amateur, with Rodríguez multi-tracking to duet with himself – keeping nuanced stumbles and asides. Each of the albums included a reflective sequence of powerful, sometimes bleak, songs rooted in cameos of individual lives. The whole process was a political statement in itself, a wooing of small audiences back to basics.

In the early 1990s, a new and more critical generation found a voice in the highly articulate songwriter **Carlos Varela**. His songs expressed the troubles of Cuban society and the frustrations of the island's youth, without much recourse to metaphor. His song "Guillermo Tell" (William Tell), for example, had a direct warning to the old generation of politicians: "William Tell, your son has grown up/And now he wants to shoot the arrow/It's his turn now to prove his valour/Using your very own bow!" Musically, Varela fluctuates between the old-style acoustic treatment of Milanés and Rodríguez and a rock (often heavy rock) backing. Recently he has recorded in Spain, producing material with a modern Spanish rock feel.

Jan Fairley

A fuller version of this article appears in
The Rough Guide to World Music: Vol. 2
– the Americas, Asia and Pacific.

Cuban sport

Since the 1959 revolution Cuba has achieved a level of sporting success that would make any country proud, consistently finishing amongst the top ten in the Olympic Games' medals tables, the biggest test of a country's sporting prowess. Yet Cuban sportsmen and women keep unusually low profiles, attracting far less media attention than many of their foreign counterparts. Uniquely, this nation of just 11 million people has reached the highest international standards in a great many sports, but has remained outside of the professionalization and commercialization that have transformed what is now a multimilliondollar industry almost everywhere else.

Cuban sport prior to the revolution

Before the political system that has spawned so many top-class athletes was established by Fidel Castro and his government, Cuba had had very few sports stars of truly international calibre. It was, however, one of the first nations to take part in the **Modern Olympic Games**, competing as one of the twenty countries present in Paris in 1900. It was at these games, the second of the modern era, and four years later in St Louis, that twelve of the fourteen Olympic **medals** collected by Cuban competitors before the revolution were won. All of those twelve were in **fencing**, a sport at which Cubans continue to excel, and the hero was Ramón Fonst. Having won the épée event in Paris, he went on to secure two further victories in St Louis, thereby becoming the first man in Olympic history to win three individual gold medals.

Cuba was also one of the three original founding members of the **Central American and Caribbean Games**, the oldest regional international sporting tournament in the world. In October 1926, 269 sportsmen from Mexico, Cuba and Guatemala took part in the inaugural championships and in 1930 Cuba staged the second of these games, when women participated for the first time.

The majority of the Cuban population, however, were alienated not only from these successes but from organized sport in general, as only the privileged classes had access to sports facilities. The sporting infrastructure was based predominantly on **private clubs**, from which black Cubans were almost always banned, reflecting the social divisions that marked society as a whole. It's no coincidence that the country's highest Olympic achievement was in fencing, a traditionally aristocratic discipline. Class determined participation in less competitive arenas, too: tennis, golf and sailing were all the exclusive domain of organizations such as the Havana Yacht Club or the Vedado Tennis Club. A large number of clubs belonged to the Unión Atlética Amateur de Cuba, a governing body for which, in order to become a member, applicants were required to supply certification including a photograph confirming their skin colour. Many of the most popular spectator sports, though accessible to a broader swathe of the population, were just as representative of the socio-political situation. The appeal of horse racing, dog racing, cock fighting, billiards and boxing derived mainly from **gambling** and, particularly during the 1940s and 1950s, was inextricably tied up with tourism and corruption. Furthermore, no government during the six decades before the revolution made any significant investment in sport. The number of teachers in physical education was just 800 in a population of ten million whilst only two percent of school children received any kind of formal physical education at all.

It was in **boxing** and **baseball** that popular sporting culture was most avidly expressed. These were genuinely sports for the masses but though Cuba had one of the world's first national baseball leagues and hosted its own boxing bouts, the really big names and reputations were made in the US. Indeed, both baseball and boxing were brought to Cuba by Americans and owe much of their popularity to American commerce and organization. With such close links between the two countries during the years of the "pseudo-republic" when a significant number of Americans lived and worked in Cuba, very few talented sportsmen went unnoticed by the fight organizers and league bosses on the other side of the Florida Straits. Almost all the biggest names in these two sports during this period – baseball players like **Tony Pérez**, **José Cardenal** and **Tito Fuentes** and boxers such as **Benny Paret** and **Kid Chocolate** – gained their fame and fortune in the US. Exploitation, particularly of boxers, was common and a significant proportion of them were simply pawns in a corrupt world of fight rigging and bribery.

Sport and the revolution

With sport prior to 1959 characterized by corruption, social discrimination and a generally poor standing in international competitions, the revolutionary government had more than enough to get its teeth into. Led by Fidel Castro himself, who has always shown a keen interest in sport, under the new regime the entire system of participation was shaken up and restructured.

The new ideology of sport

Like the Russians before them, the Cubans developed a whole new ideology around sport and its role in society. Though borrowing heavily from the Soviet model, this new ideology was very much a Cuban creation, influenced as much by the desire to make Cuba a great sporting nation as by the desire to institute social change. Rather than looking to Marx as a guide, the revolutionaries chose the ideas of Baron **Pierre de Coubertin**, the Frenchman responsible for the revival of the Olympic Games, which began their modern era in 1896. Coubertin believed that one of the reasons the Ancient Greeks had reached such high levels of social and cultural achievement was the emphasis they placed on physical activity. Rejecting the neo-Marxist argument that the competitive element of sport promotes social division and elitism, the Cubans adopted Coubertin's basic premise that participation in sport was capable of bridging differences in politics, race and religion, thus encouraging feelings of brotherhood and social equality. Believing that it is not the nature of sport but the way in which it is approached and practised that would determine its effect, the Cuban state made sport one of the priorities in the transformation of society.

Sport and physical education were incorporated into the wider revolutionary goals of education in general, and were considered inseparable from the process of development towards Che Guevara's concept of *El Hombre Nuevo* – the

New Man (see box, pp.282-83) – one of the cornerstones of Cuban communist theory. As well as promoting better health and fitness, the Cubans claim organized physical activities and games encourage discipline, responsibility, will-power, improved social communication skills, a cooperative spirit, internationalism, and generally contribute to the ethical and moral character of a person. Few governments have placed such emphasis on sport, and the right of all Cubans to participate in physical education and organized sports was even included in several clauses of the 1976 Cuban Constitution. The principal commitment – that every Cuban has the right to practice sport and should be guaranteed the necessary conditions to do so – paved the way for the changes made in this sphere from the very start of revolutionary change after 1959.

Sport for all

The transformation of post-revolutionary Cuban sport began in earnest on February 23, 1961, with the creation of **INDER** (National Institute of Sport, Physical Education and Recreation). Still very much an active institution today – its headquarters are in Havana's Ciudad Deportiva, next to the road to the airport – this body was directly responsible for carrying out the programmes of *masividad*, or sport for the masses, which formed the foundation of the new system. With the creation of INDER a campaign was launched aiming to diversify the number of sporting activities available to the public, to eliminate exclusivity and to involve every citizen in some kind of regular physical activity.

The "cradle-to-grave" politics of the revolution applied as much to sport as anything else, and the Cubans waste no time in introducing children to the benefits of physical exercise. Under the banner of slogans such as "the home is the gymnasium", INDER has always encouraged parents to actively pursue the physical health of their **children**, with classes in massage and physical manipulation offered for the benefit of babies just 45 days old. Early in the morning during term time, it is still common to see groups of schoolchildren doing exercises in the local parks and city squares with their teachers. These places are also where the so-called *circulos de abuelos* meet, groups of elderly people, usually past retirement age, performing basic stretches together. No section of society was to remain outside of these developments as sport and exercise became ingrained in the Cuban way of life, with many of the most significant changes taking place during INDER's first decade.

In 1966 legislation was passed guaranteeing workers paid leisure time for recreational activities and in 1967 entrance charges to sport stadiums and arenas were abolished, making not just participation in sport but also spectating a right of all Cuban citizens. (Today spectator sport is still accessible to the masses, with entry charges generally only one or two pesos.) In 1971, ten years after the creation of INDER, the success of its campaigns was tangible. In schools the number of pupils actively involved in one sport or another had risen from under 40,000 to just over a million, whilst it was estimated in a UNESCO-backed report that a further 1,214,000 people were participating in some kind of regular physical exercise.

Making champions

Mass participation in sport was to form the base of the Coubertin-inspired **pyramid** that underpins Cuban sport and accounts, to a large extent, for the tremendous success of Cuban sportsmen and women over the last thirty years. With millions of people involved in sport throughout the country at the base level of the pyramid, the subsequent levels, leading up to the summit, are determined by regional and specialized institutions set up in order to maximize the possibility of discovering potential champions. From primary schools to universities, physical education is a compulsory part of the curriculum and the progress of all pupils is monitored through regular **testing**, with results helping to determine whether or not a student can advance to the next grade of study. Thus, at as early as seven or eight years of age, the most promising young athletes can be selected for the **EIDE** (Escuelas de Iniciación Deportiva Escolar) **sports school**, of which there is one in every province. Here pupils continue with their programmes of academic study whilst their sporting progress, usually in a specific discipline, is even more closely watched. Physiological tests, trainers' reports and inter-provincial competitions all form a regular part of school life at the EIDE, where pupils remain until they are fifteen or sixteen. The best EIDE pupils are then selcted for the **ESPA** (Escuelas Superiores de Perfeccionamiento Atlético)

schools, one stage below the Equipo Nacional – the National Team – at the top of the pyramid. Using this structure the Cubans have demonstrated the reciprocal relationship between the top and the bottom of the pyramid: mass participation produces world champions and, in turn, success in international competitions encourages greater numbers to practise sport.

The nurturing of potentially world-class athletes is taken so seriously in Cuba that each individual sport has to be officially sanctioned before it is recognized as suitable for competition standard. The basic principle behind this is specialization and since the revolution the Cubans have made sure each of their major sports is developed to a high international standard before another is introduced. Specialization wherever possible has characterized the approach INDER has adopted to achieving success, with very little left to chance. Under the auspices of INDER, a National Institute for Sports Medicine has been developed as well as a publishing house producing books by authors who have themselves acquired expertise through the **coaching** courses imparted through INDER. Many of the coaches in Cuba during the first two decades of the revolution were supplied by other Communist-bloc countries, but as time has worn on INDER has had time to train its own experts, most of them at the Instituto Superior de Cultura Física "Comandante Manuel Fajardo" in Havana. Cuban coaches have had almost as much success as the athletes they have trained, working in over forty countries, particularly Spain and throughout Latin America.

The Fidel Castro factor

Just as few governments have shown the kind of interest and involvement in sport that the Cuban government has demonstrated since 1959, so there are even fewer political leaders who have shown the personal commitment to sport that Fidel Castro has always had. He has made numerous speeches over the years, demanding that Cubans achieve more in international competitions, lauding Cuban performances at major championships, and generally promoting participation in sport and sporting excellence. One such speech, in 1959, preempted the creation of INDER, and many of Castro's goals for Cuban sport became the objectives of that organization. He has, on more than one occasion, involved himself in disputes over scandals implicating

Cuban sports stars, and rarely misses the chance to greet a winning team's homecoming, from an overseas tournament.

This enthusiasm stems from Castro's own sporting prowess, attested to in photographs in museums and restaurants around the country depicting the Cuban leader making cameo appearances at baseball and basketball games, as well as on the football field and in numerous other physical activities. His involvement, however, goes well beyond political gimmickry, and can be traced back to his high school days at the Belen school in Havana. Here he played in the basketball and baseball teams, and in 1944 was voted the top high school athlete in the country. In his early university years he continued to play basketball and baseball as well as training as a 400-metre runner. Famously, in his first year at the University of Havana, he challenged the president of the Students' Union to settle a point of contention over a boxing match. It is Castro's belief that his own background in sports had a major influence on his later life, and he has said that had he not been a sportsman he would never have been a revolutionary, asserting that it was his physical training as an athlete that had allowed him to fight as a guerrilla in the revolutionary war.

Given his conviction that sport played so significant a role in his own personal development, it is hardly surprising that Castro put it so high on the agenda in the first reform programmes of the revolution. Even before the creation of INDER, he was calling for Cuba's poor record in international sport to be rectified and laying out his vision of how this could be done. As early as January 1959, within a month of the rebel victory, Castro made a lengthy speech in the Ciudad Deportiva and declared: "I am convinced that sporting activity is necessary for this country. It's embarrassing that there is so little sport . . . The Cuban results in international competitions up until now have been shameful."

It would be shortsighted to suppose that there has been no political motivation behind Castro's commitment to sport. However, despite the role sport has played as an encouragement to nationalism and therefore as a prop to the regime, no one in Cuba has been more insistent than Castro that the system should be free of exploitation and that everyone should enjoy the right to participate. He continues to place immense importance on sport and considers the achievements in sport since the revolution a matter of intense pride, as evidenced in his public outrage at the confiscation of medals from four Cuban athletes at the 1999 Pan American Games. Describing the results of the tests that found traces of steroids in three weightlifters and cocaine in the high jump world record holder, Javier Sotomayor, as "a colossal lie", he personally appeared in a two-day televised hearing, demanding that the medals be returned.

World beaters

Compared with just fourteen Olympic medals by 1959, Cuba's plethora of golds, silvers and bronzes since looks even more impressive. It has also come to dominate a number of sports, with one of the best homegrown baseball leagues in the world and a national team with a phenomenal record over the last two decades.

In the biggest test of a nation's sporting prowess, the **Olympic Games**, the Cubans have been among the top ten in the medals tables since 1976, when they ranked eighth at the Montreal Olympics. Despite finishing fourth in the Moscow Games in 1980, Cubans consider their finest performance to have been at the Barcelona Olympics in 1992, when their fourteen gold medals helped them to place fifth in the final rankings, ahead of countless other, far wealthier countries. The result in Moscow was tarnished by the stigma of not having competed against some of the best sporting nations in the world, notably the United States, which chose to boycott the tournament.

Unsurprisingly, rivalry between Cuba and **the US** is intense whenever they meet, whatever the sport. With diplomatic relations between the two countries formally abandoned in 1961, sport has provided one of the main battlegrounds on which they have met face to face. Whilst the Cold War ensured that the US did not compete in Moscow, it also kept Cuba out of the Los Angeles and Seoul Olympics, leaving them itching to test their might against the Americans in 1992. Though, as at every other Olympic Games, the US ranked higher in the medals tables, the Cubans have enjoyed some of their sweetest victories over Olympic clashes. They took particular satisfaction when their baseball team beat the US at their own game on the way to winning the baseball final in the 1996 Atlanta Olympics.

It has been at the Olympics that some of the best-known and most successful Cuban sports-

Baseball

Ironically, the most American of sports is also the most Cuban, and **baseball** stands out as one of the few aspects of US culture which the revolutionaries continued to embrace after 1959. It was introduced to the island in the late 1800s by American students studying in Cuba and by visiting sailors who would take on the local workers in Cuban dockyards. The first officially organized game took place between the Matanzas Béisbol Club and the Havana Béisbol Club on December 27, 1874. Frowned upon by the Spanish colonial rulers, who even banned the game for a period, the sport really took off following the Spanish-American War, which ended in 1898 and saw control of the island pass effectively into US hands. A national league was established but the Major League in the US dominated the fortunes of the best players. Cuban and American baseball developed in tandem during the prerevolutionary era, as the island became a supply line to the US teams with players like Adolfo Luque, Conrado Marrero, and Miguel Angel González, who coached the World Series-winning St Louis Cardinals team, amongst the numerous Cubans to be won over by Major League riches. These were almost exclusively white players, as black Cubans suffered discrimination in both countries and were mostly restricted either to the black leagues or the Cuban league, in which Habana, Almendares, Marianao and Santa Clara were the only teams competing.

Since 1959 Cuban baseball has transformed itself from the stepchild of the US Major League to one of the most potent, independent forces in the game. The **national league** now consists of sixteen teams instead of four and has gone from professional to amateur without losing any of the excitement that characterizes its hottest confrontations. The national team dominates

international baseball and has done so since the early 1980s, winning Olympic titles and unbeaten in the **Intercontinental Baseball Cup** – the baseball world championships – since 1983. Whilst the national team has made the biannual baseball world championships a celebration of Cuban sporting achievement, the big question that remains is whether Cuba's amateurs can hold their own against the professional players of the US, who up until recently have played no part in international competitions. The Sydney Olympics of 2000 has changed that, but the first test came in 1999 when the Baltimore Orioles made an unprecedented visit to Cuba to take on the national team. In a good-spirited game the visitors stole a 3-2 victory but perhaps more significant than the result was the visit itself, characterized by a friendly rivalry and a mutual respect in defiance of the political antagonism between the two nations.

That Cuban players are amongst the best in the world is in little doubt, a point sorely proven by a number of Cuban nationals who have escaped Cuba and signed huge contracts with **Major League** clubs. Among the big names are Rolando Arrojo and Rene Arocha, but the attention in recent years has focused on the Hernández brothers. Having signed a six-million-dollar contract with the Florida Marlins, Liván Hernández took the team to World Series victory and was named MVP (Most Valuable Player), whilst his brother Orlando, who was denied a place in the Olympic team that went to Atlanta 96, followed him by signing for the New York Yankees. By no means all the best Cuban players have left, however, with Omar Linares probably the most famous name to have rejected Major League offers in favour of staying in Cuba.

men and women have made their mark on the rest of the world. One of the first was **Alberto Juantorena,** who remains the only man in Olympic history to win both 400-metre and 800-metre events, which he did in Montreal in 1976. It was during the same era that the best Cuban boxer in history reigned supreme, **Teófilo Stevenson**, three times Olympic champion and one-time potential opponent of Muhammad Ali.

Stevenson was prevented from fighting the self-proclaimed "greatest of all time" by the governing body of the sport during the 1970s, which ruled it illegal for an amateur to fight a professional. Even Ali himself, in a visit to Havana in 1996, admitted that had the two ever met it would have been a close-run contest. Unable to compete in the professional fight extravaganzas which make all the headlines in boxing, the

Olympic Games have been for Cuban boxers the best opportunity to show the rest of the world what they're made of, as they regularly take home a clutch of medals. In the 1990s **Javier Sotomayor**, known as "El Príncipe de las Alturas" – The Prince of Heights – was recognized as the best high jumper in the world, holder of the world record and gold medal winner in Barcelona. The decade unfortunately finished on a sour note for him when, in the 1999 Pan American Games, he was allegedly found to have taken cocaine the night before he competed. Nevertheless, Sotomayor, along with the long jumper **Ivan Pedroso** and the 800-metre specialist **Ana Fidelia**, are only the most recent winners in a long line of Cuban track and field athletes, amongst the most repected in the world over the last thirty years.

Countless other sports and sporting disciplines have given Cuba world champions, including volleyball, wrestling and weightlifting, whilst this small island nation has made the result of the **Central American and Caribbean Championships** – in which Mexico, Colombia, Venezuela and Puerto Rico compete – a foregone conclu-

sion, having finished first every time since 1966. Perhaps even more impressive is Cuba's habitual second place, beaten only by the US, in the **Pan American Games**, a championship contested by all the countries of the American continent.

Conspicuous by its absence from Cuban successes in sport is **soccer**. The Cuban team has never qualified for the World Cup, though they came reasonably close to going to France 98 before Jamaica knocked them out of the tournament. Support for the game is increasing, the government well aware of the benefits of improving the national standard at the most popular sport in the world. France 98 was watched by more people on the island than any other World Cup before it, and the popularity of soccer since the tournament has visibly increased. Local parks and fields are now nearly as often host to soccer matches as baseball games, and though at an organized level there is a long way to go, with the national baseball and basketball leagues attracting far more attention and greater crowds than the soccer equivalent, the grass roots of the game have already been laid down.

Books

There has been more written on Cuba than perhaps any other Latin American country, with numerous titles devoted to unravelling the intricate politics between the US and Cuba. These make compelling – if sometimes heavy-going – reading, while a more palatable introduction to Cuban culture and politics can be gained through the cornucopia of fiction by Cuban writers both contemporary and classic, much of it translated into English and widely available. There are also plenty of novels written in English by exiled Cubans and non-Cubans, most famously Ernest Hemingway and Graham Greene. Travel writing and photography are also well represented – some of the best coffee-table photographic books can be bought in Cuba itself.

History and politics

Juan M. de Aguila, *Cuba: Dilemmas of a Revolution* (Westview Press). A good reference book for students of the revolution, with well-selected topics and plenty of useful subheadings. While it's concerned more with the questions that the revolution has raised rather than the story of what actually happened, the patttern of historical events still forms the framework of the intelligent, balanced discussions.

Leslie Bethell (ed), *Cuba: A Short History* (Cambridge University Press). Somewhat incomplete and at times lacking in coherence, this history nevertheless covers well some periods, such as the two decades prior to the 1959 revolution.

Simon Calder and Emily Hatchwell, *Cuba In Focus: A Guide to the People, Politics and Culture* (Latin American Bureau, UK; Interlink Publishing, US). A succinct overview of the country and its history, touching on a lively variety of different subject areas, from race to tourism, all dealt with intelligently and in just enough detail to be informative. Small enough to read from cover to cover on the plane.

CIA Targets Fidel (Ocean Press). A word-for-word reproduction of a CIA report compiled in 1967 and declassified in 1994, detailing the various plots that were hatched in the US, some in coordination with the Mafia, to assassinate or depose Fidel Castro during the early 1960s. Preceding the report is an interview conducted with a former head of Cuban State Security, who reveals that the Cuban Ministry of the Interior's own files list 612 US-backed plots against Castro from 1959 to 1993, also suggesting that the same body of CIA operations was behind the assassination of John F. Kennedy. Unsurprisingly, the report makes rather tedious reading, but the candid way in which Castro's assassination is discussed is quite eye-opening.

James Ferguson, *A Traveller's History of the Caribbean* (The Windrush Press, UK; Interlink Publishing, US). A clearly explained history of the region, placing Cuba in a wider context and providing a worthwhile perspective on a number of issues common to the islands.

Guillermo Cabrera Infante, *Mea Cuba* (Faber and Faber, UK). A collection of writings on Cuba from 1968 to 1993 by a Cuban exile and opponent of the current regime. His vehement criticisms of Fidel Castro are uncompromising and can make for rather heavy reading, but there are plenty of thoughtful and eyebrow-raising commentaries from a man who is clearly passionate about his subject matter.

Franklin W. Knight, *Slave Society in Cuba during the Nineteenth Century* (o/p). A detailed and sensitively handled treatment of all aspects of slavery in Cuba, from the lives of the slaves and race relations, to the broader political and economic context in which slavery evolved. The book is packed with information and the author thankfully refrains from overintellectualizing the topic.

Luis Martínez-Fernández, *Fighting Slavery in the Caribbean: The Life and Times of a British Family in Nineteenth-Century Havana* (M.E. Sharpe). Using the well-charted experiences of an Englishman working in the foreign office and living in Cuba with his family, this is a vivid social and economic history of Cuba in the mid-nineteenth century. Full of fascinating detail about the niceties of Havanan society, the drive for abolition of slavery and plenty of observations about the city itself.

Peter Marshall, *Cuba Libre: Breaking the Chains?* (o/p). Lively and upbeat analysis of the revolution, highlighting its achievements without ignoring the mistakes. Written in 1987, it is somewhat outdated but excellent chapters on education, the economy and the management of the revolution make this an above average study.

Carmelo Mesa-Lago (ed), *Cuba after the Cold War* (University of Pittsburgh Press). Ten rather dry though highly informative essays on Cuba in the wake of Glasnost, focusing on how Cuba's destiny has been shaped by its former close relationship with the Soviet Union.

Professor José Cantón Navarro, *History of Cuba* (Cuba Editorial SI-MAR S.A.). A political overview of Cuban history through the eyes of a revolutionary historian. A somewhat revisionist and romantic version of events, but interesting nevertheless.

Louis A. Pérez, Jr., *Cuba: Between Empires 1878–1902* (University of Pittsburgh Press); *Cuba: Between Reform and Revolution* (Oxford University Press). The first is a scholarly and perspicacious account of how the United States managed to supplant Spanish suzerainty, despite Cuba's struggle for independence. Superbly researched and very readable, the second title tends towards economic issues, though it's still far from one-dimensional.

Louis A. Pérez, Jr. (ed), *Slaves, Sugar and Colonial Society* (Scholarly Resources Inc, US). An extensive collection of accounts written by predominantly US and British travellers to Cuba during the nineteenth century. Divided into eight chapters, each covering a different topic, from religion to crime, as well as sugar and slavery, many of the essays are intriguing not just for their reflection of Cuban society during the period, but also for the insights into the cultural background of the writers themselves.

Robert E. Quirk, *Fidel Castro* (W.W. Norton). An impressively detailed biography of the Cuban

president, at times quite critical of its subject matter but without the kind of thoughtless Castro-bashing that other commentators indulge in.

Roger Ricardo, *Guantánamo, The Bay of Discord: The Story of the US Military Base in Cuba* (Ocean Press). A brief history of the role of Guantánamo Bay in the ongoing standoff between the US and Cuba.

Julio Le Riverend, *Breve Historia de Cuba* (Editorial de Ciencias Sociales, Cuba). Written by one of Cuba's leading historians, and also available in English, at times this history lapses into political rhetoric and revolutionary propaganda but it does provide some useful insights as well as information often missed by non-Cuban authors of the country's history.

Geoff Simons, *Cuba: From Conquistador to Castro* (Macmillan, UK). An incisive and thought-provoking history of Cuba, which aims to convey an understanding of events within their wider context, such as the religious climate in Europe during the Spanish colonization of Cuba. The writing is spiced up by the author's boldness in expressing his anti-imperialist views and his scathing account of US politics and capitalism.

Hugh Thomas, *Cuba or the Pursuit of Freedom* (Da Capo Press). Written with a right-wing slant, this authoritative and exhaustive history of Cuba from 1762 to the present day is meticulously researched, full of fascinating facts and immensely readable despite its epic proportions.

Stephen Williams, *Cuba: The Land, the History, the People, the Culture* (Prion). A highly enjoyable and easy-going coffee-table read decorated with a lively collection of illustrations and photographs.

Culture and society

Raudol Ruiz Aguilera, *El Deporte de Hoy* (Editorial Científico-Técnica, Cuba). Written by one of the leading figures in sport administration in Cuba since the revolution, much of this book is dedicated to a discussion of the forces at work in modern sport, such as commercialization and the use of performance-enhancing drugs. Not a particularly stimulating read, but gives an interesting insight into the Cuban philosophy of sport, including speeches made by Fidel Castro.

Jonathan Futrell and Lisa Linder, *Up in Smoke* (Conran Octopus, UK). An artistically presented guide to the culture of cigar production and smoking, with a chapter dedicated to Cuba, as well as advice on cigar etiquette, what to look for in a cigar and a selection of recommended smokes.

Guillermo Cabrera Infante, *Holy Smoke* (Faber and Faber, UK; Overlook Press, US). A pompous and entertaining tribute to the Havanan cigar, full of painful puns and obscure references.

Ian Lumsden, *Machos, Maricones and Gays* (Latin American Bureau, UK; Temple University Press, US). One of the few available books that discusses homosexuality in Cuba. A thorough and sensitive treatment, covering the history of homophobia in Cuba and such complex issues as the Cuban approach to AIDS.

Robin D. Moore, *Nationalizing Blackness: Afrocubanismo and Artistic Revolution in Havana, 1920–1940* (University of Pittsburgh Press). A clear and compelling analysis of the cultural and artistic role of black Cubans during an era of prejudice. A good introduction to black culture in Cuba.

Pedro Peréz Sarduy and Jean Stubbs (eds), *AfroCuba: An Anthology of Cuban Writing on Race, Politics and Culture* (Latin American Bureau, UK; Ocean Press, US). Essays and extracts written by black Cuban writers covering religion, race relations, slavery, plantation culture and a fascinating variety of other topics. This anthology contains a wide variety of writing styles with excerpts from plays, novels, poems and factual pieces but some of the quality of the texts is lost in the occasionally stilted translations.

Sue Steward, *Salsa: Musical Heartbeat of Latin America* (Thames and Hudson, UK). Tracing the roots of *salsa* and examining its place in its various home territories, from Miami to London, with three chapters concentrating specifically on Cuba.

Travel writing

Carlo Gébler, *Driving through Cuba: An East-West Journey* (o/p). Down-to-earth account of the author's journey around the island, covering most of the major tourist destinations, prior to the collapse of trade with the Soviet Union. Straightforward writing and unpretentious observations of Cuban life and customs, sprinkled with historical references.

Che Guevara, *The Motorcycle Diaries* (Fourth Estate, UK; Verso, US). Written before he met Fidel Castro, this lively read portrays a side to Che rarely discussed or revealed. The book follows his motorcycle tour of South America with his friend and fellow doctor Alberto Granado. Amusing but rarely gripping, a large part of the book's appeal is the contrast it casts with Che's later life.

Louis A. Pérez (ed), *Impressions of Cuba in the Nineteenth Century: The Travel Diary of Joseph J. Dimock* (Scholarly Resources, Inc.). An elaborate first-person account of many aspects of Cuba, including the lives of slaves, Spanish and Creoles. At times unwittingly comic, it is as revealing of Cuba as it is of the opinionated stuffed-shirt author.

Alan Ryan (ed), *The Reader's Companion to Cuba* (Harcourt Brace and Co., US). Twenty-three accounts by foreign visitors to Cuba between 1859 and the 1990s, including trips to Havana and Santiago de Cuba by Graham Greeene and fascinating observations on race relations by Langston Hughes. A broad range of writers, from novelists and poets to journalists and naturalists, cover an equally broad range of subject matter, from places and people to slavery and tourism.

Stephen Smith, *The Land of Miracles: A Journey Through Modern Cuba* (Little, Brown, and Co). Entertaining accounts of all the important aspects of Cuban culture from classic cars and Santería to love hotels and Guantánamo are surpassed by Smith's ability to pinpoint the foreigner's experience in Cuba.

Photography and architecture

Juliet Barclay and Martin Charles, *Havana: Portrait of a City* (o/p). A graceful social history of the city filled with intriguing vignettes complemented by skilful photography.

Alexandra Black and Simon McBride, *Living in Cuba* (Scriptum Editions, UK). Essentially a photographic portrait of the interiors of houses and other preserved colonial buildings around Cuba. The book does a fine job of displaying Cuba's vibrant architectural heritage but, despite its title, shows very little of the environment in which everyday life unfolds. A little like a museum handbook, in nonetheless splendid style.

Gianni Costantino, *Cuba: Land and People* (Ediciones Gianni Costantino, Italy). Sold in bookstores throughout Cuba, this collection of mostly postcard-style photography is a relatively dispassionate depiction of Cuban society, predominantly covering cities, landscapes and architecture, with the occasional street scene.

Walker Evans, *Havana 1933* (Thames & Hudson, UK; Pantheon, US). An exceptional set of photographs taken by Walker Evans, a US photographer commissioned to visit Cuba to supply pictures for a book entitled *The Crime of Cuba* by Carleton Beals. A highly evocative portrayal of 1930s Havana, illustrating, amongst other facets of the culture, the poverty of the time.

La Habana Colonial (Dirección de Planificación Física y Arquitectura, Cuba). Detailing over one hundred colonial mansions, churches, squares and other constructions around Havana; each entry consists of a photograph and an explanation of history and architectural merit. One of the most authoritative guides on the subject, including a fascinating little history of how the city developed.

María E. Haya, *Cuba La Fotografía de Los Años 60* (Cuba Fototeca de Cuba). A collection of definitive photographs by Raúl Corrales, Ernesto Fernández, Mario García Joya, Alberto Korda and Osvaldo Salas of the revolutionary struggle and the early years after its triumph. Iconic and atmospheric, they are a moving tribute to the era's optimism.

Tania Jovanovic, *Cuba ¡Que Bola! a photographic essay* (Ocean Press). Through lucid and evocative black-and-white portraits Jovanovic captures the exuberance, camaraderie and *joie de vivre* of Cuba perfectly.

Fiction

Edmundo Desnoes, *Memories of Underdevelopment* (Rutgers University Press). In this novel set in 1961 the jaded narrator takes the reader through early revolutionary Cuba after his family has fled for Miami. Its bleak tone and unflinching observations are in stark contrast to the euphoric portrayal of the era generally offered by the state.

Alejandro Hernández Díaz, *La Milla* (Pinos Nuevos, Cuba). A short novel about two men who try to make the ninety-mile journey from Cuba across the Florida Straits to the US. Thought-provoking and relatively accessible to non-native speakers.

James Ferguson (ed), *Traveller's Literary Companion: The Caribbean* (In Print Publishing Ltd, UK; Passport, US). This literary anthology's chapter on Cuba is an erudite introduction, blending the most renowned, respected and revealing writers on Cuba, both national and international. Amongst the nineteen diverse extracts literary giants Ernest Hemingway and Guillermo Cabrera Infante are represented, alongside lesser-known authors including Edmundo Desnoes and seminal Cuban poet Nicolás Guillén.

Cristina García, *Dreaming in Cuba* (Ballantine, US). Shot through with wit, García's moving novel about a Cuban family divided by the revolution captures the state of mind of the exile in the States and beautifully describes a magical and idiosyncratic Cuba.

Graham Greene, *Our Man in Havana* (Penguin). Greene's atmospheric 1958 classic is a satirical romp through the world of espionage and despotic duplicity in the runup to the revolution. Unequalled entertainment.

Ernest Hemingway, *To Have and Have Not; The Old Man and the Sea* (both Arrow, UK; Scribner, US). The first is a stark novel full of racial tension and undercurrents of violence, with a plot concerning rum-running between Cuba and Key West in the 1930s. The second is the simple, powerful account of an epic battle between an old fisherman and a giant marlin. Set in Cuban waters and the fishing village of Cojímar, this novella won Hemingway the Nobel Prize for literature in 1954.

Pico Iyer, *Cuba and the Night* (Quartet Books, UK; Vintage, US). Against a backdrop of the Special Period Iyer's bleak and claustrophobic tale of a jaded Western man's affair with a Cuban woman captures the pessimism, cynicism and ambiguity of such relationships in Cuba.

Juana Ponce de León and Esteban Ríos Rivera (eds), *Dream with No Name* (Seven Stories Press). A poignant and revealing collection of contemporary short stories by writers living in Cuba and in exile. Mixing the established talent of Alejo Carpentier, Reinaldo Arenas and Onelio Jorge Cardoso with the younger generation of writers represented by Jacqueline Herranz Brooks and Angel Santiesteban Prats, the anthology covers a diversity of subjects from rural life in the 1930s to lesbian love in modern Cuba.

Language

IDIOM AND SLANG

Since the collapse of trade with the Soviet Union English has replaced Russian as the second language of Cuba. However, standards are still pretty low and relatively few Cubans speak English fluently, many not at all. This won't stop some people trying to practise what they know with anyone willing to listen, and shouts of "My friend" or "Where you from, man?" echo incessantly around the streets of Habana Vieja.

Learning a few basic phrases in Spanish will prove invaluable, especially if you use public transport, when asking for information is the only way you'll get any. Cuban Spanish bears noticeable resemblance to the pronunciation and vernacular of the Canary Islands, one of the principal sources of Cuban immigration during the colonial era. Students of Castilian Spanish may find themselves a little thrown by all the variations in basic vocabulary in Cuba (see opposite). Though the language is full of Anglicisms and Americanisms, like *carro* instead of *coche* for car, or *queic* instead of *tarta* for cake, the Castilian equivalents are generally recognized and making yourself understood should be easier than understanding other people yourself. Things aren't made any easier by the common Cuban habit of dropping the final letters of words and changing the frequently used *-ado* ending on words to *-ao*.

Despite these areas of confusion, the rules of pronunciation for all forms of Spanish are straightforward and the basic Latin American model applies in Cuba. Unless there's an accent, all words ending in d, l, r and z are stressed on the last syllable, all others on the second last. All vowels are pure and short.

A somewhere between the A sound in "back" and that in "father".

E as in "get".

I as in "police".

O as in "hot".

U as in "rule".

C is soft before E and I, hard otherwise: *cerca* is pronounced "serka".

G works the same way: a guttural H sound (like the ch in "loch") before E or I, a hard G elsewhere: *gigante* becomes "higante".

H is always silent.

J is the same sound as a guttural G: *jamón* is pronounced "hamon".

LL is pronounced as a Y: *lleno* is therefore pronounced "yeno".

Ñ is as in English, unless it has a tilde (accent) over it, when it becomes NY: *mañana* sounds like "manyana".

QU is pronounced like the English K.

R is, technically speaking, not rolled but you will frequently hear this rule contradicted.

RR is rolled.

V sounds more like B: *vino* becomes "beano".

Z is the same as a soft C: *cerveza* is thus "servesa".

Idiom and slang

Cuban Spanish is rich in idiosyncratic words and phrases, many borrowed from English, often misinterpreted and given their own unique slant, with some comic-sounding results for native English-speakers. Far from being a bastardization of English or Castilian Spanish, however, language in Cuba is as heterogeneous as the history and culture that spawned it, with notable influences from the West African languages brought over through the slave trade and, more recently, the involvement of the US in the island. Some of the slang is common to other Latin American countries, particularly Puerto Rico, whilst there are all sorts of *cubanismos* unique to the island.

Basic Cuban vocabulary

A number of everyday Cuban words, particularly for items of clothing, differ completely from their Castilian equivalent. These are not slang words, but equate to the same kind of differences that exist between North American and British English.

el blúmer	knickers
la camiseta	vest
el carro	car
el chubasquero	kagoule
el chor	shorts
la guagua	bus
el jonrón	home run in baseball
el ómnibus	long-distance bus
el overol	dungarees
el pitusa	jeans
el pulover	T-shirt
el queik	cake
el saco	a suit
los tenis	trainers, sneakers
el yin	jeans

Popular expressions and slang

Some of the terms below, such as *barbacoa*, have emerged because of uniquely Cuban practices, while others reflect aspects of Cuban culture, such as the destigmatization of referring to people by their skin colour or racial characteristics.

Asere A commonly heard term, similar to "mate" or "buddy", but often used as an exclamation.

Barbacoa The term given to the popular Cuban practice of creating two rooms from one by building in a floor halfway up the wall.

Bárbaro/a Used both as an adjective and a noun to refer to something or someone as outstanding, but also used as a way of saying "Excellent!" or "That's great!"

Barro Dollar or dollars.

Chance Literally "chance" and often heard in the expression *Dame un chance*, "Give me a chance!"

Chao A common way of saying goodbye.

Chino/a A person with facial characteristics commonly found in Chinese people.

Chivatón A grass, an informer.

Chopin Appropriation of the word "shopping", used to mean a dollar shop. *Voy a la chopin para comprarme un pitusa*, "I'm going to the dollar shop to buy myself some jeans."

Coger lucha To get stressed out or upset.

¿Cómo andas? How's it going?

Compañero/a Very popular expression since the 1959 revolution, used by both young and old alike, and literally meaning "comrade" but equivalent to "friend", "mate" or "pal" and also acceptable as a formal address to a stranger.

Numbers and days

1	*un/uno/una*	16	*dieciséis*	1000	*mil*
2	*dos*	20	*veinte*	2000	*dos mil*
3	*tres*	21	*veitiuno*		
4	*cuatro*	30	*treinta*	first	*primero/a*
5	*cinco*	40	*cuarenta*	second	*segundo/a*
6	*seis*	50	*cincuenta*	third	*tercero/a*
7	*siete*	60	*sesenta*		
8	*ocho*	70	*setenta*	Monday	*lunes*
9	*nueve*	80	*ochenta*	Tuesday	*martes*
10	*diez*	90	*noventa*	Wednesday	*miércoles*
11	*once*	100	*cien(to)*	Thursday	*jueves*
12	*doce*	101	*ciento uno*	Friday	*viernes*
13	*trece*	200	*doscientos*	Saturday	*sábado*
14	*catorce*	201	*doscientos uno*	Sunday	*domingo*
15	*quince*	500	*quinientos*		

SPANISH LANGUAGE BASICS

BASICS

yes, no	*sí, no*	open, closed	*abierto/a, cerrado/a*
please, thank you	*por favor, gracias*	with, without	*con, sin*
where, when	*dónde, cuando*	good, bad	*buen(o)/a, mal(o)/a*
what, how much	*qué, cuanto*	big	*grande*
here, there	*aquí/acá, allí*	small	*pequeño/a, chico/a*
this, that	*esto, eso*	more, less	*más, menos*
now, later	*ahora, más*	today, tomorrow	*hoy, mañana*
	tarde/después	yesterday	*ayer*

GREETINGS AND RESPONSES

Hello, Goodbye	*Hola, Adiós*	I (don't) speak Spanish	*(No) Hablo español*
Good morning	*Buenos dias*	My name is . . .	*Me llamo . . .*
Good afternoon/ night	*Buenas tardes/noches*	What's your name?	*¿Como se llama usted?*
See you later	*Hasta luego*	I am English	*Soy inglés(a)*
Sorry	*Lo siento/discúlpeme*	. . . American	*americano(a)*
Excuse me	*Con permiso/perdón*	. . . Australian	*australiano(a)*
Pleased to meet you	*Mucho gusto*	. . . Canadian	*canadiense(a)*
How are you?	*¿Como está (usted)?*	. . . Irish	*irlandés(a)*
I (don't) understand	*(No) Entiendo*	. . . Scottish	*escosés(a)*
Not at all/ You're welcome	*De nada/ por nada*	. . . Welsh	*galés(a)*
Do you speak English?	*¿Habla (usted) inglés?*	. . . New Zealander	*neozelandés(a)*

NEEDS – HOTELS AND TRANSPORT

I want	*Quiero*	Give me. . .	*Deme. . .*
I'd like	*Quisiera*	(one like that)	*(uno así)*
Do you know. . .?	*¿Sabe. . .?*	Do you have. . .?	*¿Tiene . . .?*
I don't know	*No sé*	. . .a room	*. . .una habitación*
There is (is there)?	*(¿) Hay (?)*		

Coño Often shortened to *ño*; equivalent in usage and vulgarity to "shit".

Cursí Roughly equivalent to "corny".

Empatarse To get it together with someone romantically or sexually.

En candela Fucked up or useless.

Estar puesto/a To fancy or be attracted to someone. *¿Estás puesto pa' ella?*, "Do you fancy her?"

Fula Dollar or dollars.

Fulano/a So-and-so, what's-his/her-name; used to refer to someone without knowing or specifying their name. *Fulano me dijo . . .*, "So-and-so told me . . .".

Guapo A criminal or street hustler-type character.

Gusano/a A hostile term for a Cuban refugee; also denotes a counter-revolutionary.

¿Gusta?, ¿Gustas? Most commonly used to ask someone arriving at a meal, "Would you like some?"

Irse para afuera To go abroad.

Jabáo Describes a person with physical characteristics not usually found on people of that skin colour, eg a blonde-haired person with thick, bushy eyebrows.

Maceta A player or hustler; indicates wealth acquired illegally.

Monada A pejorative term for a group of policemen.

. . .with two beds/double bed	. . .con dos camas/cama matriomonial
It's for one person	es para una persona
(two people)	(dos personas)
. . .for one night	. . .para una noche
(one week)	(una semana)
It's fine, how much is it?	¿Está bien, cuánto es?
It's too expensive	Es demasiado caro
Don't you have anything cheaper?	¿No tiene algo más barato?
Reception	Carpeta
Can one. . . ?	¿Se puede. . ?
. . .camp (near) here?	¿. . .acampar aquí (cerca)?
Is there a hotel nearby?	¿Hay un hotel aquí cerca?
How do I get to. . .?	Por dónde se va a. . .?
Left, right, straight on	Izquierda, derecha, derecho
Where is. . .?	¿Dónde está. . .?
. . .the bus station . . .	el terminal de buses
. . .the train station	. . .la estación de ferrocarriles
. . .the nearest bank	. . .el banco más cercano
. . .the post office	. . .el correo
. . .the toilet	. . .el baño
Where does the bus to. . . leave from?	¿De dónde sale la guagua para. . .?
Is this the train for Havana?	¿Es éste el tren para Habana?
I'd like a (return) ticket to. . .	Quisiera pasaje (de ida y vuelta) para. . .
What time does it leave (arrive in. . .)?	¿A qué hora sale (llega en. . .)?
What is there to eat?	¿Qué hay para comer?
What's that?	¿Qué es eso?
What's this called in Spanish?	¿Como se llama este en español?
What time is it?	¿Qué hora es?
It's one o'clock	Es la una
It's two o'clock	Son las dos
Quarter past two	Dos y cuarto
Half past two	Dos y media
Quarter to three	Tres menos cuarto

Moña A general term for swing and hip-hop music.

Pa' Shortened version of *para – Voy par' afuera.*

Papaya Tourists should be careful with this word, used as commonly to refer to female genitalia as to the fruit.

Pepe A tourist.

Pila A lot, a load. *Hay una pila de gente aqui,* "There's a load of people here."

Pinga Literally "penis", but commonly heard in the expression *De pinga,* meaning "Fuck off!" or "Shit!". *Está de pinga* can mean either "It's shit" or "It's superb", depending on the way it's used.

Prieto/a Dark-skinned.

¿Qué bolá? "What's up?", "How's it going?"

Socia/a Equivalent to "mate" or "buddy".

¿Te cuadra? "Does that suit you?"

Tonga A lot.

Trigueño/a Light-brown skinned.

Voy echando "I'm out of here", "I'm off".

Ya Has a number of meanings but is frequently heard as a form of agreement, equivalent to *vale* in Spain.

Yuma Foreigner.

Yunta Close friend.

Glossary

AGROMERCADO A peso market selling fresh produce

APAGÓN A blackout

ARTESANÍA Arts and crafts

ASERE mate/pal

AUTOPISTA Motorway. There is only one motorway in Cuba, running most of the length of the country, referred to as *el autopista* or marked on maps as *Autopista Nacional*

BALNEARIO Health spa

BARRO Dollar or dollars, eg *Tres barro*

BICITAXI Three-wheeled bicycle taxis

BODEGA A peso general store only open to those with a corresponding state-issue ration book

BOHIO Thatched huts as made and lived in by pre-Columbian peoples on the island

BOLSA NEGRA Black market

BUCEO Diving

CABILDO Town council during the colonial era

CAMBIO Bureau de change

CAMELLO Juggernaut-style bus

CAMION Private-run trucks that travel the inter-province routes in lieu of state buses when there are petrol shortages

CAMPISMO Cuban equivalent to a campsite, usually with concrete cabins rather than tents

CARNÉ DE IDENTIDAD Identity card

CARRETERAL Highway; main road

CARRO Car

CASA DE CAMBIO Often kiosks but sometimes more like banks, these are for the express purpose of changing dollars into pesos

CASA PARTICULAR House with one or more rooms available to rent to tourists

CDR (Committee for the Defence of the Revolution) Neighbourhood watch schemes devised to root out counter-revolutionaries

CICLOTAXI See *Bicitaxi*

CIMARRON Escaped slave

COGER BOTELLA To hitchhike

COLA Queue

COMIDA CRIOLLA Traditional Cuban food

CORDILLERA Mountain range

CRIOLLO/A A pre-independence term to describe a Cuban-born Spanish person; also used to describe something as specifically or traditionally Cuban

DÍAS ALTERNOS Every other day (used on bus and train timetables)

DIVISA Hard currency or US dollars

EMBALSE Reservoir

EN EFECTIVO In cash

FINCA Ranch; country estate

GUAGUA Local bus

GUAJIRO/A Rural person; sometimes used to express a lack of education or sophistication

GUARDABOLSO Cloakroom for bags, usually at the entrance to dollar shops

GUAYABERA A lightweight shirt, often with four pockets

HABANERO/A A native of Havana

HABANOS Cuban cigars

INGENIO Sugar refinery

JINETERA Sometimes used to mean prostitute but generally refers to any woman using tourists for material or financial gain

JINETERO Male hustler who specifically targets tourists

MALECÓN Seaside promenade

MAMBÍ, MAMBÍSES Member of the nineteenth-century rebel army fighting for independence from Spain

MIRADOR Place, usually at the top of a hill or mountain, from where there are good views

MOGOTE Boulder-like hills found only in Pinar del Río, particularly in Viñales

MONEDA NACIONAL National currency (pesos)

MUNICIPIO Political division of a city equivalent to a borough or electoral district

ORISHA A deity in Afro-Cuban religions like Santería

PALADAR Restaurant run in the owner's home

PALENQUE A hideout or settlement occupied by runaway slaves during the colonial period

PENINSULAR/ES Spanish-born person living in Cuba prior to independence

PLAYA Beach

PONCHERA Puncture repair and bicycle maintenance, usually privately run from a shed or the front room of a house

REPARTO Neighbourhood or area of a city. Also apartment blocks mainly built since the revolution

SALA DE VIDEO Sometimes a state-run venue but more often a room in a house where films are shown on a video

TALLER Workshop

VEGA Tobacco farm

VEGUERO Tobacco farmer

VILLA Village complex

VITRALES Arched stained-glass windows, unique to Cuba

ZAFRA The sugar harvest

Index

Stay in touch with us!

ROUGH*NEWS* is Rough Guides' free newsletter. In four issues a year we give you news, travel issues, music reviews, readers' letters and the latest dispatches from authors on the road.

ROUGH GUIDES: Travel

Amsterdam
Andalucia
Australia

Austria
Bali & Lombok
Barcelona
Belgium &
  Luxembourg
Belize
Berlin
Brazil
Britain
Brittany &
  Normandy
Bulgaria
California
Canada
Central America
Chile
China
Corfu & the
  Ionian Islands
Corsica
Costa Rica
Crete
Croatia
Cyprus
Czech & Slovak
  Republics
Dodecanese &
  the East Aegean

Dominican
  Republic
Ecuador
Egypt
England
Europe
Florida
France
French Hotels &
  Restaurants
  1999
Germany
Goa
Greece
Greek Islands
Guatemala
Hawaii
Holland
Hong Kong &
  Macau
Hungary
India
Indonesia
Ireland
Israel & the
  Palestinian
  Territories
Italy
Jamaica
Japan
Jordan

Kenya
Lake District
Laos
London
Los Angeles
Malaysia,
  Singapore &
  Brunei
Mallorca &
  Menorca
Maya World
Mexico
Morocco
Moscow
Nepal
New England
New York
New Zealand
Norway
Pacific
  Northwest
Paris
Peru
Poland
Portugal
Prague
Provence & the
  Côte d'Azur
The Pyrenees
Rhodes & the
  Dodecanese

Romania
St Petersburg
San Francisco
Sardinia
Scandinavia
Scotland
Scottish
  highlands and
  Islands
Sicily
Singapore
South Africa
South India
Southwest USA
Spain
Sweden
Syria

Thailand
Trinidad &
  Tobago
Tunisia
Turkey
Tuscany &
  Umbria
USA
Venice
Vienna
Vietnam
Wales
Washington DC
West Africa
Zimbabwe &
  Botswana

AVAILABLE AT ALL GOOD BOOKSHOPS

ROUGH GUIDES: Mini Guides, Travel Specials and Phrasebooks

MINI GUIDES

Antigua
Bangkok
Barbados
Big Island of
  Hawaii
Boston
Brussels
Budapest

Dublin
Edinburgh
Florence
Honolulu
Jerusalem
Lisbon
London
  Restaurants
Madrid
Maui
Melbourne
New Orleans
Rome
Seattle
St Lucia

Sydney
Tokyo
Toronto

TRAVEL SPECIALS

First-Time Asia
First-Time
  Europe
Women Travel

PHRASEBOOKS

Czech
Dutch

Egyptian Arabic
European
French
German
Greek
Hindi & Urdu
Hungarian
Indonesian
Italian
Japanese

Mandarin
  Chinese
Mexican
  Spanish
Polish
Portuguese
Russian
Spanish
Swahili
Thai
Turkish
Vietnamese

AVAILABLE AT ALL GOOD BOOKSHOPS

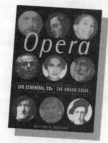

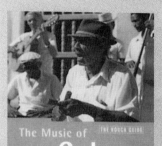

Under 30s' Travel cover

Your only worry is where to land next

Ready to take off round the world? Before you go, make sure you're fully equipped with under 30s' Travel cover from HSBC. If you're heading off for between 3 to 13 months, call the number opposite for instant cover.

Then the rest of your trip should be plain sailing. Lines are open 8am to 10pm Monday to Saturday (excluding public holidays).

0800 299 399

HSBC

YOUR WORLD OF FINANCIAL SERVICES

Issued by HSBC Bank plc

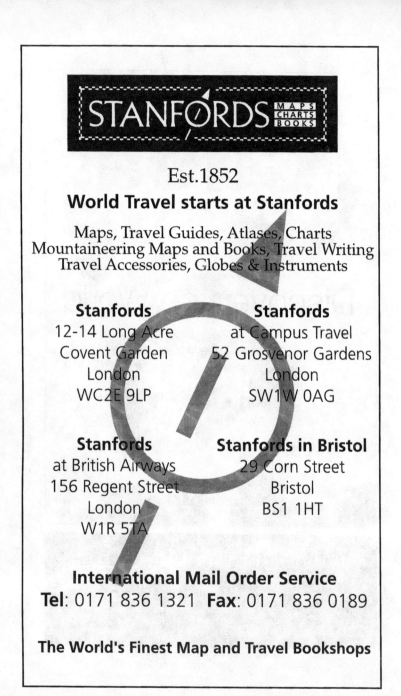

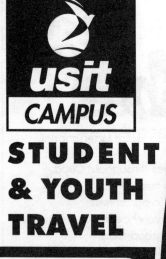